PERFORMANCE, MEMORY, AND PROCESSIONS IN ANCIENT ROME

THE *POMPA CIRCENSIS* FROM THE LATE REPUBLIC TO LATE ANTIQUITY

JACOB A. LATHAM

University of Tennessee, Knoxville

CAMBRIDGE
UNIVERSITY PRESS

CAMBRIDGE
UNIVERSITY PRESS

One Liberty Plaza, 20th Floor, New York NY 10006, USA

Cambridge University Press is part of the University of Cambridge.

It furthers the University's mission by disseminating knowledge in the pursuit of education, learning, and research at the highest international levels of excellence.

www.cambridge.org
Information on this title: www.cambridge.org/9781107130715

First published 2016

Printed in the United States of America by Sheridan Books, Inc.

A catalogue record for this publication is available from the British Library.

Library of Congress Cataloguing-in-Publication Data
Latham, Jacob A., 1974– author.
Performance, memory, and processions in ancient Rome : the *pompa circensis* from the Republic to Late Antiquity / Jacob A. Latham.
New York, NY : Cambridge University Press, 2016. | Includes bibliographical references.
LCCN 2016015481 | ISBN 9781107130715 (hardback)
LCSH: Politics and culture – Rome. | Processions – Rome. | BISAC: HISTORY / Ancient / General.
LCC DG81 .L29 2016 | DDC 306.20937–dc23
LC record available at https://lccn.loc.gov/2016015481

ISBN 978-1-107-13071-5 Hardback

To FVML, TTML, and KBFL with infinite love

CONTENTS

FIGURES

MAPS

References to specific points or landmarks on maps are indicated by their respective number or letter; for example, the reference Map 1.1 indicates building 1 on Map 1.

ABBREVIATIONS

Authors and titles of ancient texts have been abbreviated, whenever possible, according to the *Oxford Classical Dictionary* fourth edition. Other commonly used abbreviations are listed below. For each quotation of an ancient text, the edition has been provided either by an abbreviation of the series in which it appears or by the last name of the editor and the last name of the translator, if any, has also been given.

ACW	Ancient Christian Writers
AE	L'Année épigraphique
BMRRC	Eleanor Ghey and Ian Leins, ed., with contribution by M. H. Crawford, 2010. *A Catalogue of the Roman Republican Coins in the British Museum, with Descriptions and Chronology Based on M.H. Crawford, Roman Republican Coinage* (1974): www.britishmuseum.org/research/publications/online_research_catalogues/rrc/roman_republican_coins/roman_republican_coinage.aspx
BNP	Mary Beard, John North, and Simon Price, 1998. *Religions of Rome: Volume 1, A History*. New York: Cambridge University Press
CCCA	Corpus Cultus Cybelae Attidisque
CCSL	Corpus Christianorum Series Latina
CIL	Corpus Inscriptionum Latinorum
CJ	Paul Krueger ed. 1892. *Codex Iustinianus, Corpus Iuris Civilis* vol. 2. Berlin: Weidmann
CSEL	Corpus Scriptorum Ecclesiasticorum Latinorum
CTh	Theodor Mommsen and Paul Meyer, ed. 1905. *Theodosiani libri XVI cum constitutionibus Sirmondianis et leges novellae ad Theodosianum pertinentes*. Berlin: Weidmann
DOCLRE	Philip Grierson and Melinda Mays, ed. 1992. *Catalogue of Late Roman Coins in the Dumbarton Oaks Collection and in the Whittemore Collection:*

	From Arcadius and Honorius to the Accession of Anastasius. Washington, D.C.: Dumbarton Oaks Research Library and Collection
D-S	Charles Daremberg and Edmond Saglio, ed. 1877–1919. *Dictionnaire des antiquités grecques et romaines*. Paris: Hachette
EDCS	Epigraphik-Datenbank Clauss-Slaby: www.manfredclauss.de/gb/index.html
FC	Fathers of the Church
Gnecchi	Francesco Gnecchi, 1912. *I Medaglioni romani*, 3 vols. Milan: Ulrico Hoepli
ICUR	Inscriptiones Christianae Urbis Romae, new series
ILS	Inscriptiones Latinae Selectae
Imperii insignia	Thomas Schäfer, 1989. *Imperii insignia, sella curulis und fasces: Zur Repräsentation römischer Magistrate*. Mainz: Verlag Philipp von Zabern
Kontorniat-Medallions	Andreas Alföldi, Elisabeth Alföldi-Rosenbaum, and Curtis Clay, 1976–1990. *Die Kontorniat-Medaillons, Antike Münzen und geschnittene Steine 6*. Berlin: de Gruyter
LCL	Loeb Classical Library
LSA	Last Statues of Antiquity: http://laststatues.classics.ox.ac.uk/
LTUR	Eva Margareta Steinby, ed. 1993–2000. *Lexicon topographicum urbis Romae*. Rome: Quasar
MGH	Monumenta Germaniae Historica
MGH:AA	Monumenta Germaniae Historica: Auctores antiquissimi
OCT	Oxford Classical Texts
P-A	Samuel Platner and Thomas Ashby, 1929. *A Topographical Dictionary of Ancient Rome*. Oxford: Oxford University Press
PL	Patrologia Latina
RE	August Friedrich von Pauly, Georg Wissowa, Wilhelm Kroll, and Kurt Witte, ed. 1894–1963. *Paulys Real-encyclopädie der classischen Altertumswissenschaft*. Stuttgart: J. B. Metzler
RIC	Harold Mattingly, Edward Sydenham, C. H. V. Sutherland, and R. A. G. Carson, 1923–2007. *Roman Imperial Coinage*. London: Spinks

Richardson	Lawrence Richardson, 1992. *A New Topographical Dictionary of Ancient Rome*. Baltimore, MD: Johns Hopkins University Press
Roman Statutes	Michael Crawford, 1996. *Roman Statutes*. 2 vols. London: Institute of Classical Studies, University of London
Ronke	Jutta Ronke, 1987. *Magistratische Repräsentation im römischen Relief: Studien zu Standes- und statusbezeichnenden Szenen*. Oxford: BAR
Ryberg	Inez Scott Ryberg, 1955. *Rites of the State Religion in Roman Art*. Ann Arbor: University of Michigan Press for the American Academy in Rome
Trionfi romani	Eugenio La Rocca and Stefano Tortorella, ed. 2008. *Trionfi romani*. Milan: Electa
Teubner	Bibliotheca scriptorum Graecorum et Romanorum Teubneriana
TTH	Translated Texts for Historians
Visualizing Statues	Visualizing Statues in the Late Antique Roman Forum: http://inscriptions.etc.ucla.edu/

ACKNOWLEDGMENTS

Historical research may, at times, seem like a solitary endeavor, though it is a communal effort every step of the way. So, it is my great pleasure to convey my gratitude to many of those who helped to make this book possible. This project first took shape at the University of California, Santa Barbara (UCSB) under the thoughtful guidance and with the gracious support of my mentor and friend Christine Thomas and Hal Drake, whose sage advice and quick wit remain much appreciated. I would like to extend my appreciation to my fellow graduate students, especially William Robert and Ellen Posman, and also to Ann Bermingham, then director of the Interdisciplinary Humanities Center at UCSB, whose postdoctoral lifeline aided many caught by the great recession.

Research for this project began during a year as an Arthur Ross Pre-Doctoral Fellow at the American Academy in Rome with Carmela Vircillo Franklin as director, a stimulating experience that continues to impact my work. A summer seminar funded by the National Endowment for the Humanities allowed me to return there. To live and learn in the city of Rome was, of course, a true pleasure, and I would like to thank many of those who made those idyllic sojourns in the Eternal City so impactful: John Bodel, Kim Bowes, Eleanor Winsor Leach, Michele Salzman, and Simonetta Serra, whose continuing support has proved essential over the years. Eve D'Ambra, Hendrik Dey, Carlos Galvao-Sobrinho, Pat Geary, Jeremy Hartnett, Peter Mazur, Ann Vasaly, and many others also made those times worthwhile in so many ways.

At the University of Tennessee (UT), I have happily landed in a congenial scholarly environment. Special thanks to Christine Shepardson for her indefatigable willingness to help a colleague, to Gregor Kalas, whose generosity and scholarship has been greatly influential, and to Jay Rubenstein for his wonderful wit. Members of the Late Antiquity Faculty Research Seminar at UT, including Matthew Gillis, Thomas Heffernan, Gregor Kalas, Maura Lafferty, and Christine Shepardson, read and helpfully commented on a couple of chapter drafts. Financial support from the UT Graduate School afforded me an opportunity to return to Rome, while a fellowship year with some brilliant colleagues at the UT Humanities Center, under the directorship of Thomas Heffernan, truly transformed this project. In addition, the Department of History with Ernest Freeberg as Head, the Marco Institute directed by

Thomas Burman, and the UT Humanities Center generously provided greatly needed financial support to cover publication costs.

Colleagues and friends from elsewhere have also generously contributed their time and effort. Eva Diaz read the entire manuscript with an intent eye, helping me to see a new perspective on this project. Douglas Boin and Eric Orlin graciously offered their time, providing important and challenging insights that have greatly improved this work. My thanks also to the reviewers and editorial staff of *History of Religions*, especially Kenneth Yu, for their comments and suggestions on an article based on some of the material from Chapter 2. Robin Jensen and Lee Jefferson patiently edited an essay based on some of the material in Chapter 6. My great thanks, too, go to the anonymous readers of Cambridge University Press. Their carefully considered comments spurred a tremendous amount of thought and new research. I also greatly appreciate the comments and advice from audiences at the Archaeological Institute of America, in particular panel organizers Maggie Popkin and Susan Ludi Blevins, and the Society of Biblical Literature, especially colleagues in the Art and Religions of Antiquity program unit, Zsuzsanna Gulacsi, Felicity Harley-McGowan, Lee Jefferson, Robin Jensen, Ellen Muehlberger, and Michael Peppard.

I would also like to extend my thanks to those who helped to secure photographs of the objects published in this book – truly a substantial task. Daria Lanzuolo (Deutsches Archäologisches Institut Rom) endured countless emails and questions and more, while Kim Bowes and Kristine Iara (American Academy in Rome) provided essential logistics. Liz Kurtulik and Gerhard Gruitrooy (Art Resource) and Iain Calderwood (British Museum Images) were tremendous assets. Thanks also to Florian Kugler (Vienna KHM), Marta Zlotnick (Dumbarton Oaks), Dr. Agnes Schwarzmaier (Antikensammlung Altes Museum, Berlin), Laura Minarini (Museo Civico Archeologico di Bologna), Anna Santucci (Università degli studi di Urbino "Carlo Bo"), Kata Endreffy (Museum of Fine Arts, Budapest), Annetta Alexandridis (Cornell University), Ina Seiler (Deutsches Archäologisches Institut: Architekturreferat), Graham Nisbet (Hunterian Museum), Maria Daniela Donninella (Museo Nazionale Romano), Emma Dodd (Numismatica Ars Classica), Jan Krämer (Römisch-Germanisches Museum), Steven Tuck (Miami University), Annewies van den Hoek (Harvard University), Tomislav Bilić (Archaeological Museum Zagreb), the Bibliothèque nationale de France, the Fitzwilliam Museum, the Victoria and Albert Museum, and the Digital Library of Falvey Memorial Library at Villanova University.

To end, I would like to convey my immeasurable gratitude to my family. My much missed mother, Barbara; father, Michael; sister, Katy; and brother, Daniel, have long supported (and teased me about) my work. I dedicate this book to my partner, Francesca, and our two wonderful children, Teague and Keira.

INTRODUCTION

But I won't delay you any longer: I know how tedious I find the circus procession.
Seneca the elder, *Controversiae* 1 *praefatio* 24[1]

Power serves pomp. This Geertzian maxim remains especially true for ancient Rome, whose officials and rulers spent inordinate amounts of time and money on some extraordinarily pompous pomp – in particular on its three great *pompae* (processions): the triumph (*pompa triumphalis*), the public funeral procession (*pompa funebris*), and the circus procession (*pompa circensis* or *circensibus, circensium ludorum, circensi*, or *circi*).[2] But of the three, only one was performed multiple times each year in front of crowds that may have topped 150,000, at least during the high empire. From the late republic to late antiquity, the immensely popular chariot races in the Circus Maximus attracted enormous crowds, offering an unparalleled opportunity for public munificence and political patronage. Conducting a spectacular parade through the monumental heart of Rome to the Circus and its anxious crowds, the president of the games achieved considerable public visibility – a key prize in the battle for honor and glory. At the same time, this very same procession was one of Rome's most hallowed religious ceremonies, hedged with ritual rules and regulations whose violation could lead to dire consequences. That is, the *pompa circensis* was fundamentally a *pompa deorum* – a procession of gods made present or represented in various ways in a performed theology. Each carefully choreographed performance conducted the gods to the games in a ludic atmosphere oscillating between gravity and levity and "resonance and wonder" – rhythmically alternating between serious and austere public self-presentation and sexual and transgressive antics, between reminiscences and connections to memories, places, and practices and the singularity of show-stopping spectacle.[3]

The proud sponsor of the games, the *praeses ludorum*, seems to have led this dazzling procession of gods from the temple of Capitoline Jupiter (the seat of Roman sovereignty); down into the Roman Forum; to the *vicus Tuscus*, which passed through the Velabrum into the Forum Boarium; and finally toward the plebian temple of Ceres on its way to the Circus Maximus, where the wildly popular races entertained the gods and their fellow Romans. After placing the gods in the *pulvinar*, a kind of sacred "loge," the sponsor performed a sacrifice before signaling the start of the first race. From the opening procession to the last race, massive crowds gathered thanks to the beneficence of the game-giver, thronging crowds whose presence and (possibly) gratitude benefitted the patron of the games in turn – a ritual alchemy that transformed financial capital into honor and esteem. Apart from the accolades garnered by the game-giver, the late republican circus parade, in both its participants and its itinerary, fashioned an image of Rome as the senate and Roman people with their gods (SPQR+gods) – one of the most enduring symbols of the city – reveling in the pleasures of *aurea Roma*, golden Rome. Troops of young Roman men, arranged with military precision according to their census status, marched with the game-giver and porters conveyed glittering ritual vessels, while masses of ordinary and not-so-ordinary Romans lined the streets, crowded on steps and balconies, or watched the *pompa* with impatience from their seats. The itinerary mirrored this effect: starting at the gilded temple of Jupiter, the guarantor of Rome's empire, the procession passed through the monumental and historical core of Rome, a landscape of memory, ending at the equally gilded temple of Ceres, protectress of the people, before it entered the Circus whose seating constructed its own, indiscrete image of Roman society.

This republican image of Rome was greatly attenuated but never fully obscured during the course of the empire. Emperors regularly intervened in the procession even as they built an imperial Rome alongside and on top of the republican city. Images and symbols of Julius Caesar appeared in the *pompa* during his own lifetime, which transgressed the boundaries of religious and social scruple and so figured among the reasons for which Caesar was assassinated. Subsequent emperors, especially Augustus and Tiberius, who set the pattern for the next few centuries, were more circumspect, allowing only deified predecessors or deceased members of the imperial household to appear in the procession. Similarly, imperial monuments increasingly and overwhelmingly dominated the itinerary. Triumphal arches and imperial cult temples dotted the route, often marking its major turning points. Nevertheless, Rome's most important and oldest temples and sanctuaries were rebuilt or renovated (often lavishly to be sure) following religious principles, conserving the cultural memory which these monuments embodied. The Circus also achieved massive size and luxurious décor. Its previously promiscuous seating was progressively made hierarchical and structured. Nonetheless, gods and Romans still gathered for fun and games – and sex and violence. That is, despite a tremendous capacity to unleash brute force, Roman emperors were constrained by the traditions, expectations, and memories of the *pompa circensis* as well as those of the games. The imperial procession was founded upon its republican forebears, maintaining some of its memory within the new order.

This coherence between procession and itinerary fractured in late antiquity. The procession itself was arguably reduced to imperial imagery alone (statues of Victory and the emperors) in the aftermath of Christianizing legislation, at least in official versions and imperial representations, which increasingly focused on the figure of the imperial game-giver. Nonetheless, some sub-imperial images suggest the continuing transport of the traditional gods into, perhaps, the early fifth century CE. Moreover, in the early to mid fifth century CE, the circus procession may have been "Christianized" by the inclusion of Christian symbols – a *pompa Dei* replacing the *pompa deorum*. The itinerary reveals a similarly complicated situation. It prominently featured a number of newly restored republican edifices including temples and sanctuaries, while ignoring, it seems, imperial cult temples and triumphal arches, though emperors were still made present through a copious collection of statuary. The variety of processions, the competing monuments, and the fissure between procession(s) and itinerary produced a multiplicity of Romes marked by traditional civic religion, aristocratic memory (hearkening back to the republic), imperial power, and, eventually, Christianity, as the titular church of Anastasia would be built along the parade route by the late fourth century CE. It is impossible to judge when the last *pompa circensis* was performed at Rome, though it seems reasonable to suggest that some variant of a circus procession endured as long as the consulship and the circus games, both of which fade in the mid sixth century CE.

Though vast quantities of ink have been spilled on both the triumph and the public funeral, the circus parade has languished in relative scholarly neglect, even though it may have been the most often repeated of the three.[4] During the republic and early empire, a *pompa circensis* was only certainly performed before votive games, the *ludi Romani*, *ludi Apollinares*, *ludi Megalenses*, and *ludi Augustales*, though it seems reasonable to conjecture that other public games – like the *ludi Plebeii* and *ludi Ceriales*, as well as games attached to the early imperial cult – would also have been introduced by a ludic procession.[5] And so by the late first century BCE, a *pompa circensis* was performed at least three times a year, and quite possibly more than double that. In the early to mid second century CE, during the course of a twenty-four-year career, Diocles, the self-declared "most distinguished of the charioteers," competed in 4,257 races, of which he won 1,462, with 110 of those coming in the first race *a pompa* (after the procession), the most prestigious and lucrative race of the games.[6] On average, Diocles won the race *a pompa* nearly five times per year, which strongly implies that five circus processions took place each year – and likely more. If Diocles won the race *a pompa* at the same rate that he won other races (almost one of every three), a not unreasonable assumption, then Diocles may well have competed on average in thirteen races *a pompa* each year, suggesting that at least thirteen *pompae circenses* were conducted every year during the high empire. The numbers are merely suggestive, though they signal the sheer number of repetitions of the circus procession each year.

Such repetition may well have helped the *pompa circensis* to seep into everyday language. In the late first century BCE, Gaius Licinius Stolo, a dinner guest in Varro's *Res rustica*, feared that he had arrived late to a banquet at the temple of Tellus: "'Keep your spirits up,' replied Agrius [another banqueter], 'for not only has that egg which shows the last lap of the chariot race at the games in the circus not been taken down, but we have not even seen that other egg which usually heads the procession (*pompa*) at dinner.'"[7] The races in the arena opened with a procession and ended when the last egg was lowered (or raised or removed), while the parade of food at dinner kicked off with an egg.[8] This metaphorical culinary procession seems to go back to Plautus (ca. 254–184 BCE) – who not infrequently riffed on the spectacle of the circus procession – one of whose characters marveled at his good fortune to enjoy a procession of sturgeon, a *pompa acipenseris* not a *pompa circensis*. Macrobius, in the early fifth century CE, ostensibly quoted the Plautine sturgeon procession, before turning to a high imperial piscine parade. Sammonicus, an antiquarian of medical lore and tutor to Geta and Caracalla, praised the traditional spread of Septimius Severus, in which sturgeon had again achieved its ancient pride of place at the table. However, apparently "it was served by garlanded servants to the sound of a flute, as if it were the procession (*pompa*), not of a delicacy, but of a god."[9] At its core, the *pompa circensis* transported the gods from the temple of Capitoline Jupiter (or some other temple[s]) to the Circus, and so this *pompa numinis* (procession of divinity), in which a sturgeon was escorted to dinner, may well have called to mind that more obvious and fitting procession of gods.

Despite its repetition and metaphorical value, the circus procession has received comparatively cursory attention in scholarship on the games, spectacles, circuses, daily life, and Roman religion, usually consisting of a brief discussion of an excursus by Dionysius of Halicarnassus, the longest and most important portrayal of the procession, and a few other literary and iconographic sources.[10] Even though the *pompa circensis* was likely performed more often, both the *pompa triumphalis* and the *pompa funebris* were seemingly more politically consequential, their spectacle more captivating, and their place in the

Roman social imaginary larger. Indeed, some scholars lean on the elder Seneca's impatience with the procession to dismiss it as a grudgingly tolerated delay before the real show, the races themselves.[11] The evidence for the procession is also problematic: meager (by comparison with the triumph, with which the circus procession competed poorly in Roman cultural memory), varied, and often ambiguous or imprecise, though perhaps no more so than the evidence for any other ritual, ceremony, or spectacle.

I HISTORY IN THE SUBJUNCTIVE

The "grand procession of Ptolemy Philadelphus" poses similar problems. The procession itself took place in the early third century BCE (ca. 270s–260s).[12] The parade was then featured in Callixeinus of Rhodes' *On Alexandria* probably from the second century BCE. Callixeinus' version survives only as a "fragment" in Athenaeus' *Deipnosophistae* ("Scholars at the Table") from the late second century CE. It seems unlikely that Callixeinus witnessed the event himself, though, if it had been at all as he imagined, it would most probably have lived on in Alexandrian communicative (or social) memory, lingering in the stories of the elderly who may have heard about it from their own grandparents. Callixeinus may also have had access to Ptolemaic archives in which some sort of parade protocol may have been stored with "the records of the Penteteric festivals" – perhaps a list of participants and spectacles in order of appearance.[13] Athenaeus then quoted, or paraphrased, or abridged, or embellished the work of Callixeinus.

Along similar lines, Dionysius of Halicarnassus, writing in Rome at the end of the first century BCE, penned the longest extant description of the *pompa circensis*. To bolster his argument about Rome's Hellenistic origins, he based his version on the (no longer extant) work of Fabius Pictor from the late third century BCE, instead of his own eyewitness testimony. It appears that Fabius Pictor claimed to offer an account of a procession from the beginning of the Roman republic (early fifth century BCE), for which no festival archive can be claimed – though eventually ritual protocols would be inscribed on stone, as a ex post facto memorial. Nonetheless, this description may offer insight into the performance dynamics of the procession, even as it also came to frame, for some readers/hearers, the experience and remembrance of the *pompa circensis*.[14]

By contrast, Ovid seems to have based his color commentary on the litany of gods parading around the Circus, the second-longest passage on the procession, on his own firsthand observations.[15] However, Ovid was an inveterate conjurer of elusive and, at times, illusionary presences or realities – his *pompa circensis* was as much his own invention as a play on a procession actually witnessed.[16] Moreover, as John Henderson has noted, "Ovid embedded the *pompa circensis* in his erotica . . . [in which] the *pompa* does its work of escorting us forward onto the field of play, and ushering in what is officially billed by the poet as 'The greatest show on earth.'"[17] In Ovid, the *pompa circensis* was both a real event and a poetic vehicle, which, in either case, may have had nothing to do with chariot racing. Though elegiac poetry may, at first (and even second) glance, seem distant from the hard knock life of early imperial Rome, and though Ovid, as a poet, was likely more concerned with artistic, technical, and emotional effects – language, sound, and affect – than historical description, elegy as a genre was in fact deeply enmeshed in Roman urban life. And Ovid seems to have been particularly attracted to its voluptuous array of public ceremonial.[18] Ovid's evocations of the *pompa circensis* were set in a still licentious world of the Circus, whose seating increasingly mirrored Rome's stratified social sphere. Even so, the elegiac lover "Ovid" fervently recommended the cramped, intimate informality of the Circus where Venus appeared to aid amorous adventurers. Ovid's poetry thus offers an engaged, seemingly personal "reading" of the Circus, one that lurks below imperial politics and even official civic religion. His poetic and quite possibly tendentious portrayals of the *pompa circensis* appear in the midst of a playful and serious interrogation of the Circus Maximus, conjuring the magic of the procession, even if not the procession itself.

Whatever their difficulties as "evidence," Ovid's poetry and Dionysius' history taken together seem to capture the imaginative productivity of the procession in a manner reminiscent of the relationship between metaphor and narrative outlined by Paul Ricoeur. Metaphor has the power "to redescribe a reality," while narrative is "the privileged means by which we re-configure our confused, unformed, and at the limit mute temporal experience."[19] On the one hand, metaphors (and processions) are creative juxtapositions in which one thing is seen as another. Like a metaphor, the *pompa circensis* conjured a certain image of the complexities and multiplicities of Rome (an act of the social imaginary).[20] Viewed in this way, poetry may have been especially well-suited to explore what one might call the productivity of procession: its effects on participants and spectators, its constellations of meanings, institutional entanglements, and symbolic networks. On the other hand, narratives (and also processions) may order and organize a confusing welter of (urban) experience. Narrative emplotment (typically) arranges its material in a linear trajectory, much as the circus procession ordered and organized an impressive array of humans and gods into a hierarchical display and strung together certain temples, sanctuaries, monuments, civic spaces, and institutions, all with their associated cultural memories, into a linear itinerary – the parade route. Processional paths in particular could be considered the spatial equivalent to narrative, a way to make meaningful and sequential linkages.[21] In the end, as Ricoeur makes clear, "one vast poetic sphere ... includes metaphorical utterance and narrative discourse."[22] Both metaphor and narrative are poetic in the sense that they

1. *Tensa* of Jupiter Optimus Maximus: denarius, ca. 87 BCE: obverse: [D]OSSEN and reverse: L RVBR[I]]

2. *Tensa* of Juno: denarius, ca. 87 BCE: obverse: DOS and reverse: L RVBRI

are acts of *poeisis*, a creative act of the imagination – much as the procession was a creative performance.

Along similar lines, visual imagery, in the absence of labels, captions, or other clues, remains intractable. For example, in ca. 87 BCE an otherwise unknown moneyer, L. Rubrius Dossenus, minted a series of coins with an image of a member of the Capitoline triad, either Jupiter, Juno, or Minerva, on the obverse and an enigmatic vehicle on the reverse (Figures 1–3).[23] In each instance, the vehicles are driverless, single-axle *quadrigae* (four-horse chariots) decorated with "acroterial" sculptures – Victory with a wreath or Victory driving a *biga* (two-horse chariot) – and symbolic imagery on the sides: a lightning bolt for Jupiter and an eagle clasping a lightning bolt for Juno and Minerva. Unlike other numismatic representations of so-called "triumphal" *quadrigae* in which gods or *triumphatores* tower over chariots with low, swooping profiles, these vertically oriented, rectilinear chariots, with their inverted

3. *Tensa* of Minerva: denarius, ca. 87 BCE: obverse: [DOS] and reverse: L RVBRI

triangular tops, stood well above the heads of their horse train.[24] In short, the iconography suggests different vehicles. Their distinctive shape, "pedimental" ornamentation, visual hierarchy (relative size indicating relative importance), relief decoration (lightning bolts and eagles), as well as obverse images intimate that these obscure vehicles may have been *tensae*, sacred chariots that carried the symbols of the gods to the circus.[25] Without explicit corroboration, the identification of these vehicles as *tensae* must remain tentative, though reasonable. Perhaps the mysterious L. Rubrius Dossenus had been or would be an aedile, who helped to organize some of the civic games in which the *pompa circensis* figured so prominently – which may explain this elusive act of self-aggrandizement, but one in keeping with other "aedilician" coin-types.[26] The celebration of the Capitoline triad during one of its most conspicuous public appearances in the circus procession may also explain the later Trajanic restoration of these same coins at least as well as any vague "triumphal" associations would do.[27]

The vexing issue of identification complicates most if not all of the visual evidence for the *pompa circensis*. A representation of any particular procession, even the triumph, tends to look a great deal like representations of any other procession – a confluence likely prompted as much by artistic convention as by the semi-independent co-development of processional traditions, a common idiom of spectacle, or a ritual *koine*.[28] If an image could be tied to a specific structure or monument, context might offer a hint as to the nature and subject of the representations. Unfortunately, many, perhaps most, of the relevant images float free from any concrete context, and so literary evidence, with all its attendant difficulties, must necessarily provide the (all too tenuous) clues for identification. In the end, even if specific identifications are mistaken, the images offer a sense of how ancient Roman patrons, artists, and viewers communicated, represented, and understood the performance of processions. They offer a sense of the sensorium of procession.

Moreover, images transformed individual performances, singular events, into enduring visual commemorations – turning actions into memories.[29] Depictions of the *pompa circensis* inevitably condensed and so perhaps distorted the procession as performed, but they also shaped and were shaped by ways of seeing such processions. Representations of processions were influenced by earlier imagery even as they commemorated a specific performance and molded its remembrance in such a way that could affect future performances, or at least expectations and interpretations of future performances. Much the same may be said about the literary evidence. Fabius Pictor may well have invented a *pompa circensis* out of whole cloth and Dionysius may have further falsified that description with his own interventions. Even so, the description may have become normative, impacting the ceremonial expectations of literate Romans and so also subsequent processional performance. Processional performances were remembered and re-shaped in representations in image and text, archives of Roman cultural memory and potential resources for new performances.

In addition to such (standard) difficulties, evidence for the *pompa circensis* is scattered widely, ranging from texts (including history, poetry, apologetic, law, and epigraphy) to sculpture, mosaic, and coins as well as (other) archaeological materials. And so by necessity, any examination of the procession that wishes to be something other than an exegesis of Dionysius of Halicarnassus (which is nevertheless necessary) must necessarily reconstruct the procession in some way or another. In short, some kind of ideal-type seems unavoidable – an ideal-type that need not be a fanciful assemblage which piles up all extant evidence, no matter how distant in time, space, genre, or media. An ideal-type may be more Weberian in spirit, if not exactly to the letter: a tool of analysis that does not smooth away the differences between different kinds (or dates) of evidence, but one that seeks to highlight certain key features of the procession within a restricted time and place.[30] Such an ideal-type demands a wide range of research protocols, as the admittedly exiguous evidence – found in a surprisingly wide variety of materials – must be examined according to germane methods. Ciceronian rhetoric differs from antiquarian commentary; imperial law differs from a papyrus circus program. The chronological range and variety of the evidence can be used to chart the development of the procession and its representations – one of the goals of this study – rather than a compressed, anachronistic imaginary ideal-type.

Part I aims to reconstruct an ideal-type of the late republican circus procession (ca. 200–45 BCE) before Caesar's fateful interventions, based on evidence largely limited to the late republic or within its communicative, as opposed to cultural, memory. Communicative (or social) memory includes orally or informally communicated memories often of direct experiences, which tend to fade in eighty to one hundred years, while cultural memory may endure, even if unused, for millennia housed in rituals, texts (even histories), places, and monuments – a distinction akin in many ways to functional and storage memory.[31] For example, the stories that the old folks of Alexandria may have heard from their grandparents about the grand procession of Ptolemy II would be communicative memory, stories usually lost in the passage of time. The penteteric festival records or, better, the texts of Callixeinus and Athenaeus are archives of cultural memory, enduring memory resources even now.

This memory-driven circumscription of the evidence may, at times, lead to some (seeming) oddities. For example, Juvenal and Tertullian are both essential witnesses to the crown worn by the *praeses ludorum* – a crown whose history may well extend back into the republic.[32] Pompey was authorized to wear triumphal attire and a golden crown at the circus games.[33] Nonetheless, the crown of a *praeses ludorum* in a *pompa circensis* was not explicitly mentioned until the high empire. The crown may have been subsumed under the most august clothing of those who led the *tensae* (led a circus procession) or conducted a triumph in Livy's phrase, but it did not warrant special mention – the crown was not yet an essential element of the recollection of the circus procession.[34] The situation, if not also the dress, of the game-giver changed in the high empire and so the crown of the *praeses ludorum* is deferred to a discussion of elites in the imperial circus procession, when such distinction may have mattered more in lower-stakes battles for visibility.

Its hermeneutical limitations notwithstanding, there seems to have been a similar conception of communicative memory in ancient Rome, particularly with respect to its transmission and duration. According to Tacitus, Tiberius feared a disturbance at the funeral of Augustus in 14 CE, as had happened at the funeral of Julius Caesar nearly sixty years prior, so he deployed soldiers to ensure its orderly performance. "Those who had seen personally or who had heard from their parents about that day of still undigested servitude and of freedom served up again unsuccessfully, when the slaughter of the dictator Caesar seemed to some the worst of acts, to others the finest," chuckled at such precautions, for Augustus had long lived in peace as princeps.[35] Whatever its historicity, the scene does suggest that the memory of the late republic could endure in oral memory passed down from parent to child. However subjectively remembered and inconsistently transmitted, Tacitus imagined that direct memories of the funeral of Caesar lasted into the reign of Tiberius. Tacitus also had Marcus Aper, in a dialogue set during the reign of Vespasian, insist that there may still be someone living who had heard Cicero in *viva voce* before he died in 43 BCE, for "there is a sum of one hundred and twenty years from the death of Cicero to the present, the life span of one man."[36] Though far-fetched as a realistic lifespan, Tacitus seems to suggest that Cicero's oratory was still within the limits of lived, oral (or communicative) memory one hundred and twenty years later. The recollection of his rhetorical performances had not yet transitioned to a world of texts and cultural memory – it had not yet become myth.

By restricting the evidence as much as possible to that produced in the city of Rome before the advent of Caligula (37 CE), this ideal-type hopes to capture something of the texture of a late "republican" circus procession between Fabius Pictor and Dionysius: how it might have been experienced, interpreted, or remembered. Part I is not, then, a history of the circus procession in the republic; it does not take stock of the development of the *pompa* over time, a difficult prospect given that the sources are in fact overwhelmingly late republican or early imperial (ca. 50 BCE to 50 CE).[37] And so, this study has bracketed the issues of origins and early history in favor of an analysis of the procession as it appeared and was remembered in the period when the evidence was produced – in other words, an ideal-type of the circus procession at Rome ca. 200–45 BCE.[38] Assuredly, this ideal-type does not correspond to any actually performed procession – though hopefully it illuminates or coheres with an actual performance. But then again, an ideal-type is a tool of analysis, not description. It aims to take account of the constituent elements and organization of the procession, its grammar, syntax, and signification, its basic contours, and its practical logic, not to recount any particular performance. In addition to sketching what are hopefully the salient characteristics of a generic (in the sense of characteristic and common or non-specific) late-republican *pompa circensis*, it also offers a point of comparison with the changes wrought first by imperial autocracy and then by late-antique fragmentation. In other words, Part I presents a semiotic analysis of the phenomenology of the procession (a thick description), while Part II tackles its historical development from Julius Caesar to late antiquity. In the end, however, any history of the *pompa circensis* is necessarily written in the subjunctive – it is conditional, provisional.

II IDIOMS OF SPECTACLE BETWEEN HELLENISM AND IMPERIALISM

In addition to illustrating the evidentiary problems that harry the study of ancient processions, Athenaeus also offers a window onto another issue bedeviling the study of Roman public ceremonies: Hellenic influence. According to the dining sophists, Antiochus IV, "wishing to outdo [L. Aemilius] Paulus in magnificence" – whose spectacular victory celebration in 168 BCE at Amphipolis had already acquired a degree of fame – staged an impressive set of games in the mid 160s BCE at Daphnae in the suburbs of Antioch which opened with a procession that was so lavish that the sophists could only cursorily trace its contours.[39] In this case, however, Athenaeus' source,

Polybius, was a contemporary of the events (though not a witness). Some of Polybius' own history survives, though not this section: again it is known only from Athenaeus, who again may have faithfully transmitted the "fragment." Polybius' (or Athenaeus') rather extravagant description of the procession with "a hundred chariots drawn by six horses and forty drawn by four horses, and then a chariot drawn by four elephants and another drawn by a pair, and finally thirty-six elephants in single file with their housings" seems fantastical – though just the sort of thing a self-aggrandizing autocrat would do.[40]

Regardless of its (possible) rhetorical exaggeration, the description raises the thorny question of influence. The grand procession of Ptolemy II and other over-the-top productions of the Hellenistic kings are "often assumed to have influenced, directly or indirectly, the form, grandeur, and artifice of the Roman triumph," as Mary Beard has noted.[41] In this particular case, however, Antiochus sought to surpass Roman spectacle in a procession "headed by five thousand men in the prime of life armed after the Roman fashion and wearing breastplates of chain armour."[42] Rome may have looked to Greece and Etruria for inspiration, but as its republican empire expanded and its coffers swelled, Rome developed its own, semi-independent spectacle traditions, often outstripping, even if only in sheer opulence and repetition, their forebears.[43] Roman processions like the *pompa circensis* may have, eventually, influenced Hellenistic ones as much as they were influenced by them.

Nonetheless, Dionysius of Halicarnassus, in his numerous editorial additions to Fabius Pictor's description, tirelessly insisted that the *pompa circensis* drew on Greek heritage. Athletes dressed only in loin-clothes followed the custom "as it was first done by the Greeks."[44] The martial dancers took their choreography from "a very ancient Greek custom."[45] The satyr dancers performed "the Greek *sikinnis*."[46] Even the iconography and organization of the gods followed Greek models, and the sacrifices at the conclusion of the procession were "performed according to the customs established by the Greeks with reference to sacrifice."[47] Undoubtedly, prestigious Greek models influenced Roman processional practices. Equally certainly, the Etruscans also provided Rome with some of its spectacle machinery.[48] However, at some point, seemingly in the second century BCE, Rome began producing ever more spectacular ceremonies based on its own traditions and in competition with memories of past performances, whose magnificence would only intensify with the further growth of empire and the advent of emperors.

The tangled lines of influence become more complicated when considering the relations between Roman processions. As Dionysius noted, "even at the funerals of illustrious persons I have seen, along with the other participants, bands of dancers impersonating satyrs who preceded the bier and imitated in their motions the *sikinnis*, and particularly at the funerals of the rich."[49]

Furthermore, "the triumphal entrances also show that raillery and fun-making in the manner of satyrs were an ancient practice native to the Romans, for the soldiers escorting a victory celebration had license to lampoon and jeer the most distinguished men, even generals."[50] To be sure, there was a great deal of shared ground among Rome's great *pompae*, but should such overlaps (for example, the Jupiterian appearance of both the *triumphator* and the *praeses ludorum*) necessarily imply that the *pompa circensis* was originally a continuation of the triumph, as Mommsen argued long ago, starting out from where the triumph ended?[51] Even if an evolutionary origins theory has been challenged, why should the triumph be taken as the main motor of processional spectacle? After all, the triumph was an exceedingly rare spectacle, whose production depended upon the talents of performers, professionals, and others whose training, traditions, and skills would have been developed at (not to mention their gainful employment depended upon) more regularly occurring ceremonies – like the *pompa circensis*.

Perhaps Rome's three great *pompae* should be seen as semi-independent adaptations of a Roman dialect of a Mediterranean *koine* of spectacle.[52] Though there was a good bit of cross-pollination across the full range of Roman public ceremonies, each of the three great *pompae* seems to have developed its own traditions based on its own performance histories and in response to its own changing historical contexts.[53] The circus procession may be envisioned as a long line of magistrates, contestants, and performers leading the gods to the circus; the triumph as a train of booty and weapons leading the general and his army to Capitoline Jupiter; and the funeral as a solemn (and satirized) procession of ancestral masks leading the deceased in the honored position toward the end to a burial site. That is, the grammar and syntax of each procession, its participants and their order and organization, depended upon whose escort the *pompa* provided: the *pompa circensis* escorted the gods to the circus, the *pompa triumphalis* took the *triumphator* to the Capitol, while the *pompa funebris* traveled from the deceased's home to the Forum and finally to a burial location somewhere beyond the *pomerium*. The impulse toward wonder, toward spectacle, may have similarly varied. The magistrate and the aediles who organized and paid for the games would certainly have sought to attract large crowds, but the repetition of the circus procession, from three to fourteen times per year, may have curbed the impulse toward or at least the expenditure on extravagant display, to a degree at any rate. By contrast, the relative infrequency of the triumph seems to have demanded over-the-top spectacle financed by the often-stupefying profits of conquest, while the funeral procession needed to balance visibility with grief (or at least the expected funereal appearance). It seems clear, then, that the *pompa circensis*, which drew upon a common idiom of spectacle, warrants an examination on its own terms.

III RITUAL RHYTHMS OF THE *POMPA CIRCENSIS*

The *pompa circensis* was first and foremost a ritual performance.[54] Although a multivalent and contested concept, the term "ritual performance" signals that each circus procession was a distinct skilled production, guided by tradition but open to innovation, and fundamentally interactive – a joint creation of participants and spectators. In other words, each iteration of the *pompa circensis* was a singular affair, an ephemeral event which varied each time it was staged; an arresting spectacle designed to attract attention; patterned and improvised; determined by rules and religious scruples but open to change; and conditioned by the dialectical relation between performers who might seek to showcase new talents and an audience whose expectations could not be wholly disappointed and whose reactions (excitement, boredom, apathy, anger) determined its success or failure. Unquestionably, the proposed ideal-type of a republican (-ish) *pompa circensis* – with its emphasis on the traditions, rules, and regulations that framed each performance – necessarily elides much of this variability. Persistent attention to ritual failures and historical developments attempts to counter this inevitable tendency, offering a glimpse of both the individuality of each performance as well as the adaptation of tradition.[55]

Attention needs to be paid to ritual rules, especially when they are broken, as well as what might be termed performance principles – the broad characteristics that seem to apply (more or less) to each performance without impairing the possibility of variation. First, the circus procession, like the other Roman *pompae*, was strongly marked by an alternation between gravity (hierarchy, structure, consensus, authority) and levity (license, sexuality, intoxication, violence). As is commonly held, processions were often weighty political affairs, offering a kind of civic self-representation, displaying a specially structured image of the city to the city itself. The *pompa circensis*, however, was also the introduction to the *ludi* (games), and so its levity helped to fashion the ludic space in which the games unfolded. A similar play between resonance and wonder animated processional performance.[56] On the one hand, the performance reached beyond its frame to evoke or to connect to other rituals, places, practices, and memories (resonance). On the other hand, each performance also aimed at posterity, a place in Roman cultural memory, by means of exceptional and overwhelming spectacle (wonder) – fighting a battle against repetition which may have inured audiences to spectacular charms. In short, the performance of the circus procession was both serious and seriously fun, porous and singular, memorable or perhaps forgettable.

And finally, memory (individual and collective, communicative and cultural), though not really a performance principle, haunted the procession and its itinerary. Each participant had her own individual memories, based upon the various social frameworks of memories which she inhabited, that she brought to the performance.[57] These personal, as it were, or individual memories greatly determined the sorts of resonances any one person would have with civic, collective, or cultural memories (histories, images, symbols of Rome's past housed in places, buildings, monuments, ritual practices) as the procession traversed a landscape of memory from the Capitol to the Circus. This interaction between individual performer, her memories, and the itinerary, with its dense historical associations, produced an image of the city – a symbolic cityscape, but also, to a lesser degree, a kind of mental map of Rome's monumental core. The *pompa circensis* was an act of place-making, socially, culturally, and even physically.[58] In the end, the *pompa circensis* can be imagined as a *pompa hominum*, a parade of people consisting of the *praeses ludorum*, his entourage, contestants, and performers; a *pompa deorum*, a long line of gods represented in various forms; and an itinerary traversing some of Rome's most storied spaces, all animated by the dialectical oscillation between gravity/levity and resonance/wonder and also the weight of cultural memory, which allowed a Roman, whether participant or spectator, to locate herself in the imagination and on the ground.

Part I sketches the main features of the *pompa circensis*, its participants and itinerary, to develop a Weberian-inspired ideal-type of the *pompa circensis* as it might have been experienced, remembered, or imagined (all much the same thing in retrospect) in or just after the late republic. Chapter 1 opens with an analysis of the longest extant description of a *pompa circensis*, the processional protocol first penned by Fabius Pictor and later taken up by Dionysius of Halicarnassus, before turning to a detailed examination, not to say exegesis, of the *pompa hominum* (the non-divine participants in the procession), the impulse toward wonder (that is, efforts to render the procession and its itinerary memorable and spectacular), and the attendant risks and ritual failures of the "republican" *pompa circensis*. Chapter 2 turns to the *pompa deorum*, the long procession of gods represented or made present in various ways, and its performed theology – that is, the ways in which the procession imagined the gods and their relations with humanity as the procession unfolded. Chapter 3 tackles the itinerary, a landscape of memory, and its potential resonances for processional participants, which fashioned an image of Rome, both a symbolic representation, and, possibly, a concrete navigational aid. Altogether, the parade of people and gods and its itinerary of memory constitute the ideal-type of the circus procession as it emerged by the end of the republic or in its communicative memory.

Part II sets the ideal-type in motion, so to speak, assessing the imperial transformation and elite maintenance of the procession from Julius Caesar to its gradual disappearance sometime in late antiquity. Chapter 4 charts the interventions of the emperors in the procession: the inclusion of deified emperors and the imperial special dead, whose honors were calqued on those of the traditional gods, and the construction and reconstruction of buildings and monuments along the itinerary, which was caught between the restoration of memory and imperial aggrandizement. Chapter 5 takes a peek behind the veil of imperial power, first analyzing failed imperial performances, and then the continuing role of "ordinary" humans from political elites to processional professionals. Chapter 5 then analyzes ludic processions outside Rome and considers the history of the (amphi-)theater processions, offshoots of the *pompa circensis* whose even more meager evidentiary base allows for little more than a simple description. Chapter 6 treats the impact of Christian rhetoric and imperial law on the *pompa circensis* in late antiquity, which was arguably reduced to images of the emperors and Victory at the official level. However, some sub-imperial imagery still featured the traditional gods, while the itinerary featured the conspicuous restoration of a number of republican buildings – but not, it seems, imperial (cult) ones – and the construction of a Christian church in the monumental heart of the city. From its origins to its end, the *pompa circensis* seems to have continuously catalyzed the alchemical process by which financial capital became symbolic, by which power poured itself into pomp. Moreover, whatever its transformations, the circus parade seems to have remained a procession of gods, even if only imperial ancestors (not to say deified Christian emperors) and, possibly, the Christian God.

PART I

An ideal-type between the republic and memories of the republic

ONE

POMPA HOMINUM

Gravity and levity, resonance and wonder, ritual failure

After the armed choruses, bands of dancers playing satyrs came in procession . . . [who] mocked and mimicked the earnest dances, transforming them into rather comical affairs.

Dionysius of Halicarnassus, *Roman Antiquities* 7.72.10[1]

To judge from the rhetorically charged description of Dionysius of Halicarnassus, the *pompa circensis* worked simultaneously to put the Roman world in order in a reassuring representation of hierarchical consensus and to dissolve that order in ludic performance.[2] The procession opened with a *pompa hominum* (a parade of people) – a phrase calqued on Ovid's *pompa deorum* (a procession of gods) – whose regimented ranks of young Roman men in their parade best were mirrored by the legally stigmatized superstars of the arena, the charioteers, and the sexualized bodies of nearly naked athletes, while serious and warlike dancers served as a foil for frolicking groups of satyrs and Sileni.[3] In short, the procession continually shifted between gravity, marked by structure and solemnity, and levity, characterized by license and sexuality – at least in Dionysius' suspiciously regular, alternating sequence. Still, the oscillation between gravity and levity seems to have been one of the basic rhythms of the procession – a phrase intended to capture the dialectical nature of its performance: regulated by rules but still open to innovation.

The *pompa circensis* was also shaped by a creative tension between resonance and wonder and the ever-present risk of ritual failure. Ritual performances are not isolated or self-contained. Rather, they are bound up with historical, institutional, and even personal relations, negotiations, appropriations, and conflicts. As it traversed an itinerary through some of the most hallowed spaces of ancient Rome, the *pompa circensis* resonated with other rituals, ceremonies, processions, or even places, to paraphrase Stephen Greenblatt.[4] In other words, the circus procession reached beyond its performative boundaries to connect its participants, both human and divine, to other people, other practices, other places, and other times, conjuring the past, present, or even the future.[5] During any performance, echoes of collective civic memory and individual personal recollections, the opportunities and constraints of present circumstances (for example, social position, profession, gender, "ethnicity"), and the expectations and fears of future prospects would have (differentially) reverberated with every participant and spectator.[6] It is assuredly impossible to trace every or even many of the cacophonous echoes that would have resounded as the *pompa circensis* trailed its way through Rome, nonetheless it is possible to suggest at least a few of the potential resonances, especially for the participants, who, at least, can be known to some degree.

Some of these resonances would have emerged from the employment of an idiom of spectacle common to many Roman processions – links with the triumph featuring most prominently. Like the triumph, the *pompa circensis* sought to overwhelm spectators with sheer sensorial spectacularity. Spectacle, like wonder and unlike resonance, aims "to stop the spectator in his or her tracks, to convey an arresting sense of uniqueness, to evoke exalted attention," to invoke Greenblatt again.[7] As a spectacle, each iteration of the *pompa circensis* sought isolated singularity, to be an impressive and incomparable production whose fame would live on in cultural memory, in the texts of poets and historians, and in images public and private.[8] Of course, any particularly successful spectacle that so awed its audience would quickly become part of a more general repertoire upon which future spectacles could draw. It would establish a new web of associations and connections that the initial wonder had sought to cut. A miserable flop might more easily inscribe itself in Roman cultural memory than many ostensible triumphs.

That is to say, efforts to render the procession more spectacular, more memorable, in order to accrue a larger dividend of symbolic capital were risky. An audience might stand spellbound. Or it might reject, mock, or, worse still, simply ignore such attempts.[9] Furthermore, the procession, though subject to the flux and variability of any performance, was ensnared by a variety of regulations and traditions, whose violation could invalidate or simply vitiate the ceremony – even as the maintenance of some of these rules could seemingly compensate for an otherwise poor or even a failed performance. Even though ritual obligations constrained the *pompa circensis*, there were risks concomitant with any performance. Even if properly performed according to the expectations of tradition, even if spectacularly produced, a given procession may still fail to captivate its spectators. For example, there is no reason to believe that the procession before the *ludi Romani* of 168 BCE was not properly conducted. It also seems likely that the organizers would have attempted to mount a striking show. Nonetheless, after the first race "the people, in an instant forgetful of the spectacle, rushed down into the middle [of the race-track]" to hear the official report of a battle with Perseus declaring an overwhelming Roman victory.[10]

In the end and despite its shortcomings, Dionysius' long digression on the *pompa circensis*, which likely presents a procession that was never actually performed, might well express the essential rhythms of the processions. That is to say, Dionysius (based on Fabius Pictor) may have outlined a basic grammar, syntax, and process of signification, an ideal-type (to use Weberian language), or even a ritual *habitus*, a non-conscious pattern of practice in Bourdieu's terminology, from which any particular performance could have been produced.[11] These grammatical and syntactical elements – the participants, both human and divine, and their hierarchical order – as well as the rhythms of the procession (the alternation of gravity and levity, the oscillation between resonance and wonder, and the ever-present risk of ritual failure) could have constituted a basic pattern, *la langue*, from which any given iteration, *la parole*, could be generated, as it were.[12] In this way, Dionysius may be a (somewhat) reliable, if not also partial in every sense, guide to the general shape of the *pompa circensis* from its first emergence in the literary record around 200 BCE to its last performance in late antiquity – even as that shape changed over time and from one performance to the next. According to Dionysius, the *praeses ludorum* seems to have led the way, at the head of the *pompa hominum*, followed by a select coterie of the young men of Rome, contestants and athletes in the games, bands of dancers, and a group carrying ritual vessels and incense burners which introduced the *pompa deorum*.

I "RITUALS IN INK": DIONYSIUS OF HALICARNASSUS[13]

> For I promised at the end of the first book, which I composed and published concerning their origin, that I would confirm this thesis [that Romans are Greek colonists] by countless proofs, bringing forward their ancient customs, laws, and practices, which they have preserved down to my own time just as they received them from their ancestors. . . . Among these the first and the most authoritative of all are, I am persuaded, the things done by each city concerning the gods and divinities, that is ancestral worship.
>
> Dionysius of Halicarnassus, *Roman Antiquities*. 7.70.2–3[14]

Any analysis of the circus procession must depend substantially upon a digression penned by Dionysius of Halicarnassus, a Greek author writing a history of Rome while in residence in the city during the late first century BCE.[15] However, this description may be best characterized as a ritual in ink –

a rhetoric of ritual, not the ritual itself. Moreover, it is a ritual in ink with an agenda:

> Since I have come to this section of the history, I do not believe that it is necessary to pass over the things completed by [the Romans] at the festival, not so that my narrative might become more elegant by grasping at theatrical additions and flowery words, but so that something of the necessary matters might be confirmed: that the peoples who had joined in colonizing the city of the Romans were Greeks from the most renowned places and not, as some believe, barbarians and homeless.[16]

Even though Dionysius provided the longest account of a *pompa circensis*, he expressly offered it as the best proof that Romans were, in fact, Greeks, a motive which likely impacted his portrayal. Unfortunately, the late republican or early imperial games which he witnessed had long been influenced by Hellenistic culture. So Dionysius turned to an earlier source, the venerable Fabius Pictor, whose work predated the Roman conquest of Greece and was, according to Dionysius at any rate, uncontaminated by undue Greek influences. "I will produce ... evidence [from before Roman overseas conquests] ... using Quintus Fabius [Pictor] as my authority and needing no other proof at all. For the man is the most ancient of those who have written about Roman affairs, providing proof not only from what he heard, but also from what he himself knew."[17] Interspersed throughout the lengthy extract from Fabius Pictor, Dionysius offered his own comments and explanations, demonstrating the Greekness of certain Roman practices through substantial quotation from Homeric texts. Despite the commentary and Homeric excerpts, Dionysius may still have depended "almost word for word on the work of Fabius Pictor."[18] Although no independent text by Fabius Pictor has survived, Dionysius gave the impression, at least, that the earlier text had been faithfully transmitted, rendered, or paraphrased.

Fabius Pictor, in turn, purported to have described a very early – but not, seemingly, the earliest – circus procession, performed at the games (490 BCE) vowed by Aulus Postumius during the battle of lake Regillus when the last of the historical-mythical Etruscan kings who attempted to regain Rome was defeated.[19] Primordialist claims aside, he may actually have described the (much) later procession that preceded the annual *ludi Romani*. Even though a few Roman rituals would be detailed in writing, at least after the fact, for example the *acta* of the Arval Brethren or the Secular Games, it seems unlikely that any detailed account of this early circus parade existed almost three centuries later – though the early Roman annalistic tradition, on which extant histories like those of Livy and Dionysius depended, may have been broadly reliable.[20] A late-sixth-century BCE relief, with its staid line of chariots and attendants on foot from an archaic temple found at the foot of

4. Archaic terracotta relief with chariot procession, ca. 525–500 BCE

the Capitoline hill, suggests the kind of modest processional production values (or habits of visual commemoration) that early Rome could sustain (Figure 4). Though, admittedly, the simple composition of this archaic relief would not have been out of place in late-republican visual culture (for example, Figures 5, 6, and 8).[21]

Moreover, Fabius Pictor was a Hellenizing Roman, who wrote a kind of historical *apologia* for Rome in Greek, which was then used by a later Greek historian, Dionysius, to prove Rome's Greek heritage.[22] One may then reasonably doubt the accuracy of both texts. Fabius Pictor may have fabulated an ideal *pompa circensis* based on Greek models and contemporary Roman practice ("what he himself knew"), while Dionysius of Halicarnassus may have exaggerated the Greek elements to prove his thesis.[23] In other words, Fabius Pictor and Dionysius may have created a kind of Baudrillardian simulacrum, a copy without an original that very possibly came to serve as an authorizing archetype for later processions – even (other) textual ones, perhaps inspiring Vergil and Ovid, both near contemporaries of Dionysius, as well as Statius in the late first century CE.[24] In his *Thebaid* (ca. 92 CE), Statius described a green circus-like valley populated by a nearly numberless crowd. While awaiting the chariot races, the crowd watched a procession of sacrificial animals, followed by sculpted likenesses of heroic ancestors, divine and human, which evoked but also differed from the *pompa circensis* conjured by Fabius Pictor-Dionysius.[25]

Apart from the literary and historical complexities of Dionysius' *Roman Antiquities*, one should, in general, exercise a healthy skepticism with all descriptions of rituals. Such descriptions served the specific purposes of the author and so need to be situated within the "interpretative strategy" of the text.[26] Descriptions of rituals were a representation, an interpretation with interests that could stand at odds with historical "accuracy." For example, many accounts of the triumph attempt to impress their readers with inventive depictions of the staging, the sheer spectacle of the procession and its spectators, to the detriment of precise description.[27] In short, authors and texts shaped rituals. Even the basic act of narration would have organized and ordered the performance, during which neat divisions and classifications would have been impossible to maintain. And so, the nearly clinical unfolding of a textual procession may be the result of an exercise of order, the work of description rather than ritual.[28]

Even if only a mere representation of the parade, Dionysius' digression would have had to adhere to the expectations of his elite, literate audience (both Greek and Roman), which suggests that it would have both cleaved closely to Fabius Pictor's "original," however imaginary, and bore a family resemblance to contemporary processions. Even if Fabius Pictor-Dionysius did not accurately recount the actual program of a very early *pompa circensis*, their description may have been shaped by and may have shaped Roman expectations and Roman (literary) memories. In other words, the narrative could have been effected by "real" performances or a collective remembrance of such performances even as it could have effected subsequent performances and memories. That is, the text need not have described any particular *pompa circensis* to offer a kind a grammar and syntax of the ceremony, an account of its customary components and their order, as well as its rhythms. After all, the specifics of the ritual would certainly have changed from one performance to the next and over time. As a ritual, the circus procession may have been marked by repetition and rules, but as a performance this supposedly invariant act would have been a singular, ephemeral event, different from other iterations. Fabius Pictor-Dionysius may have captured something of the ritual traditions which guided any given performance.

In the end, a "ritual in ink" may, arguably, "translate" a spectacle performance into a textual representation or creatively repeat a ritual practice in a textual venue, so that a textual analysis of textual sources may still hope to engage with Roman ritual performance – or at least its reception and remembrance, as experience and interpretation are always already entangled.[29] That is, even if *merely* literary, the description of Fabius Pictor-Dionysius may still serve as a register of the concrete historical performances witnessed by its authors, as an expression or interpretation of the performance codes that governed processional production, and as a reflection upon those performance codes, to paraphrase, once again, Stephen Greenblatt.[30] And so, although this text cannot be read as a direct representation of historical reality, it still engaged extra-textual social and cultural relations and processes.[31] What is more, republican and imperial protocol officers had assuredly read or at least heard about the procession of Fabius Pictor-Dionysius – one generation's "bogus protocol" may become the next generation's ritual tradition.[32] The *pompa circensis* as conceived by the father of Roman history, Fabius Pictor, even if at secondhand from Dionysius, could have become a prestigious (literary) model which influenced those who financed, organized, and presided over the games.

II GRAVITY, LEVITY, AND RITUAL RESONANCE IN THE *POMPA HOMINUM*

"Those holding the greatest authority"

After justifying Fabius Pictor as his source and the *pompa circensis* as his example, Dionysius continued with a description of the procession: "Before beginning the contests, those holding the greatest authority arranged a procession in honor of the gods from the Capitolium through the Forum to the Circus Maximus."[33] Even though aediles (and after 22 BCE praetors) typically organized the public games, it seems that a consul, praetor, or even a specially appointed dictator – a magistrate with *imperium* – presided over the republican games: orchestrating the *pompa circensis*, performing the sacrifices, and signaling the start of the races.[34] By the early fourth century BCE, according to Livy, whichever magistrate piloted the *pompa circensis* was conspicuously dressed in "the most majestic garments of those who conduct the *tensae* or celebrate a triumph" and mounted on a chariot, probably a *biga* (a two-horse vehicle), at the head of the procession – probably.[35] Unfortunately, Dionysius did not precisely locate the president of the games, though by beginning his narration with the *praeses ludorum* he implied, at least, that such a magistrate led the way.[36]

The "most majestic" ensemble of the president of the games presents difficulties in untangling the relationship between the *pompa triumphalis* and the *pompa circensis*.[37] The similarities between the two processions may be explained "genetically," having a common origin or genealogical development, though by the fourth century BCE the two processions would likely have been at least semi-independent. Or perhaps the two processions had (more or less) independent origins, whose performances converged as Rome developed its own dialect of a Mediterranean-wide *koine* of spectacle, especially in the mid republic.[38] The coalescence of spectacle traditions would only accelerate during the empire and late antiquity when both the *adventus* ceremony and the circus procession became "triumphal" – or, perhaps better, more spectacular.[39] Whatever the "original" relationship between the two, they both exploited a common idiom of spectacle: the president of the games and the *triumphator* both dressed in august attire and drove a chariot along a somewhat shared itinerary.

Nevertheless, attention to ritual "function" and syntax reveals important differences.[40] Although drawing upon a shared vocabulary of sartorial and vehicular distinction, the triumph escorted the triumphant general, a kind of avatar of Jupiter, to Rome's sovereign god, while the circus procession conducted the gods from the same temple of Jupiter (and perhaps from other temples during games in honor of other gods) to the Circus. The *triumphator* occupied the most honored position near the end of the triumph on a *quadriga*, while the president of the games, also apparently a (lesser) avatar of Jupiter, seemingly led the *pompa circensis* on a *biga*, granting the gods the most distinguished place.[41]

Wherever the *praeses ludorum* was positioned and whatever the "origins" of his dress, it seems likely, though by no means certain, that lictors and perhaps others, potentially colleagues or even clients, escorted him from the Capitol to the Circus – a secondary but still important honor. To process in public, surrounded by crowds of colleagues and clients, was an honor for one and all and one eagerly sought and carefully stage-managed.[42] Though on foot, the lictors with their *fasces* and the others in their dazzling togas would assuredly have been prominent, though still overshadowed, perhaps quite literally, by the president towering above them in his chariot.[43] In order to impress the crowds and their elite peers, the entourage (and perhaps also other participants) may have adopted a pompous walk to fit the pompous occasion – perhaps some ostentatious gait, like Piso's supposedly monstrous and aggressive walk, which was worthy of a *pompa*, according to Cicero's invective, at least.[44]

One of two related but non-contiguous blocks from a fragmentary late-republican travertine relief – perhaps commissioned by the very magistrate who had presided over the games – seems to memorialize just such a scene, even while underscoring the uncertainty and ambiguity of the evidence (Figure 5).[45]

5. Two related travertine reliefs depicting a *pompa circensis*, ca. 50 BCE

On the first block, damaged on both ends, an *auriga* (or possibly a wingless Victory) drives a *biga* toward the right, followed by two trumpeters and a single *ferculum*-bearer in a short tunic, whose *ferculum* and co-bearers have unfortunately been lost. The second block, whose intact left side still has its decorative cornice, shows the end of this register of the relief. Four lictors amble to the right, preceding four well-heeled figures in togas, one seemingly a young man, a group which apparently stood at the end of procession. This group may represent the game-giver and his entourage, the likely option, the priests and magistrates who marched just before the gods, or even the officials who accompanied the sacrificial animals who, in Dionysius' description, seem to have brought the procession to its conclusion.

The identification of the figures, their overall location within the procession (especially if the visual narrative extended over multiple registers, not uncommon in Roman visual culture), and whether or not the tableau represents a *pompa circensis* at all remain unknowable. Without inscriptions or other overt clues, such scenes remain unyielding to precise interpretation. Moreover, this compressed and multivalent representation of a complex ritual inevitably simplified or may have even deliberately distorted the actually performed procession. If the frieze comes from a funerary monument, the visual narrative may have been purposely configured to highlight the deceased by placing him in a more visually prominent location. That is, the image may have conformed to the dictates of commemoration instead of ritual obligation. And so, the scene, if it is a *pompa circensis*, may or may not conform to the description offered by Dionysius, whose digression may or may not accurately represent processional protocol. At any rate, on at least one reasonable reading, the (upper) left corner of the relief tentatively suggests a group of lictors, the president of the games, and his entourage all on foot and all dressed in their finest togas.

The procession proper was only the most prominent element in the spectacle for the *praeses ludorum*. "When the procession was brought to completion, the highest [officials] and priests to whom belonged the hallowed task sacrificed oxen straightaway."[46] Dionysius described at some length the sacrificial procedure in order to quote also at some length its supposed Homeric antecedent. Unfortunately, however, he did not locate either the sacrificial victims and their associated officials, priests, and cultic attendants (*victimarii* and *popae*) in the procession or the site of the sacrifice in the Circus. Nonetheless, it seems reasonable to suggest that this group processed at the very end of the parade, perhaps after the gods, to an altar just in front of the *pulvinar*, where the images and symbols of the gods were installed. Wherever in the Circus the sacrifices took place, the ritual would likely have been conducted in full view of the spectators, rendering the *cura deorum* (care of the gods) palpably plain to all in attendance. Indeed, this sacrifice seems to have been sufficiently prominent for at least one of its sacrificial attendants, a *popa*, to have been infamously associated with the Circus Maximus.[47]

Finally, once the procession and sacrifices were successfully concluded, the most anticipated moment of the entire ceremony arrived. The president of the games may have driven his chariot to the *carceres*, the starting gates, from which he would give the signal to start the races.[48] Ennius, as quoted by Cicero, could compare the breathless anticipation of the crowd waiting for the results of the augural contest between Romulus and Remus with the precise instant "when the consul is about to give the sign to start the race, while everyone eagerly watches the mouths of the *carceres* out of whose painted jaws the chariots soon will come."[49] As the magistrate stood next to the gates either on the arena floor or perhaps on an elevated platform, the enormous crowd was *his*, awaiting *his* signal – an event worthy of remembrance. A late-republican relief now in the Vatican Museums represents this very moment in a single, temporally compressed scene: the president of the games flanked by a lictor stands to the left with his left arm raised, poised to give the start signal, while to the right a *quadriga* has already burst forth from the starting gates.[50] With the signal and perhaps also a trumpet blast, the eagerly anticipated races were on.[51] Or as Ovid would have it:

> Now they've cleared the course. The praetor's starting the first race.
> Four-horse chariots. Look – they're off.[52]

From the opening procession to the last race, massive crowds gathered at the beneficence and so also to the benefit of the *praeses ludorum* – a ritual alchemy that transformed financial resources into symbolic capital, the honor and esteem so valued by republican elites.[53]

"Boys on the verge of manhood"

Following the presiding magistrate (possibly) and his probable entourage, the pride of the Roman youth, whether on horseback or on foot, paraded with military precision:

> At the head of the procession, boys on the verge of manhood and of the right age to take part in the procession led the way: on horseback those whose fathers met the financial requirements to be equestrians, on foot those who would serve in the infantry; the first in troops and squadrons, the second in divisions and companies as if going to school.[54]

In other words, these young men were arranged according to their census classifications in which wealth determined hypothetical military liabilities. The young men from wealthier and so more powerful families who would serve as cavalry were to ride in front, while the young men from poorer families who would serve as infantry walked behind.

According to Dionysius, this display was meant to impress strangers with the number and virtue of the flower of the Roman youth – though by the late first century BCE the infantry recruited little from the populace of the city of Rome. Even if its military coloring had faded by the end of the republic, sons of senators and equestrians on horseback and, perhaps, sons of clients of the organizers of the games on foot could still have made a splendid display, trailing behind the *praeses ludorum*.[55] It may be that these young men, especially the elite young men, functioned like an honor guard in the late republic – much like the ephebes of the Greek east – a troop that would feature ever more prominently as a ceremonial corps in imperial Rome.[56] Even if its composition changed from Fabius Pictor to Dionysius, nonetheless, a hierarchically arranged selection of Roman youth – sons of elite peers and clients arranged according to census ranking – could still have participated in the parade.

Though ranks of young Roman men might well have impressed foreigners, the punctiliously arrayed youth may also have served as a mechanism of Roman self-representation. These youth, as described by Dionysius, were arranged according to socio-religious categories produced in another ritual: namely the census, a quinquennial ritual that classified the entire populace of Rome according to wealth and concomitant military obligations. The census arguably represented Rome according to a sociological grid, a system of knowledge that encompassed the entire city, whose abstract social categories were made concrete both in the census and also the *pompa circensis*.[57] Both ceremonies ritually mapped and performed Roman social identity. In other words, ancient (elite) Romans imagined and produced the contours of their own society in the census, which, in a kind of redundancy – perhaps something like a stronger form of resonance – the *pompa circensis* re-employed. The procession then embodied, displayed, and disseminated this ritual image of Rome to the city itself, or rather to the spectators, through its dramatic performance.[58] In effect, the entire (imagined, but not imaginary) city marched from the Capitol to the Circus Maximus as the processional performance itself made the sociological grid real and effective – even if the military service these categories also represented were increasingly less significant to inhabitants of the capital. Both the census and the *pompa circensis*, in this limited way, were the will to power of a form of social knowledge. And so, in this sense, the procession was as much a representation of the city to itself (and also to foreigners) as the city's production or re-production.[59]

"The charioteers followed"

The competitors, charioteers, and other athletes who would participate in the games followed this marching image of Roman social structure. Dionysius, following Fabius Pictor, maintained: "The charioteers followed after [the

Roman youth] driving four horses or two or unyoked horses. After them came the competitors in both the light and heavy athletic events, their bodies naked except for a covering over their loins."[60] The presence of athletes in a procession set in the earliest days of the republic, however, seems to contradict a tradition reported by Livy according to which M. Fulvius Nobilior provided games in 186 BCE in which "a contest of athletes was then for the first time made a spectacle for the Romans."[61] The inconsistent traditions may be resolved – perhaps Livy only referred to purely Greek athletic competitions – but it does call into question the historical accuracy of Fabius Pictor, whose primordial procession may well have been a more recent confection.

At any rate, with the arrival of the charioteers and athletes, gravity gave way to levity – a basic rhythm of the entire procession: an assertion of structure and order followed by its inversion or parody. In the ludic space of the *pompa circensis*, the contestants, precisely divided into their own hierarchies of honor and prestige, founded on skill, risk, and wealth (prize amounts), presented a strange but strong parallel to the Roman youth in front of them.[62] The ranked contestants, among whom a certain proximity to warfare (or rather its simulation) also reigned, represented a kind of reversal or even a distorted reflection of the Roman youth. The fresh flush of youth, perhaps embarrassed, perhaps thrilled, perhaps displaying just the right touch of elite ennui, gave way to experienced professionals or perhaps terrified boys determined or desperate to win fame and money; military dress was replaced by the charioteers' close-fitting, belted tunics and caps or even the athletes' simple loincloths; and a socio-military hierarchy gave way to celebrity, as the superstars of the arena, the *quadriga*-drivers, led their section.

Agitatores (*quadriga*-drivers) came first, followed by the other *aurigae* (charioteers), and then the rest of the lesser competitors and athletes trailed behind – each attended, perhaps, by his own support staff, flag-bearers, groomsmen, or other sporting personnel.[63] As these infamous athletes (the charioteers) were the main draw of the greatest show in the Roman world, a late republican *praeses ludorum* unsurprisingly chose to include a (well-known?) charioteer driving a *biga* in the visual commemoration of his games (Figure 5).[64] On the first block of the pair of late-republican travertine reliefs, a charioteer drives his *biga* to the right followed by trumpeters and a *ferculum*-bearer. It would seem that a *biga*-driver was as important as the gods and the game-giver as emblems of the circus procession – at least in this relief.

The equine competitors, the horses, were also popular and so it seems plausible that savvy organizers of the games would have included them and their full panoply in the procession. Another late-first-century BCE relief (though from northern Italy) depicts a pair of horses each accompanied by a young man in a cap (an *auriga*?) and trailed by a lictor lead four togate figures toward the right where a pair of *togati* awaits them (Figure 6).[65] Though the

6. Procession of horses accompanied by riders and lictors flanked by *togati*, limestone, late first century BCE

relief does not seem to represent a *pompa circensis* – indeed its train of horses and attendants could have featured in a number of ceremonies – it does offer some sense of how the parade of contestants might have looked. An early imperial lamp (50–100 CE) conjures up a similar scene, though one more clearly derived from chariot racing. A porter bearing a sign, likely listing the horse's name and wins, headed a victory procession, followed by what appears to be a groom guiding the lead horse of the triumphant chariot team accompanied by three supporters or perhaps support staff, one of whom might be the winning charioteer with his arms upraised while the other two hold palm branches (Figure 7).[66] From the early empire to late antiquity, statues of particularly successful charioteers may even have been carried on *fercula* in the procession (Figures 78–79 in Chapter 6).[67]

7. Lamp with a horse led in a post-race victory procession, pottery, 50–100 CE

"Numerous choruses of dancers"

The ludic atmosphere escalated as troops of dancers followed hard on the heels of these ranks and rows of boys and competitors. Much as Greeks regarded Dionysus as a foreign god, even though he was thoroughly Greek, Romans imagined the first group of dancers as foreigners, fancifully deriving the name *ludiones* (players) from *Lydioi* (Lydians), who settled in Italy and became Etruscans – from where they came to Rome.[68] After all, no true (elite, male) Roman would dance – "for no one sober dances at all, unless he is completely insane."[69] Far-fetched etymologies aside, the ascribed alterity of the *ludiones* seems apt since they introduced the other; the *ludiones* opened the way to the ludic space in which the games took place. Equally, one may say that the *ludiones* opened the way for the sacred, as shortly after the dancers, the gods themselves would appear.

Among this group of dancers, order and precision reigned:

> Numerous choruses of dancers divided into three groups followed the contestants – the first consisting of men, the second boys, and the last children – behind whom flutists blowing old-fashioned short pipes, as happens even at this time, and cithara-players striking seven-stringed ivory lyres and instruments called "barbita" followed closely.[70]

With this band of dancers, the rhythm of the procession seems to return to the military solemnity of the Roman youth – levity gave way in its turn to gravity as the notorious contestants in the games yielded to "the bellicose and serious dance" of the *ludiones*.[71] These martial *ludiones* sported "crimson tunics fastened with bronze belts, swords hung at their sides, and they carried spearheads that were shorter than average length. The men also had bronze helmets adorned with remarkable crests and feathers."[72] Elsewhere, Dionysius described these "leaders of the procession," "clothed in remarkable tunics and helmets, holding swords and bucklers, marching in file."[73]

In another mid-first-century BCE fragmentary relief probably from Rome, what appear to be two armed dancers (*ludiones*) wearing crested helmets, one holding a shield and a short rod, stand to the right, followed by a lyre player (*fidicen*) who looks out toward the viewer and a pair of double flute-players (*tibicines*), with what appears to be a group of three prisoners at the left (Figure 8).

8. *Ludiones* leading musicians followed by captives in a triumph, marble, mid first BCE

9. *Ludio*-herald with a *sidus Iulium* on the shield: denarius, 17 BCE: obverse: AVGVST DI-VI F LVDOS SAE

Though this image likely represents a triumph (or an ovation) – the musicians had donned crowns and the "barbarian" prisoners of war had their arms tied behind their backs – it may also serve to illustrate the importance of these serious and martial dancers with their musical accompaniment.[74] They, like the *praeses*, gods on *fercula*, and competitors, warranted visual commemoration as symbols of a procession. *Ludiones* in their iconic garb could even serve as shorthand for the games as a whole – much as the proper performance of a single member of this troop could render legitimate games that were otherwise a ritual failure. For the *ludi Saeculares* in 17 BCE and again in 88 CE, Augustus and then Domitian had coins minted depicting, seemingly, a lone *ludio* dressed in a tunic, wearing a helmet decorated with feathers, and holding a round shield (and a caduceus in 17 BCE) as a synecdoche for the entire festival (Figure 9).[75] A group of young *ludiones* anxiously awaiting their turn to march may also feature on an Augustan monument commemorating these same Secular Games – or perhaps some triumph or other – to judge from a mid-sixteenth-century CE drawing.[76]

In addition to their attire (helmets, shields, and spears), the choreography of the *ludiones* also inculcated a martial atmosphere. "One man guided each group of dancers, a man who displayed the forms of the dance to the rest and was the first to represent the quick military steps, for the most part in a rhythm of four beats."[77] That is, the dance itself imitated military gestures with its careful execution and use of weapons. Moreover, such militarized movement echoed the Roman youth, who were ranked and arranged in military order. The *ludiones* also resonated with the martial precision of the youth in yet another way: both groups were faking it. The Roman youth were arranged according to their (merely) potential and (only) theoretical future roles in the military *as if* heading to the practice fields. Similarly, the *ludiones* imitated war by gesture and costume, but they were not (necessarily) soldiers and the *ludi* were not battle. The *ludiones* were professional players, whose "dummy-weapons," cut shorter than usual, gave away the game – as illustrated, perhaps, by the short staff *ludio* in Figure 8.[78] The *pompa circensis* was a performance in a full sense: the Roman youth engaged in what may have been a non-conscious performance of their social identities, simulating their progress to the training grounds; while the *ludiones* presented a carefully choreographed display of skill, playing at being soldiers.[79]

Moreover, much as the Roman youth were ordered according to their ceremonially conferred census status, this first chorus of dancers evoked a separate set of ritual performers, the Salian priests. Dionysius insisted that the song and dance, as it were, of the Salian priests were clearly distinct from those of the *ludiones*; that is, the Salian priests seem to have performed distinct choreography and sung a distinct hymn. Nonetheless, their martial attire seems to have been strikingly similar. In fact, *ludiones* and Salian priests are difficult to distinguish in iconographical sources, which present a confused collection of undifferentiated armed dancers, whose precise identities or affiliations cannot be known.[80] Despite such superficial similarities, it seems that the Salians and *ludiones* were as different as their social statuses: the Salians, a prestigious group of priests, were elite free men singing a distinctive hymn, while the *ludiones* were lower class professional players.[81] Like the Roman youth, these dancers may have appeared grave at first glance, but they were also quite light, quite playful. Likewise, while the charioteers may have seemed light, their competitions were seriously popular and seriously grave, that is deadly. This was also true of the next group of dancers, the sartyrs and Sileni, who may also seem, at first glance, to have been merely lighthearted.

"Bands of dancers playing satyrs"

Much as the hierarchically organized competitors reflected and distorted the solemn image of Roman society presented by the Roman youth, the group of dancers who followed the martial *ludiones* explicitly lampooned their "bellicose and serious dance."

> After the armed choruses, bands of dancers playing satyrs came in procession, performing the Greek *sikinnis*. Those portraying Sileni wore woolly tunics, which some call "rustics," and were covered in flowers of every kind; while those who appeared as satyrs wore girdles around their loins and goatskins with their locks of hair standing straight up on their heads and other such things. These [dancers] mocked and mimicked the earnest dances, transforming them into rather comical affairs.[82]

If the martial dancers opened the door to the ludic, the satyrs and Sileni kicked it down. As monstrous and common companions of the god Dionysus, satyrs, mythical young men with goat legs, and Sileni, typically older men with horse ears, were apt figures to turn the city upside down, inciting an atmosphere of license and abandon. Their ridicule of the serious and somber – the rigid marching order of the youth echoed in the warlike dance of the *ludiones* – dissolved in laughter the carefully constructed distinctions which military and ritual discipline had produced. The satyrs not only burlesqued the martial choreography of the first chorus, their gyrations may also have been absurdly and comically sexual, suggestive, and seductive, which Dionysius' supposedly prude sensibility forced him to gloss over.[83] If the athletes reflected Roman social structure (embodied by the youth) as if in a fun-house mirror, that mirror now shattered: there was no structure, there was no order. Assertions of order and structure, of hierarchy and solemnity, were outmatched by disorder, dissolution, chaos, laughter, and a bit of sexualized mischief.[84]

Comical and sexual levity was a regular feature of Roman rituals. As Dionysius himself noted, soldiers "escorting a victory celebration had license to lampoon and jeer the most distinguished men, even generals."[85] Famously, Caesar's army had warned "the men of Rome, look out for your wives; we're bringing the bald adulterer [Caesar himself] home."[86] Dancers playing satyrs and Sileni even performed their salacious routines during the funeral processions of the powerful, a perhaps strangely carnevalesque accompaniment to a somber and serious (but also highly political) affair. Even so, as a public display, funerary obsequies, as might be expected, drew upon a common idiom of spectacle, of which a rhythm of gravity and levity was a particularly prominent feature.[87] After the circus procession, the wild dance of the satyrs and Sileni may well have continued during the games themselves, with musicians and dancers entertaining the crowds during the lull between the races or other events – a means for these paid performers to earn their keep and, of course, something to keep the *furor circensis* on a low boil.[88]

In addition to its festive burlesque, common to the triumph and the funeral procession, the ribaldry of the satyrs and Sileni also resonated strongly with the drunken sexuality and bawdy violence of the Lupercalia. During this festival, the *luperci*, elite young men girt in only goatskin loincloths, according to Dionysius, or perhaps just a goatskin cloak or even nothing at all, ran through the center of Rome whipping those that they encountered with goatskin thongs.[89] In a further ritual crossover, some of the young men on horseback may also have been (or would be) *luperci*, a sacred service of the Roman equestrians whose wild romp through the city seems to have covered some of the same ground as did the *pompa circensis*.[90]

"Censers in which incense and frankincense were burned"

The final section of the *pompa hominum* seems designed to prepare the way for the gods who would follow.

> After these bands of dancers, a crowd of cithara players and many flute players passed by; and after them, the men who attended the censers in which incense and frankincense were burned along the entire route and the men bringing silver and gold ritual vessels, both sacred and civic.[91]

Flutes and lyres announced the imminent arrival of the gods. Incense offerings – with incense perhaps purchased on the *vicus Turarius* (Incense Street), as the *vicus Tuscus*, a street on the itinerary, would sometimes be known in the late empire – invited them to appear: a typical preparatory ritual which commonly preceded a sacrifice, though it was also sometimes a sacrifice in its own right, and a traditional way to escort divine images.[92] Finally, gold and silver ritual vessels, an element of Ovid's *aurea pompa*, which were probably carried by priestly *apparitores* supervised by aediles dressed in purple togas, constituted the final element of the parade of people.[93] Cicero may have had such a dazzling display in mind when he repeated an adage about Socrates' reputed disaffection for wealth: "When a great quantity of gold and silver was being carried in a procession, Socrates said, 'How much there is I do not need!'"[94] In sum, the *pompa hominum* presented a double alternation of gravity and levity – Roman youth mirrored by contestants, and *ludiones* lampooned by satyrs and Sileni – that loosened the grip of traditional social mores and created a ludic environment, into which incense-bearers and attendants bearing sacred and civic vessels led the sacred. Accompanied by vibrant strains of music and trailing after plumes of perfumed smoked in which luminous glimmers of silver and gold glinted in the Roman sun, gods and humans were conducted from the gilded temple of Capitoline Jupiter to the cramped and boisterous Circus Maximus.

III WONDER: SPECTACLE AND THE *POMPA CIRCENSIS*

The political culture of the Roman republic, characterized by an elite peer competition for honor and glory (and offices), "was in many ways a culture of spectacle . . . a culture of seeing and being seen" – but "if Being, for the ancient Romans, was being seen, being seen was a basic existential risk."[95] To be noble (*nobilis*), elite Romans needed to be conspicuous – known, notable, and above all visible in the right way.[96] Cicero mocked Piso's supposed Epicurean distaste for public self-display by having an imagined Piso declare: "vanity, mere vanity . . . to chase applause, to be borne through the city [in triumph], to wish to be conspicuous," when one should rather have sought such honored visibility.[97] To produce a spectacular set of games was a common tactic to achieve such distinction. As Cicero also contended, "magnificent [games] are expected from the very best men in their year of aedileship."[98] As aediles, Julius Caesar and Marcus Bibulus lavished the city with a dazzling set of games, some jointly financed, others paid for solely by Caesar. As a result, "Marcus Bibulus . . . suffered the same fate as Pollux, for just as the temple in the Forum that was sacred to the twin brothers was simply known as the temple of Castor, so the munificence of [Marcus Bibulus] and Caesar was spoken of simply as Caesar's."[99] Every aedile apparently sought to awe his audience with wonder, in Greenblatt's phrase, to capture the rapt attention of the crowds of Rome with a show-stopping performance, as it were, that would endure in Roman cultural memory.[100]

The *pompa circensis* was not immune from this urge toward spectacle. From the "triumphally" accoutred president of the games and his pompous entourage to the martial and mad choreography of the choruses of dancers and the smoking censers and glittering processional vessels, all accompanied by the blare of music, the *pompa circensis* was designed to make an impression, to impress, perhaps especially, the elite peers of the president himself and to inscribe itself in the archive of cultural memory.[101] Unfortunately, it is difficult to outline a history of the spectacle of the *pompa circensis*, the sources are rather limited and only suggestive. Nonetheless, one may surmise that as the games were elaborated and expanded and the Circus Maximus was formalized and monumentalized, the procession too would have received a certain spectacular articulation.[102]

To draw attention and to attract the desired crowds to the subsequent *ludi*, the *pompa circensis* drew upon an idiom of spectacle shared with the triumph and other Roman rituals. At times, the *pompa circensis* could, in fact, draw directly on triumphal precedent in an effort to heighten its visibility. The grand, though sporadic, spectacle of the triumph could lead to innovations in the oft-repeated *pompa circensis*. After all, a good show was a good show. According to Livy, in the late fourth century BCE, just when public ceremonies burgeoned in Rome and also in the Hellenistic east, aediles took inspiration from a recent triumph in order to embellish their own productions:[103]

> The dictator [Papirius Cursor], by decree of the senate, celebrated a triumph, whose greatest sight by far was furnished by the captured armor. So magnificent was its appearance that the gilded shields were divided among the owners of the banking houses in order to decorate the Forum. From this, it is said, was born the custom of the aediles adorning the Forum whenever the *tensae* were conducted [in a circus procession]. So the Romans made use of the remarkable armor of their enemies to honor the gods.[104]

The aediles, perhaps opportunistically, but certainly sensibly, took advantage of an impressive precedent to create an even more stunning itinerary – an adaptation of triumphal spectacle that would have underscored the already evident resonances between the two processions.

Caesar, too, targeted spaces that were along the *pompa circensis* itinerary for a spectacular, but temporary, makeover : "besides the Comitium, Forum, and basilicas, he also decorated the Capitol with arcades built for the occasion, in which part of the equipment for his shows was displayed in great profusion."[105] To be fair, Caesar's adornment of these places served the actual games, some of which would have taken place in the Forum, as much as or even more so than the procession. Likewise, at a later set of gladiatorial contests, "Caesar when dictator stretched an awning over the whole of the Roman Forum, as well as the Sacred Way from his mansion, and the slope right up to the Capitol."[106] The awning would have served whatever procession introduced the games as well as, more importantly, the games themselves. At some point during the republic or early empire, similar provisions were extended to the parade itinerary itself, when the senate "decreed that the route of the procession should be covered with an awning."[107]

It was not enough to festoon the itinerary with shields, arches, and awnings. The procession itself seems to have been ever more lavishly produced. However, the aediles' efforts may have triggered a spectacle arms race, as it were, provoking in turn a parody from the pen of Plautus, a near contemporary of Fabius Pictor. A scene from *The Little Carthaginian*, in which Milphio supposedly translates the Carthaginian Hanno explaining in Punic why he had come to Rome, deftly lampoons the impulse toward wonder.

HANNO: Mi uulech ianna?
AGORASTOCLES: Why has he come?
MILPHIO: Can't you hear? He states that he wants to present African mice to the aediles for the parade at the games.[108]

Of course, an aedile, as an organizer of the games and as a conspicuous participant in the procession, would have liked to cut as fine a figure as wealth and imagination would allow. Even though the desire for visibility seems to have gone too far at times, nevertheless aediles continued to risk ridicule in the pursuit of distinction. In the late republic, "as wealth increased, elegance followed religion in the games": for example, "M. Scaurus [curule aedile in 58 BCE] brought on the parade, previously dressed in scarlet tunics, arrayed in specially chosen costume."[109] Without the *praeses ludorum*'s vehicular distinction, this aedile sought sartorial prominence, so that he would stand out both from tradition and, quite possibly and perhaps more importantly, his colleague.

Similar attempts at show-stopping wonder continued under the empire, when unsurprisingly the *pompa circensis* achieved its most flamboyant form as a vehicle for imperial display and imperial cult. However, not every imperial spectacle needed to be ostentatious. Some could be rather humble, though still demonstrating the scope of imperial power. Columella, writing in the mid first century CE, observed that "recently we ourselves were able to see, among the exhibits of the procession at the games in the Circus, a man of the Jewish race who was of greater stature than the tallest German."[110] Mice and tall Jewish men might not match gilded shields, specially constructed arcades, or streets covered with awnings, but one can sense the earnest efforts of the *curatores ludorum*, whether aediles, praetors, consuls, or emperors to make their games memorable in part by producing a stunning procession to introduce them. One can only imagine the spectacular opening procession that Caesar had arranged for his "infamous" aedilician games when "by lavish provision of theater shows, processions, and banquets, he washed away all memory of the ambitious efforts of his predecessors in the office."[111] However, even autocrats and emperors had to play by the rhythms of procession, no matter how loosely. Otherwise, even autocrats risked ritual failure.

IV RITUAL FAILURE IN THE *POMPA HOMINUM*

Hanno's African mice underscore another essential element of ritual performances in general and Roman rituals in particular. Ritual performances are "both fundamentally *interactive* and inherently *risky*. . . . The risk at the bottom line is that the performance will 'fail.'"[112] Such failure may be technical – the awnings may collapse or the mice may run away, for example – or, more importantly, a matter of rules, regulations, or performance: a rite rife with procedural errors or misfires of all sorts, an ineffective ritual that failed to secure the desired results, or an "infelicitous" or inauthentic performance, that is a poor, unmoving, impenetrable, or insincere performance instead of an incorrect one.[113] Participants, performers, and above all spectators constantly evaluate ritual – often informally and non-consciously – against whatever customs, norms, and expectations may apply.[114] To judge from Plautus' parody, it would seem that some felt that the procession had become a bit excessive and so needed to be taken down a notch or two even if only rhetorically – or rather theatrically. Others, especially the elites themselves who financed this ever-escalating contest, may have rather appreciated the efforts and ingenuity of the aediles. And so, just as a ritual performance and its reception is multifold and perspectival, so too are the ways that it could fail: in degrees from minor mistakes to full-blown disasters or even in different ways to different people. Such failures reveal the essential contours of a ritual, bringing into high relief features that were seen as essential by at least some members of the group, whether participants or spectators. Such failures also demonstrate the stakes of the performance: after all, if the ritual did not matter, neither would its failure.

To address some of these types of ritual failure, ancient Roman religion had its own methods: expiation and especially *instauratio* (repetition). *Instauratio* primarily resolved procedural errors, rituals that had been interrupted or incorrectly performed, by repeating the failed ritual in whole or in part – apathy or ridicule sufficed for a poor performance. On occasion, however, a ritual failure was only discovered after the fact, when the rite failed to produce the desired outcome, namely the *pax deorum*, the goodwill of the gods. Almost by definition, a properly conducted ritual produced the proper result; therefore a ritual that failed to secure the *pax deorum* was a failed ritual, even if "properly" performed. As Clifford Ando has argued, Roman religion was "founded upon an empiricist epistemology: cult addressed problems in the real world, and the effectiveness of rituals – their tangible results – determined whether they were repeated, modified, or abandoned."[115] Roman *ludi* fundamentally aimed to secure the goodwill of the gods which in turn would ensure Roman success (the tangible result). For that reason, they were prone to ritual failure, often with catastrophic consequences. Ritual failures during the course of the games, and during the *pompa circensis*, resulted in military defeat, plague, and other tragedies.[116] The procession of the gods, with the subsequent sacrifice, was the central religious element of the entire festival. A mistake during its performance vitiated the whole games, while its correct execution could compensate for errors elsewhere during the *ludi*. Moreover, these failures offer insight into what mattered to a Roman sense of ritual spirituality: in the parade of people, the performance of music and dance and the behavior of the aediles, and in the *pompa deorum*, the treatment of the gods.

In fact, Dionysius' digression based on Fabius Pictor was framed by an account of a *pompa circensis* polluted by an impious crime: the dancing had gone horrifically wrong – a ritual failure whose early republican *mise-en-scène* and wide diffusion demonstrates its status as an *exemplum*.[117] Prior to the discovery of this ritual failure, Rome was beset by prodigies – monstrous births, frenzied women prophesying calamity, and a pestilence that killed cattle, all obvious signs of a failure to secure to the *pax deorum*. No explanation was to be found until an enfeebled Titus Latinius, a modestly wealthy farmer, was carried on a litter into the senate house, where he informed the assembled fathers about a dream that he had had. In this dream, Capitoline Jupiter appeared to him and said: "Go, Latinius, and tell the citizens that they did not give me an auspicious lead dancer in the most recent procession, so that they might dedicate and complete the festival again from the beginning. For I have not accepted these."[118] Though the senators were convinced, they stood still in uncomprehending silence until one of them connected the dream to an incident that had occurred right before (temporally) and right in front of (spatially) the *pompa*. A prominent citizen, having ordered the punishment and execution of one of his slaves, forced his other slaves to drag the victim through the city, including the Circus according to Livy, as they scourged him.[119] The slave's outstretch arms were lashed to a wooden beam as he stumbled in front of the *pompa circensis*, bloodied and naked.[120] As Dionysius described it: "The slave, overpowered by such violence, both shouted ill-omened cries, which the pain induced, and also made indecent movements due to the torture."[121] Apparently the monstrous proximity of the tormented motions and the agonized shrieks of the tortured slave to the choreography and music of the *ludiones* revolted Jupiter, who communicated his divine disgust through prodigy and pestilence. In the end, a more lavish procession and more opulent games were dedicated in order to repeat and so to expiate the failed ones.[122]

One could not hold the games, and thus one could not honor the gods properly, without a proper performance by the dancers. Conversely, if only one of these *ludiones* danced faultlessly, the entire games, whatever their defects, could be judged religiously valid. A Roman proverb, which was connected either to the *ludi Apollinares* or the *ludi Megalenses*, asserted "All is well when the old man dances."[123] Whatever its origins, Roman tradition eventually understood the phrase to mean that the error-free dancing of the *ludiones*, even just one, during the procession or perhaps during an interlude of the circus games could avoid an *instauratio*.

The performance not only of the dancers but also of the musicians and even of the aediles and others was positively fraught with danger. The ritual was risky – especially the highly regulated handling of the *tensae* (processional chariots that were used only, it seems, in the *pompa circensis*).[124] According to Cicero,

> If the *ludius* [dancer] has stood still or if the flute player has suddenly become mute, if the boy whose father and mother are still alive [*puer patrimus et matrimus*] has not kept to his *tensa* or has let a rein slip, or if the aedile made a mistake in the formula or handling of the sacred vessel, then the games have not been performed according to the rite, and so the errors are expiated and the feelings of the immortal gods are placated by an *instauratio* of the games."[125]

All might have been well if the old man continued to dance, but a miscue by a musician, a misstep by a boy guiding a *tensa*, or a mistake by the aedile required redress. Christian authors would later tease "pagan" Romans about their overly fastidious, religious scruples. Moreover, one could argue that the Romans employed the *instauratio* procedure to extend the run of particularly popular theater pieces – especially those of Plautus. Although a deliberate mistake would remain inexpiable and so could have been a particularly difficult stigma for a public figure, one can imagine the possibility of creative solutions to satisfy religious consciences and to court popular acclaim.[126]

A further anecdote from Dionysius may suggest the rather dire risks associated with this ritual – even if it was not a ritual failure *per se*. In 500 BCE, a year when "nothing worthy of remembrance occurred" according to Livy, Dionysius noted that one of the consuls, Manius Tullius, who had just helped stop a plot to restore the final Tarquin to power, "fell from his sacred chariot in the Circus itself during the procession at the sacred games called after the name of the city [*ludi Romani*], and died the third day after the procession."[127] There is no hint of any ritual impropriety and no mention of an *instauratio* – remarkable considering that the *praeses ludorum* died during the very performance of the procession. It would seem that the president of the games was marginal to the procession as a religious performance – his death, or at least this death, did not impact the validity of the games – while *ludiones*, young boys, and aediles were at its center. It is also important to note that this fatal circus procession before the *ludi Romani* was said to have taken place ten years before that "recorded" by Fabius Pictor. Perhaps the successful, and expensive, repetition of the failed games due to its horrifically brutalized dancer provided a more compelling context for Dionysius' excursus on Fabius Pictor's elaborate *pompa circensis*.

Finally, sometimes potential ritual failures, or at least risky situations, could be avoided beforehand. According to Livy, in 202 BCE the Tiber overran its banks and flooded the Circus Maximus, preventing the *ludi Apollinares* from taking place at their usual location. And so the games were moved to an alternate location northeast of the city outside the porta Collina, a gate in the Servian walls on the Quirinal hill.

> On the very day of the games, however, after a sudden clearing the procession, already on its way to porta Collina, was recalled and directed into the Circus when word was received that the water had retired from it. Restoration of its normal scene to the customary spectacle added to the delight of the people and to the throngs who attended the games.[128]

Perhaps one might very tentatively ascribe some small portion of that popular delight to the return not only to the traditional location of the games, with its superior spectator facilities, but also to the return to traditional ritual practice.

Though his digression on the *pompa circensis* is tenuous, if not also tendentious, as history, Dionysius, and before him Fabius Pictor, would have had to conform his description of the *pompa circensis* to contemporary readers' expectations in order to appear accurate or at least plausible. So even though the description may be an idealized and ahistorical "ideal-type," it may still correspond to the rhythm of the procession, offering insight into how the procession may have been structured – its elements, its framework, its production values – without needing to tally exactly with any particular iteration. In short, Fabius Pictor and Dionysius may convey the grammatical and syntactical "rules," according to which a given performance of the *pompa circensis* could have been enunciated. Much as the circus and its games were an assembly of humans and gods, the *pompa circensis* consisted of two sub-sections, a *pompa hominum* which comprised, at the simplest level, the magistrate(s) charged with producing and presiding over the games, their entourage, the contestants, and the bearers of the ritual paraphernalia; and a *pompa deorum* which escorted the gods to the arena (Chapter 2). These basic "grammatical" elements were ordered and organized according to processional "syntax" and performance principles – an alternation between gravity and levity as well as resonance and wonder, with an ever-present risk of ritual failure or infelicitous performance. These elements, organization, and principles seem to have constituted the basic rhythms of the *pompa circensis*, its grammar or notes, and its syntax or composition, which may have served in turn to produce any number of different tunes, as it were, while remaining recognizable as a circus procession.

In the imagined (not to say imaginary) version of Fabius Pictor-Dionysius, the president and his entourage seemingly led the way, followed closely or, perhaps better, accompanied by young Roman men organized according to census status and arrayed in military formation. The charioteers and athletes then appeared arranged according to their own hierarchy of status and celebrity – a distorted echo of the earnest young men right in front of them. The alternation of gravity and levity was repeated by the choruses of dancers and musicians that followed – martial movements were mocked by sexualized satyrs and Sileni. At the end of the parade of people, more musicians accompanied the aediles and their assistants who carried the ritual vessels to the Circus for the performance of the sacrifice, as well as censer bearers whose perfumed smoke introduced the *pompa deorum* with which the procession concludes.

As the procession, oscillating between gravity and levity, traversed the city, most of the participants recalled or resonated with other rituals or ceremonies – echoes that may well have magnified and extended the authority and visibility of all the rituals involved. The president of the games dressed in a manner similar to those who celebrated triumphs, while driving a two-horse chariot instead of a *quadriga*. The Roman youth were organized according to their fathers' census qualifications. The armed dancers recalled the Salians, while the satyrs and Sileni appeared in funeral processions and might well have conjured up the riotous disorder of the Lupercalia, in which some of the young elite men might participate.

Some of these resonances may have originated as attempts to render the procession more spectacular by borrowing elements from other spectacles – most notably the triumph, though such "borrowings" were not confined to the triumph. Despite the risks of ritual failure, as Plautus comically suggested, such attempts would accelerate in the late republic and early empire under the autocrat Julius Caesar and then the early emperors – with unequal success. Aggrandizement and immoderate pageantry always courted disaster. Even during the empire, the procession was hemmed in with rules, regulations, traditions, and even audience expectations, whose demands needed to be met, at least in part. Even though ritual anxieties and taboos constrained the procession in certain ways, it also remained open to innovation, whether mice from Africa or, eventually, deified emperors, empresses, and others from the imperial special dead.

TWO

POMPA DEORUM

Performing theology, performing the gods

But here's the procession. Everybody hush.
Give them a hand. The golden procession's here.

Ovid, *Amores* 3.2.43–44[1]

The *pompa circensis* was fundamentally a religious ceremony: at its core, it was a *pompa deorum*, or "a procession packed with ivory gods" that crowded and distinguished the Circus as it paraded along the arena floor.[2] Its purpose, as it were, was to escort the gods from the Capitoline temple of Jupiter, or possibly some other temple, to the Circus Maximus to witness "the greatest show on earth."[3] Upon their arrival, the massive crowd would both maintain reverent silence, so that no untoward word would be heard – except for the amorous suitor "Ovid," who maintained a running commentary despite his own admonition – and applaud and cheer with vigor and verve, so that whatever words were actually spoken would not vitiate the ritual.[4] Devout silence, prudently accompanied by some form of white noise, was a common element of Roman rituals: "at public celebrations of religious rites, the command, 'Favor your tongues,' was typically given," according to Cicero.[5] As Seneca explained: "'be favorable with your tongues.' This expression is not derived, as many imagine, from '*favor*' in the sense of 'applause,' but enjoins silence in order that the sacrifice may be performed according to ritual without the interruption of an ill-omened word."[6] Customarily, as the elder Pliny noted, an attendant "was put in charge to maintain a strict silence; a piper plays so that nothing but the prayer is heard."[7] Such strictures seem to have held sway in the Circus Maximus, where tens if not hundreds of thousands of people were enjoined to observe a sacred silence with their mouths even as they were to greet noisily and enthusiastically the arrival of the gods with their hands.

This seemingly carefully orchestrated ritual response greeted an array of gods, who were represented or made present in varying ways, fashioned from a variety of materials, transported by various means, and organized hierarchically and relationally in a kind of pantheon that likely varied depending upon occasion and context.[8] Though analytically separable, representation, material of manufacture, transportation, and organization came together in the *pompa circensis* to offer a kind of performed theology, in contrast to an emphasis on the discursive articulation of belief (theology) common to many philosophies and religions. As is commonly accepted, ancient Roman civic religion emphasized orthopraxy, the meticulously correct performance of ritual, at the expense of orthodoxy to such an extent that one could argue that the Romans could *think* whatever they wanted, so long as they *did* the right thing.[9] That is not to say that Romans did not have "beliefs" or engage in theological discourse.[10] Nonetheless, the rules, meanings, and interpretations of Roman civic religion seem to have been primarily communicated in practice and performance, rather than discursively in a distinct, formal educational setting. Varro, a first-century BCE polymath whose articulation of a three-fold theology constitutes one of the most important sources on Roman religious thought, admitted the limited appeal of philosophical theology and the unreliability of poetic theology, whose authority was rather feeble in any case. Nevertheless, judgments about the divine world were formed and performed to large audiences – not necessarily textually or discursively, but ritually, spatially, and visually: that is, in civic cult, Varro's third and most prominent theological category. In other words, much authoritative religious thought at Rome was performed: ancient Roman civic religion ritually constructed its theology, which the *pompa deorum* rather dramatically demonstrates.

In the *pompa circensis*, a seemingly conscientiously chosen selection of deities, "a taxonomy of divine representation," appeared as *simulacra* (anthropomorphic statues) borne on *fercula* (litters) and as *exuviae* (symbols, attributes, or relics) conveyed in *tensae* (processional chariots).[11] On the one hand, the *simulacra* presented the gods as fellow citizens who came to enjoy the races, while, on the other, the *exuviae* demonstrated divine alterity. In addition, the procession offered more theatrical modes of supernatural representation – large wooden *effigies* (puppets) of folkloric figures and stilt-walkers imitating deities, both of which directly engaged the audience with bawdy banter. Consequently, from this ritual procession one can extract two different modes of divine representation: naturalistic (or anthropomorphic) statues and abstract (or symbolic) tokens, each of which seemingly corresponded to a particular species of divine–human relationship, in which the gods appeared as familiar in a human guise or as foreign represented by emblems of their power. Moreover, supernatural figures, the wooden puppets and stilt-walkers, titillated and terrified the audience.

In short, the *pompa circensis* staged an implicit and embodied theology, an act of thinking and doing – a *savoir-faire*, not simply a *savoir-penser*.[12] And so all ritual participants, including spectators, could gain a religious education by watching the procession, in which divine images and symbols traversing an itinerary overwhelmed by cultural memory communicated something essential about the organization, activity, and meaning of the divine world. While written or even more broadly discursive theology seems have been rather limited and isolated in ancient Rome, nevertheless, in ritual, the image and imagination of the gods was as rich, complex, and paradoxical as anywhere.

I RELIGIOUS EDUCATION AND PERFORMED THEOLOGY

Rome's elites assuredly had "beliefs" and engaged in theological discourse. Indeed, Varro outlined three modes of theology (*tria genera theologiae*): natural or philosophical, mythical or poetical, and civil or civic.[13] However, according to Varro, as ostensibly quoted centuries later by Augustine of Hippo, "our [Roman] ears more readily tolerate [philosophical theology] within the walls of a lecture-hall than in the forum outside."[14] Unsurprisingly, Augustine critiqued Varro for accepting the segregation of "real" theology and, worse, the public parade of mythical theology, "with its monstrous lies so utterly loathsome":

> [Varro] banished this kind of discourse [philosophical natural theology] from the marketplace, in other words from the public, and shuts it up within the walls of the schools. . . . So much for the god-fearing ears of the people, even the Romans among them! They cannot stomach the arguments of the philosophers concerning the immortal gods, yet the songs of poets and the performances of actors, which invent fictions against the dignity and nature of the immortal gods . . . they not merely stomach but even rejoice to hear.[15]

For Augustine, only philosophical discourse on the gods counted as true theology, as "reasoning or speech concerning divinity," and its truths should trump popular poetic discourse, a common complaint of philosophically minded theologians ever since Plato advocated the revision and even censorship of Homer and Hesiod.[16]

Even so, mythical theology appeared everywhere, unfortunately in Augustine's opinion: in texts, images, and above all the theater. In fact,

Augustine "could [have] document[ed] these [mythological travesties] from written accounts, but there is no need; they are paraded every day in song and dance in the theaters."[17] The *ludi scaenici* (theater shows) were an essential and nearly ubiquitous part of public celebrations of the gods.[18] At any given festival, theatrical performances could extend for days – and so their dramatic, mythological theology would have reached a broad swathe of the Roman people. Myth may not have been not central to sacrifice or the other core rituals of Roman civic religion, but it was fundamental to the festival as a whole.[19] However, as Varro says – according to Augustine – this dramatically polysemic and entertaining, "fabular . . . [or] fabulous" theology could be rather bluntly criticized as "mendacious fables."[20]

In general, as Greg Woolf argues, "the authority of Roman theological texts (or texts about religion) was *relative* rather than absolute." Both "poetic and philosophical texts that dealt with the gods . . . might become respected and emulated, yet always remained open to criticism and (potentially at least) to replacement."[21] In the end, neither abstruse philosophical speculations, with their limited appeal, nor "lewd" mythological productions, with their broader allure, exercised the kind of authority ascribed to Christian theology, for example – perhaps because neither philosophy nor poetry had sacred scriptures upon which to base their claims and to assert their urgency. By contrast, challenges to civic rituals performed under the authority of Rome's magistrates and under the guidance of its priests were discouraged. In fact, the *tria genera theologiae* may have emerged precisely to insulate the necessary performance of civic cult, which secured the goodwill of the gods, from the potentially disruptive effects of philosophy and poetry.[22]

Even though the proper performance of civic cult was valued and perhaps protected, it remains a bit of a problem to envision how the Romans learned anything about their civic religion. With a paucity of formal (or even semi-formal) religious educational institutions or frameworks for the creation and dissemination of religious knowledge, such material was transmitted primarily through the family or via public ceremonies.[23] As Arnaldo Momigliano noted, "we have to face in Rome . . . a strange absence of information about religious education. . . . [I]t is arguable that in Rome . . . the way to find out about religious practices was to be taken around or, if grown up, to go around the city."[24] In the words of "Piso," an Academic-Platonic persona of Cicero who was attempting to demonstrate humanity's innate instinct for learning:

> Do we notice how children cannot be deterred even by a beating from studying and inquiring into the world around them? Drive them away, and back they come. They delight in knowing things. To learn things fills them with joy. Processions, games, and spectacles of any sort hold them spell-bound and they will endure hunger and thirst so as to be able to watch them.[25]

Though one may doubt the purely educational value of Rome's *pompae*, *ludi*, and *spectacula*, and so also children's desires to see them, nonetheless for "Piso" these public religious displays constituted part of the curriculum. Children learned by watching and doing ritual.

In short, "Much of what a Roman 'knew' was 'performative knowledge'" or perhaps also experiential or even habitual.[26] That is, much like the *habitus* as conceived by Pierre Bourdieu, Roman religious education was seemingly mimetic, non-conscious, and largely non-discursive.

> So long as the work of education is not clearly institutionalized as a specific, autonomous practice, so long as it is the whole group and a whole symbolically structured environment, without specialized agents or specific occasions, that exerts an anonymous, diffuse pedagogic action, the essential part of the *modus operandi* that defines practical mastery is transmitted through practice, in the practical state, without rising to the level of discourse.[27]

In Roman civic religion, there were few if any formal or institutional settings for expressly religious instruction. Religious knowledge was transmitted in the act of performing rites, rituals, and ceremonies.[28] In other words, as Mary Beard, John North, and Simon Price insist, Rome's "processions, festivals and celebrations were one of the ways of educating these new citizens in the meaning of Roman life and history, providing a map of Roman-ness for those who had not inherited this knowledge."[29] Discursive theology was not a core element of Roman public cult, but processions were.

Although Romans systematically and discursively investigated religion, according to Beard, North, and Price, works like those of Varro "were not part of internal priestly discourse *within* religion or directly related to ritual performance; they were commentaries *on* religion from an external standpoint."[30] To be sure, writing and words also featured prominently *within* religious cult – for example, the Sibylline books, memorials of the Arval Brethren, petitions or vows, public calendars, so-called magical texts, and essential and often solidly practical prayers. Nonetheless, discursive *theology* still occupied only a limited place, and so one should look elsewhere for Roman "theology" and its inculcation.[31] In particular, one needs to pay attention to the mode of theology which seemingly most concerned Varro: civic theology or the analysis of Roman traditional, public civic cults. The regulations of sacrifices, the spatial arrangements of sanctuaries, and the deployment of images and imagery produced and disseminated an "unwritten" or "material" theology – a theology that Varro attempted to capture in his "theology of practice."[32] At Rome, theology was embedded and embodied in sacred places and ritual practice – theology was material and especially performed. In short, Roman civic theology was produced in the most "perceptible" aspects of civic religion – theater shows, dancing and music, festivals and fairs, art, debates, dedications, pilgrimages, and above all processions, perhaps the most prominent, visible, accessible, and venerable means of "attracting crowds."[33]

Though surely a contested term, performance rather compellingly positions a ritual procession as a singular event in a specific context in which skillful performers and a primed audience interact in a patterned and improvisational manner.[34] As a ritual, a procession may be marked by repetition and rules, but as a performance this supposedly invariant act is shown to be a one-off, ephemeral event, different from other iterations.[35] As Jörg Rüpke puts it, "Individual enactments of a ritual are not simply mere repetitions of an eternally fixed ritual but conscious attempts of historical individuals to do a ritual, to repeat an honoured pattern, to perform it to and for others in a specific situation, in a particular place."[36] One performs a script (that itself may change) but one also improvises a performance (within a set of rules or traditions).[37]

The dialectical relationship between continuity and change highlights a second essential aspect of performance: it is "fundamentally *interactive*."[38] Ritual performers may extemporize, but within certain bounds. To violate audience expectations too vigorously courts danger. That is, in a performance, as distinct, perhaps, from a spectacle, the audience or spectators are participants who play an active role in its success or failure.[39] A ritual performance may well provide an aesthetically pleasing pageant to watch, but the viewers always constitute an essential element of the performance itself. Both ritual conventions and audience expectations constrain ritual performances, which nonetheless remain open to adaptation.

Performance, constituted by skilled inventions within customary limits and engaged interaction between performers and audiences, may be considered auto-poetic – in other words, a framed or ritualized spatial and embodied activity that captures its participants, captivates its audience, and so creates its own reality. A well-executed "performance seems more real than everyday life." In general, "it is part of the work of rituals and performances to bring about such realities and presences."[40] In the present case, the performance of the *pompa circensis* conjured the presence of the gods in the city streets and at the games. In the end, "performances, whether ritual or dramatic, create and make present realities vivid enough to beguile, amuse or terrify."[41] And so, performance emphasizes the emotional, physical, sensory, and aesthetic dimensions of processions that may otherwise get lost in a textual analysis based largely on textual evidence. A performance may be captivating, it may be boring, but it always involves the entire sensorium.[42]

II PERFORMING THE GODS

During the course of the procession, regimented ranks of young Roman men gave way to the superstars of the arena, and bands of martial players yielded to burlesque dancers, followed by a stunning group of gold and silver ritual vessels whose glittering radiance was enchantingly obscured by perfumed clouds of incense, out of which the *pompa deorum* appeared at last. With this extended introduction, which may have spurred the lamentations of the elder Seneca, the spectators were now ready for the event. They were prepped and prepared, taken to another place where the gods themselves would manifest – "the city became totally Jupiterian," at the *ludi Romani* at least.[43]

> Last of all, icons of all the gods came in procession, borne on men's shoulders, bearing the same forms as those fashioned by the Greeks, with the same attire, the same tokens, and the same gifts which each [divine] inventor and benefactor hands over to humanity.[44]

Fercula *and* simulacra

In the position of honor toward the end of the procession, anthropomorphic images of the gods, which, unsurprisingly given Dionysius' aims, conformed to the representational and iconographical conventions of the Greek (and also Roman) deities, were borne on *fercula*, a type of stretcher or litter, carried by groups of paid laborers or perhaps devotees.[45] Of course, just because Dionysius had an agenda does not necessarily mean that he was wrong – a great deal of iconographical evidence seems to corroborate that anthropomorphic imagery was indeed carried in what are most likely circus processions.[46] These anthropomorphic images of the gods, made from various materials (ivory or plaster), were quite possibly miniature versions of cult statues, some perhaps specially manufactured for each new iteration of the circus procession.[47]

Such imagery had been long familiar at Rome, Varro's assertion of early Roman aniconism notwithstanding.[48] This manner of imagining or this modality of representing the gods was familiar to most Romans as part of their lived experience. According to one of Cicero's Skeptic personae:

> From childhood we have come to know Jupiter, Juno, Minerva, Neptune, Vulcan, Apollo, and the rest of the gods by the appearance that painters and sculptors wanted; and not only their appearance but also their equipment, age, and attire – but [the gods did not appear in this way] to the Egyptians, or Syrians, or almost all of the barbarian lands.[49]

To a Roman, anthropomorphic images of the gods were common – because, according to one of Cicero's Epicurean personae, the gods really did share human form – even if culturally specific.[50] Other peoples imaged their gods in other ways, which for some intellectual elites, such as, it would seem, Lucilius (second century BCE), Varro, and Cicero (or at least his "Skeptic"), implied that the gods were not their statues and that statues were frauds – though even Cicero could refer to statues of the gods directly by name *as if* they were gods, at least in polemical contexts.[51] This sometime elision between deity and image, even among elites, reveals the striking impact of a ritualized mode of seeing facilitated by naturalistic imagery, a visuality in which the gods were and were not their statues at the same time.[52] Naturalizing images of the gods referred to, referenced, represented, and even presenced the gods in complicated ways.[53]

However ambiguous, such imagery brought the gods into a world of human relations. Such imagery allowed proximity to the gods, as a mean-spirited, but also poignant, caricature by the Stoic philosopher Seneca, later picked up by Augustine (again), shows:

> But make your way to the Capitol, and you will be mortified at the lunacy on show, at the tasks which pointless madness imposes on itself. One man supplies the names [of his devotees] to Jupiter, and another announces the hours to him. One is a washer and another anoints him (in fact, he merely imitates anointing with pointless movements of his arms). Some women there dress the hair of Juno and Minerva; they take their stand at a distance not merely from the statue but also from the temple, working their fingers as though arranging hair; other women are in attendance, holding a mirror. There are men there calling on the gods to stand surety for them; others submit their briefs and acquaint them with their legal cases. One moth-eaten old fellow, earlier a learned troupe-leader, would perform a daily mime on the Capitol, as if the gods were taking delight in watching him, now that the men of the time had ceased to do so. Every type of artist settles there to present their work to the immortal gods.[54]

Hostile polemic aside, this rant makes clear that anthropomorphic imagery offered a medium by which worshippers could create or invent rather personal and even intimate relationships with a divinity – relations that Varro, according to Augustine, and a Skeptic persona of Cicero unsurprisingly ascribed to the supposedly superstitious.[55] One should, however, not overestimate the relational component – a gap, both physical and intellectual, stood between the worshippers and the deity as well as between the statue and the deity, offering ample space for reflection and debate on the nature of humanity and divinity. Naturalistic imagery seems to have enabled a tender, complex, and also paradoxical play between divinity, image, and devotee.[56]

In the *pompa circensis*, paradoxical divine images carried all their ambiguity with them as they crossed the city. Their standard Greek (and Roman) iconography may have rendered the gods (made present in/as/by/through their statues) more easily identifiable, but it did not resolve their complexities. Perhaps, in part, to control such ambiguity, the *fercula*-borne anthropomorphic images were also organized, it seems, into a pantheon of the twelve Olympian Greek gods (a variable category).[57] Dionysius, following Fabius Pictor it would seem, insisted that "Zeus, Hera, Athena, Poseidon, and the others whom the Greeks count among the twelve gods" were specially featured.[58] Dionysius thus discerned a rather canonical and quite Greek arrangement of the most prominent of the Olympian gods, enumerated according to their Greek names. If, however, one "translates" Zeus, Hera, Athena, and Poseidon into Latin, one may see the Capitoline triad of Jupiter, Juno, and Minerva followed by Neptune. The possible (or even probable) prominence of the Capitoline gods nicely corresponded to the possible purpose of the games, which may have been the *ludi Romani* in honor of Rome's patron deity, Jupiter Optimus Maximus (along with his temple mates, Juno and Minerva), suggesting that Dionysius (and Fabius Pictor) might have seen truly despite his (their) Greek lens.

However, such a grouping of twelve Olympian gods seems to have made its appearance at Rome for the first time in 217 BCE when the Sibylline books commanded a *lectisternium*, in which "there were six *pulvinaria* [couches] set out in plain sight: one for Jupiter and Juno, a second for Neptune and Minerva, a third for Mars and Venus, a fourth for Apollo and Diana, a fifth for Vulcan and Vesta, a sixth for Mercury and Ceres."[59] If the tradition reported by Livy is accurate, then Fabius Pictor (as transmitted by Dionysius), who most likely witnessed this *lectisternium*, may not have been able to resist ascribing this arrangement of the gods to one of the earliest *pompa circensis*. Alternatively, even if the gods were not structured according to the Olympic twelve *ab origine* (from the very beginning), it may have become standard or normative to do so by the end of the third century BCE when Fabius Pictor penned his description.

Whatever the case, Ovid presented a different order from perhaps a different set of games, or perhaps from his own imagination:

> First comes Victory, wings outstretched.
> Goddess, grant me victory in love!
>
> Neptune next. Salute him, sailors.
> Not for me the ocean – I'm a landlover.
>
> Soldiers, salute Mars. I'm a disarmer,
> All for peace and amorous plenty.
>
> There's Phoebus for the soothsayers, Phoebe for the hunters,
> Minerva for the master craftsmen.
>
> Farmers can greet Bacchus and Ceres,
> Boxers pray to Pollux and knights to Castor
>
> But I salute the queen of love and the boy with the bow.
> Venus, smile on my latest venture.[60]

Of course, the speaker of a poem praising the Circus as an apt location for erotic encounters would praise Venus and could imagine that the goddess herself responded encouragingly to his efforts to hit on the girl next to him: "A lucky sign – the goddess nodded."[61] It is, however, possible that the goddess did actually (physically) nod – her bearers may have tilted the *ferculum* upon entering the Circus so that the goddess could greet the assembled crowd. Or perhaps, the natural swaying movement of Venus' *ferculum* as its bearers carried it through the arena made it seem as if she were nodding. In any case, Ovid was not alone in construing the motion of litter-borne images as divine communication or even prophecy.[62] Moreover, one of Horace's satires condemns a local notable who "would inch along like someone carrying Juno's *sacra*," which suggests that those who carried the *sacra* and by extension those who bore the *fercula* adopted a particular walk for the *pompa*, perhaps a nod to ritual formality and physical necessity – those things were heavy.[63] Whatever the reason, the pompous deportment of processional professionals seems to have been proverbial.

Neither the Dionysian nor the Ovidian arrangement may have ever been used or even have been visible, if only because the authors very possibly arranged their lists for their own purposes. Nonetheless, if ritual obligation and correct performance were the core of Roman spirituality (with its strong emphasis on ritual exactitude), then it seems likely that there would have been some kind of order, some ritual construction of theology.[64] That is, the *pompa circensis* had to be performed correctly, which included, one may imagine, the correct configuration of the gods. In fact, a fragmentary relief from an early-first-century CE sepulchral monument commemorating a set of municipal gladiator games offered by a *triumvir Augustalis* suggests that Fabius Pictor-Dionysius and Ovid might both have presented a reasonably faithful description of a *pompa deorum*. On one fragment of this relief, a winged Victory in a chariot, similar to one later conjured by Plutarch, appears to lead a *pompa deorum* with Mars, possibly, in a *biga* close behind, while on a second, contiguous fragment Jupiter and Juno stand on *fercula* with Minerva, who would have almost certainly trailed behind, cut off at the break (Figure 10).[65] All told, Victory seems like an apt choice to head a procession of gods to the arena where the contests would determine the victors and the vanquished. Equally, the organization of the opening procession could have reflected a number of theological factors including the requirements of a particular festival, like the *ludi Romani* which starred Jupiter, Juno, and Minerva, according to Dionysius.

The arrangement of the gods likely changed over time, and, moreover, the flux and flow of the procession may have made any theological ordering difficult to detect. The spectators may simply have seen the gods pass by in a rapid rush, as in Dionysius' description of the rest of the gods who followed the Greek twelve:

10. Ludic procession before *ludi Augustales*, marble, mid first century CE

> Kronos, Rhea, Themis, Latona, the Fates, Mnemosyne, and all the others who have temples and sanctuaries among the Greeks; and next, those coming into existence after Zeus seized power according to the mythic traditions, Persephone, Eileithyia, the Nymphs, the Muses, the Seasons, the Graces, Dionysus; and those who became demigods whose souls are said to have ascended to heaven after they had left their mortal bodies and to have obtained for themselves honors similar to those of the gods, such as Heracles, Asclepius, the Dioscuri, Helen, Pan, and countless others.[66]

This long train of gods who themselves followed an equally lengthy parade of people may well have generated devout respect, bored contempt, anxious anticipation, or all three together, any of which would have impacted the spectators' ability and willingness to engage thoughtfully with the circus procession's embodied theology. That is, even if skillfully produced and meticulously organized, the performance of the procession would not have captivated everyone at every moment – even the arrival of the gods need not have always generated pious enthusiasm.

Even if they do not cohere, the texts of Dionysius and Ovid suggest that the *pompa* somewhat messily organized the gods into a taxonomy of divine representations, a set of theological categories.[67] According to Dionysius' interpretation, the twelve Olympian gods (itself an unstable category) led the way, though he only named Zeus (Jupiter), Hera (Juno), Athena (Minerva), and Poseidon (Neptune). In other words, the Capitoline triad of Jupiter, Juno, and Minerva, whom these games and so also this *pompa circensis* honored, figured most prominently among the distinguished Olympian gods. Poseidon-Neptune ranked fourth in the list, perhaps due to his connection to horses, chariot racing, and the Circus Maximus itself.[68] Fabius Pictor-Dionysius imagined the rest of the gods organized according to their very Greek, poetically inspired theogonic generations: Kronos and the generation of gods who had preceded Zeus, followed by Persephone and other gods who emerged after

Zeus achieved sovereignty. At the bottom of the divine rankings stood demigods, mortals who had attained divinity. The material of manufacture of these images may have emphasized such theological classifications: Victories were apparently plaster, while the traditional gods were ivory, though perhaps some were marble or some other stone.[69]

Ovid, by contrast, offered a significantly shorter list of deities, with the goddess Victory at its head. The remaining nine gods then appeared with seemingly no discernible rank or order, with the exception of Venus, of course, who needed to bring up the rear so that she could nod her approval at the Ovidian lover's exploits. Apart from the seemingly elaborate choreography (and also the hard, sweaty work) of the *fercula*-bearers, whose sway "Ovid" took as Venus' approval of his romantic endeavors, one should also note that Jupiter (and Juno for that matter) did not appear in this evocation of a *pompa circensis*. Perhaps Jupiter's stereotyped devotees (possibly Roman political elites) were all too easily or too dangerously caricatured. Rather than Fabius Pictor-Dionysius' ranked list based on existing theological categories, which as it happens also signals the power of Greek poetic, mythical theology, Ovid insistently connected each god to a single profession (including his persona "Ovid," who seems to have been a professional lover), which both highlights the social nature of divine–human relations and the possibility of very individual responses to the procession. That is, Fabius Pictor-Dionysius' description inscribed the procession of gods in a hierarchical list based on Greek mytho-poetic models, while Ovid drew attention to the interlocking interactions between gods and humans.

Even though the pantheons handed down by Dionysius or Ovid may never have appeared in any actual performance, their textual evocations may stand as examples of the kinds of theological organization presented by the producers of the games and the types of theological activities spectators might have engaged in as the procession wound its way around the arena floor. It is quite plausible, if not probable, that each festival obligated a certain order (which may have changed over time), or perhaps the game-giver, as author of the games, could have determined his own order within certain limits, enforced by tradition and even the threat of spectator violence. Equally as possible, each and every spectator could have forged his or her own personal order out of the litany of gods marching down the street. In each case, every attempt at order and organization reveals something about the hierarchy and even relations among the gods and between divinity and humanity. No matter the composition of the gods or its visibility, the presumably careful, even if merely imagined, organization of the gods would have simultaneously arranged them hierarchically in ranks as well as relationally according to their common connections.[70]

Tensae *and* exuviae

In addition to anthropomorphic statues (*simulacra*) borne on *fercula* likely arranged in some sort of pantheon, the gods appeared in other forms in the *pompa circensis*. There were other ways of representing, presencing, or picturing the gods – modalities about which Dionysius remained silent. In particular, Dionysius omitted the *exuviae* – perhaps, initially, *struppi* (crowns or effigies woven from branches) or, more certainly, symbols, attributes, or relics of the gods – that were carried inside *tensae*: "vehicle[s] of the gods," that is, processional chariots that seem to have been used (almost) exclusively in the *pompa circensis*.[71] Perhaps, these relics borne by sacred vehicles, chariots made from precious materials and stored in their own temple or shrine (an *aedes tensarum* or *sacrarium*) on the Capitol (at least those of the Capitoline triad), were so distinctly Roman that Dionysius could not read them as Greek, even with the help of Homer.[72] Or perhaps Fabius Pictor, who was almost certainly familiar with *exuviae* and *tensae*, had simply omitted them from his description. Whatever the reason, this omission seems especially egregious since Livy, a contemporary of Dionysius, could employ the phrase "when the *tensae* were conducted" as a synecdoche for the circus procession as a whole – a usage maintained by Suetonius well over a century later, when he wrote that Augustus "led the *tensae*," meaning that the emperor presided over a *pompa circensis*. Almost another century later, Tertullian again used the same formulation.[73]

Not only could the *tensae* symbolize the *pompa circensis*, but they might also endow the itinerary with meaning. Cicero, in a polemic against Verres, excoriated the notorious villain by insisting that he had committed the most grievous sacrilege: Verres had failed to repair the *vicus Tuscus* adequately, endangering gods and humans alike. "The repair of that road, the route for *tensae* and processions [*pompae*], you have reinforced so thoroughly that you would not risk going over it yourself."[74] Cicero may well have exaggerated both Verres' incompetence and the associations of the street with *tensae* and the *pompa circensis*. Even if Cicero inflated the connection, he still deployed it on three separate occasions to stress the supposed turpitude of Verres, which suggests that Cicero at least found them compelling and/or that he believed that he could exploit Roman religious sympathies. What is more, Cicero seems to have developed such a fondness for "pathetic reference[s] to the *tensae*" that an opposing counsel in another court case attempted to prevent the trial from coinciding with the games so that Cicero would have no reason to mention them. The gambit failed: Cicero teased Laterensis by mentioning the *tensae* two more times in the very same passage.[75]

According to Verrius Flaccus (an Augustan-era scholar whose work Festus abridged in the second century CE, which Paul the Deacon subsequently epitomized in the late eighth century CE), "Sinnius Capito [a younger contemporary of Varro] says that the vehicle in which the symbols [*exuviae*] of the gods are carried to the *pulvinar* [a sacred 'loge'] in the Circus during the circus games is called a *tensa*. It was made from both ivory, according to Titinius [early second century BCE] in his Bearded Man, and silver."[76] Though perhaps also an elite mule-drawn vehicle in the mid republic according to Titinius, again, by the late republic *tensae* seem to have been reserved for the *pompa circensis*.[77] Accompanied by a boy with both parents still living (a *puer patrimus et matrimus*) and perhaps another attendant to ensure proper ritual performance, four horses pulled each *tensa*, a two-wheeled chariot, whose façade evoked a temple gable often with acroterial statuary gracing its peak and whose sides were elegantly decorated with relief sculptures that were seemingly related to either the god to whom the *tensa* was dedicated or the symbols held within.

For example, L. Rubrius Dossenus minted a series of *denarii* in 87 BCE whose reverses depict what seem to be the *tensae* of the Capitoline triad, whose busts appear on the obverses (Figures 1–3).[78] Though the identification of these chariots remains contested – unsurprisingly given the lack of any explicit tag – their distinctive shape (boxy and vertically oriented), scale (towering above the horses), ornament, and the lack of a driver distinguishes these vehicles from numismatic images of so-called triumphal chariots, with their triumphant drivers and low sweeping curves. The strict profile rendering of the "*tensae*" makes it difficult to assess the shape of their façades, though the inverted triangular top is an odd feature for a chariot, which is unfortunate since a pediment seems to be the closest thing to an unambiguous iconographic indicator of a *tensa*.[79] The acroterial statuary (a flying Victory holding a wreath or a Victory driving a *biga*) echoes Ovid's Victory who led the *pompa deorum*, while the symbols adorning the sides (a lightning bolt for Jupiter, or an eagle grasping a lightning bolt in its claws for Juno and Minerva) reinforce the identification with the Capitoline triad. In other words, the iconographical features of these numismatic "*tensae*" both differs from "triumphal" chariots and suggests a connection to the circus procession. These enigmatic vehicles also conform to subsequent imperial-era *tensa* iconography, or at least with imperial imagery taken as representations of *tensae* – like a fragmentary Augustan or early imperial terracotta plaque that may represent a *tensa* to judge from its pediment and ornament. Its façade is decorated by images of the Capitoline triad (Juno, Jupiter, and Minerva from left to right) to whom the *tensa* may have belonged, with Mercury, Hercules, and a Victory on the long side (again from left to right) (Figure 11).[80]

In addition to the ambiguities surrounding their identification, the reason or occasion for their puzzling numismatic appearance also presents difficulties. Aediles were largely responsible for financing and organizing the games – and a few "aedilician" coin-types seemingly advertised the would-have-been *cura ludorum* of failed candidates for the post. Perhaps this mysterious L. Rubrius Dossenus had stood or would stand for an aedileship and so signaled his unrealized or potential generosity by trading on the robust late-republican associations

INV 4355

11. Terracotta relief depicting a *tensa*, Augustan or early imperial, ca. 25 BCE–50 CE

between the *ludi*, the *pompa circensis*, and the *tensae* – an elusive and allusive act of self-aggrandizement, but one in keeping with other "aedilician" coin-types. Whatever the motivation for their initial issue, these issues were sufficiently striking that Trajan had them restored in the high empire.[81]

However important the *tensae* themselves were, their contents, the *exuviae*, were equally significant. If anthropomorphic divine images allowed worshippers to forge an often-intimate relation with divinity, the *exuviae*, by contrast, demanded distance and generated alienation. The *exuviae* were kept out of sight and secret until their installation in the *pulvinar*. Transgression courted divine anger: gazing on the *sacra* resulted in a plague, while handling the *exuviae* led to one of the worst military disasters in Roman collective memory.[82] The gods, in their symbolic form as sacred and secret objects, did not want to be spied upon or touched as they traveled to the Circus and so it seems that a *nomenclator* needed to announce the arrival of the relevant god.[83] Once at the Circus, however, these sacred objects – perhaps cultic objects (something like relics of use or touch) or the symbols or attributes by which each god was identified (i.e. the lightning bolt of Jupiter) – and almost certainly also the *fercula*-images, were ceremonially installed on chairs for the *exuvaie* (a *sellisternium*) or couches for the *simulacra* (a *lectisternium*) in the *pulvinar*, an elevated platform (and a later a temple-like structure) from which the gods and eventually some of the emperors enjoyed the races.[84] The *exuviae* seem to have functioned like Greek *xoana*, archaic and perhaps also aniconic cult statues. According to Pausanius, writing in the second century CE, these primitive, strange, and disconcertingly supernatural statues differed dramatically from ordinary, anthropomorphic cult images. *Xoana* were not normally on view; rather they "oscillate[d] between the two extremes of 'being kept secret' and 'being shown in public,'" as did the *exuviae*. Their display in public could have seemed "like an 'unveiling' of a mysterious and fearful reality."[85]

Jupiter and the other gods were present as their *simulacra* on *fercula* and as their *exuviae* or *sacra* carried in *tensae*. This duality has been and still is explained as an artifact of historical evolution: the symbols were supposedly the first Roman medium for representing the gods in the aniconic early Rome of Varro's philosophizing conceit; anthropomorphic images only came later.[86] However, the two modes of making the gods present had long, if not always, co-existed at Rome. Rather than emerging successively, they more likely worked contemporaneously to fashion different kinds of relations between humans and gods.[87] On the one hand, the statues made present the gods *as if* they were fellow citizens who had, just like the rest of the crowd, left their homes to view the games. These images made the gods more familiar, more like family.[88] On the other hand, the *exuviae*, the sacred symbols, demonstrated divine alterity: the gods were not human; they existed in other ways, uncircumscribable by human social relations. The distinct modes of transport further underscored the differences between these modalities of divinity: human *fercula*-bearers carried the gods in full view to the arena, whereas horses drawing cars bore the wholly other sacred symbols.

Folkloric figures

This double image of the gods, as familiar and foreign, was supplemented by another, more theatrical means of representing the supernatural, the other-than-human. Even combined, the lengthy lists of both Dionysius and Ovid ignore "folkloric figures," *effigies* like Manducus, a grotesque "devil" who gnashed his large teeth, Citeria, a silly chatterbox, and Petreia, a stumbling drunkard, as well as stilt-walkers who seemingly imitated the more wild side of the divine – the only extant examples of what might have been a larger group of preternatural performers who likely appeared in all manner of public celebrations.[89] Whatever these figures may have been – neither deities, nor humans – their performance seems to have spiced up what was already a ludic and sacred procession with a pinch of the paranormal.

Though the evidence for these *effigies* is especially tenuous, they seem to have formed a group of colossal, terrifying, and amusing wooden puppets carried in the *pompa circensis*.[90] According to Paul the Deacon's early medieval epitome of Festus' high-imperial version of Verrius Flaccus' early imperial encyclopedic text, which quotes a mid-republican play by Plautus, "An effigy of Manducus was accustomed to go in the procession of the ancients among other ridiculous and dreadful [*effigies*], gaping its great jaws widely and making tremendous noise with its teeth ... at the games."[91] A mid-fifth-century CE grammarian defined Manducus as "a huge, wooden figure of a human being, which was wont to move its jaws at the circus games as if chewing."[92] Likewise, Paul the Deacon, Festus, and ultimately Cato (234–149

BCE) noted that a loquacious effigy of Citeria was carried in a procession to the games, chatting up the crowd as she went.[93] Finally, Petreia, a drunken old hag, also staggered along in an unspecified provincial parade.[94] Taken together, the precarious evidence suggests that a group of outsized, wooden puppets performed their antics in the circus procession.

Along similar lines, stilt-walkers might have stridden along in the parade next to the gods with their huge steps imitating the wild dance of Aegipan (Goat-Pan), perhaps the Roman god Silvanus. However, their placement, not to mention their presence, in the *pompa circensis* remains entirely arguable, though such entertainers seem to have plied their trade at both theatrical shows and circus games.[95] If these "gods" on stilts did appear in the procession, which seems entirely plausible, their antics and even their costumes may have skillfully echoed the sexualized satire of the burlesque dancers, the satyrs and Sileni.

Whatever these ridiculous and terrifying figures were, their alternating frightening and humorous engagements with the crowd recall contemporary anthropological descriptions of séances, in which spirits, dead ancestors, spirits of certain places, or even deities, teased and terrified their audience. For example, among the Kaluli of Papua New Guinea according to Edward Schieffelin, a female spirit named "Daluami was rather forward and provocative, and conversations with the young bachelors of the community often evoked lewd and ribald repartee, accompanied by howls of laughter throughout the longhouse."[96] Citeria might well have engaged the spectators with similarly bawdy banter. By the same token, it seems plausible to imagine any one of these folkloric figures engaging or addressing the audiences of the *pompa* in equally provocative ways.

The traditional gods, whether as statues or symbols, may have been carried along in the procession rather quietly even if ostentatiously – after all the *fercula*-bearers seem to have had a processional walk, which may have allowed "Ovid" to imagine Venus nodding her approval of his flirtations, and the *tensae* were ivory and silver. By contrast, these *effigies* clattered and chattered with the crowds, perhaps stumbling into or even stepping high over them. In a third modality of presencing or representing the uncanny (or even the divine in the case of the stilt-walkers), these spirited images moved, talked, and interacted with the audience in a kind of "theater, where theater meets magic – the weirdness and intoxication – of a ritual ... [which] adds to rather than eliminates the *mysterium tremendum*" of the divinities, to borrow the words of Michael Taussig, who leaned on those of Rudolf Otto.[97] Assuming that these supernatural spirits chomped, chatted, staggered, and stepped alongside the (other) representations of the gods, then all at once in one and the same procession, the gods are presented as fellow citizens and powerful others in a playful and terrifying paranormal performance.

In the end, the double presence of the gods, as anthropomorphic images on *fercula* and sacred symbols in *tensae*, arranged in some more or less visible manner suggests that the performed theology of the *pompa circensis* articulated a familiar set of theological categories. On the one hand, their marching order – whatever form of representation the gods took – would have suggested hierarchical relations between divinities and the powers or spheres of activity with which they were associated. In other words, the procession presented a pantheon. On the other hand, the anthropomorphic images (*simulacra*) of the gods borne on *fercula* enabled certain kinds of social relations that seemingly emphasized imminence and presence, while the concealed symbols (*exuviae*) drawn in sacred chariots (*tensae*) underscored transcendence and absence. Moreover, *effigies* of supernatural figures and stilt-walkers imitating deities muddied the waters to ensure that these neat dichotomies, imminence-transcendence and presence-absence, got a bit dirty. That is, the *pompa circensis* staged a "debate" concerning the nature of divinity and divine–human relations as well as the (im-)possibility of representation, generating paradoxical theological categories that bear a striking resemblance to those which would haunt late ancient Christian discursive theological thought as it sorted out the incarnation and its own cult of icons.[98]

III REGULATIONS AND RITUAL FAILURE IN THE *POMPA DEORUM*

Dancing back and forth between gravity-levity and resonance-wonder, and emerging out of the smoky haze of burning incense, the passage of the gods through Rome transformed the city and the Circus into a ludic space in which gods and humans could interact.[99] But the creation and maintenance of this ludic space was itself governed by regulations – every game has its rules. In particular, the proper care and handling of the gods as they traversed the city seems to have been garrisoned by ritual restrictions and riddled with anxieties, most of which focused on the *tensae* and *exuviae*.

In fact, the very name *tensa* may derive from its ritual use. According to Cicero, a *puer patrimus et matrimus*, a boy whose parents were both living, needed to hold fast to the *tensa* without letting go of the reins.[100] Plutarch, just after relating the awful story of the tortured slave whose agonized gestures Jupiter found so appalling, noted among the more "petty" ritual regulations observed by the Romans that the horses who drew the *tensae* needed to maintain their pace even as one holding the reins could not grab them with his left hand.[101] *Tensa*, then, could have been derived from the act of reaching out (*tendo*) to grasp or to hold (*teneo* or *tango*) the reins and to maintain contact with the *tensa*.[102]

Along with the *puer matrimus et patrimus*, there seem to have been other attendants charged with the care of the *tensae* – specifically a *tensarius*.

A tantalizing "fragment" from Accius (late second to early first century BCE) quoted by Nonius Marcellus in the late fourth or early fifth century CE in his *De compendiosa doctrina* notes that "some of them fit bridles to the *tensa* and to the mouth of the horses," while an altar to Sol Invictus was erected in the late second century CE by a *nomenclator tensarum iugaris* – perhaps an individual who yoked the horses and announced the *tensa* of Sol.[103] An elusive verse from the Augustan-era author Grattius suggests that even the horses employed to draw the *tensae* through the city needed to meet certain qualifications: "but the herds of Cyrrha, sacred to you Phoebus, have earned great honor, whether the need be to yoke a light chariot or to pull our *tensae* to the shrines."[104] While the evidence is obscure, it does suggest that a specifically appointed individual (or individuals) was (were) responsible for properly yoking specially chosen horses to a *tensa* at the shrines or temples where they were housed, or perhaps while the sacred chariots were assembling at the *aedes tensarum*, the shrine which housed the *tensae* on the Capitoline.[105] This same individual (or these same individuals) may have then accompanied the *tensa* in the procession to announce the deity whose symbols or attributes sat inside.

Similarly, the *fercula* may have been borne by specially chosen individuals. Even though much of the evidence suggests that those who carried *fercula* "come from those whose lot it is to bear loads [i.e. day-laborers or slaves]," priests and/or devotees of the apropos deity may have cultivated divine goodwill by hoisting a heavy *ferculum*, which swayed as it traveled and bowed the support staves when stopped, up on their shoulders.[106] The *galli*, eunuch devotees of Magna Mater, were said to have carried their goddess on their "soft necks."[107] A number of inscriptions refer to *lecticarii* (litter-bearers) of named deities, Jupiter Dolichenus and Jupiter Optimus Maximus specifically, which suggests that these individuals carried their gods.[108] Of course, there are many, many more *lecticarii* who were simply hired help for the wealthy (above all for the imperial family).[109] Furthermore, three inscriptions mention a Bellona *pulvinensis*, Bellona of the *pulvinar*, which has commonly been understood to signal a temple in which Bellona rested upon a sacred couch (*pulvinar*), either in the Vatican or near the circus Flaminius.[110] However, *pulvinensis* may refer to the place that Bellona occupied in the *pulvinar* at the Circus Maximus.[111] Perhaps these devotees had been honored with the responsibility of carrying a specially manufactured processional image of their goddess in the circus procession – a duty worthy of a funeral epitaph. In fact, L. Lartius Anthus was a *cistophorus* of Bellona *pulvinensis*, a bearer of the *cista* of Bellona, and so perhaps he also bore a *ferculum*.[112] Finally, an augur from north Africa donated a decorated litter (*lectica*) to Bellona, though of course that does not mean that he carried it.[113] Altogether, it is not unlikely that cultic adherents carried at least some deities, in particular those from "imported" cults, while traditional Roman civic gods, except possibly Jupiter Optimus Maximus, were typically in the hands of paid haulers.

Whether devotees or laborers, it seems that either the weight of the divine burden or perhaps a relentless urge toward "wonder" led to a very distinctive, languid, tottering gait. According to Cicero in his *De Officiis*, one "should take care not to employ an effeminate lingering in our gait, lest we seem like *fercula* in procession."[114] By late antiquity, the peculiarities of the processional *fercula* had become a topos, but an illuminating one – if not simply a neat intertextual refrain. In the late fourth century CE, bishop Ambrose of Milan commented in a text modeled after Cicero's, "there are people who walk so slowly that they appear to be imitating the sort of contrived movements which actors make, or even the motions of statues nodding on *fercula* at processions: with every step they take they look as though they are observing some vague, imaginary rhythm."[115] Whatever his other talents, Ambrose was certainly a keen observer of public, social-identity performance. Ambrose refused a man entry to the priesthood because "he carried himself physically in a way that was totally unseemly," and he even fired a priest "for the cocky way in which he walked was painful for [Ambrose] to behold."[116] Around the same time, Jerome criticized the arrogant, bloated souls of the uncaring rich and their pompous behavior by comparing them to *fercula* in procession – a comparison that he would employ rather frequently.[117] For both Ambrose and Jerome, to saunter like *fercula* in procession was a sure sign of a "bad" Christian, and worse a bad ascetic, whether monk or virgin.[118] From Cicero and Ovid to Ambrose and Jerome, it seems that the *fercula*-bearers were at least thought or imagined to have performed their duty with a certain altogether appropriate pomposity.

Unfortunately, the extant evidence only offers scant traces of the complex apparatus of devotees, ritual personnel, and paid laborers who organized, produced, and performed in the *pompa circensis*. Even so, their intricate operations were strictly regulated, even down to the sway of the *fercula* perhaps. To transgress the rules always risked ritual failure. Whoever attended the *tensae* or bore the *fercula* needed to take every precaution to ensure the proper conduct of the procession. Even the horses had to follow the rules. "If the *puer patrimus et matrimus* has not kept to his *tensa* or has let a rein slip," or "if one of the horses drawing the sacred chariots called *tensae* gives out; or again, if the one who holds the reins [seemingly either the *puer* or the *iugaris* if there was one] takes hold of the reins with his left hand, [the Romans] decree that the procession be renewed."[119] Even if the attendants had performed their duties properly, there were further taboos that could be violated.

That is, a properly performed ritual may fail, if its audience or even its producer violated its obligations. For example, the processional route was decorated with an awning at some point during the republic or perhaps early empire. That awning was, however, spurred by a failed ritual.

> Verrius Flaccus reports that when the Roman people were in the grip of a plague and an oracle said it was happening because the gods "were being looked down upon," the city was seized by anxiety because the oracle was opaque; and it came to pass that on the days of the circus games a boy was looking down on the procession from a garret, reporting to his father the arrangement of the secret sacred objects [*secreta sacrorum*] he saw in the cart's [*pilentum*] coffer. When his father told the senate what happened, it decreed that the route of the procession should be covered with an awning.[120]

If looking down upon the *sacra* instigated a plague, holding them led to one of the worst military defeats in the Roman historical imagination.

> It was believed that consul Varro met with such misfortune in his battle with the Carthaginians at Cannae because of Juno's wrath by reason of his having as aedile in charge of the circus games [in 220 BCE] placed an exceptionally handsome boy actor in the *tensa* of Jupiter Best and Greatest to hold the *exuviae*. Some years later this act was recalled to memory and sacrificially expiated.[121]

The gods, in their symbolic form as sacred and secret objects, did not want to be spied upon or handled as they traveled to the Circus. A *puer matrimus et patrimus* and perhaps also a *nomenclator* accompanied the *tensa* to avoid, as far as possible, ritual failure, which could trigger death, disease, and defeat, but happenstance and poor executive decisions cannot always be avoided.

Other prodigies related to both the *tensae* and the *fercula* could signal divine displeasure with less traumatic consequences. At the *ludi Romani* in 187 BCE, "a badly fixed mast in the Circus fell on a statue of Pollentia and shattered it."[122] The senate, moved by religious scruple, voted to add one day of games. Additionally, in place of the destroyed statue two new ones were to be set up, one of which would be gilded. Though the original statue may have been erected on a wooden column on the central barrier, it is also possible that the statue of Pollentia was carried in a *pompa circensis* to the *pulvinar*. The pole or beam that fell on the statue could have held an awning that covered the *pulvinar*, at this time most likely a raised wooden platform which housed the gods at the games.[123] Yet other prodigies betrayed civil disturbances, which seemingly also roiled the heavens. In 42 BCE, as a sign of the cosmic struggle between the "liberators," Cassius and Brutus, and the second triumvirate, primarily Antony and Octavian, "a *tensa* of Athena [Minerva] while returning to the Capitol [presumably to the *aedes tensarum*] from the races in the Circus was dashed to pieces."[124] This prodigy seems simply to signify universal unrest, on earth and in heaven. Another omen presaged the ultimate defeat of Cassius and Brutus. In that same year, according to Julius Obsequens, "A boy, while he was carried in a *pompa* dressed as Victory, fell from the *ferculum*," in what seems to have been a military procession in camp of Cassius, though the setting is unclear. If a boy holding the *exuviae* led to the disaster at Cannae, then it should have been obvious that dressing a boy up as a goddess would not turn out well. Seemingly describing the same procession, Plutarch and Cassius Dio, however, assert that a statue of Victory simply fell to the ground as a portent of defeat when its bearer, a boy, slipped.[125] Whether a ritual failure or an omen, processions in general, and the *pompa circensis* in particular, seem to have been an important index of cosmic unrest throughout the civil wars at the end of the first century BCE. After defeating the assassins of Caesar, Antony and Octavian then turned on each other, during which struggle "the *tensa* of Zeus [Jupiter] was demolished in the arena at Rome," as divine disquiet continued to march in step with human strife.[126]

As portrayed by Dionysius, the circus procession continually oscillated between gravity and levity, between solemnity and laughter, between structure and sexuality. Young Roman men arranged according to military rank were followed by charioteers and contestants ranked according to their own hierarchy of status and celebrity and three choruses of armed dancers were lampooned by bands of dancers playing satyrs and Sileni. This oscillation helped to mark or frame the games as special, as distinct from everyday life. The impulse toward wonder or spectacle aided these efforts, in particular and most importantly for the *pompa deorum*, the parade of gold and silver ritual vessels and censers billowing perfumed smoke, which invited the gods to join. In the ludic space traced by the *pompa circensis*, gods and humans could assemble together to enjoy the games.

This ludic space was also something of a classroom. The *pompa circensis* was an important moment in which power and divinity was performed and thought about.[127] Each enactment of this ephemeral event performed theology in the interactions between divinity, (re-)presented in various ways, and humanity. The grammar and syntax of the *pompa deorum* – that is, its modes of divine representation and the organization and order of divine images and symbols – enunciated a contingent understanding of the divine world and its relation with the human; understandings and relations that could change with each iteration or according to individual experience and predilection, as Ovid suggested. The gods appeared in the procession as anthropomorphic statues carried on *fercula* and as symbols secreted away in *tensae*, augmented by supernatural folk figures and stilt-walkers imitating gods. In other words, the other-than-human appeared as familiar and approachable, alien and distant, and terrifying and ridiculous. These various modes of presencing the gods or the supernatural were themselves ordered and organized into pantheons, at least in the texts of Dionysius and Ovid. Any such arrangement, however, would have likely been scattered in disarray once the procession began, and so might or might not have been visible to an audience that could have formulated its own pantheons according to its own ways of seeing – intent, execution, and reception need not correspond.

To these performed axes of theological differentiation, one could also add mode of transportation: *simulacra* on *fercula* carried by human bearers or *exuviae* in *tensae* drawn by four horses underscored the different modalities of presencing the gods. Even material of manufacture – plaster Victories and ivory (and perhaps also marble) gods – may have emphasized divine hierarchies. All of these distinctions, indeed the entire procession, was regulated by tradition and religious scruple. The curriculum, as it were, of this public, performative theological education was not put together haphazardly. Ritual attendants, devotees, Roman officials, and apparently even horses all had a part in ensuring a proper performance. Ritual failure could be devastating, resulting in plague or military disaster. Ancient Rome may not have had a distinct, formal setting for discursive religious education; nonetheless, its public ceremonies, rituals, and especially processions offered a robust, yet subtle and complex, performed theology.

And yet, this religious education, this theological performance, with its various modes of divine (re-)presentation, its hierarchical organization, and its distinctions of transport and material of manufacture does not fully capture the work that the *pompa circensis* performed. Once again there is another notable lacuna in Dionysius' description: in 45 BCE, Julius Caesar and subsequently deified Roman emperors and empresses as well as deceased members of the imperial family began to process with the traditional gods in the *pompa circensis*. That is, the double image of the *dei* (traditional gods), as familiar and foreign, was itself doubled by the eventual inclusion of the *divi* (deified emperors and empresses), who appeared in the procession doubled as statues carried on *fercula* or borne on carts drawn by up to four elephants and symbols carried in *tensae* – or statues in *carpenta*, a cart drawn by mules, and/or elephant *biga* for deified empresses. During the early empire, at least, the performance of the *pompa circensis* would continue to articulate the changing nature and relations between power and divinity. In the late empire, by contrast, such performed theology gradually, over the course of centuries, withered in the face of the burgeoning discursive theology of an imperially supported Christianity.

THREE

ITER POMPAE CIRCENSIS

Memory, resonance, and the image of the city

We have a city founded by auspice and augury; there is no place in it that is not full of religious obligations and of gods; the days are not more fixed for the traditional sacrifices than are the places in which they are performed.

Livy 5.52.2[1]

In a famous speech set in the aftermath of the Gallic sack of Rome in 390 BCE, Livy – whose history was shaped by Roman topography even as his stories gave it significance (a *monimentum* which endowed monuments with meaning) – had Camillus, hero of the republic, forcefully argue against abandoning a ruined Rome in favor of a still-standing Veii.[2] Camillus insisted that the proper observance of Roman civic religion required the proper rituals to be conducted at the proper times in their proper places – a reflection, perhaps, of heightened early imperial anxieties over the displacement and dissolution of (elite) Roman identities, which were so relentlessly tied to the lovingly remembered places of Rome.[3] Even if empire amplified concerns about dislocation, Roman historical and religious traditions had long emphasized emplacement – Roman authors were quite attached to the peculiarities of places.[4] As Cicero had a literary Atticus concede, "we are affected in some mysterious way by places about which cluster memories [*vestigia*] of those whom we love and admire."[5]

At Rome, such sentimental attachment to place was closely tied to what one might call cultural memory – collective, historical consciousness, a stream of tradition reified in rituals, images, places, monuments, and texts.[6] And the itinerary of the *pompa circensis* may be considered an archive of cultural memory, encompassing some of the most historically saturated terrain of the republican (and even imperial) city. Traveling from the Capitol through the Forum, along the *vicus Tuscus* in the Velabrum, and then through the Forum Boarium to the Circus Maximus, the *iter pompae circensis* (my own confection) constituted a landscape of memory that was central to (elite) Roman identity (Map 1). The itinerary comprised much of what could be called Rome's urban armature, a series of connected, monumental public spaces, rather than the more typical broad, colonnaded avenues.[7] This "armature" was significant in part because a historian like Livy wrote about it, rhetorical exercises required a rehearsal of a canned history set in it, and an orator like Cicero referenced it – discursive practices that all functioned as frameworks of collective memory.[8] In addition, this "armature" continued to matter because it continued to be animated by all manner of practices, ceremonies, and rituals. As Diane Favro has argued, "ritual events such as parades or contemporaneous celebrations experientially linked disparate urban sites, imbuing them with collective meaning."[9] As the circus procession traversed its landscape of memory, the ritual performance conjured a vast pageant of Rome's past embodied by practices, places, and monuments.

To put it another way, the performance of the *pompa circensis* could generate linkages between the participants and the itinerary, spinning dense webs of associations, in which history, tradition, and topography were enmeshed. Linked by cultural memory, such public or collective resonances formed a symbolic, ritual topography – in short, an image of the city.[10] Much as the *pompa circensis* performed theology in an act of ritual education, it also performed Rome – or at least one version and vision of it, stringing together certain places, buildings, and monuments (as well as select institutions, social identities, and individuals) in a single itinerary plucked from the swarming mass of ancient Rome.[11] The procession and itinerary, with its multitude of memories and meanings, privileged and displayed to participants and spectators alike what was supposed to be essential – at least, according to the contingent history and traditions of the procession as well as the religious scruples and the political struggles that governed its performance.

Within this epic staging of Rome's cultural memory, individual echoes could also resonate. That is, the procession could have helped to make the itinerary meaningful to both participants, who would travel the entire route, but see only their section of the procession, and also spectators, who likely witnessed the performance from a single location, though they could watch the entire parade. The exiguous evidence, however, only allows for some limited speculation about the experiences of the participants, about whose social identities or professions at least a little may be known. Political elites, sons of equestrians, contestants, paid performers, and even paid laborers can be imagined to have felt any number of personal, political, ritual, historical, and

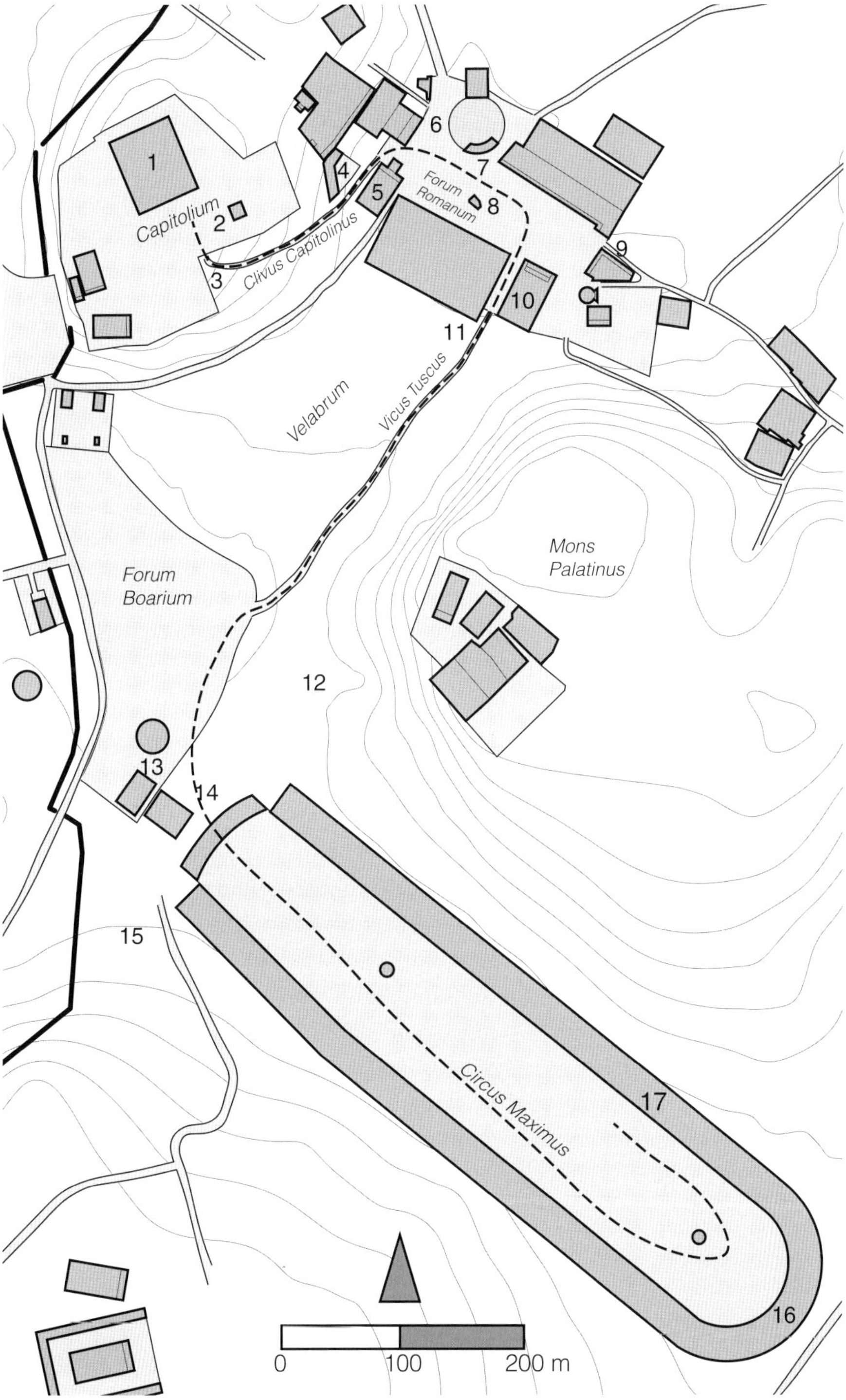

Map 1 The "republican" itinerary of the *pompa circensis*, drawn by Marie Saldaña

collective resonances at any number of the crowded and celebrated places along the itinerary. Moreover, the processional itinerary seems to have framed the participants' experiences in two ways. On the one hand, the linear itinerary ordered and organized Roman topography, history, and memory in a single intelligible, sequential pattern – not unlike the structured and hierarchical image of Roman society embodied by the cortege itself.[12] On the other hand, an insistent series of repetitions – of temples, arches (*fornices*), columns, and even fig trees – may have collapsed this linear parade of (collective and individual) memory places, producing a kind of utopian, ludic space in which beginning and end have folded in on themselves.

In many respects, then, the procession performed (or forged) an image of the city as conceived by Kevin Lynch.[13] Built from idiosyncratic and subjective urban experiences, an image of the city, whether public (that is, widely held) or individual, functioned as a scaffold of knowledge, a political and symbolic topography, and a framework for activity, a mental map. The play between a meticulously arranged (and then playfully dis-arranged) cortege, a kind of urban cross-section, and an itinerary that privileged certain places could be said to construct a scaffold of knowledge or even a representation of the city – a traditional understanding of processional performance, but no less important for that.[14] More specifically, the *pompa circensis* seems to have conjured Rome as two intertwined symbolic cityscapes, two highly condensed and very traditional images of the city: *aurea Roma* and, above all, the senate and Roman people with their gods (SPQR+gods). There are also a few rather tenuous hints that this image of the city could also have been a framework for activity, a navigational aid. After all, the metaphorical string of memory places, prominent landmarks and public squares, was also an actual pathway, a real route through the city. And so the social, symbolic "map" could also have been a navigational one, an image of the city in the full sense, with which a spectator could place herself in Rome – in both its political and symbolic topography and physical landscape. In the end, the *pompa circensis* was a means of place-making that drew together memory, people, and place to help one navigate Rome's complex social life, its vertiginous and competitive political culture, and its baffling labyrinth of streets and alleys in the imagination and on the ground.

I AN ITINERARY OF COLLECTIVE MEMORY

"Camillus" (or at least Livy) as well as "Atticus" (or at least Cicero) would seemingly have well understood the sentiments of "Marco Polo" as imagined by Italo Calvino:

> As this wave of memories flows in, the city soaks it up and expands. A description of Zaira as it is today should contain all of Zaira's past. The

> city, however, does not tell its past but it contains it like the lines of a hand, written in the corners of streets, the gratings of windows, the banisters of steps, the antennae of lightning rods, the poles of the flags, every segment in turn marked with scratches, indentations, scrolls.[15]

Like an imagined Zaira, narratives of an equally imagined, but also historical, Rome were traced and re-traced, layered deeply on its monuments, and written and re-written on its streets, buildings, and public spaces like a palimpsest.[16] Indeed, most cities to one degree or another house their histories in their buildings, places, and streets. As the urban historian M. Christine Boyer remarks, "addressed to the eye of vision and to the soul of memory, a city's streets, monuments, and architectural forms often contain grand discourses on history."[17] This seems to have been especially true at Rome, where according to Catharine Edwards "in the republic, at least, the city itself was Rome's chief historical text."[18] The heroes of the republic who were commemorated with monuments were also lionized in texts creating a complex interplay between place and narrative.[19] The city, then, staged history in a double sense: the cityscape functioned as the theater in which historical action took place, and later the city "remembered" or "rehearsed" that history in its statues, monuments, and even rituals. In other words, history shaped the city, even as the city shaped its history. History (*historia*) was, in many ways, public memory (*memoria publica*), collective memory that all Romans (or at least elite Romans) were obligated to remember.[20] And so, the city functioned, in many ways, as a framework of public memory.

Analogously, much as Roman myths and also Roman histories were, among other things, stories of place and housed in places, so too Roman civic religion was a religion of place(s).[21] At Rome, sanctuaries and temples were not only ritually constituted spaces for the performance of ritual, but also monuments of memory and history.[22] For example, the Lupercalia commemorated the hoary days of a real and really imagined archaic Rome at the very spot, the Lupercal, where according to tradition the twins Romulus and Remus were supposed to have suckled.[23] That is, narrative and ritual constituted Rome's landscape of memory as much as buildings and monuments, even as Roman history and Roman religion were embodied and embedded in places, buildings, and monuments.[24] These embodied and embedded memories lay dormant until re-activated by human actors and actions, like processions which, as Karl-Joachim Hölkeskamp puts it, "moved from one meaningful location to the next, thereby galvanizing memories and reinvigorating the nexus of associations that attached Rome's contemporary urban topography to her past."[25] Processions were one of the frameworks of cultural memory, a practical and material buttress for the inter-subjective remembrance of Roman traditions.[26] Or, following Michel de Certeau, as a procession traversed its itinerary, it strung together peoples and institutions, monuments and spaces, and landmarks and pathways, as well as historical associations and memories, into a coherent, and linear, performed narrative.[27]

In other words, the performance of the *pompa circensis* narrated, in a manner of speaking, a kind of history of Rome from the city's archive of cultural memory – yet another way in which the procession could make Romans out of participants and spectators alike.[28] Perhaps for this reason, Dionysius of Halicarnassus, for whom the circus procession demonstrated Rome's Greek origins, all too cursorily sketched the itinerary "from the Capitolium through the Forum to the Circus Maximus." Rome's "landscape of memory thronged with monuments of power" was perhaps too thoroughly rooted in the soil.[29]

The only securely attested itinerary of the *pompa circensis* began on the Capitoline hill, possibly within the sanctuary of Capitoline Jupiter where an *aedes* or *sacrarium tensarum* (or two) stood. It is difficult to overestimate the importance of the Capitol, and especially the Capitoline temple which housed "the father, the king of gods and men."[30] From its inauguration, the temple was, in Livy's words, "the citadel of empire and head of the world," and remained "the citadel and Capitolium, the seat of the gods, the senate, and the head of public judgment" throughout the republic (and even into the late empire).[31] As "Camillus" continued his appeal on behalf of Rome, he gestured to the Capitol itself:

> Here (*hic*) is the Capitol, where men were told, when of old they discovered a human head, that in that place should be the head of the world and the seat of an empire; here (*hic*), when the Capitol was being cleared with augural rites, Juventas and Terminus, to the vast joy of your fathers, refused to be removed.[32]

Just as Juventas, whose shrine may have sat just before the cella of Minerva, and Terminus, possibly in the cella of Jupiter himself, refused to move, forecasting an eternally youthful, ever-expanding empire, so too should the Romans stay put. To abandon the Capitol was to abandon Rome and Roman identity. The Capitol was a kind of weather vane; it's fortunes were an index of Rome's fortunes. Moreover, the Capitol, as a kind of sanctuary of cultural memory, sheltered Roman history in its accumulation of statues, votives, inscriptions, and other dedications.[33]

The procession then wended its way down the *clivus Capitolinus* to reach the "hallowed ground" of the Roman Forum – another key site of collective memory.[34] During the republic, one could argue that the Forum Romanum was still an active "*milieu de mémoire*, [a] setting in which memory is a real part of everyday experience," rather than an ossified "*lieu de mémoire*" that it may have become under the empire.[35] The republican Forum was the central stage of Roman political theater in a double sense: both an interactive museum of

Rome's glorious past, with an increasing number of monuments and honorific statues, and the beating political heart of the state.[36] Again contemplating the power of place, Cicero conjured a Marcus Piso who, struck deeply by Athens, remarked that "one's emotions are more strongly aroused by seeing the places that tradition records to have been the favorite resort of men of note in former days, than by hearing about their deeds or reading their writings." Athens certainly stirred "Marcus Piso," but the impact of places on memory was not confined to its storied sites. For "Marcus Piso," "even the sight of our senate-house at home (I mean the Curia Hostilia, not the present new building, which looks to my eyes smaller since its enlargement) used to call up to me thoughts of Scipio, Cato, Laelius, and chief of all, my grandfather, such powers of suggestion do places possess."[37] The Forum could summon both cultural memory in the form of heroes of the republic like Scipio and personal or familial memory, in this case Marcus Piso's grandfather. Indeed, the space of the Forum ran deep in semantic overlays, allowing for countless individual reverberations to echo in the larger landscape of Roman public memory.

The circus procession continued onto the *vicus Tuscus*, "the street of *tensae* and processions."[38] This ancient street, in turn, passed through the Velabrum, "where now the processions are wont to defile to the Circus, [while previously] there was naught but willows and hollow canes" in the Ovidian imagination.[39] As it turns out, archaeological evidence tends to confirm that the Velabrum was a floodplain and an active port and industrial, commercial area, nearly bereft, it seems, of the kind of political collective memory that marked the Forum. However, the area teemed with primordial mnemotopoi (memory places) like the Lupercal, where sluggish floodwaters deposited Romulus and Remus, and the Ara Maxima in honor of Hercules, attributed to Hercules himself (or Evander, or his followers) – a demi-god among countless others who also appeared in the *pompa circensis* according to Fabius Pictor-Dionysius.[40]

The procession then finally arrived at the Circus Maximus carved out of the hollow between the Palatine and Aventine hills, where according to tradition Romulus abducted the Sabine women during Rome's first games. The altar of Consus, whom the inaugural games honored, was not only one of the Circus' many mnemotopoi, cult sites of primordial antiquity, but it also served as a boundary marker for the so-called Romulean *pomerium*. And so the Circus was a legendary and liminal space, a place altogether fitting for "the social intercourse of gods and humans."[41] In the end, the landscape of memory from the Capitol to the Circus was dominated by some of the most politically potent and religiously significant places, storied moments, and treasured memories of the republic. Nonetheless, even a paid dancer playing a satyr could potentially see himself in this symbolic topography.

II RESONANCE AND REPETITION

From the Capitolium through the Forum to the Circus Maximus.

Dionysius of Halicarnassus, *Roman Antiquities* 7.72.1[42]

On any given day, the streets of (late) republican Rome overflowed with its vast population.[43] To address such congestion, the so-called *Lex Iulia Municipalis* forbade *plostra* (or *plaustra*) within the city during the day with few exceptions, one of which notably exempted "*plostra* . . . for the *pompa* of the *ludi circenses*." Though *plostrum/plaustrum* typically referred to a slow, heavy wagon, in the case of the *pompa circensis*, the word's semantic range seems to have included *tensa*, as suggested by a passage from Tertullian, admittedly written centuries after the regulations in question, where *tensa* and *plaustrum* were synonymous: "Even if one draws only one *tensa*, nevertheless it is the *plaustrum* of Jupiter."[44] And so the *pompa circensis* and possibly its sacred vehicles (or at least heavy carts connected to the games) were given legal sanction to occupy the streets, when normally access was restricted – an important indicator that the procession constituted a special event, a ritualized moment. In addition, crowd control measures would have been required to carve out space for the procession to pass – lictors may have hacked open a space just before the procession which quickly closed behind or perhaps the entire itinerary had been cleared in advance.[45] In either case, both the legal sanction to drive *plaustra/tensae* through the city during otherwise forbidden hours and the employment of crowd-control measures ensured that the *pompa circensis* was exceptional: for everyone, participants and spectators alike.

Perhaps such discontinuity with daily experience – or ritualization – would have prepared the participants to be more attentive to whatever resonances there may have been between themselves, their experiences, and the itinerary, a few possibilities of which will be sketched in what follows. What "Lucius" noted for classical Athens, "wherever we go, we tread on some historical memory," seems to hold equally true for Rome, if the participant was paying attention.[46] The ritualization of a stroll through town (that is, the *pompa circensis*) might have predisposed the participants to feel the full weight of the itinerary; not only its structured and hierarchical linearity, but also its repetition of temples, arches, columns, trees, and even honorific statues – repetitions which may have uncannily collapsed space.

Capitolium

The citadel and Capitolium, the seat of the gods, the senate, and the head of public judgment.

Livy 5.39.12[47]

The sheer, outsized importance of the Capitoline temple seems to have matched its overawing, colossal size, likely from its first foundation

(Map 1.1).[48] According to the Roman mytho-historical imagination (that is, legend), "with prophetic anticipation of the splendor which the place was one day to possess, [Tarquinius Priscus] laid foundations for the temple of Jupiter on the Capitol."[49] Though its construction was ostensibly initiated during the royal period under Tarquinius Priscus and continued by Tarquinius Superbus, who sought to build "a temple of Jupiter so great that it would be worthy of the king of gods and humans, the Roman empire, and the majesty of the place itself," it was founded in 509 BCE, contemporaneously with the Roman republic itself.[50] Subsequently, as Catharine Edwards notes, "this one hill and particularly its temple could be made to stand for the city as a whole and even for the entire Roman empire."[51] The endurance of its form and function, its very architecture and also its rituals, were a sign and symptom of the continuity of Rome, Roman power, and Roman identity. Indeed, scrupulous efforts were made to reproduce or to seem to reproduce the original architectural form, rituals, and even contents of the temple of Capitoline Jupiter, notwithstanding certain allowable upgrades (or corruptions).[52]

The Capitol was so central to Rome's political and religious life that the poetic imagination could conflate it with Rome itself. For Vergil, "so long as the house of Aeneas [the Roman people] dwells on the Capitol's unshaken rock, and the Father of Rome [Augustus and his line] holds sovereign sway," his poetry would be remembered.[53] Likewise, Horace's poetry would continue to reap the praise of posterity "as long as the pontifex climbs the Capitol with the silent [Vestal] virgin."[54] The temple and its rituals stood literally and figuratively at the heart of Rome and Roman identity. The supposedly limitless power of Roman imperium originated on its steep peaks, which figuratively dominated Roman topography (it was not Rome's largest hill), and washed out over the world in waves. Cicero, perhaps a bit hyperbolically, characterized the Capitol, temple and hill, as "the citadel of all nations" and "the citadel of all peoples."[55] For Livy, it was the "citadel of empire and the head of the world."[56] In Ovid's imagination, "When from his citadel Jupiter looks upon the whole globe, nothing but the Roman empire meets his eye."[57] The *urbs aeterna* (the eternal city) was guaranteed by the temple of Capitoline Jupiter, whose fortunes served as a synecdoche for the fortunes of Rome, the city and its empire: ruin of the Capitol meant the death of the empire.[58]

By the Augustan era, if not earlier, at least one *sacrarium* (shrine) or *aedes* (temple) for *tensae* existed somewhere within the *area Capitolina* (Map 1.2). A small number of military *diplomata* attest that they were affixed to the left, exterior wall of an *aedes tensarum* (*in Capitolio ad latus sinistrum aedis thensarum extrinsecus*, as the formula goes), one of which refers to an older *aedes tensarum* (*thesarium veterem*), implying that there were more than one.[59] This sacred building or these sacred buildings almost certainly housed the *tensae* of the Capitoline triad and perhaps also (some of the) other deities (at least those with shrines on the Capitol) who were borne in the *pompa circensis*. And so, the Capitol, the center of Roman imperium and the barometer of Rome's fortunes, also housed some of the organizational apparatus for the circus procession – that is, the Capitol was not only the ideological origin of the Roman empire, but also the practical origin of a circus procession.

The Capitol and the temple of Capitoline Jupiter may also have had individual resonances for some of the participants. For example, on January 1, the *processus consularis* took place: "in spotless garments a procession wends to the Tarpeian towers; the people wear the color of the festive day; and now new rods of office lead the way, new purple gleams, and the illustrious ivory chair feels a new weight."[60] That is, the consuls-elect, clad in spotless togas and accompanied by groups of equestrians, were conducted in procession from their respective homes to the Capitol, where they oversaw the required sacrifices and then presided over their first session of the senate. Sometime that same year, one of these same consuls (or perhaps a praetor or even a specially appointed dictator) along with, perhaps, the sons of some of the equestrians who had participated in the *processus consularis* would return to the Capitol to lead the circus procession. Perhaps the game-giving consul would have remembered his inauguration, when all the eyes of Rome (or at least a selection of its elites) were upon him, as they were now when a much greater crowd would witness his triumphant, as it were, progress through Rome as and under the auspices of Jupiter Optimus Maximus, who also appeared in the procession in/as his statue and symbols.[61] Other political players may well have brought similar emotional and political investments to the Capitol as they prepared to parade to the Circus Maximus.

On March 17, it was traditional, though by no means mandatory or even generally practiced, for free-born young men, having just donned the *toga virilis* for the first time, to make their adult public premiere by processing with family and friends to the Forum and then the Capitol, where the newly made man performed a sacrifice to (probably) Capitoline Jupiter and Juventas, who also received a coin.[62] For the elite, this entry into public life – after which, for example, one-time Augustan heirs Gaius and Lucius "could take part in councils of state" – was also a political rite of passage, fraught with danger and so carefully orchestrated.[63] Many of these same young men may have previously participated in the *pompa circensis* – or perhaps the youth in the procession were those who had recently attained their *toga virilis*. A few of these same young men could hope to return to the Capitol on January 1 as consul-elect or in his entourage. In the end, the same divine power that conferred authority on Rome's leading magistrates also created its body politic by guiding its future leaders to adulthood. And so the place where at least one *pompa circensis* was organized was also one of the places where Rome as a socio-political entity was produced.

The procession would have then left the *area Capitolina* somewhere near the *fornix* of Scipio Africanus, erected in 190 BCE, an arch at the beginning of the itinerary that would echo those in the Forum in middle and in the Circus Maximus at the end (Map 1.3). This monumental arch – decorated with seven gilded statues, two equestrian figures (or at least horses), two marble basins, and possibly reliefs commemorating Scipio's triumph (making the arch a site of memory) – may have fronted (more commonly accepted) or, more dramatically, straddled the *clivus Capitolinus*, and so served as a monumental entrance to Capitol itself.[64] It is possible that a *fornix* erected by the *gens Calpurnia*, the so-called *fornix* of Calpurnius built before 133 BCE, competed with that of Scipio, though its location is uncertain and it might not have been visible from the procession.[65] Another victory monument, a *columna rostrata* (a column outfitted with ships' prows), was erected on the Capitol to honor M. Aemilius Paulus' victory over the Carthaginians in 255 BCE – and was destroyed by lightning in 172 BCE.[66] Even if this column was not visible from the procession (Livy did not give its exact location) and even if its relatively short-lived presence precluded strong resonances with other victory monuments (duration of overlap would seem to affect ritual echoes), similar columns would dot the itinerary. The short-lived column also suggests a salutatory caution: the precise lifespan of many monuments is difficult to determine and so the itinerary's potential resonances and repetitions must remain tentative suggestions. The procession would have continued down toward the Forum along the *clivus Capitolinus*, a road likely constructed at the same time as the Capitoline temple itself, a road built for processions (most notably the triumph, of course).

As the *clivus Capitolinus* neared the Forum, it passed between the *porticus deorum consentium* (portico of the Harmonious Gods) and the temple of Saturn. First constructed in 174 BCE when the *clivus Capitolinus* was also first paved with hard stone, the portico was seemingly dedicated to a Roman version of the twelve Olympian gods, "twelve *dei consentes* whose gilded images stand by the Forum," presumably somewhere in the precinct defined by the portico (Map 1.4).[67] This sanctuary and its pantheon may be associated with the *lectisternium* performed in 217 BCE, in which the twelve so-called Olympian gods seemingly appeared together for the first time as a group at Rome, an event which may have have influenced Fabius Pictor, almost assuredly a witness of this *lectisternium*, or perhaps Dionysius in retrospect.[68] Whichever way the currents of influences flowed, the performed theology of the procession, in which the gods may have been organized according to a Greek pantheon, or, at least, were imagined to have been organized into the Greek twelve, would have echoed the theology in images housed in this sanctuary.

As the *clivus Capitolinus* wrapped around the stairs of the temple of Saturn, the fulcrum of the itinerary as it entered the Forum, another ritual echo would have resounded (Map 1.5). Saturn, a deity whose venerable cult seems to have stretched into legendary prehistory and whose temple was dedicated shortly after that of Jupiter Optimus Maximus, appeared both in the procession, in/as an image borne on a *ferculum* (and possibly also as a symbol carried in a *tensa*), and in his temple, in/as his cult statue filled with olive oil – oil which may have preserved the statue, which was made from ivory like its avatar on a *ferculum* (or was the cult statue itself carried in the *pompa circensis*?).[69] The god's presence in the procession mirrored his presence in the temple, intensifying and magnifying, one may imagine, the power of the god. Would the *fercula*-bearers have tilted their litter so that their Saturn could greet Saturn in his temple?

Forum Romanum

[W]ider intercolumniations should be distributed around the spectacles . . . and balconies should be placed on the upper floors.

Vitruvius, *On Architecture* 5.1.2[70]

The procession would seemingly have proceeded through the Forum Romanum along its southern edge, perhaps the via Sacra – though typically the northern route through the Forum has been considered the Sacred Way.[71] The Forum, after it had been filled and elevated above flood levels, was saturated with historical memory and political weight.[72] But here too, the overwhelming mass of collective, civic significance left room for more individual resonances as "Marcus Piso" could wax nostalgic about the old senate house, which conjured memories of republican heroes, his grandfather among them.[73] Moreover, the Forum also offered ample room for the procession and even seating for spectators on the steps of its temples and basilicas and its open space – a relative rarity elsewhere along the itinerary.[74]

According to Vitruvius, the Roman habit of producing gladiatorial games in the Forum meant that its architectural frame needed to accommodate as many spectators as possible, and so the wider intercolumniations and balconies. Of course, such provisions could have been used for any spectacle in or passing through the Forum. For example, Verrius Flaccus, as abridged by Festus, contended that the *Maeniana* (the balconies mentioned by Vitruvius) were named after the censor Maenius, who first erected posts in the Forum beyond the columns to provide elevated seating for the spectacles.[75] A *columna Maenia*, a victory monument probably erected in the Northern corner of the Forum in 338 BCE, was (much) later imagined, by the third-century CE scholar Pomponius Porphyrio – and seconded by a late-antique scholiast – as a most ingenious and prodigal seat (Map 1.6). "[Maenius] is said to have reserved for himself a column from his house that had a view of the Forum, when it was sold, from which he could watch the gladiatorial games. For this reason it was called the column of Maenius."[76] Setting aside this fantastical viewing platform, ad hoc or temporary seating was erected in the Forum on a number of occasions, namely gladiatorial combats and triumph(s).[77] Though no purpose-built seating is specifically mentioned for the *pompa circensis*, such accommodation seem entirely plausible, even if nowhere attested.

Even if the column of Maenius had never, in fact, been used as a viewing platform, it would have, nonetheless, added to the monumental staging of the procession. Much like the *fornix* of Scipio may have competed for attention with the *fornix* of Calpurnius on the Capitol, this column would have competed with the neighboring column of Duilius, erected after 260 BCE on or perhaps near the rostra – a partner with the one Duilius erected in front of the Circus by the starting gates (Map 1.7).[78] This kind of repetition of arches and columns, an unremitting accumulation of architectural forms which may have been a bit surreal (depending, of course, on whether or not or for how long the monuments overlapped), could have contributed to the collapsing of mundane space, from which a ludic space could emerge.

In this ludic space enhanced by, one may imagine, the thundering applause of spectators, the Forum may have occasioned a number of personal or individual resonances alongside or within Roman cultural memory. For example, "Marcus Piso's" reminiscences about the curia and his grandfather may have had a parallel in the procession. The *praeses ludorum*, members of his probable entourage, any of the elite Roman youth, or even the aediles may have had the pleasant experience of seeing a statue of themselves, a family member or ancestor, or some personally important hero of the republic in that other population, "the most plentiful population of statues" erected in the Forum and other prominent places.[79] Such an encounter could have spurred family (and civic) memory within the framework of civic (and family) memory. An imagined, youthful "Cicero," agreeing with "Marcus Piso," allowed that "it is a common experience that places strongly stimulate the imagination and vivify our ideas of famous men," before noting that he could almost summon a vision of Carneades (214–129/8 BCE), founder of the New (Platonic) Academy, in his exedra based on his well-known (sculpted) likeness.[80] That is, place and image may evoke cultural memory, especially perhaps in a special, ritualized context like the *pompa circensis*.

It is possible that some consul, or even a praetor, dictator, aedile, or senator found himself face to face with himself, or at least his own statue on the Capitol or in the Forum, both *loci celeberrimi*, famous and frequented places and highly prized as locations for public honors – probably an amiable, but perhaps also an uncanny experience with one's double, not wholly unlike the insistent repetitions of architectural forms.[81] M. Aemilius Lepidus, for example, was honored with a statue for outstanding bravery while a boy (ca. 200 BCE), so when consul in 187 BCE and again in 175, it is possible that he would have passed his own statue, if he led a *pompa circensis*. The father of the Gracchi had a statue erected seemingly in the mid 170s BCE, so again it is possible that when he was consul again in 163 he would have seen his statue from a *pompa circensis*. The sons of Q. Fabius Maximus may have seen their father's statue sometime after it was erected – such a sight could be very affecting as Gaius Gracchus wept in front of his father's statue after his brother's murder.[82] Additional examples, however, are difficult to adduce given the paucity of evidence as well as the fact that Rome's second population was occasionally culled. In 179 BCE, statues were removed from the Capitoline, while in 158 BCE "unauthorized" statues, that is, ones erected without some form (explicit or merely tacit) of official approval, were removed.[83] Nonetheless, it seems reasonable to suggest that at the end of the republic, should a Marius, a Sulla, a Pompey, or a Caesar have led a *pompa circensis*, then very likely they would have passed by one or more of their sizable population of doubles. The same would have held for the stars of republic who shone a little less brightly in the firmament of the late-republican political sky. Around 84 BCE, for a short period of time statues of M. Marius Gratidianus graced all the districts – and public spaces. He was a praetor then.[84] If one then adds the elite youth and the aediles, then the possibility of such a personal and potentially uncanny resonance during the procession becomes a very real and important possibility.

There were, of course, other statues in the Forum. In particular, the procession would have passed by an odd statue in the middle of the Forum standing near a fig tree, a counterpart to another such fig tree further along the itinerary in the Lupercal (yet another potentially surreal repetition): a statue of a pot-bellied, hirsute satyr, wearing nothing at all except a pair of boots and a wreath or perhaps a so-called Phrygian cap (*pileus*), holding a wineskin over his left shoulder with his right arm raised up in the air, as depicted on the reverse of a denarius minted by L. Censorinus in 82 BCE (Map 1.8 and Figure 12).[85] This statue, the satyr Marsyas, was regularly set up in *fora* of free cities (*civitates liberae*).[86] This symbol of freedom (*libertas*) could also be seen as a sign of license (*libertas*), redolent in many ways of the satyrs and Sileni, who mocked and mimicked the serious, martial choruses with their sexualized choreography. Perhaps these burlesque dancers, with their relative surfeit of clothing, goat-skins and manes, tunics and flowers, recognized a kin in the naked, and likely intoxicated, Marsyas, whose licentiousness one could imagine the satyrs and Sileni celebrating with a dance around the statue.[87] Ritual resonances need not have been confined to the rarified heights of the Roman elite, even if such echoes are now hard to hear.

A little further along the itinerary, the *fornix Fabianus* may have straddled the via Sacra – a repetition of previous *fornices* that may have been visually emphasized should the gaze of a participant have panned from this arch in the Forum to catch a glimpse of the *fornix* of Scipio on the Capitoline out of the corner of her eye as the procession turned right onto the *vicus Tuscus* (Map 1.9). Built sometime after 120 BCE and restored in 57 BCE by the aedile Q. Fabius Maximus (perhaps in part in anticipation of this moment during the procession), the arch (the first of its kind in the Forum) not only contributed to the potentially uncanny reduplication along the itinerary, it also helped maintain Roman cultural memory, embodied by the statues of illustrious members of the *Fabii* (including the original builder and triumphator Q. Fabius Maximus Allobrogicus), *Aemilii*, and *Cornelii*, which stood on the attic.[88] Indeed, all known republican *fornices* and even honorific columns were bearers of cultural memory, monuments to a victorious individual, family, and state.

12. Marsyas statue in the Forum and column with a statue of Victory in the background: denarius, 82 BCE: reverse: LCENSOR

As the procession left the Forum, it arrived at the temple of Castor and Pollux, which was dedicated in the earliest years of the republic – just like the temples of Jupiter Optimus Maximus and Saturn. The temple honored the twin horsemen gods for their assistance in defeating the forces of the final Tarquin, the victory which also occasioned the early *pompa circensis* supposedly described by Fabius Pictor and transmitted by Dionysius, in which the Dioscuri figured among the other demi-gods (Map 1.10).[89] The temple of the Dioscuri, also like the temple of Capitoline Jupiter, was decorated with antefixes featuring a wide-eyed satyr or Silenus with a somewhat menacing glare, intense smile, and beard who nevertheless appears a bit comical with a bulbous nose, which would have looked down upon his human counterparts dancing below.[90] The robust resonances between the Dioscuri, the temple, and the procession as well as the repetition of early republican temples and, moreover, architectural decoration could certainly have contributed to a ludic atmosphere.

What is more, in remembrance of the victory which ushered in the republic, Roman knights – who, in Ovid's enumeration of the gods in the *pompa circensis*, were especially fond of the Dioscuri – would ride past the temple on their way to the Capitol in an annual review on July 15. According to Dionysius of Halicarnassus:

> But above all these things [other commemorations of the Dioscuri] there is the procession performed after the sacrifice by those who have a public horse and who, arrayed by tribes and centuries, ride in regular ranks on horseback, as if they came from battle, crowned with olive branches and attired in the purple robes with stripes of scarlet which they call *trabeae*. They begin their procession from a certain temple of Mars built outside

> the walls [on the via Appia], and going through several parts of the city and the Forum, they pass by the temple of Castor and Pollux, sometimes to the number even of five thousand, wearing whatever rewards for valor in battle they have received from their commanders, a fine sight and worthy of the greatness of the Roman dominion.[91]

Dionysius' version of this horse parade, which is thought to have originated in the mid republic, seems to have been the reinvigorated and reinvented Augustan procession, a ritual which became an important element of imperial elite collective identity.[92] From exile, Ovid "recalled" riding by the temple of the Dioscuri as Augustus himself reviewed the equites.[93] Equestrians often featured prominently in public ceremonies (like the *processus consularis*) – much like their sons, who also seem to have formed a kind of elite militarized performance corps.[94]

In fact, Dionysius described both the elite youth in the circus procession and the equestrians in the *transvectio equitum* in strikingly similar terms: riding in regular ranks, in troops and squadrons or tribes and centuries, as if going to the training ground or returning from battle, both groups purportedly presented a fine spectacle of military might. Additionally, as the equestrian youth passed the temple of the Dioscuri in a *pompa circensis*, they imitated or even anticipated the *transvectio equitum* of their fathers. The reverberations between the two spectacles are pervasive: historical associations with the foundation of the republic, participants with their performative resonances, and their itineraries (the circus procession began where the *transvectio equitum* ended, the temple of Capitoline Jupiter) with their architectural repetitions. As the *pompa circensis* continued, it turned south onto the *vicus Tuscus*, the "Etruscan Way," which ran from the Forum Romanum through the Velabrum to the Forum Boarium.

Velabrum

> The wicked throng of the *vicus Tuscus*[95]
>
> Horace, *Satire* 2.3.228

The "route for *tensae* and processions," in Cicero's phrase, stretched "from the statue of Vertumnus to the Circus Maximus."[96] Vertumnus, an Etruscan god who stood at the head of the Etruscan Way (*vicus Tuscus*), did not seemingly appear in the *pompa circensis*, but, as Propertius would have it, he was content to enjoy the throng (*turba*) (Map 1.11). Horace's "wicked throng (*turba*)," bankers and artisans, but also Plautus' "men who sell themselves," may have been matched by a vile smell from the cloaca Maxima, whose course was seemingly altered to accommodate the *signum Vertumni* and which paralleled the *vicus Tuscus* for a short stretch near the Forum.[97] It is possible that "the stench of the cloaca Maxima, the salt taste of sweat, and the hum of insects locate[d] the wanderer turning a corner of the Basilia Iulia and heading into the *vicus Tuscus*." And so, the sacred sewer, "one of

Rome's most solid but dubious glories," may have made all the more urgent the incense and perfume that burned before the gods.[98] However, the cloaca Maxima might not have been quite so noxious even when it was open to the air, and by the second century BCE its vaulting would have mitigated any fetor.[99] In any case, the street of *tensae* and processions stretching from the statue of Vertumnus to the Circus was still a pungent path: "a street where they sell frankincense and perfumes and pepper," according to Horace.[100]

While resonances between procession and itinerary have been conjectural up to now, associations between the circus parade and the *vicus Tuscus*, one of Rome's oldest paved streets, and even the Velabrum as a whole seem more concrete.[101] Cicero, for instance, repeatedly drew a connection between the *pompa circensis* and the *vicus Tuscus* in his repeated denunciations of Verres. "Has anyone walked along the road from the statue of Vertumnus to the Circus Maximus without being reminded of your [Verres'] rapacious greed at every step he took? The repair of that road, the route for *tensae* and processions, you have reinforced so thoroughly that you would not risk going over it yourself."[102] Though assuredly sensationalized for rhetorical effect, Cicero was so taken with the alleged sacrilege of "this shameless maker of profit at the expense even of the wheels of the *tensae*" that he invoked it again just after calling on Castor and Pollux, whose temple sat at the beginning of this street, to witness Verres' depravity: "Hear me, every god who is borne in a *tensa* to behold our festival gatherings at the appointed seasons; for it was to fill his purse, not to uphold the dignity of that solemn rite, that Verres saw to the making and repairing of the way by which you go."[103] Indeed, Cicero seems to have had a well-known penchant for "pathetic reference[s] to the *tensae*" in order to play on the religious sympathies of a jury, and in the case against Verres such a strategy depended on an association between procession and street.[104]

As it happens, the "Velabrum, a most famous [and frequented] spot of the city," through which the *vicus Tuscus* passed, was also linked to the procession.[105] In response to the strange sight of a barefoot matron at the festival of Vesta, an old woman from the neighborhood explained the practical origins of the custom to "Ovid": "Where now the processions are wont to defile through the Velabrum to the Circus, there was nothing but willows and hollow canes."[106] That is, the Velabrum had been a swamp. Plutarch (mid second century CE) offered a different association between the procession and the Velabrum, in what seems to be a riff on a ritual failure noted by Verrius Flaccus, which was later picked up by Macrobius. "This spot is now called the Velabrum . . . because from that point on, the street leading to the hippodrome [Circus Maximus] from the Forum is covered over with sails by the givers of public spectacle, and the Roman word for sail is 'velum.'"[107] Although Macrobius did not name the street that was to be covered with an awning to prevent spectators from looking down on the gods, the *vicus Tuscus* is a likely candidate. And so, as Plutarch insisted, this street may really have been covered to protect the gods from the spectators and the spectators from the sun – a luxury the spectators would not enjoy at the racing arena.[108]

As the *vicus Tuscus* neared the Forum Boarium, the procession would have passed near the Lupercal, where Faustulus, as legend (or cultural memory) would have it, discovered the she-wolf suckling Romulus and Remus under a fig tree (*ficus ruminalis*) (Map 1.12).[109] A grove may once have stood in the sanctuary, though by the late republic apparently one lone fig tree remained, along with, surprisingly, its twin near the statue of Marsyas in the Forum. The fig tree in the Lupercal would seem to have the advantage of location as a marker of authenticity, but both trees may in fact have been judged the authentic *ficus Ruminalis* (or its sacred descendant). Perhaps the tree in the Forum was a memory clone of the one in the Lupercal, which itself could be construed both as a memorial of and as "identical" to the original legendary one. However one parses the confusing and conflicting traditions about the *ficus ruminalis*, it would seem that duplication, repetition, and so in a way identification, could collapse space (and time). When a processional participant proceeded from the Forum to the Lupercal only to be confronted by the "same" tree with (possibly) the "same" bronze sculptural group (of the suckling she-wolf), one may imagine a rather powerful experience of déjà vu.[110]

Indeed, at the Lupercal such repetitions and resonances abounded. Much as the burlesque dancers bore a certain resemblance to Marsyas, whose statue stood near the Forum fig tree, these same dancers also recalled the naked or scantily clad *luperci*, fully nude or dressed perhaps in a goatskin cape or loincloth as they ran through the city whipping or perhaps simply touching spectators with goatskin thongs.[111] Even though called *ludii* (players) by Varro, according to Tertullian, "because in play they run hither and thither," the *luperci* did not dance like the *ludiones* (also players) – instead they may have beat a path around the Palatine, ran to and fro in the Velabrum, Forum, and Velia, or simply ran back and forth from the Lupercal to the Forum from fig tree to fig tree.[112] Despite the differences, the dress of the *luperci* and their drunk and disorderly deportment seemingly echoed both the sexual tricks of the satyr dancers and the liberty and license of Marsyas.

The Lupercal, Lupercalia, and *luperci* had, perhaps, a louder resonance for the sons of Roman knights, who rode at the head of the procession. These young men, who could anticipate reprise performances in the *processus consularis* and the *transvectio equitum*, would comprise the two teams of drunken *luperci*, running amok (semi-)naked through the city – a slightly less dignified public appearance perhaps, but one that was likely more fun. As Valerius Maximus noted, "the younger members of the equestrian order filled Rome twice annually with a showing of themselves": first during the Lupercalia, when they were "carried away by the merriment of a feast and large draughts of wine" and again during the *transvectio equitum* in which "knights, wearing the purple coat [*trabea*], ride past on the Ides of July."[113] "Statues in the dress of the *luperci*" may have been a recent innovation according to Pliny the elder, nonetheless many knights during the early empire had these two peak moments commemorated on their grave memorials (though some honorands may have died before performing one or both of the ceremonies, which, in sadness, signals their importance).[114] Though the Lupercalia had long been an equestrian festival, Augustan reforms of the *ordo equester* and its public role assuredly amplified the import of the festival, which would remain an important, if much changed, festival to the end of antiquity.[115]

In the end, the Lupercal and the Lupercalia could have resonated with many processional participants. On the one hand, the dress (or its lack) and deportment of the *luperci* as well as the *ficus ruminalis*, the one(s) in front the Lupercal and/or in the Forum near the statue of Marsyas, recalled the burlesque dancers. On the other hand, the Lupercalia, like the *transvectio equitum* connected to the temple of Dioscuri at the other end of the *vicus Tuscus*, pointed to the sons of equestrians who rode at the head of the *pompa circensis*. Indeed, the Lupercalia, *transvectio equitum*, and also, it would seem, the *pompa circensis* were among the fundamental rituals of the equestrian order.

Aedes Cereris

After the Lupercal, the *pompa circensis* would have entered the Forum Boarium, the so-called cattle market – though it may have been named after a colossal gilded bronze bull from Aegina which marked the *pomerium* – where yet more crowds could gather, especially on the steps of monuments dedicated to Hercules: two temples (possibly) and the *Ara Maxima* (the great altar) just in front of the starting gates (Map 1.13).[116] Even Hercules himself, in/as his cult statue, might have looked on as he in/as his processional statue passed by. In addition, a pair of honorific columns awaited the procession. In 439 BCE, L. Minucius Augurinus may have been the first to be honored by the people with a statue on a column, which stood outside the *porta Trigemina* across from the starting gates – a monument seemingly evoked on a denarius minted by two descendants of the honorand.[117] About two hundred years later, C. Duilius erected a second column, a *columna rostrata* just like that in the Forum, which stood "in front of the Circus on the side with the doors" and may have marked the ceremonial entrance to the as yet underdeveloped Circus (Map 1.14).[118]

And finally, just before entering the arena, the *pompa circensis* would almost certainly have faced "the most beautiful and magnificent temple" of Ceres, Liber, and Libera, the plebian triad, which stood "near the turning posts of the greatest of hippodromes [Circus Maximus], having been erected above the starting gates themselves."[119] Though the temple cannot be located with certainty, ancient authors repeatedly placed it at, near, or next to the Circus Maximus, and so it was almost certainly visible to the participants as they entered the Circus (Map 1.15).[120] The temple of the Capitoline triad and this temple dedicated to the plebian triad offered apt bookends to the procession, which began at the fount of Roman aristocratic power and ended at the seat of plebian authority.[121] Both temples seem to have shared common construction techniques ("continuous wooden beams as architraves"), design features ("straddling, top-heavy, low, broad"), roofline décor ("pediments decorated with terracotta or gilded bronze statues in the Etruscan fashion"), and perhaps even a homologous floor plan with three *cellae*.[122] Also like the temple of Jupiter Optimus Maximus, as well as those of Saturn and the Dioscuri, the temple of Ceres was dedicated during the early years of the republic in 493 BCE with (reputedly) a first-of-its-kind-in-Rome bronze cult statue of Ceres, which in conjunction with the gilded statues (possibly) on its pediment helped the *aedes Cereris* to fill the itinerary of the golden procession with yet more ostentation.[123]

At either end of the itinerary stood a magnificent, archaic, Etruscan-style temple, one with a chryselephantine cult statue (eventually), the other a well-polished bronze, each neatly balancing the other. Such similarities would have highlighted the differences. At the beginning of the itinerary, sitting high on the Capitol, the citadel, in the center of the city, Jupiter Optimus Maximus took the oaths of newly inaugurated consuls, while at its end, at one point even beyond the *pomerium*, at the foot of the Aventine hill in the low-lying *vallis Murcia*, Ceres housed plebian magistrates, their archive, and treasury. Jupiter oversaw the coming-into-political adulthood of young elites, while Ceres offered asylum and bread to the poor.[124] Moving from the temple of the sovereign god to that of the plebian protector, the *pompa circensis* offered an image of Rome as *Senatus Populusque Romanus* (SPQR), an enduring symbol of Rome from the republic (when Cicero used some form of it well over one hundred times) until late antiquity, when it was inscribed on the Aurelian walls during an early-fifth-century CE restoration.[125] The procession, however, did not simply imagine Rome as SPQR, but as SPQR plus the gods (SPQR+gods) – a particularly fitting image of the city as the careful cultivation of the gods made possible the city of Rome and its empire – who were embodied in their temples and made present in the procession by their images and relics.

Circus Maximus

> They come to see, they come that they, themselves, may be seen.
>
> Ovid, *The Art of Love* 1.99[126]

Though Ovid wrote this about the theater, people watching, flirtation, and perhaps more was equally a hallmark of "the Circus, where the greatest part of the people displays itself," as Seneca the younger pointed out – and, of course, "the people put on a much better show," as Horace knew.[127] Indeed, "Ovid" fervently recommended the cramped, intimate informality of the Circus where Venus appeared to aid amorous adventurers:

> The spacious Circus offers chances galore
> No need, here, of private finger-talk, or secret signals
> Nods conveying messages:
> You'll sit right beside your mistress, without let or hindrance
> So be sure to press against her whenever you can –
> An easy task: the seating-divisions restrict her,
> Regulations facilitate contact.[128]

As the lover "Ovid" noted elsewhere:

> It's not the horses that bring me here
> though I hope your favorite wins.
>
> To sit with you and talk with you is why I've come –
> I've come to tell you I'm in love.
>
> If I watch you and you watch the races
> We'll both enjoy watching a winner.[129]

According to Suetonius, Augustus "chastised and regulated the most disorderly and unrestrained habits of the spectators," so that "the seating at the arena can be seen as an ideological map of the social structure of the Roman state," in the words of Erik Gunderson.[130] But such precise seating regulations seem to have applied only to the theaters and amphitheaters – at least at first. "Ovid" protested to his suspicious lover that "at the theater I've only to glance at the back rows / and your jealous eye pin-points a rival," which suggests that despite physical segregation (elite men in the front and women in the back), the theater remained a good pick-up spot.[131] By contrast, he sarcastically suggested that one "Destroy the Circus! The license of the Circus is not safe: here a girl may sit next to a strange man."[132] The Circus (much like the circus procession) seems to have retained its ludic, sexual atmosphere, despite Augustus' efforts – though Claudius and Nero may have been more, though never wholly, successful.[133] Eventually, senators and equestrians were granted the first several rows, but co-ed seating appears to have remained a feature at the races.[134]

Before the procession even entered the Circus, the blaring, brassy notes of horns, the boisterous strains of stringed instruments, and the rhythmic stamping of dancers' feet would have announced its imminent, epiphanic entrance through the starting gates (*carceres*).[135] Like the arena in general, the starting gates were only first made monumental by the early second century BCE, when they may have been an imposing *oppidum*, a wooden "town" with towers from which or, more probably, a simple wooden palisade next to which the game-giver could give the start signal for the first race.[136] As the gods passed through the *carceres*, the spectators – knee-to-knee with the opposite sex as Ovid would have it – were supposed to erupt in applause: "Give them a hand. The golden procession's here."[137] Each individual may have applauded the arrival of his or her favorite god(s), but altogether the collective applause of tens or hundreds of thousands of hands would have been staggering.[138] That is, even if Ovid conjured a poetical arrival, the crowd was in fact expected to cheer the gods, and also the *praeses ludorum*, as they entered the arena and circled the track. For example, in the mid first century CE the emperor Claudius "would rise up with the rest of the crowd, paying his respects with word and gesture."[139] Nonetheless, despite such expectations, or even ritual requirements, the crowd could deviate from tradition to good effect when necessary.[140]

Like the city through which the procession passed, the *vallis Murcia*, in which the Circus Maximus was built, housed memories, legends, and cults – notably, three temples on the Aventine slope: a temple of Sol, a god with the sole extant *nomenclator tensarum*; a temple of Juventas, who also enjoyed a shrine in Capitoline temple; and a temple of Summanus, possibly built in response to a lightning strike which decapitated his statue on the pediment of the Capitoline temple.[141] Though the temples of Juventas and Summanus might have stood just outside the circus proper, even so they were, probably, still visible at least until the erection of permanent seating in the late republic, and so would have linked the Capitol, though only by memory in the case of Summanus, and the Circus. This possibly uncanny folding of the procession's beginning onto its end may have evoked "memories" of a primordial and liminal circus valley, which, according to T. P. Wiseman, was imagined as "a conceptual landscape of woods, caves, and springs, the haunt of wild, licentious creatures, nymphs and satyrs, Faunus and Pan."[142] After its wild and mysterious mythological prehistory, the Roman mytho-historical imagination envisioned the origins of the Circus marked by sociality, sexuality, and violence when Romulus' inaugural games in honor of Consus, which brought together Romans and their neighbors, served as an infamous pretext to abduct (to rape) the Sabine women.[143] Perhaps strangely, or not, this moment from the legendary foundation of the city remained an important element in the Roman cultural memory of the Circus – and the continuing connection between spectacle, sexuality, and violence may help to explain the enduring attraction of the arena.[144]

These lurid, primeval memories may have invigorated more mundane and physical etiologies of the Circus. According to Varro, the arena "was called the Circus Maximus, because, being the place where the games are performed, it is built up *circum* 'round about' for the shows, and because there the procession (*pompa*) goes and the horses race *circum* 'around' the turning posts."[145] That is, the procession traced the design of the Circus itself, carving a track parallel to the Aventine hill, before curving around the first turning post to reach the *pulvinar* on the Palatine side. In short, according to Varro, the procession established by its itinerary the very space of the games – a less seductive origin story to be sure.[146] Architectural repetition may have aided such efforts, the procession may have passed yet another *fornix* as it rounded the first *meta* (turning post) (Map 1.16). In 196 BCE, L. Stertinius erected a monumental arch adorned with gilded statues possibly in the south curve of the Circus – the oldest such arch on record and the first known manubial monument – contemporaneous, its seems, with the monumentalization of the *carceres*.[147]

Finally, having rounded the first *meta*, the procession entered the home stretch, arriving at the *pulvinar*, seemingly a simple elevated wooden platform covered, perhaps, by an awning that served as the sacred loge of the gods (Map 1.17). Likely located in the first several rows of seats, the *pulvinar* is first attested in the mid first century BCE, but it likely existed (much) earlier.[148] Wherever, whenever, and however it was constructed, once the procession had completed its circuit, the *exuviae* were installed in the *pulvinar* according to Sinnius Capito, a contemporary of Varro – possibly on chairs and probably alongside the divine images borne on *fercula* installed on couches.[149] As a late-antique scholion on Horace would have it, "*pulvinaria* [including, one supposes, the *pulvinar* in the Circus] used to be called either couches or platforms of the gods, on which the divinities stood, so that they might seem more conspicuous" – that is, so that the gods might appear more imposing and might be more easily seen.[150] At last, after the installation of the gods and the sacrifice in their honor, the greatest show on earth could begin. The *praeses ludorum* would seemingly ride to the starting gates, next to or on top of which he would stand in order to give the start signal: "straining, they [the competitors] await the signal, while throbbing fear and passion for glory drain each bounding heart. Then, when the clear trumpet sounded, all at once they shot forth from their starting places," to borrow Vergil's evocation of the boat race at Anchises' funeral games, which in turn had seemingly borrowed from the chariot races themselves.[151]

From the Capitol to the Circus, the itinerary of the *pompa circensis* processed through a landscape of cultural memory, producing a continual and continually evolving interplay between procession and place. Though saturated with collective, civic significance, individual participants from the gods to the game-giver, sons of equestrians, and also paid performers could potentially have heard echoes between their own experiences and the memories and monuments along the way – ritual, historical, political, and even personal resonances. To parade images and symbols of the gods past their own temples multiplied their powerful presence. In an analogous, intricately self-referential fashion, the interaction between procession and itinerary could have amplified the connections, not only between the peak ceremonial moments of elite life (the *processus consularis* and the *transvectio equitum*), but also between the burlesque and playful aspects of public life – for example, the satyrs' resemblance to both

Marsyas, symbol of *libertas* (liberty and license), and the equestrian *luperci*. The procession did not, however, only tap into the cultural memory and cultural capital of prestigious places like the Capitol and the Forum. The performance of the procession seems also to have endowed the *vicus Tuscus*, the route of *tensae* and processions, and the Velabrum with special significance and even to have carved out, at least symbolically, the very track of Circus.

Moreover, even as the itinerary forged a linear path, a linear narrative, through the city, repetitions of architecture (early republican temples, *fornices*, and columns), cult sites (Juventas and Summanus, once on the Capitol and then later in the Circus), flora (the fig trees), and even participants (in the form of their doubles, honorific statues and the statue of Marsyas) can be imagined to have collapsed space, to have folded the end back onto the beginning. By such means, the procession produced the space in which the games themselves could unfold to the utmost pleasure of gods and humans alike. Equally, one could argue that the performance of the *pompa circensis* as it traversed an itinerary of collective memory produced an image of the city.

III IMAGING ROME ON THE GROUND AND IN THE IMAGINATION

> For while we were wandering and straying as if strangers in our own city, your books led us home, as it were, so that we might finally recognize *who* and *where* we were.
>
> Cicero, *Academica* 1.9[152]

Though perhaps a bit shopworn these days, Kevin Lynch's concept of the "image of the city" remains an important conceptual tool with which to analyze ancient cities.[153] The sprawling mass of late republican Rome resisted distillation (and so comprehension) with its vast, overawing public, monumental spaces and its equally enormous labyrinth of alleys, small streets, apartment complexes, and elite housing. There were no ready symbols or simple means of understanding its massive totality: Rome was difficult to map or image.[154] Lynch's image of the city seems to offer a handle on Rome's often overwhelming built environment that accords well, it appears, with ancient urban experience. On the one hand, the urban image is most commonly and practically a navigational aid: "Way-finding is the original function of the … image. … [It may] act as an organizer of activity." As one moves around the city, an experiential image forms, which is necessarily subjective "not sustained, but rather partial, fragmentary, mixed with other concerns." That is, the urban image functions as a personal, and so limited, rough and ready mental map – though a large group may share a broadly similar public image, based on individual experiences of the same paths, edges, districts, nodes, and monuments. In short, an image of a city helps to identify *where* one is, as Cicero would have it. On the other hand, "the image is valuable not only in this immediate sense in which it acts as a map for the direction of movement; in a broader sense it can serve as a general frame of reference within which an individual can act, or to which he can attach his knowledge. . . . It is an organizer of facts and possibilities . . . [and] may [also] be a basis for the ordering of knowledge."[155] In other words, the image of a city may also help to establish *who* one is. The image of the city offers both a framework for practice and a scaffold of knowledge.

Lynch's image of the city, a concept which is at once both real and practical and imagined and conceptual, bears a clear connection to what Cicero wrote regarding Varro's antiquarian efforts. Indeed, Varro's work may well have helped some Romans to place themselves in the city in a variety of senses from physical to social and cultural locations.[156] By and during the late republic, the city of Rome had undergone massive changes in every sphere – cultural, social, economic, physical – all of which demanded an urgent response as "the city of Rome, along with Roman citizenship, lay at the core of Roman identity."[157] To be lost implied not only physical disorientation, but also the dissolution of tradition and self, against which Andrew Wallace-Hadrill argues republican Rome had limited powers of redress. Just as there were little to no institutional frameworks for a specifically civic religious education, there were equally few means by which an ancient Roman or a visitor to Rome could have oriented him- or herself in the city and its traditions. And so, Varro's antiquarian researches may be viewed as an anxious attempt at place-making, a desperate effort to provide a kind of urban image, by which Romans could locate themselves topographically, socially, and religiously, the last of which seems to have been quite prominent.[158] In many ways, the *pompa circensis* complemented Varro's explorations by tracing some of the social, cultural, political, and religious contours of the city in its very performance.[159] The circus procession also offered ways to navigate Rome's confusing welter of urban experience – both on the ground and in the imagination.

Way-finding in republican Rome

Informal means of navigation were essential in ancient cities, for which there were no practical maps (no folding, hand-held ones), no evidence for systems of numbering, and few named streets.[160] Even if a street was formally named, street signs, which demand a certain level of literacy, did not seemingly develop in a (somewhat) systematic way until the Middle Ages.[161] City gates were often named, as were city districts, but such identifications had only limited use for navigation. In the absence of formal navigational aids, directions must have been given by means of topography (hills, valleys, rivers), prominent landmarks (large streets, temples, and fountains), more humble locales (shops and bars), or even personal associations (so-and-so's home or the place where so-and-so works). In the early second century BCE, the playwright Terence offered a particularly amusing, and often cited, example of such urban way-finding – albeit a comically and intentionally misleading one.[162]

> DEMEA: Tell me the place, then.
> SYRUS: Do you know the portico down that way (*pointing*) by the market?
> DEMEA: Of course I know it.
> SYRUS: Go past it straight up the street. When you get to the top, there's a downhill slope in front of you; run down there. Then there's a shrine on this side (*pointing*) and not far away there's an alley.
> DEMEA: Which one?
> SYRUS: The one by the large fig tree.
> DEMEA: I know it.
> SYRUS: Proceed down this.
> DEMEA: But there's no way through.
> SYRUS: Of course not. Blast! You must think I've lost my senses! My mistake. Go back to the portico. In fact this is a much shorter route and there's less chance of losing your way. You know the house of that wealthy Cratinus?
> DEMEA: Yes.
> SYRUS: When you've passed this, turn left, go straight down the street, and, when you get to the temple of Diana, go right. Before you come to the city gate, right by the pond, there is a bakery, and facing that a workshop. That's where he is.[163]

Even if this particular instance of way-finding deliberately deceived the one it was ostensibly supposed to help, nonetheless this exaggerated scene grasps something essential about navigating any ancient city, particularly Rome. To get around town, one needed to develop a set of way-finding aids (shrines, porticos, trees, bakeries, ponds): a process that could be aided by rituals, which may be understood as practices akin to, but differentiated from daily acts, which could nevertheless function as paradigms of sorts for daily life.[164] Processions did, after all, plot real, navigable pathways through the city, even though they more obviously served as a kind of civic self-representation.

By tying places together and by focusing attention on one particular route, a procession helped one to picture the city, to understand its coherence or pattern – an act of imagination that helped to construct an image of the city.[165] The circus parade featured one such path by which one could place oneself in the city topographically and even in other ways.[166] The very visible and often repeated *pompa circensis* – indeed, perhaps Rome's most often repeated public procession – linked some of the most important pathways (the *clivus Capitolinus* and *vicus Tuscus*), skirted along edges (for example, between the Velabrum and the Palatine), united districts (Forum, Velabrum, Forum Boarium), lined up nodes (Capitol, Forum, Circus), and highlighted landmarks (temples, *fornices*, columns, and statues) of classical Rome – the five essential elements of urban navigation in Lynch's image of the city. The proposition that the circus procession could assist urban way-finding may seem far-fetched or at least redundant – after all, there were plenty of navigational aids to signal its itinerary without reference to the procession. However, Plautus, whose *Poenulus* (*The Little Carthaginian*) so neatly mocked the pageantry of the *pompa circensis* with its African mice, also seemingly undermined the gravity of the procession by caricaturing its itinerary as a gallery of rogues and scoundrels, for the most part at least. "The colorful walk through the Forum that introduces the fourth act of Plautus' *Curculio* (4.1.467–481) is an impious itinerary on a clearly designated course," according to Eleanor Leach – a course that, in fact, followed the itinerary of the *pompa circensis*, at least in part.[167]

> I'll show you where you'll find each sort of man in town,
> To save you the trouble of tracking them down, be it men of virtue
> You seek, or men of vice, men with and without morals.
> If you need a man to perjure an oath, the Comitium's the place;
> But for liars and braggarts, go to the shrine of Venus Cloacina.
> Wealthy husbands incautious with cash haunt the Basilica –
> There too the busiest hookers and the pimps who strike the deal.
> Members of the dinner clubs you'll find in the Fish-market.
> Gentlemen stroll at the end of the Forum, men of money;
> In the center, near the Canal, linger the pure pretenders.
> Above the Lacus Curtius the slanderers gather, bold
> Malicious men who brazenly accuse the innocent
> But who themselves make truer targets for their charges.
> At the Old Shops are those who lend or borrow money,
> And others behind the Temple of Castor – trust them at your peril.
> On Tuscan Way, men who sell themselves;
> In the Velabrum, bakers, butchers, and soothsayers,
> And swindlers, or those who rent the stalls for swindlers' work.[168]

From the Comitium just in front of the curia of the senate, down the via Sacra past the cloaca, and the basilica; and then back to the Lacus Curtius to the *taberna veteres* and the temple of Castor and Pollux, Plautus' choragus verbally, and visually by gesture one assumes, moved the audience through the Forum from Northwest to Southeast twice, first along the northern edge, and then along the southern. Most of this impious itinerary would have been visible to both the actors and the audience, which could have been seated in some of the locations just named since it is likely that this play was initially staged in the Forum itself. After the second "trip" through the Forum, the Plautine itinerary turned past the temple of Castor, following the *vicus Tuscus* into the Velabrum, and so escaped sight. It may seem strange that this performed "map," which elided, as

Timothy Moore argues, "the distinctions between the imaginary world presented on stage and the 'real world' of Rome," would guide the audience beyond its field of vision.[169] Perhaps Plautus simply wanted to amplify the tension between imagined and real.

Or perhaps Plautus had a "real" itinerary in mind, which his pen portrait neatly satirized much as the satyrs and Sileni mocked the *ludiones*, the martial dancers. After all, Plautus' choragus twice moved the audience through the Forum in the same direction as the procession would have, before exiting onto the *vicus Tuscus* (the "street of *tensae* and processions") and continuing into the Velabrum ("where now the processions are wont to defile to the Circus") – both seemingly endowed with special significance by the *pompa circensis*.[170] One can just imagine the proud north African mice turning on the *vicus Tuscus*, dutifully trooping along, until perhaps the offal of the cloaca Maxima distracted them. Whether or not Plautus targeted the *pompa circensis* a second time (if the itinerary had continued all the way to the Circus one could be more certain), the passage does at least suggest that a processional itinerary like that of the *pompa circensis* could impact urban way-finding – or at least that it was (in-)famous enough to be lampooned.[171] The itinerary of the *pompa circensis* may be envisioned like a string on which Plautus or anyone could thread the beads of practical navigation. By such means, an ancient Roman could know *where* she was.

As the Plautine itinerary suggests, the only securely known itinerary of the *pompa circensis* from the Capitol to the Circus forged a privileged pathway through the city, elevating the processional route over myriad others. If there were other itineraries for other games, like the *ludi Apollinares* or the *ludi Megalenses*, or alternative itineraries when the temple of Capitoline Jupiter or even the Forum were under construction and so inaccessible, then such privileged pathways would have multiplied. The very prominence of the itinerary could have been useful, though clearly limited, in urban way-finding: if, for example, one was in the Forum and needed to find the metal working shop near the *pulvinar*.[172] Even so, the performance of the procession would have more readily affected how elements along the itinerary were perceived or remembered. Traversing a landscape of cultural memory, the *pompa circensis* generated linkages between processional participants and the urban environment in an act of performed place-making. By turning the spaces of Rome into known places, the *pompa circensis* could be said to offer a means of knowing the city.

Symbolic cityscapes: SPQR+gods and aurea Roma

As a linear emplotment of spaces, places, buildings, and monuments, the itinerary of the *pompa circensis* can be construed as an image of the city akin to those used in urban way-finding, even if it was not, in fact, employed in practical situations – though, there was also a fruit vendor with a stall near the *pulvinar* who could be found by reference to this itinerary.[173] The linearity of the itinerary, which arranged its elements in sequence, also mirrored in a way the hierarchical composition of the cortege. In both cases (itinerary and cortege), the procession put the city in order. At the same time, a rhythm of gravity and levity, solemnity and mockery, familiarity and alterity regulated the performance of the *pompa circensis*, whose fluctuations and reversals turned the city upside down and inside out. The repetition of temples, columns, *fornices*, doubles (honorific statues), and fig trees complemented this ludic performance by collapsing space to create a singular, temporary festival sphere in which the games could unfold. In other words, the webs of significance and networks of associations generated by the rhythms of the performance and the relentless repetitions of the itinerary added another layer of complexity to the ritual: it was linear and looped, serious and comical. Moreover, if the cortege and itinerary forged an image of the city as a framework for practice, then, in one and the same passage through the city, processional performance and topographical resonances and repetitions combined to produce twin images of the city as a scaffold of knowledge: namely SPQR+gods (the senate and Roman people, one of the most enduring symbols of the city, together with the gods) and *aurea Roma* (golden Rome).

On the shield of Aeneas, Vergil placed Augustus at the head of a very traditional image of Rome, "with the fathers [senators] and people, the penates, and the great gods."[174] Though mentioned less frequently than simple variations on SPQR, Cicero often invoked "the immortal gods, the senate, and Roman people," not necessarily in that order, on his own or his client's behalf.[175] The *pompa circensis* conjured this same image of Rome in both its participants and itinerary. According to Fabius Pictor and Dionysius, the game-giver with, probably, an elite entourage, sons of equestrians on horseback, aediles and other magistrates accompanied by regular Romans on foot, charioteers and athletes, performers, and paid laborers marched from the heights of the Capitol, seat of empire, site of consular inauguration; through the political heart of Rome, the Forum; to commercial zones of the Velabrum and Forum Boarium; passing by (visually, at least) the plebian temple of Ceres; finally to arrive at the Circus in the low-lying *vallis Murcia*, where masses of Romans of all ranks (which were, eventually, seated according to rank) watched, perhaps impatiently, the arrival of the *pompa circensis*. From imperial power to plebian asylum; from political elites to day laborers; from gravity (the Capitol and Forum and their high-stakes politics) to levity (the Circus with its violence and sex); from high to low physically, socially, and ideologically (from the perspective of the literate elite at least), the choreography of the *pompa circensis* and its itinerary embodied or encapsulated Rome's hierarchical social relations.[176]

The very order of the procession underscored this hierarchy: the gods occupied the place of honor toward the end of the procession, while the *praeses ludorum* seemingly led the way in his chariot, a secondary but still prestigious position, and the aediles on foot introduced the gods, a tertiary placement, with ordinary Romans in between.

To emphasize power and politics, however, may undervalue religious piety: the seating arrangements of the Circus mirrored, to a degree, social status, but the Circus was also a place for spectacle and the social intercourse of humans and gods.[177] For Livy, chariot races in honor of the gods suited the bellicose nature of the ancient Romans. However, in 364 BCE, in the face of an unrelenting plague, the Romans organized the third *lectisternium* in the city's history "in order to petition for the peace of the gods." When the *lectisternium* failed to secure divine goodwill, the Romans then "gave way to superstitious fears, and, among other efforts to placate the wrath of the gods, are said also to have instituted *ludi scaenici*," which also failed to produce the desired results.[178] Theater shows were a symptom of decline for Livy, but the addition of *ludi scaenici* to the traditional *ludi circenses* as a means of securing the *pax deorum* signals the firm belief, the knowledge even, that the games honored the gods. In fact, even the location of the theater "for the festive days of the games of the immortal gods" should be chosen with great care, according to Vitruvius.[179]

Cicero's self-aggrandizing rhetoric nicely captures both the political importance of the games and the asymmetrical relations between gods and humans, in which humans offer games for the gods' pleasure, while the gods in turn are supposed to grant their favor. "I am to celebrate with utter zeal and reverence the most sacred games of Ceres, Liber, and Libera; I am bound to render Lady Flora favorably disposed to the people and the Roman plebs by the renown of her games; I am to celebrate those most ancient games, which were the first to be called Roman, of Jupiter, Juno, and Minerva in the most worthy and devout fashion."[180] As aedile elect, Cicero was indeed to ensure the *cura ludorum* which maintained the *pax deorum*. Or, as Ovid imagined it: "The country folk used to come to the city for the games, but that honor was given to the gods, not to [popular] enthusiasms."[181] Though the erotic stage productions during the Floralia assuredly achieved a certain notoriety (which may well have been the very kind of renown that Cicero had in mind), the games themselves were, in general, marked by a balance of gravity, levity, and piety.[182]

In fact, many Christian polemicists felt compelled to draw attention to the assumption that the gods enjoyed or felt honored by the games, which Roman "pagans" simply took for granted. For Arnobius (ca. 300 CE), it was an absurd commonplace: "it is said that the gods are honored by these things [the games]."[183] Not only were the gods honored by the games, they even at times demanded them, according to Augustine.[184] But Arnobius simply could not believe that:

> Jupiter, called by you the supreme god and founder of all things, set out from heaven to see geldings competing in speed and tearing off the seven laps . . . and rejoiced that they passed, were passed, plunged headlong on their necks, turned up on their backs with their chariots; that others were dragged along and lamed, their legs broken.[185]

Seemingly in spite of (or perhaps even because of) such lurid violence among other attractions, the games were "rightly given gifts" to the gods, who were imagined to enjoy them just as much as their human fellow citizens and who, in exchange for lavishly produced *ludi*, might, for example, stem an epidemic or lend aid in war.[186] In short, the *pompa circensis*, the games it introduced, and the arena in which they took place performed and presented Rome, the city and its citizens, as SPQR+gods – a symbolic image of the city which was also an urban cross-section by which one may have found one's way in Rome's social labyrinths.[187]

The itinerary as a scaffold of knowledge offered another conceptualization of Rome – another way for the Romans to understand *who* they were. By describing the circus parade as a "golden procession," Ovid juxtaposed the parade, the city, and its empire through a nebulous series of associations.[188] The *aurea pompa* – marked by the gleaming gold of its ritual vessels – traversed an itinerary littered with gold, beginning at the golden temple of Capitoline Jupiter, in a ritual performance which evoked and embodied *aurea Roma*, golden Rome.[189] Of course, *aurea Roma* often indexed empire, conquest, and even moral decline, as Ovid noted: "There was coarse simplicity before: now Rome is golden, and possesses the vast wealth of the conquered world."[190] Indeed, Augustan-era authors often deployed this contrast between Rome's putative rustic origins and its current opulence, most famously Vergil: "the Capitol, golden now, then rough with woodland thickets," but also the elder Seneca: "Once these hills stood bare; among such wide-flung walls there is nothing more distinguished than a low hut, though above it shines out the Capitol with its sloping roofs, gleaming in pure gold."[191] Though golden Rome could signal imperial decadence and decline, gold suited Rome and its immortal occupants well, as Ovid himself conceded: "We, too, are tickled by golden temples, though we approve the ancient ones. Grandeur suits a god."[192]

However, the golden procession and its itinerary were gilded well before the age of emperors (though not before empire or imperial ambition). In fact, the "golden Capitol" had long been gold – even its first recorded dedication in 495 BCE was a golden crown.[193] In 193 BCE, aediles placed gilded shields in its gables; in 142 BCE, the ceiling was gilded; while after the fire in 83 BCE, the temple was rebuilt with gilded bronze roof tiles and the terracotta statue was probably replaced with a chryselephantine imitation of Pheidias' Olympian Zeus.[194] By 27 BCE, according to Vitruvius, gilded bronze statues (possibly) graced the pediment of the temple of Capitoline Jupiter as well that of Ceres.[195] The Capitoline temple would, of course, receive ever more resplendent décor under the emperors (like Domitian's gilded bronze doors) – until its gradual despoliation beginning in the late fourth century CE – but "the gleaming Capitol" stood already in the republic.[196] Which might have been a problem: as the elder Seneca complained, "when poor, we had quieter times. With a gilded Capitol [after 83 BCE] we waged civil wars."[197] The rest of the republican itinerary also had its (lesser) share of gold: for example, the gilded statues on the *fornices* of Scipio and Stertinius, and the twelve gilded statues in the portico of the Harmonious Gods, all erected in the second century BCE.

The *aurea pompa* originated in the *aurea Capitolia*, which itself was an index of *aurea Roma*, the city and the empire. This metaphorical association, which sees the *aurea pompa* as *aurea Roma*, also implies "being as," in the terminology of Paul Ricoeur.[198] In this sense, the golden procession was golden Rome, a sign, symbol, and even symptom of Rome's imperial majesty (or decay). Dionysius' comment that troops of Roman youth rode or walked in the *pompa circensis* so that strangers might be impressed by their number and beauty may apply equally to the procession as a synecdoche of Rome and to the version or vision of the city that it represented to or, better, performed for itself. Cicero had Socrates complain about how much gold there was that he did not need passing by in procession, but gold, and particularly a golden procession marching through a gilded city, nonetheless, suited the gods', the Romans', and Rome's grandeur.[199] All together, the circus procession fashioned a multivalent image of Rome, an image that was at once both practical and symbolic: it organized activity and ordered knowledge, in Lynch's phrase. Or in Cicero's terms, the *pompa circensis*, like Varro's antiquarian place-making efforts, were a means for ancient Romans to recognize *where* and *who* they were.

IV AN IDEAL-TYPE BETWEEN THE REPUBLIC AND MEMORIES OF THE REPUBLIC

The first three chapters have constructed a kind of "ideal-type" of the *pompa circensis* as it emerged (primarily though not exclusively) from the texts, images, and urban environment of the republic and (what is now called) the early principate. Through the reigns of Augustus and Tiberius, many still thought that they lived under a *res publica restituta* (a restored republic) and many worked very hard "to remember" the republic, such that the early empire appeared as its continuation not its replacement.[200] That is, rather than an ahistorical ideal-type that piles up all extant evidence, no matter how distant in time, space, genre, or media, or an ethical ideal-type that imagines affairs as they *ought* to have been, this portrait of the *pompa circensis* collates chronologically (and geographically) restricted evidence into a rough-edged pattern for analytic and expressive purposes, in a Weberian spirit if not exactly to the letter. This ideal-type attempts both to assemble the evidence without erasing its differences and disjunctions and to present an image of the procession that might cohere with the experiences, interpretations, and recollections of a late-republican or early imperial viewer, that might square with the traditions and expectations of a contemporary (plus or minus a communicative memory generation, approximately eighty years) of Dionysius of Halicarnassus. This ideal-type, then, may be compared to a mosaic: it aims to present a picture of a late-republican *pompa circensis*, while preserving the individuality of the disparate evidence, its tessellation, and leaving gaps where the tesserae have fallen off. In short, by necessity this ideal-type draws upon a wide range of evidence to highlight a few key aspects of the procession and by intention it attempts to avoid excessive "filling the gaps" and "ungarbl[ing] the garbled evidence," risks that every reconstruction runs, as Mary Beard has argued.[201]

An ideal-type in this sense is a scholarly construct, a necessary act of the imagination (which is not thereby imaginary) that sketches the practical logic or language of the *pompa circensis*: its grammar (or its components: *praeses*, Roman youth, athletes, dancers, gods, arches, columns, Capitol, Forum, etc.), its syntax (order, organization, itinerary), and its signification (how its grammar and syntax come together in performance: gravity and levity, resonance and wonder, memory and place).[202] At the same time, this construct also seeks to communicate or express the logic of the procession in a clear and coherent way: aided by unavoidable attention to certain features for simplicity and clarity – a state of affairs also demanded by the exiguous but (barely) adequate evidence. As such, it is not a description of any particular performance of the *pompa circensis*, but rather an outline of the traditions, expectations, and interpretations that may have guided any given performance and its reception. Put bluntly, "[an ideal-type] is not a *description* of reality but it aims to give unambiguous means of expression to such description," as Max Weber insisted.[203]

Moreover, the literary procession of Fabius Pictor-Dionysius, upon which this ideal-type necessarily leans heavily, could have become tradition in its own right, an unthought influence on processional production and reception not unlike Bourdieu's *habitus*:

> systems of durable, transposable dispositions, structured structures predisposed to function as structuring structures, that is, as *principles which generate and organize practices* and representations that can be objectively adapted to their outcomes *without presupposing a conscious aiming at ends* or an express mastery of the operations necessary to attain them. Objectively "regulated" and "regular" without being in any way the product of obedience to rules, they can be collectively orchestrated without being the product of the organizing action of a conductor.[204]

In other words, the description of Fabius Pictor-Dionsyius could have affected subsequent performances to the extent to which it was accepted as authoritative – and Dionysius, at least, thought he could trade on the authority of Fabius Pictor. Assuming that the description was read and accepted as an ancient *pompa circensis*, the text could have shaped tradition, becoming an unthought principle with which to generate and organize practice. Literary representations of the procession, including Fabius Pictor-Dionysius but also Cicero and Ovid, could have subtly shaped both the organizational protocols of the aediles and the expectations, imaginations, and memories of (literate) spectators.

And so, if this ideal-type comes anywhere near what a late-republican/early-imperial spectator may have seen, experienced, imagined, and remembered (inseparable acts in this case), then it may also offer a gauge to measure subsequent historical change.[205] In other words, though this ideal-type is first and foremost a tool of analysis and communication, it can also throw the transformations of the imperial era into sharper relief. Such an ideal-type is then nothing more than a research tool that hopefully remains adequate to the evidence and useful as an interpretation – if not or when it is not, it should be discarded as Weber contended.

In schematic terms and for heuristic purposes, the procession can be separated into three components, which would have been melded in performance: a *pompa hominum*, a *pompa deorum*, and an *iter* (itinerary), which were linked by an over-arching set of performance principles – gravity and levity, resonance and wonder, memory and place. In this version of a "republican" *pompa circensis*, the *pompa hominum* consisted of elites (the *praeses ludorum* and *curatores ludorum*, the magistrate with imperium who presided over and the aediles and others who produced the games) with their "entourages" (Roman youth, other magistrates, and lictors); competitors (charioteers, athletes, and other contestants in the games); entertainers (dancers and musicians); and support staff (censer bearers and those who carried the ritual vessels). The *pompa deorum* comprised the gods (represented, transported, and performed in a variety of ways), other supernatural figures (folkloric figures and stilt-walkers imitating deities), and sacrificial victims (oxen accompanied by priests and cultic attendants). And the itinerary encompassed a linear pathway (from the Capitoline temple high on the citadel to the arena low in the valley between the Palatine and Aventine hills) marked by repetition (temples, *fornices*, columns, and fig trees) and resonance (both personal or individual and also public or collective).

These three constituent components (the grammar and syntax) were then animated by a cluster of performance principles (the process of signification): the constant oscillation between gravity and levity (authority and hierarchy dissolved in laughter and sexuality), resonance and wonder (connectivity and show-stopping spectacle), and memory (tradition, cultural memory, and even familial or personal memory embodied in texts, rituals, and places). As the procession of humans and gods traversed the itinerary, a landscape of memory, numerous individual images of the city (based on individual resonances and experiences) would have emerged, in addition to a public, or collective image, a version and vision of Rome as powerful and united: *aurea Roma*, a golden Rome fit for the gods and worthy of empire, composed of the utterly traditional SPQR+gods – the senate (or the elite more broadly) and the Roman people (everyone else) and the gods. In short, the golden procession conserved a traditional, and so significant, image of "republican" Rome.

These symbolic images of the city could have facilitated multiple modes of way-finding. As a scaffold of knowledge, the procession may have allowed an ancient Roman to imagine *who* she was, her "location" within the symbolic universe of Roman society (that is, *aurea Roma* and SPQR+gods). As a framework for practice, the symbolic "map" may also have been a practical one – in an informal, Terentian, or even Plautine form of way-making. The itinerary traveled some of Rome's most prominent and earliest paved streets (like the *clivus Capitolinus*, the road through the Forum, and the *vicus Tuscus*); connected some of its most important districts (the Forum and Velabrum); and strung together some of its most notable nodes (Capitolium and the Circus). Moreover, at each major turn and all along the itinerary sat temples, shrines, and statues: at the beginning Jupiter Optimus Maximus; in the middle Saturn, Marsyas, the Dioscuri, and the Lupercal; and at the end, next to the Circus above the starting gates, Ceres. In short, the *pompa circensis* produced a complex, symbolic, mental map by which an ancient Roman could determine her social, political, and perhaps also physical location – so that she could at last recognize *who* and *where* she was, to paraphrase Cicero once again.

In conclusion, this ideal-type hopefully captures something of the consistent logic or language, the inevitable performance variability, and the significance(s) of a "republican" circus procession. Ideally, so to speak, it also offers a template to chart the changes wrought by autocracy. The performed image of republican Rome would be greatly attenuated, though never eliminated, by autocrats and emperors, who built an imperial Rome alongside and on top of the republican city and its memory. Though memories of the republic would endure, the procession would not remain unchanged: as Rome, its institutions, people, and built environment, changed during the course of the empire, so too would the *pompa circensis*.

PART II

The *pompa circensis* from Julius Caesar to late antiquity

FOUR

"HONORS GREATER THAN HUMAN"

Imperial cult in the *pompa circensis*[1]

What is a god? The exercise of power. What is a king? God-like.

Papyrus Heidelberger G 1716[2]

The imperial cult in the Greek east (and also in the much of the Latin west for that matter) seems to have served as a means of imagining Roman power – emperors, like gods, were foreign, powerful beings who could exercise their authority at a distance and with whom one must establish some kind of relationship.[3] Imperial cult created a place for Roman imperium within long-established forms of Greek civic life, forging relations between center and periphery, links which varied as local traditions varied.[4] Even at Rome, Ittai Gradel argues that "ruler cult was the traditional republican response to monarchy, whether the monarch was Jupiter or Caesar" – even if the boundary between humanity and divinity was not quite as easily elided as this model demands. Divinity may have been an absolute, not a relative category, in theory at least.[5] Ambiguous distinctions between traditional and imperial gods notwithstanding, ruler cult formulated the nature of autocratic power in stark terms: "What mattered was power."[6] As the Greek maxim put it: divinity was power and the emperor was like divinity. And so, even though the imperial gods (*divi*) were consistently differentiated (though not wholly different) from the traditional deities (*dei*), imperial cult offered a means to imagine and even to negotiate with imperial power.

That is to say, imperial cult established a relationship: the acceptance of god-like honors on the part of the emperor entailed reciprocal, but asymmetrical exchange with those who offered the honors – a responsibility met by the living emperor on behalf of the *divi*.[7] This deeply traditional, politico-religious protocol obligated the emperor to his subjects and the subjects to the emperor in a manner reminiscent of Maussian gift-exchange – an exchange that comprised social and political relations and religious traditions and attitudes as much as economic traffic.[8] For example, those who devised honors for the autocrat Caesar felt "that he would be reasonable" in terms of what sorts of honors he would accept and, one suspects, that he would reciprocate with favors and privileges.[9] The hallowed or religious honors exceeding or contrary to the human that were granted to Caesar and subsequently to Roman emperors, empresses, and family members were a model for practical action, for both ruler and ruled, a means to express and perform reciprocal relations between unequal partners.

Dionysius of Halicarnassus arrived at Rome "at the time Augustus Caesar put an end to the civil war [30/29 BCE]," and lived through part of the process by which the republic was gradually translated into the principate.[10] He was thus perfectly positioned to see an imperial system of honors and obligations blossom under the tutelage of the first emperor. All the same, his search for the Greek origins of Rome as well as the Augustan "restoration of the republic" seems to have occluded certain realities of early imperial Rome.[11] And so the description of the *pompa circensis* that Dionysius adapted from Fabius Pictor made no mention of the burgeoning imperial interventions in the circus procession, even though under Julius Caesar the *pompa circensis* had already been mobilized as a means of imagining and relating to power – albeit with rather uneven results. The appearance of a living Caesar in the procession (or rather his statue and symbols) seems to have violated tradition and unsettled audience expectations. Subsequent rulers, notably Augustus, were more circumspect, allowing only deceased emperors or members of the imperial household to appear in the procession. Moreover, honors for the imperial gods were both clearly modeled after and visibly distinguished from those for the traditional gods, in a way that both "respectfully" differed from and pompously competed with the traditional gods. Even so, some, both "pagan" and Christian, remained ill at ease with rulers who "have been appointed priesthoods and other pageantry: *tensae*, chariots [*currus* (*elephantorum*)], *solisternia* [relics displayed on thrones], *lectisternia* [divine images displayed on couches], festivals, and games."[12] Divine honors in the *pompa circensis* remained a delicate negotiation.

Although assuredly augmented by an impulse toward spectacle and wonder, imperial cult in the *pompa circensis* showed an odd mixture of dutiful respect and striking innovation, which seems to have allowed the maintenance of some republican tradition. Octavian (eventually the emperor Augustus) paid homage to Caesar with a *simulacrum* on a *ferculum* and *exuviae* in a *tensa*, honors clearly patterned after divine ones, while Tiberius' postmortem commemoration of Augustus subtly and yet blatantly differentiated the new *divus* from the *dei*. Just like the traditional gods, *divus* Augustus was honored with a *tensa*. But instead of a *simulacrum* on a *ferculum*, his statue sat atop a cart pulled by four elephants (a *currus elephantorum* or, perhaps, an *armamaxa*). This *currus elephantorum* occupied something of an ambiguous space in the procession's ritual construction of theology. On the one hand, it drew a "humble" distinction between the image of *divus* Augustus and the traditional gods on *fercula*. On the other hand, the *currus elephantorum* was a raw, spectacular assertion of imperial power. The *divus* was properly distinguished from the *dei*, but the sheer size and grandeur of this display subverted any pious distinction between deified humans and traditional gods.[13] The elephant *quadriga* pushed the limit of traditional expectations, while seemingly remaining within the bounds of the acceptable.

A similar finesse would be employed for other deceased members of the imperial house. An emperor warranted a *tensa* and a *currus elephantorum*, while a male member of the imperial *domus* seems to have rated only a statue, likely borne on a *ferculum* either at the head of the entire procession or at the head of the *pompa deorum* accompanying Victory. Deceased female members of the imperial household, including empresses, received yet different honors – a *carpentum*, a two-wheeled, roofed cart drawn by mules, in which sat a statue of the honorand, though eventually some empresses and other imperial women earned an elephant cart, albeit a *biga* instead of a *quadriga*. And so, over the course of the first century CE, a rough pattern of honors emerged in which imperial honorands were internally differentiated among themselves and externally distinguished from the traditional gods – even if this same distinction also made the *divi* present in a rather more spectacular manner. Whatever the theological status of these imperial divinities, the humbly arrogant difference seems to have assuaged the religious scruples of the Roman people – that or the threat of massive imperial retaliation – even as it reconfigured, in part and perhaps only for some, the divine world whose goodwill was so important for a flourishing human society.

These divine-like (and -unlike) honors were both a matter of memory (a postmortem verdict on the exercise of power), and so part of the asymmetrical, but reciprocal relations between emperors and elites, and also dynastic, fashioning ties between the deceased and the living ruler. After Caesar's funeral, the cultivation of *divus Iulius* in the *pompa circensis* became an important vehicle for Caesar's heir, Octavian-Augustus, to forge dynastic links to his adoptive father, who, as a god, could no longer appear in more traditional familial (and so also dynastic) contexts like the aristocratic funeral procession.[14]

Later emperors followed the Augustan precedent: they used the *pompa circensis* to honor the memory of their predecessors and to construct imperial lineages into the late second century CE, after which this particular configuration of imperial cult(ural) memory seems to have broken down.[15]

Much as imperial cult honors were calqued on those of the traditional gods, ostentatious display notwithstanding, the itinerary of the imperial *pompa circensis* was built upon the republican one, even as imperial restorations and *de novo* imperial construction overlaid an even more glittering city on top of its republican forebear. One the one hand, the most important archaic temples along the itinerary were assiduously and even lavishly maintained. Despite their opulence, the restoration of some of Rome's most sacred sites demonstrated a certain respect for the past – especially in the case of the temple of Capitoline Jupiter, which was continually and sumptuously restored on the very (memory) traces (*vestigia*) of the original. Similarly, the massive Tiberian temple of the Dioscuri might have loomed over the Forum, but it still honored the twin horsemen demi-gods who helped to save the republic at lake Regillus. On the other hand, an impressive amount of new imperial projects dotted the itinerary – especially triumphal arches and imperial cult temples. From the arch of Nero somewhere in the middle of the Capitol and the temple of divine Vespasian in the Forum to the temple of divine Augustus in the Velabrum and the arch of Titus in the sphendone of the arena, new imperial monuments sat at nearly every turning point of the procession. Among the participants (human and divine) and along the itinerary, the imperial performance of the *pompa circensis* demonstrated a careful conservation of the past and a respectful cultivation of (certain aspects of) republican memory alongside spectacular and impressive imperial self-assertions, resulting in a kind of hybrid image of the city. SPQR+gods endured, but with an autocratic princeps at the head of SPQR, and imperial *divi* eclipsing the traditional gods.

I IMPERIAL GODS IN THE *POMPA CIRCENSIS*: FROM CAESAR TO THE SEVERANS

Dynastic beginnings: Julius Caesar

"Caesar having ended the civil wars hastened to Rome, honored and feared as no one had ever been before. All kinds of honors were devised for his gratification without stint, even those that were greater than human – sacrifices, games, statues in all the temples and public places."[16] In response to Caesar's nearly unprecedented stature, he was granted honors equal to the gods, *isotheoi timai*, elevating him above the merely human.[17] According to the third-century CE Greek senator and historian Cassius Dio, in 45 BCE the senate decreed "that an ivory statue (*andrias*) of [Julius Caesar] and later that a whole car should appear in the procession at the games in the Circus, together with the cult statues [*agalmata*] of the gods," among Caesar's myriad honors whose nature, number, and chronology remain a bit intractable.[18] That is, Caesar would be presented and represented in much, but not exactly, the same ways as the traditional gods: an ivory image (an *andrias*, in contrast to the *agalmata* of the gods) on a *ferculum* and later a processional vehicle (*tensa*) which would have carried his *exuviae*, perhaps relics like "his golden chair and his crown set with precious gems and overlaid with gold [which was] carried into the theaters in the same manner as those of the gods."[19]

13. Caesar's curule chair and crown: denarius, 42 BCE: reverse CAESAR DIC PER

In fact, this very same crown was borne to the theater, and even the Circus, where it was displayed on a curule chair after Caesar's murder, as suggested by a denarius minted in 42 BCE by Octavian that shows a *sella curulis* inscribed with *Caesar Dic(tator) Per(petuo)*, on which rests a laurel crown (Figure 13).[20] Indeed, about a decade later in 31 BCE, during a set of *ludi scaenici*, "a madman rushed into the theater at one of the festivals and seized the crown of the former Caesar and put it on, whereupon he was torn to pieces by the bystanders."[21] This same crown was also present at horse races held in honor of Augustus' birthday in 13 CE, when "a madman seated himself in the chair which was dedicated to Julius Caesar, and taking his crown, put it on."[22] And so, to judge from its subsequent use as *exuviae* displayed on a chair (*sellisternium*) at both the theater (and so transported in a *pompa theatralis*) and the racing arena (and so transported in a *pompa circensis*), it seems reasonable to conjecture that a living Caesar's crown would have been the *exuviae* borne in his *tensa*.

While his *tensa* may only have featured in postmortem processions, Caesar's ivory statue appeared during his life, perhaps twice – once in the company of Quirinus and a second time next to Victory – as well as after his assassination.[23] Among the improvised honors granted to Caesar as part of the Parilia in 45 BCE, Caesar's ivory image may have been borne next to that of Quirinus, in whose temple a statue of Caesar stood.[24] Such an honor in the hallowed procession to the Circus was not, however, simply accepted. During what seems to have been a separate performance of the circus procession also in 45 BCE, perhaps during the *ludi victoriae Caesaris* or more likely the *ludi Apollinares*, a statue of Caesar was carried next to Victory.[25] But, as Victory led the gods into the arena, the crowd deviated from the prescribed ritual by refusing to clap for the gods lest they also applaud Caesar. Cicero was delighted.[26] Instead of the customary wild applause, there was silence, stark silence – and, of course, the normal hum of a crowd of thousands.

This ceremonial setback did not, it seems, stop Caesar from pursuing or accepting further honors. Sometime after the ivory statue, the senate voted that a *tensa* for Caesar should be drawn in the circus procession.[27] His image and symbol or relic should then have been displayed together in the *pulvinar* at the Circus, an indiscrete display about which Cicero may have complained several months after Caesar's death.[28] Rather than establishing a relationship between Caesar and his subjects, these "excessive honors . . . a *tensa* and a *ferculum* in the circus procession," amongst others that "were greater than is right for mortals," alienated a number of senators, who then conspired to kill him.[29] That is, Caesar's over-the-top and heavy-handed formulation of his absolute power seems to have short-circuited the anticipated gift exchange – perhaps his honors that exceeded the human placed Caesar beyond normative human social relations, a lesson that Octavian-Augustus apparently learned.

Assassinated for honors too close to those of the traditional gods as well as, of course, other sins against the republic, his death and funeral ironically raised Caesar into "the ranks of the gods, not only by formal decree but also by the conviction of the common people."[30] In a cleverly orchestrated performance at the *ludi circenses* during the Parilia in 44 BCE, Caesar's ivory statue may have once again been carried to the Circus Maximus with the other gods. Instead of stony silence, however, Caesar's supporters or at least his mourners, including even Cicero's nephew, wore garlands, which they removed as a sign of remembrance. According to Stefan Weinstock, "as had been decreed they also wore wreaths in Caesar's honour and carried his ivory statue in the procession of the gods. But when the statue arrived in the Circus they took off their wreaths as a sign of mourning and lamented Caesar's fate."[31] A remarkable turn of events.

Apart from this possible appearance of Caesar's statue in the circus procession, Mark Antony repeatedly stymied Octavian's attempts to place Caesar's crown and chair in the Circus and at the theater.[32] However, an "astronomical windfall," a comet that appeared in the sky during games in honor of Caesar in July 44 BCE, was taken as Caesar's soul ascending to the heavens, thereby emphatically making the case for Caesar's divinity, or at least it would do so eventually.[33] Almost two years later, on January 1, 42 BCE (not coincidentally the same year the denarius with an image of Caesar's curule chair and crown was minted), Antony and Octavian, along with Lepidus, deified Caesar with all the accoutrements:

> a shrine to him, as hero, in the Forum, on the spot where his body had been burned, and [they] caused an image of him [an *agalma*], together

> with a second image, that of Aphrodite [Venus], to be carried together in the procession at the chariot races. . . . Moreover, they forbade any likeness of him to be carried at the funerals of his relatives – just as if he were in very truth a god – though this was an ancient custom and was still being observed.[34]

As an officially recognized god, Caesar could no longer appear in a *pompa funebris* – in fact, Caesar's image did not appear in Augustus' funeral, just as Augustus' would not appear in funeral processions after his death and deification.[35] Instead, Octavian-Augustus cultivated a dynastic link with his adoptive father in part by means of the *pompa circensis*, which seems to have served as a substitute for a *pompa funebris*. In place of a more traditional funerary, dynastic ritual, the circus procession became a means to parade publically one's deified ancestors, *divi* and *divae*, and other imperial special dead.

In addition to his image to be carried next to Venus, Caesar was also honored with a *tensa*, which had been decreed during his lifetime, but seems to have appeared in procession only after his death – perhaps a particularly important honor given the likely complexities of fabricating a cult for the new god.[36] Caesar's *exuviae* (his crown installed on a *sella curulis*) appeared on coins in 42 BCE (Figure 13), but only in 32–29 BCE, did Octavian's mint issue a series of coins whose reverses feature what appears to be a *tensa*.[37] This tall, boxy, and driver-less chariot with a prominent pediment – the key iconographic marker of a *tensa* – towered over its horse train. On its façade stood a relief of Jupiter with Victory on its flank, while a galloping *quadriga* served as an acroterial ornament (Figure 14).[38] This coin-type bears the legend *Caesar Divi F* ("Caesar son of the god," that is Octavian son of divine Caesar), suggesting that this sacred *tensa*, if that is what it was, belonged to Julius Caesar, upon whose divinity Octavian

14. *Tensa* of *divus* Julius Caesar: aureus, ca. 32–29 BCE: reverse: CAESAR DIVI F

15. *Tensa* of *divus* Julius Caesar: denarius, ca. 18 BCE: reverse: CAESARI AUGUSTO

16. *Tensa* of *divus* Julius Caesar with aquila: denarius, 18 BCE: obverse: CAESARI [AVG] VSTO and reverse: SPQR

was trying to capitalize. In 18 BCE, a very similar vehicle appeared on coins minted in Spain within some of which was mounted an aquila, possibly the legionary standards that Crassus had lost in 53 BCE and that Augustus had regained in 20 BCE (Figures 15 and 16).[39] Augustus may have placed the recently returned standards in Caesar's "*tensa*" during the circus procession to signal the completion of unfinished business – as was widely reported, Caesar had planned to take on the Parthian empire.[40]

Numismatic catalogs often blandly refer to this "*tensa*" as a "triumphal" or empty, "slow" *quadriga* (in other words, a driver-less chariot whose horses appear to be walking). However, its iconography (tall, rectilinear, with a pediment and figural decoration) distinguishes the numismatic "*tensa*" of Caesar from other more clearly identified triumphal chariots, which are typically equal in height to or shorter than the horse train, curvilinear, pediment-less, with abstract ornament and often, but not always, a driver. These iconographical differences do not necessarily mean, of course, that this vehicle was a *tensa*. Even so, this obscure chariot seem a suitable candidate for the *tensa* that had been decreed to Caesar during his own lifetime and that likely carried his crown to the Circus after his death. Given the frequency with which the *pompa circensis* was performed, it should occasion no surprise that Octavian-Augustus may have made maximum use of this spectacle to trumpet his deified father. If the identification is sound, then Octavian-Augustus honored his deified father in the exact same manner as the traditional gods, revealing a dutiful respect for Roman religious tradition even as he courted transgression by rendering Caesar and Jupiter, for example, cultically equivalent.

On at least one further occasion, Augustus struck a similar balance between custom and impropriety, "when he was giving votive games in the Circus he happened to fall ill and led the procession of *tensae* reclining in his litter [*letica*]."[41] On the one hand, Augustus piously completed his vow by conducting the procession of gods on their *fercula* and in their *tensae* to the arena. He may have appreciated the pageantry: the elite entourage, likely a company of young equestrians, the competitors in the games, dancers, musicians, magistrates, folkloric figures, and supernatural performers on stilts.[42] On the other hand, the *letica* which bore Augustus in the procession could not have been too dissimilar from the *fercula* on which sat the images of the gods – even in normal circumstances a litter was an arrogant mode of travel. In general, Augustus retreated from Caesar's overly bold self-assertions, making better use of traditional options for self-display as a game-giver and parading his father as a pious *divi filius*. Still, he also sought to awe the circus crowds with spectacle, with wonder, so that their applause might even eclipse the first race.[43]

Indeed, Augustus was seemingly well attuned to the value of "soft-power," as advocated by a fictional early-third-century CE Maecenas who counseled "Octavian" to "adorn this capital with utter disregard of expense and make it magnificent with festivals of every kind."[44] About a century after his death, posterity recognized the skill and scale with which Augustus deployed the resources of the *ludi*. In Suetonius' judgment, "in the frequency, variety, and magnificence of the games he provided he outdid all who had gone before."[45] The frequency with which games were given also signals the frequency of the circus procession. Though, the *pompa circensis* did not compete well with the triumph in Roman cultural memory, nonetheless, its regular and repeated performances made it an important part of the public performance of imperial power. The persistent and pervasive power of the *pompa circensis* could slowly and steadily work its magic – and Augustus seems to have recognized its appeal.

The Augustan settlement

Even while risking ritual failure, Augustus played the part of the good princeps. Indeed, Augustus' strategic interventions in the *pompa circensis* not only forged dynastic links to Caesar which helped to secure his own authority, but also provided a model for subsequent emperors to maintain theirs. As Appian put it, Octavian "decreed divine honors to his father. From this example the Romans now pay like honors to each emperor at his death if he has not reigned in a tyrannical manner."[46] Playing the game well, managing one's public perception and political authority in the appropriate (republican) manner was rewarded with the gift of divinization. The success of Augustus' ceremonial style, a key element of the "Augustan settlement," seems to have set an invaluable precedent, especially for Tiberius, who cleaved closely, if not always successfully, to the example of Augustus.[47] This early imperial style, by

17. *Tensa* of *divus* Augustus: denarius, 68–69 CE: obverse: AVGVSTVS DIVI F and reverse: EX SC

which Augustus and Tiberius sought to safeguard their power and to establish the dynastic future of their imperial heirs, was still unsurprisingly indebted to republican ceremonial traditions, expectations, and even memories.[48] Just as Augustus honored his own divine parent, Julius Caesar, Tiberius commemorated his adoptive imperial father, making appropriate use of the opportunities offered by the *pompa circensis*. As Vellieus Paterculus insisted, "Caesar [Tiberius] deified his father, not by exercise of imperial authority, but by reverence; he did not call him god, but made him one [by ritual practice]."[49]

More specifically, Tiberius seems to have commissioned a *tensa* for Augustus, which is not, however, mentioned in textual sources. Despite that, coinage represents a *tensa* for *divus* Augustus, a standard tall, boxy chariot with a pediment and figural decoration on the reverse with a bust of the god himself on the obverse – but not until 68–69 CE during the civil wars following the fall of Nero (Figure 17).[50] However, Augustus' *tensa* was commemorated in other visual media at Rome from the Julio-Claudians to the age of Constantine, which suggests both that it was among the immediate postmortem honors for the new god and that the *tensa* continued to appear in the procession for centuries – likely the only *divus* to be honored for so long a time. Fragments of an extensive but largely lost relief cycle from the mid first century CE, possibly the reign of Claudius, which might have belonged to a monumental altar or imperial cult sanctuary, depict the naval victory at Actium, a triumphal procession, and a two-wheeled *tensa* pulled by four horses followed by, at least, two *togati* wearing laurel wreaths, one of whom holds a laurel branch (Figure 18).[51] Jupiter's eagle perches on its *fastigium* (pediment), while on the façade, decorated with a garland, Aeneas, carrying his father on his shoulder, leads his son by the hand toward a sow and her piglets and Romulus, seemingly, carries a trophy on the side. The iconography, with its clear Augustan ideological references (echoing imagery from the Ara Pacis, the Forum of Augustus,

18. "Actium" relief with *tensa* of *divus* Augustus, marble, mid first century CE

as well as Vergil's *Aeneid*), suggests, but only suggests, that the *tensa* carried *exuviae* of the deified Augustus – unlike the coin, the relief has no flip side with a bust of its owner.

An early-fourth-century CE relief may also represent the *tensa* of Augustus accompanied by four *togati*, one of whom appears to be a young man (perhaps the *puer patrimus et matrimus*) looking back at the chariot, though with a different decorative scheme. The Capitoline triad or perhaps the imperial genius flanked by Roma and Victory adorn the façade, while the side sports Augustus' *corona civica* (civic crown) flanked by two laurel trees (Figure 19).[52] Unsurprisingly, only Augustus seems to have warranted such an extended memory, if not also a ritual life. The figure (or memory) of Augustus was almost synonymous with the imperial system that he founded. And so, he was seemingly remembered in both ephemeral ritual performance (possibly) and enduring, but static, visual commemoration, each reinforcing the other's impact. By contrast, the *tensae* (and also statues) of other imperial deities may have disappeared from the procession, more or less forgotten, perhaps shortly after apotheosis, an appearance or two sufficing to forge dynastic links, or whenever their memories were no longer useful.

In addition to his *tensa*, Augustus was also honored with a statue in the procession – again, much like Caesar. In this case, however, Tiberius seems to have amplified Augustus' honors: his statue (as the legend, "to deified Augustus," declares) appeared on a large, decorated cart pulled by four elephants instead of the *ferculum* that carried the image of Caesar (Figure 20).[53] According to Pliny the elder, Lucius Metellus was the first to

19. Early-fourth-century CE *tensa* of *divus* Augustus, marble, 300–350 CE

20. Elephant *quadriga* for *divus* Augustus: sestertius, 35–36 CE: obverse: DIVO AVGVSTO SPQR

lead elephants in the train of a triumph, while Pompey was the first to harness them to the triumphal chariot, although the *porta triumphalis* was too narrow and so the great general had to content himself with the traditional four horses instead.[54] Pliny also credited Augustus with the introduction of elephant statues on triumphal monuments.[55] Whoever introduced or tried to introduce elephants into the triumph or its ex post facto commemoration, Tiberius drew upon a long tradition of spectacle in order to offer inflated honors to his august predecessor. The tactic was a success – that is, it set a precedent for subsequent *divi* and entered into Roman cultural memory. In a poem likely written early in the reign of Tiberius, Philip of Thessalonica waxed lyrically about this very vehicle: "He no longer rushes into battle turreted and irresistible, the phalanx-fighting huge-tusked elephant. Through fear he has put his thick neck to the yoke straps and draws the chariot of divine Caesar [Augustus]."[56] Indeed, by the high empire a herd of north African elephants was maintained in Latium, supervised, at least on occasion, by an imperial freedman, a *procurator ad elephantos*. The practical problem of parading four elephants side by side along the itinerary remains, especially down the relatively narrow *clivus Capitolinus* which would have required the elephants to walk single file – and so perhaps the elephant *quadriga* marching shoulder to shoulder appeared only in visual imagery but not ritual performance.[57]

Whatever the case, the *currus elephantorum* occupied an ambiguous space in the ritual construction of theology during the performance of the *pompa circensis*. On the one hand, Tiberius, or Augustus if he had planned this far in advance, "humbly" differentiated the image of *divus* Augustus from the image of traditional gods borne on *fercula*. On the other hand, the *currus elephantorum* was a raw, spectacular assertion of imperial power. *Divi* assuredly differed from *dei*, relative gods differed from absolute ones, or, perhaps better, imperial gods differed from traditional ones, but the sheer size and grandeur of this display subverted any humble, pious distinction between deified humans and gods. The elephant car pushed the limits of traditional expectations, while seemingly remaining within the bounds of the acceptable, a delicate balance at which Augustus so excelled and which Tiberius attempted (not entirely successfully) to maintain.

Innovation into tradition: the Julio-Claudians

Both Augustus and Tiberius employed the *pompa circensis* and its representations to forge dynasty links, to legitimate their rule, and to foster a certain image of imperial rule in Roman cultural memory. However, the imperial circus procession was, it seems, contested territory in a battle over memory. "Good" emperors were deified and subsequently featured in ceremonies like the *pompa circensis*. More importantly, their appearance in the procession was commemorated in image and text, archives of cultural memory whose curation was split between emperors and aristocrats. What is more, postmortem inclusion in the *pompa circensis* could enhance the image of an empress long since departed or even rehabilitate the memory of one who had been condemned (exiled) in life. "Bad" emperors, by contrast, suffered all manner of memory sanctions – nasty biographies in Suetonius, for example, or their erasure from public memory, their blatantly chiseled out names in inscriptions and disfigured faces in imagery left to stand as a negative example, an anti-monument.[58] "Bad" emperors also appear to have been beset by ritual failures in the *pompa circensis* while ruling (at least in retrospect) and did not, of course, appear in the procession after death. In many ways, the *pompa circensis* indexed imperial rule. As a result, the oft-repeated *pompa circensis* seems to have become a favored tool in the construction of imperial memory, as Tiberius' extension of processional honors to the imperial family more widely, all the while remaining within accepted limits, suggests. Non-deified members of the imperial house could have appeared in a funeral procession, a more traditional dynastic mechanism, but the *pompa circensis* took place more often and, importantly, allowed all the imperial special dead, both *divi* and non-deified members of the imperial house, to appear together in one and the same performance. In this way, the *pompa circensis* might outstrip the *pompa funebris* as a means to manufacture dynastic assemblages.

Here as elsewhere, Augustus himself may have set the precedent. Still, the long, conservative reign of Tiberius, who rather resolutely adhered to the Augustan settlement, transformed precedent into a more or less established pattern.[59] After the death of his nephew Marcellus in 23 BCE, "[Augustus] ordered that a golden image, a golden crown, and a curule chair should be carried into the theater at the *ludi Romani* and should be placed in the midst of the officials in charge of the games."[60] Despite the fact that this passage seems to refer only to a *pompa theatralis* and *ludi scaenici* (theater shows) in the eponymous theater of Marcellus, it is possible that Augustus could have honored Marcellus in a manner very similar to Caesar. Deified Caesar was given a crown at the theater and a crown and a statue in the Circus, which were, it seems, placed among the traditional gods, while Marcellus' golden (not ivory) image (*eikon* not *agalma*) and gilded (but seemingly not bejeweled) crown were placed among the organizers of the games. Such differences notwithstanding, the case for Marcellus' crown displayed on a chair at the theater and at the Circus finds some slight support in Tertullian, who, while lamenting the patent idolatry of all the *ludi*, mentioned thrones and crowns among the apparatus of the circus procession.[61]

Whether or not Marcellus' image and crown appeared in the *pompa circensis*, after the death of Tiberius' nephew Germanicus in 19 CE, the many honors given the deceased included his *sella* placed in the theaters among the Augustal priests – much along the lines of Marcellus.[62] In addition, "an ivory image [of Germanicus] should precede at the circus games" during imperial celebrations – honors which were modeled, at least in part, after those conferred earlier on Gaius and Lucius (grandsons and adopted heirs of Augustus who died in 4 CE and 2 CE respectively), with whose statues the ivory equestrian statue of Germanicus seems to have been stored in the temple of Concord. Although the extent to which Germanicus' honors imitated those of Gaius and Lucius cannot be firmly determined, it is possible that these young princes appeared in a *pompa circensis* about twenty years earlier.[63] Even if images of Marcellus, Gaius, and Lucius were not honored in the circus procession, Germanicus' ivory statue (*effigies*) certainly processed to the arena, most likely borne on a *ferculum*, on the model of Caesar, alongside Victory at the head of the *pompa deorum* – though it could just as easily have found a home anywhere in the parade, perhaps even at its very front.[64]

Later, in 23 CE, the same honors "were decreed to Drusus' memory as [had been decreed] for Germanicus," and so an ivory image of Tiberius' son was also carried in the circus parade.[65] Initially, processional honors may have been given a bit indiscriminately to male members of the imperial household, if Marcellus' statue and crown did appear in the *pompa circensis*. But during the reign of Tiberius, the circus ritual seems to have been routinized to a degree. Male family members, who had not, after all, been deified, were only commemorated with statues most likely borne on *fercula*, while the gods, whether traditional or imperial, received both statues on *fercula* or *currus elephantorum* and *exuviae* in *tensae*.

Women of the Julio-Claudian dynasty would also be honored in the *pompa circensis*, although probably not under Tiberius. In 22–23 CE, by decree of the Senate, Tiberius issued a coin to honor Livia, the widow of Augustus, perhaps after her recovery from an illness.[66] On the obverse, the coins show a *carpentum* – a prestigious "processional carriage" drawn by two mules, whose use had been largely restricted to priests and Vestal virgins, and then matrons, only eventually to be monopolized by imperial ladies.[67] Although it is possible, but unlikely, that Livia's *carpentum* was "enrolled among the processional wagons of the *pompa*" during her lifetime, every other example of a *carpentum* in the *pompa circensis* seems to have occurred posthumously.[68] Livia and some subsequent empresses were granted *carpenta* during their lifetimes, but Livia's image is first securely attested in the *pompa circensis* (on a *currus elephantorum*) only under Claudius, under whom Livia was also deified. Indeed, Claudius' mother, Antonia, who had previously received all of Livia's honors, was only awarded a *carpentum* after her death – suggesting much the same for Livia. Moreover, Tiberius seems to have been stingy with honors for his mother, all of which suggests, at least, that Livia's *carpentum* did not feature in the circus parade while the empress lived.[69] After Tiberius, however, female members of the imperial household were commemorated with images in *carpenta* in the circus procession.

Indeed, shortly after having laid Tiberius to rest, Caligula arranged funerary commemorations for his mother, Agrippina the elder who had died in exile, among which "he prescribed . . . more grandly still, circus games in honor of his mother and a carriage [*carpentum*] in which she [her statue] might be transported in the procession."[70] A victim of intrigue at Tiberius' court, Caligula strikingly employed the *pompa circensis* to rehabilitate the memory of his mother, instead of what may have been the more customary option, the *pompa funebris*. As a means to maintain her remembrance, Caligula also had issued coins dedicated "to the memory of Agrippina" (*memoriae Agrippinae*), which depict a *carpentum* with a barrel-vaulted roof supported by caryatids, whose façade recalls, perhaps, a *struppus* (a crown woven from laurel branches) or, better, an aedicula or shrine built to protect a statue (Figure 21).[71] Much as the *fastigium* or pediment on the front of the *tensa* evokes a temple façade to suggest the divinity contained within, the shrine-like shape of the *carpenta* may also signal the status of the statue inside.

Subsequently, "by senatorial decree [Caligula] heaped upon his [living] grandmother Antonia whatever honors had been bestowed upon Livia

21. *Carpentum* of Agrippina I: sestertius, 37–41 CE: reverse: SPQR MEMORIAE AGRIPPINAE

Augusta."[72] In this case, however, it seems more certain that Antonia, and so by extension Livia, did not receive an image borne by a *carpentum* in the *pompa circensis* while living. That was left to Claudius. Shortly after his accession, Claudius arranged public funerary ceremonies for his parents which included "for his mother [Caligula's grandmother] a carriage [*carpentum*] to transport her [image] through the Circus" – an honor which Antonia had seemingly not enjoyed previously.[73] However, Caligula was not one to follow the staid and traditional rules of imperial public ceremonial, and so perhaps Antonia (and so also Livia) had appeared in the circus procession while still living – perhaps one of the reasons for which he was judged a "mad" emperor.[74] Indeed, Caligula rather regularly flirted with ritual transgression, for example, leading, it seems, the circus procession before a set of Trojan games on a six-horse "processional chariot."[75] He even elevated his sister Drusilla above Livia, who at that time still had no (certain) honors in the procession, by having "her statue [*agalma*] brought into the Circus on a car drawn by elephants," which made her almost equal (in ritual practice) to Augustus.[76] Rather than simple imperial insanity, however, the deification of Drusilla may have aimed to overcome a "dynastic disaster" by transforming her into a symbolic genetrix of the dynasty – or in other words, Drusilla's honors may have helped to legitimate the position of this insecure princeps.[77]

After the assassination of Caligula, Claudius returned in many respects to the more conservative pattern established by Augustus and Tiberius, though certain aspects of his predecessor's ceremonial derring-do remained. Two of his wives, Messalina and Agrippina, received the privilege to use a *carpentum*. Though they used their processional carriages ostentatiously – Messalina in Claudius' triumph, and Agrippina, whose *carpentum* also features on coins, "entered the Capitolium by *carpentum*," a right once reserved for priests and sacred objects according to Tacitus – neither *carpentum* seems to have graced the circus procession while the empresses lived.[78] Claudius seems to have reserved that privilege for the honored dead, like Antonia, following the custom of the Augustan-Tiberian settlement. Even so, Claudius, on the model of the supposedly profligate Caligula, "had divine honors voted to his grandmother Livia, as well as a chariot drawn by elephants in the circus procession, like that for Augustus."[79] Now that she was deified, Livia finally had a place in the procession, a statue borne on a *currus elephantorum* like Augustus and even Drusilla, for that matter.

Perhaps, in small part, for his cultivation of what had become traditional Augustan-Tiberian ceremonial habits, "[t]he emperor [Claudius] received the state burial and all the other honors that had been accorded to Augustus."[80] Among the many awards in the deification package assembled by Nero and his mother (Claudius' final wife Agrippina), the senate approved a *tensa* which was represented on a series of coins, adorned, it seems, with images of his civic and naval crowns, which may also have been housed within the sacred chariot, with what may be Victories and other figures (Figure 22).[81] Additionally, *divus* Claudius was awarded a *currus elephantorum* on which sat two figures: Claudius, likely closest to the viewer, and probably Augustus (Figure 23).[82] Perhaps Claudius, "a butt for insults," needed protection, which Augustus had also provided while living, shielding Claudius from public scrutiny.[83] More likely, Claudius' divinization and the prominent display of Augustus and Claudius in the *pompa circensis* aimed at buttressing Nero's insecure imperium immediately after his accession.[84] With the deification of Claudius, an Augustan-Tiberian or, even more broadly, a Julio-Claudian ceremonial pattern for the *pompa circensis* was seemingly established. Divine emperors were rewarded with symbols in *tensae* and images on elephant carts. Deified imperial women, like Livia and Drusilla, were also honored with elephant carts, while other women of the imperial household were given *carpenta*. Male members of the imperial household were also provided lesser honors, typically an ivory statue on a *ferculum*, with the possible exception of Marcellus. Into the early third century CE, subsequent emperors would readily and regularly employ this pattern to forge dynastic connections and to honor relatives, though not without alteration.

22. *Tensa* of *divus* Claudius: aureus, 54 CE: reverse: EX SC

23. Elephant *quadriga* for *divus* Claudius: aureus, 55 CE: reverse: AGRIPP AUG DIVI CLAVD NERONIS CAES MATER – EX SC

Divi, divae, *and the imperial special dead from the Flavians to the Severans*

According to Suetonius, "during his final days Nero was warned in a dream to lead the *tensa* of Jupiter Best and Greatest from the sanctuary (*sacrarium*) to the house of Vespasian and then into the Circus."[85] By leading Jupiter's *tensa* from the shrine (or *aedes tensarum*) on the Capitol to the house of Vespasian and from there to the Circus, this dream "foretold" Vespasian's eventual assumption of the imperial throne – and possibly his ultimate deification. In other words, Nero was to conduct a kind of *pompa circensis* with a detour to pick up the future emperor who would replace Nero at the head of the procession – or perhaps Vespasian joined the gods directly. Vespasian would become Rome's sovereign by the favor of its sovereign god, a transfer of power signaled by the conveyance of *exuviae* in a *tensa* to Vespasian. Apparently, Jupiter also had had enough of the extravagant behavior of Nero and so sought to turn over the reins of power to one better suited.

Once in power, the Flavians made good use of the opportunities afforded by the *pompa circensis*. At some point, probably near the beginning of the dynasty, though possibly at the beginning of his own reign, Titus "dedicated a statue of [Britannicus] on horseback, made of ivory, which even now is carried in the circus procession, attending it himself on its first appearance."[86] This ivory equestrian statue – an exemplar, like that of Germanicus, for all the youthful Roman equites who may have still ridden in the procession – was probably carried on a *ferculum*, shouldered perhaps by *Augustales* or their slaves.[87] Titus would have walked alongside, an act which would have demonstrated clear and tangible connections between the new Flavian dynasty and the worthy among the Julio-Claudians. The image of Britannicus, of course, recalled the rule of his father Claudius, who had been the only other emperor deified and then honored in the *pompa circensis* after Augustus. In fact, Suetonius claimed that Claudius' divinization (and corresponding temple) was restored by Vespasian after having been cancelled by Nero – presumably sometime after Nero had outfitted a *tensa* and an elephant cart for *divus* Claudius.[88]

Titus continued to respect the (imperial) traditions of the *pompa circensis* after the death of his father, divine Vespasian, who received the last numismatic example of a *tensa*, whose pediment was decorated with a *quadriga* flanked by Victories holding wreaths and whose sides were graced by figures (perhaps gods) (Figure 24).[89] As had become customary, Titus also commemorated his deified father with a decorated *currus elephantorum*, on which deified Vespasian sits alone, clutching a long scepter in his right hand and a miniature statue of Victory in his left, reminiscent of the image of deified Augustus (Figure 25).[90] Titus even maintained the traditional, but not wholly stable, imperial hierarchy of honors when he dedicated a *carpentum* "to the memory of Domitilla" (*memoriae Domitillae*) or "to Domitilla [wife of] the Emperor Caesar

24. *Tensa* of *divus* Vespasian: aureus, 80–81 CE: obverse: DIVVS AVGVSTVS VESPASIANVS and reverse: EX SC

Vespasian Augustus" (*Domitillae Imp. Caes. Vesp. Aug.*) (Figure 26).[91] By offering his mother a *carpentum*, clearly on the model of Agrippina and Antonia, Titus observed the more conservative honors due an imperial woman who had not been an empress (she died before Vespasian took power), adhering closely to the prescriptions of imperial ritual tradition.

25. Elephant *quadriga* for *divus* Vespasian: sestertius, 80–81 CE: obverse: DIVO AVG VESP

After Titus' short-lived reign, Domitian also conformed to the more conservative tradition of posthumous honors, initially at least. Shortly after the death of Titus' daughter Julia in the later 80s CE, Domitian awarded *diva* Julia a *carpentum* seen on coins minted in 90–92 CE (Figure 27).[92] At about the same time, however, Domitian, seemingly not content with customary honors – perhaps because he had been inappropriately close to his niece or because he felt responsible for her death – conferred an elephant *biga* on *diva* Julia, whose image held a scepter and a stalk of wheat or perhaps a branch (Figure 28).[93] A *biga*, as opposed to a *quadriga*, may suggest a modicum of restraint. Emperors warranted elephant *quadrigae*, while empresses, and

26. *Carpentum* of *diva* Domitilla: sestertius, 80–81 CE: obverse: MEMORIAE DOMITILLAE SPQR

Drusilla, rated an elephant cart with an unknown number of draft animals. Julia's honors may, then, have recalled Caligula's model. Although Domitian transgressed the traditional pattern of honors, he seems to have instituted a new, albeit less obvious, articulation of difference: *divi* would receive elephant *quadrigae* and *tensae*, while imperial women were granted elephant *bigae* and/or *carpenta*. This manner of expressing distinctions among the imperial special dead would continue throughout the second century CE and into the third, though not, of course, without rather frequent exception.

In fact, the very next deified emperor to appear in the *pompa circensis, divus* Nerva, was only awarded an elephant *biga*, not a *quadriga*, according to a restored coin re-minted by his adopted heir and successor, Trajan (Figure 29).[94] Trajan then returned, if only temporarily, to the older pattern when he provided a barrel-vaulted *carpentum* drawn by two mules for his sister, *diva* Augusta Marciana, on the occasion of her deification. There may, however, have been some confusion at the mint. On one of the coin types, a tall, boxy, *tensa* with a pediment and figural ornament has replaced the barrel-vaulted *carpentum*, though it is still drawn by mules (Figure 30).[95] To add to the profusion (not to say confusion) of honors, *diva* Marciana eventually received an elephant *biga* on which she sat perhaps as a kind of Vesta with a scepter and a patera (Figure 31).[96] Even the "good" emperors did not always conform to tradition. Admittedly, the tradition was neither

27. *Carpentum* of *diva* Julia: sestertius, 90–91 CE: obverse: DIVAE IVLIAE AVG DIVI TITI F SPQR

28. Elephant *biga* for *diva* Julia: aureus, 90–91 CE: obverse: DIVA IVLIA AVGVSTA

29. Elephant *biga* for *divus* Nerva: aureus, ca. 102–117 CE: obverse: DIVVS NERVA and reverse: IMP CAES TRAIAN AVG GER DAC P P REST

30. *Carpentum-tensa* of *diva* Marciana: aureus, ca. 113 CE: obverse: DIVA AVGVSTA MARCIANA and reverse: CONSECRATIO

systematic nor perfectly regular: there was a range of options with which an emperor could honor the imperial special dead.

Strangely, no extant evidence indicates that Trajan or even his successor Hadrian was commemorated in the circus parade. Antoninus Pius, however, actively intervened in the ceremony to honor his wife, Faustina I (the elder), rather effusively.[97] According to the sometimes unreliable, though less so for the second century CE, *Historia Augusta*, the senate voted her games, a temple, and statues of gold and silver. Perhaps one of these many statues hid within her *carpentum* as it rode to the circus – only to encounter "her statue" that Antoninus Pius had "placed in all the circuses" (Figure 32).[98] When not jostling along in a *pompa circensis*, this *carpentum* may have been displayed on a platform on the stairs of the temple of Antoninus Pius and Faustina, not far from the only

31. Elephant *biga* for *diva* Marciana: denarius, 113 CE: obverse: DIVA AVGVSTA MARCIANA and reverse: EX SENATVS CONSVLTO

32. *Carpentum* of *diva* Faustina I: aureus, 141–161 CE: obverse: DIVA AVGVSTA FAVSTINA and reverse: EX SC

known itinerary of the circus parade, though probably screened from view.[99] Antoninus Pius also honored his wife with an elephant *biga*. On some coin-types, *diva* Faustina appears dressed, perhaps, as Ceres holding a scepter and a sheaf of grain; on others her statue sits beneath a kind of aedicula, a flat canopy supported by columns which protected and framed the *diva* under the inscription AETERNITAS (Figures 33 and 34).[100] On yet other coins, *diva* Faustina I appears in the guise of Magna Mater conveyed in a cart by two lions, perhaps a reference to the *pompa circensis* of the *ludi Megalenses*, or perhaps a depiction of the *lavatio* procession in which the statue of Magna Mater was escorted to the Almo, a Tiber tributary, for a ritualized washing.[101] If elephants were really made to pull carts through the city, then *perhaps* securely chained lions were too – though the images seems symbolic, rather than commemorative.

The aedicula, a shrine and framing device, was characteristic of most Antonine elephant carts, whether for a *divus* or a *diva*, with the notable exception of the elephant *quadriga* of deified Antoninus Pius himself.[102]

33. Elephant *biga* for *diva* Faustina I as "Ceres": sestertius, 141–161 CE: obverse: DIVA AVGVSTA FAVSTINA and reverse: EX SC

34. Elephant *biga* for *diva* Faustina I enshrined: sestertius, 141–161 CE: obverse: DIVA FAVSTINA and reverse: AETERNITAS

Marcus Aurelius consecrated his imperial colleague Lucius Verus with an elephant *quadriga*, on which a statue of the *divus* rests under an aedicula (Figure 35).[103] Marcus Aurelius then provided an elephant *biga* for his deified wife, Faustina II (the younger), whose statue also sits under a shrine-like structure.[104] A still living Faustina II also seems to have been granted a *carpentum* by Antoninus Pius to judge from the last numismatic version of this processional vehicle.[105] Whether or not it appeared in the *pompa circensis* during her lifetime remains an open question, but perhaps it did after her deification in imitation of her mother. In honor of his son, Verus, Marcus Aurelius decreed that "a golden image should be carried to the circus games in procession [during the games for Jupiter Optimus Maximus]," on the model of Germanicus.[106] In general, both Antoninus Pius and Marcus Aurelius honored the imperial special dead, especially spouses, in what had become the amplified high imperial pattern of honors: an elephant *quadriga* for an emperor,

35. Elephant *quadriga* for *divus* Lucius Verus enshrined: sestertius, 169 CE or later: obverse: DIVVS VERVS and reverse: SC CONSECRATIO

an elephant *biga* for an empress, and a statue for male members of the household.

The notorious Commodus honored his father, Marcus Aurelius, with the customary elephant *quadriga*, on which sat a statue under the Antonine aedicula.[107] After this nod to the *mos maiorum*, Commodus – consumed, it seems, by Hercules-mania – had a lion skin and a club (something like Herculean *exuviae*) borne before him as he marched through the streets. These same *exuviae* "were placed on a gilded chair in the theaters [and so perhaps also the Circus], whether he was present or not."[108] After the assassination of Commodus, Septimius Severus eventually wrested control of the empire from a number of rival claimants after a protracted and deeply contentious civil war. Faced with a situation similar to that of the Flavians, Septimius Severus turned to the *pompa circensis* to link his reign with previous regimes. In this case, Septimius Severus paid tribute to Pertinax, a short-lived successor of Commodus, by ordering that "a golden image of Pertinax should be carried into the hippodrome [Circus] on a car drawn by elephants," an act which was subsequently commemorated on a medallion (Figure 36).[109]

The traditional gods

Though *tensae*, *carpenta*, and *currus elephantorum* for new imperial deities were commonly introduced into the circus procession, the traditional gods still appeared and, on occasion, new ones could be added. Indeed, the enduring cult of the traditional gods and their continued presence in the *pompa circensis* made similar imperial honors possible. For example, a terracotta relief from the Augustan period or early empire seems to show the boxy, gabled *tensa* of

36. Elephant *quadriga* for *divus* Pertinax enshrined: bronze medallion, ca. 193 CE: obverse: DIVVS PERTINAX PIVS PATER and reverse: AETERNITAS

the Capitoline triad, who grace the façade, while Mercury, Hercules, and Victory adorn the long side (Figure 11).[110] Similarly, Trajan had the L. Rubrius Dossenus coins with the "*tensae*" of the Capitoline triad re-issued with the addition of a legend reminding the viewer of the emperor's conquests (IMP. CAES. TRAIAN. AVG. GER. DAC. P. P. REST.), perhaps an effort to recall the virtues of the republic, which his own reign supposedly revivified after the depravity of Domitian (see Figures 1–3, which show the republican issues).[111] To have re-minted these coins, or any coins, strongly suggests that at least some Romans paid attention to coin imagery and that the memory of the republic and its ritual traditions still mattered. The re-minted *denarii* of L. Rubrius Dossenus may well have conjured, for a few at least, a continuous history of the circus procession from Fabius Pictor-Dionysius' early republican version to the present day, in which the "*tensae*" of Jupiter, Juno, and Minerva stood for the very continuity of (republican) Rome. In short, the Trajanic-restoration coins appealed to Roman cultural memory, for which the performance of the *pompa circensis* served as a social framework of collective remembrance.

In addition to the continuing presence of the Capitoline triad, a few traditional gods may have joined the circus procession. For example, Augustus may have introduced something like a *tensa* of Ceres, a cylindrical car which held ears of grain, perhaps in reference to his re-organization of Rome's subsidized food program (the *annona*) (Figure 37).[112] The iconography of this vehicle conforms neither to triumphal chariots nor *tensae*, though its vague associations with Ceres, or rather agricultural fertility, suggest some sort of ritual chariot, functionally similar, at least, to a *tensa*. In 79 CE, Titus may have re-introduced, or at least re-represented, a very similar "*tensa*" for Ceres for very similar reasons.[113] In the wake of Hadrian's massive temple to Venus and Rome and prompted by the nine-hundredth birthday of the city,

37. "*Tensa*" of Ceres (Augustus): denarius, ca. 19 BCE: reverse: CAESAR AVGVSTV[S]

38. *Tensa* of Roma (Antoninus Pius): bronze medallion, 147–148 CE: reverse: ROM

Antoninus Pius introduced a more standard-looking *tensa* for Dea Roma, whose statue may grace the peak of the pediment flanked by laurel branches (Figure 38).[114] Beneath the pediment, in which sat a globe, the façade is inscribed with ROM, while the side panel depicts the she-wolf suckling Romulus and Remus in the Lupercal, recalling, of course, Rome's foundation legends and the Lupercal, by which the *tensa* would have passed as it traveled along the *vicus Tuscus*.

Perhaps most infamously, the emperor Marcus Aurelius Antoninus (218–222 CE), better known as Elagabalus, priest of the deity Elagabal, caused something like a *tensa* in honor of his deity to appear in something like a circus procession – a *pompa deorum* from the Palatine to the god's suburban sanctuary with its adjoining circus. The *quadriga*, which holds the large conical sacred stone of Emesa, differs from the (other) *tensae* – much as Ceres' "*tensa*" differs from standard gabled ones. In fact, it adheres closely to "triumphal" iconography, with its low, swooping contours. Moreover, the "*tensa*" – either rung about with four parasols (or rather cultic standards) or moving in the direction of a star – openly displays (rather than hides) the aniconic embodiment of the god (akin to Greek *xoana* and Roman *exuviae*) festooned with an eagle (Figures 39 and 40).[115] In some ways, then, this vehicle functioned like a *tensa*, a *quadriga* to transport abstract divine presence, though its appearance obviously and unsurprisingly differed: Emesa would have had its own ritual traditions and idiom of spectacle.[116] On its own, the addition of a god to something like a *pompa circensis* followed a well-worn path. Elagabalus, however, went further in his devotions when he conducted a *pompa deorum* to Elagabal's suburban sanctuary: he himself led the "*tensa*" as a *puer patrimus et matrimus* would have done for the other gods in a more traditional *pompa circensis*.

39. "*Tensa*" of Elagabal surrounded by "parasols" or cultic standards: aureus, 218–219 CE: obverse: IMP C M AVR ANTONINVS P F AVG and reverse: SANCT DEO SOLI ELAGABAL

> The god was set up in a chariot studded with gold and precious stones and driven from the city to the suburb. The chariot was drawn by a team of six large, pure white horses which had been decorated with lots of gold and ornamented discs. No human person ever sat in the chariot or held the reins, which were fastened to the god as though he were driving himself. Antoninus ran along in front of the chariot, but facing backwards as he ran looking at the god and holding the bridles of the horses. He ran the whole way backwards like this looking up at the front of the god. But to stop him tripping and falling while he was not looking where he was going, lots of sand gleaming like gold was put down, and his bodyguard supported him on either side to make sure he was safe as he ran like this. Along both sides of the route the people ran with a great array of torches, showering wreaths and flowers on him. In the procession, in front of the god, went images of all the other gods and valuable or precious temple dedications and all the imperial standards or costly heirlooms. Also the cavalry and all the army joined in. After the god had been conducted and installed in the temple, the emperor carried out the festival sacrifices described above.[117]

Following in broad strokes the traditional practice of the *pompa circensis* as conjured by Fabius Pictor-Dionysius, Herodian construed the procession as a *pompa deorum*, introduced, perhaps, by the gold and silver vessels of the gods and the state (that is, "temple dedications" and "imperial standards or costly heirlooms"), while the "images of all the other gods" formed a pantheon headed by Elagabal, the honorand in the most prestigious position at the end. The procession was also something of an Ovidian *aurea pompa*: the chariot was "studded with gold," the six white horses (though the coins show only four) were "decorated with lots of gold," and even the sand gleamed like gold. Moreover, the procession even recalled the *pompa hominum*: "the cavalry and all the army" participated very much on the model of Fabius Pictor-Dionysius' regimented youth on foot and on horseback. Most strikingly, however, Elagabalus' own behavior strongly evoked that of a *puer patrimus et matrimus*, who had to maintain contact with the *tensa* and keep hold of the reins (possibly with his right hand only). Elagabalus also took great pains to escort his god properly, running backwards to keep his attention fixed on his god, holding the bridles, but not the reins, and ensuring that he did not fall down with the help of other attendants.[118] Perhaps a ritual failure would have resulted should Elagabalus have violated any of these rules – again much like a *pompa circensis*.

40. "*Tensa*" of Elagabal with star: aureus, 220–221 CE: reverse: CONSERVATOR AVG

In the end, Elagabalus' procession may simply have inflected a common practice with his own local, priestly traditions. It seems plausible that other emperors would have prominently featured their preferred god(s) in the *pompa circensis*. It is equally possible that the itinerary of the circus procession varied to accommodate other origination points, like the temple of the games' honorand, and other destinations, that is, racing tracks other than the Circus Maximus. Therefore, however ostentatious Elagabalus may have seemed, he may have been acting within the accepted boundaries of Roman public ceremonial.

II AN IMPERIAL PALIMPSEST: THE ITINERARY FROM AUGUSTUS TO SEPTIMIUS SEVERUS

Much as imperial cult honors in the *pompa circensis* were calqued on those of the traditional gods, the itinerary, though vastly transformed during the first three imperial centuries, still conserved Roman cultural memory which stretched (however selectively) from the hoary days of archaic Rome and the venerated republic to the imperial present. The relevance of the republican senate as a political institution waned, even as memories of the republic and its political culture remained essential resources for Roman elite identity formation, as a group and individually, into late antiquity.[119] On the one hand, the itinerary of the *pompa circensis* witnessed the restoration of many of Rome's most ancient temples, sanctuaries, basilicas, and, unsurprisingly, the Circus itself. These imperial renovations maintained the presence of the past, from whose power and prestige the imperial present drew (some of) its own authority.[120] On the other hand, the emperors came to dominate the itinerary in the same overwhelming and conspicuous manner that they dominated the city of Rome as a whole, with massive new monumental construction projects, which steadily accumulated over the course of centuries. In many ways, imperial building projects along the itinerary radically re-shaped the environment through which the procession passed, re-shaping memories and resonances, and so also the symbolic image of the city.[121]

The imperial impact on the city was indeed proverbial – after all, Augustus famously "boasted he had found a city of brick and left it a city of marble" – transforming a supposedly squalid town into a gleaming, imperial megalopolis, even though earlier monuments and memories remained vital and visible.[122] Augustus' contemporaries seem to have agreed – or at least one contemporary, whose career was deeply indebted to the emperor. According to Vitruvius, Augustus "cared . . . about the provision of suitable public buildings; so that . . . the majesty of empire was expressed through the eminent dignity of its public buildings."[123] This keen regard for Rome's built environment ensured that the Augustan building projects would "correspond to the grandeur of [Rome's] history and would be a memorial to posterity."[124]

In other words, though thoroughly re-built (again and again), ancient republican edifices, now glittering imperial monuments (like the temples of Capitoline Jupiter, the Dioscuri, and Ceres) still lined the itinerary. They were now joined, however, by wholly new (imperial cult) temples and (triumphal) arches which transformed Rome's urban image without entirely obliterating the republican one. Resonance and repetition tied to republican cultural memory could still have constituted a part of the processional experience, even as the repetition of new imperial structures would have placed the ludic space created by the procession and its itinerary under the auspices of a seemingly eternal imperial victoriousness.[125] Even though imperial Rome after Augustus may have been more image-able and so navigable, as evidenced by the systematically organized *vici* (neighborhoods) with their attendant festival, the Compitalia, the panoptic and monumental Severan marble map (and its predecessors), and the late-antique regionary catalogs (even though they may be closer to medieval *mirabilia* literature than bureaucratic texts), the circus procession continued to perform an image of Rome whose symbolic roots sank deep into its historical topography.[126] New forms of urban knowledge and social organization did not vitiate the need for and indeed the production of images of the city by other means. Imperial Rome could be imagined in new ways, but the formation of processional images continued unabated.

Indeed, as the striking *pompa deorum* of Elagabalus suggests, a *pompa circensis* could potentially follow any number of itineraries, which would have proliferated variations on the image of Rome. For example, the gods would have been present at games held at other circuses, like the circus Vaticanus (*Gaii et Neronis*), circus Varianus (the destination of Elagabalus' procession), or the circus of Maxentius equipped with a large, monumental "*porta pompae*" and a *pulvinar.*[127] Moreover, the circus procession may have set out from the temple of the deity in whose honor the games were produced, including the temples of the imperial *divi*. So, it is certainly possible that "all the new temples built for *divi* and *divae* were involved in the *pompa circensis*, because the imperial images, which paraded in the *pompa*, were placed there and thus had to be carried out from there," as Patrizia Arena has argued.[128] It is certainly possible that there were different itineraries for games in the Circus Maximus, but it is also possible that all necessary images, symbols, or vehicles were transported to the Capitolium, which already housed some processional equipment in one or more *aedes tensarum*. In the end, the path from the Capitol through the Forum, Velabrum, and Forum Boarium to the Circus Maximus remains the only securely attested route, and so the sole itinerary considered here.

The restoration of cultural memory in imperial Rome

Ancient Rome, like every city, continually decayed and so continually needed to be renovated.[129] Monuments along the itinerary were rebuilt, restored, enlarged, and enhanced. These renovations and restorations, which at times almost amounted to new construction, attest to the power and persistence of the past – especially when religious scruples determined, to a degree, the scope of allowable reconstruction. For example, according to Dionysius of Halicarnassus, after the temple of Jupiter Optimus Maximus burned in 83 BCE, it was assiduously "erected upon the same foundations, and differed from the ancient structure in nothing but the costliness of the materials"[130] (Map 2.1). Tacitus told a similar tale: after its dedication at the beginning of the republic, "the vast resources of the Roman people that came later would rather decorate than enlarge [the Capitoline temple]. It was laid out again on the same traces (*vestigia*)," after its destruction in 83 BCE.[131] Cicero also expressed approval, albeit in a rhetorical context which prompted its exaggeration, of this lavish restoration. He even approved of the manner in which it was restored, "as it was done by our ancestors," while Pliny the elder reported that reactions to the rebuilt temple varied, which suggests that at least some Romans were concerned that restoration might erase the traces, the memory, of the archaic temple.[132] Perhaps to assuage such anxiety, Augustus publicly declared his reverence for tradition in his *Res gestae*, insisting insisted that he "rebuilt the Capitoline temple ... incurring great expense ... without any inscription of [his] name" – even though this rebuilding may been a rather thoroughgoing renovation.[133]

In 69 CE, "The saddest and most shameful crime that the Roman state had ever suffered since its foundation" occurred, according to Tacitus' lurid account, "the home of Jupiter Optimus Maximus, founded with due auspices by our ancestors as a pledge of empire ... was destroyed by the mad fury of

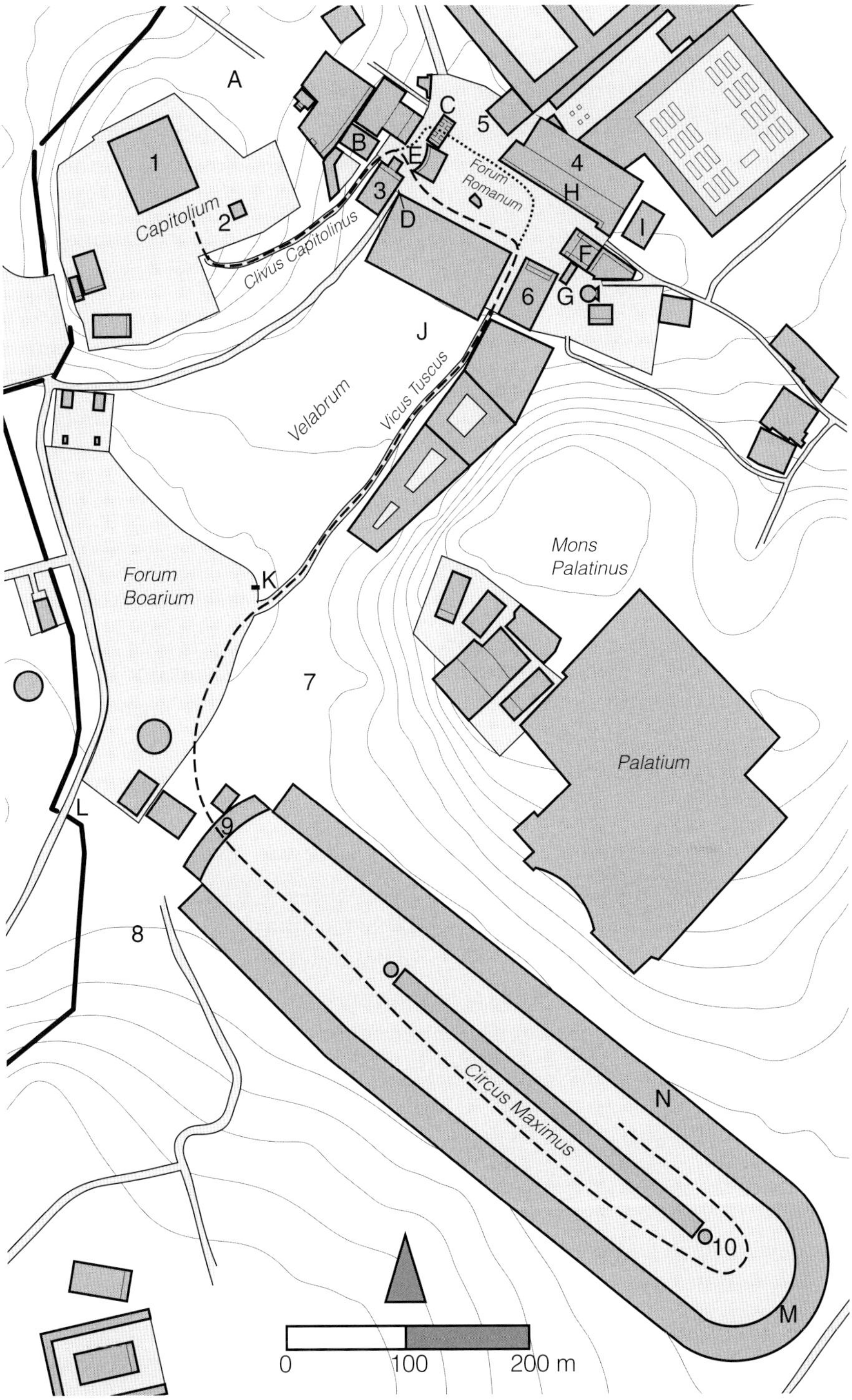

Map 2 The imperial itinerary (ca. 44 BCE–235 CE) of the *pompa circensis*, drawn by Marie Saldaña

emperors."[134] Before the temple was once again rebuilt, the haruspices (Etruscan diviners) determined that "the new temple should be erected on exactly the same site as the old (*vestigia*): the gods were unwilling to have the old plan changed."[135] Nonetheless, "the temple was given greater height than the old: this was the only change that religious scruples allowed, and the only feature that was thought wanting in the magnificence of the old structure."[136] In 80 CE, the temple burned yet again, only to be even more extravagantly rebuilt by Domitian (at enormous expense) with gilded bronze roof tiles and doors and Pentelic marble columns. But unlike Augustus, who had not added his name to the temple, Domitian inscribed his name alone with no mention of previous builders, an egregious erasure of memory by a "mad" emperor, though to be fair Domitian may have been following the example of his father, Vespasian.[137]

However profligate the décor and whoever took credit, the temple was seemingly always rebuilt (or imagined to have been rebuilt) on the very traces (*vestigia*), in the very memory of the original. Still, its periodic destruction must have destroyed some of its cultural memory, which had been archived in votives, inscriptions, and statues held in the sanctuary.[138] Despite destruction and reconstruction, the continuing ritual role of the Capitoline temple in political and domestic life helped maintain its place in Roman memory. The *processus consularis* at Rome would end, it seems, at the Capitol for as long as the city hosted consuls.[139] Even the Roman initiation into manhood, the assumption of the *toga virilis*, may still have taken place on the Capitol, as it had traditionally, though the temple of Mars Ultor was now included in some manner.[140] And, most importantly in the present context, at least one *aedes tensarum* stood in the *area Capitolina* by the first century CE, and so the *pompa circensis*, at least on occasion, still originated on the Capitol (Map 2.2).

As part of his prodigious efforts to transform Rome from a city of bricks into one of marble, "[Augustus] often exhorted other prominent men, so far as the resources of each permitted, to beautify the city with monuments, whether new or restored and improved. At that time, many men undertook many projects; for instance ... the Temple of Saturn by Munatius Plancus [in 42 BCE]" (Map 2.3).[141] Unlike the Capitoline temple, which was hedged by religious restrictions, the temple of Saturn seems to have been rebuilt on a grander scale in addition to its more impressive decoration. Such alterations would certainly have impacted, but would not necessarily have severed cultural memory. In fact, during the early empire an altar to Saturn still stood in front of the temple, an altar which was originally erected, or so the story goes, in mythical pre-history by either the Pelasgi or Hercules with an expedition of Greeks.[142] And so, despite a temple rebuilt to match the grandeur of empire, the site (temple and altar) remained dedicated to Saturn as it had been from a time before Rome was Rome.

Similarly, despite its seeming decline from a living, political "milieu de mémoire" during the republic to a dead "lieu de mémoire, in which a residual sense of continuity remains," under the emperors, the Forum also embodied a tension between republican myth-memory and imperial innovation.[143] On the one hand, the Twelve Tables seem to have been preserved in their original form and location, affixed to the rostra in front of the curia, until the triumviral period at least.[144] On the other hand, the curia and the rostra both were re-oriented – the curia was shifted to align with the Forum Iulium, while the rostra now faced the open space of the Forum. Julius Caesar (and Augustus) also replaced the basilica Sempronia built in 170 BCE behind the *tabernae veteres* along the southern edge of the Forum with the basilica Iulia. Similarly, a basilica Paulli, commonly known as the basilica Aemilia, begun by L. Aemilius Paullus before the mid 50s BCE but dedicated by his son, L. Aemilius Lepidus Paullus, in 34 BCE, replaced the basilica Fulvia (built behind the *tabernae novae*), dedicated in 179 BCE, erasing the name of its founder, M. Fulvius Nobilior, even as it seems to have re-used the "original antique columns." (Map 2.4).[145] In 22 CE, M. Aemilius Lepidus spent "his own money to consolidate and decorate the basilica of Paulus, an Aemilian monument ... [part of a still continuing] custom of public munificence ... [which] revived his ancestral honor," an act of sheer willingness that maintained familial memory in the Forum – in the tradition of Marcus Aemilius who had "set up portrait-shields in the basilica Aemilia" in 78 BCE, an initial act, it seems, of the re-branding the building.[146]

In 58 CE, "the *ruminalis* tree in the Comitium, which 830 years before had protected Remus and Romulus in their infancy, had shriveled, its twigs dead and its trunk dying out, was held as a prodigy, until it revived with new growth." (Map 2.5).[147] Somehow this fig tree, which should have shaded the Lupercal where the twins were supposedly suckled and a where a *ficus ruminalis* once (or still) stood, ended up in the Forum. The (elite) Romans may have had a strong attachment to place, but it seems that, at times, they were also willing to re-place or replicate. Whatever the case, the tree, which had nearly died, sprouted new growth – much like, of course, memories of the republic. Remembrance of the Dioscuri even found new life, when their monumentally rebuilt temple in the southwestern corner of the Forum was re-dedicated in 6 CE in the name of Tiberius and his brother Drusus, styling the imperial brothers as Dioscuri redux (Map 2.6).[148] If the Forum was a mirror of the state, then the imperial Forum assuredly offered an imperial reflection, but with a still shimmering aura of the republic.[149]

The Lupercal, somewhere along the *vicus Tuscus* at the foot of the Palatine hill near the Circus, may have remained quaintly rustic in memory of the rescue of Romulus and Remus; for which reason Augustus may have correctly claimed to have built it (*feci*), while he only claimed to have rebuilt or restored (*refeci*) the Capitoline temple (Map 2.7).[150] Nevertheless, the site seems to have retained a vestige of its primeval charm, as Ovid noted: "there was a tree: traces [or memories (*vestigia*)] remain."[151] The newly developed Lupercal, haunted still by its fabled past, also proved an apt location at which to preserve the memory of Drusus Caesar with a golden equestrian statue, linking Rome's legendary foundation to the Augustan dynasty.[152]

Near the end of the itinerary, the temple of Ceres was also restored, likely in line with the imperial renovations of the temples of Jupiter, Saturn, and the Dioscuri in terms of scale and décor (Map 2.8). In 17 CE, "[Tiberius] dedicated shrines of the gods which, destroyed by age or fire, had been projects of Augustus': [for example] that to Liber, Libera, and Ceres near the Circus Maximus, which A. Postumius as dictator had vowed."[153] Imperial magnificence need not completely overwhelm republican memory, at least for one like Tacitus; indeed, such splendor might even enhance it.

The Circus itself provides an attenuated example of the juxtaposition of republican memory and imperial prodigality. The arena began to be monumentalized during the second century BCE, but Caesar and Augustus gave the Circus its definitive form. According to Cassiodorus in the early sixth century CE, "Augustus, lord of the world, raised a work equal to his power, and laid out a construction [the Circus Maximus] in the Murcian valley that is a marvel even to the Romans."[154] Augustus himself, however, only claimed to have "built (*feci*) the *pulvinar* at the Circus Maximus," perhaps only now replacing a simple wooden platform with a proper stone temple (*naos*) (Map 2.N).[155] Pliny the Younger credited Trajan, of course, with "the vast façade of the Circus [which] rivals the beauty of temples, a fitting place for a nation that has conquered the world, a sight to be seen on its own account as well as for the spectacles there to be displayed: to be seen indeed for its beauty."[156] Like Augustus, however, Trajan also seems to have advertised his efforts humbly, in the style of a *civilis princeps*. According to Cassius Dio, "[Trajan] was so high-minded and generous that, after enlarging and embellishing the Circus, which had crumbled away in places, he merely inscribed on it a statement that he had made it adequate for the Roman people."[157] Other emperors also worked to enlarge and adorn this cavernous arena, an increasingly important political site where the emperor could meet the people.[158] Claudius "adorned the Circus Maximus with marble *carceres* and gilded *metae*."[159] In the early third century CE, Caracalla seems to have added a loge above the starting gates from which the *praeses ludorum* would preside over an increasingly ritualized start to the races (Map 2.9).

Even as the emperors transformed the arena into an imperial monument, the legendary past continued to haunt the low-lying *vallis Murcia*, named for a deity whose shrine may have stood on the edge of track, its very location a sign of its revered antiquity. Across the track, the altar of Consus, the god to whom Romulus dedicated that infamous set of games during which the young Sabine women were kidnapped, sat enclosed (probably) within the first turning post at the southern curved end (the so-called sphendone) (Map 2.10). At this very spot, it seems, the rape of the Sabines was re-enacted during the empire, its sexual violence surely magnifying the mad *furor* of the crowd – at least a medallion minted under Antoninus Pius suggests as much. On the reverse of this medallion, the Sabine women "loosely based on the standard visual topoi of erotic pursuit" flee their captors, while the *meta* looms in the background (see Figure 86, a fourth- or early-fifth-century CE medallion based on the Antonine prototype). This image, the first depiction of the rape of the Sabines in an explicitly built-up (as opposed to a primitive) Circus Maximus, recalled Rome's (sexualized) foundation story in an erotic "historical" dramatization that fit perfectly the ludic atmosphere of the games.[160]

And so, even at the sites that emperors most transformed, like the Circus, the cultural memory of legendary Rome remained. Indeed, the continuing power of these memories and the potent symbolic topography of which they were a part helps to explain, in some measure, the insistent siting of *de novo* imperial monuments in the midst of this enduring landscape of memory. The (mytho-historical and republican) past mattered and the (imperial) present harnessed it. Or, in other words, historical (and not-so-historical) resonances still echoed within the image of the city projected by the imperial *pompa circenis.*

Deus praesens: *imperial cult temples and triumphal arches*

Emperors were not, however, merely content to lean on the power of the past to assert their authority in the present, important though that was. Following Augustus, who claimed to have "revived many exemplary ancestral practices ... and handed down to later generations exemplary practices for them to imitate," the "good" emperors respected the past, even as they attempted to master Roman cultural memory.[161] That is, "good" emperors not only renovated venerable temples, they also built wholly new structures, in particular imperial cult temples to honor deified predecessors and to secure dynastic links as well as triumphal arches to celebrate military victories and imperial victoriousness. In this way, *de novo* imperial construction mirrored the *pompa circensis*, which recalled the legendary and republican past even as it honored the imperial special dead and celebrated the present emperor, the *deus praesens*, the present god.[162]

Following the itinerary from the Capitol to the Circus: according to Tacitus, thanks to Corbulo's capture of Artaxata in 58 CE, "Nero was hailed as 'commander' ... and there was a decree of statues and arches (*arcus*)," one of which was erected in 62 CE "in the middle of the Capitoline hill" somewhere – in the tradition of the *fornices* of Scipio and Calpurnius (Map 2.A).[163] Numismatic imagery shows an arch with a single bay and a triumphal *quadriga* atop the attic story, but unfortunately offers no clues about its precise location.[164] This arch may have been dismantled upon Nero's death – or perhaps the fire in 69 CE which destroyed the Capitoline temple also obliterated it. After Nero, Domitian "put up so many vaulted passageways and arches (*arcus*) on such a great scale, with four-horsed chariots and triumphal insignia, in every part of the city that on one of them someone wrote in Greek: 'Arci' [Enough!]," at least according to Suetonius.[165] Unfortunately, that great arbiter of imperial memory provided no topographical indications for those arches, but given the itinerary of the *pompa circensis* from the Capitol through the Forum, Velabrum, and Forum Boarium to the Circus Maximus, it would not be surprising if one of them favored the procession with its presence, at least until they were torn down shortly after his death.[166]

Near the bottom of the *clivus Capitolinus*, tucked in between the portico of the Harmonious Gods and the temple of Concord, where the statues of Lucius, Gaius, and Germanicus were exhibited when not on parade, the temple of deified Vespasian was constructed, whose divine imperial presence was magnified by his statue and relics (*exuviae*) in the procession (Map 2.B). As the procession curved around the temple of Saturn and descended into the Forum, the imposing triple arch of Septimius Severus with its gilded bronze six- or eight-horse chariot (time-honored attic ornament) loomed (Map 2.C).[167] Septimius Severus' sons, Geta and Caracalla, may have shared his chariot, or perhaps they flanked it with their own equestrian statues; though of course Geta's statue would have been removed from the attic story, much as his name was chiseled off the attic inscription.[168] The viewing platform atop the column of Maenius seems to be a figment of the late-antique imagination, but archaeological evidence reveals that the arch of Septimius Severus had galleries along the attic story most likely for use during spectacles and processions. Senators or other elites might have trudged up the narrow staircase in order to watch the spectacle from the narrow balcony, so that they themselves might also be a spectacle in their own right, or perhaps support staff scattered flowers, while musicians played from its heights.[169]

After having rounded the temple of Saturn, the procession would have confronted another triumphal arch that rose into the Roman skyline. A triumphal arch of Tiberius sat "next to the temple of Saturn," wedged, perhaps, between the temple of Saturn and the basilica Iulia (Map 2.D).[170] In between the arches of Septimius Severus and Tiberius, and just behind the Caesarean-Augustan rostra at the northwestern end of the Forum, Augustus, as *curator viarum* (superintendent of roads), erected "a gilded column at which all the roads that intersect Italy terminate" (Map 2.E).[171] From the so-called Miliarium Aureum (the golden mile-marker), the imaginary starting point of the vast Roman road network, the procession traveled from the center outward, no longer to the edge of or even beyond the *pomerium*, but still away from the symbolic center.

As the emperors inexorably impressed their image on the city of Rome, opportunities for aristocratic public display correspondingly constricted. For example, after having utterly destroyed "some statues of famous men which Augustus had moved from the Capitoline precinct to the Campus Martius because of the lack of space ... [Caligula] issued orders banning the future erection of any statue or image to a living man unless authorized or initiated by himself."[172] It would seem that Caligula's orders were not entirely effective, as a short while later Claudius needed once again to clear out Rome's second population and to issue similar regulations concerning public statuary:

> In view of the fact that the city was becoming filled with a great multitude of images (for any who wished were free to have their likenesses appear in public in a painting or in bronze or marble), Claudius removed most of them elsewhere and for the future forbade that any private citizen should be allowed to follow the practice, except by permission of the senate or unless he should have built or repaired some public work; for he permitted such persons and their relatives to have their images set up in the places in question.[173]

While statues of emperors multiplied exponentially and monopolistically, statues honoring lesser mortals became increasingly rare in public, though they could still populate domestic or private places.[174] And so whenever an emperor led a circus procession, it was a near certainty that he would encounter his double somewhere: on the Capitol, in the Forum Romanum, or nearly anywhere along the itinerary.[175] By contrast, a non-imperial *praeses ludorum* or other participant was unlikely to encounter his or even a family member's double. The sheer quantity (and scale) of the imperial population of statues and their resonances with imperial images and symbols in the procession may have been deafening.

The amplification of imperial presence may have been especially overwhelming at the eastern end of the Forum, where monuments of the Julio-Claudian dynasty piled up *en masse*. Here, in 29 BCE during the festivities for his Actian triumph, Augustus dedicated the temple of *divus* Julius, "on the spot where his body had been burned" (Map 2.F).[176] (And so, when *divus* Julius was transported in a circus procession, would the doors of his temple have been open, so that Caesar could see himself in the procession from the temple and in his temple from the procession?) The temple only cemented the significance of that spot, which had already been marked by impromptu monuments in the immediate aftermath of Caesar's funeral (44 BCE): a column, and possibly an altar, which were quickly destroyed only to be replaced, it seems, by another column, "a solid pillar of Numidian marble almost twenty feet high," and another altar, where for some time afterwards sacrifices were made, vows undertaken, and disputes settled by oaths to Caesar and which may have been conserved as a memory monument within the rostra of the later temple.[177]

Also during his Actian triumph, a triple triumphal arch was dedicated to Augustus somewhere in the Forum.[178] Ten years later, in 19 BCE, another arch was erected for Augustus in honor of the return of the standards lost to the Parthians at the battle of Carrhae in 53 BCE – standards which may have been placed in Caesar's *tensa* in the procession. This second arch seems to have been located "next to the temple of *divus* Julius" and the soon-to-be restored temple of the Dioscuri, straddling what may have been the via Sacra, where the remains of a foundation of a triple arch have been found (Map 2.G).[179] If the Parthian arch stood on the southern flank of temple of deified Caesar, perhaps the Actian arch stood on its northern one.[180] Or perhaps the Actian arch was later remodeled as the Parthian arch.[181] Or maybe the Actian arch was at the other end of the Forum. Just to the north of the temple of Caesar stood the *porticus Gai et Luci*, which seems to have been a portico in front of the basilica Aemilia re-dedicated in honor of the prematurely deceased imperial heirs, or perhaps a monumental double-arched entry to the Forum, reduplicating or even displacing the still-standing *fornix Fabianus* (Map 2.H and Map 1.9).[182] Whatever the case, the republican *fornix* would have been shunted (further) aside by the erection of the temple of *divus* Antoninus Pius and *diva* Faustina I, on whose steps, perhaps, Faustina's *carpentum* was displayed (Map 2.I).

Whatever the precise disposition of the monuments at the eastern end of the Forum, it provided a grandiose Caesarean-Augustan backdrop in front of which Tiberius delivered his eulogy of Augustus, standing "in front of the temple of *divus* Julius."[183] In fact, this funeral rite condensed and embodied a history of the early Julio-Claudian dynasty: from the death and divinization of Caesar to the triumph(s) of Augustus, with (perhaps) a generous recapitulation of the history of Rome's triumphs in the form of the *fasti Capitolini* (*Triumphales*); the memorialization of the one-time imperial heirs Gaius and Lucius; and the public oratory of the new princeps Tiberius, who also restored the adjacent temple of the Castori, mourning his predecessor and adoptive father during a funeral that witnessed the making of *divus* Augustus.[184]

After having passed through the valley of monuments and the forest of statues in the Forum, the procession continued onto the *vicus Tuscus*, where the temple of divine Augustus sat just south of the basilica Iulia (Map 2.J). This temple may have faced the *vicus Tuscus*, and so perhaps its cult statue could gaze upon the procession as it passed – much like Caesar's, Saturn's, or those of the Dioscuri. Or perhaps the temple was oriented toward Capitoline Jupiter, whose temple and statue may have been the model for *divus* Augustus' – a pointed repetition of architectural and sculptural forms.[185] Further along the *vicus Tuscus*, the procession proceeded past the so-called Arch of the Argentarii, a monumental doorway to Forum Boarium, whose Severan imagery (memory sanctions against Geta and others included) recalled the arch of Septimius Severus in the Forum (though the "arch" in the Forum Boarium was post and lintel and so not arched) (Map 2.K).[186] Just before entering the arena, the procession would have witnessed another example of the declining "custom of public munificence." The so-called arch of P. Lentulus Scipio and T. Quinctius Crispinus Valerianus, consuls in 2 CE, seems to have been a massive rebuilding of the porta Trigemina, a gate in the Servian walls not far from the *carceres*, into a monumental triple arch (Map 2.L). In an interesting twist of memory, the late-antique regionary catalogs recorded its republican name, porta Trigemina, and not those of its imperial "restorers."[187]

At last, the procession arrived at the Circus Maximus, which became, perhaps, a kind of microcosm of empire – or at least it was re-built to suit Rome's imperial grandeur.[188] Once in the arena, "a conclave of demons," according to Tertullian in recognition of the sheer number of its sacred places, the procession – greeted by the thunderous applause of the increasingly hierarchized but also "mad, disorderly, blind, and excited" spectators – followed the counter-clockwise course of the track. Passing alongside the central barrier with its altars, shrines, statues, columns, statues atop columns, and obelisk, the *pompa circensis* continued to the semi-circular end where an arch celebrating Titus' conquest of Judea was erected in the center of the sphendone, possibly replacing the *fornix* of L. Stertinius (Map 2.M).[189] Having rounded the first *meta*, which sheltered the altar of Consus, the procession arrived at the *pulvinar*, the sacred edifice directly across the track from the finish line, built by Augustus to house the images and symbols of the gods, replacing, it seems, a simpler wooden structure (Map 2.N).[190] The Augustan *pulvinar*-temple seems to have been positioned close to the arena floor, while under Domitian perhaps or Trajan it may have been re-built further up in the seats. After its monumentalization, the *pulvinar* seems to have become sufficiently prominent that it served as a toponym, an urban way-finding device. For example, the wife of an early imperial fruit vendor memorialized her late husband, C. Julius Epaphra, and his fruit stand which stood in the Circus Maximus in front of the *pulvinar*, on a funerary inscription. Similarly, Tiberius Claudius Sabinus was commemorated by a group of metal workers who also advertised the distinctive location of their shop near the *pulvinar*.[191]

The *pulvinar* even had its attractions for emperors. Augustus, for one, was not immune to the possibilities of such a conspicuous seat. From time to time, Augustus actually "watched the games sitting in the *pulvinar* with his wife and children."[192] It would seem that on occasion the *pulvinar*, which otherwise housed divine relics and statues, also served as a kind of imperial loge from which Augustus and his family might enjoy the races in the company of the gods, both traditional and imperial.[193] Pushing the limits of the acceptable, much as he had done by leading a *pompa circensis* on a *lectica*, Augustus employed the *pulvinar* to display not only his power and prominence, but also his traditional and familial, not to say dynastic, piety.

For the Julio-Claudians, at least, it may have been something of a tradition for members of the imperial family to take in the chariot races from the *pulvinar*. After giving the signal to start the first race after the *pompa*, the imperial game-giver may have ridden along the outside edge of the track to the *pulvinar* so as to remain continually before the eyes of the crowd.[194] Such exposure, though, posed risks. Augustus hoped that Claudius would "not do anything to make himself conspicuous or an object of ridicule," while presiding over the games of Mars Ultor in 12 CE. Accordingly, Augustus did "not wish [Claudius] to watch the circus games from the *pulvinar*, for he would be conspicuous, exposed in front of the spectators."[195] Whether or not Claudius made use of the *pulvinar* at that point, he may have done so as emperor when "he would commend [his son Britannicus] to the people at the games, holding him on his lap or in front of him; and [Claudius] would invoke good omens for him, with the approval of the applauding crowd."[196] Nero also tried to take advantage of the visibility of the *pulvinar*, with unfortunate results. Domitian, by contrast, may have secreted himself in an "emperor's box (*cubiculum*)," perhaps a room of the *domus Flavia* from which he watched the games and the spectators without the discomfort of the audience's reciprocal gaze, while Trajan was praised for "sitting among the people," which may be a rather inventive take on Trajan's reconstruction of the *pulvinar*, during which the *pulvinar* may have moved from the senatorial seats along the track up into the cheap seats, as it were.[197]

From the first century BCE through the third century CE, the emperors intervened in the *pompa circensis* in fairly traditional, even if spectacular ways. As officially consecrated gods, duly recognized by the Roman senate, *divi* and *divae* had rightful places in the procession, carefully if ostentatiously distinguished from the traditional gods. The traditional gods were both companionably present in their statues on *fercula* and mysteriously distant in their *exuviae* hidden within *tensae*. Deified emperors were also doubled as symbols and statues. However, imperial statues were borne not on *fercula* but elephant *quadrigae*, a wondrous sight which came to overshadow numismatic *tensa* imagery, unattested after Vespasian, as a symbol of the imperial circus procession. Of course, statues of the gods (both traditional and imperial) also littered the itinerary – on arches and columns, and in temples. At first, deceased imperial women warranted only *carpenta*, though eventually they too were honored with elephant carts – not *quadrigae*, but *bigae* to distinguish them from the *divi*. Male members of the imperial house consistently rated statues, likely borne on *fercula*. Of course, only the imperial special dead were to be honored in the procession, the appraisal of which was seemingly contested between emperors and aristocrats.

This basic pattern of honors endured from Octavian-Augustus to the Severans, after which point this particular configuration of the imperial cult waned during the so-called third-century crisis. As long as the Augustan-Tiberian settlement held, its ceremonial framework seems to have allowed the *pompa circensis* to function, in part, as a kind of substitute *pompa funebris*, as emperors could manufacture imperial genealogies by parading the appropriate "ancestors." Only *divus* Augustus, whose *tensa* and *currus elephantorum* might have appeared in the procession for centuries, seems to have floated above the contingent demands of dynastic politics. Despite, the prominence of deified emperors and empresses in the procession, or, at least, in its textual and visual representations, the traditional gods continued to be paraded to the Circus Maximus. Indeed, imperial cult honors were both modeled after and drew their power from the traditional cult of the gods. Without the traditional gods (and in late antiquity the Christian God perhaps), the imperial *pompa circensis*, robbed of its religious purpose, might truly have degenerated into that noisome spectacle scorned by the elder Seneca.

A similar dynamic, drawing upon the past while dominating the present, was at work along the itinerary. From the opulently restored temple of Jupiter Optimus Maximus to the temples of Saturn, the Castori, and even Ceres, and also from the massive basilicas and the population of statues in the Forum to the vast monumental valley that was the Circus, imperial renovations, which often amounted to *de novo* construction, graced the route from the Capitol to the arena. Even so, primordial and republican history remained housed in these monuments, even after their lavish imperial restorations. The sheer grandeur of imperial rebuilding may have stretched traditional expectations, but connections to the past were not thereby broken. In the end, the emperors seem to have attempted to channel the potency of the landscape of memory that the procession traversed. The emperors also sited new monuments along this same itinerary, most notably a series of triumphal arches, whose form and function followed that of the republican *fornices*, and an array of temples to deified emperors. The transformation of the *pompa circensis*, both its participants and itinerary, transformed the processional image of Rome. Nonetheless, the efficacy and attraction of the *pompa circensis* still depended upon its traditional foundation: the transport of the gods through the city to the Circus, which not even the emperors could change – not until late antiquity, at least, when the religious environment had sufficiently changed to necessitate a (partial) transformation of the procession. In short, the urban image of Rome performed by the imperial *pompa circensis* was not so different from its republican predecessor(s) – SPQR+gods traversed the glittering *aurea Roma*, though now a princeps dominated SPQR, imperial gods upstaged traditional ones, and imperial monuments further gilded the golden city.

FIVE

BEHIND "THE VEIL OF POWER"

Ritual failure, ordinary humans, and ludic processions during the high empire[1]

In this matter [of placating the people], processions [*pompae*], *carpenta, tensae*, and *exuviae* consecrated by our ancestors, and even elephants (who appeared in peacetime as the Roman people never used them in the line of battle) were employed in nighttime spectacles.

Fronto, *Principia Historiae* 20[2]

Like Juvenal's more famous critique of the residents of Rome and their satisfaction with bread and circuses (*panem et circenses*), Fronto also recognized the power of fodder and fun when he asserted that "[Trajan] knew that the Roman people were held by two things above all, the *annona* and spectacles. Imperial rule was accepted for its games just as much as more serious matters."[3] A one-time sponsor of the games and fervent race fanatic, who once despite debilitating pain in his hand had himself carried to the Circus, Fronto well understood the power of the games.[4] But Fronto also recognized the importance of ritual and pageantry and so he added customary elements of the circus procession, *carpenta, tensae, exuviae*, and even elephants, to the more usual emoluments. That is, for Fronto the *pompa circensis* was not an overly long introduction, but rather a key component of the relationship between the emperor and his subjects as staged in the arena – a relationship that could, at times, be a bit rocky.[5] Though on occasion it might have seemed that the autocrats of Rome wielded absolute authority, attempts to exercise that authority and to perform imperial power could always be challenged, even if only by the weapons of the weak – silence, dissimulation, innuendo, indifference.[6] In the *pompa circensis*, even emperors faced the risk of ritual failure.[7] Moreover, the *pompa circensis* could also signal the failure or, more pointedly, the impending demise of an emperor – if only in retrospect in the battle over memory.

Along the same lines, though emperors appear to have dominated the *pompa circensis*, there were still "ordinary" (that is, non-imperial) elite game-givers (consuls, praetors, and others) who continued to seek honor and glory through their conduct of the games – much as they had during the republic.[8] Why else would Claudius have had to regulate the repetition of the games due to supposed religious fault (*instauratio*)? Why else were sub-imperial ludic processions commemorated in stone and baked clay (terracotta)? Elites continued to compete for what was left of the spotlight, even during the empire visibility conferred honor. Though these elites were clearly beneath the imperial gaze, they could still compete for status and the *pompa circensis* still offered an arena for that contest. The same holds true outside the imperial metropole. Seemingly throughout the Latin west, local elites deployed the spectacle of the circus procession in their own contests for honor and prestige.

The significance of the circus procession may also be gauged by its "progeny," ludic processions that seem to have derived from the *pompa circensis*. The *pompa theatralis* (theater procession) seems to have first emerged in Rome in the first century BCE, sometime after which a *pompa amphitheatralis* (amphitheater procession) also developed. This *pompa (amphi-)theatralis* was then performed, seemingly, wherever Roman (amphi-)theaters were built. For example, some municipal *Augustales* (priests, often freedmen, of the cult of the emperors) commemorated their provision of *munera*, which commonly included some reference to or even a full-fledged depiction of the procession that preceded the games. Indeed, a certain respect for the *pompa circensis* seems to have extended even into the humbler levels of the populace, including the not-so-humble charioteers, some of whom bragged about the number of palms (victories) won after the procession (*a pompa*) – a signal of the procession's religious significance which endowed the first race with something of its import. The bright glare of imperial spectacle could blind a spectator to these sub-imperial investments in the *pompa circensis* (and its "offspring"), but it seems fair to say that the circus procession mattered as both political spectacle and religious ritual to many and for a very long time.

I IMPERIAL RITUAL FAILURE

The exercise of power demands a certain amount of reciprocity – even in autocratic regimes. That is, even Caesar, who was "honored and feared as no one had ever been before," was still constrained by (an assuredly unequal) relation with those whom he attempted to rule.[9] And so, when Caesar allowed his statue to appear in a circus procession next to Victory, the ritual failed as the audience, or at least the elites within it, refused to accept the statue. Rather than greet the arrival of the procession with the obligatory thunderous applause, the circus crowd remained silent – or at least some of them did.

After he heard the news, Cicero gloated: "What a delightful letter! Though that procession is distasteful enough. . . . The people are behaving splendidly in refusing to applaud Victory because of her undesirable neighbor [the statue of Caesar]. . . . The procession puts me off."[10] Instead of a cacophony of clapping hands, accompanied by piously silent mouths, the *pompa circensis* seems to have been met by quiet hostility – or perhaps rather the indifferent, low-level murmuring of tens of thousands of people.

Cicero's victory, as it were, was short-lived. And though Caesar (and Cicero for that matter) was not too much longer lived, shortly after his demise this ritual failure was transformed into a resounding success. In a skillfully choreographed performance at the Parilia after his death, Caesar's ivory statue seems to have been borne once again in the *pompa circensis*. Instead of stony silence, however, Caesar's supporters wore wreaths which they removed as a sign of mourning. Even Cicero's nephew, "our Quintus crowned at the Parilia," "had worn [a crown] in Caesar's honor and laid it aside in mourning."[11] This act must have been particularly disappointing to Cicero, who, even after Caesar's death, continued to harp on the overreaching honors granted to the late dictator. While haranguing Mark Antony for failing to meet his religious obligations, Cicero rhetorically demanded: "What greater honor had Caesar attained than to have a *pulvinar*, a *simulacrum*, a temple gable [*fastigium*], a *flamen*? . . . You ask whether I approve of the *pulvinar*, [the *simulacrum*], the *fastigium*, the *flamen*. Certainly not, none of it has my approval."[12] The first two taken together (*pulvinar* and *simulacrum*) seem to signal the *pompa circensis* and so apparently Cicero remained put off by the procession. In the end, even if Cicero's contestation of Caesar's processional honors ultimately failed, the circus procession was still an important political pageant and a hallowed religious ritual, whose rules, regulations, and traditions constrained even Octavian-Augustus.[13]

Although he successfully overcame Mark Antony's initial reluctance to display Caesar's crown and chair, which resulted from the celestial stroke of luck that was Caesar's comet, a couple of years later Octavian imperiously interfered with a *pompa circensis* with nearly fatal results. In 40 BCE, possibly at the *ludi Plebeii*, the huge crowds gathered "at the games in the Circus honored by loud applause the statue of Poseidon [Neptune] carried in the procession," to signal their support for Sextus Pompeius, the son of Pompey the Great who had identified himself with Neptune and whose navy had disrupted Rome's grain supply, and a détente with the triumvirate (Mark Antony, Lepidus, and Octavian).[14] Such variation in the applause ritual (silence or intense clapping) served as a means for the mass of ordinary Romans to communicate with their rulers.[15] In this case, the message was apparently received as Octavian seems to have countered the crowd's strategic use of the processional ritual with his own, rather direct, counter tactic. As tensions between the *tresviri* and Sextus

Pompeius escalated and after he lost a fleet to a storm, Octavian declared "that he would attain victory even against the will of Neptune and the next time circus games were held, he had the *simulacrum* of the god removed from the religious procession."[16] In turn, the people reacted even more forcefully.

> When on certain days [the statue of Neptune] was not brought out, they took stones and drove the magistrates from the Forum, threw down the statues of [Octavian and Antony], and finally, when they could not accomplish anything even in this way, they rushed violently upon [Octavian and Antony] as if to kill them.[17]

While Octavian pleaded with the angry mob, Antony roused the troops to put down the riot. Avid applause, that is symbolic resistance, prompted, in part, the removal of Neptune from the procession, which left the crowd with little choice but to resort to physical protest, violence – though conceivably the crowd could have fetched Neptune and carried his image on its own.[18]

This episode suggests that the organizers of the games had some license to alter the procession. However, any alteration was risky – a changed ritual could be a failed ritual. The production of the procession and its reception together comprised the ritual: organizers and audience co-created it in each new performance.[19] Though assuredly marked by a certain regularity, the *pompa circensis* could vary from one iteration to the next and a sophisticated Roman audience could respond, positively or negatively. All of these examples – the silence that greeted Caesar at first, the gesture of mourning after his death, the loud applause for Neptune, and his subsequent removal – put into evidence the sheer power of this sacred procession, which late-republican rulers, like Caesar and Octavian, seem to have (partially) understood and tried to marshal as a means of (re-)producing and (re-)presenting a certain vision of Rome. The *plebs romana* was equally as sensitive to adaptations of the ritual imagination of the city and could also respond in a variety of ways.[20]

Subsequently Octavian-Augustus, eventually alerted to the perils of ritual performance, especially its reception, wanted to limit Claudius' exposure during his presidency of the games in honor of Mars Ultor for fear of ridicule, though as emperor Claudius certainly made himself very visible (and likeable it seems) at the Circus.[21] Visibility was not always a boon, however, as Nero might have realized after he was publically humiliated at the Circus – to judge from an anecdote reported well after the fact. After having murdered his mother, according to rumor at any rate, a *pompa circensis* stopped short, refusing it seems to join the defiled Nero in the *pulvinar*. According to Cassius Dio, "the elephants which drew the cart of Augustus, when they had entered the Circus and proceeded as far as the senators' seats, stopped at that point and refused to go any further."[22] This story may well have been the basis of Cassiodorus' observation, in the early sixth century CE, that elephants wisely discriminate between a good princeps and a tyrant.[23] The opportunity for public self-display in the parade and at the arena was always matched by the prospect of public criticism, ridicule, or, more devastatingly, indifference. It seems that enduring traditions, religious scruples, and popular expectations stemming from the republic continued to guide the production and reception of the *pompa circensis*. Emperors like Nero (and even Octavian-Augustus) flouted such customs at their own peril.

Despite an elephantine ritual failure, Nero still deployed the *pompa circensis* in unconventional and self-aggrandizing ways. After his triumphal return from Greece and his performance of (something like) a triumph, Nero seems to have put on something like a *pompa circensis* (much as Elagabalus would almost two centuries later): "When [Nero] had finished these ceremonies [during his triumphal return from Greece], he announced a series of horse races, and carrying into the Circus these crowns [which he had 'won' in performance competitions at Greek religious festivals] as well as all the others that he had secured by his victories in chariot-racing, he placed them round the Egyptian obelisk." Though not strictly speaking a ritual failure, perhaps this travesty of a *pompa circensis*, in which Nero paraded his own crowns as *exuviae*, as well as the religious scruples of elephants compelled the people (elites and otherwise) to say enough to Nero, as eventually they would to Domitian.[24]

The performance of the circus procession and its attendant rituals, the installation of images and symbols in the *pulvinar* in particular, also continued to provide more general portents, as they had during the republic.[25] Vespasian's rule, and so also Nero's demise, was foretold in one of Nero's dreams in which he conducted the *tensa* of Capitoline Jupiter, and thus also Jupiter's imperium, from the *sacrarium* on the Capitol to the home of Vespasian and then to the Circus.[26] Statues of Victories installed in the *pulvinar* not only presaged the death of Septimius Severus, but also the death and "*damnatio memoriae*" of Geta as well as the instability of Caracalla, at least according to the late-fourth-century CE *Historia Augusta*.

> On the day of the circus games, when three little plaster Victories holding palms were erected in the customary way, the one in the middle, which held a globe inscribed with [Septimius Severus'] name, was struck by a gust of wind, fell down from the podium in an upright position and remained on the ground in this posture; while the one on which Geta's name was inscribed was dashed down and completely shattered; and the one which bore Bassianus' name [i.e. Caracalla] lost its palm and barely managed to keep its place, such was the whirling of the wind.[27]

Caracalla's own fate was foretold when, according to Cassius Dio, "at the horse race held in honor of Severus' reign the statue of Mars, while being borne in the procession, fell down."[28] Though typically the more heavily regulated *tensae* were the medium of divine communication, in this case the statue of Mars fell from a *ferculum* as a sign of Caracalla's imminent demise. In the end, the *pompa circensis* remained structured according to traditional expectations and rules, which could be bent if not broken, even by the emperors. To alter the ritual grammar or syntax could mean a failed performance. And so these omens, assuredly invented (that is, discovered *and* made up) after the fact, signaled a breach (both political and religious) by the deceased, whether Nero or Caracalla. Moreover, these invented portents depended upon the traditional machinery of the *pompa circensis* to underscore the depravity of these emperors in a backward-looking battle for memory.

Of course, a failed ritual required a repetition (an *instauratio*) of the *pompa circensis* and the games, either in whole or in part – part of Roman civic religion's "empiricist epistemology" which addressed ritual failure directly and practically.[29] Though Rome's "practical" religious scruples aimed to secure the goodwill of the gods, they also created opportunity: an accidentally-on-purpose ritual failure risked divine displeasure, but it also afforded an extension or repetition of popular entertainments. According to Cassius Dio, early imperial game-givers took such egregious advantage of traditional religious obligations that Claudius had to rein in their exuberance.

> It had been the custom that if any detail whatsoever in connection with the festivals was carried out contrary to precedent, they should be given over again, as I have stated. But since such repetitions were frequent, occurring a third, fourth, fifth, and sometimes a tenth time, partly, to be sure, as the result of accident, but generally by deliberate intent on the part of those who benefited from these repetitions, Claudius enacted a law that the equestrian contests in case of a second exhibition should occupy only one day; and in actual practice he usually prevented any repetition at all. For the schemers were not so ready to commit irregularities now that they gained very little by doing so.[30]

As a religious ritual, the procession and the subsequent games were one of the means by which the peace of the gods was secured. If the *pompa circensis*, in particular, or some other facet of the games, in general, failed to propitiate the gods, they would let the Romans know – via plague, military disaster, disturbing portents. And so a failed ritual, even if done accidentally-on-purpose or occasioned by an imagined or inconsequential mistake, needed to be re-performed properly. An intentional fault was technically inexpiable, but probably difficult to prove. Moreover, the gods seem to have been inclined to look the other way more often than not (after all, there were likely dozens or even hundreds of technical errors in any performance of the circus procession) and so perhaps the visibility was worth the (possible but unlikely) cost.

To preside over the circus games, to lead the procession, to sacrifice to the gods before an audience of tens of thousands, to start the wildly popular races, and to sit before the eyes of the entire audience afterwards was a magnificent opportunity to achieve distinction, *nobilitas* (notability). Such prominence came with its own risks, of course – both on earth and in the heavens.

II "ORDINARY" HUMANS IN THE *POMPA CIRCENSIS*

While the emperors dominated the procession at their own risk, ordinary humans could still preside over the games – also at their own risk, which included Juvenal's satirical contempt. Indeed, the most celebrated image of a high imperial game-giver, driving a *biga*, dressed in triumphal attire, carrying a scepter, with a crown held over his head by a public slave, appears in Juvenal's amusing and scathingly sarcastic portrait of an overly pompous magistrate and his pretentious retinue of pretenders:

> What if [Democritus] had seen our praetor standing conspicuously up there in his tall chariot, in the thick of the Circus dust, wearing the tunic of Jupiter, with Tyrian hangings of an embroidered toga falling from his shoulders and a huge crown so big around that no neck is strong enough for it? In fact, a public slave holds it, sweating profusely, and – so the consul [the *praeses*] doesn't get too pleased with himself – he rides in the same vehicle. Throw in the bird that soars from his ivory scepter, the horn-players there, here the escort in long lines walking ahead of him and the snowy white citizens at his bridle, transformed into friends by the handouts buried inside their purses.[31]

The game-giver, here a praetor or a consul, dressed much like a triumphant general, as was already the case during the republic. For the first time, however, he was explicitly described wearing a crown, held by a public slave, though that too *may* have been the case during the republic. At least, a slave customarily held a gold Etruscan crown above the head of republican *triumphatores* according to Pliny the elder, a crown that may also have been part of the august attire of those who led the *tensae*.[32] During the high empire, this same "triumphal" honor was first ascribed to the *praeses ludorum*, who, according to Tertullian, wore an Etruscan crown "distinguished by gems and oak leaves of gold like Jupiter's" and a toga *palmata* to lead the *tensae*.[33] Tertullian also noted that during the triumph someone stood behind the victorious commander in his chariot to remind him of his humanity: "Look behind you! Remember that you are human!"[34] It would seem that the golden out-sized Etruscan crown could really go to one's head – for which reason one needed Juvenal's seemingly silent slave: to hold the crown and to humble the game-giver. Additionally, the game-giver now carried an ivory scepter surmounted by an eagle ("the bird that soars from his ivory scepter"), another bit of triumphal paraphernalia, which those who led the *tensae* during the republic *may* also have held.[35]

Riding in a chariot was a republican tradition. Emperors celebrating consulships seem to have driven a *quadriga* – to judge from late-first to late-fourth-century CE numismatic imagery of imperial consular games – or even a six-horse chariot, as Caligula seems to have done at the *lusus Troiae*.[36] By contrast, it seems that republican and now imperial elites drove *bigae*. Pliny the elder remarked that "the custom of erecting memorial chariots with two horses in the case of those who held the office of praetor and had ridden round the Circus in a chariot is not an old one."[37] During the republic, the elite may have aimed at a victory monument or even a triumph, while during the empire the game of honor and glory seems to have been played for lower stakes. Rather than scaling the Capitoline hill as an avatar of Jupiter, it appears that the imperial Roman elite settled for leading the *pompa circensis* as a different, but lesser, avatar of Jupiter – an act which then warranted a new form of commemoration: a statue of the *biga*, presumably with the sub-imperial *praeses ludorum* holding the reins. A Renaissance drawing of the so-called Maffei relief, dated anywhere from the second to the fourth century CE, seems to capture this Juvenalian game-giver: the praetor, dressed in a toga, steers a *biga* along the central barrier, while a "slave" holds a crown above his head and a crowd acclaims his arrival (Figure 41).[38] The image omits the scepter and the toga appears to be rather plain, but otherwise it accords with the literary evidence from Pliny, Juvenal, and Tertullian.

Emperors, consuls, and praetors rated chariots, while lower-ranked game-givers seemingly walked. For example, the tribunes of the plebs at the inaugural *ludi Augustales* "were to enjoy triumphal clothing in the Circus, while riding in a chariot was not permitted."[39] Otherwise, the *pompa circensis* during the maiden *ludi Augustales* was reputedly conducted according to

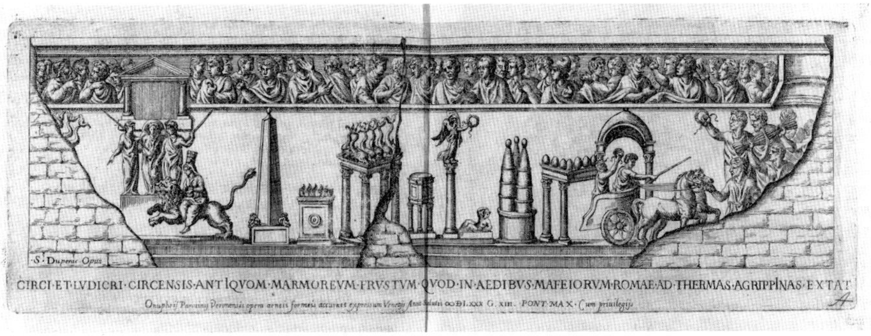

41. Early-modern drawing of a *praeses ludorum* and attendant holding a crown on a *biga* (Maffei circus relief), original second–fourth century CE

tradition. But when the praetors took responsibility for the Augustal games, the *praeses ludorum*, clothed in triumphal vestments with a scepter in hand, would have, once again, driven a *biga*, accompanied by, perhaps, a slave holding an Etruscan crown.[40]

The so-called Maffei relief also omitted the president's entourage, of which Juvenal also provides the earliest, extant, description, though some sort of retinue was almost certainly a republican tradition. During the high empire, at least, a lengthy escort, likely comprised of lictors and perhaps also clients, led the way, while "friends," political allies or perhaps men of like rank dressed in their brilliant white parade-best, walked next to the chariot, accompanied by a troop of trumpeters to announce brazenly his arrival. A late-third-century CE fragment of a sarcophagus lid may portray a fraction of this tableau (Figure 42).[41] A stern-faced bearded magistrate in a toga stands in a chariot, decorated with what seems to be images of the Capitoline triad, gesturing grandiosely with his right hand while grasping a scepter adorned with a bust

42. Third-century game-giver with entourage, marble, late third century CE

close to his chest with his left. A second *togatus*, a young man, trails directly behind, accompanied by an older man, while another young man guides a horse alongside the chariot. Though by no means certain, the scene seemingly presents the head of a sub-imperial circus procession: the game-giver in a chariot holding a scepter, accompanied his entourage composed of two men of various ages and, seemingly, ranks and escorted by a young man on horseback. The young *togatus* may have been the game-giver's son, the older man, seemingly wearing a tunic, may have been a client, while the young rider suggests that the sons of equestrians (or other elites) continued to play an important role in public ceremonial.[42]

However much Juvenal mocked it, such accoutrement (triumphal attire, scepter, crown, chariot, entourage, and musicians), was certainly appropriate for the *pompa* and the pandemonium which awaited the *praeses ludorum* once he entered the Circus. Juvenal's contemporary, the younger Pliny preened before the emperor and the senate while delivering a panegyric, in which he celebrated his suffect consulship, held in conjunction with Trajan as ordinary consul. Picturing what may have been a *pompa circensis* for some set of games during his tenure, Pliny evoked his future passage through the city and perhaps also the Circus itself: "It will be our lot to mount (beneath your own eyes) a chariot even nobler than usual, and amid the cries of good omen and clamor of competing vows offered in your presence, we will be carried along gladly, unable to judge from which quarter the louder cheering strikes our ears."[43] Juvenal, in fact, conjured a similar scene, explicitly set in the commotion of the Circus Maximus, from which an elderly "Juvenal" was happily absent, enjoying instead a virtuous meal at home with a friend: "Meanwhile, the tiers of spectators are celebrating the Idaean ritual of the Megalesian *mappa* [*ludi Megalesia*], and the praetor is sitting there as if in a triumph, prey of the nags and, if I may say so without offending a populace too huge to count, today the whole of Rome is inside the Circus."[44] Though a praetor might well have bankrupted himself to finance this profligate potlatch, such outlays of financial capital were still seemingly worth the investment – the returns of symbolic capital were considerable. Rome was his, for a day.

At a set of imagined funeral games, Silius Italicus evoked the moment after the funerary rites were concluded, but before the races had begun: "Even before the starting gate was unbarred, the excited crowd surged to and fro with a noise like the sound of the sea, and, with a fury of partisanship, fixed their eyes on the doors behind which the racers were standing."[45] Just over a century later, Tertullian acerbically ridiculed the same moment, highlighting, of course, its mad frenzy and gross immorality (to Tertullian at least):

> Look at the populace coming to the spectacle – already mad, already disorderly, already blind, already excited about its bets. The praetor is too slow for them; with their eyes always on his urn, they are tossed about with the lots. And then, they wait hanging in anxious suspense for the signal. One frenzy, one voice! (Recognize their frenzy from their empty-mindedness.) "He has thrown it," they shout.[46]

Though Tertullian penned his caustic description as a critique and though both he and Silius Italicus depended on a literary tradition that extended back centuries to Ennius (early second century BCE), both scenes forcefully convey the intensity of those tense moments after the procession but before the first race as the praetor slowly and perhaps even dramatically chose lots to determine the starting gate assignments. The crowd, numbering tens if not hundreds of thousands and overwrought with anticipation, avidly followed his every move. In a political culture that still prized visibility – that continued to compete for honor, glory, and prestige – such moments were to be savored.[47]

So long as public visibility defined elite distinction and so long as massive crowds gathered at the races, the *pompa circensis*, one the most spectacular stages in the Roman theater of power, and its attendant introductory rituals would continue to matter. And such performances would continue to be commemorated. In the late empire (third–fourth centuries CE), a *praeses ludorum* proudly displayed that impatient moment before the start signal was given: in the upper left, the game-giver, holding a scepter in his left hand, stands in the loge above the *carceres*, poised to throw the *mappa*, surrounded by his entourage including a lictor, even as a race seems to have come to its conclusion in the arena below with the winning charioteer saluting the game giver. The relief presented a synopsis of the entire pageant: procession, start signal, and, of course, the races (Figure 43).[48] Indeed, the *praeses* clutching a *mappa* in his hand, ready to give the signal, would increasingly dominate circus imagery in the late empire, displacing even representations of the gods, traditional and imperial.

Other areas of the procession were also assuredly affected by the passage of time – for example, the youthful cavalry and infantry of Fabius Pictor-Dionysius may have given way to an elite equestrian ceremonial corps, while particularly successful charioteers (or the god Sol) may have been honored with statues carried on *fercula* (Figures 78–79).[49] Sometime during the long decades between Fabius Pictor and Dionysius, the martial dancers (*ludiones*) may have stopped dancing in the procession, though they would still have walked. In the early second century CE, Hadrian may well have re-organized the *pompa circensis* by renewing theses martial dances.[50] The evidence is ambiguous to be sure. Dionysius himself witnessed the martial dancers "clothed in remarkable tunics and helmets, holding swords and bucklers, marching in file," which *may* indicate that during the Augustan age they no longer danced. But he also noted that martial dancing (by the Salian priests and the *ludiones*) was still an

43. Third-century game-giver throwing *mappa* with first race already underway, marble, third–fourth century CE

important Roman tradition, during the procession to the Circus and to the theater. Moreover, Dionysius had sufficient experience with both the Salian priests and the *ludiones* to develop a comparison of their choreography.[51] Whether they danced or not, *ludiones* continued to appear in a number of ludic contexts. For Domitian's Secular Games in 88 CE, an extensive set of coin types was produced, including several with a single, armed *ludio* on the reverse.[52] In a similar vein, a Flavian-era relief shows three *ludiones* in tunics with crested helmets, spears, and shields in a representation of an unknown ceremony – though the *ludi Saeculares* seems like a good bet (Figure 44).[53] Two adolescent, or at least short, shield-carrying *ludiones* also appeared on a medallion produced for the *ludi decennales* of Antoninus Pius.[54] Therefore, it would seem that the armed *ludiones* remained an important part of many public rites, even if their performance history cannot be charted in detail. Perhaps, the appeal of the *ludiones* waned in the face of the competition from the burlesque satyr dancers may have added fauns and maenads to their salacious steps.[55]

Whether or not (or in whatever way) the dancers were affected, Tertullian noted, more or less in passing in a rant against the supposed idolatry of the *pompa circensis*, a new addition to the procession: *collegia* were now found in the cortege, along with priests and magistrates, traditional participants.[56] The presence of *collegia* in an imperial-era circus procession is unsurprising: professional associations regularly participated in public ceremonies throughout the Roman empire. Much like the equestrian class, *collegia* were increasingly included in imperial ceremonies as an index of their social

44. *Ludiones* with spears and shields, marble, ca. 88 CE

belonging and their assent to the Roman imperial order. Though no *collegia* members with their banners or flags (*vexilla*) seem to have appeared in a *pompa circensis* at Rome specifically, their likely participation finds support from their involvement in other civic processions like funeral rites, triumphs, and *adventus* ceremonies – the earliest of which seems to have been the funeral of Pertinax, whose golden image also appeared in a circus procession.[57] The increasing prominence of such associations within Roman urban life may have necessitated yet another amendment of the processional image of the city – SPQR+gods might still have served as short-hand, so long as one understood that the senate was led by the emperor, the Roman people included the *collegia*, and the gods, the *divi*.

Processional performers from the *praeses* to the satyr dancers and even the *collegia* surely took center stage, but behind the curtains lurked an enormous production staff. The circus procession, much like the games, was a massive undertaking, whose equally massive apparatus remains largely invisible.[58] According to Suetonius, Augustus "honored with his concern all the different sorts of people involved in providing different varieties of games for the public."[59] Unsurprisingly, Augustus paid specific attention to the contestants and magistrates, though he may also have deigned to consider the processional staff. As it turns out, Tertullian's invective against the spectacles, which casually mentioned the presence of *collegia* in the circus procession, may identify one such staff member. Tertullian, probably sarcastically, asserted that the masters of ceremonies for both the *pompa circensis* and the *pompa theatralis* were a *dissignator* or a *designator* (an "undertaker") and a *haruspex* (a "diviner").[60] A *designator* did choreograph funeral processions, managing the participants and their equipment.[61] However, a passage from Plautus, epigraphic evidence, and a late-antique scholion on Horace suggest that they also served as theater ushers.[62] What is more, they apparently functioned as referees at athletic contests – and so they might have been professional spectacle administrators of sorts.[63] It makes sense that some professional(s), called not entirely improbably a *dissignator* by Tertullian, would have orchestrated the *pompa circensis*. And it makes sense that those individuals would also have worked a number of similar public events in a number of different but related capacities. Unfortunately, the bright lights of imperial politics, ancient habits of commemoration, and accidents of evidentiary survival confined such professionals to obscurity offstage.

III THE *POMPA CIRCENSIS* OUTSIDE ROME AND THE *POMPA* (*AMPHI-*)*THEATRALIS*

The pompa circensis *outside Rome*

Though the best evidence for the *pompa circensis*, such as it is, comes from Rome, similar processions to introduce the circus games almost certainly took place wherever circuses were built. Once again, Tertullian provided unequivocal but hostile evidence for the existence of a "provincial" circus procession:

> But rather more pompous is the pomp of the circus, to which the term *pompa* properly belongs. The *pompa* (procession) comes first and proves in itself to whom it belongs with a train of images (*simulacra*), a troop of statues (*imagines*), chariots (*currus*), *tensae*, elephant carts (*armamaxae*), thrones (*sedes*), crowns (*coronae*), and relics (*exuviae*). What sacred rites, what sacrifices, come at the beginning, in the middle, at the end; what guilds (*collegia*), what priesthoods, what offices are astir – the men of *that* city [Rome] know where the conclave of demons has settled. If less elaboration is bestowed on it in the provinces, where there is less to spend, still all the shows of the circus everywhere must be attributed to their origin, must be examined at their source. For the little rivulet from its spring, the tiny shoot from its first leaf, has in it the nature of its origin. Let its splendor, let its modesty look to it – a circus procession (*pompa circi*) of whatever kind offends god. Even if the images are but few in procession, just one is idolatry; even if one draws only one *tensa*, nevertheless it is

> the *plaustrum* of Jupiter; any idolatry in any form, meanly equipped, moderately rich, splendid, is still reckoned idolatry in its guilt.[64]

Despite the polemic, Tertullian identified essential characteristics of the *pompa circensis: simulacra* of the gods, statues (of the emperors perhaps), chariots possibly ridden by the *praeses ludorum* or Charioteers, *tensae*, and possibly elephant carts (*armamaxae*), along with chairs on which crowns and other *exuviae* were displayed once the procession arrived at the arena. Members of professional associations, priests, and magistrates also appeared in the *pompa* and performed its religious rites. Moreover, this same ritual was also performed in the provinces, according to Tertullian – even if at a lesser scale and with some unsurprising variation. As a fellow north African and near contemporary, Apuleius, noted, "other elements of the *sacra* [apart from music and dance] differ greatly and variously by region: the formations of processions . . . likewise images (*effigies*) and relics (*exuviae*) of the gods, all of which are customary and established in accordance with the tradition of each place."[65] So the "same," but different procession preceded circus games everywhere, it would seem – especially the western Latin provinces.

In Spain during the late republic, local luminaries erected a column to the *genius* of New Carthage and then produced a procession as well as a set of games (*pompam ludosque*).[66] At about the same time, the *Lex Coloniae Genetivae Iuliae*, or at least the Flavian copy of Julius Caesar's foundation law for the colony at Urso in Spain, mandated that sacrifices and a display of gods on *pulvinaria* take place during the circus games.

> Whoever shall be IIvir, aedile, or prefect of the colonia Genetiva Iulia . . . according to the decree of the decurions during his own year will see that games in the circus, sacrifices, and *pulvinaria* [couches for the gods] take place, as the decurions shall have decided and decreed anything about those matters, that is the election of *magistri*, the celebration of games in the circus, the organization of sacrifices, and the preparing of *pulvinaria*.[67]

The combination of circus games, sacrifices, and *pulvinaria* strongly suggests that a procession would have introduced the races, in which images of the gods would be taken from their temples to the circus where they would be installed on couches (*pulvinaria*) from which the gods could watch the games with the rest of the citizens of the colony. To speculate a bit further: a lack of chairs or thrones *might* mean that only statues of the gods, and not their *exuviae* which seem to have been displayed on chairs, were paraded to the arena at Urso – a reflection, perhaps, of local religious customs as decreed by the decurions. Or, if *exuviae* were transported, they could have been included with divine images under *pulvinaria* as a blanket term covering both a *lectisternium* (divine images displayed on couches) and a *sellisternium* (relics displayed on chairs or thrones).[68]

Later during the reign of Tiberius, a local citizen and his mother were apparently given exceptional privileges during circus games, *pulvinaria*, and other festivals at Cumae. Though the inscription is lacunose, the honorands seem to have been given permission to wear laurel crowns during the circus procession.[69] In the second century CE at Formia, Titus Acilius Publius left a bequest of 100,000 sesterces for the production of one (or possibly more) *tensa(e)* for Minerva constructed from 100 pounds of silver.[70] The cost, and perhaps also the number of *tensae*, may indicate that Minerva was an especially favored goddess of the patron and/or the town. *Tensae* also appeared from the late first to the third century CE on modest, mass-produced lamps found throughout the western Roman empire – where "Roman"-style chariot racing and its attendant ceremonial were particularly concentrated.[71] These lamps, which seem to have been produced in large-scale operations and may have been sold at the arena as a kind of souvenir, strikingly commemorated the races with an image of a single *tensa*, instead of, say, a charioteer or even a victory parade with the winning horse (Figure 45; compare with Figures 7 and 77).[72] The gods, including imperial ones, in a *pompa circensis* seem to have been popular in other "minor" arts as well, namely jewelry – as an undated gem now in Berlin with a carving of what seems to be deified Livia's *currus elephantorum* may demonstrate (Figure 46).[73] And so, for some race fans the *pompa deorum*, symbolized by a lone *tensa* or *currus elephantorum*, best memorialized the circus games – instead of images of the races or other athletic contests.

45. Terracotta lamp with a *tensa*, ca. first–second century CE

The pompa *(*amphi-*)*theatralis

Just as a *pompa circensis* preceded the *ludi circenses*, a *pompa theatralis* opened the *ludi scaenici* and a *pompa amphitheatralis* ushered in the *munera*.[74] Both the *pompa theatralis*, which seems to have developed in the early to mid first century BCE, and the *pompa amphitheatralis*, which first appeared about a century later in the early first century CE, appear to have been spin-offs of the *pompa circensis* – though they too must have quickly developed their own semi-independent traditions. Indeed, Tertullian, an interested observer of Roman spectacle, suggested that all the games (chariot races, theater shows, animal hunts, gladiatorial combats) shared a common spectacular array, including an introductory procession: "The equipment [of all the games whether for the

46. Gem with elephant *quadriga* of Livia/Ceres, first–third century CE

gods or the dead] must be the same because of the common guilt of idolatry which founded them. . . . Even the pageantry is the same, marching to the theater from the temples and altars, from that wretchedness of incense and blood, to the tune of flutes and trumpets, led by the two most polluted masters of ceremonies at funerals and religious rites: the *dissignator* and the *haruspex*."[75] Religious polemic aside, it seems that Tertullian was correct: the pageantry was similar on the way to the circus or (amphi-)theater.

Their ritual grammar and syntax (the participants and their organization) as well as their signification (ritual rhythms) – an oscillation between gravity (structure and solemnity) and levity (disorder and frivolity), and also between resonance (a penchant to reach beyond the ritual frame) and wonder (a tendency toward singularity or show-stopping spectacle) – seems have been comparable, though assuredly not the same, as these ludic processions shared a common purpose: to escort the gods to the games with the appropriate accompaniment – the sponsor of the games, his entourage, contestants or participants in the games, and entertainers – with all due pomp. However, by comparison with the relatively ample though scattered and difficult evidence for the *pompa circensis*, the evidence for the procession to the theater of whatever sort is downright meager, sufficient for only a bare, synoptic sketch – an idealizing ideal-type, one might say, rather than the circumscribed, analytical one that this study attempts to assemble for the circus procession.[76] At any rate, the limited extant evidence suggests that *pompae (amphi-)theatralis* were, in many ways, smaller-scale versions of a *pompa circensis* (if only because the same professional staff were likely involved), with appropriate adaptations to suit the genre and venue of the spectacle in question – to argue much more would verge on sheer speculation.

A now lost early- or mid-first-century CE relief in honor of a municipal magistrate, but probably carved at a workshop in Rome, seems to offer some confirmation of Tertullian's polemic: to wit, the processions that preceded both *ludi circenses* and *ludi scaenici* were, in fact, similarly organized. In the upper register, a *histrio* (a player, actor, and/or dancer) and a chorus of young men escort a magistrate, the *editor ludorum* presumably, who is accompanied by a female dancer and followed by musicians playing pan pipes and double flutes with lictors trailing behind (Figure 47).[77] The procession files through a theater, or at least in front of a *scaenae frons*, while a vigorous chariot race unfolds in the lower register. This dual imagery suggests an ingenious visual economy in which the relief may do double duty by memorializing both processions (represented by the *pompa theatralis* in the upper register) and both sets of games (symbolized by the theater stage and, especially, the races). In the end, whether a *pompa theatralis* or *circensis* or some conflation of the two, this local variant of a *pompa ludorum* seems to include many of the same participants as the *pompa circensis* outlined by Fabius Pictor-Dionysius: a *praeses ludorum* with an entourage (the chorus of young men and lictors), contestants or performers (the *histrio*), and dancers and musicians.

The seeming presence of a *histrio* (an actor) on the relief suggests that those who appeared in the games (contestants or performers) also customarily appeared in the procession that preceded them, a hint which finds some corroboration from hostile sources. In the early fifth century CE, a caustic remark from Augustine on celebrations in honor of Caelestis intimates that the performers in those games, who may have produced a set of erotic skits, processed to the goddess' temple: while standing "in front of the shrine itself," he witnessed or rather ogled "a whorish procession here and the virgin goddess there."[78] About a century earlier, Arnobius may well have had a similar procession of prostitutes in mind, when he wondered whether the goddess Flora felt honored by "the migration from the brothels to the theaters."[79] Looking past their vitriolic, mean-spirited, schoolboy snickering, Arnobius and Augustine may well have witnessed performers parading to the temple or theater, or wherever the shows took place – after all, processions were supposed to attract attention and these participants may well have done double duty as contestants (like the charioteers and actors) and as (erotic) entertainment (very much like the satyrs and Sileni). Such provocatively choreographed processions may well have been a staple of erotically colored games. For example, in the mid second century CE Apuleius conjured a scene in which "[Lucius still in the form of an ass] was led to the theater with a crowd of people cheering in procession following," before he narrowly escaped his pornographic stage debut.[80] Satyrs, Sileni, and erotic performers of all sorts

47. Ludic procession in a theater with chariot races below, marble, early to mid first century CE

may well have regularly featured in ludic processions, which were both serious public performances and seriously fun.

Dionysius of Halicarnassus confirmed another overlap among ludic processions: martial dancers (*ludiones*) appeared in both, at least, on occasion, at Rome.

> This dancing after the manner of the Curetes was a native institution among the Romans and was held in great honor by them, as I gather from

> many other institutions and especially what takes place in the processions both to the Circus and to the theaters. For in all of them young men clothed in remarkable tunics and helmets, holding swords and bucklers, march in file.[81]

All told, it seems that the ceremonial apparatus of the *pompa hominum* (parade of people) in the theater procession was analogous to that of circus, at least to judge from the very tenuous evidence. A magistrate or sponsor of the games with his entourage (young men, perhaps, and lictors), contestants or performers, dancers and entertainers (martial and female dancers), and musicians seem to have performed in both. The entertainment venue, however, may have dictated certain accommodations. The game-giver and his entourage may have processed to the theater on foot rather than in a chariot or on horseback – perhaps a practical issue, as riding into a theater may have been difficult, though triumphal processions, whose rarity may have demanded extraordinary effort, seem to have done so. By the same token, the genre of spectacle determined, in part, the participants in the procession. Actors and perhaps also (erotic) dancers/pantomimes took part in the *pompa theatralis* and subsequently performed in the theater shows, instead of the charioteers who featured so prominently in the circus procession and, of course, the races that followed.

What is more, much like the *pompa circensis*, the *pompa theatralis* was also fundamentally a *pompa deorum*: it, too, served to conduct the gods from their altars and temples to the theater as Tertullian bitterly lamented. It seems that *ludi scaenici* at Rome were at first performed in close proximity to or even directly in front of a temple, whose stairs could then double as seating. In the case of the *ludi Megalenses*, for example, the theater shows were said to have taken place on the Palatine "before the temple in the very sight of Magna Mater."[82] Accordingly, there would have been no need for a *pompa theatralis* as the divine honorand was already "present." The earliest (potential) evidence for a *pompa theatralis*, a "fragment" from Varro's *Eumenides* written in the early to mid first century BCE, emerged not long after the earliest examples of freestanding temporary stages. In the passage, the protagonist was lured to the sanctuary of Magna Mater by the entrancing sounds emanating from it. "When [he] got there, [he] saw a crowd of Galli in the temple, raving about and singing their hymn in zealous confusion, while the aedile was putting on the statue a crown he had brought back from the theater."[83] Though the reading of the passage remains contested, it is plausible that Magna Mater was (re-)presented by her turreted crown at the theater and that the aediles supervised the handling of the relic, much as they did the sacred vessels in the *pompa circensis*. Also in early to mid first century BCE, a few aediles, perhaps spurred by their new role in the pageantry of the theatrical shows, minted coins, an uncommon occurrence, featuring Magna Mater with her mural crown on the obverse, and on the

48. Cast of a relief with the temple of Magna Mater in the background, on which a chair and crown sit in the center of the pediment, marble (original), mid first century CE

reverse (of two of the three types) a curule chair to advertise their role in the production of the *ludi Megalenses*.[84]

A mid-first-century CE imperial relief may likewise allude to the *pompa theatralis* of the *ludi Megalenses*, or perhaps some other Metroac ritual which included a *sellisternium*.[85] The relief, perhaps from a Claudian altar monument similar to the Ara Pacis, pictures the Palatine temple of Magna Mater, on whose pediment the goddess, represented by her mural crown, rests upon a mantle-draped *sella* (Figure 48).[86] This relief may well accurately present the façade. Alternatively, it may rather portray key moments in the ritual and iconographic life of the cult to identify the temple by visual shorthand – such ambiguity characterizes most if not all of the visual evidence for any Roman procession. In either case, the veiled throne and crown may well refer to the procession to and enthronement at the theater during the *ludi Megalenses*, when a number of famous plays had their debut.[87] A late-second or early-third-century CE altar now in the Fitzwilliam Museum at Cambridge University offers a striking image of what this procession might have looked like (Figure 49).[88] Four litter-bearers dressed in so-called Phrygian attire, long pants and a conical cap – perhaps multiple avatars of Attis, the goddess's consort, or Metroac devotees – carry a *ferculum* on which rests a throne with a conch-shell back flanked by two further figures dressed just like the *ferculum*-bearers. This throne, however, does not hold

49. Metroac altar or box with relief showing four figures carrying a *ferculum* with a throne, marble, second–third century CE

the Great Mother's mural crown, but rather a *cista mystica*, an enclosed wickerwork chest that would have held *sacra* of some sort.

Putting the evidence together, an inevitable necessity in the study of Roman ceremonial, it seems that after the construction of the first stand-alone, temporary theaters, Magna Mater's mural crown (or *cista mystica*) was paraded from her temple on a throne borne on a *ferculum* to the theater where it would have been installed so that the Great Mother could enjoy the show. As it turns out, the goddess may have been entertained by a theatrical version of her own legends. After detailing Magna Mater's momentous and miraculous arrival at Rome, in which an unjustly slandered Claudia Quinta freed the goddess's boat from muddy shallows at the mouth of the Tiber as a sign of her innocence, "Ovid" rather sheepishly admitted, "It's extraordinary, but attested by the stage."[89] Whatever the show, Magna Mater would likely have had a good view as her chair was probably placed in the orchestra, nearby or even among the senatorial seats – visible to the audience, which might have been reassured by the presence of goddess watching the show, even as she was watched by an audience that also watched the show.[90]

In short, like the *pompa circensis*, the *pompa theatralis* was a *pompa deorum*. Also like the circus procession, the theater procession would include *divi* (deified emperors) beginning, of course, in the late republic with Julius Caesar. Along with his honors in the circus procession (*tensa* and *ferculum*), the senate voted that "[Caesar's] golden chair and his crown set with precious gems and overlaid with gold should be carried into the theaters in the same manner as those of the gods."[91] Although Mark Antony and his allies briefly delayed the enthronement of Caesar's crown at the games, Octavian-Augustus eventually succeeded in honoring his adoptive father at both the Circus and theater, an act commemorated on a coin-type in 42 BCE, which Trajan had re-minted nearly one hundred and fifty years later (Figure 13, Augustan original).[92] Indeed, Caesar's chair and crown were displayed at the games throughout the reign of Augustus. Moreover, transgressive treatment of these Caesarean *exuviae* were (retrospectively at least) understood as ominous prodigies. In 31 BCE, as a sign of the impending war between Antony and Octavian, "a madman rushed into the theater at one of the festivals and seized the crown of the former Caesar and put it on, whereupon he was torn to pieces by the bystanders."[93] Similarly, in 13 CE, another madman put on the crown of Caesar during Augustus' birthday games. In this case, the madman lived, but Augustus died the next year. In the end, the presence of the gods, whether traditional or imperial, was thought to secure the *pax deorum* and so any sacrilege was both an omen and could trigger a strong (and savage) reaction – fortified to be sure by strong political sentiments – much as Augustus' attempt to omit Neptune from the circus procession was met by fierce and violent opposition.[94]

Augustus continued to honor the imperial special dead in the *pompa theatralis*, just as he had in the *pompa circensis* – a pattern that Tiberius dutifully followed just as he had with the circus procession. In 23 BCE, after the death of Marcellus, "[Augustus] ordered that a golden image of the deceased, a golden crown, and a curule chair should be carried into the theater at the *ludi Romani* and should be placed in the midst of the officials in charge of the games."[95] Marcellus' honors clearly echoed those of the traditional gods (and also Julius Caesar), but he had not been deified, and so his statue and symbol were placed with the game-giver and the organizers, not the gods. In 19 CE, Tiberius granted Germanicus a similar posthumous honor according to the *Lex Valeria Aurelia* as transmitted by the *tabula Hebana*.

> During the Augustal Games, [when the benches of the Brotherhood] are placed in the theaters, curule chairs of Germanicus Caesar [with oak garlands] should be placed among them [in his remembrance] of that priesthood, and these chairs [should be brought out of] the temple of

> divine Augustus, when it will have been finished, [and in the meantime] they should be stored in and brought out of [the temple] of Mars Ultor, and whoever [will see to it that] the games listed above are carried out, he should [also see to it that the chairs are placed in the theaters] and, when they are to be put away, that they are put away in the temple.[96]

According to the law, Germanicus' curule chairs were to be housed in the temple of Mars Ultor until the completion of the temple for divine Augustus, from where it would join a *pompa theatralis* to be ushered to the theater. Tacitus, probably based on this law, confirmed that "curule seats set up in the places of the Augustal priests, and, above them, oaken crowns" were decreed in honor of Germanicus, but he did not identify the venue. The theater may have been understood, since immediately after commenting on the chair and crowns, Tacitus disclosed that Germanicus' ivory statue, which seems to have been stored in the temple of Concord, would appear in the circus procession.[97] Just four years later, Tiberius' son Drusus was granted the same honors as had been decreed for Germanicus: namely chairs among the *Augustales* at the theater and an ivory image in the circus procession.[98] Even "gilded chairs for both [Tiberius and the 'Sharer of His Cares,' Sejanus] [were] brought into the theaters," seemingly in Tiberius' absence, though Sejanus was at Rome.[99] Similar honors extended even to municipal elites – again in parallel with the *pompa circensis*. Also during the reign of Tiberius, C. Cupiennius Satrius Marcianus may have been honored at Cumae with a statue (or perhaps he erected a statue to Tiberius), or perhaps more likely (if this honor pertained to a theater procession) he was granted a chair placed in the theater in addition to the right to wear a crown during the circus procession and the races.[100]

After the death of Faustina the younger, the senate ordered "that a golden statue of Faustina should be carried into the theater, on every occasion when the emperor [Marcus Aurelius] was to be a spectator, and placed in the special section from which she was wont, when alive, to view the games, and that the most influential women should sit around it."[101] Strangely, the deified Faustina did not find a place among the gods, but rather among the aristocratic women with whom she would have customarily sat, much like Marcellus, Germanicus, and Drusus who also seem to have been placed among colleagues not divinities. Equally as odd, Faustina was not made present by a relic, for example a crown, but rather by a golden statue. However, her presence in the theater procession coheres to a certain degree with honors for *divae* in the *pompa circensis*, in which they received a statue borne either in a *carpentum* or more emphatically on an elephant *bigae*, but not a *tensa* with *exuviae* – honors both distinguished from and lesser than deified emperors. Commodus seems to have grasped the malleability and (megalomaniacal) value of the theater procession as he had his "lion-skin and club [his Herculean '*exuviae*'] placed on a gilded chair in the theaters," potentially including the amphitheater.[102] After Commodus' excessive public self-display, Septimius Severus returned to a more traditional style of commemoration and divinization, when, in addition to a *currus elephantorum* in the *pompa circensis* in honor of Pertinax, "he ordered that three thrones in honor of [Pertinax] should be borne into the other theaters," again possibly including the amphitheater.[103]

An Augustan-Tiberian settlement seems to have established a hierarchy of honors that became more or less traditional, though not obligatory, for the circus and theater processions. The similarities in the pattern of divine honors seems a result of a common idiom of spectacle and a shared dynastic function. That is, the theater procession, like the circus procession, seems to have served in lieu of a funeral procession, in which gods were not supposed to appear. Moreover, the often repeated ludic *pompae* offered more opportunities to forge dynastic links, in a ritual that might have penetrated civic collective memory as effectively as a grandiosely staged funeral. Indeed, such persistent similarities between the circus and theater processions were readily apparent to Tertullian, an inveterate critic of Roman public culture, who with mocking incredulity observed that "even your kings are appointed priesthoods and other pageantry: *tensae*, chariots [*currus* (*elephantorum*)], *solisternia* [relics displayed on thrones] and *lectisternia* [divine images displayed on couches], festivals, and games."[104] Symbols and images of deified emperors were transported by *tensae* and elephant carts and displayed on chairs and couches at festivals, games, and shows and so, unsurprisingly, the pageantry to the circus and to the theater drew substantially, but not completely, upon the same idiom of spectacle.

Though Pertinax seems to be the last individual honored in a *pompa theatralis* (as well as with the last extant example of a *currus elephantorum*), theater processions seem to have continued well into late antiquity. In the late fourth century CE, an elusive allusion in bishop Ambrose of Milan seems to draw upon the supposedly vain pageantry of the theater procession (as well as the theater and processions in general), while a more definite one in Ausonius, in a meditation on dreams, conjures a vision of "the procession [or the pomp] of the spacious theater," before the sleeping mind jumps to arena where the dreamer is butchered.[105] Even though the *ludi scaenici* were utterly depraved – at least in the heated rhetoric of Christian polemic – in 537 CE, the emperor Justinian issued *Novella 105: De consulibus*, which constitutes what appears to be the last, albeit very circumstantial, suggestion of the continuation of a *pompa theatralis*, of some sort.[106] According to the *novella*, consuls were limited to seven processions or public appearances (ἡ πρόοδος/*processus*) during their tenure in office: "the fifth procession leads to the theater, [to a show] called 'harlots,' where there are buffoons on stage with choruses of tragic actors and theatrical dancers."[107] If erotically themed shows and their (possible) introductory procession took place in the second Rome, it is possible that a similar procession introduced similar shows in the old Rome. Despite a long tradition of Christian rhetoric against all the games (composed by a very "select" group of Christians), erotic performances like "Harlots," possibly preceded by a procession, were organized by Christian consuls for the pleasure of a largely Christian audience.[108]

Much like the *pompa theatralis* seems to have developed concomitant with the fabrication of stand-alone theaters, a *pompa amphitheatralis* might have been produced for the unveiling of the Flavian amphitheater, the first permanent amphitheater in Rome. During the inauguration of the Colosseum, Titus seems to have organized a procession of informers who had just been cudgeled in the Forum, a particularly brutal species of the amphitheater procession, seemingly an semi-independent offshoot of both the circus and theater parades. According to Suetonius, Titus ordered "[the informers and their instigators] to be thoroughly beaten with whips and cudgels in the Forum and last of all paraded in the arena of the amphitheater."[109] Martial commemorated what seems to be the same parade, which he would have seen in person: "a company dangerous to peace and inimical to placid tranquility, ever harrying hapless wealth, was led in parade and the vast arena did not have room enough for the guilty."[110] As part of the extended opening ceremonies, this parade of informers was unlikely to have been repeated.[111] Such exigencies, however, surely impacted all procession performances, which needed to adapted to specific circumstances, and so no one representation of a procession (like that of Fabius Pictor-Dionysius) represents all iterations.

Bracketing such inevitable variability, which is largely impossible to trace at any rate, it seems that Rome's various ludic processions drew upon a common spectacle vocabulary, in part because they "served" a common purpose. Like the *pompa circensis* and *pompa theatralis*, the *pompa amphitheatralis* was fundamentally a procession to escort the gods to the games with all due pomp. And so, in addition to a parade of civic nuisances, Titus and Domitian also appear to have staged a version of a *pompa theatralis* in which *exuviae* were processed on chairs or thrones to the Colosseum, where they were displayed – at least if a number of Flavian coin-types depicting *sellisternia* (ceremonies in which objects were displayed on chairs or thrones) pertain to the dedication of the amphitheater, which seems eminently plausible.[112] The precise referent of the images on the reverses, if there was one, is unsurprisingly imprecise. The reverses show various objects on draped thrones or chairs: a winged lightning bolt (*fulmen*) to represent Jupiter and a helmet for Minerva (or Mars) it would seem, but no symbol for Juno to complete the Capitoline triad (Figures 50 and 51).[113] Other, even more ambiguous, objects were also represented: one, a wreath on a *sella curulis* quite likely for divine Vespasian (who was explicitly mentioned in the legend of a few of Domitian's issues); two, a triangular-shaped frame adorned with palmettes and/or sheafs of grain above a draped throne; and, three, a semi-circular arched frame typically decorated with crescents but on occasion with sheafs of grain, again on a few Domitianic issues, also on a draped throne (Figures 52–54).[114]

50. Draped seat with winged lightning bolt: aureus, 80 CE: obverse: IMP TITVS CAES VESPASIAN AVG P M and reverse: TR P IX IMP XV COS VIII P P

51. Draped seat with Corinthian helmet: aureus, 80–81 CE: obverse: CAESAR DIVI F DOMITIANVS COS VII and reverse: PRINCEPS IVVENTVTIS

52. Curule chair with wreath: aureus, 80 CE: obverse: IMP TITVS CAES VESPASIAN AVG P M and reverse: TR P IX IMP XV COS VIII P P

The triangular and semicircular frames may be differently arranged *struppi* (laurel branches woven into specific shapes): the triangular form recalling, perhaps, the pediment of a temple or *tensa* in honor of the *divi*, the semicircular frame somewhat reminiscent of a shrine, aedicula, or façade of a *carpentum* for a *diva* – though any allusion to a *tensa*, which seemingly refers to a temple façade, or a *carpentum*, pointing to a aedicula, could refer to the gods in general, traditional and imperial. Or maybe they simply were the backs of the thrones.[115]

Whatever these coins were to supposed to represent, Trajan had restored a set of hybrid coins with deified Vespasian or divine Titus on the obverse and an enthroned lightning bolt of Jupiter on the reverse, which suggests that such numismatic imagery suitably reflected the specific achievements of the Flavian dynasty, among which the Colosseum certainly loomed large.[116] Later in the second century CE, Antoninus Pius had minted a similar coin type for Rome's nine-hundredth birthday on which an enthroned thunderbolt appeared on the reverse – in addition to his Dea Roma *tensa* coin-types.[117] To be sure, not every representation of a *sella* or a draped throne on which sat symbols or ambiguous shapes needs to have represented a *pompa* (*amphi-*)*theatralis*. Nonetheless, these coin types do provide some sense of a *sellisternium*, the

53. Draped seat with triangular frame (with palmette and wheat stalks): denarius, 80 CE: reverse: TR P IX IMP XV COS VIII

54. Draped seat with semicircular frame (with three crescents): aureus, 80 CE: obverse: IMP TITVS CAES VESPASIAN AVG P M and reverse: TR P IX IMP XV COS VIII P P

55. Ludic procession before *munera*, marble, Julio-Claudian

installation of the gods on chairs and thrones at banquets, theaters, arenas, and the Circus Maximus, where such chairs were seemingly exhibited on the *pulvinar*.[118] In fact, the Colosseum may have had its own *pulvinar* from which the gods, traditional and imperial, enjoyed the shows.[119]

Though the *pompa amphitheatralis* may not have developed at Rome until the Flavians, it seems to have been performed earlier elsewhere in Italy. Even before the inauguration of the Flavian amphitheater, municipal magistrates and *Augustales* in the mid first century CE commemorated their patronage of *ludi* and *munera*, which often included references in text and image to the procession which kicked off the games. Before two different sets of games for Apollo in the Forum at Pompeii, Aulus Clodius Flaccus, a *duovir*, presented a procession, perhaps to conduct Apollo from his temple adjacent to the Forum to a special viewing stand (something like a *pulvinar*), or perhaps the animals and athletes filed past the god in his temple, where he remained to watch the games.[120] A Julio-Claudian-era relief from the necropolis at the Porta Stabia of Pompeii, and possibly from the funerary monument of Cn. or N. Clovatius, suggests how a *pompa* that preceded the *munera* might have looked (Figure 55).[121] In the top register, two lictors lead a procession, followed by three trumpeters. Behind the musicians, four porters carry a *ferculum* on which two smiths, apparently, ply their trade (perhaps indicating the participation of a *collegium*). On the heels of the *ferculum*, the *editor* and his entourage appear (the first member of which carries a *tabula* likely announcing the games, while the second holds a palm for the victor), followed by a long line of gladiators or possibly arena staff carrying armor. The procession closes with one further horn player and two contestants or grooms leading horses dressed in fine style. Though the lone *ferculum* appears to carry smiths at work instead of a deity, the gods did have a place in this kind of procession. The amphitheater at Avenches, like the Colosseum at Rome, perhaps, may preserve traces of a kind of *pulvinar* or sacred loge for the gods (and perhaps also the sponsors of the games). A monumental terrace above one of the axial entries could have housed and displayed the gods, including imperial ones, while they attended the show.[122]

55. (cont.)

Other imagery related to the *munera* and its procession seems to confirm that much of the apparatus of the *pompa deorum* (as well as the *pompa hominum*) also appeared in the *pompa amphitheatralis*. In the mid first century CE at Amiternum, a *triumvir Augustalis* commemorated what seems to be the procession conducted before *munera* that he had sponsored – an important moment of public visibility for an emperor, senator, or *Augustalis* (Figure 10).[123] The relief is fragmentary, but one of the remaining fragments shows Victory driving a chariot accompanied by four *togati* – two adults and two youths apparently, who may be further *Augustales*, the persons charged to ensure the proper conduct of the gods in the procession (*pueri patrimi et matrimi* with adult attendants), or perhaps the game-giver and his entourage – with, seemingly, Mars, piloting a chariot whose horses were handled by an attendant (a *tensarius* of sorts, perhaps), following behind.[124] The adjoining fragment reveals statues of Jupiter and Juno borne on *fercula* accompanied by two further *togati*. The two remaining fragments show musicians as well as a group of gladiators already engaged in combat. Reminiscent of the doubled presence of the gods in the *pompa circensis* as statues on *fercula* and *exuviae* in *tensae*, the gods in this *pompa amphitheatralis* were also made present on *fercula*, but in place of or perhaps in addition to *tensae*, Victory and Mars were imaged as actually present, *as if* guiding their own chariots to the arena – though the diminutive size of the horses gives away the game.[125]

A *sevir Augustalis* named Marcus Valerius Anteros Asiaticus similarly and nearly contemporaneously commemorated himself on his own conspicuously original funerary monument in Brescia in northern Italy (Figure 56).[126] The narrative relief along the bottom edge of the panel depicts moments from the deceased's career, which seemingly come from the same public ceremony that must have been a particular high point. At the left, a pair of boxers square off next to a statue of a divinity, possibly a Mercury erected by Anteros Asiaticus himself in response to his appointment to the college. To the right of the boxers, a sacrifice takes place over which the deceased himself likely presided. In the center, the *collegium* with Anteros Asiaticus likely occupying the central seat distributes gifts to their fellow citizens (a *congiarium*). Finally, at the far right, two lictors lead the *collegium* in a procession which would have

56. Tomb monument of M. Valerius Anteros Asiaticus (cast), marble (original), mid first century CE

57. Tomb monument of C. Lusius Storax, marble, early first century CE

preceded the *congiarium*, sacrifice, and games. Yet another contemporary relief of an Augustal priest, now in Chieti, represents C. Lusius Storax also at a *congiarium* in the triangular pediment, which would have preceded the *munera* depicted in the lower register (Figure 57).[127] On this relief, however, the procession and sacrifice that preceded the games were only signaled tangentially by the musicians who flanked the central tribunal: *tibicines* on the left side and *cornicines* on the right. Unsurprisingly, the grave monuments

58. Magistrates with lictors and *fercula* carrying deities in an amphitheater procession, marble, mid second century CE

of M. Valerius Anteros Asiaticus and C. Lusius Storax foreground the generous donations of "bread and circuses," as it were, by their honorees. Nonetheless, the procession which introduced the contests also had a (secondary or even tertiary) place.

On occasion, the *pompa amphitheatralis* could feature more prominently; see the sculpted balustrades of the amphitheater at Capua from the second century CE, for example. One relief depicts four togate figures, one of whom climbs the stairs to enter, it seems, the seating area, where he will preside over the spectacles, while two other men and a pair of lictors continue on, their duty as escort seemingly completed. Another panel clearly depicts two *fercula* bearing deities, perhaps the Tyche of Capua with her mural crown on the left and, mostly likely, Mars on the right (Figure 58). Other panels also seem to offer scenes from the procession: more *fercula* images, which are too fragmentary to identify their burdens; a line of Tychai (or women and a man impersonating Tychai); an ambiguous four-wheeled cart (with a *divus*?) whose purpose is opaque; and a sacrificial scene. Two further reliefs may even show the sanctuaries of Mars (whose statue also seems to have been borne on a *ferculum*) and Minerva, from which processions to this amphitheater may have originated.[128]

Like the other ludic processions, the *pompa amphitheatralis* seems to have continued into late antiquity, at least at Rome. In the late fourth or early fifth century CE, Prudentius complained that "those dreadful spectacles, [including] the procession in [or the pomp of] the amphitheater," endured among the many "pagan" errors that still haunted Rome, though the *munera* may have come to an end in the following decades.[129] Even with the decline of gladiator combat, the pageantry of the *pompa* might even have endured into the mid sixth century CE. Justinian's *Novella* 105, which outlined the spectacles to be offered during a consulship, suggests a procession or public display prior to *venationes*, animal hunts, during the third and fourth public events of a given consular year – which at Rome, at least, may still have included an opening procession.[130]

The *pompa circensis* seems to have been the first and most pompous of the ludic *pompae*. The *pompa theatralis* and subsequently the *pompa amphitheatralis* were seemingly less spectacular and smaller-scale offshoots with, of course, necessary adaptions. In all three ludic processions, the sponsor of the games and his entourage (often political allies and young men it seems) featured prominently, though in the (amphi-)theater processions this group appears to have processed on foot, rather than in a chariot or on horseback. Contestants or performers (charioteers, actors, stage dancers, or gladiators) also seem to have appeared in such processions – charioteers guiding or driving their chariots, stage performers executing their choreography, and gladiators, perhaps, with their panoply. Similarly, martial dancers, miming military movements with their dummy weapons, and satyrs and other burlesque performers, teasing the crowds, may have participated in circus and theater processions. Processions, after all, were meant to attract attention and so suggestive choreography might well have been a staple of every ludic parade. And finally, these ludic processions escorted the gods, both traditional and imperial, to the appropriate venue – though in the theater processions, it seems that the gods were represented only (or rather most often) by their *exuviae*, which may have rested on chairs borne on *fercula*, while both *exuviae* and/or *simulacra* were seemingly carried to (some) amphitheaters, at least on occasion.

With such variation, the performed theology of these ludic processions surely also varied – the gods would have been made present in different media and transported in different ways, all resulting in a myriad of pantheons and theological possibilities. To a certain degree, the exigencies of architecture may have dictated this diversity: the circus had a large track around which a large number of *fercula* and *tensae* could process, while the more confined theater and, to a lesser degree, amphitheater may have ruled out similarly abundant displays – though the amphitheater, a doubled theater, procession seems to have offered a more robust performed theology, though still without *tensae*. The honors for imperial gods could seemingly ignore such practical limitations as the the imperial special dead could be made present by statues and/or symbols – a humbly arrogant distinction reminiscent of the conceited humility with which imperial *divi* were distinguished from the traditional *dei* in the *pompa circensis*.

In addition to a shared ritual grammar, the constitutive elements from which the ludic processions were produced (game-giver and entourage, contestants/performers, entertainers, and gods), they also seem to have shared a ritual syntax, order and organization, and signification, a similar set of rhythms that orchestrated any performance. The hierarchical, public self-presentation of a *praeses ludorum* like Cicero at the Floralia, for example, may have been comically twinned by erotic performers trailing behind, who might also have marched according to their own system of rank with an *archimimus/a* leading the way.[131] That is, an oscillation between gravity (order, structure, authority) and levity (disorder, mockery, sexuality) probably marked the (amphi-)theater procession as much as it did the circus parade. In much the same way, this shared idiom of ludic spectacle suggests an alternation between resonance – in which the procession reached out beyond its performative boundaries to connect to other rituals, ceremonies, histories, and even places – and wonder, show-stopping, awe-inspiring spectacularity. For example, if the Flavian *sellisternium* coin-types commemorated the inauguration of the amphitheater, then perhaps reverse images of a lone elephant signal both its participation in the games as well as the procession beforehand. Martial insisted that an elephant would "feel our god," indicating perhaps that an elephant carried divine Vespasian in the *pompa amphitheatralis* in some ceremony for the opening of the Flavian amphitheater.[132] Elephants, of course, recall both the triumph and the circus procession, but an elephant in the Colosseum carrying or pulling a god may have been wondrous.

Roman ludic processions may also have shared one further concern: proper ritual performance. All ludic processions seem to have escorted the gods to the games, which required that proper procedure – or at least tradition – be followed, lest the ritual fail. Although most of the extant evidence for ritual failure and its correction, *instauratio*, centered on the *pompa circensis* and its attendant rituals, an array of ceremonial customs and ritual traditions might also have surrounded the (amphi-)theater procession, the installation of the gods in the theaters, and the subsequent sacrifice. The pair of portentous madmen who put on Caesar's crown suggests that religious scruple also hedged the *pompa (amphi-)theatralis* – and so expiation would likely have been required after the brutal dismemberment of the first madman. Deviation, improvisation, and innovation risked ritual failure, which would have required (at least some degree of) repetition. Of course, that may well have been the point: repetition could help to court popular favor, so long as allegations of purposeful sacrilege – a stain that could not be removed – could be avoided.[133]

Though the scattershot evidence for the *pompa (amphi-)theatralis* supports only an idealizing ideal-type (as opposed to the heuristic ideal-type posited for the late-republican circus procession), it seems that the (amphi-)theater processions followed a similar historical arc. The (amphi-)theater procession seems to have first emerged in the late republic (or early empire) to conduct the gods from their temples to temporary (and eventually permanent) free-standing (amphi-)theaters. During the empire, imperial gods and the honored dead of the imperial house were included in a variety of ways. Other developments are seemingly untraceable. Nonetheless, as the games, shows, and spectacles changed, so too would its opening procession. For example, gladiators would no longer have appeared in the amphitheater procession after the end of gladiatorial combat in late antiquity. However the procession developed, and it assuredly changed over time and even from one performance to the next, such ludic processions seem to have endured for as long as the *ludi* themselves did, as suggested by *Novella* 105 which prescribes a public appearance or procession before "Harlots" and the *venationes*.

In the end, Tertullian was right: circus processions were performed in western municipalities and a similar parade preceded both *ludi scaenici* and *munera*. Outside of Rome, sponsors of the games may not have had the resources of empire with which to outfit their productions. Nonetheless, both in the capital and elsewhere the procession was still an important political performance for those organizing and financing the chariot races, theater shows, or gladiatorial combats. Tertullian was also right concerning the religious nature of these *pompae*, though he reviled it as idolatry. Despite local traditions and regional differences, ludic processions at Rome and in the west shared the same basic function: to transport the gods to the games, where the show entertained divinity and humanity together. Indeed, the religious character of the *pompa circensis*, at least, seems to have spilled over into the "main event." That is to say, the circus parade seems to have lent its significance to the races themselves – especially the first race *a pompa* ("after the procession").

IV "AND THE HORSES, FLEET AS THE WIND, WILL CONTEND FOR THE FIRST PALM"[134]

After the long line of gods was finally installed in the *pulvinar* (or some similar structure) and after the magistrates and priests sacrificed to the gods, the *editor* at last signaled the most eagerly anticipated race of the day, the *maxima spectacula*, "the greatest show on earth," which also offered the biggest purse and the first palm of the games.[135] It seems that only the most experienced drivers and the best horses competed in this race – perhaps because the horses had not yet settled after the procession or perhaps so that the best horses could race again.[136] However, the name of the race, *a pompa* ("after the procession"), rather suggests that pious sentiment also contributed to its importance.[137]

To compete in the race *a pompa* was a signal honor for charioteers. Indeed, the self-proclaimed "most distinguished of the charioteers," whose records "surpass the *agitatores* of all the factions who ever participated in the contests of the circus games," Gaius Appuleius Diocles, reviewed his illustrious career in this way (ca. 122–146 CE): "In sum: he drove a *quadriga* for 24 years, started 4,257 races, won 1,462 times, 110 times after the *pompa*."[138] Not only does this précis offer some sense of the number of times each year a *pompa circensis* would have been performed in the mid second century CE (on average, at least, thirteen), but it also offers some sense of what the procession may have meant to ordinary Romans.[139] For Diocles, the race *a pompa* seems to have been the most important race, victories in which he listed first in the enumeration of his triumphs. What is more, Diocles' ranking of his victories seems to confirm what a "souvenir" lamp with an image of a *tensa* or a cameo with *diva* Livia on an elephant *biga* suggests: the procession mattered.

Similarly, another eminent charioteer, Publius Aelius Gutta Calpurnianus, also commemorated the number of races that he had won *a pompa*. On a monument which he erected in his own honor, he listed his 1,127 palms according to the faction for which he was driving. In this list, he presented the total number of victories and number of times he won the largest purses first. Then at the head of the types of races that he had won (for example, one-, two-, three-, or four-horse chariots), he numbered the races he won "after the procession": four times with the Whites, thirty-five times with the Blues (only the extraordinary six-horse chariot win was listed before), and six times with the Greens – apparently he never won the race *a pompa* for the Reds.[140] In short, for two of Rome's most accomplished charioteers, the race *a pompa* was the most important race, to be listed first before the others, which seemingly reflects something of the prestige of the procession itself. Perhaps it was especially auspicious to win the first race when one could be assured of the gods' full and enthusiastic attention. Victories in the race *a pompa*, as part of an especially successful career, may even have earned a charioteer like Diocles or Gutta Calpurnius a statue in the *pompa circensis* itself, as a near contemporary terracotta suggests (Figure 78).

Over the centuries, the *pompa circensis* had accumulated significant traditions. Julius Caesar and Octavian-Augustus seem to have run headlong into its bulwarks of venerable custom, after which Augustus, at least, showed greater respect for its ritual obligations. Likewise, subsequent emperors seem to have conscientiously maintained the traditional honors of the gods in the procession – at least, no other emperor seems to have removed one of the traditional gods in a fit of pique (the gods would eventually be removed from the procession, but for other reasons). Indeed, the preservation of processional honors for the traditional gods made imperial cult honors possible. Moreover, the proper conduct of the *pompa circensis* and the games themselves, of course, offered an unparalleled opportunity for public self-display by emperors and their families – an opportunity that had to be carefully managed if it was to be successful, as Nero (probably posthumously) learned. That is to say, imperial ritual failures and other extraordinary events (prodigies) related to the *pompa circensis* joined the arsenal by which deceased emperors were judged and their memories shaped. Or, in other words, the traditions of the *pompa circensis* and its place in the Roman cultural imaginary offered a venue for the negotiation between ruler and ruled, in which even autocrats found themselves constrained, a bit, by the rules of the game (at least in retrospect).

What is more, the emperors' careful conservation of the customs of the *pompa circensis* maintained it as a platform for sub-imperial elite display. Imperial respect for and investment in the circus procession meant that one of the important theaters in the republican battle for honor and glory remained available for imperial elites in their continuing status competition. This contest may now have been fought under the eyes of emperors, but it was still fought. Both emperors and elites continued to enjoy the stage afforded by the procession, even if the figure of the emperor (both the living ruler and select predecessors) dominated the spotlight. Praetors and other elites could still savor the deafening cheers and applause of the massive crowds as they circled the arena. Their performance of the sacrifices still proved their role in maintaining the peace of the gods. They could relish the anxious expectation and tense silence as starting gates were allocated just before the start signal was given. The procession also provided the masses of non-elites in the procession similar visibility. Competitors, contestants, and performers still featured prominently. Martial dancers still strutted through the streets, while the sartyrs and Sileni seem to have added maenads and fauns to their bawdy performance. Also during the empire, it seems that professional *collegia* joined the procession, though their participation remains speculative. The whole show would have been choreographed under the watchful eye of some master of ceremonies, perhaps Tertullian's so-called undertaker, who would have assuredly felt pleased during a well-received performance.

The *pompa circensis* was not simply an overly long introduction as the elder Seneca would have it. In fact, it seems to have appealed greatly to a wide swathe of the Roman world. Provincial elites lavished their lesser resources on this procession – for example, outfitting a silver *tensa(e)* for Minverva – not only because it may have been enshrined in law (for certain colonies at least), but also because it was a spectacle worth producing and also worth commemorating afterwards. Moreover, some elements of the circus procession's idiom of spectacle seem to have been employed in other ludic processions, the *pompa theatralis* introducing the *ludi scaenici* and the *pompa amphitheatralis* which opened the *munera*. In all three cases, a carefully choreographed procession escorted the sponsors of the games with their entourages, competitors or performers, and gods to the appropriate spectacle venue. These *pompae deorum* which launched the games could in fact signify the festival as a whole for the many race fans who took home lamps decorated with an image of a *tensa*, and even for the owner of the cameo depicting Livia's *currus elephantorum*. In short, the *pompa circensis*, from which the most prestigious race of the greatest show on earth took its name, remained an essential political pageant and a hollowed religious ritual for emperors, elites, charioteers, and other ordinary Romans.

SIX

THE *POMPA CIRCENSIS* IN LATE ANTIQUITY

Imperialization, Christianization, restoration

Although all superstition must be completely eradicated, nevertheless, it is Our will that the buildings of temples situated outside the walls shall remain untouched and uninjured ... since from them is provided the regular performance of long-established amusements [shows, circus games, and contests] for the Roman people.

Codex Theodosianus 16.10.3[1]

Standing at the head of a long Christian rhetorical tradition, Tertullian, around the turn of the third century CE, insisted, "We [Christians] renounce your spectacles as heartily as we do their origins, which we know lie in superstition.... We have nothing to do in speech, in sight, or in hearing with the madness of the circus, the shamelessness of the theater, the savagery of the arena."[2] Of course, not every Christian adhered to Tertullian's puritanical loathing of the common, sensory pleasures of Roman civic life or even accepted his authority to define normative Christianity, but beginning with Tertullian and continuing into late antiquity a stream of Christian polemic would repeatedly and mostly futilely attack the spectacles of the circus, theater, and arena. Despite such efforts, "the madness of the circus" and the other spectacles continued at Rome and Christians of all stripes continued to attend them into the sixth century CE, when the economic, social, and cultural structures that had enveloped the games seem to have disappeared in the course of Justinian's "re-conquest" of Italy (ca. 535–554 CE). Even though Christian rhetoric did not put an end to the games, it seems to have had a forceful effect on how the games were framed – especially by Christian emperors, who had a particular interest in satisfying both Christian opinion makers, who were seemingly unanimous in their opposition, and their other subjects, the vast majority of whom, regardless of religious affiliation, took pleasure in a robust array of shows and spectacles. Late-antique emperors could not dispense with what had become the central arena of imperial display, but they could argue in law that the games had been freed from superstition (typically sacrifice and image devotion) and were thus "safe" as ancestral amusements, as "secular" affairs unencumbered by "idolatrous" religiosity.

While the re-interpreted games could continue largely unaltered during the *longue durée* of late antiquity, the *pompa circensis* was seemingly more deeply affected by the slowly changing religious landscape – though its actual practice is difficult to determine. Much of the traditional public ceremonial system remained in place into the fifth and even sixth centuries CE, even as vociferous criticisms from various Christian authors, in particular bishops, and the steady pressure of imperial legislation must have had a slow, cumulative effect on traditional practices. As public entertainments remained a central mechanism in the perpetual negotiations between ruler and ruled and an essential element of elite distinction, the *pompa circensis* at Rome seems to have continued into the fifth century CE, and quite possibly beyond. But a *pompa deorum* became increasingly difficult to produce in a world whose public sphere, rhetoric, urban symbolism, and built environment were ever so slowly, but steadily marked by Christian rituals, language, symbols, and buildings – in short, the circus procession changed in a Christianizing empire. To judge from rather meager and far-flung evidence, over the course of the fourth century CE the *pompa circensis* seems to have been reduced to a procession of imperial images and Victory – at least in its imperial iterations. That is, imperial representations of the *pompa circensis* focused more and more on the imperial *praeses ludorum* at the expense of the rest of the procession: the traditional gods, in particular, but also the *divi* and the other imperial special dead.

Though the tectonic re-interpretation of the games as simple ancestral amusements may have been a response to Christian criticisms, the shift from gods to game-givers in imperial imagery seems to have been the result of evolving imperial ideology and ruler cult. During the course of the third century CE, the system by which deceased emperors and empresses were deified seems to have gradually broken down as senatorial prestige which had sanctioned official apotheosis ebbed and high-imperial court ceremonial was disrupted. Even the term *divus* may have devolved into a simple title, meaning little more than "of blessed memory" with a semantic range overlapping *sanctus* (holy), rather than divinity, or at least it could have been construed as such to accommodate Christian emperors in an enduring, but altered, imperial cult.[3] Modified forms of imperial cult endured with all of their local variety in fourth-century CE Rome and beyond.[4] New Christian *divi* were made and even honored with games, but no Christian emperor was honored with a temple in Rome – indeed, no imperial cult temple whatsoever seems have been built in Rome after Pertinax's in 193 CE, though Gordian I and II were supposedly voted one in the mid third century CE according to the *Historia Augusta*.[5] However it was reconfigured and however it varied locally, imperial cult figured differently in the construction of late-antique imperial power and representations of the traditional and imperial gods in the *pompa circensis* seem to have been a casualty of that shift. Over the course of the third, fourth, and into the early fifth centuries CE, concomitant with the advent of an imperial Christianity, the imperial cult slowly changed and so too, it seems, did the *pompa circensis* which was first "secularized" or "imperialized" and then, possibly, "Christianized."

These shifts in interpretation and representation (if not also practice) built upon earlier precedents. The games had long been considered pleasures, though not necessarily mere pleasures, while sponsors always sought to be remembered. In late antiquity, however, this understanding of the games and this manner of commemorating the circus procession came to dominate imperial rhetoric and imagery, while much, but not all, sub-imperial imagery conformed to imperial visual culture. Despite Christian polemic and imperial law, there is some evidence which suggests that, on occasion, the *pompa circensis* continued to be a *pompa deorum* until the end of the fourth century CE – at least at Rome. In some cases, the *pompa circensis* may have been performed in a traditional manner – or at least imagined or remembered as such. In the end, the late-antique *pompa circensis* developed something of a split personality – torn between Christian rhetoric, imperial coercion, and the weight of republican memories.

The only securely attested itinerary of the *pompa circensis* reveals a similar tension. During the late republic and early empire, there was a certain coherence between procession and itinerary. The republican *pompa circensis* performed a traditional image of the city (SPQR+gods) as it marched along an itinerary whose monuments clearly manifested republican political culture. Much the same held for the urban image performed during the imperial *pompa circensis*, which was superimposed on a still visible but attentuated republican one.[6] This harmony between procession and itinerary seems to have broken down in late antiquity. The procession itself was arguably reduced, for the most part, to imperial imagery in the aftermath of Christianizing legislation, while the itinerary featured a number of newly restored republican edifices including temples and sanctuaries – restorations which seem to have ignored imperial cult temples and triumphal monuments. The fracture between procession and itinerary produced a multiplicity of Romes: aristocratic (hearkening back to the republic), traditional (including a *pompa deorum*), imperial, and, eventually, Christian as the titular church of Anastasia would be built along the parade route by the late fourth century CE. If the procession was to perform an image of the city, it needed to accommodate a limited, but burgeoning, Christian public presence. In fact, in the mid fifth century CE, the *pompa circensis* may even have been "Christianized" with the transport of Christian symbols in the train. The *pompa deorum* may have become a *pompa Dei.*

I *POMPA DIABOLI*: CHRISTIAN RHETORIC AND THE *POMPA CIRCENSIS*

You [Christians] do not go to see the spectacles, you take no part in the processions . . . you abhor the sacred contests.

Minucius Felix, *Octavius* 12.5[7]

Caecilius, the "pagan" interlocutor in an early-third century CE "dialogue" written by the Christian apologist Minucius Felix, accused Christians of leading unnecessarily miserable lives, of which avoiding spectacles, processions, and games was an unequivocal symptom. At the end of the "dialogue," Octavius, the Christian protagonist, proudly admitted what Caecilius had intended as an accusation: "we [Christians] rightly keep aloof from wicked amusements, your processions and spectacles."[8] Tertullian, an older contemporary of Minucius Felix, voiced similar sentiments when he insisted "we [Christians] do not gather at the spectacles."[9] Elsewhere, however, Tertullian openly debated other Christians who did, in fact, attend games, shows, and other spectacles. Seemingly these Christians did not share Tertullian's dogmatic religious scruples. Or perhaps they toned down their Christian identity in order to get along in mainstream Roman culture. To judge from Tertullian, it would seem that some of these supposedly "simpler or more punctilious" Christians squared attendance at the games with their religious affiliation by noting the absence of an explicit biblical prohibition – "abstinence in this matter [the spectacles] is not specifically and in so many words enjoined upon the servants of God" – and whatever was not forbidden was allowed.[10] Even worse, according to Novatian writing at Rome later in the third century CE, "Among the faithful and those who lay claim to the dignity of a Christian calling, some find no shame – no shame, I say – in vindicating, from the heavenly scripture, the vain superstitions that are intermingled in the spectacles."[11] Throughout late antiquity, Christian authors and church councils condemned traditional spectacles and festivals – often with tremendous angst concerning Christian attendance and even participation.[12] Christian rhetoric regularly excoriated the games and those (Christians) who would attend them, attempting to draw a bright line between the acceptable and unacceptable – a boundary line that remained contested even as it shifted over the centuries.[13]

Though not quite as egregious as either "the shamelessness of the theater" or "the savagery of the arena," still the "madness of the circus" was often singled out in Christian polemic.[14] In a tortured argument, Tertullian insisted that even though places could not defile, nonetheless there are places where no good Christian should go for fear of defilement. "If as a sacrificer and worshipper, I enter the Capitolium or the temple of Serapis, I fall from god – just as I should if I am a spectator in the circus or the theater."[15] Though the circus or theater itself could not technically pollute, "the common guilt of idolatry" stained the circus and theater games as well as its spectators.[16] Following Tertullian closely, Novatian, a Roman presbyter and then counter-bishop of Rome, condemned not only the idolatry of the games, but also the vanity of the races themselves:

> How vain are the contests themselves, the quarreling over colors, vying over different chariots, resounding acclamations over mere marks of prestige, the rejoicing that one horse was faster than another, the grieving that one ran too slow, trying to reckon the age of a beast, becoming acquainted with the consuls under whom the horses ran, ascertaining their different ages, pinpointing their breed, recalling even their grandsires and great-grandsires. Isn't this whole matter a waste of time – or rather, shameful and despicable![17]

Approximately a century and a half later, Ammianus Marcellinus, probably a "pagan," agreed that circus races were a terrific waste of time – they "permit nothing memorable or serious to be done at Rome."[18] But at least the circus was better than the theater or the amphitheater in the shrill arc of Christian invective.

Both Tertullian and Novatian began their criticisms of Roman spectacles with the circus games before continuing with the theater shows and ending with gladiatorial combat – moving from bad to worse and then worst. This trilogy of depravity became a staple of late-antique Christian moralizing. For example, Ambrose evoked wasteful extravagance with the image of men who financed "circus games, theatrical shows, and gladiatorial *munera*," squandering their inheritance in a vain bid to win popular favor.[19] Also in the late fourth century CE, Jerome riffed on Tertullian when he insisted that all Rome's spectacles were clear signs of its corruption, which the virtuous (according to his definition) would avoid: "Let Rome keep her bustle for herself, the savage arena, the madness of the circus, the profligacy of the theater." Similarly Augustine, a little over a quarter of a century later, contended that demons, that is ancient Mediterranean traditional gods, and their supposedly misguided devotees took pleasure in "the various indecencies of the theaters, in the insanity of the circus, in the cruelties of the amphitheater."[20] In the early seventh century CE, Isidore of Seville again isolated the same Tertullianic triad: "the insanity of the circus, the indecency of the theater, the cruelty of the amphitheater, and the brutality of the arena" – with, seemingly, a double attack on gladiators and animal hunts (in the amphitheater and arena) to underscore the magnitude of their infamy.[21]

The circus procession also figured in this polemic, beginning again with Tertullian: "But rather more pompous is the pomp of the circus, to which the term *pompa* properly belongs. The *pompa* (procession) comes first."[22] Tertullian's especially ostentatious *pompa circensis* seems to have inspired what would become a very common Christian tag – *pompa diaboli*, the "pomps [or processions] of the Devil" renounced during Christian baptism.[23] For Tertullian, "a circus procession (*pompa circi*) of whatever kind offends God."[24] Indeed, in his condemnation of the *pompa circensis* Tertullian noted that "the men of *that* city [Rome] know where the conclave of demons has settled" – that is to say, the *pulvinar* in which the gods were installed and before which, likely, a sacrifice was conducted (in addition, of course, to the statues, shrines, and temples elsewhere in the arena).[25] In the end, the phrase *pompa diaboli*, initially a condemnation of the circus procession and by extension all Roman spectacle, eventually came to include the entire world and its sinful allures, especially idolatry, within its semiotic ambit.[26]

About a century later, Arnobius and Lactantius continued to condemn the circus procession. Arnobius ridiculed what he took to be the exaggerated ritual scruples of Roman traditional religion, scoffing at the taboos surrounding the *pompa circensis*, in particular the overly fastidious, to Arnobius at any rate, regulations governing dancing, music, and the *puer patrimus et matrimus*.

> If at the solemn games and sacred races the dancer has halted, or the musician suddenly becomes silent – you all cry out immediately that something has been done contrary to the sacredness of the ceremonies; or if the boy termed *patrimus et matrimus* let go of the thong in ignorance, or could not hold to the *tensa*.[27]

In a common Christian strategy of which Augustine's *City of God* is only the most illustrious example, Arnobius exploited the very words of classical authors to condemn Roman traditional religion. In this case, Arnobius misconstrued the reverent (and polemical) observations of Cicero so that the ritual prescriptions would appear absurd and even hypocritical.[28]

Lactantius – who had studied under Arnobius and later served as a tutor to Crispus, Constantine's oldest son – also made use of classical tradition, specifically Valerius Maximus, to demonstrate how silly and superstitious the Romans were supposed to be. "Every time danger threatens, the demons [that is, the traditional gods] claim they are angry on some stupid and trivial ground, as Juno was with Varro, because he had placed a pretty boy in the *tensa* of Jupiter to carry his relics (*exuviae*), and that was why the Roman name was nearly wiped out at Cannae."[29] Rather than signaling a pious emphasis on ritual performance, the hallmark of Roman spirituality, for Lactantius, this episode highlighted the sheer and wanton caprice of the traditional gods. Lactantius, however, also feared, to a certain extent, the power of (a circus?) procession to attract attention, which was after all one of its primary "functions." Lactantius argued that if the so-called wise, like Cicero, engaged in the error of cultivating divine images, "all the more so the ignorant masses, who rejoice in meaningless *pompae* and gawp at everything like children, delighted by frivolities and enchanted by pretty *simulacra* [divine images]."[30] It seems that Lactantius believed that the very spectacle of a procession, a *pompa deorum* with an array of gods, could capture the religious imagination of the crowd, which was to the literate elite (whether "pagan" or Christian) always notoriously susceptible to such persuasion – even though the crowds of Rome had on several memorable occasions exercised a great deal of discretion concerning the *pompa circensis*.[31]

Jerome, in 374 CE, employed the image of a game-giver in a *pompa aurea*, perhaps a golden *pompa circensis* (but more likely a triumph), as the very symbol of empty worldliness: "Anyone whosoever may glow with gold and brilliant metals, [silver and gold] may glitter from the trappings of the processional *fercula*."[32] Many wasted their time seeking honor and glory by leading a *pompa*, but for Jerome, love and friendship could not be bought. Shortly thereafter, in the early fifth century CE, Paulinus of Nola insisted that a Christian wedding must be free from similar idolatrous performances. "There must be no crazed *pompa* through the city where Christ dwells."[33] Also in the early fifth century CE, Bachiarius, an itinerant ascetic, described depraved contemporaries as those "who are truly caught in a net of vices, and, that is, submissively find pleasure in their enemies' hunts, even while exposed in the seats, and there for a long stretch of time fattened at the *pompa*."[34] Just a bit later, in the mid fifth century CE, Salvian, a presbyter from Marseille, numbered "processions, athletes, tumblers, pantomimes, and other monstrosities" among the insidious snares of demons, though "[he] would speak only about the impurities of the circuses and theaters."[35] Even Caesarius of Arles in the early to mid sixth century CE denounced "all spectacles whether furious, cruel, or shameful [as] pomps of the Devil (*pompae diaboli*)," a nod seemingly to the Tertullianic origins of the phrase as a condemnation of the circus procession and games.[36]

In the face of deeply entrenched habits of "idolatrous" spectacle, Novatian tried to argue, a bit idealistically, that "a Christian has better spectacles ... [namely] the beauty of world."[37] Augustine would also insist that Christians had other spectacles, but ones as brutal, in a way, as the games themselves: "a splendid spectacle offered to the eyes of the mind is a spirit whole and unbroken while the body is torn to pieces."[38] For Augustine, the image of Perpetua and Felicitas, maimed and killed in the arena, was unsurpassed: "What could be sweeter than this spectacle?"[39] Earnestly, though somewhat horrifically, Augustine contended that martyrdom, which was often emplotted in the course of bloody and furious Roman spectacles, offered Christians a kind of pious counter-show. Despite a Christian alternative of sorts, many Christian Romans seem to have remained loyal to traditional spectacles.

In other words, attempts to dissuade Christians from the spectacles or to channel the desire for spectacle in a different direction do not seem to have been as successful as Christian authorities, bishops and preachers, might have wanted. From Tertullian to Caesarius of Arles, Christian rhetoric regularly inveighed against the games – even as Christians continued to attend them. There were likely many ways to square attendance at the games with Christian identity, if such an accommodation was needed – ancient Christianity was multiform not monolithic.[40] Christian rhetoric painted those who attended games as less than fully Christian, while Christians who did attend the games may have had a different understanding of their religious commitments. A Christian need not have assented to Tertullian's, Novatian's, or Augustine's definition of Christianity, but if one did, such a Christian might have "deactivated" her religious identity in order to get along in Roman society.[41] However it was justified, if it needed to be justified, Christians regularly attended the *ludi*, perhaps even those who would become or were already priests and bishops.

For example, in a portrait of priests behaving badly seemingly targeting Ambrose, a career politician turned bishop of Milan, Jerome complained that Ambrose's or anyone's hasty elevation to the episcopacy would have left him unfit and ill-prepared: "yesterday a catechumen, today a pontifex [bishop]; yesterday in the amphitheater, today in church; in the evening at the circus, in the morning at the altar; a little while ago a patron of actors, now a consecrator of virgins."[42] As a governor of Aemilia in northern Italy, Ambrose would likely have sponsored games before which, one may imagine, he led a procession, perhaps carrying some Christian symbol to inoculate himself against the *pompa diaboli*. Somehow, it seems, Ambrose rendered Christianity compatible with high office – though Jerome remained skeptical. Augustine, likewise, insisted that a convert to Christianity "has turned away from the circus, from the theater, from the amphitheater." Nonetheless, he had to admit that such Christians were "few in comparison to the larger crowds in attendance [at the shows]."[43] Augustine again admitted that "there are many who do not lead lives consistent with the baptism they received: look how many baptized Christians have today chosen to crowd into the circus rather than this basilica!"[44] About a half-century later, bishop Leo I of Rome protested that "more effort is spent on demons than on the apostles, and the insane spectacles draw greater crowds than the shrines of martyrs."[45] Indeed, Leo's concerted efforts to convince Romans to dance to the rhythms of episcopal public worship instead of those of Roman civic time were frustrated by the entrenched habits of the aristocracy.[46] Also in the mid fifth century CE, Salvian, too, complained that "countless thousands of Christians . . . run wild in the circuses. . . . The churches are empty, the circus packed!"[47] What was worse, according to Salvian, "to Christ, then (O monstrous madness!), to Christ we offer circuses and mimes."[48]

II *VOLUPTATES*: IMPERIAL LAW AND THE "SECULARIZATION" OF THE *LUDI*

For Roman aristocrats, the games remained an essential weapon in the battle for honor and prestige. Indeed, this contest may have only become more consequential and more perilous in late antiquity. In the absence of emperors, who typically resided elswhere, the senatorial aristocracy and other elites became more powerful than they had been for centuries – at least in the city itself – while their overriding obsession with status, regardless of religious affiliation, was as intense as ever.[49] Their political *cursus* was largely confined to offices in the city, Italy, and nearby provinces, culminating in the urban praetorship of Rome. Even so, aristocratic influence far outstripped the constitutional role of the senate or the offices held by its members.[50] Much of this power and influence was the result of immense fortunes, stemming from far-flung landholdings throughout the empire.[51] This vast wealth allowed "the senate – the better part of the human race," according to Symmachus – to patronize a lavish calendar of games and spectacles, preserving the Roman heritage industry upon which aristocratic distinction was in part based.[52]

The public games continued to attract large crowds of all stripes, offering an unparalleled opportunity for public display and patronage.[53] As a result, its profligate patronage of traditional *ludi* allowed the Roman aristocracy to convert some of its economic wealth into symbolic capital.[54] In 401 CE, Symmachus, a well-known adherent of Rome's traditional religions, shelled out an incredible 2,000 lbs. of gold on the praetorian games of his son – in addition to the arduous labors that he invested in the production of the games, which needed to surpass those that he had organized for his son's quaestorship. A short while later, in 415 CE, the games that the Christian senator Maximus arranged for his son (probably the future consul and emperor Petronius Maximus) cost *double*, upwards of 4,000 lbs. of gold – an amount equal to the yearly cash incomes of the richest senators.[55] Such extreme expenditures were part of the alchemy by which mere wealth was transformed into honor and glory. As Apronianus Asterius, consul 494 CE, rather openly put it in a poem he wrote in a manuscript of Vergil:

> I provided banners in the Circus and erected a temporary stage on the *euripus*, so that Rome might rejoice and hold games, races, and different sorts of wild beast shows. Three times did I earn cheers, three times the people sang out my praises in the theater. My fortune vanished into my fame, for such losses bear the fruit of glory. Thus do the games preserve the expenditure of my riches, and the single day that saw three spectacles

> will last, and hand on to Asterius to a lively future, Asterius who spent the wealth he had won on his consulship.[56]

As long as consuls continued to be named, aristocratic traditions of munificence would maintain classical spectacle.[57] Indeed, the last (non-imperial) consular appointment in 541 CE nearly coincides with the last known senatorial inscriptions (ca. 521 CE) and *venationes* (523 CE) in the Colosseum, as well as the last known games in the Circus Maximus, seemingly given by the Ostrogothic king Totila in 549 CE.[58] The on-going provision of games served to assert traditional values – sheer willingness and public visibility – and ended when the aristocrats who fashioned their distinction through those traditions disappeared, seemingly a casualty of Justinian's "re-conquest" of Italy. Coincidentally, Procopius unduly accused Justinian of causing the closure of theaters, hippodromes, and wild beast shows – procopius was not entirely wrong, at least as far as the city of Rome was concerned.[59]

If "sheer willingness" was lacking, the emperors attempted to ensure that the games would go on. Not every aristocrat could afford the contest for civic glory and so in the mid fourth century CE, elites "were compelled to come to the city of Rome with the funds which are demanded for the production of theatrical performances, the games of the circus" – a law which seems to have been at least partially rescinded in the early fifth century CE.[60] Those who failed to fulfill their spectacle duties would face penalties – even though emperors and also elites like Symmachus were concerned that the Roman aristocracy plan for and moderate its ludic expenditures for fear of bankruptcy.[61] So eager were emperors to ensure a steady program of public spectacle that in the late fourth century CE even *sacerdotales*, civic priests both "pagan" and Christian, were allowed to return to Carthage to preside over games at their own discretion. Though permitted to preside over games at Carthage, these *sacerdotales* were not to linger for long after the opening procession, a synecdoche for the games themselves: "whoever will have come to Carthage for the procession [or for the general pomp (*pompa*)] of that day will depart from the city within five days to return to their own homes."[62] After all, the emperors also wanted to ensure that each municipality continued to enjoy its traditional festivities as well.[63]

Imperial rule still depended, at least in part, on the proverbial bread and circuses, as the association between the games and imperial victoriousness also attests.[64] The Roman people demanded games and good emperors gave them. As Symmachus recounted in *Relatio* 6 (384 CE), in which he prodded the emperors to deliver on their promise of shows and games, the riotous Roman people "regard [the spectacles] as owed. . . . And so [the Roman people] beg your Clemencies, after granting those subsidies which your generosity has made towards our sustenance, should furnish also the enjoyment (*voluptates*) of chariot races and dramatic performances to be held in the Circus and Pompey's theater."[65] The late-fourth-century CE *Historia Augusta* often praised past emperors for offering games even *in absentia*, seemingly in the hopes of motivating contemporary rulers: Marcus Aurelius "while absent from Rome left forceful instruction that the amusements (*voluptates*) for the Roman people should be provided for by the richest *editores*"; likewise Septimius Severus, "though away [from Rome], gave games."[66] Theodoric the Ostrogothic king of Italy, whose capital was Ravenna, was later praised as a second Trajan or even a Valentinian "for giving games in the Circus and amphitheater."[67] For good reason, it seems, Ammianus Marcellinus contemptuously named the "Circus Maximus, the temple" of "the idle and indolent plebs."[68]

In fact, inhabitants of Rome and Carthage seem to have been especially infected by a fever for spectacles. Augustine complained that a theater mania "shrouded the minds of those poor wretches in such darkness, and defiled them so foully that even now that the city of Rome was laid waste [during the sack of 410 CE], those in the grip of that plague who managed to reach Carthage as refugees were at the theaters each day, raving for the performers."[69] Not long afterwards Quodvultdeus, bishop of Carthage, expressed unqualified disgust that "the spectacles are frequented daily: daily the blood of men is poured on the ground, and the voices of the mad clatter in the circus," even though the Vandals were on the verge of taking the city in 439 CE.[70] Shortly after the fall of Carthage, Salvian in Gaul echoed that horror: "The barbarian peoples were sounding their arms around the wall of Cirta and Carthage and the church of Carthage still went mad in the circuses and reveled in the theaters."[71] Unsurprisingly, the games continued under the Vandals, who had learned a few lessons in Roman statecraft.[72] Augustine, Quodvultdeus, and Salvian each had rhetorical targets in mind, nonetheless there seems to have been a widespread passion for the games. As a result, no emperor could dispense with the games, nor would he want to toss them aside.

In short, despite the relentless assault of Christian rhetoric against the mindless, bloodthirsty spectacles, the games ever remained an especially important stage for the performance of civic and imperial politics.[73] Christian criticisms had about as much impact as their classical, largely philosophical, predecessors: not much.[74] This is not to say that such invective had no effect. After Constantine, when Christian emperor followed Christian emperor, with the notable exception of the short-lived Julian (361–363 CE), Christianity first became a recognized and licit religious practice, then the favorite of the imperial house, and eventually the "official" religion of empire. As a result, Christian authorities, in particular bishops, were positioned to exercise a degree of influence over the emperors, which means that Christian criticisms of the *ludi* gained some force, but only some.[75] In effect, the emperors were caught in a double bind. On the one hand, as Christians, the emperors felt compelled to acknowledge, if not exactly to obey, the dictates of Christian opinion makers. On the other hand, Christian emperors and the aristocracy, whether "pagan" or Christian, deeply coveted the stage that the games offered. In order both to appease critics and to allow the games to continue, a two-pronged imperial strategy developed: to modify in modest ways the practice of the games, and at the same time to re-interpret them. In the first place, the practice of the games was seemingly "de-sacralized" with the prohibition of sacrifice, blood sacrifice in particular, the very emblem of "pagan superstition," as well as image devotion – even as "pagan" holidays were demoted concomitantly with the elevation of Christian ones.[76] Secondly, the games were re-interpreted, re-framed as both purely secular entertainments and venerable Roman custom.[77]

Throughout late antiquity, emperors repeatedly issued laws condemning sacrifice, which simultaneously reveals the limits of law (its jurisdictional and practical limitations), as well as the imperial desire to set the boundaries of the acceptable.[78] In 341 CE, Constantius II (or rather his quaestor, legal writer) shrieked "superstition shall cease; the madness of sacrifices shall be abolished."[79] This law, though it claimed a no-longer-extant Constantinian precedent, was the first in a series of laws targeting sacrifice – a series which continued into the mid sixth century CE.[80] The cultic traditions of sacrifice, which apparently offended imperial, Christian sensibilities, were now labeled superstition – a normative term whose definition, however, shifted according to individual perspective. That is to say, superstition would not necessarily signal the same kinds of practices or attitudes to a so-called "pagan" and a Christian.[81] Image devotion faced a similar ban. In 356 CE, Constantius II insisted that all those who should "devote their attention to sacrifices or to worship images" would be subject to capital punishment.[82] This law, too, stood at the head of a long procession of similar laws that subjected image devotion to various legal restrictions.[83]

Once sacrifice and image devotion were outlawed, on the page at least, then even divine images in a temple could "be measured by the value of their art rather than by their divinity."[84] According to same legal logic, the proscription of offensive practices neutralized public celebrations – the banning of sacrifice and image cult ostensibly rendered the games religiously innocuous.[85] In 399 CE, festal assemblies and banquets could continue, "but without any sacrifice or any accursed superstition."[86] An earlier law of Constantius II made clear that without "superstition," here studiously ill-defined, some temples at Rome and their related games were harmless:

> Although all superstitions must be completely eradicated, nevertheless, it is Our will that the buildings of temples situated outside the walls shall remain untouched and uninjured ... since the origin of games or circus shows or contests sprung from some of these temples.[87]

This stream of prohibitions against sacrifice, image worship, and superstition more generally may be connected to the demotion of "the ceremonial days of pagan superstition" which lost their status as legal holidays in the late fourth century CE.[88] A comparison of the chronograph of 354 CE with the calendar of Polemius Silvius about a century later (448/449 CE) suggests that this law (and other factors) did indeed undermine the traditional religious roots of the games – some the *ludi* seem have been stripped of their religious associations, the *ludi Megalesiaci* and *ludi Cerealici*, for example, became simply *ludi*, though other "pagan" festivals, like the Lupercalia, remained.[89]

In conjunction with the legal rhetoric and, eventually, the practice of desacralization or "secularization" of the games, a series of laws progressively limited the days on which games could be held. In particular, Christian holidays, like Sunday, were protected from games to give Christian celebrations a monopoly on the public's attention, so that they would not have to compete with the arena or theater. In 392 CE, Valentinian II, Theodosius, and Arcadius declared that "contests in the circuses shall be prohibited on the festal days of the sun [Sundays], *except* on the birthdays of our Clemency, in order that no concourse of the people to the spectacles may divert men from the reverend mysteries of the Christian law."[90] In 399 CE, a similar ruling was issued, which repeated the exemption for shows in honor of an imperial *natalis*.[91] Shortly thereafter, additional Christian holidays were given monopoly protection. In 405 CE, "out of respect for religion We provide and decree that on the seven days of Quadragesima and on the seven paschal days . . . and also on the birthday [Christmas?] and on Epiphany spectacles shall not be produced."[92] Four years later, in 409 CE, the Sunday exemption for games in honor of imperial anniversaries was eliminated.[93] In 469 CE, the complete monopoly of the Lord's Day in the civic calendar was reconfirmed: "On this religious day, We permit no one to be detained by obscene pleasures. Let no theater show or circus contest or sad spectacle of wild beasts claim that day for themselves. Even if the solemn celebration should fall on our imperial anniversary or birthday, [the imperial celebration] should be postponed."[94]

As a further measure to inoculate the games from Christian criticism, late-antique imperial laws repeatedly referred to them as silly amusements, about which one need hardly fuss, or even as long-standing custom, hallowed by antiquity.[95] *Voluptates*, however, had long served as a (somewhat) derogatory or at least a condescending synonym for the games or spectacles.[96] After the death of Germanicus, Tacitus had Tiberius cynically urge the people of Rome to "revert to their usual formalities and, because the spectacle of the Megalesian games was approaching, resume even their pleasures."[97] Despite his encouragement at that time, Tiberius was seemingly a bit stingy with spectacles. Again according to Tacitus, "hungry for entertainment, people streamed in [to an amphitheater near Fidenae], having been kept far from their pleasures during the command of Tiberius," which intensified the tragedy when the poorly built amphitheater collapsed.[98] Later in the second century CE, Apuleius fulsomely lampooned the "public pleasures," gladiatorial combats in this case, provided by Demochares, "People-Pleaser."[99]

This usage seems, in fact, to have been widespread. An early imperial patron from Aquileia was honored for his production of pleasures for the people; a mid imperial local notable from Praeneste was granted an honorific statue for the pleasures (including gladiatorial games) that he gave to the people; in 214 CE Gabinia Hermiona was commemorated for her civic benefactions including "a field which is called a circus for the pleasure of the people [that] she remitted to the city (*res publica*)" of Dougga in Africa Proconsularis; and in the early third century CE, L. Caecilius, a Roman equite also from Africa Proconsularis, was honored for the unspecified pleasures that he had provided.[100] Also in the early third century CE, Tertullian could refer to the rigors of a true Christian life, as he militantly envisioned it, as "these pleasures, these spectacles," which he then compared to circus games, while Minucius Felix had his "pagan" interlocutor Caecilius accuse Christians of denying themselves "respectable pleasures," meaning processions, games, and spectacles.[101] A rescript issued by Diocletian and Maximian promised the restoration of the pleasure of the games, while the late-fourth-century CE *Historia Augusta* repeatedly referred to games, shows, and spectacles as pleasures.[102]

In short, the Christian emperors of late antiquity and their legal staffs did not invent the rhetoric of games, shows, and spectacles as pleasures or amusements, but they did employ the trope rather extensively. After all, it suited their purposes very well. In the law of 342 CE, Constantius II declared that extramural temples freed from superstition "shall remain untouched and uninjured. . . . Since from them is provided the regular performance of long established amusements (*priscarum sollemnitas voluptatum*) for the Roman people."[103] And so, this one law presents the complete logic of the late imperial re-interpretation of the games: the elimination of superstition (ostensibly meaning sacrifices and image devotion, but left undefined) and the re-framing of the games as simple, traditional pleasures. As with Constantius II's rulings against sacrifice and image worship, this law too heads a long line of legislation that characterized public games, shows, and spectacles of all sorts as pleasures and/or as customary – indeed the antiquity of the games had long been used to defend them.[104] The diversion of "horses for the customary contests" from public "amusements" was prohibited.[105] If the people of Campania wanted "horses for amusements," they would need to contribute "the necessary, ancient, and customary payment" for the games at Rome.[106] The emperors expected the *iudices* at Rome to be "present at the festivities of the shows, as is the custom, and elicit the favor of the people by delights."[107]

In what amounts to another, more succinct and precise, summary of the legal logic concerning the games, in 399 CE Arcadius and Honorius decreed that "according to ancient custom, amusements shall be furnished to the people, but without any sacrifice or any accursed superstition."[108]

By 414 CE, a *tribunus voluptatum*, a "tribune of amusements," had been created for the city of Rome, most likely, and charged with the *ludi scaenici*, particularly the supervision of its performers.[109] This office also had early imperial precursors, perhaps most notoriously Tiberius' "post with the responsibility for pleasures," though there were also other (real) officials with similar titles charged with various aspects of the games.[110] What is more, two (of the six known) *tribuni voluptatum* were buried in churches in Rome in the early sixth century CE: one in S. Pietro, the other in S. Lorenzo *fuori le mura*. It would seem that the rhetoric of amusements or pleasures readily accommodated a Christian sensibility, even if some Christian preachers saw through the supposed subterfuge.[111]

Stripped of sacrifices and shorn of image devotion (though not necessarily the images themselves) by law, the *ludi circenses*, and all types of games, shows, and spectacles, were re-interpreted, at least rhetorically if not also in practice, as the neutral, not to say secular, and customary amusements of the people. Even so, to avoid the ire of ecclesiastical firebrands, the emperors also forbade games on many Christians holidays, including all days of the sun, Sundays – even games in honor of imperial anniversaries would be postponed. By such devices, emperors and elites, whether "pagan" or Christian, could continue to provide an astonishing array of games and shows, all still introduced, it seems, by a ludic procession of some sort. However, if an analysis of the late-republican and imperial *pompa circensis* must be written in the "historical subjective" – hedged with may, might, seems, apparently – a study of the late-antique *pompa circensis* can hardly be written at all. Without much textual evidence, the late-antique *pompa circensis* often emerges from inference, comparison, and even informed speculation. Still, nestled within the extended process by which the games were re-imagined as traditional "secular" pleasures, the increasingly exiguous evidence for the late-antique circus procession at Rome affords, at least, a plausible account.[112]

III EMPERORS AND VICTORY: THE *POMPA CIRCENSIS* IN LATE ANTIQUITY

In his panegyric on the fourth consulship of Honorius, Claudian declared that "triumph always attends your consulship and victory your *fasces*."[113] This association between triumph, victory, and the consulship seems to have also found expression in the ritual procession that opened the consular games – at least in many of its official commemorations. The conjunction of the emperor as consular game-giver, Victory, and public spectacle was strikingly represented

59. Elephant *quadriga* with consular Maxentius: follis, 308–310 CE: obverse: IMP C MAXENTIUS P F AVG and reverse: FEL PROCES CONS III AVG N

on a series of coins minted under Maxentius (306–312 CE) to commemorate the joys of his consulship – FEL[IX] PROCESS[VS] CONSVLAT[VS]. On the reverses, the emperor is either shown on foot in recollection of his consular procession (*processus consularis*) or on a chariot in remembrance of the *pompa circensis* performed before his consular games – a *quadriga*, a six-horse chariot, or even more spectacularly an elephant *quadriga* above which, in the numismatic imagination, a Victory flies to crown the imperial consul (Figure 59).[114] Unsurprisingly, the late-imperial consular *pompa circensis* and the late-imperial *processus consularis* took on triumphal overtones – indeed a number of actual triumphs took place on January 1 and all three processions shared some of the carnivalesque atmosphere and pageantry of a New Year's festival.[115]

Even though Constantinian propaganda portrayed the defeat of Maxentius at the Milvian bridge as the liberation of Rome from an evil tyrant, nonetheless Constantinian numismatic imagery followed in Maxentius' footsteps.[116] Constantine had minted coins on which he and Constantius II drive an elephant *quadriga* accompanied by lictors under the auspices of the eternal glory of the senate and the Roman people (AETERNA GLORIA SENAT[VS] PQR); while on another version Victory replaces Constantius on the elephant *quadriga* and crowns a triumphant Constantine (Figure 60).[117] Indeed, this imagery, an elephant *quadriga* on which stood an emperor to represent or commemorate what appears to be a *pompa circensis* before the consular games, seems to have been a tetrarchic innovation. Diocletian and Maximian, crowned by Victory, appear together on an elephant *quadriga* accompanied by lictors on a medallion to commemorate Diocletian's third and Maximian's first consulships in 287 CE – even though they did *not* in fact lead a *pompa circensis* together (Figure 61).[118] *Currus elephantorum* carry deified emperors on early imperial coinage, but by the late third century CE living

60. Elephant *quadriga* with consular Constantine and Constantius: gold medallion, 326 CE: obverse: FL IVL CONSTANTIVS NOB C and reverse: AETERNA GLORIA SENAT PQR

emperors driving elephant *quadrigae* replace the *divi* – a shift in the representation or remembrance of the *pompa circensis* from the gods to the game-giver.

61. Elephant *quadriga* with consular Diocletian and Maximian crowned by Victory: gold medallion, 287 CE: reverse: IMPP DIOCLETIANO III ET MAXIMIANO CCSS

This shift, however, has its roots in the late first century CE, when images of the processional vehicles of the traditional and especially imperial gods still flourished.[119] Representations of a consular emperor (signaled by legend, attire, and/or paraphernalia) in a horse *quadriga* were first coined, it seems, early in the reign of Vespasian, when he appears in a *quadriga* with both Titus and Domitian, whose heads just top the peak of the chariot – some with the legend COS (consul) and TR POT (tribunician power) on the reverse (Figure 62).[120] Given the need to appear as legitimate heirs of the Augustan principate and to repudiate Neronian excesses, an emphasis on traditional republican office combined with lavish public patronage was simply savvy politics. Coins showing a consular Vespasian standing alone on a *quadriga* were also minted, as were similar images of Titus and Domitian (Figure 63).[121] To celebrate his fourteenth to seventeenth consulships, Domitian, as emperor, issued a series of similar coin types, on which he drives a *quadriga* decorated with Victory, connecting consular authority, public munificence, and triumphal associations.[122]

This type of consular imagery continued into the second century CE, even as imagery of the *divi* in the *pompa circensis* multiplied. For example, several of Trajan's consulships were commemorated with an image of the emperor

62. *Quadriga* with consular Vespasian and Caesars: denarius, 69–71 CE: obverse: IMP CAESAR VESPASIANVS AVG and reverse: IMP

63. *Quadriga* with consular Vespasian: aureus, 72–73 CE

driving a *quadriga*, whose sides are often decorated by Victory erecting a trophy.[123] In 140 CE, Antoninus Pius and his two heirs, Marcus Aurelius and Lucius Verus, drive a *quadriga* under a legend commemorating his third consulship (COS III) (Figure 64).[124] Also during the reign of Antoninus Pius, similar coin-types celebrated the consular games of Marcus Aurelius.[125] As emperors, Marcus Aurelius and Lucius Verus together or Lucius Verus alone were commemorated in a like manner.[126] Marcus Aurelius then honored Commodus in 176 CE with comparable imagery – first father and son together and then Commodus by himself.[127] Commodus continued the pattern as sole emperor, minting analogous coins of himself, sometimes with Victory offering him a crown, adding another "triumphal" element to the spectacle.[128]

Coin imagery picturing the emperor crowned or accompanied by a Victory proliferated during the third century CE, when the traditional forms of Roman imperial cult were disrupted. It seems that hard-pressed emperors seeking legitimacy could no longer count on the deification of their predecessors to assert their (dynastic) authority. Instead, emperors increasingly turned to an older "republican" model of authority, by presenting themselves as consular game-givers following Flavian precedent. In 204 CE, Caracalla was first represented alone on a *quadriga* – while Septimius Severus was still alive – but after the death of his father and the murder of his brother Geta, Caracalla was shown crowned by Victory who now stood with him in the *quadriga* (Figure 65).[129] Several other

64. *Quadriga* with consular Antoninus Pius and Caesars: aureus, 140–144 CE: obverse: ANTONINVS AVG PIVS P P and reverse: COS III TR POT

65. *Quadriga* with consular Caracalla crowned by Victory: sestertius, 213 CE: obverse: M AVREL ANTONINVS PIVS AVG BRIT and reverse: P M TR P XVI IMP II COS IIII P P SC

members of the Severan dynasty were also shown on coins or medallions honoring their consular games, including the unfortunate Geta, but also Macrinus, Elagabalus, and Severus Alexander, one of whose coin-types has soldiers acting as grooms – a martial escort that would become more common in such scenes.[130]

After the Severans and throughout the so-called third-century crisis, emperors deployed the imagery of the consular *pompa circensis* to buttress their tenuous authority, including the first of the "soldier-emperors," Maximinus I Thrax.[131] Gordian III minted similar coins for his second consulship in 241 CE – and one of his more striking medallions may depict him leading the *pompa circensis* (or perhaps a "triumph") in the Circus itself. In front of the *euripus* with its flanking *metae* and towering obelisk, six athletes (boxers and gladiators or soldiers) occupy the foreground; a hybrid chariot race comprised of a *biga* and a *quadriga* runs behind the barrier; while lictors lead the emperor's six-horse chariot in the far back

66. Circus scene with Gordian III in procession: copper alloy medallion, 244 CE: obverse: IMP GORDIANVS PIVS FELIX AVG and reverse: P M TR P VII COS II P P

plane – a fair summary of both the *pompa* and *ludi* (Figure 66).[132] Philip the Arab, crowned by Victory and accompanied by soldiers, and his son appear together in 248 CE; Trebonius Gallus and Volusian in 252 CE as well as Gallienus (both as joint ruler with his father Valerian and later on his own), Carinus, Numerian, and Postumus also appear in a like manner.[133] Under the legend GLORIA ORBIS COS IIII (and later V), Probus appears on a six-horse chariot with Victory holding a crown, while Mars and Virtus (or possibly soldiers or lictors) hold the reigns and four palm bearers walk behind. Probus also seems to have made a less dramatic entrance on a simple *quadriga* accompanied by Victory and led by soldiers.[134] After Probus, tetrarchic imagery memorably represents Diocletian and Maximian "virtually" leading a *pompa circensis* driving an elephant *quadriga* – seemingly the first image of its kind.

Under Constantine, however, the imagery of the imperial, consular game-giver added one more variation to the repertoire. Several coin types from Constantinople and Nicomedia depict Constantine, Constantius II, or Constans standing in a horse *quadriga* holding a scepter in his left hand, while scattering coins with his right, a representation of the *sparsio*, a distribution of largesse, during the consular *pompa circensis* (Figure 67).[135] This particular consular-*sparsio* procession image under the legend *Gloria Romanorum* was regularly re-used during the fourth century CE: by Constantius II in 346 CE, Valentinian I, Valentinian II, and even the "usurper" Eugenius in 393 CE.[136]

At the end of the fourth century CE, the image of an emperor (or emperors) in a *quadriga* seems to have faded, only to be replaced by another visual commemoration of the imperially sponsored consular games – namely, an emperor seated on a curule chair holding a *mappa*, ready to signal the start of the first race. This shift in representation may reflect the ceremonial habits of the new Rome, Constantinople, where the hippodrome was directly connected to the imperial palace, which allowed emperors to appear almost epiphanically at the racetrack,

67. *Quadriga* with consular Constantius II distributing coins (*sparsio*): gold medallion, 335 CE: obverse: DN CONSTAN-TIUS NOB CAES

68. Diocletian holding a *mappa*: silver AES, ca. 305: obverse: D N DIOCLETIANO BAEATISSIMO SEN AVG and reverse: PROVIDENTIA DEORVM QVIES AVGG

obviating the import of other "preliminary" rituals. *Mappa* imagery, however, appears to have emerged sometime after Caracalla's renovation of the *carceres* in the early third century CE when a loge for the *praeses ludorum* over the starting gates is first attested (for example, Figure 43).[137] After the late third century CE, it would become common to see an emperor dressed in consular robes holding a *mappa* on the obverse of coin-types, as seen in an early example under Diocletian, who holds an olive branch in his right hand and a *mappa* in his left (Figure 68).[138] Similar numismatic imagery (and, subsequently, analogous representations on ivory consular diptychs) exploded after Diocletian, eventually becoming synonymous with the games.[139]

In 537 CE, this synthesis of ritual and symbolism (procession, races, *mappa*, and *sparsio*) was nicely summarized by Justinian's *Novella* 105, promulgated shortly before the last known circus games in Rome. According to *Novella* 105, consuls might distribute silver – the emperor Marjorian had previously abolished the *sparsio*, though earlier laws had allowed ordinary consuls to give golden gifts – during their seven processions or public appearances (ἡ πρόοδος/*processus*) and the accompanying shows and games. The first *processus* was the consular *processus*, the inauguration ceremony which at Rome traditionally included a procession to the Capitol on January 1, while the second and sixth *processus* were horse races, spectacles now dubbed μάππα/*mappa*, which suggests a procession to or a public appearance at the racetrack where the consul would drop a *mappa* to start the races. And so, if a consular *processus* at the hippodrome took place in the new Rome, perhaps some kind of circus procession survived in the old one. The chariot races may have been an utter and wanton waste of resources, according to Christian critics, but at least they were not as blatantly immoral as theater shows, like "Harlots," though both types of *ludi*, perhaps along with their *pompae*, may have survived at Rome until the mid sixth century CE.[140]

69. Theodosius II and Valentinian III enthroned and holding cruciform scepters and *mappae*: solidus, 425–429 CE: reverse: SALUS REI PUBLICAE

All together, the scant and ambiguous evidence intimates that some sort of traditional Roman pageantry continued to precede the games into the sixth century CE. However, in the early to mid fifth century CE, there was another transformation of circus imagery and so possibly one further alteration of the *pompa circensis*. In 425 CE, when Valentinian III acceded to the throne, Theodosius II minted several coin types showing the two emperors in consular robes, holding *mappae* and a cruciform scepters (Figure 69).[141] In 430 CE and several times thereafter, Valentinian III had a coin minted in Rome (or Ravenna) showing him alone in consular robes holding a *mappa* and a cruciform scepter (Figure 70).[142] If these coins represent symbols that the emperor carried during a *pompa circensis*, then it would seem that something like *exuviae* of Christ, the cross, had made its way into the procession, transforming the *pompa deorum* (procession of the gods) into a *pompa Dei* (procession of God). If circus games could be offered to Christ – much to Salvian's horror: "O monstrous madness!" – then Christian symbols (*exuviae*) could plausibly appear in a circus procession. The Christian God, made present by Christian symbols, might have been escorted to the Circus with all due pomp. This particular conjunction of symbols (*mappa* and cruciform scepter) and so also a possible *pompa Dei* proved persistent in the western Mediterranean until the early sixth century CE, when the last consul, Anicius Faustus Albinus Basilius, appeared on his consular diptych with a cross tipped scepter in his left and a *mappa* in his right (Figure 74).[143]

70. Valentinian III holding a *mappa* and cruciform scepter: solidus, 435 CE: obverse: D N PLA VALENTI-NIANVS P F AVG and reverse: VOT X – MVLT XX

This shift from the gods (both traditional and imperial) to the emperor and Victory and eventually Christian symbolism might not have been mere representation. It might also have reflected (or even inspired) changes in performance practices. However, given the scarcity of textual evidence for the late-antique *pompa circensis*, that hypothesis must remain hypothetical. According to John Malalas, writing in the mid sixth century CE, during the inaugural circus games of Constantinople in 330 CE, Constantine staged a kind of *pompa circensis*.

> He had another statue made of himself in gilded wood, bearing in its right hand the Tyche of the city, itself gilded, which he called Anthousa. He ordered that on the same day as the anniversary race-meeting this wooden statue should be brought in, escorted by soldiers wearing cloaks and boots, all holding candles; the carriage should march around the turning post and reach the pit opposite the imperial *kathisma* [something like a *pulvinar*], and the emperor of the time should rise and make obeisance as he gazed at this statue of Constantine and the Tyche of the city.[144]

The ceremony is obviously a species of the *pompa circensis*, in which a gilded statue of Constantine holding the Tyche of Constantinople (or possibly a Victory) stood on a chariot accompanied by an entourage of soldiers seems to have constituted the entire procession. Like Julius Caesar nearly four centuries earlier, Constantine placed his own statue in a *pompa circensis*. However, unlike the statue of Caesar, whose presence among the gods repelled certain Roman religious sensibilities, the statue of Constantine seems to have wholly replaced the gods – both traditional and imperial. Moreover, Constantine's statue was to be greeted with reverence (worship one might say), rather than stony silence, by subsequent emperors, who seem to have enjoyed the dynastic linkages afforded by an "imperialized" and/or "secularized" *pompa circensis*. It seems that Constantine, like Augustus, enjoyed an extended ceremonial afterlife.[145] Notably, the possible excision of the traditional gods by the first Christian emperor took place at Constantinople, where emperors did not have to contend with a powerful aristocracy jealous of its traditions.[146]

Even at Rome, however, a similar process might well have occurred, at least in some iterations. In 384 CE, Symmachus, during his tenure as urban prefect, wrote to thank the emperors for their lavish provision of games, before which "a *pompa* led royal elephants through packed herds of noble horses," which suggests that deified emperors were still conducted on elephants carts. It also suggests that the young men on horseback, competitors with their horses, or perhaps even *tensae* drawn by specially chosen horses, once considered sacred to Apollo, still appeared in the procession.[147] If the *pompa deorum* had been reduced to a *pompa Constantini* or, more broadly, a *pompa divorum* at Constantinople, it is possible that something similar occurred at imperially sponsored games at Rome, in accordance with late-imperial law and contemporary coinage. Yet, it is also possible, that the *tensae* were still conducted.

The continuing presence of imperial imagery (and seemingly also imperial gods) in the circus (and, probably, also the circus procession) was enshrined in a law in 425 CE. The law insists that whenever imperial statues were displayed in the circus "they shall demonstrate that Our divinity and glory live only in the hearts and secret places of the minds of those who attend. A worship in excess of human dignity shall be reserved for the Supernal Divinity."[148] Unsurprisingly, imperial statues were to be displayed at the games – such visibility remained an important component of imperial authority – but they were not to be worshipped or (mis-)taken for gods. Law, however, would have had a limited effect on such practices (acclamation, veneration, and worship can be hard to distinguish), not to mention attitudes. And so, some seem to have maintained an imperial cult as a way to relate to imperial power. After all, an emperor, Christian or otherwise, was still powerful, god-like. All told, the very limited evidence suggests that imperial game-givers or presidents of imperial games led a pared down *pompa circensis* comprised of an escort of soldiers and statues of the reigning emperor as well as the *divi*, which were subsequently installed in the circus – perhaps in the *pulvinar*.

That is, the circus procession could still be used as a stage for imperial public display, once its traditional cult religiosity was neutralized, as imperial law demanded. Though seemingly dominated by the emperors, some of the traditional ceremonial apparatus would have endured – in particular, the contestants or performers at the games, like Augustine's parading prostitutes, or Victory, who regularly appeared in numismatic representations of the imperial consular games.[149] In fact, four extant circus programs from Egypt dating from the late fifth to the sixth century CE suggest that a parade of religiously innocuous Victory or Victories was the entire procession. All four programs open with what seems to be an invocation of good fortune, followed by (a display of) Victory/Victories – or perhaps acclamations along the lines of "go team" (*Nika*!) – after which the programs diverge slightly.[150] Two of the programs have a procession directly following Victory, which may indicate that a statue of Victory was processed (P. Oxy. 79.5215 and P. Harrauer 56). The other two programs put the first race immediately after Victory, while the procession comes third (P. Oxy. 34.2707 and P. Bingen 128). A procession remained on the program in late-antique Egypt, but it seems to have been demoted. No longer a pious procession to introduce the games, the *pompa circensis* was apparently a secondary spectacle like rope-dancers or mimes. It may also have been reduced to a procession of Victories, though one may suppose that local dignitaries, competitors/performers (for example, charioteers, athletes, rope-dancers, and mimes), and imperial representations would have been included.[151] Something broadly similar may have held for Rome also: a procession consisting of, for the most part, the sponsor carrying, eventually perhaps, Christian symbols; competitors and performers; Victory, whose statue may have remained in the senate house even after her altar was removed and whose statues also stood on columns in the Circus itself; and representations of both the reigning emperor and the imperial special dead.[152]

IV THE SUB-IMPERIAL *POMPA CIRCENSIS* IN LATE ANTIQUITY

Imperial representations of the *pompa circensis* increasingly focused on the consular *praeses ludorum* in a *quadriga*, a vehicle once reserved for the triumph, while the procession seems to have constricted to a parade of Victory and imperial images with some of the traditional cortege still included. This shift in representation (if not also performance) was echoed at sub-imperial levels. The so-called Maffei relief, which prominently features a *praeses ludorum* and an attendant holding a crown on a *biga* heading toward the eager circus crowds, may well stand at the head of a late-antique stream of sub-imperial imagery that emphasizes the game-giver. This relief, in turn, seems to draw upon republican cultural memory resources (upon which imperial imagery also drew), which had seemingly languished like an eddy in "the stream of tradition"– for example, the first-century BCE travertine reliefs with, possibly, the game-giver among the four *togati* in the second fragment (Figures 5 and 41).[153]

After his tenure as ordinary consul in 331 CE, Junius Bassus commissioned a scene drawn from both imperial and republican streams of tradition to decorate his domestic basilica. In a magnificent polychrome mosaic, Bassus memorialized what seems to have been a peak moment of his political career when he led a *pompa circensis* in a *biga* – *quadrigae* were reserved for emperors – dressed in *toga picta* with an entourage of four horsemen dressed in circus faction colors and holding elongated basket-like instruments (see cover image).[154]

A (non-imperial) consular *praeses ludorum* driving a *biga* in a procession surrounded by figures symbolic of the circus games recalls the republican competition for honor and glory, while the striking frontality of the image with Junius Bassus leading the procession right at the viewer evokes tetrarchic or Constantinian numismatic imagery (Figures 60–61 and 67). Indeed, other scenes from this mosaic, now lost and known only from drawings, also seem to follow the imperial model – a *sparsio*, for example.[155] As a sign of the times, perhaps, Junius Bassus also chose representatives of the circus factions to serve as his entourage. Young equestrians may have once performed that role, but the equestrian class was seemingly in a slow decline after Constantine's expansion of the senate, while the circus factions attained heightened visibility and enlarged ceremonial roles in late antiquity.[156]

"Consular" diptychs similarly show the impact of late imperial trends. On these prestige gifts – commissioned by consuls to commemorate their achievement and seemingly intended as gifts to friends, associates, political allies, and even emperors – a depiction of the honorand seated holding a *mappa* in his right hand was very common.[157] An early, possibly the earliest, western example shows either Postumius Lampadius (suffect consul 396 CE), most likely, or Rufius Caecina Felix Lampadius (suffect consul 426 CE) holding a *mappa* in his right hand, while sitting majestically in the loge above the *carceres*, presiding over chariot races which appear in a vivid scene in the lower register (Figure 71).[158] The other candidate for the earliest western consular ivory, to judge from a mold of a now lost diptych from 408 CE of ordinary consul Anicius Auchenius Bassus, also shows the honorand holding the *mappa* in his right hand and a scepter with imperial portrait busts in his left, if that is one reverses the mold (Figure 72).[159]

In a late western example, Rufius Gennadius Probus Orestes, consul in 530 CE, sits in the central register flanked by Roma and Constantinopolis, holding a *mappa*, while diminutive figures play out a *sparsio* scene below. More importantly, a cross appears prominently in the upper register, a first for western diptychs, though Probus (consul 406 CE) held a standard surmounted by a chi-rho with a Christian slogan on the banner. Though the cross simply floats at the top, it may reflect, like the numismatic imagery of Theodosius II and Valentinian III, the eventual Christianization of circus ceremonial by the inclusion of Christian symbols (Figure 73).[160] The diptych of the last (non-imperial) consul, Anicius Faustus Albinus Basilius, in 541 CE more compelling evokes the Christianization of the *pompa circensis*. Basilius clutches a *mappa* in his right hand as he stands next to Roma and a crossed-tipped scepter in his left, while a chariot race unfolds below (Figure 74). With this scepter in hand, Basilius, who held his consulship at Rome, just might have led a circus procession.[161]

The *mappa* also appeared in other media. Two full-size marble statues (speculatively Symmachus and his son Memmius) from the late fourth or

71. "Consular" diptych of Lampadii, ivory, 396 or 426 CE

early fifth century CE, now in the Centrale Montemartini, dramatically capture the tense moment before the first race – their right arms raised, poised to throw the *mappa* (Figure 75).[162] In sum, such *mappa* imagery condensed the whole pomp and circumstance of the consular inauguration from the *processus* to the *pompa* to the *ludi*, for which reason it appealed to emperors and elites. Such imagery also transformed a fleeting moment of agonized anticipation – when the crowd, riveted to every movement of the sponsor, held its breath as it waited for the doors to open – into a fixed and enduring memorial.[163]

Though much sub-imperial imagery conformed to the norms of imperial representation, another type of semi-public, semi-private prestige gift also with a limited circulation – namely Roman "contorniate" medallions (souvenirs distributed at the games and on other occasions) – could but did not always diverge from imperial models. Following imperial precedent, a contorniate medallion of 433 CE shows the consul, and eventual emperor, Petronius Maximus, whose father, perhaps, paid 4,000 lbs. of gold for his praetorian

72. African Red Slipware mold of consular diptych of Anicius Auchenius Bassus, 408 CE

73. Consular diptych of Rufius Gennadius Probus Orestes, ivory, 530 CE

74. Consular diptych of Anicius Faustus Albinus Basilius, ivory, 541 CE

games, seated holding a *mappa* in his right hand and an eagle-tipped scepter in his left with sacks of money (possibly) in the exergue (Figure 76).[164] Another medallion – minted between 350 and 400 CE and perhaps commissioned by Asturius, the charioteer named in the legend, to commemorate a particularly successful set of races or perhaps a particularly successful career – seems to show an *auriga* (Asturius) led by a groom in a *pompa circensis* on the obverse, while the same charioteer, shown frontally, conducts a victory lap on the reverse (Figure 77).[165] Even though the sponsor of the games (whether emperor or aristocrat), like Petronius Maximus, dominated the spotlight, it seems that charioteers (and likely other sub-elite participants) similarly prized their participation in the circus parade, much as they seem to have cherished winning the first race *a pompa* (after the procession).[166]

What is more, honorific statues of victorious charioteers may also have been carried on *fercula* in subsequent circus processions, as a late-first or early-second-century CE terracotta "Campana" plaque picturing four *fercula*-bearers carrying a *biga* driven by an *auriga* (or a wingless Victory or Sol) suggests (Figure 78).[167] Along similar lines, a mid-fourth-century CE sarcophagus lid of unknown provenance seems to depict an *agitator* (or a soldier) carrying the banner of his faction (or his troop) leading a group of *ferculum*-bearers, whose load consists of a *quadriga*, whose driver, perhaps a charioteer (or again perhaps the god Sol), has unfortunately broken off. This sarcophagus

75. Two (paired) statues of an older and a younger *praeses ludorum* about to throw a *mappa*, marble, 375–400 CE

76. Contorniate medallion of consul Petronius Maximus: 433 CE: obverse: D N VALENTINIANVS P F AVG and reverse: PETRONIVS MAX-SIMUS V C CONS

lid, like the mosaic of Junius Bassus and the medallion of Asturius, may index the increasing prominence of racing professionals (factions and charioteers) in late antiquity and their continuing investment in circus ceremonial or, equally as likely, the continued presence of the traditional gods in the procession (Figure 79).[168]

77. Contorniate medallion of a charioteer (Asturius) in a circus and a victory procession: 350–400 CE: obverse: ASTVRI NIKA BOTROCALES and reverse: A-ST-VRI NIKA CVPIDO

78. Terracotta "Campana" plaque of an *auriga* or Sol driving a *quadriga* carried on a *ferculum*, mid first–early second century CE

In fact, other Roman contorniate medallions hint that the traditional gods still appeared in the *pompa circensis* up through the late fourth century CE – a possibility which also finds some corroboration in contemporaneous funerary imagery. Many contorniate medallion-types from fourth-century CE Rome show Isis and other Egyptian gods on the reverse. More specifically, from Constantius II to Gratian (from 337–383 CE) several of these medallions depict

79. Sarcophagus cover fragment with a charioteer or Sol in a *quadriga* on a *ferculum*, marble, mid fourth century CE

80. Contorniate medallion of Constantius II (for his consular games?) with a chariot carrying Isis on the reverse: 352–355 CE: obverse: ON CONSTAN–TIUS PF AVG

Isis in a chariot drawn by two mules, sometimes accompanied by Anubis, on their reverses – a vehicle which may be some kind of cross between a *carpentum* and a *tensa*.[169] And most importantly, one type from this group represents Constantius II in consular robes holding a scepter and possibly a *mappa* on the obverse, and so perhaps the reverse image of Isis in a chariot pulled by two mules was meant to recall the circus procession (Figure 80).[170]

Funerary imagery from a more private sphere, the family and the household, appears to corroborate the presence of the traditional gods in the *pompa circensis* – at least until the end of the fourth century CE. A funerary relief now housed in Foligno dated anywhere from the end of the second to the mid fourth century CE depicts a race in the Circus Maximus with the sponsor of the games

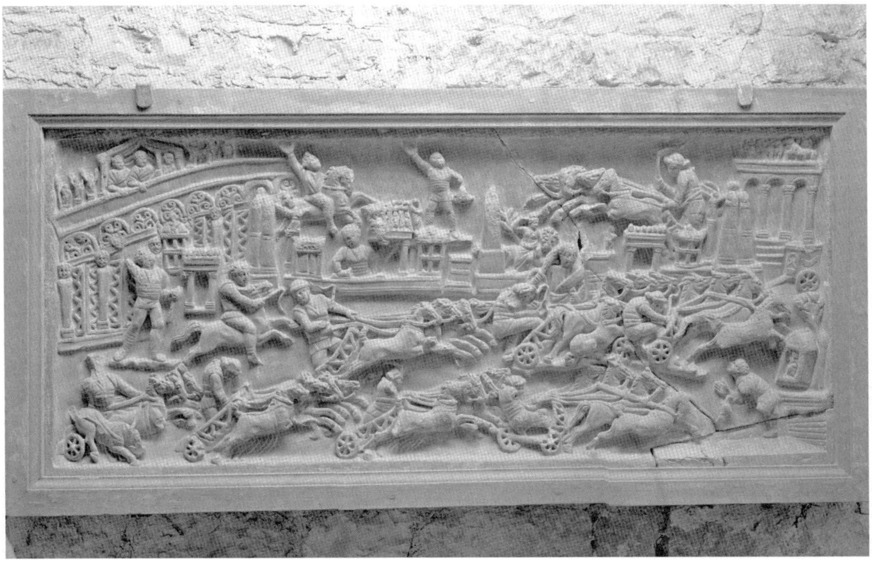

81. Late imperial relief with a game-giver seated in loge, marble, third–fourth century CE

seated in the loge above the starting gates in the upper left corner (Figure 81).[171] In the middle of the right edge, a square-shaped chariot, often considered a *tensa* decorated with a wreath on the front and a garland on the side, stands at the foot of a monumental arch, likely the arch of Titus. Its prominent location, seemingly on the track itself, may indicate that this "*tensa*" belonged to the divine honorand of the games. Its square shape coheres with "standard" *tensa* iconography, but its lack of a pediment and non-figural decoration weakens the argument. A sarcophagus lid from fourth-century CE Rome now in the British Museum more certainly represents what seems to be a *tensa*, accompanied by a young man, who may possibly have been a *puer patrimus et matrimus*. Its height (standing above its horse *quadriga*), boxy shape, pediment, and figural decoration fully correspond to the proposed iconographic markers for a *tensa* (Figure 82).[172] The façade sports a nude image of Jupiter holding a staff in his right hand and a scepter in his left, while the Dioscuri stand in a canonical pose, shoulder to shoulder gripping the bridles of their horses with one hand and cradling staffs with the other, on the long side. In many respects, this *tensa* resembles an early-fourth-century CE sarcophagus lid, which also depicts a *tensa*, quite possibly Augustus', accompanied by a young togate figure who looks back at the vehicle, again possibly the *puer patrimus et matrimus*, and three older, bearded *togati*, one of whom may be the *tensarius* (Figure 19).[173]

A Roman sarcophagus from the second half of the fourth century CE offers what appears to be a wider view of a late-antique *pompa circensis* during the *ludi Megalenses*. Two lions leap in front of an enthroned Magna Mater, who balances a drum on her left leg, atop a *ferculum*, while trumpeters and

82. Sarcophagus lid fragment with *tensa* drawn by four horses and guided by a youth, marble, fourth century CE

a Victory on a second *ferculum* follow behind. On the left hand side of the uninscribed central panel two togate figures (the sponsors perhaps) face the viewer, followed by an elephant *quadriga*. Unfortunately, the relief broke off just after a bearded attendant who accompanies the cart (a lictor with the *fasces*?), and so the occupant of the *currus elephantorum* (likely a deified emperor) has been lost (Figure 83).[174] To judge from this sarcophagus lid, both traditional and imperial gods may have continued to grace the circus procession, at least during the Megalesian games – at least in funerary commemoration.

A second fragmentary, fourth-century CE funerary relief of unknown provenance but probable Roman manufacture may offer further evidence for the continued appearance of Magna Mater – in this case made present by her black stone – in a *pompa circensis*. Victory, whose wings are visible at the right and whose presence suggests a circus procession, leads the cortege, followed by two lictors accompanying a cart drawn by two mules. A diminutive figure guides the mule *biga*, on which two togate magistrates sit, after which comes a *ferculum* on which a small *naiskos* shelters what seems to be the aniconic image of the Great Mother (Figure 84).[175] Despite the seemingly unorthodox mode of transport for those who may have been the sponsors of the games and the *ferculum* for the aniconic image of Magna Mater instead of a *tensa*, the relief has many of the hallmarks of a traditional *pompa circensis*.

One final image, another ivory relief panel, suggests that the imperial *divi* continued to feature in the *pompa circensis* – or rather that deification could still be represented by a *pompa circensis*. The panel, commissioned by the Symmachi

83. Sarcophagus lid fragment with Magna Mater, Victory, and an unknown *divus* in a *pompa circensis*, marble, 350–400 CE

84. Relief with magistrates on a chariot and an aniconic Magna Mater in a *naiskos* on a *ferculum*, marble, mid fourth century CE

85. Ivory diptych with three scenes: *pompa circensis*, funeral pyre, and apotheosis, early fifth century CE

(whose monogram appears in the top center) in the early fifth century CE may commemorate the famous Quintus Aurelius Symmachus (ca. 340–402 CE) (Figure 85).[176] The diptych appears to depict three moments in the process of *consecratio*.[177] In the middle ground, a statue of the deceased, likely an emperor or perhaps Symmachus himself, drives a horse *quadriga* which sits atop a funeral pyre, next to which two eagles, traditional signs of heavenly ascent, soar skyward. At the top, two winged figures carry the deceased aloft toward five *divi* (or ancestors), who await his arrival. Then, following the likely chronological order of the funeral rites, another image of the deceased sits enthroned under an aedicula on a *currus elephantorum* in the foreground – a scene which clearly evokes numismatic imagery of Antonine *divi*, and so also the *pompa circensis* (Figures 34–35).[178] Whoever the deceased may have been, the panel points to the enduring power of traditional imperial rituals (among them the *pompa circensis*) and/or their iconography to commemorate and honor the dead.

Two literary sources may offer some meager corroboration of the visual imagery. A passage from Macrobius' *Saturnalia*, written in the early to mid fifth century CE though set in the late fourth century CE, in which "the cult image of the god of Heliopolis is carried on a *ferculum*, like the images of the gods in the procession at our circus games," shows that Macrobius could imagine, at least, that a traditional *pompa circensis* could have taken place in late-fourth-century CE Rome.[179] At about the same time, Peter Chrysologus of Ravenna (433–450 CE) decried idolatrous New Year's celebrations, in which "gentiles ['pagans'] ... haul, draw, and drag their gods about."[180] In another sermon condemning New Year's festivities, Chrysologus lamented that "the whole procession (*pompa*) of demons arrives" on the kalends of January, when

> a full-fledged workshop of idols is set up.... They fashion Saturn, they make Jupiter, they form Hercules, they exhibit Diana with her young servants, they lead Vulcan around roaring out tales of his obscenities, and there are even more, whose names must be left unmentioned, since they are hideous monsters.[181]

Much of this polemic against "pagan" depravity accords with the traditional *pompa circensis*: images of gods conducted through the city, some of which interacted with the crowd and others of which were monstrous, akin to the folkloric figures like Manducus. Peter Chrysologus, however, targeted what seems to have been a masquerade, a game in which people dressed up as the gods and paraded publicly and merrily around town.[182] Even so, if the gods could appear in a public masquerade, in which some gods were hauled, in mid-fifth-century CE Ravenna, then the gods could also have appeared in a *pompa circensis* at Rome in the fourth or early fifth century CE.

All together, a difficult and tenuous collection evidence seems to suggest that, on occasion, a *pompa circensis* was still performed (or at least commemorated) in a traditional manner with divine images (anthropomorphic and aniconic) on *fercula, exuviae* in *tensae*, and *divi* on *currus elephantorum*. Other performances likely conformed to imperial law and practice – and there is little reason to believe that such divergent choices were always contentious. The late ancient Roman aristocracy, whether "pagan" or Christian, appears to have been more interested in class distinction than religious confrontation.[183] Moreover, aristocratic identity remained enmeshed in the city's classical heritage, and so Roman traditions were maintained for a surprisingly long time.[184] So, while Constantine may have excised the traditional gods from the circus procession at Constantinople, at Rome the *pompa circensis* may still have conducted the gods to the games into the late fourth century CE. Eventually imperial and ecclesiastical pressure and the slow attrition of the late classical elite affected the performance of the circus procession at Rome. Its final incarnation may have been similar to the "secular," imperial version: a procession of emperors and Victories possibly led by the game-giver and his entourage, the contestants, dancers, and musicians. As the *pompa deorum* was slowly but steadily imperialized and even Christianized, the *pompa hominum* could have survived relatively undisturbed, as is suggested by a group of contorniate medallions issued during the reign of Valentinian III (the same Valentinian who may have conducted a *pompa Dei* replete with Christian symbols) with a dancer or even groups of dancers holding wreaths on the reverses.[185]

V RESTORING THE "REPUBLIC": THE LATE-ANTIQUE ITINERARY

> The Romans love their city above all the men we know, and are eager to protect their entire ancestral legacy and to preserve it, so that nothing of the ancient glory of Rome may be obliterated. Even though they lived long under barbarian [Ostrogothic] sway, they preserved the buildings of the city and most of its adornments, those which could withstand so long a lapse of time and such neglect through the sheer excellence of their workmanship. Furthermore, all the memorials of the race that were still left are preserved even to this day, among them the ship of Aeneas, the founder of the city, an altogether incredible sight.
>
> Procopius, *History of the Wars* 8.22.5–7[186]

While the *pompa circensis* may have been "secularized" or imperialized and then perhaps Christianized, the late-antique itinerary seems to tell a different story (Map 3). Much of the traditional and only known itinerary from the Capitol to the Circus witnessed a good bit of the increasingly rare restorations in late antiquity – the Forum in particular, unsurprisingly.[187] What may be surprising is that the restorations seem to have concentrated on buildings with republican and even traditional religious associations, largely ignoring, it seems, the imperial monuments, arches, and temples, which had come to dominate the city and the itinerary.[188] Imperial monuments still stood and imperial statues were erected along the itinerary, along with, eventually, a Christian church. Still, restorations at Rome seem to have favored the republic.

In late antiquity, restoration was something like a sacred tenet of urban life, enshrined in law and rhetoric.[189] In 364 CE, the emperors Valentinian and Valens informed the urban prefect Lucius Aurelius Avianius Symmachus that "none of the judges shall construct any new building within the eternal city of Rome if the order therefor of Our Serenity should be lacking. However, we grant permission to all to restore those buildings which are said to have fallen into unsightly ruins."[190] A little over a decade later, a second law echoed those

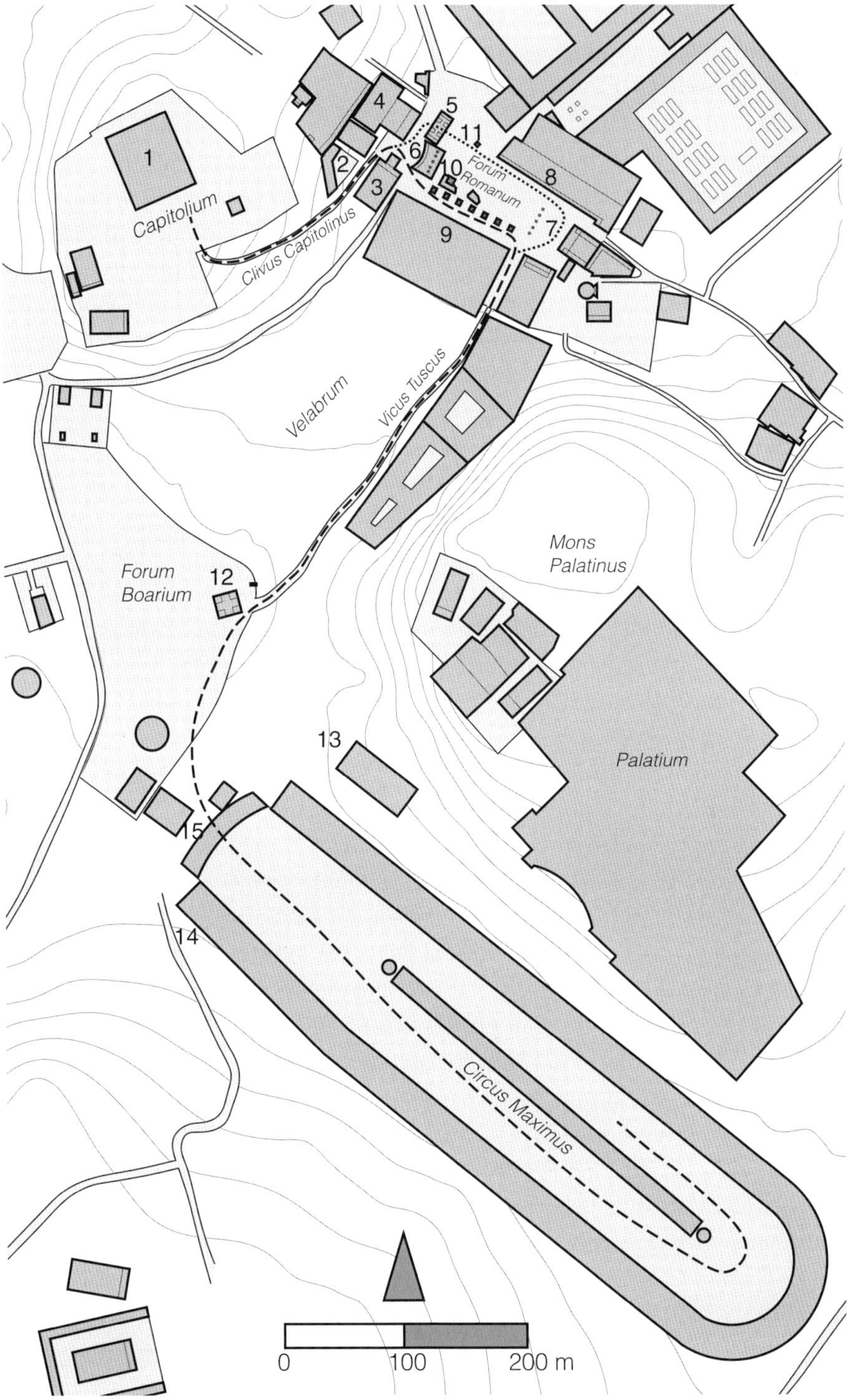

Map 3 The late-antique itinerary of the *pompa circensis* (ca. 235–mid sixth century CE), drawn by Marie Saldaña

sentiments: "No one of the prefects of the city or other judges whom power has placed in high position shall undertake any new structure in the renowned city of Rome, but he shall direct his attention to improving the old."[191] Nazarius, an early-fourth-century CE rhetor, rather fulsomely praised the restorations of Constantine, which outshone even the glory of the ancients: "All the most celebrated things in the city gleam with new work, and not only are those which have been worn out through age distinguished with renewed splendor, but the very ones which were formerly considered the most magnificent betray the unseemly parsimony of the ancients now that they shine with golden light."[192] Even during the sixth-century CE Gothic war, the eastern Roman general Belisarius supposedly wrote to the Ostrogothic king, Totila, urging him to spare "the greatest and the most noteworthy" city out of regard for its astonishing longevity and magnificent patrimony.[193] On the other side of the conflict, the Roman senator Cassiodorus had the Ostrogoth king, Athalaric, exhort urban denizens of southern Italy, seemingly, to return to their homes: "let the cities return, then, to their original glory."[194] Restoration of the past was deeply valued, but restoration at Rome was also limited and selective, often guided, it seems, by reverence for republican tradition.

Although the temple of Jupiter Optimus Maximus was the seat of empire and the glittering center of Roman public religion, it was not seemingly restored (Map 3.1). Nonetheless, the Capitol still loomed large in the image and imagination of late-antique Rome.[195] For some (both "pagans" and Christians), the temple could still be imagined in traditional terms; for others (Christians) it had fallen into ruined desuetude. On the one hand, in the late fourth century CE, Ausonius recalled the "golden roofs of the Capitol."[196] Ammianus Marcellinus, a near contemporary, had Constantius II stand awe-struck when he saw "the sanctuaries of Tarpeian Jupiter, which surpassed [all things] much as things divine excel those of earth." Indeed, for Ammianus, no monument could top the majestic Serapeum except "the Capitolium, with which revered Rome raised herself to eternity."[197] Even in the early sixth century CE, Cassiodorus still imagined the temple of Jupiter Optimus Maximus as a splendid sanctuary, a marvel of antiquity: "To ascend the lofty Capitol is to see all other works of human ingenuity surpassed."[198] On the other hand, as a backhanded testament to the power of the temple, several Christian authors felt compelled to denigrate or even eulogize it. In the early fourth century CE, Lactantius insisted, "their Capitol, the capital, that is, of all their state religion, is simply a meaningless memorial."[199] In the late fourth century CE, Jerome contended that "the gilded Capitol seems dirty," as the people have abandoned the temples to run to the shrines of marytrs.[200] Prudentius, too, fantasized about crowds forsaking Jupiter's altar for the tomb of Peter or the Lateran basilica.[201] For Paulinus of Nola, "the summit of the Capitol shakes and totters [from the blows of sacred shouts]. Dilapidated images in deserted temples tremble, struck by holy voices."[202] The temple was either a magnificent monument or a defeated relic.

To the rhetorical bifurcation, one may add the equally rhetorical, but perhaps more believable, history of the despoliation of the temple. At the end of the fourth century CE, the temple seemingly began its slow decline when Stilicho impiously, according to Zosimus, removed the gilding from the doors.[203] The roof, certainly restored and re-gilded over the years, appears to have survived until 455 CE, when Gaiseric, king of the Vandals, "plundered the temple of Jupiter Capitolinus and tore off half the roof. This roof was of bronze of the finest quality and, as a thick layer of gold had been poured over it, it shone as a magnificent and wonderful spectacle."[204] Later in 571 CE, Narses, an eastern Roman general, performed what is often considered the last recorded act of pillage when he removed, it seems, statues from the temple.[205]

In any case, by the end of the sixth century CE, the golden temple was golden no more. Its declining physical state, however, belies its enduring symbolic and ritual importance. In the later years of Constantine's reign, Ceionius Rufius Albinus successfully lobbied the emperor for senatorial control over membership in the senate at Rome. For that triumph of "republican" (or at least senatorial) autonomy, Albinus was awarded a statue on the Capitol by the senate – an exceptional site for an exceptional honor. Moreover, the dedicatory inscription explicitly celebrates the restoration of a republican prerogative that had been abrogated by Julius Caesar 381 years earlier.[206] Thereafter, any senatorial *praeses ludorum* might have smiled at the statue, as he led a *pompa circensis* down from the Capitol. Late-antique game-givers may also have been struck by the sheer endurance of ritual tradition on the Capitol. Republican privileges which had survived only in cultural memory could be restored, while some traditions, like the *processus consularis*, were continuously maintained. Jerome, writing from Palestine, imagined a procession conducted by the "arch-pagan" Praetextatus, whose outlines suggest a *processus consularis*, even though Praetextatus, ordinary consul designate, died before his inauguration.

> A few days ago the highest of all the dignitaries walked before [Praetextatus], as he ascended the peaks of the Capitol, almost as if he had triumphed over defeated enemies, received with applause and celebration by the Roman people.[207]

Although Praetextatus never performed his *processus consularis*, nearly 150 years later Boethius consoled himself with the memory of the consular procession of his two (Christian) sons, the last known consular procession at Rome:

> If genuine happiness ever comes from the affairs of mortals, could the weight of any crowding ills, however great, obliterate the memory of the glory you experienced when you saw your sons borne from your house together as consuls, in the crowd of senators and the throng of the rejoicing populace?[208]

Though Boethius did not explicitly name the Capitol, choosing to emphasize instead his own speech given in the curia, the Capitol was still the likely destination of this consular procession. In short, the Capitoline temple, which had been repeatedly re-built on the traces (or memories) of the original during the republic and empire, may not have been restored in late antiquity, but the Capitol remained a symbolic center for the aristocracy of Rome, whether "pagan" or Christian.

Proceeding down the *clivus Capitolinus*, a number of notable late-fourth-century CE restorations flanked the itinerary: the *Porticus dei consentes* and the temple of Saturn (Map 3.2 and 3.3). As urban prefect in 367/8, Praetextatus (with senatorial and possibly imperial approval) restored the unassuming portico to its "ancient form," but with mismatched spoliated columns and capitals, which may have been intended as a visible, material restoration of memory. This portico had previously housed gilded statues of the twelve gods, and in the late fourth century CE it still sheltered *sacrosancta simulacra* (sacrosanct divine images).[209] Just across the *clivus*, "The senate and Roman people restored [the temple of Saturn], which was destroyed by a fire," likely in the late fourth century CE.[210] At the end of the *clivus Capitolinus* where it enters the Forum, "the senate and Roman people (SPQR) restored the temple of Concord, after it collapsed from old age, with effort and care to a better and more splendid state" (Map 3.4).[211]

Strikingly, three republican sanctuaries of the traditional gods warranted some of the increasingly rare late-antique renovations. Moreover, despite the passage of time (as signaled by mismatched spolia, columns, capitals, bases, and architraves, from which the temples were restored), these restorations show that the past, even the republican past, could be restored. Equally importantly, all three restorations frame the *clivus Capitolinus*, which seems to have remained an important processional way, probably (or possibly) for the *pompa circensis* or other processions, like the *processus consularis*.[212] Indeed, this traditional processional way may have extended to the other end of the Forum, if the podium of the temple of Dioscuri was restored in the late fourth century CE.[213] Restored "pagan" temples may, then, have bookended the Forum at the end of the fourth century CE. If the traditional gods still appeared in the procession, which seems possible, then resonances between processional and temple images could still have echoed during the performance of at least some circus processions.

The restoration of traditional civic temples seems to have been part of a larger trend, in which the memory of the republic, in a sense, was restored. The republican Forum may have been a living *milieu de mémoire*, while the imperial Forum may have degenerated into a museum of power, a fossilized *lieu de mémoire*.[214] In late antiquity, the Forum may have been refigured as an archive of cultural memory as Roman aristocrats sought to re-assert long dormant traditional republican values by selective restoration. Cities, buildings, and monuments are always decaying and are only ever selectively restored.

Those choices, in turn, reveal a great deal about the priorities and values of those who made them – especially when resources are limited.[215] Of course, even without (evidence for) restoration, monuments could endure in some form or another, like the temple of Vespasian, whose inscription was still legible to an anonymous early medieval visitor, or even the mid-republican column of Maenius, which still stood at the end of the fourth century CE (Map 3.5).[216] More typically, however, simply to survive the sheer passage of time (in addition to fires, wars, sacks, and other calamities) a building required restoration. And so, the renovation of buildings and structures with republican resonances seem to have recalled an aristocratic, republican past, even in the midst of on-going imperial domination.[217] Like an eddy in "the stream of tradition," to invoke Jan Assmann once again, the republican heritage of the Forum was a largely unmoving and unused cultural memory resource during the early empire, for the aristocracy at least – a resource that re-joined the mainstream in late antiquity.[218]

In 303 CE, five columns – representing, perhaps, the reigning *Augusti* and *Caesares* flanking Jupiter (visually linked to his temple above) – were erected on the Augustan rostra at the western end of the Forum Roman to celebrate the *decennalia* of the tetrarchy (Map 3.6). At the same time, at other end of the Forum the Diocletianic rostra was erected, which sported a twin set of five columns – perhaps Hercules flanked by imperial *genii* (Map 3.7). Both rostra were renovated again during late antiquity – the Augustan rostra may have been extended by the tetrarchs or perhaps by the urban prefect Ulpius Iunius Valentinus in 470 CE with the addition of the so-called rostra Vandalica, while the Diocletianic rostra was restored by the urban prefect Lucius Valerius Septimius Bassus in 379/383 CE.[219] Along the same lines, the senate house itself, the curia Iulia, was rebuilt first by the tetrarchs and then again after the sack of 410 CE.[220] Not only was the senate house rebuilt multiple times, but during the course of the fourth century CE a senatorial compound was established, comprising (some combination of) an *atrium Libertatis*, an *atrium Minervae* (the *Chalcidium* perhaps), a *secretarium Senatus*, whose fifth-century CE renovation conspicuously called attention to its late-fourth-century CE aristocratic foundation, and an area called *ad Palmam* or *Palma aurea*.[221] Though the tetrarchic columns and their statuary towered over the two rostra, both the re-constructed rostra and the curia with its surrounding complex embodied republican political culture, emphasizing public oratory, whose ideals still shaped late-antique aristocratic identity. For example, the inscribed statue base of Lucius Aurelius Avianius Symmachus, father of the more famous Quintus Aurelius Symmachus, from the forum of Trajan praised his "authority, wisdom, and eloquence."[222]

Memories of Roman traditions were also recalled by the persistent practice of erecting, moving, and re-erecting statues.[223] In the Forum, most of these statues were imperial, unsurprisingly, but they were also elite dedications, artistic installations, and even statues of "pagan" deities. During the reign of Maxentius (306–312 CE), a statue was dedicated "to Mars *Invictus*, our father, and the founders of his eternal city," on April 21, the anniversary of Rome, near the lapis Niger, considered the legendary tomb of Romulus.[224] Such antiquarian sensibilities were common in Maxentian public display and unsurprising in the early fourth century CE.[225] Strikingly, in the last quarter of the fifth century CE a *simulacrum* of Minerva was re-erected by a Christian (probably) after it had been destroyed when the roof of the *atrium Minervae* collapsed. The statue may have been re-erected as an emblem of "the [restored] happiness of our times," or as a symbol of the senate, but the use of the term *simulacrum*, which had traditionally signaled a divine image, allows for the possibility, at least, of pious ("pagan") sentiment.[226] In the late fourth century CE, bishop Ambrose of Milan complained that Rome was crowded with such "pagan idols": "Are they ['pagan' senators] not satisfied with the baths, the colonnades, and the streets, all crammed with divine images (*simulacra*)?"[227] Many of these *simulacra* would have long survived among "the most plentiful population of statues" erected and re-erected in the Forum and elsewhere – and individual responses to these statues undoubtedly varied: from apathy, to respect, to curation.[228]

In fact, the basilica Iulia and (possibly) the portico of the basilica Aemilia, which formed the long sides of the Forum, seem to have housed elaborate statue installations, works of art perhaps (rather than honorific statues), which were taken from less-trafficked places or perhaps even dilapidated buildings elsewhere in Rome. Unfortunately the statues do not survive, but some of them were seemingly attributed to famous Greek sculptors, Praxiteles, Polyclitus, and Timarchus.[229] In an effort to preserve Rome's patrimony, Fabius Titianus (urban prefect 339–341 CE) "curated" a large collection of statues in the Forum, which may have been installed in the portico of the basilica Aemilia – a portico which was likely restored in the early fifth century CE (after the sack of 410 CE), even though the basilica proper was left in rubbled ruin (Map 3.8).[230] The restored portico with its array of statues would have maintained the elegant appearance of the Forum despite straitened circumstances. A generation or so later, Gabinus Vettius Probianus, urban prefect in 377 CE probably (or possibly 416 CE), claimed to have completely restored the basilica Iulia, a "celebrated location" in which he placed a good-sized statue assemblage (Map 3.9).[231] Probianus also re-erected four further statues, whose inscriptions do not provide their location, but which may have been housed in the portico of the basilica Aemilia (or the basilica Iulia).[232] A similar concern for the heritage of Rome endured into the late fifth century CE, when Flavius Macrobius Plotinus Eustathius, prefect of the city, transported a statue (probably) from an abandoned or hidden place to a location near the curia.[233]

On rare occasions, the aristocracy of Rome could even be honored in the central space of the Forum, though most non-imperial honorific statues were erected in the forum of Trajan. For example, just prior to or shortly after his death in 384 CE, Praetextatus, who restored the *Porticus dei consentes* with its sacrosanct divine images, received a statue in the Forum.[234] However, most non-imperial dedications in the Forum honored the western empire's strongmen, *magistri militum* like Stilicho and Aetius, who often seemed to dominate their emperors. Exceptionally then, Petronius Maximus before he ascended to the imperial throne, a Rufius, and a couple of other individuals were given such honors in the fifth century CE, when, despite a regular imperial presence in the city, imperial dedications went into a steep decline.[235] Such dedications could be tremendously affecting, it seems, triggering, for example, a cascade of filial devotion. In the early fifth century CE, Rutilius Namatianus "was shown a statue of his revered father, erected by the Pisans in their forum. The honor done to his late parent made [Namatianus] weep: tears of a saddened joy wet [his] cheeks with their flow."[236] Should any *praeses ludorum* have passed by some relative, one of the fortunate few honored in the Forum or on the Capitol, tears may not have come, but pride seems a likely response.

Despite the careful, but limited, restoration of republican memory, the central space of the Forum remained a venue for imperial public display, especially in the fourth century CE, for which there is epigraphic evidence of statues for every emperor, except Jovinian.[237] In addition to the matching sets on the two *rostra*, seven further column-statues were also erected in the early fourth century CE, which pace the façade of the basilica Iulia. Around this same time, early to mid fourth century CE, an eighth columnar statue was erected in the central paved area on axis with the Argiletum. This column would receive the last-known imperial dedication in Rome in 608 CE, when Smaragdus, the exarch of Ravenna, re-dedicated the column with a statue of the reigning emperor Phocas (Map 3.10). The overwhelming majority of the imperial statues were concentrated in the open space in front of the curia framed by the arch of Septimius Severus and the basilica Aemilia: where both Constantine and Constantius received equestrian statues and a Theodosian monument displayed statues of Theodosius I, his mother Thermantia (the only woman to be so honored), as well as Valentinian II and Arcadius (Map 3.11).[238] In the fifth century CE, imperial dedications sharply declined; seemingly only Marcian and Avitus received statues, leaving greater scope for non-imperial public display, especially by the *magistri militum*.[239]

As a result, Roman aristocrats in the *pompa circensis* may well have experienced dissonant resonances: building restorations and cultural displays along the edges of the Forum embodied the memory of an illustrious republican past, while the statuary in the open space of the Forum, whether of emperors or generals, would have been an insistent reminder of late-antique political realities. Stilicho, by contrast, may have rather enjoyed the uncanny experience of seeing his double, a statue erected in 398 CE after the defeat of Gildo, either when he was consul in 400 CE (though he seems to have been at Rome infrequently at that point) or perhaps when he rode with Honorius in the same chariot during an *adventus* in celebration of the emperor's sixth consulship in 404 CE.[240] What would many fifth-century CE western emperors, who were often resident in Rome, have thought when they paraded by illustrious predecessors like Theodosius, but were not themselves honored? In general, few statues were granted in the fifth century CE in the Forum or anywhere in Rome for that matter, and fewer still in the sixth century CE when the statue habit (as well as, probably, the *pompa circensis*) waned.[241]

After leaving the Forum, the procession wended its way through the Velabrum to the Forum Boarium and the Circus, where two notable new constructions and a significant reconstruction would have greeted the cortege. If the *ianus quadrifrons* in the Forum Boarium was indeed the arch of *divus* Constantine mentioned in fourth-century CE regionary catalogs, then the deified emperor and the goddesses Roma, Juno, Minerva, and Ceres, who graced the four keystones, along with whatever statuary occupied the forty-eight niches, could watch the *pompa circensis* and its imperial imagery pass by (Map 3.12). Moreover, like the arch of Septimius Severus, this *ianus* also had an interior staircase and so also, perhaps, a platform for processional staff or spectators.[242] Perhaps more consequentially, not far from the arch and in the vicinity of the Lupercal – whose festival (Christian) Roman aristocrats continued to patronize into the late fifth century CE if not beyond – the *pompa circensis* would have passed near its first and probably only Christian edifice, the *titulus Anastasiae* (Map 3.13).[243] This *titulus* must have existed by the episcopacy of Damasus (366–384 CE), who is credited with some of its painted decoration, though it may been founded much earlier – possibly in 326 CE by Constantine's sister, Anastasia, for whom the *titulus* might have been named.[244] Even if the church had an impressive imperial pedigree, it had a rather minimal visual presence, built a short distance from the parade route within the imperial compound on the Palatine. It was, however, a herald of things to come. To hearken back to the past: directly across the *vallis Murcia*, a Symmachus restored the temple of Flora on the other side of the Circus, whose massive bulk visually separated church and temple (Map 3.14). This temple restoration, like those in the Forum, testifies to the enduring strength of Roman traditional religions into the late fourth century CE.[245] In the end, the (possible) arch of deified Constantine, the *titulus Anastasiae*, the Lupercal, and the temple of Flora, nicely capture the late-antique *pompa circensis* caught between "paganism" and Christianity, between aristocratic tradition and imperial power.

The procession then arrived at a piazza that may have been called the *duodecim portae* (twelve gates) by the fourth-century CE regionary catalogs after the adjacent *carceres* (Map 3.15).[246] After Caracalla's restoration of the starting gates, visual evidence strongly suggests that a larger, central entry was constructed, through which the procession could enter the arena and over which a loge was built for the *praeses ludorum* (see Figures 43 and 81).[247] The early-fourth-century CE circus of Maxentius was equipped with a large central gate, which suggests that its model, the Circus Maximus, would have also been similarly outfitted.[248] Moreover, it seems that this central gate was ceremonial, constructed for the *pompa circensis*. According to a mid-third-century CE graffito, the seventh cohort of firefighters, whose remit may have included the Circus, provided lamps *ad porta ad pompas* ("for the processional gate"), a tenuous but tantalizing hint that the central gate may have been a *porta pompae*.[249] Ausonius, in the late fourth century CE, noted that at the start of a race all the gates would fly open, "except the middle one that opens onto the stadium," which may have been reserved for the procession.[250] In the mid fifth century CE, Sidonius Apollinaris mentioned a "gateway and seat of consuls" flanked by six doors on either side, referring, it seems, to the ceremonial central gate and loge at the Circus in Rome.[251]

Entering the arena through this processional gate, "the clamor of the adoring people," would have greeted the game-giver, like the emperor Honorius in 404 CE, whose "thunderstruck ears [would] resound with the noise of the Circus," in the words of Rutilius Namatianus, who may even have conducted a *pompa circensis* during his tenure as urban prefect in 414 CE.[252] Such acclamation and popular approval cemented the consensus between the emperor and his subjects, and also between the elite and the people. Unsurprisingly, then, late-antique emperors took care to maintain the arena – at least through the fourth century CE.[253] Constantine "completed the decorations [begun under Diocletian] in the Circus Maximus in a marvelous fashion," with "lofty porticoes and columns glowing red with gold."[254] According to Ammianus Marcellinus, Constantius II finished his father's work by transporting and erecting a giant obelisk dedicated to Sol on the *euripus* (a feat celebrated by the versified dedicatory inscription), which was "capped by a bronze globe gleaming with goldleaf" – a globe which was destroyed by lightning and replaced by a gilded bronze torch.[255] This torch may have been among the rich bronze decorations mentioned by the *Expositio totius mundi et gentium*, a text first written in the mid fourth century CE.[256] The regionary catalogs and fourth-century CE visual imagery conjure the *euripus* filled with columns, statues, shrines, and altars, whose maintenance would have been part of the regular maintenance of the Circus itself.[257] The urban prefects, who seem to have had an office or archive in or near the Circus Maximus, performed some of this upkeep, erecting statues and overseeing structural repairs, into the fifth century CE.[258]

Unfortunately, little remains of the Circus Maximus, and so its architectural integrity and also its possible Christianization – for example, the addition of Christian symbols, especially crosses, or even a church building – are open questions, though very few Christian edifices were built in spectacle buildings.[259] Textual references to the Circus and chariot races continue until 549 CE, when Totila offered the last known races in the Circus Maximus. Its continuing use suggests the track and seating, at least, as well as the adornments (statues, shrines, temples), perhaps, were maintained in usable, even if not perfect condition into the sixth century CE – indeed, Cassiodorus' lavish description of the Circus and the races seems to presume it.[260] As the temple of the people, in Ammianus Marcellinus' contemptuous phrase, the Circus would have remained a priority target of the increasingly rare restorations in late antiquity. More positively, the Circus, like the Forum, remained a central site of Roman cultural memory. In fact, late-antique contorniate medallions still place (a re-enactment of) the rape of the Sabine women at the first *meta*, a scene first staged during the reign of Antoninus Pius (Figure 86).[261] The rape of the Sabines with its violent sexuality, so well suited to the Circus, and its connection to Rome's primordial origins long remained an important component of Roman collective identity. In thanking the emperors for "the noisy excitement in the valley of Murcia," Symmachus insisted that games still mattered to the Romans – after all, "the circus attractions furnished spouses from their neighbors!"[262]

86. Contorniate medallion of the rape of the Sabine women: 350–400 CE: reverse: SABINAE

In general, archaeological and textual evidence suggest the perdurance of a traditional, though altered, processional itinerary, and so also the continuation, if not also the continuity, of the *pompa circensis* throughout the fourth and early fifth centuries CE and perhaps even into the sixth – like the *pompa (amphi-)theatralis* preceding shows like "Harlots" and *venationes*, which also seems to have endured, in Justinianic law at least.[263] The traditional gods were eventually excised from the procession and the concluding sacrifice banned, but the rest of the traditional panoply of game-givers, entourage, competitors and performers, entertainers, Victory, and deified emperors persisted. The itinerary also suggests a transformation of the *pompa circensis* – a fissure between procession and itinerary. Even though representations of the emperor seem to have dominated both the procession and the central space of the Forum, at least during the fourth century CE, late-antique restorations indicate a re-assertion of republican sensibilities: the renewal of republican memory in the form of traditional cult sanctuaries, the senate, rostra, basilicas, and, of course, the Circus itself – at the expense of, it seems, imperial monuments. In other words, the late-antique aristocracy of Rome restored the very sorts of buildings and monuments most closely associated with its republican Roman heritage. The foundation of the *titulus Anastasiae* along the *vicus Tuscus* sometime in the fourth century CE represents another fault line between procession and itinerary, a further fracturing of the coherence between procession, itinerary, and memory, even as it seems to have been a harbinger of things to come: if Valentinian III did in fact carry a cruciform scepter in a *pompa circensis*.

The "republican" *pompa circensis*, with its hierarchically arranged cortege and itinerary from the temple of Jupiter Optimus Maximus, the font of Roman power, to the temple of Ceres, a plebian asylum, and ultimately the Circus, performed Rome as SPQR+the gods – a traditional image of Rome. Starting with Julius Caesar and the ensuing Augustan settlement, the imperial special dead came to dominate the procession by sheer numbers and over-awing spectacularity. Sheer monumentality matched ritual spectacularity, as imperial buildings, in particular imperial cult temples and triumphal arches, engulfed the high imperial itinerary. In short, from the first century BCE to the third century CE, the *pompa circensis* spun a tale of imperial Rome, ruled by the image and power of the emperor.

At the same time, beginning in the late first and picking up steam in the third century CE, *pompa circensis* imagery shifted from the gods, especially imperial ones, to the imperial game-giver. This process of imperialization, a component of, it seems, the third-century CE reconfiguration of imperial power, was also a means of secularization, in which the traditional gods and rituals were eliminated and which may have resulted in the Christianization of the procession with a Christian emperor leading something like a *pompa Dei* in place of the traditional *pompa deorum*. Though imperialization-secularization-Christianization seems to have developed in response to a crisis of imperial authority, this same process may also have addressed the critiques of Christian opinion-makers, whose rhetoric was able to exercise some influence over the emperors and so also over public ceremonial.

The late-antique itinerary seems to contradict, in part, imperialization-secularization-Christianization. Imperial monuments that once dominated the path were most likely still extent and imperial statues still dominated the open space of the Forum. It is striking, however, that the temples of Saturn, Concord, and Flora (and possibly the Dioscuri), the portico of the Harmonious Gods, statue collections flanking the Forum, and venerable civic structures, like the curia and its surrounding complex, the portico of the basilica Aemilia, the basilica Iulia, and the Circus were restored in what must have been a very selective process. This assertion of late-classical aristocratic power, and republican memory, may well have allowed the the *pompa circensis* to keep its traditional form when the traditional gods were paraded, on some occasions at least. In short, the Roman aristocracy maintained certain Roman traditions, at least sometimes, as well as certain traditional monuments, which were central to the construction of its identity.

In the end, the unity between procession and itinerary shattered due to the implicit opposition between the demands of Christian emperors and the desires of the late-classical Roman aristocracy, itself a conflicted group with varying priorities. Thus, a multiplicity of images of Rome emerged in the fourth and fifth centuries CE, one imperial upheld by emperors and office-holders, one traditional cultivated by the aristocracy, and one Christian patronized by a mixture of emperors, elites, and, one assumes, bishops. Among these competing visions of Rome, it seems that the imperial image dominated the fourth century CE, while the traditional one may have gained ground during the fifth, with a burgeoning Christian public presence running in third. This competition to define Rome changed sharply during the sixth-century CE Justinianic re-conquest of Italy (and subsequent Lombard invasions), which dealt a devastating blow to aristocratic wealth, and with it aristocratic power and prestige, and also eroded imperial authority at Rome. Most of what had survived of classical Rome (games, offices, festivals) seems to have disappeared in the choking fog of decades of war, leaving the bishop of Rome as the last man standing, as it were, free to develop a new processional image of the city.[264]

A circus procession of sorts, though, may have continued for as long as a Roman (even if a Byzantine) emperor produced spectacles in an arena. In the late twelfth century CE, rabbi Benjamin of Tudela traveled to Constantinople on his way to Jerusalem and beyond, where he witnessed an odd Christmas festival or perhaps an interesting wedding celebration in the hippodrome:

> Every year on the anniversary of the birth of Jesus the king gives great entertainment there. And in that place men from all the races of the world come before the king and queen with jugglery and without jugglery, and they introduce lions, leopards, bears, and wild asses, and they engage them in combat with one another; and the same thing is done with birds. No entertainment like this is to be found in any other land.[265]

A parade of the nations of the world represented Byzantine power and influence, a serious piece of political theater; the jugglers offered simple fun and wonderment; while the trained animals contributed blood and violence – all hints of the traditional pageantry of the circus procession. But did the representatives of the nations, the jugglers, and wild animals process through the city? Or did they simply parade along the arena floor, much as the (Byzantine) emperor himself directly accessed the hippodrome from the palace? Did the pageantry of the hippodrome define Constantinople as the circus procession did Rome?

CONCLUSION

The *pompa circensis* was at one and the same time a spectacular political pageant and a hallowed ritual performance. The sponsor of the games escorted the gods (traditional and/or imperial) or perhaps even the Christian God from the relevant sanctuary(-ies) to the appropriate entertainment venue. In the circus procession, an otherwise mundane walk through town was ritualized, differentiated from the everyday. Crowded streets would have been cleared as the *praeses ludorum* conducted the procession dressed in august, not to say "triumphal," attire accompanied by an entourage whose composition may have varied widely: Roman youth divided according to census status, political allies, magistrates, clients, lictors, and/or even soldiers. To draw (even more) attention to the games that followed (whether chariot races, theater shows, gladiatorial combat, or animal hunts), competitors, contestants, performers, even animals appeared in the parade in their full regalia, so to speak – horses and chariots, arms and armor, bare loincloths, or perhaps even less. To ensure maximum publicity, dancers, musicians, and, likely, other entertainers performed as well – martial dancers executing their precise choreography, burlesque dancers playing satyrs and Sileni, perhaps maenads and fauns, and also jugglers or buffoons. All this to introduce the gods, who occupied the position of honor toward the end of the procession.

Preceded by gleaming, glittering gold and silver ritual vessels, the gods themselves appeared like an epiphany out of a haze of burning incense and perfume. Victory seems to have led a long train of gods, represented or made present in a number of ways, each of which demanded a distinct mode of transport: ivory *simulacra* (divine images) on *fercula* (litters borne on the shoulders of porters who may have been devotees or perhaps more likely paid laborers); and *exuviae* (relics or symbols) secreted away within *tensae* (sacred chariots almost exclusively reserved for the *pompa circensis*). Surrounding the solemn procession of gods, folkloric figures stumbled, bumbled, and rumbled, chatting up they crowd as they passed, while stilt-walkers imitating deities (*grallatores*) may have captured the wilder side of divinity. In other words, the *pompa deorum* performed a theology in which the gods and/or the other-than-human appeared as familiar and approachable (*simulacra*), as distant and inaccessible (*exuviae*), or as terrifying and titillating (folkloric figures and *grallatores*), all arranged in something like a pantheon by the very marching order of the procession itself. Once at the Circus, the divine images seem to have been installed on couches (a *lectisternium*) and the relics on chairs (a *sellisternium*) in the *pulvinar*, before which, possibly, a sacrifice was performed to inaugurate the games.

The order and organization of the participants from the game-giver to the gods may constructively be considered the grammar and syntax of the "republican" procession, a kind of ritual pattern from which specific performances could be produced – much like linguistic "rules" (or habits) may generate any number of utterances (or practices). This pattern may also be construed as a kind of ideal-type: not an assertion of how the procession should have been performed, but rather an outline of the components, principles, and traditions upon which any given *pompa circensis* could have drawn – in short, a sketch of the practical logic of the "republican" procession based, in this analysis, as much as possible on evidence from the republic or within its communicative memory. Indeed, the Roman social imaginary (as represented, for example, by Cicero and Livy) had its own sense of an ideal-type of the *pompa circensis*, its own sense of the procession's rules, whose violation risked divine displeasure. Dancers needed to dance; musicians needed to play; attendants of the *tensae* needed to guide the sacred chariots. Fortunately, there was a procedure to correct any infraction – *instauratio*, a repetition of the procession and games in whole or in part. In other words, this ideal-type, this exploration of the grammar, syntax, and signification of the procession, this précis of its practical logic, aims to offer some sense of how a *pompa circensis* could be performed according to Roman expectations in the late republic, not necessarily how any particular *pompa circensis* was actually performed. Performances could vary; performances could fail; performance could be corrected.

Even though any particular performance would have differed from any other in myriad ways, any given performance would have been recognizable as a species of *pompa circensis*. Each iteration of the procession resulted from the patterned and improvised actions of skilled performers (*praeses ludorum*, satyrs and Sileni, stilt-walking imitators of divinities, and even *fercula*-bearers with their distinctive gait) and their interactions with an audience (both divine and human), whose expectations and responses greatly impacted the performance. And so, the *pompa circensis* unfolded according to certain rules, but it was never a simple repetition. Each performance seems to have been marked by a play between gravity (for example, the sponsor's serious public performance) and levity (the sexualized play of the burlesque dancers), but the specific forms that this oscillation took would have varied depending on circumstance – perhaps a particular magistrate served as a better foil for the antics of the satyrs. The procession was also a spectacle, but one that reached beyond its stage, alternating between resonance and wonder. As a spectacle, the procession sought to overawe the spectator with its wondrous and singular pomposity, but it also resonated in a variety of ways with other rituals, places along the itinerary, and memories for participants and audiences alike. Such performative indeterminacies may well be the hallmark of Roman civic processions: whether a triumph, funeral procession, circus procession, or other. The mundane world of work-a-day Rome would have been transformed by the play between gravity and levity, between resonance and wonder – by festive sights, sounds, and smells. In short, the circus procession (like other processions) was a performance in the round, as it were, embracing the full sensorium.

This may have been particularly true for the participants, who traveled the entire itinerary. The itinerary played an active role; it was not a mere stage. During the republic, and indeed into late antiquity, the road from the Capitol to the Circus traversed a linear path over some of the most historically dense and memory-laden terrain of ancient Rome. It was also marked by a striking repetition of archaic temples (some constructed in the "same" architectural style), commemorative arches (*fornices*) and columns, and even fig trees. The same was true of imperial Rome, when the itinerary was littered with imperial cult temples and triumphal arches. In the festival atmosphere of the procession, such repetitions may well have seemed surreal: space may have appeared to collapse or to have folded in on itself. The experience of such persistent repetition may have been echoed, for some, in an encounter with Rome's second population – the vast collection of statues dotting Rome's most frequented and famous places. Among this population of statues, some participants may have come across their own, a family member's, or even a friend's double – likely a pleasant experience, but perhaps also an uncanny one, as Freud would have it. Similar resonances may have stirred the memory of every participant at some point along the itinerary. The *praeses ludorum* could have recalled his *processus consularis* on the Capitol; his escort of Roman youth on horseback may well have anticipated their *transvectio equitum* as they passed the temple of the Dioscuri; the burlesque dancers may have appreciated their resemblance to the statue of Marysas in the Forum or to the *luperci*, who would have drunkenly burst forth from the Lupercal (and who might have comprised some of the young men who rode in the circus procession); and even the most experienced *agitator* may have felt a tingle of excitement as the procession approached the starting gates and the first race *a pompa* (after the procession) neared.

As the procession ranged over this landscape of memory from the heights of the Capitol, seat of empire and home to the gilded temple of Jupiter Optimus Maximus, to the low-lying *vallis Murcia* where the plebian temple of Ceres sat adjacent to the starting gates, it seems to have conjured collective or civic resonances. Much like other processions, the *pompa circensis* was a civic self-representation – a means by which the city, so to speak, represented (a certain version of) itself to itself. In the present case, the circus procession produced an image of the city as golden Rome (*aurea Roma*) comprised of the senate and Roman people plus the gods (SPQR+gods), in both its hierarchically arranged cortege and itinerary littered with gilded monuments that traveled from high to low physically, politically, socially, and ideologically. In addition to this symbolic image that sought to capture the entire city, the procession just might have produced a more practical one. A colorful passage from Plautus tantalizingly hints that the itinerary of the *pompa circensis*, which strung together some of the most prominent pathways, districts, and landmarks of ancient Rome, might have played a part in urban way-finding. It might have aided the development of mental maps by which to navigate the city.

All of the above (and, indeed, what follows below) has been written in the historical subjunctive. Though grounded in a careful consideration of the extant evidence, this study is necessarily tentative, hedged by "should," "might," "seems," and "appears." Such caution is due in part to the nature of performance, in part to the limits of historical analysis, in part to the elusive nature of "experience," which seems to be accessible only after the fact in representation and interpretation, and in part to the limited evidentiary base, which is scattered and often ambiguous and difficult. Literary sources, like Cicero, Dionysius of Halicarnassus, and Ovid, may explicitly address the *pompa circensis*, but for their own reasons and ends which impact their (re-)presentation, interpretation, and/or remembrance of the procession. Similarly, even if an visual image can be ascribed with some certainty to this or that type of procession, or this or that specific performance, Roman visual culture had its own rules and traditions that would have substantially shaped the image's composition, content, and appearance. And so, literary and visual sources would seem to offer glimpses of the various ways a procession could be received, interpreted, and remembered, rather than a transcription or a representation of any particular performance – the "experience" of which would be unrecoverable anyway.

The so-called documentary sources, laws, inscriptions, and papyri also have their own limitations. They may offer a window on conditions affecting production or document that a procession took place, on occasion with some detail, but they do not, as a result, capture the full performance. The *Lex Coloniae Genetivae Iuliae* seems to have mandated a procession with no protocol for its performance, while Aulus Clodius Flaccus organized two otherwise un-described processions before *munera* in the forum at Pompeii. The Theodosian Code contains a number of laws which, in theory, would have affected the *pompa circensis*, but any direct impact has to be inferred. Late-antique papyrus circus programs from Egypt simply note that a procession of some sort might have taken place. Even if a full procession protocol were extant, whatever it prescribed would have surely been subject to the normal exigencies of performance and historical change.

And so any specific performance or experience of the procession seems to be inaccessible, while a heuristic ideal-type and a general arc of development seems possible. On occasion, the evidence offers precious insight into this or that performance: it went through or by this or that place; a statue of Julius Caesar appeared in this procession; Neptune was purposely omitted from that one. Nonetheless, the evidence most often demands a carefully demarcated ideal-type, an analytic reconstruction that does not fill in the gaps or gloss over ambiguity or contradiction. This kind of ideal-type may then provide a basis for an examination of the procession's historical trajectory. In other words, a reconstruction need not be whimsical or entirely ahistorical. A careful analysis of the disparate evidence may cobble together an image of the procession that adequately represents its horizons of possibility, the grammatical and syntactical "rules" that guided, but did not determine, the performance of any particular procession. This ideal-type of the procession may then serve as a baseline from which to evaluate change. Certain changes, like the inclusion of the *divi*, stand out, but others, like the potential modifications to the choreography of the *ludiones*, remain harder to track, while continuities typically went unmentioned. The procession also varied from one performance to the next. Some performances could be more traditional (or even appear downright anachronistic in an attempt to cleave to Roman heritage), others more innovative. It also assuredly developed over time – in all cases, though, the procession still needed to be identifiable as *pompa circensis*.

And so, unsurprisingly, it seems that elements of the "republican" ideal-type continued into the empire, maintaining continuity amid change. Imperial and elite game-givers surrounded by an appropriate entourage and followed by contestants, competitors, performers, and entertainers still led the gods to the games along the same itinerary (at least for the *ludi Romani*) – even if one imperial *praeses* did so carried on a litter and another driving a six-horse chariot, and even if some itineraries may now have included imperial cult temples. However, the *pompa deorum* was now filled with deified emperors and empresses (*divi* and *divae*), whose honors were both calqued on and differentiated from the traditional gods. The *divi* were honored with *exuviae* in *tensae* like the traditional gods, but in place of a *ferculum*, some *divi* received massive and spectacular elephant *quadrigae* to draw their *simulacra* to the Circus, where they would have been installed in the *pulvinar* with the traditional gods. Deified empresses, other imperial women, and even non-deified imperial men similarly featured in the circus procession, though with lesser honors. The itinerary tells a similar story of enduring "republican" tradition and domineering imperial power. The route from the Capitol to the Circus was increasingly marked by imperial monuments, most notably imperial cult temples, triumphal arches, and statues. Even imperial renovations and reconstructions were often so lavish and extensive that they nearly amounted to new construction. Nevertheless, many of these massively rebuilt public buildings were still remembered for their republican pedigrees – especially the temples and above all the temple of Jupiter Optimus, which was thought, at least, to have always been rebuilt on the same foundations, the same footprints or memories (*vestigia*) as the "original."

The imperial *pompa circensis* was thus built upon its republican predecessor, even though a steady accumulation of imperial opulence – indeed, emperors seem to have been especially attracted to the production of "wonder" – would have nearly overwhelmed this republican heritage. The traditional gods still appeared in the procession, emperors were constrained (to a degree) by its traditions (its logic), and elite game-givers still competed for honor and visibility in their conduct of the procession and, of course, the games. In fact, the procession to the arena was sufficiently valued as a means of distinction that two spin-off ludic processions seemingly developed from it: the procession to the theater seems to have emerged in the late republic, while the one to the amphitheater first appears in the early empire. These (amphi-)theater processions appear to have been close kin to the circus procession, though with necessary adaptations to accommodate different venues. The Circus was larger, with a wide track for a processional route, while (amphi-)theaters offered more constricted space for processional spectacle. The *pompa circensis* was also prized by the competitors in the games: a couple of Rome's most decorated charioteers prominently commemorated the number of races won *a pompa* ("after the procession") among their accomplishments. In the fourth century CE, one charioteer may have pictured himself in the *pompa circensis* on a celebratory medallion. Other Romans, too, seem to have appreciated the circus procession – at least, inexpensive lamps produced on a large scale with an image of a lone *tensa* could serve as souvenir for a day at the races, instead of, say, a victorious charioteer or a favored horse.

Some of this traditional apparatus would ultimately disappear in late antiquity. In particular, the traditional gods seem to have been a casualty of Christian rhetoric aimed at the games in general and, at times, the *pompa circensis* specifically; or rather, a victim of imperial law designed to address such criticisms in some way so that the games could go on. Even before image cult and sacrifice were prohibited by law (even if not in practice), numismatic representations of the circus procession shifted from the traditional and above all imperial gods to the imperial game-giver. In late antiquity, an image of an emperor as consul leading a circus procession often on an elephant *quadriga* displaced the *currus elephantorum* of the imperial gods – though it seems that *divi* may still have traveled to the circus on such vehicles in actual processions. This process of imperialization (the dominance of processional imagery, if not also the procession itself, by emperors) seems to have both preceded and enabled a process of secularization, in which image cult and sacrifice were eventually excised (first in law, and then eventually in practice) so that certain Christian sensibilities might be assuaged. Imperialized and secularized processions and games could thus continue. As it turns out, imperialization-secularization may also have paved the way for Christianization – the transport of Christian symbols, namely the cross, in the procession – possibly transforming a *pompa deorum* into a *pompa Dei*.

Despite these shifts in representation and practice at an imperial level, some elites on some occasions still seem to have produced something like a traditional procession, traditional gods and all – if only in memory, in the visual commemoration of the performance. Even among the shifting tides of late antiquity, there was a degree of continuity – the complexities of which the late-antique itinerary readily demonstrates. In the late third and early fourth centuries CE, the Forum was massively reconstructed after a devastating fire, at which point it seems to have taken on its most imperial visage. Throughout the fourth century CE, statues of emperors dominated the open space of the Forum. At the same time, Roman magistrates targeted buildings with venerable republican pedigrees or associations, sanctuaries and temples, as well as the rostra and the curia, for a surprisingly large number of the increasingly rare restorations in late antiquity. Republican tradition began, in some ways, to compete with imperial power. Eventually, the Christian church at Rome would join this competition. In the fourth century CE, the *titulus Anastasiae*, the first Christian church building erected along the itinerary, might have resonated with the possible early-to mid-fifth-century CE addition of Christian symbols to the procession – other churches would, of course, be built in areas once traversed by the procession, but only after it was no longer performed. And so, the late-antique procession and its itinerary seem to have embodied a multiplicity of images of Rome – traditional, imperial, and Christian – as the procession came to its end.

The *pompa circensis*, possibly the most-often performed procession in ancient Rome, had a long and continuous performance history – stretching, it seems, from the early republic to late antiquity. Over that long history, it is important to note that despite inevitable and even desirable variation, any given performance of the procession seems to have remained within certain parameters, remaining legible as a *pompa circensis* – even in late antiquity when it may have been limited to the *praeses*, his entourage, and contestants leading Victory and imperial imagery (likely statues of the living emperor, but possibly also certain *divi*) to the arena. The procession remained a coherent species, even as historical developments demanded change. Adaptation allowed the circus procession to continue to serve as a crucible in which links between divinity and humanity, ruler(s) and ruled, citizens and the city, and collective memory and collective identity were forged and re-forged. For that reason, the circus procession offers a valuable prism through which to assess the changing intersections of religious performance, cultural memory, and civic identity in ancient Rome. The *pompa circensis* both shaped and was shaped by how Romans understood themselves, their society, and their city – in the imagination and on the ground.

NOTES

Introduction

1. *Sed iam non sustineo diutius vos morari: scio quam odiosa res mihi sit circensibus pompa* (LCL).
2. In order: Sen. *Controv.* 1, *praef.* 24; Columella, *Rust.* 3.8.2; Macrob. *Sat.* 1.23.13; Suet. *Iul.* 76.1, *Claud.* 11.2, and *Tit.* 2; and Tert. *Spect.* 7.5.
3. Greenblatt, "Resonance and Wonder."
4. On the circus procession, see esp. Piganiol, *Jeux romains*, 15–31; RE sv *pompa* col. 1985; Versnel, *Triumphus*, 94–115; Thuillier, "Denys d'Halicarnasse"; Clavel-Lévêque, *L'Empire en jeux*, 40–45; Devallet, "*Pompa circensis*"; Dupont, "*Pompa* et *carmina*"; Jannot, "danseurs de la *pompa*"; Bernstein, *Ludi publici*, esp. 41–48, 85–96, and 254–268; Lo Monaco, "In processione al Circo"; Doukellis, "Από την έννομητάξη"; and Arena, *Feste e rituali*, 53–102, in addition to other (sections of) essays addressing the procession, e.g. Nelis-Clément, "Pompes et circonstances," 61–70.
5. Votive: Dion. Hal. *Ant. Rom.* 7.72.1–13 (perhaps the *ludi Romani*) and Suet. *Aug.* 43.5; *Romani*: Dion. Hal. *Ant. Rom.* 5.57.5; *Apollinares*: Livy 30.38.10–11; *Megalenses*: Ov. *Fast.* 4.391; and *Augustales*: Tac. *Ann.* 1.15.2. Latte, *Römische Religionsgeschichte*, 248, would add the *ludi Plebeii*; Beacham, *Spectacle Entertainments*, 22 n. 36, the *ludi Cerealia*; and see pp. 108–117 on Caesar and Augustus in the *pompa circensis*.
6. See pp. 180–181.
7. Varro, *Rust.* 1.2.11: *Bono animo este, inquit Agrius. Nam non modo ovom illut sublatum est, quod ludis circensibus novissimi curriculi finem facit quadrigis, sed ne illud quidem ovom vidimus, quod in cenali pompa solet esse primum* (trans. adapted Hooper/Ash LCL).
8. On the eggs in the circus, see Humphrey, *Roman Circuses*, 260–262.
9. Macrob. *Sat.* 3.16.2: a *pompa* which brought an *acipenser* to the table and *Sat.* 3.16.8: *a coronatis inferretur cum tibicinis cantu, quasi quaedam non deliciarum sed numinis pompa* (trans. Kaster LCL).
10. Many works treat the procession insightfully, but briefly: e.g. Friedländer, "jeux," 278–283; Balsdon, *Life and Leisure*, 245 and 316; Hönle and Henze, *Römische Amphitheater und Stadien*, 89–92; Humphrey, *Roman Circuses*, passim; Beacham, *Spectacle Entertainments*, 21–23 and 42; Dupont, *Daily Life in Ancient Rome*, 207–209; BNP 40–41, 59, 262, 383: fig. 8.3; and Scheid, *Introduction to Roman Religion*, 107.
11. E.g. D-S sv Circus (p. 1193); and Auguet, *Cruelty and Civilization*, 126–128.
12. From a large literature, see Rice, *Grand Procession of Ptolemy* (dating the procession to 280–275 BCE); Foertmeyer, "Dating of the Pompe" (275/4 BCE); Wikander, "Pomp and Circumstance"; Walbank, "Two Hellenistic Processions" (279/8 BCE); Hazzard, *Imagination of a Monarchy*, 60–79 (262 BCE); Thompson, "Philadelphus' Procession"; and Bell, *Spectacular Power*, 119–138.
13. Ath. 5.197C–203B, at 197D: τὰς τῶν πεντετηρίδων γραφὰς (LCL). See Beard, *Roman Triumph*, 167–173, esp. 168–169, who critiques Rice, *Grand Procession of Ptolemy*, esp. 138–150, on the accuracy of the description; and Hazzard, *Imagination of a Monarchy*, 64–66, who accepts the existence, detail, and accuracy of the records.
14. See further pp. 21–25.
15. Ov. *Am.* 3.2.43–56; and see also *Ars am.* 1.147–148 and *Fast.* 4.391 and 6.405.
16. Hardie, *Ovid's Poetics*, esp. 1–61.
17. Henderson, "A Doo-Dah-Doo-Dah-Dey," 53.
18. Welch, "Elegy and the Monuments," esp. 109–114; and also Thomas, "Ovid at the Races."

19. Ricoeur, *Time and Narrative*, 1.xi.
20. Davis, *Parades and Power*, 1–22 on parades, power, and social relations.
21. See de Certeau, *Practice of Everyday Life*, 91–130; and Favro, *Urban Image*, 1–23, following Lynch, *Image of the City*.
22. Ricoeur, *Time and Narrative*, 1.xi.
23. BMRRC #348.1–3.
24. Compare Figures 1–3 with BMRRC #326.1, 367.3–5, and 402.1; and Crawford, *Roman Republican Coinage* #358.1 and 367.1–2, all labeled triumphal chariots, which resemble gods in *quadrigae* and humans in *bigae*, e.g. BMRRC #350.1 (Jupiter), 352.1 (Victory), 354.1 (Minerva), and 404 (togate figure on a *biga*). See further Latham, "Representing Ritual," 202–205 (figures 1–3) on numismatic images of *tensa* and triumphal chariots.
25. See further pp. 57–58, on the "*tensae*" of Dossenus, and pp. 111–112 on imperial *tensae* and triumphal chariots.
26. Crawford, *Roman Republican Coinage*, 729.
27. RIC 2 Trajan #777–779 (see p. 129)
28. Madigan, *Ceremonial Sculptures*, 41–45, notes the difficulties in assigning images to a specific procession.
29. See remarks by Hölscher, "Transformation of Victory into Power," on triumphal imagery; and La Rocca, "Art and Representation," on the roles of the patron, subject matter, and artistic training.
30. See further pp. 98–101; and Itgenshorst, *Tota illa pompa*, 13–41, esp. 13–14 and 30, for whom ideal-type describes idealized and anachronistic imperial-era descriptions of republican triumphs.
31. Out of a large literature, see A. Assmann, *Cultural Memory and Western Civilization*, 119–134, on functional and stored memory; J. Assmann, *Cultural Memory and Early Civilization*, 6–7 and 34–41, *Religion and Cultural Memory*, 1–4 and 24–30, and "Communicative and Cultural Memory," on communicative/cultural memory; and Erll, *Memory in Culture*, esp. 28–37 and 53–61, surveying both.
32. Versnel, *Triumphus*, 73–77.
33. Vell. Pat. 2.40.4.
34. See pp. 25–26 and also pp. 152–153.
35. Tac. *Ann.* 1.8.6: *qui ipsi viderant quique a parentibus acceperant diem illum crudi adhuc servitii et libertatis inprospere repetitae, cum occisus dictator Caesar aliis pessimum, aliis pulcherrimum facinus videretur* (ed. LCL, trans. Woodman), on which see Woodman, "Not a Funeral Note"; Gowing, *Empire and Memory*, 28–30; and Sumi, "Topography and Ideology," 227–229.
36. Tac. *Dial.* 17.3: *centum et viginti anni ab interitu Ciceronis in hunc diem colliguntur, unius hominis aetas* (ed. LCL, trans. Benario), on which see Gowing, *Empire and Memory*, 114–115. Evans-Pritchard, "From *The Nuer*," argued that oral cultures had a collective memory of approximately 100–120 years, beyond which the past became undifferentiated myth. See also J. Assmann (n. 31 above) on the "floating gap" between the recent and the mythical past.
37. See Piganiol, *Jeux romains*, 15–31; and esp. Bernstein, *Ludi publici*, esp. 41–48, 85–96, and 254–268, and "Complex Rituals," for such a history.
38. See BNP 1–18 on the origins and early history of Roman religion; and Itgenshorst, *Tota illa pompa*, who employed a similar, but more restricted circumscription of evidence for the republican triumph.
39. Ath. 5.194c: βουλόμενος τῇ μεγαλοδωρίᾳ ὑπερᾶραι τὸν Παῦλον (trans. Gulick LCL) and 5.195A, on which see Walbank, "Two Hellenistic Processions," 125–129; and Bell, *Spectacular Power*, 138–150.
40. Polyb. 30.25.11 (= Ath. 5.194f): ἔξιππα μὲν ἦν ἑκατόν, τέθριππα δὲ τετταράκοντα, ἔπειτα ἐλεφάντων ἅρμα καὶ συνωρίς. καθ᾽ ἕνα δὲ εἵποντο ἐλέφαντες διεσκευασμένοι τριάκοντα καὶ ἕξ (trans. Paton/Walbank/Habicht/Olson LCL). Diod. Sic. 31.16 (according to a seemingly reliable tenth-century CE excerpt) sketchily covers the same material. On Hellenistic processions more generally, see Chaniotis, "Processions in Hellenistic Cities."
41. Beard, *The Roman Triumph*, 168; and see also Itgenshorst, "Roman Commanders."
42. Polyb. 30.25.3 (= Ath. 5.194d): καθηγοῦντό τινες Ῥωμαϊκὸν ἔχοντες καθοπλισμὸν ἐν θώραξιν ἁλυσιδωτοῖς, ἄνδρες ἀκμάζοντες ταῖς ἡλικίαις πεντα κισχίλιοι (trans. Paton/Walbank/Habicht/Olson LCL). See Edmonson, "Cultural Politics," on the complex interactions between Greece and Rome regarding public spectacle.
43. See Orlin, *Foreign Cults in Rome*, 137–161, on *ludi* as Roman celebrations.
44. Dion. Hal. *Ant. Rom.* 7.72.2: ὡς ἐξ ἀρχῆς ἐγίνετο παρ᾽ Ἕλλησιν (LCL).

45. Dion. Hal. *Ant. Rom.* 7.72.7: Ἑλληνικὸν ... πάνυ παλαιὸν ἐπιτήδευμα (LCL).
46. Dion. Hal. *Ant. Rom.* 7.72.10: τὴν Ἑλληνικὴν ... σίκιννιν (LCL).
47. Dion. Hal. *Ant. Rom.* 7.72.13 (chapter 2 nn. 44, 58, 66) and 7.72.16: κατὰ νόμους ἐγίνετο τοὺς ἀμφὶ θυσίαν ὑφ' Ἑλλήνων κατασταθέντας (trans. Cary LCL).
48. Thuillier, "Denys d'Halicarnasse," "Les jeux," and *Le sport dans la Rome antique*, 15–36, on Etruscan influence on the games; and Bonfante Warren, "Roman Triumphs and Etruscan Kings"; and Versnel, *Triumphus*, esp. 255–303, on Etruscan influence on the triumph.
49. Dion. Hal. *Ant. Rom.* 7.72.12: εἶδον δὲ καὶ ἐν ἀνδρῶν ἐπισήμων ταφαῖς ἅμα ταῖς ἄλλαις πομπαῖς προηγουμένους τῆς κλίνης τοὺς σατυριστῶν χοροὺς κινουμένους τὴν σίκιννιν ὄρχησιν, μάλιστα δ' ἐν τοῖς τῶν εὐδαιμόνων κήδεσιν (trans. Cary LCL).
50. Dion. Hal. *Ant. Rom.* 7.72.11: δηλοῦσι δὲ καὶ αἱ τῶν θριάμβων εἴσοδοι παλαιὰν καὶ ἐπιχώριον οὖσαν Ῥωμαίοις τὴν κέρτομον καὶ σατυρικὴν παιδιάν. ἐφεῖται γὰρ τοῖς κατάγουσι τὰς νίκας ἰαμβίζειν τε καὶ κατασκώπτειν τοὺς ἐπιφανεστάτους ἄνδρας αὐτοῖς στρατηλάταις (trans. adapted Cary LCL).
51. Mommsen, "Die *ludi Magni* und *romani*," an argument that Östenberg, "*Circum metas fertur*," esp. 314–318, repurposes to suggest an alternate triumphal route. See also Versnel, *Triumphus*, 101–115; and Bernstein, *Ludi publici*, 31–35 on Mommsen; and pp. 25–26, on the triumph and circus procession.
52. Bell, *Spectacular Power*, tends in the direction of a common classical Mediterranean culture of spectacle. Gailliot, "place de l'*editor*," 3–4, suggests a parallel but reciprocal development of the triumph and circus procession.
53. Versnel, *Triumphus*, 94–131; Beck, "Züge in die Ewigkeit"; and Hölkeskamp, "Rituali e cerimonie," "Pomp und Prozessionen," and "Hierarchie und Konsens," compare the three different processions.
54. See Östenberg, *Staging the World*, 6–12, on the triumph as spectacle.
55. On performance, see p. 49; and on ritual failure, see pp. 39–42, 61–65 and 147–152.
56. See Chapter 1 Introduction (pp. 19–21), on gravity/levity and resonance/wonder.
57. Halbwachs, *On Collective Memory*, pioneered social frameworks of memory, on whom see J. Assmann, *Cultural Memory and Early Civilization*, 21–33; Erll, *Memory in Culture*, 14–18; and Olick, Vinitzky-Seroussi, and Levy, "Introduction," 16–25.
58. See Valli, "I percorsi delle processioni," on processions and urban space; and Chapter 3.

One *Pompa hominum*

1. μετὰ γὰρ τοὺς ἐνοπλίους χοροὺς οἱ τῶν σατυριστῶν ἐπόμπευον χοροὶ ... κατέσκωπτόν τε καὶ κατεμιμοῦντο τὰς σπουδαίας κινήσεις ἐπὶ τὰ γελοιότερα μεταφέροντες (LCL).
2. On structure and unity, see Clavel-Lévêque, *L'Empire en jeux*, 40–45, and "L'espace des jeux," 2439–2446; Bernstein, *Ludi publici*, esp. 254–268, and "Complex Rituals," 228–229; and Beck, "Züge in die Ewigkeit." On ludic performance, see Versnel, *Triumphus*, esp. 255–270; Devallet, "*Pompa circensis*"; and Dupont, "*Pompa* et *carmina*." Doukellis, "Από την έννομη τάξη," addresses both.
3. Ov. *Am.* 3.2.61: *pompamque deorum* (LCL).
4. Greenblatt, "Resonance and Wonder," 42; and see also Boin, *Ostia in Late Antiquity*, 192.
5. See Chaniotis, "Rituals between Norms and Emotions," on connections formed in ritual; and Davis, *Parades and Power*, 9–12, on temporality in processions.
6. J. Assmann, *Religion and Cultural Memory*, esp. 1–4, and *Cultural Memory and Early Civilization*, esp. 21–33, discusses ties between neurologically based individual and culturally based collective memories.
7. Greenblatt, "Resonance and Wonder," 42.
8. Bergmann, "Introduction."
9. Lim, "In the 'Temple of Laughter,'" on audience reception.
10. Livy 45.1.8: *repente immemor spectaculi populus in medium decurrit* (LCL).
11. See Graf, "What Is New about Greek Sacrifice?" esp. 116–117, for apposite remarks on reconstructing the grammar of sacrifice. Weber, "'Objectivity' in Social Science," esp. 89–106, on ideal-types; Bourdieu, *Outline of a Theory of Practice*, 72–95 and 159–197, and *Logic of Practice*, 52–97, on *habitus*. See further, pp. 9–11 and 98–101.

12. The metaphors (grammar, syntax, *langue, parole*) borrowed from linguistics are not meant to read ritual as language *per se*.
13. Section title from Barchiesi, Rüpke, and Stephens, ed., *Rituals in Ink*.
14. ὑπεσχόμην γὰρ ἐπὶ τῷ τέλει τῆς πρώτης γπαφῆς, ἣν περὶ τοῦ γένους αὐτῶν σθνταξάμενος ἐξέδωκα, μυρίοις βεβαιώσειν τεκμηρίοις τὴν πρόθεσιν, ἔθη καὶ νόμιμα καὶ ἐπιτηδεύματα παλαιὰ παρεχόμενος αὐτῶν, ἃ μέχρι τοῦ κατ᾽ ἐμὲ φυλάττουσι χρόνου οἷα παρὰ τῶν προγόνων ἐδέξαντο ... ἐν αἷς πρῶτα καὶ κυριώτατα πάντων εἶναι πείθομαι τὰ γινόμενα καθ᾽ ἑκάστην πόλιν περὶ θεῶν καὶ δαιμόνων πατρίους σεβασμούς (LCL).
15. On this digression, see Gabba, *Dionysius and the History of Archaic Rome*, 134–138; and esp. Schultze, "Dionysius of Halicarnassus."
16. Dion. Hal. *Ant. Rom.* 7.70.1: Ἐπεὶ δὲ κατὰ τοῦτο γέγονα τῆς ἱστορίας τὸ μέρος, οὐκ οἴομαι δεῖν τὰ περὶ τὴν ἑορτὴν ἐπιτελούμενα ὑπ αὐτῶν παρελθεῖν, οὐχ ἵνα μοι χαριεστέρα γένηται προσθήκας λαβοῦσα θεατρικὰς καὶ λόγους ἀνθηροτέρους ἡ διήγησις, ἀλλ ἵνα τῶν ἀναγκαίων τι πιστώσηται πραγμάτων, ὅτι τὰ συνοικίσαντα ἔθνη τὴν Ῥωμαίων πόλιν Ἑλληνικὰ ἦν ἐκ τῶν ἐπιφανεστάτων ἀποικισθέντα τόπων, ἀλλ᾽ οὐχ, ὥσπερ ἔνιοι νομίζουσι, βάρβαρα καὶ ἀνέστια (LCL).
17. Dion. Hal. *Ant. Rom.* 7.71.1: ποιήσομαι ... τὴν τέκμαρσιν ... Κοΐντῳ Φαβίῳ βεβαιωτῇ χρώμενος καὶ οὐδεμιᾶς ἔτι δεόμενος πίστεως ἑτέρας· παλαιότατος γὰρ ἀνὴρ τῶν τὰ Ῥωμαϊκὰ συνταξαμένων, καὶ πίστιν οὐκ ἐξ ὧν ἤκουσε μόνον, ἀλλὰ καὶ ἐξ ὧν αὐτὸς ἔγνω παρεχόμενος (LCL).
18. Gabba, *Dionysius and the History of Archaic Rome*, 89. Schultze, "Authority, Originality and Competence," agrees that Dionysius was quite reliable.
19. Dion. Hal. *Ant. Rom.* 5.57.5 mentions one set in 500 BCE.
20. On sources for early Rome, see Cornell, *Beginnings of Rome*, 1–30. On written records of ritual, see Scheid, "Rituel et écriture à Rome"; and Rodríguez-Mayorgas, "*Annales Maximi*," 245–252.
21. Mura Sommella, "L'area sacra di S. Omobono," 71–82; Coarelli, *Foro Boario*, 222–224; Cristofani (ed.), *La grande Roma* #5.1.28–30; Massa Pairault, "Aspects idéologique des *ludi*," 268–269; and Adornato, "L'area sacra di Omobono," 816–818. Both Fulminante, *Urbanisation of Rome and Latium Vetus*, 66–104; and Hopkins, "Creation of the Forum," 52–54, argue that archaic Rome would have been impressive. See also Chapter 3 n. 48.
22. Beck, "Fabius Pictor, Quintus."
23. Piganiol, *Jeux romains*; and Thuillier, "Denys d'Halicarnasse," 576, question the reliability of the description; while Thuillier, "Les jeux," notes an overemphasis on Greece to the detriment of Etruria; and Itgenshorst, *Tota illa pompa*, 13–30, argues that imperial-era Greek descriptions of republican processions are typically idealized rather than historical.
24. Baudrillard, *Simulacra and Simulation*, 1–42. Vergil and Dionysius may have both had their interest piqued by Augustan performances according to Nelis and Nelis-Clément, "Vergil, *Georgics* 1.1–42," paragraph 12.
25. Stat. *Theb.* 6.255–295, on which see Lovatt, "Statius on Parade."
26. Buc, "Ritual and Interpretation," 186. See also Buc, *The Dangers of Ritual*, esp. 1–12; tempered by Koziol, "Review Article."
27. For apposite remarks on the triumph, see Beard, "The Triumph of the Absurd," "Writing Ritual," and esp. *Roman Triumph*.
28. On this point, see Clavel-Lévêque, *L'Empire en jeux*, 40–45; and Darnton, *Great Cat Massacre*, 107–43 ("A Bourgeois Puts His World in Order"), for just such an exercise.
29. Elsner, *Roman Eyes*, 34–38, on the textual repetition of ritual.
30. Greenblatt, *Renaissance Self-Fashioning*, 3–7.
31. See apposite comments by Rebillard, *Christians and Their Many Identities*, 5–6.
32. Ogilvie, *Commentary on Livy Books 1–5*, 149.
33. Dion. Hal. *Ant. Rom.* 7.72.1: Πρὶν ἄρξασθαι τῶν ἀγώνων, πομπὴν ἔστελλον τοῖς θεοῖς οἱ τὴν μεγίστην ἔχοντες ἐξουσίαν, ἀπὸ τοῦ Καπιτωλίου τε καὶ δι᾽ ἀγορᾶς ἄγοντες ἐπὶ τὸν μέγαν ἱππόδρομον (LCL).
34. Livy 8.40.2–3: Aulus Cornelius appointed dictator to start the races, and 27.33.6: Titus Manlius Torquatus named dictator to produce games. On the consul as *praeses ludorum* and aediles as *curatores ludorum*, see

Salomonson, *Chair, Sceptre and Wreath*, 58–61; Bernstein, *Ludi publici*, esp. 58–78, and "Complex Rituals," 224–225; and Pina Polo, "Consuls as *curatores pacis deorum*," 108–112, and *Consul at Rome*, 44–52. Piganiol, *Jeux romains*, 17, argues that aediles presided over annual games, while dictators and consuls over votive ones, against which see Versnel, *Triumphus*, 130.

35. Livy 5.41.2: *augustissima vestis est tensas ducentibus triumphantibusve* (LCL). On the chariot, see Livy 45.1.7; Dion. Hal. *Ant. Rom.* 5.57.5; and Plin. *HN* 34.20: praetors in *bigae*, on which see further pp. 153–154. On visibility, see Hölkeskamp, "Roman Republic as Theatre of Power."
36. Abaecherli, "*Fercula, carpenta*, and *tensae*," 8; and Gailliot, "impiété volontaire?" and, at greater length, "place de l'*editor*," argue that the game-giver came later in the procession, based in large part on assumed parallels with the triumph and processions in the *ludi Saeculares*. Though the evidence is ambiguous, the game-giver at the head of the procession is commonly accepted: e.g. Versnel, *Triumphus*, 262; Jannot, "danseurs de la *pompa*," 57; Beck, "Züge in die Ewigkeit," 100; Bernstein, "Complex Rituals," 228; Arena, *Feste e rituali*, 55; Pina Polo, *Consul at Rome*, 45; and Rüpke, *Religion in Republican Rome*, 30. Piganiol, *Jeux romains*, 17, did not locate the *praeses*.
37. See Piganiol, *Jeux romains*, 75–91; Bernstein, *Ludi publici*, 31–51; Rüpke, *Religion in Republic Rome*, 65–67; and pp. 12–13.
38. Rüpke, "Public and Publicity."
39. MacCormack, *Art and Ceremony*, 17–89, on the "triumphalization" of the *adventus*.
40. See Rüpke, "Triumphator and Ancestor Rituals," 256–259, on the difference between the president of the games and the *triumphator* during the republic. Of course, there are marked similarities which cannot be ignored, on which see Versnel, *Triumphus*, 101–115 and 129–131, and "Red (Herring?)," a critique of Rüpke. On ritual syntax, see Hölkeskamp, "Rituali e cerimonie," "Pomp und Prozessionen," and "Hierarchie und Konsens," who also compares the triumph and circus procession.
41. Scheid, "Le flamine de Jupiter," 221–224, on the possibility of multiple figurations of Jupiter in the circus procession and triumph.
42. Auliard, "La composition du cortège triomphal"; and Östenberg, "Power Walks."
43. Jones, "Processional Colors," argues that processional colors were different from everyday dress.
44. Cic. *De fin.* 2.77: faking an impressive walk; and on Piso's walk: Cic. *Sest.* 19 and *Pis.* 24, on which see Corbeill, *Nature Embodied*, 118–119; and O'Sullivan, *Walking in Roman Culture*, 12 with 59–64 on the entourage of elites. See also Gailliot, "place de l'*editor*," on the (probable) entourage. On the distinct bearing of *fercula*-bearers, see pp. 53 and 62–63.
45. Ryberg, 36 (a triumphal procession and a wing-less Victory); while the consensus is a charioteer: Ronke #11; *Imperii insignia* B15; Holliday, *Origins of Roman Historical Commemoration*, 182–185; Fless, "Römische Prozessionen," #82; and *Trionfi romani* I.3.1.
46. Dion. Hal. *Ant. Rom.* 7.72.15: Συντελεσθείσης δὲ τῆς πομπῆς ἐβουθύτουν εὐθὺς οἵ τε ὕπατοι καὶ τῶν ἱερέων οἷς ὅσιον (LCL).
47. Cic. *Mil.* 65: *popa . . . de circo maximo* (LCL), on which see Nelis-Clément, "métiers du cirque," esp. 270–272, for staff related to the procession.
48. Livy 45.1.7: a consul mounting a chariot after giving the start signal, suggesting that he rode to the gates, on which see Versnel, *Triumphus*, 131. On the start signal, see Marchet, "*Mittere mappam*"; and pp. 89 and 155–156, for other evocations of the race start.
49. Cic. *Div.* 1.107–108: *consul quom mittere signum volt, omnes avidi spectant ad carceris oras, quam mox emittat pictis e faucibus currus* (trans. adapted Falconer LCL).
50. Ronke #153 (mid first century CE); *Imperii insignia* B17 (mid first century BCE); and Holliday, *Origins of Roman Historical; Commemoration*, 185–186 (mid first century BCE). Marcattili, *Circo Massimo*, 160–162, argues for monumental *carceres* in the late third century BCE; while Humphrey, *Roman Circuses*, 153–154 and 171–172, argues for the mid first century CE.
51. Marchet, "*Mittere mappam*," 295–297; and Nelis-Clément, "cirque romain et son paysage sonore," 445.
52. Ov. *Am.* 3.2.65–66: *maxima iam vacuo praetor spectacula circo / quadriiugos aequo carcere misit equos* (ed. LCL, trans. Lee).

53. See Veyne, *Bread and Circuses*, esp. 208–228; Flaig, *Ritualisierte Politik*, 232–242, on *ludi* as political ceremony and symbolic capital; and Wiseman, *Remembering the Roman People*, 157–164, on value of games for the game-giver.
54. Dion. Hal. *Ant. Rom.* 7.72.1: ἡγοῦντο δὲ τῆς πομπῆς πρῶτον μὲν οἱ παῖδες αὐτῶν οἱ πρόσηβοί τε καὶ τοῦ πομπεύειν ἔχοντες ἡλικίαν, ἱππεῖς μὲν ὧν οἱ πατέρες τιμήματα ἱππέων εἶχον, πεζοὶ δ᾽ οἱ μέλλοντες ἐν τοῖς πεζοῖς στρατεύεσθαι· οἱ μὲν κατ᾽ ἴλας τε καὶ κατὰ λόχους, οἱ δὲ κατὰ συμμορίας τε καὶ τάξεις ὡς εἰς διδασκαλεῖον πορευόμενοι (LCL), on which see Piganiol, *Jeux romains*, 18; and Bernstein, *Ludi publici*, 255–257.
55. Taylor, "*Seviri Equitum Romanorum*," contends there was no infantry parade by the Augustan era.
56. On ephebes in processions, see e.g. Connelly, "Ritual Movement," 317 and 319–320; Rogers, *Sacred Identity of Ephesos*, 67–69 and 112; and Nijf, *Civic World*, 193. On the ceremonial role of the early imperial equites, see Demougin, *L'ordre équestre*, esp. 150–156 and 250–258; and pp. 81–82.
57. Hopkins, "Violence to Blessing," beautifully captures this aspect of the census; an interpretation followed by Marco Simón, "Ritual Participation and Collective Identity." For an analysis of the whole process, see Nicolet, *World of the Citizen*, 49–88, and *Space, Geography, and Politics*, 123–147.
58. On processions as communication and publicity, see Beck, "Züge in die Ewigkeit," 90–100, emphasizing social hierarchy and integration; and Rüpke, "Public and Publicity" and *Religion in Republican Rome*, esp. 37–42.
59. Davis, *Parades and Power*, 1–22.
60. Dion. Hal. *Ant. Rom.* 7.72.2: τούτοις ἠκολούθουν ἡνίοχοι τὰ τέθριππά τε καὶ τὰς συνωρίδας καὶ τοὺς ἀζεύκτους ἵππους ἐλαύνοντες· μεθ᾽ οὓς οἱ τῶν ἀθλημάτων ἀγωνισταὶ τῶν τε κούφων καὶ τῶν βαρέων, τὸ μὲν ἄλλο σῶμα γυμνοί, τὸ δὲ περὶ τὴν αἰδῶ καλυπτόμενοι (LCL).
61. Livy 39.22.2: *Athletarum quoque certamen tum primo Romanis spectaculo fuit* (LCL), on which see Piganiol, *Jeux romains*, 19–20, for whom the Livian passage casts doubt on Fabius Pictor-Dionysius; while Thuillier, "Denys d'Halicarnasse"; and Crowther, "Greek Games in Republican Rome," attempt to reconcile the seemingly contradictory traditions.
62. See Thuillier, *sport dans la Rome antique*, 126–127, on chariot racing hierarchy; and, on charioteers, Horsmann, *Wagenlenker*; and more briefly Junkelmann, "On the Starting Line," esp. 86–89; Potter, "Entertainers," 312–327; and Bell, "Roman Chariot Racing," 495–498.
63. See Nelis-Clément, "métiers du cirque," esp. 270–287, on processional and circus professionals, and "cirque romain et son paysage sonore," 440, on race support staff.
64. See Leppin, "Between Marginality and Celebrity," on charioteers' ambivalent status.
65. Ronke #12 (a funeral procession); and *Imperii insignia* C66 (a kind of awards ceremony).
66. Bailey, *Catalogue of Lamps* Q961. See also Decker and Thuillier, *sport dans l'antiquité*, 211 and fig. 124; and Figure 77.
67. See pp. 211–214.
68. Dion. Hal. *Ant. Rom.* 2.71.4; Val. Max. 2.4.4; and Tert., *De spect.* 5.2, on *ludiones* from Lydians. On *ludiones*, see Jannot, "danseurs de la *pompa*," esp. 58–62; Dupont, "Ludions, *lydioi*," and "*Pompa* et *carmina*," 77–78; and Tagliafico, "Ludiones."
69. Cic. *Mur.* 13: *nemo enim fere saltat sobrius, nisi forte insanit* (LCL), on which, see Naerebout, "*Reich Tanzt*," esp. 148–150.
70. Dion. Hal. *Ant. Rom.* 7.72.5: Ἠκολούθουν δὲ τοῖς ἀγωνισταῖς ὀρχηστῶν χοροὶ πολλοὶ τριχῇ νενεμημένοι, πρῶτοι μὲν ἀνδρῶν, δεύτεροι δ᾽ ἀγενείων, τελευταῖοι δὲ παίδων, οἷς παρηκολούθουν αὐληταί τε ἀρχαϊκοῖς ἐμφυσῶντες αὐλίσκοις βραχέσιν, ὡς καὶ εἰς τόδε χρόνου γίνεται, καὶ κιθαρισταὶ λύρας ἑπταχόρδους ἐλεφαντίνας καὶ τὰ καλούμενα βάρβιτα κρέκοντες (LCL).
71. Dion. Hal. *Ant. Rom.* 7.72.10: τῆς ἐναγωνίου τε καὶ κατεσπουδασμένης ὀρχήσεως (LCL).
72. Dion. Hal. *Ant. Rom.* 7.72.6: χιτῶνες φοινίκεοι ζωστῆρσι χαλκέοις ἐσφιγμένοι, καὶ ξίφη παρηρτημένα, καὶ λόγχαι βραχύτεραι τῶν μετρίων· τοῖς δ ἀνδράσι καὶ κράνη χάλκεα λόφοις ἐπισήμοις κεκοσμημένα καὶ πτεροῖς (LCL).
73. Dion. Hal. *Ant. Rom.* 2.71.4: οὗτοι τῆς πομπῆς ἡγεμόνες and, from the previous sentence, χιτωνίσκους ἐνδεδυκότες ἐκπρεπεῖς κράνη καὶ ξίφη καὶ πάρμας

ἔχοντες στοιχηδὸν πορεύονται (LCL). Based on this passage, Piganiol, *Jeux romains*, 21, concluded that the *ludiones* no longer danced by the early empire; Boyancé, "À propos de la *satura*," 15–17, agrees, but notes that the *ludiones* still appeared in public celebrations; while Jannot, "danseurs de la *pompa*," 62, contrasts the decline of the *ludiones* with the popularity of the burlesque dancers. See further pp. 156–157.

74. Bacchielli, "Un rilievo della collezione Castelli-Baldassini"; followed by Santucci, "Rilievo frammentario," suggests Roman provenance. Beard, *Roman Triumph*, 221–222, calls the prisoners barbarians after Fless, "Römische Prozessionen," #72. See further Fless, *Opferdiener und Kultmusiker*, 28–31 (pl. 10.2).

75. See pp. 40–41, on *ludiones* and *instauratio*; RIC 1^2 Augustus #339–340 (Figure 9); and RIC 2.1^2 Domitian #595–602. Piganiol, *Jeux romains*, 22 n. 1, suggested they were *ludiones*; which Boyancé, "À propos de la *satura*," 15–16; and Turcan, *Religion Romaine*, vol. 2, 39–40, accept. See esp. Sobocinski, "Visualizing Ceremony," 587–590, on the *ludio* in coinage for the Secular Games.

76. Fless, *Opferdiener und Kultmusiker*, 28–30 and #46 (pl. 9.1–2), and "Römische Prozessionen," #73.

77. Dion. Hal. *Ant. Rom.* 7.72.6: ἡγεῖτο δὲ καθ' ἕκαστον χορὸν εἷς ἀνήρ, ὃς ἐνεδίδου τοῖς ἄλλοις τὰ τῆς ὀρχήσεως σχήματα, πρῶτος εἰδοφορῶν τὰς πολεμικὰς καὶ συντόνους κινήσεις ἐν τοῖς προκελευσματικοῖς ὡς τὰ πολλὰ ῥυθμοῖς (LCL).

78. Sen. *Ep.* 117.25: *remove ista lusoria arma* (LCL), on which see Garelli-François, "Ludions, homéristes ou pantomimes?"

79. See Goffman, *Presentation of Self in Everyday Life*, esp. 17–76; and Carson, *Performance*, esp. 11–55, on social performance.

80. Dion. Hal. *Ant. Rom.* 2.71.4; and, on imagery of armed dancers, Fless and Moede, "Music and Dance," esp. 253–256.

81. Jannot, "danseurs de la *pompa*," 67, on the social status of the *ludiones*.

82. Dion. Hal. *Ant. Rom.* 7.72.10: μετὰ γὰρ τοὺς ἐνοπλίους χοροὺς οἱ τῶν σατυριστῶν ἐπόμπευον χοροὶ τὴν Ἑλληνικὴν εἰδοφοροῦντες σίκιννιν. Σκευαὶ δ' αὐτοῖς ἦσαν τοῖς μὲν εἰς Σιληνοὺς εἰκασθεῖσι μαλλωτοὶ χιτῶνες, οὓς ἔνιοι χορταίους καλοῦσι, καὶ περιβόλαια ἐκ παντὸς ἄνθους· τοῖς δ' εἰς Σατύρους περιζώματα καὶ δοραὶ τράγων καὶ ὀρθότριχες ἐπὶ ταῖς κεφαλαῖς φόβαι καὶ ὅσα τούτοις ὅμοια. Οὗτοι κατέσκωπτόν τε καὶ κατεμιμοῦντο τὰς σπουδαίας κινήσεις ἐπὶ τὰ γελοιότερα μεταφέροντες (LCL).

83. Jannot, "danseurs de la *pompa*," 66–67.

84. On reversal with its sexuality and toilet humor, see Bahktin's seminal contribution, *Rabelais and His World*, 196–277. For ancient Rome, see Versnel, *Inconsistencies in Greek and Roman Religion*, 2.136–227; and Beard, *Laughter in Ancient Rome*, esp. 59–69, critiquing Bakhtin.

85. Dion. Hal. *Ant. Rom.* 7.72.11: ἐφεῖται γὰρ τοῖς κατάγουσι τὰς νίκας ἰαμβίζειν τε καὶ κατασκώπτειν τοὺς ἐπιφανεστάτους ἄνδρας αὐτοῖς στρατηλάταις (LCL).

86. Suet. *Caes.* 51: *Urbani, servate uxores: moechum calvom adducimus* (ed. LCL, trans. adapted Edwards), on which see Beard, *Roman Triumph*, 247–249. See also App. *Pun.* 66.

87. Dion. Hal. *Ant. Rom.* 7.72.12; and see pp. 12–13. On funeral rites, see Flower, *Ancestor Masks and Aristocratic Power*, 97–121; and Bodel, "Death on Display."

88. Simpson, "Musicians and the Arena"; Péché and Vendries, *Musique et spectacles dans la Rome antique*, 75–100; Nelis-Clément, "métiers du cirque," 289–290; and Maclean, "People on the Margins," 583–584. I borrow the phrase *furor circensis* from Bell, "Roman Chariot Racing," 499.

89. Loincloth: Dion. Hal. *Ant. Rom.* 1.80.1; cloak: Just. *Epit.* 43.1.7; and naked: Cic. *Phil.* 3.12, Varro, *Ling.* 6.34, and Verg. *Aen.* 8.663, on which see Porte, "Note sur les *luperci nudi*." On the similarity of the burlesque dancers and the *luperci*, see Piganiol, *Jeux romains*, 23–25. For a striking discussion of the Lupercalia, see Hopkins, "Violence to Blessing."

90. Veyne, "Iconographie de la *transvectio equitum*"; Wiseman, "God of the Lupercal"; Rebecchi, "Per l'iconografia"; and Tortorella, "*Luperci* e *Lupercalia*." On the "route," see p. 84.

91. Dion. Hal. *Ant. Rom.* 7.72.13: Μετὰ δὲ τοὺς χοροὺς τούτους κιθαρισταί τ' ἀθρόοι καὶ αὐληταὶ πολλοὶ παρεξῄεσαν· καὶ μετ' αὐτοὺς οἵ τε τὰ θυμιατήρια κομίζοντες, ἐφ'

ὧν ἀρώματα καὶ λιβανωτὸς παρ' ὅλην ὁδὸν ἐθυμιᾶτο, καὶ οἱ τὰ πομπεῖα παραφέροντες ἀργυρίου καὶ χρυσίου πεποιημένα τά τε ἱερὰ καὶ τὰ δημόσια (LCL).

92. Cic. *Verr.* 2.4.77: the goddess Diana of Segesta escorted with burning incense, on which see Cancik and Cancik-Lindemaier, "Truth of Images," esp. 54–55. On incense in processions, see Atchley, *History of the Use of Incense*, 46–60, esp. 46–47; Burkert, *Greek Religion*, 62 and 73; and Scheid, *Introduction to Roman Religion*, 79–83; and, on the *vicus Turarius*, LTUR sv *vicus Tuscus*; and Holleran, *Shopping in Ancient Rome*, 57.
93. Ov. *Am.* 3.2.44; pp. 97–98, on *aurea pompa*; and, on the aediles, Cic. *Har. resp.* 11.23 (sacred vessels); Dion. Hal. *Ant. Rom.* 6.95.4: (purple robe and an ivory chair); and Val. Max. 2.4.6 (scarlet cloak), with Gailliot, "impiété volontaire?" 92–93.
94. Cic. *Tusc.* 5.32.91: *Socrates, in pompa cum magna vis auri argentique ferretur:* Quam multa non desidero! *inquit* (trans. King LCL).
95. Flower, "Spectacle and Political Culture," 322; and Barton, "Being in the Eyes," 221. On aristocratic culture and visibility, see further Parker, "Observed of All Observers"; Rosenstein, "Aristocratic Values"; Flower, "Elite Self-Representation in Rome"; Hölkeskamp, "Republic as Theater of Power"; and Jenkyns, *God, Space, and City*, 1–53.
96. Bell, *Spectacular Power*, esp. 1–23.
97. Cic. *Pis.* 60: *Inania sunt ista . . . captare plausus, vehi per urbem, conspici velle* (trans. adapted Watts LCL).
98. Cic. *Off.* 2.57: *ut splendor aedilitatum ab optimis viris postuletur* (trans. adapted Miller LCL), on which see Beacham, *Spectacle Entertainments*, 1–91.
99. Suet. *Caes.* 10.1: *Marcus Bibulus, evenisse sibi quod Polluci; ut enim geminis fratribus aedes in Foro constituta tantum Castoris vocaretur, ita suam Caesarisque munificentiam unius Caesaris dici* (ed. LCL, trans. Edwards).
100. On memory in republican political culture, see Flower, *Art of Forgetting*, 51–55.
101. See Bergmann, "Introduction," on interaction, memory, and innovation; and Scott, *Domination and the Arts of Resistance*, 66–69, on the elite as the target audience.
102. See Coleman, "Spectacle," on the difficulties of a history of spectacle; Bernstein, *Ludi publici*, 254–268, on the *pompa* re-shaped in a Greek mold, and "Complex Rituals," 227–231, on the elaboration of the games.
103. See Rüpke, "Public and Publicity," on fourth-century BCE ceremonial.
104. Livy 9.40.15–17: *Dictator ex senatus consulto triumphavit, cuius triumpho longe maximam speciem captiva arma praebuere. Tantum magnificentiae visum in iis, ut aurata scuta dominis argentariarum ad forum ornandum dividerentur. Inde natum initium dicitur fori ornandi ab aedilibus cum tensae ducerentur. Et Romani quidem ad honorem deum insignibus armis hostium usi sunt* (trans. adapted Foster LCL).
105. Suet. *Caes.* 10.1: *praeter Comitium ac Forum basilicasque etiam Capitolium ornavit porticibus ad tempus extructis, in quibus abundante rerum copia pars apparatus exponeretur* (ed. LCL, trans. Edwards).
106. Plin. *HN* 19.6.23: *Caesar dictator totum forum Romanum intexit viamque sacram ab domo sua et clivum usque in Capitolium* (trans. Rackham LCL).
107. Macrob. *Sat.* 1.6.15: *placuisse velari loca ea qua pompa veheretur* (trans. Kaster LCL); and see also pp. 58; 64 and 83–84.
108. Plaut. *Poen.* 1010–1012: HAN *mi uulech ianna?* AGO *quid venit?* MIL *non audis? mures Africanos praedicat in pompam ludis dare se velle aedilibus* (trans. slightly adapted Melo LCL).
109. Val. Max. 2.4.6: *Religionem ludorum crescentibus opibus secuta lautitia est . . . translatum antea punicis indutum tunicis, M. Scaurus exquisito genere vestis cultum induxit* (trans. Shackleton-Bailey LCL).
110. Columella, *Rust.* 3.8.2: *nuper ipsi videre potuimus in apparatu pompae circensium ludorum Iudaeae gentis hominem proceriorem celsissimo Germano* (trans. adapted Ash LCL).
111. Plut. *Caes.* 5: καὶ ταῖς ἄλλαις περί θέατρα καὶ πομπὰς καὶ δεῖπνα χορηγίαις καὶ πολυτελείαις τὰς πρὸ αὐτοῦ κατέκλυσε φιλοτιμίας (trans. Perrin LCL).
112. Schieffelin, "On Failure and Performance," 60 (italics in original) and 66; and see also "Problematizing Performance," esp. 198.
113. Schieffelen, "Introduction," lays out a concise model of ritual failure. The phrase "infelicitous performance" comes from the pioneering study by Grimes, "Infelicitous Performances and Ritual Criticism," who uses the concept broadly (see esp. 110–116 for his taxonomy).

114. See esp. Grimes, *Ritual Criticism*, on ritual evaluation; and also Hüsken, "Ritual Dynamics and Ritual Failure."
115. Ando, *Matter of the Gods*, 13.
116. Monti, "*Instauratio ludorum*."
117. Dion. Hal. *Ant. Rom.* 7.68.1–7.69.2 and 7.73.5; Cic. *Div.* 1.26.55; Livy 2.36.1–8; Val. Max. 1.7.4; Plut. *Coriol.* 24.1–25.1; Min. Fel. *Oct.* 7.3 and 27.4; Arn. *Adv. nat.* 7.39 and 7.41–43; Lactant. *Div. Inst.* 2.7.20–21; August. *De civ. D.* 4.26; and Macrob. *Sat.* 1.11.3–5, all mention this episode with some variations, on which see Bernstein, *Ludi publici*, 85–96; and Gailliot, "impiété volontaire?" 90. See pp. 63–65, on ritual failure in the *pompa deorum*.
118. Dion. Hal. *Ant. Rom.* 7.68.3: Ἴθι, Λατίνιε, καὶ λέγε τοῖς πολίταις ὅτι μοι τῆς νεωστὶ πομπῆς τὸν ἡγούμενον ὀρχηστὴν οὐ καλὸν ἔδωκαν, ἵνα ἀναθῶνται τὰς ἑορτὰς καὶ ἐξ ἀρχῆς ἑτέρας ἐπιτελέσωσιν· οὐ γὰρ δέδεγμαι ταύτας (LCL).
119. Livy 2.36.1.
120. Dion. Hal. *Ant. Rom.* 7.69.1; and Plut. *Coriol.* 25.1.
121. Dion. Hal. *Ant. Rom.* 7.69.2: ὁ δ᾽ ἐν τοιᾷδε ἀνάγκῃ κρατούμενος ἐβόα τε φωνὰς δυσφήμους, ἃς ἡ ἀλγηδὼν ἐβούλετο, καὶ κινήσεις διὰ τὴν αἰκίαν ἀσχήμονας ἐκινεῖτο (LCL).
122. Dion. Hal. *Ant. Rom.* 7.73.5 (after the long digression).
123. Serv. *Aen.* 8.110: *salva res est, saltat senex* (Teubner) during circus games possibly of Apollo in 211, and 3.279: *omnia seconda, saltat senex* (Teubner), which links more or less the same adage to Magna Mater. See also Fest. 436L: *salva res* <*est dum cantat* [*saltat*?]> *senex* (Teubner), during theatrical games, on which see Caldelli, "Associazioni di artisti," 141–146. See, Salzman, *On Roman Time*, 287–288; and Bernstein, *Ludi publici*, 89, on the adage.
124. On *tensa* regulations, see pp. 61–65.
125. Cic. *De har. resp.* 11.23: *An si ludius constitit aut tibicen repente conticuit aut puer ille patrimus et matrimus si tensam non tenuit, si lorum omisit, aut si aedilis verbo aut simpuvio aberravit, ludi sunt non rite facti, eaque errata expiantur et mentes deorum immortalium ludorum instauratione placantur* (trans. adapted Watts LCL), on which see Lenaghan, *Commentary*, 118–119. Gailliot, "impiété volontaire?" focuses on the game-giver and ritual, but religious scruples made demands on most participants and even spectators.
126. See n. 117 above and pp. 188–189, for Christian criticisms; Owen, "Plautus' *Stichus*," 386, citing Taylor, "Opportunities for Dramatic Performances," on the repetition of successful plays; Monti, "*Instauratio ludorum*," and Gailliot, "impiété volontaire?" on religious obligation; and Scheid, "délit religieux," esp. 121–124, and "Expiation of Impieties," on religious faults generally.
127. Livy 2.19.1: *nihil dignum memoria actum* (trans. adapted Foster LCL); and Dion. Hal. *Ant. Rom.* 5.57.5: Μανίου δὲ Τυλλίου θατέρου τῶν ὑπάτων ἐν τοῖς ἱεροῖς καὶ ἐπωνύμοις τῆς πόλεως ἀγῶσι κατὰ τὴν πομπὴν ἐκ τοῦ ἱεροῦ πεσόντος ἅρματος κατ᾽ αὐτὸν τὸν ἱππόδρομον, καὶ τρίτῃ μετὰ τὴν πομπὴν ταύτην ἡμέρᾳ τελευτήσαντος (trans. Cary LCL).
128. Livy 30.38.11–12: *Ceterum ludorum ipso die subita serenitate orta pompa duci coepta ad portam Collinam revocata deductaque in circum est cum decessisse inde aquam nuntiatum esset; laetitiamque populo et ludis celebritatem addidit sedes sua sollemni spectaculo reddita.* (trans. Moore LCL).

Two *Pompa deorum*

1. *Sed iam pompa venit – linguis animisque favete! / tempus est plausus – aurea pompa venit* (ed. LCL, trans. Lee). See also Ov. *Am.* 3.13.29 (a similar passage) and *Fast.* 1.71 and 2.654; Hor. *Carm.* 3.1.2; Verg. *Aen.* 5.71; Tib. 2.2.2; and Juv. 12.83, on silence.
2. Ov. *Am.* 3.2.61: *pompamque deorum* (LCL), *Ars am.* 1.147: *pompa frequens caelestibus ... eburnis* (LCL), and *Fast.* 4.391: *Circus erit pompa celeber numeroque deorum* (the circus will be crowded/distinguished with a procession and a great number of gods, ed. LCL).
3. Ov. *Am.* 3.2.65: *maxima ... spectacula* (LCL), as gloss by Henderson, "A Doo-Dah-Doo-Dah-Dey," 53.
4. On silence/applause, see Gailliot, "impiété volontaire?" 94–95; and Nelis-Clément, "cirque romain et son paysage sonore," 441–442. See also Suet. *Claud.* 21.1: *cum prius apud superiores aedes supplicasset perque*

mediam caveam sedentibus ac silentibus cunctis descendisset ("first he offered supplications in the temple at the top [of the theater of Pompey] and then came down through the auditorium, while everyone sat in silence," ed. LCL and trans. adapted Edwards); and Chaniotis, "Staging and Feeling the Presence of God," exploring collective emotions.

5. Cic. *Div.* 1.102: *rebusque divinis, quae publice fierent, ut "favent linguis," imperabatur* (trans. adapted Falconer LCL), and see also *Div.* 2.83.
6. Sen. *Vit. beat.* 26.7: *"favete linguis." Hoc verbum non, ut plerique existimant, a favore trahitur, sed imperat silentium, ut rite peragi possit sacrum nulla voce mala obstrepente. Quod multo magis necessarium est imperari vobis, ut, quotiens aliquid ex illo proferetur oraculo, intenti et compressa voce audiatis* (trans. Basore LCL).
7. Plin. *HN* 28.3.11: [*custos*] *vero praeponi qui favere linguis iubeat, tibicinem canere, ne quid aliud exaudiatur* (trans. Jones LCL).
8. On gods and/in/as statues, see Rüpke, "Representation or Presence?"; while Estienne, "Statues de dieux 'isolées,'" 83, notes that divine images were often called by the name of the deity, suggesting that "presence" may be the best metaphor; on which see also Chaniotis, "Staging and Feeling the Presence of God," on the Hellenistic east. On the difficulties of conceptualizing material representation of gods, see further Ando, *Matter of the Gods*, 21–42.
9. A sentiment forcefully argued by Scheid, *Introduction to Roman Religion*, 18–20, "Religion romaine et spiritualité," and "Les sens des rites." Scheid, "Polytheism Impossible"; and Durand and Scheid, "'Rites' et 'Religion'" also argue that Roman ritual had its own spirituality, against perceptions that Roman religion was meaningless. See further Feeney, *Literature and Religion*, 1–11 and 115–136.
10. On belief in ancient Mediterranean religions, see Linder and Scheid, "Quand croire c'est faire"; Feeney, *Literature and Religion*, 12–46, on "brain balkanization," (compartmentalized believing) following Veyne, *Did the Greeks Believe in Their Myths?* esp. 41–57; King, "Organization of Roman Religious Beliefs," on differences between Roman and Christian believing; and Versnel, *Coping with the Gods*, 539–559. On the emergence of Roman theological discourse, see Momigliano, *On Pagans, Jews, and Christians*, 58–73; Rawson, *Intellectual Life in the Late Roman Republic*, 298–316; Beard, "Cicero and Divination"; BNP 149–156; and Rüpke, "Varro's *Tria Genera Theologiae*" and *Religion in Republican Rome*, 51–61 and 172–204.
11. Feeney, *Literature and Religion*, 83.
12. Ando, *Matter of the Gods*, 1–18; and Scheid, "Hierarchy and Structure."
13. Varro in August. *De civ. D.* 6.5.1. Ando, "Ontology of Religious Institutions," 75, argues that Augustine decisively impacted Varro's works on Roman religion and so Varronian quotations will be taken from Augustine's *De civitate Dei*. On Varro's theology, see Lehmann, *Varron théologien et philosophe*; and Rüpke, "Varro's *Tria Genera Theologiae*" and *Religion in Republican Rome*, 172–185. On Augustine's polemical employment of Varro, see O'Daly, *Augustine's City of God*.
14. August. *De civ. D.* 6.5.3: *facilius intra parietes in schola quam extra in foro ferre possunt aures* (ed. and trans. adapted Walsh). Brunt, "Philosophy and Religion in the Late Republic," notes a limited interest in philosophy among the literate elite.
15. August. *De civ. D.* 6.5.5: *mendacissimum atque turpissimum* (ed. and trans. Walsh); and 6.5.4–5: *Removit tamen hoc genus a foro, id est a populis; scholis vero et parietibus clausit. . . . O religiosas aures populares, atque in his etiam Romanas! Quod de diis immortalibus philosophi disputant, ferre non possunt; quod vero poetae canunt et histriones agunt, quae contra dignitatem ac naturam immortalium ficta sunt . . . non solum ferunt sed etiam libenter audiunt* (ed. and trans. adapted Walsh).
16. August. *De civ. D.* 8.1: *de divinitate rationem sive sermonem* (ed. Walsh), cited by McGinn, "*Regina quondam* . . ." 820 n. 12, a study of theology as a term and as a practice; and Plat. *Resp.* 376e–383c.
17. August. *De civ. D.* 7.26.3: *proferremus de libris nisi cotidie cantarentur et saltarentur in theatris* (ed. and trans. adapted Walsh). On this passage and mythological theatrical shows in general, see Wiseman, *Roman Drama and Roman History*, esp. 17–24, and also "Ovid and the Stage."
18. Beacham, *Spectacle Entertainments*.
19. Scheid, "Cults, Myths, and Politics," on the limited place of myth in ritual and its importance elsewhere; and also Bendlin, "Rituals or

Beliefs?" on the cognitive, as opposed to ritual, value of Roman myth.

20. August. *De civ. D.* 6.5.1: *fabulare . . . fabulosum* and 6.5.2: *mendacissimis fabulis* (ed. and trans. Walsh). See BNP 153 on "as Varro says" as an authorizing device.
21. Woolf, "Reading and Religion in Rome," 201 (emphasis in original) and 205.
22. Ando, "Ontology of Religious Institutions," 60–64.
23. See esp. Prescendi, "Children and the Transmission of Religious Knowledge"; and also Horsfall, "Cultural Horizons of the *Plebs Romana*," 103–109, and *Culture of the Roman Plebs*, 48–63.
24. Momigliano, *On Pagans, Jews, and Christians*, 85 and 86. See also Momigliano, *On Pagans, Jews, and Christians*, 163 and 166, with similar concerns about "pagan" religious education.
25. Cic. *Fin.* 5.48: *Videmusne ut pueri ne verberibus quidem a contemplandis rebus perquirendisque deterreantur? ut pulsi recurrant? ut aliquid scire se gaudeant? ut id aliis narrare gestiant? ut pompa, ludis atque eiusmodi spectaculis teneantur ob eamque rem vel famem et sitim perferant?* (trans. adapted Rackham LCL)
26. Feeney, *Literature and Religion*, 138.
27. Bourdieu, *Logic of Practice*, 73–74.
28. Prescendi, "Children and the Transmission of Religious Knowledge," 91–92, notes a possible exception (Stat. *Silv.* 5.3.176–184); on which see also Feeney, *Literature and Religion*, 138.
29. BNP 75.
30. BNP 153 (emphasis in original).
31. See Beard, "Writing and Religion," on writing in Roman religions; Hickson Hahn, "Performing the Sacred," on prayer; and Scheid, "Hierarchy and Structure," "Religion romaine et spiritualité," and "Théologie romaine et représentation de l'action," on non-discursive Roman theology.
32. On sacrificial theology, see Scheid, *Quand croire, c'est faire* and "Roman Animal Sacrifice"; on spatial theology, Scheid, "dieux du Capitole"; on image theology, Cordier and Huet, "'théologie' en images?" and Bricault and Prescendi, "'théologie en images'?"; on art and theology, Rives, *Religion in the Roman Empire*, 32–37 and Elsner, *Roman Eyes*, 38–42; and on the theology of practice, Scheid, *Introduction to Roman Religion*, 174–176, at 176 (unwritten), Rüpke, *Religion of the Romans*, 113–116 (material), and Ando, "Introduction to Part IV," 142 (practice).
33. MacMullen, *Paganism in the Roman Empire*, 1 and 18. On publicity, see Rüpke, "Public and Publicity"; on festival theology, Scheid, "Festivals of the Forum Boarium"; and on the ubiquity of processions, Burkert, *Greek Religion*, 99–101.
34. See, from a vast literature, Carson, *Performance*, 1–7, and works cited below.
35. On formal characteristics of ritual, see Bell, *Ritual*, 138–169; and Rappaport, *Ritual and Religion*, 23–58, esp. 36–37, on invariance. On the triumph as performance, see Östenberg, *Staging the World*, esp. 6–12.
36. Rüpke, "Acta aut agenda," 25.
37. Bell, "Performance" and *Ritual*, 72–76 and 159–164. On ritual change, see Lincoln, "On Ritual, Change, and Marked Categories."
38. Schieffelin, "On Failure and Performance," 60 (italics in original).
39. See esp. Schieffelen, "Introduction"; and Bell, *Spectacular Power*, for the classical world.
40. Schieffelin, "On Failure and Performance," 67 and 64. On performance as auto-poetic, see Schieffelen, "Performance and the Cultural Construction of Reality"; and Carson, "Introduction."
41. Schieffelin, "Problematizing Performance," 194.
42. See Betts, "Towards a Multisensory Experience," on ancient Rome in the sensual round, as it were.
43. Sen. *Controv.* 1.*praef.* 24 (Introduction n. 1); and Dupont, "*Pompa* et *carmina*," 77: La Ville devient totalement jupitérienne.
44. Dion. Hal. *Ant. Rom.* 7.72.13: τελευταῖα δὲ πάντων αἱ τῶν θεῶν εἰκόνες ἐπόμπευον ὤμοις ὑπ' ἀνδρῶν φερόμεναι, μορφάς τε ὁμοίας παρέχουσαι ταῖς παρ' Ἕλλησι πλαττομέναις καὶ σκευὰς καὶ σύμβολα καὶ δωρεάς, ὧν εὑρεταὶ καὶ δοτῆρες ἀνθρώποις ἕκαστοι παραδίδονται (LCL).
45. See Feeney, *Literature and Religion*, 96–97, on processional images; and Madigan, *Ceremonial Sculptures*, esp. 39–66, on litter statues; and on *fercula*: D-S sv ferculum; Abaecherli, "*Fercula, carpenta*, and *tensae*," 1–5 (a *scholion* on Horace provides a working definition: "*fercula" sunt et pulpita, in quibus deorum simulacra tolluntur* [*fercula* are platforms on which the images of the

gods are raised up], 2); RE sv ferculum; and Pisani Sartorio, *Mezzi di trasporto*, 35–36. See further pp. 62–63.

46. On images related to the circus procession, see Abaercherli, "*Fercula, carpenta*, and *tensae*"; Fless, "Römische Prozessionen"; *Trionfi romani*, 77–80 and 147–153; and Madigan, *Ceremonial Sculptures*, 39–66 and 83–101. See pp. 7–9, on the ambiguities of visual evidence.
47. Serv. *Aen.* 6.68 notes that little images (*simulacra brevia*) were carried on litters in Egypt and Carthage, which suggests that processional images were, at times, smaller than cult images. Fishwick, *Imperial Cult in the Latin West*, 2.553–554, contends that the cult statues were carried.
48. Varro in August. *De civ. D.* 4.31.4, on which see Cancik and Cancik-Lindemaier, "Truth of Images," 46–47; Rüpke, "Representation or Presence?" 182–183; and Estienne, "Image et culte," 147–149.
49. Cic. *Nat. D.* 1.81*: a parvis enim Iovem Iunonem Minervam Neptunum Vulcanum Apollinem reliquos deos ea facie novimus qua pictores fictoresque voluerunt, neque solum facie sed etiam ornatu aetate vestitu. At non Aegyptii nec Syri nec fere cuncta barbaria* (LCL).
50. Cic. *Nat. D.* 1.46–49.
51. E.g. Cic. *Verr.* 2.4.77. On the status of divine images, see the classic analysis of Gordon, "Real and Imaginary," esp. 7–8; and also Estienne, "*Simulacra deorum*," 258–261; Feeney, *Literature and Religion*, 92–97; and Cancik and Cancik-Lindemaier, "Truth of Images," esp. 49–58.
52. Elsner, *Roman Eyes*, 1–26.
53. Vernant, "'Presentification' of the Invisible," is essential; and see also Steiner, *Images in Mind*, 79–134.
54. A fragment from Seneca, *De superstitione*, known only from its later second-level polemic usage in August. *De civ. D.* 6.10.4: *In Capitolium perveni, pudebit publicatae dementiae, quod sibi vanus furor adtribuit officii. Alius nomina deo subicit, alius horas Iovi nuntiat; alius lutor est, alius unctor qui vano motu bracchiorum imitatur unguentem. Sunt quae Iunoni ac Minervae capillos disponant longe a templo, non tantum a simulacro stantes, digitos movent ornantium modo; sunt quae speculum teneant; sunt qui ad vadimonia sua deos advocent; sunt qui libellos offerant et illos causam suam doceant. Doctus archimimus, senex iam decrepitus, cotidie in Capitolio mimum agebat, quasi dii libenter spectarent quem illi homines desierant. Omne illic artificum genus operatum diis inmortalibus desidet* (ed. and trans. adapted Walsh), on which see Feeney, *Literature and Religion*, 95; and esp. Estienne, "'dévots' du Capitole."
55. Varro in August. *De civ. D.* 4.31.4; and Cic. *Nat. D.* 1.77, on which Auvray-Assayas, "Images mentales et représentations figurées"; and Bricault and Prescendi, "'théologie en images?'" 64–65. On the power and allure of naturalistic images, see Freedberg, *Power of Images*; and esp. Elsner, *Roman Eyes*, 29–48.
56. Estienne, "Image et culte," 150–151, argues that image cult staged a debate between self and other, difference and similarity.
57. Long, *Twelve Gods of Greece and Rome*, 33–34 and 239–242, on the *pompa circensis*; and more generally Versnel, *Coping with the Gods*, 507–515.
58. Dion. Hal. *Ant. Rom.* 7.72.13: Διὸς καὶ Ἥρας καὶ Ἀθηνᾶς καὶ Ποσειδῶνος καὶ τῶν ἄλλων οὓς Ἕλληνες ἐν τοῖς δώδεκα θεοῖς καταριθμοῦσιν (LCL).
59. Livy 22.10.9: *Sex pulvinaria in conspectu fuerunt: Iovi ac Iunoni unum, alterum Neptuno ac Minervae, tertium Marti ac Veneri, quartum Apollini ac Dianae, quintum Volcano ac Vestae, sextum Mercurio et Cereri* (LCL), on which see Long, *Twelve Gods of Greece and Rome*, 33 and 235–239.
60. Ov. *Am.* 3.2.45–56: *prima loco fertur passis Victoria pinnis – / huc ades et meus hic fac, dea, vincat amor! / plaudite Neptuno, nimium qui creditis undis! / nil mihi cum pelago, me mea terra capit. / plaude tuo Marti, miles! nos odimus arma: / pax iuvat et media pace repertus amor. / auguribus Phoebus, Phoebe venantibus adsit! / artifices in te verte, Minerva, manus! / ruricolae, Cereri teneroque adsurgite Baccho! / Pollucem pugiles, Castora placet eques! / nos tibi, blanda Venus, puerisque potentibus arcu / plaudimus: inceptis adnue, diva, meis* (ed. LCL, trans. Lee).
61. Ov. *Am.* 3.2.58: *Adnuit et motu signa secunda dedit* (ed. LCL, trans. Lee). Ov. *Ars am.* 1. 135–163 (see pp. 86–87) also recommends the cramped informality of the Circus, on which see Henderson, "A Doo-Dah-Doo-Dah-Dey,"; Nelis and Nelis-Clément, "Vergil, *Georgics* 1.1–42," paragraphs 7–9; Nelis, "Caesar, the Circus and the

Charioteer," 502–503; and Welch, "Elegy and the Monuments," 109–114.

62. Serv. *Aen.* 6.68. On *fercula* movement, see p. 63
63. Hor. *Sat.* 1.3.10–11: *velut qui / Iunonis sacra ferret* (LCL), trans. and analysis O'Sullivan, *Walking in Roman Culture*, 36.
64. See, n. 9 above on Roman ritual spirituality; and pp. 39–42, 61–65, and 147–152, on ritual regulations.
65. Plut. *Otho* 4.4; Ryberg, 99–100 and fig. 48a–b (game-giver, not Mars); Ronke #4; *Imperii insignia* C48; La Regina (ed.), *Sangue e Arena* #73; Fless, "Romische Prozessionen," #83; *Trionfi romani* I.3.3; and see p. 175. For images of Victory in procession, see Ronke #37, Fless, "Römische Prozessionen," #40; and Lo Monaco, "In processione al Circo," 79–80, fig. 6.
66. Dion. Hal. *Ant. Rom.* 7.72.13: Κρόνου καὶ Ῥέας καὶ Θέμιδος καὶ Λητοῦς καὶ Μοιρῶν καὶ Μνημοσύνης καὶ τῶν ἄλλων ἁπάντων ὅσων ἐστὶν ἱερὰ καὶ τεμένη παρ' Ἕλλησι· καὶ τῶν ὕστερον, ἀφ' οὗ τὴν ἀρχὴν Ζεὺς παρέλαβε, μυθολογουμένων γενέσθαι, Περσεφόνης Εἰλειθυίας Νυμφῶν Μουσῶν Ὡρῶν Χαρίτων Διονύσου, καὶ ὅσων ἡμιθέων γενομένων αἱ ψυχαὶ τὰ θνητὰ ἀπολιποῦσαι σώματα εἰς οὐρανὸν ἀνελθεῖν λέγονται, καὶ τιμὰς λαχεῖν ὁμοίας θεοῖς, Ἡρακλέους Ἀσκληπιοῦ Διοσκούρων Ἑλήνης Πανὸς ἄλλων μυρίων (LCL). Piganiol, *Jeux romains*, 25, points out that some gods in this list date to the third century BCE.
67. Feeney, *Literature and Religion*, 83–87; and Nelis and Nelis-Clement, "Vergil, *Georgics* 1. 1–42," paragraph 10.
68. LTUR sv Consus, Ara.
69. SHA *Sev.* 22.3: plaster Victories; and Ov. *Ars am.* 1.147: ivory gods.
70. See Scheid, "Hierarchy and Structure" and "Roman Animal Sacrifice"; Guittard, "Invocations et structures théologiques"; and also pp. 148–149, a failed attempt to alter the arrangement of the gods.
71. Diom. *Ars gramm.* 1: *deorum vehiculum tensam dixerunt* (*Gramm. Lat.* 1.376.10–11); on *exuviae*: Val. Max. 1.1.16; Suet. *Aug.* 94.6; and Apul. *Met.* 11.10 and 11.29; and on *struppi*: Fest. 472L and Paul. Fest. 473L with Serv. *Aen.* 2.225. On the *tensa*, see D-S sv *tensa*; RE sv *tensa* oder *thensa*; Abaercherli, "*Fercula, carpenta,* and *tensae*," 7–11; Pisani-Sartorio, *Mezzi di trasporto*, 38–40; Szidet, *Teile eines historischen Frieses*, 24–83; Molin, "char," 292–293; Schäfer, "Römisches Relief mit Tensa"; Guidetti, "*Tensam non tenuit*"; and, with caution, Piacente, "*Peregrini ac superbi vehiculi.*" On *exuviae*, see Abaercherli, "Imperial Symbols"; Versnel, *Triumphus*, 260–261; La Rocca, "troni dei nuovi dei," 78–79; and Madigan, *Ceremonial Sculptures*, 83–101.
72. Grattius (Augustan-era), *Cynegetica* 535; and, later, Suet. *Vesp.* 5.7; and see pp. 75–76 on the *aedes tensarum*.
73. Livy 9.40.16: *cum tensae ducerentur* (LCL) and also 5.41.2: *tensas ducentibus* (LCL); Suet. *Aug.* 43.5: *tensas deduceret* (LCL); and Tert. *De corona* 13.1: *deducendas tensas* (CSEL).
74. Cic. *Verr.* 2.1.154: *quam tu viam tensarum atque pompae eius modi exegisti ut tu ipse illa ire non audeas* (trans. adapted Greenwood LCL); and also *Verr.* 2.3.6 and 2.5.186 (see pp. 81 and 83).
75. Cic. *Planc.* 83: *aliquid tensis misericordiae causa dicerem* (trans. adapted Watts LCL); and also Cic. *Har. resp.* 11.23 (see pp. 41, 61, 63, and 83).
76. Fest. 500L: *Tensam ait vocari Sinnius Capito vehiculum, quo exuviae deorum ludicris circensibus in circum ad pulvinar vehuntur. Fuit et ex ebore, ut apud Titinium in Barbato, et ex argento* (Teubner); and also Paul. Fest. 501L: *Tensa vehiculum argenteum, quo exuviae deorum ludis Circensibus in circum ad pulvinar vehebantur* (The *tensa* is a silver vehicle in which the symbols of the gods were carried to the *pulvinar* in the circus during the circus games, ed. Teubner). Serv. *Aen.* 1.17 notes that images of the gods were carried in *tensae*, but the bulk of the evidence suggests symbols or attributes.
77. Titinius frg. 140 in Non. 494L: *vende thensam atque mulos; sine* [*eam*] *pedibus grassari; confringe eius superbiam* (Sell the *tensa* and the mules; to move without it [the *tensa*] on her/his own feet, break her/his arrogance, ed. Teubner), on which see André, "Glanures," 74–75; and Manuwald, *Roman Republican Theater*, 261–262 #4.11, on Titinius. A late-fourth-century CE panegyric, Pacatus, *Pan. Lat.* II (12) 21.4, also considers a *tensa* an elite vehicle.
78. Jupiter: BMRRC #348.1; Juno: BMRRC #348.2; and Minerva: BMRRC #348.3; and Introduction nn. 23–24. On Dossenus, Wiseman, *New Men in the Roman Senate*, 257.

79. Crawford, *Roman Republican Coinage*, 362–363, argues against the *tensa* identification; as does Szidat, *Teile eines historischen Frieses*, 36–49, in part because the vehicles lack clear pediments, which, she argues, is the key marker. However, the *tensa* identification is standard: e.g. D-S sv tensa; Abaecherli, "*Fercula, carpenta,* and *tensae*," 7; Latte, *Römische Religionsgeschichte*, 249 n. 2; Turcan, *Religion romaine* vol. 2 #50; Junkelmann, "On the Starting Line"; and La Rocca, "troni dei nuovi dei," 84 n. 42. See also pp. 111–112 on *tensa* iconography.
80. Szidat, *Teile eines historischen Frieses*, 33, 50–51, fig. 14; Fless, "Römische Prozessionen," #43; Tortorella, "Processione trionfale e circense," #10.1; and see pp. 128–129.
81. See Crawford, *Roman Republican Coinage*, 2.729; and p. 129 on the Trajanic restorations.
82. Macrob. *Sat.* 1.6.15 and Val. Max. 1.1.16, on which see p. 64 below.
83. CIL 6.740 (suggests that *iugarii tensarum* led the *tensae*) = ILS 4216 = EDCS-17300881: a *nomenclator tens(arum) iugaris* of Sol Invictus, on which see D-S sv tensa; Abaercherli, "*Fercula, carpenta,* and *tensae*," 9; and Madigan, *Ceremonial Sculptures*, 85. The *Oxford Latin Dictionary* sv tensarius suggests that this *nomenclator* may be a *tensarius*, an official who attended a *tensa*.
84. Tert. *Spect.* 7.2 (see pp. 159–160) lists cult images and statues then chariots, *tensae, armamaxae* (elephant drawn carts), then thrones, crowns, and *exuviae* – that is, divine representations, means of transport, and mode of display (crowns and *exuviae* placed on chairs at the games). On the *pulvinar*, see pp. 89, 138, and 143–144.
85. E.g. Paus. 2.4.5 and 10.19.3 on uncanny *xoana*; and Vernant, "'Presentification' to Imitation," 153–155, at 155.
86. See Piganiol, *Jeux romains*, 25–26; Latte, *Römische Religionsgeschichte*, 249 n. 2; Versnel, *Triumphus*, 259; Bernstein, *Ludi publici*, 42–48; and Marcattili, *Circo Massimo*, 153, for such a view.
87. See Gordon, "Real and Imaginary," 11–13; and Feeney, *Literature and Religion*, 96–97.
88. BNP 30–41; and Scheid, *Introduction to Roman Religion*, 147–152, on citizen gods.
89. Marquardt, *Römische Staatsverwaltung*, 487–490, at 489; and Piganiol, *Jeux romains*, 26. Similar characterizations in Friedländer, "Jeux," 281; RE sv Citeria; and Latte, *Römische Religionsgeschichte*, 249.
90. Piganiol, *Jeux romains*, 26; Latte, *Römische Religionsgeschichte*, 249; and esp. Versnel, *Triumphus*, 264–266, convincingly argue that these *effigies*, which should not be confused with stock figures from Atellan farce, appeared in the circus procession.
91. Paul. Fest. 115L: *Manduci effigies in pompa antiquorum inter ceteras ridiculas formidolosasque ire solebat magnis malis ac late dehiscens et ingentem sonitem dentibus faciens, de qua Plautus ait: "Quid si ad ludos me pro manduco locem? Quapropter? Clare crepito dentibus.*" (An effigy of Manducus was accustomed to go in the procession of the ancients among other the ridiculous and dreadful [*effigies*], gaping its great jaws widely and making tremendous noise with its teeth about whom Plautus said: "What if I hire myself out somewhere as a Manducus at the games. Why? Because I make a lot of noise with my teeth, ed. Teubner). The term *effigies* could refer to an image of a god or human, on which see Stewart, *Statues in Roman Society*, 20–28; and Estienne, "*Simulacra deorum*," 258–259.
92. Lactantius Placidus, *Luctatii Placidi grammatici Glossae*, 68: *Manducum, ligneam hominis figuram ingentem, quae solet ludis circensibus malas movere quasi manducandum* (ed. Teubner). For Versnel, *Triumphus*, 265–266, this gloss clinches the case for the presence of these figures in a *pompa circensis*.
93. Paul. Fest. 52L: *Citeria appellabatur effigies quaedam arguta et loquax ridiculi gratia, quae in pompa vehi solita sit. Cato in Marcum Cae[ci]lium: "Quid ego cum illo dissertem amplius, quem ego denique credo in pompa vectitatum ire ludis pro citeria, atque cum spectatoribus sermocinaturum"* (Teubner).
94. Paul. Fest. 281L: *Petreia vocabatur, quae pompam praecedens in colonis aut municipiis imitabatur anum ebriam, ab agri vitio, scilicet petris, appellate [m]* (Teubner).
95. Paul. Fest. 86L: stilt-walkers imitating Aegipan; and [Plut.] *Para. min.* 22 (= Plut. *Mor.* 311B): Aegipan as Silvanus, on which see Gee, "Cicero's Astronomy," 526 n. 29, who notes that Cicero likely knew traditions about Aegipan as Silvanus. Arn. *Adv. nat.* 2.38 associates stilt-walkers with both theater

performances and circus games, but not necessarily the *pompa*. Piganiol, *Jeux romains*, 22–23, suggested their appearance in parade; followed by Boyancé, "À propos de la *satura*," 18.

96. Schieffelin, "Performance and the Cultural Construction of Reality," 716. See further Brown, *Mama Lola*, a classic on spirit performances.
97. Taussig, "Viscerality, Faith, and Skepticism," 246 and 250.
98. E.g. Ando, *Matter of the Gods*, 21–42 on the challenges of theorizing image cult; and also Latham, "Performing Theology," on, ever so briefly, discursive ("Christian") theology in comparison to performed ("Roman") theology.
99. Livy 2.37.9: gods and humans at the Circus, on which Scheid, *Introduction to Roman Religion*, 107.
100. Cic. *Har. resp.* 11.23 (see pp. 41 and 63); repeated by Arn. *Adv. nat.* 4.31, on which see Guaglianone "Cic. *De harusp. resp.* XI 23,3"; and esp. Guidetti, "*Tensam non tenuit.*"
101. Plut. *Cor.* 25.3: τοῦ ἡνιόχου (anyone holding the reins, ed. LCL).
102. Ps.-Asc. *Verr.* 2.1.154: *Tensae autem sunt sacra vehicula, pompa ordinum et hostiarum. Tensas alii a divinitate dici putant, alii, quod ante ipsas lora tenduntur, quae gaudent manu tenere et tangere qui eas deducunt* (*tensae* are sacred vehicles in a procession of ranks [officials] and [sacrificial] victims. *Tensae* are considered divine by some, others [emphasize a need] for those who lead the them to keep a hand on and to touch them, ed. Stangl), on which see Abaercherli, "*Fercula, carpenta,* and *tensae,*" 1 n. 1 and 7–11; Le Bonniec, "faute rituelle," arguing that the boy could not fall (based on an older reconstruction of the text); and Guidetti, "*Tensam non tenuit,*" suggesting indirect contact.
103. Accius, *Ex incertis fabulis* #39 (Non. 303L, Teubner): *Pars frena tensae atque equorum accommodant* (LCL); and p. 58 n. 83 for a *nomenclator*/*tensarius*.
104. Grattius, *Cynegetica* 533–535: *at tibi devotae magnum pecuaria Cyrrhae, / Phoebe, decus meruere, leves seu iungere currus / usus, seu nostras agere in sacraria tensas* (trans. adapted Duff LCL).
105. See pp. 75–76 on the *aedes tensarium*.
106. Madigan, *Ceremonial Sculptures*, 63–66, at 63; Macrob. *Sat.* 1.23.13 (chapter 6 n. 179): leading men carrying the gods; Abaercherli, "*Fercula, carpenta,* and *tensae,*" 2, on staves; and Frankfurter, *Religion in Roman Egypt*, 145, on priests carrying a shrine.
107. Ov. *Fast.* 4.185 *molli ... cervice* (LCL), probably not a *pompa circensis*. For other ostensible Metroac devotees as porters, see CCCA 4.42, 4.94, and 7.39, on the last of which see Figure 49 (pp. 166–167).
108. Hörig and Schwertheim (eds.), *Corpus Cultus Iovis Dolicheni* #375 (= EDCS-29200159) and #381 (CIL 6.406 = ILS 4316 = EDCS-17300559); and AE 1957 #105 = EDCS-13600181.
109. E.g. CIL 6.8872 = EDCS-18800060.
110. CIL 6.490 = ILS 4180 = CCCA 3.289 = EDCS-17300639; CIL 6.2232 = ILS 4181 = EDCS-18100946; and CIL 6.2233 = ILS 4182 = EDCS-18100947 (L. Lartius Anthus). See also CIL 4.2155 = ILS 04181b = CCCA 4.47 = EDCS-28900302: *fanatici tres a pulvinari Synethaei*.
111. See La Regina (ed.), *Lexicon Topographicum Urbis Romae – Suburbium* sv Bellonae Pulvinensis Aedes, preferring a temple in the *ager Vaticanus*, but cautioning that the *pulvinar* at the Circus Maximus cannot be discounted.
112. Strong, "Sepuchral Relief of a Priest of Bellona," 210–211; and Pietrangeli (ed.), *monumenti dei culti orientali*, 14–15.
113. ILS 3804 = EDCS-17000041, on which see Fishwick, "*Hastiferi,*" 153 n 83.
114. Cic. *Off.* 1.131: *Cavendum autem est, ne aut tarditatibus utamur <in> ingressu mollioribus, ut pomparum ferculis similes esse videamur* (ed. LCL, trans. adapted O'Sullivan, *Walking in Roman Culture*, 19). See also Abaercherli, "*Fercula, carpenta,* and *tensae,*" 2; and Corbeill, *Nature Embodied*, 118–119.
115. Ambros. *Off.* 1.18.73: *Sunt etiam qui sensim ambulando imitantur histrionicos gestus et quasi quaedam fercula pomparum et statuarum motus nutantium; ut quotienscumque gradum transferunt modulos quosdam servare videantur* (ed. and trans. Davidson).
116. Ambros. *Off.* 1.18.72: *gestus eius plurimum dedeceret ... quia velut quodam insolentis incessus verbere oculos feriret meos* (ed. and trans. Davidson).
117. Jer. *In Amos* 2.6: *tumorem animi corpus ostendat, et pomparum ferculis similes esse videantur* (the body shows the swelling of the soul, and they seem to be similar to *fercula* in

procession, ed. CCSL). See also Jer. *Adv. Iovinian.* 1.34: *incessus pomparum ferculis similis* (a gait like *fercula* in procession, ed. PL); and Jer. *Ep.* 125.16: *pomparum ferculis similes procedunt ad publicum* ([bad monks] walk like *fercula* in procession in public, ed. CSEL).

118. E.g. Ambros. *De virginibus* 1.9.54: *Cernis ut pomparum ferculis similis incedat quae se componit ut placeat, omnium in se vultus et ora convertens* (you see that the woman who sets out to be pleasing goes about like *fercula* in procession, making herself the object of everyone's glance and talk, ed. Bibliotheca Ambrosiana).

119. Cic. *Har. resp.* 11.23: *puer ille patrimus et matrimus si tensam non tenuit, si lorum omisit* (LCL) on which on which see Lenaghan, *Commentary*, 118–119; and Plut. *Cor.* 25.3: ἵππου τε γὰρ ἑνὸς τῶν ἀγόντων τὰς καλουμένας θήσσας ἀτονήσαντος, καὶ πάλιν τοῦ ἡνιόχου τῇ ἀριστερᾷ χειρὶ τὰς ἡνίας συλλαβόντος, αὖθις ἐψηφίσαντο τὴν πομπὴν ἐπιτελεῖν (trans. Perrin LCL). On ritual failure and *instauratio*, see further pp. 39–42 and 147–152

120. Macrob. *Sat.* 1.6.15: *Verrius Flaccus ait cum populus Romanus pestilentia laboraret essetque responsum id accidere quod di despicerentur, anxiam urbem fuisse, quia non intellegeretur oraculum evenisseque ut Circensium die puer de cenaculo pompam superne despiceret et patri referret quo ordine secreta sacrorum in arca pilenti composita vidisset: qui cum rem gestam senatui nuntiasset, placuisse velari loca ea qua pompa veheretur* (trans. Kaster LCL). Admittedly, Macrobius wrote *secreta sacrorum* and *pilenti* instead of *exuviae* and *tensae*. Abaercherli, "*Fercula, carpenta,* and *tensae,*" 9, suggests *pilenta* and *tensae* functioned similarly; while André, "Glanures," 74–76, argues that they were much the same thing. See also pp. 38 and 83–84.

121. Val. Max. 1.1.16: *Creditum est Varronem consulem apud Cannas cum Carthaginiensibus tam infeliciter dimicasse ob iram Iunonis, quod cum ludos circenses aedilis faceret, in Iovis optimi maximi tensa eximia facie puerum histrionem ad exuvias tenendas posuisset. quod factum, post aliquot annos memoria repetitum, sacrificiis expiatum est* (trans. adapted Shackleton-Bailey LCL). An anecdote mockingly repeated by Lactant. *Div. Inst.* 2.16.16 (see pp. 188–189).

122. Livy 39.7.8: *malus in circo instabilis in signum Pollentiae procidit atque id deiecit* (trans. adapted Sage LCL).

123. Livy 40.2.1–4: statues on columns (*columnis*) in the Circus blown over during a storm, on which see Humphrey, *Roman Circuses*, 70 and 78; and Marcattili, *Circo Massimo*, 187–191. See also pp. 89 and 143–144 on the *pulvinar.*

124. Dio Cass. 47.40.4: καὶ ὁ τῆς Ἀθηνᾶς ὀχὸς πρὸς τὸ Καπιτώλιον ἐξ ἱπποδρομίας τινὸς ἐπανιὼν συνετρίβη (trans. adapted Cary LCL). Ὁ ὀχὸς translates *tensa*, on which see Abaercherli, "*Fercula, carpenta,* and *tensae,*" 9–11.

125. Obsequens 70: *Puer in pompa Victoriae cultu cum ferretur, ferculo decidit* (LCL); Plut. *Brut.* 39.2; and Dio Cass. 47.40.8.

126. Dio Cass. 50.8.2: ὅ τε ὀχὸς ὁ τοῦ Διὸς ἐν τῇ τῶν Ῥωμαίων ἱπποδρομίᾳ συνετρίβη (trans. adapted Cary LCL).

127. Nelis and Nelis Clément, "Vergil, *Georgics* 1. 1–42," paragraph 20.

Three *Iter pompae circensis*

1. *Urbem auspicato inauguratoque conditam habemus; nullus locus in ea non religionum deorumque est plenus; sacrificiis sollemnibus non dies magis stati quam loca sunt, in quibus fiant* (LCL), on which see Edwards, *Writing Rome*, 45–52; and Levene, *Religion in Livy*, 199–202.

2. Varro, *Ling.* 6.49; and Paul. Fest. 123L on narrative and memory as monuments, on which see Jaeger, *Livy's Written Rome*, 15–29.

3. On historical memory and Roman identity, see Miles, *Livy*, 67–74; and Wallace-Hadrill, *Rome's Cultural Revolution*, 259–260. Gaertner, "Livy's Camillus," cautions against an unduly "Augustan" reading of Livy. See also Plut. *Cam.* 31–32, for another version of the Camillus story.

4. Hölscher, "Die Alten vor Augen"; and Jenkyns, *God, Space, and City*, 126–133.

5. Cic. *Leg.* 2.2.4: *movemur enim nescio quo pacto locis ipsis, in quibus eorum, quos diligimus aut admiramur, adsunt vestigia* (trans. Keyes LCL), on which Edwards, *Writing Rome*, 16–18. See also Bonjour, *Terre natale*, esp. 7–19 and 114–161, on attachment to Rome.

6. On cultural memory, see J. Assmann, *Cultural Memory*, esp. 34–41, and *Religion and Cultural Memory*, esp. 1–4 and 24–30; and pp. 9–11, on communicative and cultural memory.

7. MacDonald, *Architecture of the Roman Empire*, 2.5–31, coined the term armature; while Laurence, "City Traffic" and esp. "Streets and Facades," applies it to Rome.

8. See Edwards, *Writing Rome*, 45, on Livy; and Vasaly, *Representations*, on Cicero. Halbwachs, *On Collective Memory*, (*Les cadres sociaux de la mémoire* perhaps better rendered as *Social Frameworks of Memory*), offers the classical treatment of memory frameworks, on whom see Olick, Vinitsky-Seroussi, and Levy, "Introduction," 16–25; and J. Assmann, *Cultural Memory*, 21–33. See too Fentress and Wickham, *Social Memory*, 51–75, on narrative and collective memory.
9. Favro, *Urban Image*, 7. See also Mumford, *City in History*, 277–280, on the importance of processions; and Favro, "Street Triumphant," "Festive Experience," and "Moving Events"; and Alcock, *Archaeologies of the Greek Past*, esp. 28–32, on processions (or practices), monuments, and memory.
10. de Certeau, *Practice of Everyday Life*, 97–102; Hinard, "Rome dans Rome"; Gruet, *rue à Rome*, esp. 233–263; and, on the triumph as image of Rome, Östenberg, *Staging the World*, esp. 262–292.
11. For a similar process at Ephesus, see Rogers, *Sacred Identity of Ephesos*; Portefaix, "Ancient Ephesus"; Yegül, "Street Experience of Ancient Ephesus"; and Feldman, "Bodies in Motion."
12. See pp. 25–36.
13. Lynch, *Image of the City*, esp. 1–13 and 125–128.
14. See, e.g. Davis, *Parades and Power*, 1–22; and Bruit Zaidman and Pantel Schmitt, *Religion in the Ancient Greek City*, 105–107, on processions as representations; and Chankowski, "Processions et cérémonies d'accueil," interrogating the concept.
15. Calvino, *Invisible Cities*, 10–11, on which see Edwards, *Writing Rome*, 1; and Gowing, "Rome and the Ruin of Memory," 466–467, both of whom quote Calvino for similar purposes.
16. Elsner, "Rome as Palimpsest"; and Larmour and Spencer, "Introduction – *Roma, recepta*."
17. Boyer, *City of Collective Memory*, 31 (whose work inspired this section's title).
18. Edwards, *Writing Rome*, 30.
19. Hölkeskamp, "Images of Power," 257. See also Livy *praef.* 10–12, on which Miles, *Livy*, 8–74; Jaeger, *Livy's Written Rome*, 15–29; and Gowing, *Empire and Memory*, 22–23.
20. Gowing, *Empire and Memory*, 14–17.
21. BNP 167–174. See too MacCormack, "*Loca sancta*," on sacred place; and Smith, *Map Is Not Territory*, on religious "mapping" traditions.
22. Orlin, "Augustan Religion," 82–83; and Rüpke, "Tempel, Daten, Rituale."
23. E.g. Livy 1.4–5; Dion. Hal. *Ant. Rom.* 1.79. 5–8; and Plut. *Rom.* 3–4, on which see esp. Rodríguez-Mayorgas, *memoria de Rome*, 42–47 and "Romulus, Aeneas," 93 and 98–100, on rituals as a framework of cultural memory. As Beard, "A Complex of Times," notes, the Parilia was also concerned with memory, among its multiple valances.
24. Cancik, "Rome as Sacred Landscape," esp. 253–254. See too Laurence, "Emperors, Nature and the City," esp. 79, on ritual, conceptions of the city, and memory; and more generally, Cosgrove, *Social Formation and Symbolic Landscape*, on the idea of landscape as a way to imagine social relations and relations with nature.
25. Hölkeskamp, "History and Collective Memory," 483, which takes up themes developed at greater length in Hölkeskamp, "Capitol, Comitium und Forum," reprinted in Hölkeskamp, *Senatus Populusque Romanus*, 137–168 with a bibliographical addendum. See also, Hölkeskamp, "Images of Power."
26. See J. Assmann, *Cultural Memory*, esp. 41–44, 70–76, and 81–87 and *Religion and Cultural Memory*, 9–16; Alcock, *Archaeologies of the Greek Past*, esp. 28–32; and the debate between Wiseman, "Popular Memory"; and Hölkeskamp, "In Defense of Concepts," on Roman collective memory.
27. de Certeau, *Practice of Everyday Life*, 91–110 and 115–130.
28. See pp. 46–49 on religious education; and Larmour and Spencer, "Introduction – *Roma, recepta*," 29.
29. Dion. Hal. *Ant. Rom.* 7.72.1: ἀπὸ τοῦ Καπιτωλίου τε καὶ δι᾽ ἀγορᾶς ἄγοντες ἐπὶ τὸν μέγαν ἱππόδρομον (LCL); and Hölkeskamp, "Roman Republic as Theatre of Power," esp. 167. See further Hölscher, "Die Alten vor Augen," 189–202.
30. Enn. in Varro, *Ling.* 5.65: *divumque hominumque pater rex* (LCL); and also Enn. in Cic. *Nat. D.* 2.2.4 and 2.25.64: *patrem divumque hominumque* (LCL). See pp. 75–76 on the *aedes tensarum.*

31. Livy 1.55.6: *arcem . . . imperii caputque rerum* and 5.39.12: *arx Capitoliumque, sedes deorum, . . . senatus, caput publici consilii* (LCL).
32. Livy 5.54.7: *Hic Capitolium est, ubi quondam capite humano invento responsum est eo loco caput rerum summamque imperii fore; hic cum augurato liberaretur Capitolium, Iuventas Terminusque maximo gaudio patrum vestrorum moveri se non passi* (trans. Foster LCL), on which see Jaeger, *Livy's Written Rome*, 89–91; Feldherr, *Spectacle and Society*, 46–48, on *hic*; and Vasaly, *Representations*, on the rhetorical power of places. See Fears, "Cult of Jupiter," 9–17; and Thein, "Capitoline Jupiter," on the Capitol, the *caput*, and Terminus and Juventas.
33. Hölkeskamp, "Capitol, Comitium und Forum," 99–111 and "History and Collective Memory," 488; and F. Hölscher, "Capitol," on the memory of the Capitol over the *longue durée*.
34. Hölkeskamp, "History and Collective Memory," 485. See further, Hölkeskamp, "Capitol, Comitium und Forum," 111–126; Hölscher, "Die Alten vor Augen," 189–194 and "Forum Romanum," on the Forum and memory over the *longue durée*.
35. Nora, "General Introduction," 1, adapted to the singular, on which see Erll, *Memory in Culture*, 22–27. See also Brint and Salzman, "Reflections on Political Space," 4–7.
36. Val. Max. 9.5.ext.4 suggests that the use of a forum mirrors the larger state.
37. Cic. *Fin.* 5.1.2: *cum ea loca videamus in quibus memoria dignos viros acceperimus multum esse versatos, magis moveamur quam si quando eorum ipsorum aut facta audiamus aut scriptum aliquod legamus. . . . Equidem etiam curiam nostram (Hostiliam dico, non hanc novam, quae minor mihi esse videtur posteaquam est maior) solebam intuens Scipionem, Catonem, Laelium, nostrum vero in primis avum cogitare; tanta vis admonitionis inest in locis* (trans. Rackham LCL), on which see Favro, "Roman Forum." Jenkyns, "Memory of Rome," cautions against equating the experience of Athens and Rome for ancient Romans, but "Marcus Piso" seems to do so.
38. Cic. *Verr.* 2.1.154: *viam tensarum atque pompae* (LCL); pp. 56 and 82–83.
39. Ov. *Fast.* 6.405–406: *solent in Circum ducere pompas, / nil praeter salices cassa que canna fuit* (trans. Frazer/Goold LCL).
40. Velabrum: e.g. LTUR sv Velabrum; and Hopkins, "Creation of the Forum," 36–42; Lupercal: e.g. Ov. *Fast.* 2.381–424; LTUR sv Lupercal; Raaflaub, "Romulus und die Wölflin"; Rodríguez-Mayorgas, *memoria de Roma*, 19–39, and n. 23 above; Ara Maxima: e.g. Verg. *Aen.* 8.213–305; Prop. 4.9; LTUR sv Hercules Invictus, Ara Maxima; and Welch, *Elegiac Cityscape*, 112–132; and mnemotopoi: J. Assmann, *Cultural Memory*, esp. 44–45.
41. Livy 1.9: rape of the Sabines and 2.37.9: *coetu . . . hominum deorumque* (LCL) during a festival in, presumably, the Circus Maximus, on which see Scheid, *Introduction to Roman Religion*, 107; and Bernstein, *Ludi publici*, 266–267 and "Complex Rituals," 229. See also LTUR sv Consus, Ara; Favro, "City Is a Living Thing," on the Circus as memory site; and Green, "Gods in Circus," on the Circus as liminal space.
42. See n. 29 above.
43. Laurence, "City Traffic," esp. 87–88 and 92–99.
44. CIL 1.2^2 593 = ILS 6085 = EDCS-20000229 = *Tabula Heracleensis* 64: *plostra . . . pompam ludeis circiensibus* (*Roman Statutes*, 1.365); and Tert. *Spect.* 7.5: *etsi unam tensam trahat, Iovis tamen plaustrum est* (LCL). On this law, see Robinson, *Ancient Rome*, 73–76; Martin, "Transportation and Law"; Tilburg, *Traffic and Congestion*, 128–131; Kaiser, "Cart Traffic Flow," 174–176, and *Roman Urban Street Networks*, 23–24; and Newsome, "Making Movement Meaningful," 14–20.
45. On lictors clearing a path, see Plut. *Aem.* 32.2; and Bell, *Spectacular Power*, 218–220. Favro, "Festive Experience," 20–21, suggests both possibilities.
46. *[Q]uacumque enim ingredimur, in aliqua historia vestigium ponimus* (LCL). See Chaniotis, "Rituals between Norms and Emotions," on heightened emotions in processions; and Bell, *Ritual Theory*, on ritualization. The following references have been consulted on each site, building, or monument, which will only be cited to make a specific point: D-S; P-A; Lugli, *Roma antica* and *Itinerario di Roma antica*; Nash, *Pictorial Dictionary*; Coarelli, *Foro Romano, Foro Boario*, and *Rome and Environs*; Richardson; LTUR; Claridge, *Rome*; Gros, *L'architecture romaine*; and Romano, "Digital Augustan Rome."

47. n. 31 above. See Paradisi, *Il Campidoglio*, for the *longue durée*; Rea, *Legendary Rome*, 44–63 an overview; and nn. 30–33 above.
48. On the monumentality of the Capitoline temple, see Hopkins, "Creation of the Forum," 49–52, "Colossal Temple," and "Capitoline Temple"; and Mura Sommella, "Il tempio," who argue for monumental size and importance from its late-sixth century BCE foundation; contra e.g. Stamper, *Architecture of Roman Temples*, 6–33, and "Urban Sanctuaries," 208–213, who argues for a more modestly sized temple, but one with great symbolic value. See also, Arata, "Nuove considerazioni," who argues for smaller superstructure dimensions; and Ridley, "Unbridgeable Gaps," on the tangled historiography of the Capitoline temple.
49. Livy 1.38.7: *aream ad aedem in Capitolio Iovis ... iam praesagiente animo futuram olim amplitudinem loci occupant fundamentis* (trans. Foster LCL).
50. Livy 1.53.3: *amplitudinem Iovis templi quae digna deum hominumque rege, quae Romano imperio, quae ipsius etiam loci maiestate esset* (trans. adapted Foster LCL); Livy 2.8.6–8; Dion. Hal. *Ant. Rom.* 4.61.3; and, on the dedication year as a time-keeping mechanism, Purcell, "Becoming Historical," 26–33.
51. Edwards, *Writing Rome*, 69–95, at 70. See further Fears, "Cult of Jupiter," 43–47; Flower, "Remembering and Forgetting," 74–80; Thein, "Capitoline Jupiter" and "Augustan 'Rebuilding,'" on the building history and import of the temple.
52. Perry, "Same, but Different," on continuities; and Sobocinski, "Visualizing Architecture," on evidentiary difficulties of its reconstruction.
53. Verg. *Aen.* 9.448–449: *dum domus Aeneae Capitoli immobile saxum / accolet imperiumque pater Romanus habebit* (trans. Fairclough/Gould LCL).
54. Hor. *Carm.* 3.30.8–9: *dum Capitolium /scandet cum tacita virgine pontifex* (trans. adapted Rudd LCL).
55. Cic. *Verr.* 2.5.184: *arce omniun nationum* (LCL) and *Leg. agr.* 1.18: *arce omnium gentium* (LCL), a phrase also used at *Cat.* 4.11.
56. Livy 1.55.6, on which see Thein, "Capitoline Jupiter."
57. Ov. *Fast.* 1.85–86: *Iuppiter arce suo totum cum spectat in orbem, / nil nisi Romanum, quod tueatur, habet* (trans. adapted Frazer/Goold LCL), on which see Jenkyns, *God, Space, and Time*, 26–35, on seeing as the gods saw. See also Serv. *Aen.* 2.319: *in Capitolio enim omnium deorum simulacra colebantur* (on the Capitol, images of all the gods were offered cult, ed. Teubner), fusing religious worship and empire.
58. Hor. *Carm* 1.73.6–8; Ov. *Met.* 15.826–828; and Cic. *Cat.* 3.19–20, on which see Edwards, *Writing Rome*, 86–88; Rea, *Legendary Rome*, 52–53; and Flower, "Remembering and Forgetting"; and see further Tac. *Hist.* 3.72: and *Hist.* 4.54 (and pp. 134–136), on the consequences of the destruction of the Capitoline temple, on which see Ash, "Victim and Voyeur," esp. 229–236.
59. Grattius, *Cynegetica* 535: *in sacraria tensas* (LCL); and also Suet. *Vesp.* 5.7: *tensam Iovis Optimi Maximi e sacrario* (LCL); CIL 16.4 = ILS 1987 = EDCS-12300209; CIL 16.30 = ILS 1997 = EDCS-12300234: *the/sarium veterem*; and AE 1998 #1056 = EDCS-24400401, on which see Dušanić, "*Loci Constitutionum Fixarum*," esp. 98–99 and 105–106.
60. Ov. *Fast.* 1.79–82: *vestibus intactis Tarpeias itur in arces, / et populus festo concolor ipse suo est, / iamque novi praeeunt fasces, nova purpura fulget, / et nova conspicuum pondera sentit ebur* (trans. adapted Frazer/Goold LCL). On the consular procession, see Jullian, "*Processus consularis*"; Frank, *Scholae Palatinae*, 147–154; Meslin, *fête des kalendes*, 23–28 and 55–59; Beard, *Roman Triumph*, 277–280; Östenberg, "Power Walks"; and pp. 197–198.
61. See pp. 25–26 on the *praeses ludorum* as an avatar of Jupiter; and pp. 50–59 on statues and symbols in the procession.
62. Dolansky, "*Togam Virilem Sumere.*"
63. Augustus, *RG* 14: *interessent consiliis publicis* (ed. and trans. adapted Cooley), on which see further Amiotti, "Religione e politica"; O'Sullivan, *Walking in Roman Culture*, 56–58; and Östenberg, "Power Walks."
64. Livy 37.3.7; on which see Hölkeskamp, "Republic as Theatre of Power," 168; Hurlet, "Représentation(s) et autoreprésentation(s)," 162, emphasizing triumphal associations; and esp. Kontokosta, "Reconsidering the Arches."
65. Oros. 5.9.2.

66. Livy 42.20.1, on which see Sehlmeyer, *Stadtrömische Ehrenstatuen*, 119–120.
67. Varro, *Rust.* 1.1.4: *duodecim deos Consentis ... quorum imagines ad forum auratae stant* (LCL), on which see Long, *Twelve Gods of Greece and Rome*, 34, 101–103, and 242–243; and Livy 41.27.7 on the paving of the *clivus* and, perhaps, the construction of the portico.
68. Livy 22.10.9 (see pp. 51–52).
69. Plin. *HN* 15.32. See Connelly, "Ritual Movement," esp. 320–324; and Feldman, "Bodies in Motion," 57–58, on statues as processional participants.
70. *[C]ircum spectacula spatiosiora intercolumnia distribuantur ... maenianaque superioribus coaxationibus conlocentur* (LCL).
71. Scott, "Triple Arch of Augustus," argues that the triple arch of Augustus straddled the via Sacra.
72. See Hopkins, "Creation of the Forum," esp. 30–35 and 42–47.
73. N. 37 above.
74. Cavalier and des Courtils, "Degrés et gradins"; and Hollinshead, "Monumental Steps," on steps in ritual and processional use.
75. Fest. 120L: *Maeniana appellata sunt a Maenio censore, qui primus in fora ultra columnas tigna proiecit, quo ampliarentur superiora spectacula* (Teubner); and Isid. *Etym.* 15.3.11.
76. Porphyr. *Hor. Sat.* 1.3.21: *Hic fertur domo sua, quam ad forum spectantem habuerat, divendita unam columnam inde sibi excepisse, unde gladiatores spectaret, quae ex eo Maenii columna nominabatur* (Teubner); and Ps. Asc. *Div. Caec.* 16.50: *Maenius cum domum suam venderet Catoni et Flacco censoribus, ut ibi basilica aedificaretur, exceperat ius sibi unius columnae, super quam tectum proiceret ex provolantibus tabulatis, unde ipse et posteri eius spectare munus gladiatorium possent, quod etiam tum in foro dabatur* (When Maenius sold his house to the censors Cato and Flaccus, so that a basilica might be built there, he stipulated the right to one column for himself, above which he projected a roof from protruding boards, from which he and his heirs could watch the gladiator games, which were still produced in the Forum, ed. Stangl). Coarelli, *Foro Romano*, 2. 39–53; Richardson sv Columna Maenia; LTUR sv Columna Maenia, agree on one column erected initially in 338 BCE, which seems to have supported a statue (Plin. *NH* 34.20). Sehlmeyer, *Stadtrömische Ehrenstatuen*, 53–57, suggests that BMRRC 363.1 (Figure 12) depicts this column behind Marsyas.
77. In the second century CE, Plut. *Aem.* 32.1: platforms for a triumph in 167 BCE, and *C. Gracch* 12.3: temporary seating for gladiator combats in 122 BCE, could imagine such amenities to have existed in the mid republic. See Welch, "The Roman Arena," 69–78, on wooden amphitheaters in the Forum.
78. Plin. *NH.* 34.20; Quint. *Inst.* 1.7.12; and Serv. *ad Georg.* 3.29, on which see Sehlmeyer, *Stadtrömische Ehrenstatuen*, 117–119; and Kondratieff, "Coinage and Column," 7–10.
79. Cassiod. *Var.* 7.13.1: *populus copiosissimus statuarum* (MGH); and also Cass. *Var.* 7.15. See Sehlmeyer, *Stadtrömische Ehrenstatuen*, with a broad collection of the evidence. On statues in public spaces, see Stewart, *Statues in Roman Society*, 118–156; and Trifiló, "Power, Architecture and Community."
80. Cic. *Fin.* 5.4: *usu hoc venire ut acrius aliquanto et attentius de claris viris locorum admonitu cogitemus* (trans. Rackham LCL), on which see Gregory, "'Powerful Images,'" esp. 86–88.
81. Freud, "The 'Uncanny,'" esp. 233–238, on doubles and repetition as uncanny. Stewart, *Statues in Roman Society*, 136–140; and Newsome, "Making Movement Meaningful," 20–26, on *locus celeberrimus*.
82. Val. Max 3.1.1; Plut. *C. Gracch.* 14.4 and *Fab.* 22.6, on which see Sehlmeyer, *Stadtrömische Ehrenstatuen*, 142–143, 150–151, and 125–126.
83. Livy 40.51.3 with Plin. *HN* 35.14; Plin. *HN* 34.30; and also Stewart, *Statues in Roman Society*, 128–136, on the history of statue removal at Rome.
84. Cic. *Off.* 3.80; Plin. *HN* 33.132 and 34.27, on which see Sehlmeyer, *Stadtrömische Ehrenstatuen*, 199–201.
85. BMRRC #363.1.
86. Serv. *Aen.* 3.20: *in liberis civitatibus simulacrum Marsyae erat* and 4.58: *Marsyas, eius minister, est in civitatibus, in foro positus, libertatis indicium* (Teubner), on which see Small, *Cacus and Marsyas*, 68–92; and Habetzeder, "Marsyas in the Garden?"
87. See pp. 34–35 on the satyr dancers.
88. Kontokosta, "Reconsidering the Arches," 9 and 15–16.

89. Sumi, "Monuments and Memory," on the significance of the temple.
90. Cristofani (ed.), *La grande Roma* #3.4.1 and 3.6.1; Grønne, "Architectural Terracottas," 1.165–169; and Wiseman, *Historiography and Imagination*, 71–72, fig. 4.
91. Dion. Hal. *Ant. Rom.* 6.13.4: ὑπὲρ ἅπαντα δὲ ταῦτα ἡ μετὰ τὴν θυσίαν ἐπιτελουμένη πομπὴ τῶν ἐχόντων τὸν δημόσιον ἵππον, οἳ κατὰ φυλάς τε καὶ λόχους κεκοσμημένοι στοιχηδὸν ἐπὶ τῶν ἵππων ὀχούμενοι πορεύονται πάντες, ὡς ἐκ μάχης ἥκοντες ἐστεφανωμένοι θαλλοῖς ἐλαίας, καὶ πορφυρᾶς φοινικοπαρύφους ἀμπεχόμενοι τηβέννας τὰς καλουμένας τραβέας, ἀρξάμενοι μὲν ἀφ' ἱεροῦ τινος Ἄρεος ἔξω τῆς πόλεως ἱδρυμένου, διεξιόντες δὲ τήν τε ἄλλην πόλιν καὶ διὰ τῆς ἀγορᾶς παρὰ τὸ τῶν Διοσκούρων ἱερὸν παρερχόμενοι, ἄνδρες ἔστιν ὅτε καὶ πεντακισχίλιοι φέροντες ὅσα παρὰ τῶν ἡγεμόνων ἀριστεῖα ἔλαβον ἐν ταῖς μάχαις, καλὴ καὶ ἀξία τοῦ μεγέθους τῆς ἡγεμονίας ὄψις (trans. Cary LCL). On the *ordo* in general and the *transvectio equitum* in particular, see Nicolet, *L'ordre équestre*, esp. 70–73; and Demougin, *L'ordre équestre*, 150–156 and 250–258.
92. Livy 9.46.15; Val. Max. 2.2.9; and [Aur. Vict.] *De vir. ill.* 32.3: Capitol as destination, all ascribed its origins to Q. Fabius Rullianus and his colleague, Decius Mus, in 304 BCE; Plut. *Pomp.* 22.4–6 (a late republican version); and Suet. *Aug.* 38.3, on which see Spencer, "Rome at a Gallop," 89–97.
93. Ov. *Tr.* 2.89–90 and 2.541–542.
94. Taylor, "*Seviri Equitum Romanorum*," 158–163; Rowe, *Princes and Political Cultures*, esp. 67–84; and pp. 28–29. See also Plin. *HN* 5.19 who notes that the same olive wreaths were worn in an *ovatio* and a *transvectio equitum*.
95. *Tusci turba impia vici* (LCL).
96. Cic. *Verr.* 2.1.154 (see p. 56): *a signo Vertumni in circum maximum ... viam tensarum atque pompae* (trans. adapted Greenwood LCL).
97. Prop. 4.2; and Varr. *Ling.* 5.46, on which see Welch, *Elegiac Cityscape*, esp. 36–42; and Plaut. *Curc.* 482: *homines qui ipsi sese venditant* (LCL), on which see Papi "*turba inpia*," esp. 48–50.
98. Betts, "Towards a Multisensory Experience," 121; and Gowers, "The Anatomy of Rome," 24.
99. Hopkins, "Cloaca Maxima" and "'Sacred Sewer.'"
100. Hor. *Ep.* 2.1.269–70: *in vicum vendentem tus et odores / et piper* (LCL).
101. Nielsen, "The Forum Paving," esp. 93–101.
102. Cic. *Verr.* 2.1.154: *Quis a signo Vertumni in circum maximum venit quin is uno quoque gradu de avaritia tua commoneretur? quam tu viam tensarum atque pompae eius modi exegisti ut tu ipse illa ire non audeas* (trans. adapted Greenwood LCL). On Cicero's topographical allusions, see Vasaly, *Representations*, esp. 15–39.
103. Cic. *Verr.* 2.3.6: *ex tensarum orbitis praedari sit ausus* (trans. adapted Greenwood LCL); and Cic. *Verr.* 2.5.186: *omnesque di qui vehiculis tensarum sollemnis coetus ludorum invisitis, quorum iter iste ad suum quaestum, non ad religionum dignitatem faciundum exigendumque curavit* (trans. adapted Greenwood LCL).
104. Cic. *Planc.* 83: *aliquid tensis misericordiae causa dicerem* (trans. adapted Watts LCL). See pp. 56–59 on *tensae*.
105. Macrob. *Sat.* 1.10.15: *Velabro, loco celeberrimo urbis*; and n. 81 above on *locus celeberrimus*.
106. Ov. *Fast.* 6.405–406: *qua Velabra solent in Circum ducere pompas, / nil praeter salices cassa que canna fuit* (trans. adapted Frazer/Goold LCL). See also Varro, *Ling.* 5.43–44 and 5.156: sailing in the Velabrum.
107. Plut. *Rom.* 5.5: καλεῖται δὲ νῦν ὁ τόπος Βήλαυρον ... τὴν εἰς τὸν ἱππόδρομον φέρουσαν ἐξ ἀγορᾶς πάροδον ἱστίοις καταπεταννύναι τοὺς τὴν θέαν παρέχοντας, ἐντεῦθεν ἀρχομένους: ῥωμαϊστὶ δὲ τὸ ἱστίον βῆλον ὀνομάζουσι (trans. Perrin LCL). Macrob. *Sat.* 1.6.15 (see pp. 38 and 64).
108. Theaters (Lucr. 4.75–77 and 6.109–111; Prop. 4.1a.15; Val. Max. 2.4.6; Ov. *Ars am.* 1.103; Plin. *HN* 19.23; Mart. 14.29; and Amm. Marc. 14.6.25) and amphitheaters (Plin. *HN* 19.24; Suet. *Calig.* 26.5; and SHA, *Comm.* 15.6) were outfitted with awnings, though not the Circus, on which see Humphrey, *Roman Circuses*, 101, 122–124, and 210 with fig. 63.
109. On the Lupercal and Lupercalia, from a large literature see Hopkins, "Violence to Blessing"; Wiseman, "God of the Lupercal"; LTUR sv Lupercal; North, "Caesar at the Lupercalia"; McLynn, "Crying Wolf"; and North and McLynn, "Postscript to the Lupercalia."

110. See Hunt, "Keeping the Memory Alive"; and pp. 137–138.
111. On clothing or its lack, see Ov. *Fast.* 2.267: nude; Plut. *Rom.* 21: a loincloth; and chapter 1 n. 89.
112. Varro in Tert. *Spect.* 5.3: *quod ludendo discurrant* (trans. Glover LCL). Routes: Coarelli, "percorsi cerimoniali," 32–37, a circular lustration around the Palatine; supported by Valli, "*Lupercis nudis*," 110–120, who also admits that route may have changed; while Michels, "Topography and Interpretation," 36–44; and Ziółkowski, "Ritual Cleaning-Up," 194–210, argue for a route back and forth from the Forum to the *summa via Sacra*; and Wiseman, "God of the Lupercal," 7–8, suggesting tree to tree.
113. Val. Max. 2.2.9a: *Equestris vero ordinis iuventus omnibus annis bis urbem spectaculo sui ... epularum hilaritate ac vino largiore provecti ... trabeatos vero equites idibus Iuliis ... transvehi* (trans. Shackleton-Bailey LCL).
114. Plin. *HN* 34.18: [*effigies*] *Lupercorum habitu* (LCL), on which see Veyne, "Iconographie de la *transvectio equitum*"; Rebecchi, "Per l'iconografia"; and Tortorella, "*Luperci e Lupercalia*," on the visual evidence, some of which represents both the *transvectio* and the Lupercalia. See also, Rowe, *Princes and Political Cultures*, 72.
115. Nn. 91–92 on Augustan reforms; and Lepelley, "Du triomphe à la disparition," on the decline of equestrians. Prudent. *Perist.* 10. 161–165 and *C. Symm.* 2.862–863; and Gelasius I, *Adv. Andromachum*, suggest elite participation in the late-antique Lupercalia, on which see McLynn, "Crying Wolf."
116. Varro, *Ling.* 5.146; and Paul. Fest. 27L on the forum as cattle market; and Ov. *Fast.* 6. 477–478; Plin. *NH* 34.10; and Tac. *Ann.* 12.24 on the bronze bull.
117. Plin. *HN* 18.15 and 34.21; and BMRRC #242.1 and 243.1. Cf. Dion. Hal. *Ant. Rom.* 12.4.6: senate voted the statue; and Livy 4.16.2: the plebs did not oppose the statue.
118. Serv. *Georg.* 3.29: *ante circum ... a parte ianuarum* (Teubner); and Richardson sv Columna Rostrata C. Duilii (1): axial ceremonial entrance implied.
119. Cic. *Verr.* 2.4.108: *pulcherrimum et magnificentissimum templum* (LCL); and Dion. Hal. *Ant. Rom.* 6.94.3: ἐπὶ τοῖς τέρμασι τοῦ μεγίστου τῶν ἱπποδρόμων ὑπὲρ αὐτὰς ἱδρυμένος τὰς ἀφέσεις (LCL), on which see Spaeth, *Roman Goddess Ceres*, 82–83.
120. Vitr. *De arch.* 3.3.5: *ad Circum Maximum* (LCL); Plin. *HN* 35.154: *ad Circum Maximum* (LCL); and Tac. *Ann.* 2.49.1: *iuxta Circum Maximum* (LCL), on which see LTUR sv Ceres, Liber, Liberaque, Aedes; Aedes Cereris.
121. Le Bonniec, *culte de Cérès à Rome*, 365–367; and esp. Spaeth, *Roman Goddess Ceres*, 81–102, on the plebian character of goddess and her temple.
122. Vitruv. *De arch.* 3.3.5: *epistyliis ... materia trabes perpetuae ... varicae, barycephalae, humiles, latae, ornanturque signis fictilibus aut aereis inauratis earum fastigia tuscanico more* (LCL). Richardon sv Ceres, Liber Liberaque, Aedes suggests three *cellae* on the model of the Capitoline temple.
123. Plin. *NH* 34.15; and see pp. 97–98 below.
124. On the temple of Ceres: Varro in Non. 63L; Dion. Hal. *Ant. Rom.* 6.89.3 and 10.42.4; and Livy 3.55.7 and 13, on which see Spaeth, *Roman Goddess Ceres*, 83–90 and esp. 91–92, on the opposition between the two triads.
125. CIL 6.1188–1190 = ILS 797 = EDCS-17600826. See BNP 74 and 108–9; and pp. 94–97 below, on SPQR.
126. *Spectatum veniunt, veniunt spectentur ut ipsae* (LCL).
127. Sen. *De Ira* 2.8: *circum, in quo maximam sui partem populus ostendit* (LCL); and Hor. *Ep.* 2.1.198: [*populum*] *praebentem nimio spectacula plura* (LCL), on which see Parker, "Observed of All Observers."
128. Ov. *Ars am.* 1.136–42: *Multa capax populi commoda circus habet. / Nil opus est digitis, per quos arcana loquaris, / Nec tibi per nutus accipienda nota est: / Proximus a domina, nullo prohibente, sedeto, / Iunge tuum lateri qua potes usque, latus / Et bene, quod cogit, si nolis, linea iungi, / Quod tibi tangenda est lege puella loca* (ed. LCL, trans. Green).
129. Ov. *Am.* 3.2.1–5: *Non ego nobilium sedeo studiosus equorum: / cui tamen ipsa faves, vincat ut ille, precor. / ut loquerer tecum veni, tecumque sederem, / ne tibi non notus, quem facis, esset amor. / tu cursus spectas, ego te; spectemus uterque / quod iuvat, atque oculos pascat uterque suos* (ed. LCL, trans. Lee), on which see Henderson, "A Doo-Dah-Doo-Dah-Dey"; and Welch, "Elegy and the Monuments," 109–114.

130. Suet. *Aug.* 44.1: *Spectandi confusissimum ac solutissimum morem correxit ordinavitque* (LCL); and Gunderson, "Ideology of the Arena," 125.
131. Ov. *Am.* 2.7.3–4: *sive ego marmorei respexi summa theatri, / eligis e multis, unde dolere velis* (ed. LCL, trans. Lee).
132. Ov. *Tr.* 2.283–4: *tollatur Circus! non tuta licentia Circi est: / hic sedet ignoto iuncta puella viro* (trans. adapted Wheeler/Goold LCL).
133. See Rawson, "*Discrimina ordinum,*" 112–113 n. 174; and Henderson, "A Doo-Dah-Doo-Dah-Dey," 50, on the limited success of seating regulations at the Circus; Rose, "Spectators and Spectator Comfort," 102; and Arena, *Feste e Rituali*, esp. 103–110, on the implementation (and panoptic character) of imperial circus seating regulations; Ciancio Rosetto, "La ricostruzione architettonica," on logistics and status differentiation; and Polverini, "Donne al circo," 471–472, on women spectators.
134. Juv. *Sat.* 11.201–202; on which see Edmondson, "Public Spectacles," 44–46 and 52.
135. Nelis-Clément, "cirque romain et son paysage sonore," 440–444.
136. Varro, *Ling.* 5.153; and Paul. Fest. 201L, on which see Humphrey, *Roman Circuses*, 132–135 and 171–172; Marcattili, *Circo Massimo*, 160–161; Marchet, "*Mittere mappam,*" 295–298; and see pp. 28, 89, and 155–156.
137. Ovid, *Am.* 3.2.44 (chapter 2 n. 1).
138. See Henderson, "Doo-Dah-Doo-Dah-Dey," 53; and, on communal ceremonial emotions, Chaniotis, "Staging and Feeling the Presence of God."
139. Suet. *Claud.* 12.2: *surgens et ipse cum cetera turba voce ac manu veneratus est* (ed. LCL, trans. Edwards).
140. Cic. *Att.* 13.44.1; and Dio Cass. 48.31.5, on which see Yavetz, *Plebs and Princeps*, 18–24; and pp. 147–150.
141. Livy 36.36.5; Plin. *HN* 29.57; Cic. *Div.* 1.16, on which see Humphrey, *Roman Circuses*, 60–64 and 91–95; Favro, "City is a Living Thing," on memory; Marcatilli, *Circo Massimo*, esp. 18–135, on archaic cults; and Green, "Gods in the Circus." On the *nomenclator*, see pp. 58 and 61–62.
142. Wiseman, *Myths of Rome*, 74–80, at 80.
143. Varro, Ling. 6.20: *in Circo* (LCL); Cic. *Har. resp.* 2.12: *in Circo* (LCL); Dion. Hal. *Ant. Rom.* 2.31.2: τῷ μεγίστῳ τῶν ἱπποδρόμων (LCL); Val. Max. 2.4.4: *circensi* (LCL); and Plut. *Rom.* 14.3: ἐν τῷ μείζονι τῶν ἱπποδρόμων (LCL), all situate the story in the Circus. Ov. *Ars am.* 1.101–134, sets the story in a discourse on the theater. BMRRC #344.1 depicts the rape of the Sabines on the reverse, but at no discernible location.
144. See Plass, *Game of Death*, 30–31; and Torlone, "Writings Arenas," 414–415, on sex, violence, and games; and pp. 138–139 and 230 on the Sabine women.
145. Varro, *Ling.* 5.153: *Circus Maximus dictus, quod circum spectaculis aedificatus ubi ludi fiunt, et quod ibi circum metas fertur pompa et equi currunt* (trans. Kent LCL), a route which the triumph may also have followed at times, for which see Östenberg, "*Circum metas fertur.*" On the circus building (whose full history cannot be addressed here), in addition to standard reference works (n. 46), see Humphreys, *Roman Circuses*; Ciancio Rossetto and Bounfiglio, "Circo Massimo"; Ciancio Rosetto, "La ricostruzione architettonica"; and Marcattili, *Circo Massimo*; and, for overviews, Zarmakoupi, "Public Entertainment Structures," 46–48; Bell, "Roman Chariot Racing," 493–495; and Dodge, "Venues for Spectacle," 562–566.
146. Devallet, "*Pompa circensis*"; and Dupont, "*Pompa* et *carmina,*" 77–78, on ludic space.
147. Livy 33.27.4, on which see Humphrey, *Roman Circuses*, 69 and 100; Richardson sv Fornices Stertinii, precise location unknown; Marcattili, *Circo Massimo*, 180–187, by the *carceres*; while LTUR sv Fornices Stertinii; and Kontokosta, "Reconsidering the Arches," 13–15, at the curved end.
148. See esp. Humphrey, *Roman Circuses*, 78–83; Marcatilli, "Pulvinar" and *Circo Massimo*, 205–211; van den Berg, "*Pulvinar,*" esp. 258–266, a lexical and cultural study; and also pp. 138 and 143–144.
149. Fest. 500L; and Paul. Fest. 501L, on which see Chapter 2 n. 76: *exuviae* and statues, possibly, in the *pulvinar*.
150. Ps.-Acro, *Hor. Carm.* 1.37.3: *pulvinaria dicebantur aut lecti deorum aut tabulata, in quibus stabant numina, ut eminentiora viderentur* (Teubner), on which see Dareggi, "Genesi e sviluppo," 79–80; and Golvin, "Réflexion relative."
151. Verg. *Aen.* 5.137–140: *intenti exspectant signum, exsultantiaque haurit / corda pavor pulsans laudumque arrecta cupido. / inde ubi clara*

dedit sonitum tuba, finibus omnes, / haud mora, prosiluere suis (trans. Fairclough/Goold LCL); on which see Marchet, "*Mittere mappam*"; and see pp. 28 and 155–156.

152. *[N]am nos in nostra urbe peregrinantis errantisque tamquam hospites tui libri quasi domum reduxerunt, ut possemus aliquando qui et ubi essemus agnoscere* (LCL, emphasis added).
153. Malmberg, "Finding Your Way"; and Kaiser, *Roman Urban Street Networks*, 2–12.
154. See Edwards, "Imaginaires de l'image"; Favro, *Urban Image*, esp. 1–23 and "IconiCITY"; Vout, "Sizing Up Rome"; Wallace-Hadrill, *Rome's Cultural Revolution*, 259–275; and Holleran, "Street Life," 246–251, on the difficulties of conceptualizing the city; and Jenkyns, *God, Space, and City*, 111–141, for an exploration of how some literate Romans may have felt about Rome.
155. Lynch, *Image of the City*, 125, 126, 2, and 125–126. See too, Lynch, "Reconsidering *The Image of the City*." Favro, *Urban Image*, puts this holistic view of Lynch's theory to good use.
156. Edwards, *Writing Rome*, 4–6 and 16–18; and Spencer, "Movement and the Linguistic Turn" and "Urban Flux," on Varronian place-making.
157. Wallace-Hadrill, *Rome's Cultural Revolution*, 259.
158. Cancik, "Rome as Sacred Landscape"; BNP 75 (Chapter 2 n. 29); and Wallace-Hadrill, *Rome's Cultural Revolution*, 231–237.
159. Bayliss, "Usurping the Urban Image," argues that procession, itinerary, and history ritually produced an urban image.
160. Ling, "Stranger in Town"; Castrén, "*Vici* and *Insulae*"; and Malmberg, "Finding Your Way."
161. Camille, "Signs of the City." Ling, "Street Plaques," argues that street plaques served various, non-navigational purposes (décor, advertising, religious scruples).
162. E.g. Ling, "Stranger in Town," 211–212; Favro, *Urban Image*, 5–6; Tilburg, *Traffic and Congestion*, 49–51; Betts, "Towards a Multisensory Experience," 122; Holleran, "Street Life in Ancient Rome," 247–248; Kaiser, *Roman Urban Street Networks*, 8; and Newsome, "Movement and Fora in Rome," 295–296.
163. Ter. *Ad.* 572–584: *DEM dic ergo locum. SYR nostin porticum apud macellum hanc deorsum? DEM quidni noverim? SYR praeterito hanc recta platea sursum. ubi eo veneris, clivos deorsum vorsumst: hac te praecipitato. postea est ad hanc manum sacellum: ibi angiportum propter est, DEM quodnam? SYR illi ubi etiam caprificus magnast. DEM novi. SYR hac pergito. DEM id quidem angiportum non est pervium. SYR verum hercle. vah! censen hominem me esse? erravi. in porticum rursum redi. sane hac multo propius ibis et minor est erratio. scin Cratini huius ditis aedes? DEM scio. SYR ubi eas praeterieris, ad sinistram hac recta platea, ubi ad Dianae veneris, ito ad dextram. prius quam ad portam venias, apud ipsum lacum est pistrilla et exadvorsum fabrica: ibist* (trans. Barsby LCL). See Ter. *Ad.* 713–718 for the outcome.
164. Reversing Bell, *Ritual Theory*, on ritualization or the differentiation of "ritual" practice from quotidian practice.
165. Lynch, *Image of the City*, 1–13; and Smith, *Imagining Religion*, 53–65, and esp. *To Take Place*, esp. 47–73, on ritual as a focusing device and the ritual construction of place.
166. See Östenberg, *Staging the World*, 262–292, esp. 262–272, on the definition and dissemination of an idea of Rome in the triumph; and Feldman, "Bodies in Motion," noting the diversity of place-making in processional performance.
167. Leach, *Rhetoric of Space*, 73–143, at 74; and Plaut. *Poen.* 1012 (p. 38).
168. Plaut. *Curc.* 467–484: *commonstrabo quo in quemque hominem facile inveniatis loco, / ne nimio opere sumat operam si quem conventum velit / vel vitiosum vel sine vitio, vel probum vel improbum. / qui periurum convenire volt hominem ito in comitium; / qui mendacem et gloriosum, apud Cloacinae sacrum, / dites, damnosos maritos sub basilica quaerito. / ibidem erunt scorta exoleta quique stipulari solent; / symbolarum collatores apud forum piscarium. / in foro infumo boni homines atque dites ambulant; / in medio propter canalem, ibi ostentatores meri; / confidentes garrulique et malevoli supra lacum, / qui alteri de nihilo audacter dicunt contumeliam / et qui ipsi sat habent quod in se possit vere dicier. / sub veteribus, ibi sunt qui dant quique accipiunt faenore. / pone aedem Castoris, ibi sunt subito quibus credas male. / in Tusco vico, ibi sunt homines qui ipsi sese venditant. / in Velabro vel pistorem vel lanium vel haruspicem / vel qui ipsi vortant vel qui aliis ubi vorsentur praebeant* (ed. LCL, trans. Aicher).
169. Leach, *Rhetoric of Space*, 74; and Moore, "*Palliata Togata*," 344.

170. Cic. *Verr.* 2.1.154 (n. 38); and Ov. *Fast.* 6.405–406 (n. 39).
171. Other literary itineraries: Vergil, *Aen.* 8. 337–361; Hor. *Sat.* 1.9; Ov. *Tr.* 3.1.27–72; and Mart. 1.70, on which see e.g. Edwards, *Writing Rome*; Roman, "Martial and the City"; and O'Sullivan, *Walking in Roman Culture*, 150–152, and "Augustan Literary Tours."
172. Letzner, *Der römische Circus*, 61–67 and fig. 43, asserts that the *pompa* for the *ludi Apollinares* began at the temple of Apollo Sosianus; and Favro, "Festival Experience," 30, suggests that the *ludi Megalenses* started from Magna Mater's Palatine temple. In the fourth century CE, CTh 16.10.3 attempted to preserve certain extramural temples because games originated from them. See pp. 133–134 and 143 on the possibility of multiple imperial itineraries and shops associated with the *pulvinar*.
173. See p. 143
174. Verg. *Aen.* 8.679: *cum patribus populoque, penatibus et magnis dis* (LCL).
175. Cic. *Dom.* 58.147: *dis immortalibus ... senatui ... populo Romano* (LCL). For other references to SPQR+god(s), see e.g. Cic. *Deiot.* 2, *Har. resp.* 6.12, and *Verr.* 2.4.69; Livy 8.4.11; and Tac. *Hist.* 3.84.2. A quick search in the *Library of Latin Texts* database (Brepols) produced approximately two hundred references to some variant of SPQR between the republic and late antiquity, about half of which were from Cicero, a third of which from the *Philippics*; about 30 in Livy; and 12 in the SHA. Similarly, a quick search on EDCS turned up 51 instances of SPQR inscribed in the city of Rome. SPQR was also very popular on coinage, on which see Gallia, *Remembering the Roman Republic*, 22; and Beneš, "Whose SPQR?" 874–875 nn. 2–4, for examples.
176. See Fishwick, *Imperial Cult*, 2.550–566; and chapter 1 n. 2, on hierarchy and unity.
177. See Livy 2.37.9 (n. 41). Veyne, *Bread and Circuses*, 212, on "Piety, merrymaking, and solemnity"; and Massa - Pairault, "Aspects idéologiques des *ludi*," arguing that the games were more than simply politics or sports. On the religiosity of games and shows, see Piganiol, "Les sens religieux des jeux"; Harmon, "Religious Significance of the Games"; Gebhard, "Theater and the City"; Zaleski, "Religion and Roman Spectacle," all brief sketches; and chapter 2 on the circus procession.
178. Livy 7.2.2–3: *pacis deum exposcendae causa ... victis superstitione animis ludi quoque scaenici ... inter alia caelestis irae placamina instituti dicuntur* (trans. adapted Foster LCL) and 7.3.1–2: ritual failure. Livy regularly invoked the *pax deorum* and attempts to secure it, e.g. 3.5.14, 3.8.1, 4.30.10, 6.1.12, 6.12.7, 24.11.1, 27.23.4, and 38.46.12.
179. Vitruv. *De arch.* 5.3.1: *deorum inmortalium diebus festis ludorum* (LCL).
180. Cic. *Verr.* 2.5.36: *mihi ludos sanctissimos maxima cum cura et caerimonia Cereri Libero Liberaeque faciundos, mihi Floram matrem populo plebique Romanae ludorum celebritate placandam, mihi ludos antiquissimos, qui primi Romani appellati sunt, cum dignitate maxima et religione Iovi Iunoni Minervaeque esse faciundos* (trans. adapted Greenwood LCL).
181. Ov. *Fast.* 3.783–784: *rusticus ad ludos populus veniebat in Urbem /(sed dis, non studiis ille dabatur honor)* (trans. adapted Frazer/Gould LCL).
182. Wiseman, "Games of Flora"; and see pp. 163–164.
183. Arn. *Adv. nat.* 7.33: *Honorantur, inquit, his dii* (CSEL); and see also Lactant. *Div. Inst.* 6.20.34: *ludorum celebrationes deorum festa sunt* (celebrations of the games are feasts for the gods, ed. CSEL).
184. Aug. *De civ. D.* 1.32, a critique of the events narrated by Livy 7.2 (n. 178 above).
185. Arn. *Adv. nat.* 7.41: *Iovem, quem deum principem dicitis et rerum quaecumque sunt conditorem, qui spectatum proficisceretur e caelo cantherios de velocitate certantes, replicantes gyros septem, et ... gauderet transire, transiri, pronos et cernuos ruere, cum curribus resupinos verti, trahi alios, cruribus et claudicare praefractis* (ed. CSEL, trans. McCracken ACW). See further pp. 186–191 for Christian critiques of the games.
186. Livy 36.2.5: *donaque data recte* (LCL); and e.g. Livy 27.23.5–7.
187. Benoist, "processions," on processions and civic identity, both divine and human.
188. Ov. *Am.* 3.2.44: *aurea pompa* (LCL); and see also *Am.* 3.13.29, where Ovid evoked a procession for Juno as an *aurea pompa*, so perhaps he just liked the phrase.
189. Gernentz, *Laudes Romae*, 58–62 testimonia, on which Edwards, *Writing Rome*, 69–72.
190. Ov. *Ars am.* 3.113–114: *Simplicitas rudis ante fuit, nunc aurea Roma est / Et domiti magnas*

possidet orbis opes (trans. adapted Mozley/Goold LCL).

191. Verg. *Aen.* 8.347–348: *Capitolia ... / aurea nunc, olim silvestribus horrida dumis* (ed. LCL, trans. Edwards, *Writing Rome*, 31); and Sen. *Controv.* 1.6.4: *nudi stetere colles, interque tam effusa moenia nihil est humili casa nobilius: fastigatis supra tectis auro puro fulgens praelucet Capitolium* (trans. Winterbottom LCL).
192. Ov. *Fast.* 1.223–224: *nos quoque templa iuvant, quamvis antiqua probemus, / aurea: maiestas convenit ista deo* (trans. adapted Frazer/Goold LCL).
193. Ov. *Fast.* 6.73: *aurea ... Capitolia* (LCL); and Livy 2.22.6.
194. Livy 35.10.12 (shields); and Plin. *HN* 33.57 (ceiling and roof). On upgrades after the fire in 83 BCE, see Dion. Hal. *Ant. Rom.* 4.61.4; and Cic. *Verr.* 2.4.69; and, on the cult statue, Perry, "Same, but Different," 190–194.
195. Vitr. *De arch.* 3.3.5.
196. Hor. *Carm.* 3.3.42–43: *Capitolium / fulgens* (LCL); and see pp. 134–136, on the imperial-era Capitoline temple.
197. Sen. *Contr.* 2.1.1: *Quietiora tempora pauperes habuimus; bella civilia aurato Capitolio gessimus* (LCL).
198. Ricoeur, *Time and Narrative*, 1.xi.
199. Cic. *Tusc.* 5.32.91 (Chapter 1 n. 94).
200. See Eder, "Augustus and the Power of Tradition," (1990 and 2005); esp. Gowing, *Empire and Memory*; and also pp. 9–11 and 21–25.
201. Beard, *Roman Triumph*, 80–85, at 82.
202. Smith, *Imagining Religion*, xi: "Religion is solely a creation of the scholar's study. It is created for the scholar's analytic purposes by his [sic] imaginative acts of comparison and generalization."
203. Weber, "'Objectivity' in Social Science," esp. 89–106, at 90. However, given the limited evidence, this ideal-type of the *pompa circensis* cannot function as fully as Weber envisioned.
204. Bourdieu, *Logic of Practice*, 53 (emphasis added).
205. And so, hopefully this ideal-type is not simply an amalgamation of textual and visual representations, but it is also that.

Four "Honors greater than human"

1. App. *B. Civ.* 2.16.106: [τιμαὶ] ὅσαι ὑπὲρ ἄνθρωπον (LCL).
2. τί θεός; τὸ κρατοῦν / τί βασιλεῦς, ἰσόθεος (www.trismegistos.org/text/63490), on which see Price, "Gods and Emperors," 95. My thanks to Christopher Kelly for the reference.
3. Price, *Rituals and Power*.
4. Lozano, "*Divi Augusti*"; Brodd and Reed (ed), *Rome and Religion*, part 2; and Iossif, Chankowski, and Lorber (ed), *More than Men*, part III, on Roman imperial cult in the eastern Mediterranean.
5. Gradel, *Emperor Worship*, 54, with critiques by Levene, "Defining the Divine"; and Koortbojian, *Divinization*, esp. 23–24.
6. Gradel, *Emperor Worship*, 72; and see also Iossif and Lorber, "More than Men."
7. Gradel, *Emperor Worship*, 369: "By receiving such honours, the emperor was morally obligated to return benefactions, that is, to rule well." See also Peppel, "Gott oder Mensch?" on imperial cult as a way to temper imperial power; and Tanner, "Portraits, Power," on honorific statues and their attendant obligations.
8. Mauss, *The Gift*, esp. 39–46.
9. Dio Cass. 44.7.2: ὡς καὶ μετριάσοντα (trans. Cary LCL).
10. Dion. Hal. *Ant. Rom.* 1.7.2: ἅμα τῷ καταλυθῆναι τὸν ἐμφύλιον πόλεμον ὑπὸ τοῦ Σεβαστοῦ Καίσαρος (LCL). From an overwhelming literature on the transition from republic to empire, see Eder, "Augustus and Power of Tradition," (1990 and 2005).
11. See essays in Hurlet and Mineo (ed), *principat d'Auguste*, on the "restoration" of the republic.
12. Tert. *Ad nat.* 1.10: *regibus quidem etiam sacerdotia adscripta sunt ceterique apparatus, ut tensae et currus et solisternia et lectisternia <et> feriae et ludi* (CCSL). Sen. *Apocol.*; and Vespasian's famous quip (Suet. *Vesp.* 23.4) suggest elite ambivalence about the imperial cult. See Scheid, "Roman Animal Sacrifice," 88–90, on the distinction between traditional and imperial gods in Arval sacrifices.
13. Estienne, "*Simulacra deorum*," 266–270, argues that imperial images in traditional cult sanctuaries were subordinate, but similar to the traditional gods.
14. See Arena, "*Pompa Circensis*," and more fully *Feste e rituali*, 53–102, on the dynastic implications of the imperial *pompa circensis*.

15. Benoist, "Images des dieux," cautions against too much third-century CE discontinuity, though the third century did catalyze a reconfiguration of the *pompa circensis*, on which see Latham, "Representing Ritual"; and pp. 197–207.
16. App. *B. Civ.* 2.16.106: ὁ δὲ Καῖσαρ ἐς Ῥώμην ἠπείγετο, τὰ ἐμφύλια πάντα καθελών, ἐπὶ φόβου καὶ δόξης, οἵας οὔ τις πρὸ τοῦ· ὅθεν αὐτῷ τιμαὶ πᾶσαι, ὅσαι ὑπὲρ ἄνθρωπον, ἀμέτρως ἐς χάριν ἐπενοοῦντο, θυσιῶν τε πέρι καὶ ἀγώνων καὶ ἀναθημάτων ἐν πᾶσιν ἱεροῖς καὶ δημοσίοις χωρίοις (trans. adapted White LCL). On imperial statues at Rome, see Hitzl, "Kultstätten und Praxis," 98–104.
17. Fishwick, *Imperial Cult*, 1.21–45, on honors equal to the gods.
18. Dio Cass. 43.45.2: καὶ τότε μὲν ἀνδριάντα αὐτοῦ ἐλεφάντινον, ὕστερον δὲ καὶ ἅρμα ὅλον ἐν ταῖς ἱπποδρομίαις μετὰ τῶν θείων ἀγαλμάτων πέμπεσθαι ἔγνωσαν (trans. adapted Cary LCL). *Arma* translates *tensa*, on which see Abaecherli, "*Fercula, carpenta,* and *tensae*," 10–11; André, "Glanures," 75 n. 21; and Weinstock, *Divus Julius*, 285. Out of a vast literature on Caesar and ruler cult, see Taylor, *Divinity*, 58–77; Weinstock, *Divus Julius*, with reviews by Alföldi, North, and Versnel; Fishwick, *Imperial Cult*, 1.56–72; Gradel, *Emperor Worship*, 54–72; Bell, *Spectacular Power*, 24–51; Sumi, *Ceremony and Power*; Ferrary, "À propos de deux passages" and "À propos des pouvoirs"; and Koortbojian, *Divinization*.
19. Dio Cass. 44.6.3: ἔσ τε τὰ θέατρα τόν τε δίφρον αὐτοῦ ἐπίχρυσον καὶ τὸν στέφανον τὸν διάλιθον καὶ διάχρυσον, ἐξ ἴσου τοῖς τῶν θεῶν, ἐσκομίζεσθαι (trans. Cary LCL). On Caesar's crown, see La Rocca, "troni dei nuovi dei," 91–92; and Koortbojian, *Divinization*, 34 and 118–126. Dio Cass. 44.6.3 continues κἀν ταῖς ἱπποδρομίαις ὀχὸν ἐσάγεσθαι ("and that on the occasion of the games in the circus his chariot [*oxos* = *tensa*] should be brought in," trans. Cary LCL), distinguishing between the Circus and the theater, which argues against Arena, "Circo Massimo come microcosmo," 39–41, "*Pompa Circensis*," 79, and *Feste e rituali*, 108–110 and 134–135, who maintains that *theatron* in Dio meant both the theater and Circus. Elkins, "Procession and Placement," argues that *theatron* names the amphitheater especially, which seems too restrictive. See pp. 161–180 for further on the *pompa (amphi-)theatralis*, similar but separate processions.
20. BMRRC #497.2, on which *Imperii insignia*, 114–122 and taf. 12.10; and La Rocca, "troni dei nuovi dei," 91–92.
21. Dio Cass. 50.10.2: ἄνθρωπός τέ τις μανιώδης ἐς τὸ θέατρον ἐν πανηγύρει τινὶ ἐσπηδήσας τὸν στέφανον τὸν τοῦ προτέρου Καίσαρος ἀνείλετο καὶ περιέθετο, καὶ διεσπάσθη ὑπὸ τῶν περιεστηκότων (trans. Cary LCL). See further p. 168.
22. Dio Cass. 56.29.1: ἀνήρ τις ἐμμανὴς ἔς τε τὸν δίφρον τὸν τῷ Καίσαρι τῷ Ἰουλίῳ κείμενον ἐνιδρύθη καὶ τὸν στέφανον αὐτοῦ λαβὼν περιέθετο (trans. Cary LCL).
23. Weinstock, *Divus Julius*, 110–112, 184–186, 271, 284–286, and 367. Cf. Ferrary, "À propos des pouvoirs," 19, for whom two letters of Cicero (*Att.* 13.28.3 [LCL 299] and 13.44.1 [LCL 336]) pertain to the same procession in 45 BCE.
24. Cic. *Att.* 13.28.3 (LCL 299) May 45: *tu hunc de pompa, Quirini contubernalem, his nostris moderatis epistulis laetaturum putas?* ("And do you suppose that this figure in the procession, this fellow lodger of Quirinus', will be gratified by a sober letter like mine?" trans. Shackleton-Bailey LCL). On Caesar's statue in the temple of Quirinus, see Cic. *Att.* 12.45 (LCL 290) and 12.48 (LCL 289); and Dio Cass. 43.45.3, with Weinstock, *Divus Julius*, 184–188; Fishwick, *Imperial Cult*, 1.57–60; and Koortbojian, *Divinization*, 84–93.
25. Dio Cass. 43.45.2, on which see Weinstock, *Divus Julius*, 91, 103, 111, and 185; and Sumi, *Ceremony and Power*, 144, who convincingly argues for the *ludi Apollinares*.
26. Cic. *Att.* 13.44.1 (LCL 336): LCL gives July 14, 45 BCE, which suggests the *ludi Apollinares*; while Taylor, "Chronology of Cicero's Letters," dates the letter to July 27–31 in association with the victory games. See further pp. 147–148; and, on applause, pp. 44–45; and 87–88;.
27. Dio Cass. 43.45.2 and 44.6.3 (nn. 18–19 above), with Ferrary, "À propos des pouvoirs," 19–20.
28. Cic. *Phil.* 2.110: *pulvinar* and *simulacrum*, strongly suggesting the circus procession, on which see Ferrary, "À propos de deux passages," esp. 222–231.

29. Suet. *Iul.* 76.1: *honores ... nimios ... tensam et ferculum circensi pompa ... ampliora etiam humano* (ed. LCL, trans. adapted Edwards).
30. Suet. *Iul.* 88.1: *in deorum numerum relatus est, non ore modo decernentium, sed et persuasione volgi* (ed. LCL, trans. Edwards), on which see e.g. Taylor, *Divinity*, 77–85; Weinstock, *Divus Julius*, 346–367; Fraschetti, *Roma e il principe*, 46–59; Flower, *Ancestor Masks*, 125–126; Sumi, *Ceremony and Power*, 97–120; Benoist, *Rome, le prince*, esp. 117–122; and Koortbojian, *Divinization*, 24–27.
31. Weinstock, *Divus Julius*, 367, piecing together Cic. *Att.* 14.14.1 (LCL 368) and 14.19.3 (LCL 372), on which see also Sumi, *Ceremony and Power*, 118–119.
32. Cic. *Att.* 15.3.2 (LCL 380), Nic. Dam. F 130: 28.108; App. *B. Civ.* 3.4.28; Plut. *Ant.* 16.2; and Dio Cass. 45.6.5, on which see Weinstock, *Divus Julius*, 367–384; Toher, "Octavian's Arrival," esp. 175 and 182–183; and Sumi, *Ceremony and Power*, esp. 130–131 and 150–153.
33. Fishwick, *Imperial Cult*, 1.74. On the comet, see e.g. Plin. *HN* 2.93–94; Suet. *Iul.* 88; Dio Cass. 45.7.1; and Obsequens 68, on which see Ramsey and Licht, *Comet of 44 B.C.*; and Pandey, "Caesar's Comet," who argues that Augustus did not, in fact, capitalize on the comet/star until later in his career.
34. Dio Cass. 47.18.4: ἡρῷόν οἱ ἔν τε τῇ ἀγορᾷ καὶ ἐν τῷ τόπῳ ἐν ᾧ ἐκέκαυτο προκατεβάλοντο, καί τι καὶ ἄγαλμα αὐτοῦ ἐν ταῖς ἱπποδρομίαις μεθ' ἑτέρου Ἀφροδισίου ἔπεμπον and 47.19.2: πρὸς δὲ τούτοις ἀπεῖπον μὲν μηδεμίαν εἰκόνα αὐτοῦ, καθάπερ θεοῦ τινος ὡς ἀληθῶς ὄντος, ἐν ταῖς τῶν συγγενῶν αὐτοῦ ἐκφοραῖς πέμπεσθαι (trans. adapted Cary LCL).
35. Dio Cass. 56.34.2: Caesar's image left out of Augustus' funeral and 56.46.4: exemption for Augustus' image, on which see Taylor, *Divinity*, 96–98; Weinstock, *Divus Julius*, 393–394; Price, "Noble Funerals"; Fraschetti, *Roma e il principe*, esp. 59–70; and Flower, *Ancestor Masks*, 97–109, on republican funeral processions, and 237–246, on Augustan funerals.
36. Suet. *Iul.* 76.1 (n. 29 above). See Koortbojian, *Divinization*, on the difficulties of inventing representations of the new *divus*.
37. As Wallace-Hadrill, "Image and Authority," notes, the emperor did not design or even necessarily approve the coins. Nonetheless, moneyers presented an imperial message. See also Ando, *Imperial Ideology*, 215–228; and esp. Noreña, *Imperial Ideals*, on coinage and communication.
38. RIC 1^2 Augustus #258–259 (Figure 14). Alföldi, *zwei Lorbeerbäume*, 38–40 and *Caesar in 44 v. Chr.*, 1.147; and Szidat, *Teile eines historischen Frieses*, 31 and 61–62, take this chariot as a *tensa*. Weinstock, *Divus Julius*, 54–59; and Rich, "Augustus' Parthian Honors," 115–125 argue that they represent other honors. See Latham, "Representing Ritual," 201–205 with figures 1–3; and pp. 7–8 and 57–58, on representations of "*tensae*" in comparison with other chariots. In addition, one should compare, for example, RIC 1^2 Augustus #96–101 (= Weinstock, *Divus Julius*, pl. 6.2 and Rich, "Augustus' Parthian Honors," fig. 9.iii), RIC 1^2 Augustus #107, 109–110, and 113 (= Weinstock, *Divus Julius*, pl. 6.1 and Rich, "Augustus' Parthian Honors," fig. 9.i), and RIC 1^2 Augustus #258–259 (Figure 14) (= Weinstock, *Divus Julius*, pl. 5.15 and Rich, "Augustus' Parthian Honors," fig. 11), all empty, tall, rectilinear "*tensae*" with pediments and figural ornamentation with RIC 1^2 Augustus #108 and 111: an empty chariot with a curved façade and abstract ornament; RIC 1^2 Augustus #114–120: an flat-topped, rounded chariot with abstract ornament (= Weinstock, *Divus Julius*, pl. 6.3 and Rich, "Augustus' Parthian Honors," fig. 9.ii); RIC 1^2 Augustus #221–224: Tiberius in a low, rounded chariot; RIC 1^2 Augustus #260–261: a low and sweeping chariot driven by Victory (similar to Weinstock, *Divus Julius*, pl. 6.4–5); and RIC 1^2 #263–264: Octavian in a low, rounded chariot without pediment and with figural decoration (= Weinstock, *Divus Julius* pl. 5.16). Note: RIC 1^2 considers Augustus # 107–113 to represent the same vehicle on all the reverses, though 107, 109–110, and 113 are rectilinear with a pediment and figural decoration, while 108 and 111 are curvilinear with abstract ornament.
39. RIC 1^2 Augustus #96–101 (Figure 15) and 107, 109–110, and 113 (Figure 16). Bastien, "Remarques," 25, associates these chariots with the *pompa circensis*.
40. On the intended Parthian campaign, see e.g. Cic. *Att.* 13.31.3 (LCL 302); Vell. Pat. 2.59.4; and Suet. *Iul.* 44.3 and *Aug.* 8.2.

41. Suet. *Aug.* 43.5: *Accidit votivis circensibus, ut correptus valitudine lectica cubans tensas deduceret* (ed. LCL trans. adapted Edwards). On travel by litter, see O'Sullivan, *Walking in Roman Culture*, 71–74.
42. Suet. *Aug.* 45.1–3, on Augustus' appreciation of the games.
43. Mart. 8.11.5–6: applause obscures the start of the races; Zanker, *Power of Images*, 33–37, on *divi filius* and 85–98 on traditionalism with nn. 10–11 above; and see pp. 19–20 and 36–39 on spectacle and wonder.
44. Dio Cass. 52.30.1: τὸ μὲν ἄστυ τοῦτο καὶ κατακόσμει πάσῃ πολυτελείᾳ καὶ ἐπιλάμπρυνε παντὶ εἴδει πανηγύρεων (trans. Cary LCL), on which Gunderson, "Ideology of the Arena," 126–133; Beacham, "Emperor as Impresario"; and also Benoist, "prince, les dieux," 171–173.
45. Suet. *Aug.* 43.1: *Spectaculorum et assiduitate et varietate et magnificentia omnes antecessit* (ed. LCL, trans. Edwards).
46. App. *B. Civ.* 2.20.148: τὸν πατέρα τιμῶν ἰσοθέων ἠξίωσεν: ὧν δὴ καὶ νῦν, ἐξ ἐκείνου πρώτου, Ῥωμαῖοι τὸν ἑκάστοτε τὴν ἀρχὴν τήνδε ἄρχοντα, ἣν μὴ τύχῃ τυραννικὸς ... ἀποθανόντα ἀξιοῦσιν (trans. White LCL), on which see Taylor, *Divinity*, esp. 241–244; Fishwick, *Imperial Cult*, 1.73–82; and Hekster, "Honouring Ancestors."
47. Gradel, *Emperor Worship*, 109–139; Wallace-Hadrill, "Civilis Princeps," on the proper balance of accepting and refusing honors; and Drake, *Constantine and the Bishops*, esp. 35–71, on the game of empire.
48. Rowe, *Princes and Political Cultures*, 1–2; and Gowing, *Empire and Memory*, 28–66.
49. Vell. Pat. 2.126.1: *Sacravit parentem suum Caesar non imperio, sed religione, non appellavit eum, sed fecit deum* (trans. adapted Shipley LCL); on which see Koortbojian, *Divinization*, 21–24, stressing cultic and representational practices in deification.
50. RIC 1^2 Civil Wars #93.
51. Schäfer, "Römisches Relief mit Tensa"; and Guidetti, "*Tensam non tenuit.*" See also Szidat, *Teile eines historischen Frieses*, 5–23; Ronke #38; and Fless, "Römische Prozessionen," #75.
52. Alföldi, *zwei Lorbeerbäume*, 38 and pl. 17.1 (Severan-era); Fishwick, *Imperial Cult*, 2.555 n. 490 (Severan?); Szidat, *Teile eines historischen Frieses*, 31, 54–56, and fig. 12 (Constantinian); Ronke #187 (300–350 CE); and Fless, "Römische Prozessionen," #42 (300–350 CE).
53. Augustan elephant cart: RIC 1^2 Tiberius #56, 62 (Figure 20), and 68; Suet. *Claud.* 11.2: *currum elephantorum* (LCL); and Dio Cass. 61.16.4: ἁρμάμαξαν (LCL). Abaecherli, "*Fercula, carpenta,* and *tensae*," 10–11, notes that an elephant cart in Latin was usually *currus elephantorum* or perhaps *armamaxa* (Tert. *Spect.* 7.2). On the elephant cart, see Pisani Sartorio, *Mezzi di trasporto*, 40–41, who uses the term *pilentum*; Molin, "char," 294–298; and Arena, *Feste e rituali*, 75–76 n. 81 and 76–79. On elephants, see Toynbee, *Animals in Roman Life*, esp. 39–46; and Scullard, *Elephant*, esp. 254–259.
54. Plin. *HN* 7.139 (cf. Plin. *HN* 8.16: elephants in a triumph in 275 BCE) and *HN* 8.4; and Plut. *Pomp.* 14.4. On Pompey and elephants, see Beard, *Roman Triumph*, 7–41, esp. 17; Shelton, "Elephants, Pompey"; and Mader, "Triumphal Elephants."
55. Plin. *HN* 34.19. For elephant *bigae* on arches or driven by a living Augustus, see e.g. RIC 1^2 Augustus #280–284 and 301, with comments by Volpe and Loreti, "L'Arco di Domiziano."
56. *Anth. Pal.* 9.285 (Philip 4): οὐκέτι πυργωθεὶς ὁ φαλαγγομάχας ἐπὶ δῆριν / ἄσχετος ὁρμαίνει μυριόδους ἐλέφας, / ἀλλὰ φόβῳ στείλας βαθὺν αὐχένα πρὸς ζυγοδέσμοις, / ἄντυγα διφρουλκεῖ Καίσαρος οὐρανίου (ed. and trans. Gow and Page).
57. Juv. 12.104–106; and CIL 6.8583 = ILS 1578 = EDCS-18500230, on which see Toynbee, *Animals in Roman Life*, 47; and Scullard, *Elephant*, 199–200. See Tilburg, *Traffic and Congestion*, 78–81, on road travel and elephants.
58. Gradel, *Emperor Worship*, 286–288; Varner, *Mutilation and Transformation*; Flower, *Art of Forgetting*, 276–283, on controlling memory, and "Sévères." See also Hedrick, *History and Silence*, 89–130, on "*damnatio memoriae*" in late antiquity; Hekster, "Honouring Ancestors," on the importance of ancestry; and J. Assmann, *Cultural Memory*, 70–110, and *Religion and Cultural Memory*, 24–30, on ritual and writing as modes of cultural memory.
59. See Benoist, *fête*, esp. 246–267, and *Rome, le prince*; and Arena, "politica imperiale," on the institutionalization of ceremonial and the ritualization of imperial power.

60. Dio Cass. 53.30.6: οἱ καὶ εἰκόνα χρυσῆν καὶ στέφανον χρυσοῦν δίφρον τε ἀρχικὸν ἔς τε τὸ θέατρον ἐν τῇ τῶν Ῥωμαίων πανηγύρει ἐσφέρεσθαι καὶ ἐς τὸ μέσον τῶν ἀρχόντων τῶν τελούντων αὐτὰ τίθεσθαι ἐκέλευσε (trans. adapted Cary LCL). *Theatron* might have meant both theater and arena, but Dio did, at least at times, distinguish between the two venues and their separate honors (e.g. n. 19 above). Moreover, in the prior sentence, Dio mentioned the theater named after Marcellus, which may well be the theater in question.
61. Tert. *Spect.* 7.2: *de sedibus, de coronis* (LCL).
62. Tac. 2.83.1: does not specify the location; but the *tabula Hebana* 50–51 places them in the theater, on which see *Roman Statutes*, 521 with 531–532 and 539; Lott, *Death and Dynasty*, 111–113 and 250–251; Weinstock, "Image and the Chair"; and pp. 168–169.
63. Tac. *Ann.* 2.83.1: *ludos circenses eburna effigies praeiret* (ed. LCL, trans. adapted Woodman); a passage seemingly related to the lacunose *tabula Siarensis*: fragment (b), col. 3 (*Roman Statutes*, 518 with 529 and 536–537; and Lott, *Death and Dynasty*, 98–99 with 239). On these inscriptions broadly, see Rowe, *Princes and Political Cultures*. Arena, "*Pompa Circensis*," 78–83, and *Feste e rituali*, 61–66, argues that Marcellus, Gaius, Lucius, and Germanicus shared the same, or very similar, honors based on Dio Cass. 53.30.6, Tac. *Ann.* 2.83.1, and the *tabulae Siarensis* and *Hebana* as reconstructed by Lebek, "circensischen Ehrungen," "Kritik und Exegese," and "Intenzione e composizione."
64. Based on *praeiret* in Tac. *Ann.* 2.83.1, *praeferantur* on the *tabula Siarensis*, and *praefertur* in Suet. *Tit.* 2 (n. 86 below), Arena, "*Pompa Circensis*," 85 and *Feste e rituali*, 64–65 and 73–74, argues that imperial additions to the *pompa circensis* led the entire procession, which might be true for the un-deified imperial dead, but not seemingly so for the *divi*. A fourth-century CE relief depicts an elephant cart (seemingly reserved for *divi*) following Magna Mater and so with the traditional gods in the position of honor near the back of the procession (see Figure 83).
65. Tac. *Ann.* 4.9.2: *Memoriae Drusi eadem quae in Germanicum decernuntur* (ed. LCL, trans. adapted Woodman).
66. RIC 1^2 Tiberius #50–51, on which see Wood, *Imperial Women*, 82; and Arena, "*Pompa Circensis*," 83–84 with n. 18, and *Feste e rituali*, 76–79.
67. Isid. *Etym.* 20.12.3: *carpentum pompaticum* (OCT). On the *carpentum*, see D-S sv carpentum; Abaecherli, "Imperial Symbols," and "*Fercula, carpenta,* and *tensae*"; Lucchi, "Sul significato"; Pagnotta, "Carpentum"; Pisani-Sartorio, *Mezzi di trasporto*, 13–15 and 51–54; Molin, "char," 293–294; and Kaiser, "Cart Traffic Flow," 187–188 and 190–191.
68. Abaecherli, "*Fercula, carpenta,* and *tensae,*" 5, with which Jucker, "Zum Carpentum-Sesterz," 208; and Ginsburg, *Representing Agrippina*, 59–61, agree; while Lucchi, "Sul significato," 140 argues that it was a posthumous honor.
69. Suet. *Claud.* 11.2, *Calig.* 15.2, and *Tib.* 50.3–5; and Tac. *Ann.* 5.2.
70. Suet. *Calig.* 15.1: *instituit, et eo amplius matri circenses carpentumque quo in pompa traduceretur* (ed. LCL, trans. adapted Edwards), on which, see Wood, *Imperial Women*, 208–210; and Ginsburg, *Representing Agrippina*, 62.
71. RIC 1^2 Gaius #55; and also *Kontorniat-Medallions* #425, 604, and 240 (p. 1.215), on which see Abaecherli, "Imperial Symbols," 132–138 (*struppus*); Jucker, "Zum Carpentum-Sesterz" (aedicula); and Flower, *Art of Forgetting*, 138–143, on memory.
72. Suet. *Calig.* 15.2: *Antoniae aviae, quidquid umquam Livia Augusta honorum cepisset, uno senatus consulto congessit* (ed. LCL, trans. Edwards).
73. Suet. *Calig.* 23.2 and *Claud.* 11.2: *matri carpentum, quo per Circum duceretur* (ed. LCL, trans. adapted Edwards). Claudius also granted her the title Augusta, which she had refused while alive, suggesting that all these honors were posthumous.
74. Gradel, *Emperor Worship*, 141–159.
75. Dio Cass. 59.7.4: τὸ ἅρμα τὸ πομπικὸν (LCL).
76. Dio. Cass. 59.13.8: ἄγαλμά τε αὐτῆς ὑπ' ἐλεφάντων ἐν ἁρμαμάξῃ ἐς τὸν ἱππόδρομον ἐσήγαγε (trans. adapted Cary LCL), on which see Herz, "Diva Drusilla."
77. Wood, "Diva Drusilla Panthea," at 459; and McIntyre, "Constructing a Family," 110–113.
78. Suet. *Claud.* 17.3: Claudius' triumph; Dio Cass. 60.22.2: Messalina's *carpentum* and 60.33.

1–2 (epitome): Agrippina's *carpentum*; RIC 1^2 Claudius #103; and Tac. *Ann.* 12.42: *carpento Capitolium ingredi* (LCL).

79. Suet. *Claud.* 11.2: *Aviae Liviae divinos honores et circensi pompa currum elephantorum Augustino similem decernenda curavit* (ed. LCL, trans. Edwards).
80. Dio Cass. 61.35.2 (epitome): ἔτυχε δὲ καὶ τῆς ταφῆς καὶ τῶν ἄλλων ὅσων ὁ Αὔγουστος (trans. Cary LCL). See also Tac. *Ann.* 12.69.3; and Hekster, "Honouring Ancestors."
81. RIC 1^2 Nero #4–5, on which see Abaecherli, "*Fercula, carpenta,* and *tensae,*" 8.
82. RIC 1^2 Nero #6–7.
83. Suet. *Claud.* 8: *contumeliis obnoxius* (ed. LCL, trans. Edwards); and n. 195 below on Augustus' concerns about Claudius' visibility at the games.
84. See Osgood, *Claudius Caesar*, 242–259, on Claudius' postmortem commemoration.
85. Suet., *Vesp.* 5.7: *Neronem diebus ultimis monitum per quietem, ut tensam Iovis Optimi Maximi e sacrario in domum Vespasiani et inde in Circum deduceret* (ed. LCL, trans. adapted Edwards).
86. Suet. *Tit.* 2: *alteram [statuam] ex ebore equestrem, quae circensi pompa hodieque praefertur, dedicavit prosecutusque est* (ed. LCL, trans. adapted Edwards).
87. Madigan, *Ceremonial Sculptures*, 24, envisions a hand-held statue.
88. Suet. *Claud.* 45 and *Vesp.* 9.1, on which see Fishwick, "Deification of Claudius," who is skeptical of Suetonius; and, on the Flavian imperial cult, Rosso, "Culte imperial."
89. RIC 2.1^2 Titus #360–362, on which see Abaecherli, "Imperial Symbols," 131–132.
90. RIC 2.1^2 Titus #257–259; and also Mart. *Spect.* 20.
91. RIC 2.1^2 Titus #262–264, on which see Abaercherli, "*Fercula, carpenta,* and *tensae,*" 5 n. 81, and "Imperial Symbols," 132 n. 9; Lucchi, "Sul significato," 135; Kienast, "Diva Domitilla"; and Wood, "Who was Diva Domitilla?"
92. RIC 2.1^2 Domitian #717 and 760, on which see Wood, *Imperial Women*, 317–318, noting visual connections to coin images of Livia and Agrippina the elder.
93. RIC 2.1^2 Domitian #718; Juv. 2.29–33; Plin. *Ep.* 4.11.6; and Suet. *Dom.* 22, on which Wood, "Who was Diva Domitilla?" 51–54.
94. RIC 2 Trajan #835.
95. RIC 2 Trajan #746 (*tensa-carpentum*) and 749 (standard *carpentum*); on which see Lucchi, "Sul significato," 137.
96. RIC 2 Trajan #747 and 750. According to RIC 2 p. 479; and Lucchi, "Sul significato," 136, a *carpentum* for *diva* Sabina, Hadrian's wife, should be disregarded.
97. Mattingly, "Consecration of Faustina"; Beckmann, *Diva Faustina*, esp. 32–35, on the *carpentum* and *currus elephantorum*, pl. 18: CP1–2 and EC2–4 and pl. 19: EC5–6, EC9–12, and EC19; and Levick, *Faustina I and II*, 119–138.
98. SHA *Ant. Pius* 6.7: *imago eius cunctis circensibus poneretur* (one of the more reliable lives, ed. LCL); RIC 3 Antoninus Pius #389 and 1141.
99. Beckmann, *Diva Faustina*, 67–68.
100. "Ceres": RIC 3 Antoninus Pius #390, 1139–1140, and 1198; Shrine/Aedicula: RIC 3 Antoninus Pius #352, 1112–1113, and 1166, on which see Beckmann, *Diva Faustina*, 65–66 and figs. 5.1–2.
101. RIC 3 Antoninus Pius #1114 and 1167; chapter 6 n. 175 on the *lavatio*; and see also RIC 4.1 Septimius Severus #562, 858, and 879: Julia Domna on a lion-*quadriga.*
102. RIC 3 Marcus Aurelius #1274.
103. RIC 3 Marcus Aurelius #1507–1508.
104. RIC 3 Marcus Aurelius #1698; and Mattingly, "Consecration of Faustina," who notes that Faustina I and II were similarly honored.
105. Robertson, *Hunter Coin Cabinet* 2, Faustina II (under Antoninus Pius) #43 with pl. 83.43; though RIC 3 Antoninus Pius #1385; and Lucchi, "Sul significato," 136–137 n. 23, which were both published prior to the Hunter Coin Cabinet catalog, doubt its authenticity. A *carpentum* for Julia Domna is highly dubious, RIC 4.1 pp. 211 and 311.
106. SHA *Marc.* 21.5: *imago aurea circensibus per pompam ferenda* (LCL).
107. RIC 3 Commodus #661.
108. Dio Cass. 73.17.4 (epitome): ἐν τοῖς θεάτροις ἐπὶ δίφρου ἐπιχρύσου, εἴτε παρείη εἴτε καὶ ἀπείη, ἐτίθετο (trans. adapted Cary LCL); and SHA, *Comm.* 8.9, on which Gradel, *Emperor Worship*, 160–161; and Arena, *Feste e rituali*, 138–139. Caligula (Dio Cass. 59.24.4) had a throne on the Capitol, but only in his absence.
109. Dio Cass. (epitome) 75.4.1: χρυσῆν εἰκόνα αὐτοῦ ἐφ' ἅρματος ἐλεφάντων ἐς τὸν ἱππόδρομον ἐσάγεσθαι (trans. Cary LCL);

Gnecchi II: Pertinace 1 (p. 72), pl. 91.10; and Toynbee, *Roman Medallions*, 102.

110. pp. 57–58 with n. 80.

111. Jupiter: RIC 2 Trajan #777; Juno: RIC 2 Trajan #778; and Minerva: RIC 2 Trajan #779 (called Roma), on which see Seelentag, *Taten und Tugenden Traians*, 442–446; and Gallia, *Remembering the Roman Republic*, 217–247, esp. 238–240, who both associate the Dossenus (re-) issues with the triumph; and pp. 7–8 and 57–58.

112. RIC 1^2 Augustus #303 and 313.

113. RIC 2.1^2 (Titus under) Vespasian #1072–1074 and Titus #7–8, 24–26, and 42–43.

114. Toynbee, *Roman Medallions*, 146 and fig. 41.3; Szidat, *Teile eines historischen Frieses*, 32, 50–52, and fig. 19; and BNP 159–160 (briefly on Dea Roma).

115. Parasols: RIC 4.2 Elagabalus #143–144 (minted at Rome) and #195–197 (Figure 39); Eagle: RIC 4.2 Elagabalus # 61–62 (Figure 40 minted in Rome) and 64–65, on which see Humphrey, *Roman Circuses*, 552–557; Icks, *Crimes of Elagabalus*, 74 and fig. 7, comparing Elagabal's "*tensa*" with the Augustan "*tensa*" of Ceres; and Rowan, *Under Divine Auspices*, 164–218, esp. 203–206.

116. See RIC 4.3 Uranius Antoninus #1–2, images of the "*tensa*" minted in Emesa.

117. Herodian 5.6.6–8: τόν τε θεὸν αὐτὸν ἐπιστήσας ἅρματι χρυσῷ τε καὶ λίθοις τιμιωτάτοις πεποικιλμένῳ κατῆγεν ἀπὸ τῆς πόλεως ἐπὶ τὸ προάστειον. τὸ δὲ ἅρμα ἦγεν ἑξάπωλον, ἵππων λευκῶν μεγίστων τε καὶ ἀσπίλων, χρυσῷ πολλῷ καὶ φαλάροις ποικίλοις κεκοσμημένων, τάς τε ἡνίας κατεῖχεν οὐδείς, οὐδὲ τοῦ ἅρματος ἄνθρωπος ἐπέβαινεν, αὐτῷ δὲ περιέκειντο ὡς ἡνιοχοῦντι δὴ τῷ θεῷ. ὁ δ' Ἀντωνῖνος ἔθεε πρὸ τοῦ ἅρματος ἀναποδίζων ἐς τοὐπίσω, ἔς τε τὸν θεὸν ἀποβλέπων καὶ τοὺς χαλινοὺς ἀντέχων τῶν ἵππων· πᾶσάν τε τὴν ὁδὸν ἤνυε τρέχων ἔμπαλιν ἑαυτοῦ ἀφορῶν τε ἐς τὸ πρόσθεν τοῦ θεοῦ. πρός τε τὸ μὴ πταῖσαι αὐτὸν ἢ διολισθαίνειν, οὐχ ὁρῶντα ὅπου βαίνει, γῆ τε ἡ χρυσίζουσα παμπλείστη ὑπέστρωτο, οἵ τε προασπ- ίζοντες ἑκατέρωθεν ἀντεῖχον, τῆς ἀσφαλείας τοῦ τοιούτου δρόμου προνοούμενοι. ὁ δὲ δῆμος ἑκατέρωθεν παρέθει μετὰ παντοδαπῆς δᾳδουχίας, στεφάνους καὶ ἄνθη ἐπιρριπτοῦντες· ἀγάλματά τε πάντων θεῶν, καὶ εἴ τι πολυτελὲς ἀνάθημα <ἢ> τίμιον, ὅσα τε τῆς βασιλείας σύμβολα ἢ πολυτελῆ κειμήλια, οἵ τε ἱππεῖς καὶ ὁ στρατὸς πᾶς προεπόμπευον τοῦ θεοῦ (trans. Whittaker LCL). See also Ick, *Crimes of Elagabalus*, 72 and fig. 6 (not in RIC), on whose reverse Elagabalus stands in front of the "*tensa*," facing out towards the viewer, while he sacrifices at a small altar to his right – which gives a sense of Elagabalus leading his god to his sanctuary.

118. See pp. 61–65 on *tensa* regulations.

119. Gowing, *Empire and Memory*, argues that the (political) memory of the republic wanes after Tiberius; while Gallia, *Remembering the Roman Republic*, see its socio-cultural significance extend into the Flavian period; and see pp. 220–230 for late antiquity.

120. Boin, *Ostia in Late Antiquity*, on place and the power of the past; and Favro, "Street Triumphant" and "Moving Events," on tradition, monuments, and the triumph; and see pp. 70–73.

121. On aspects of the imperial use of public space, see Benoist, "L'espace urbain" and *Fête*, 275–331. See Flower, "Elite Self-Representation," on the imperial domination Roman public life.

122. Suet. *Aug.* 28.3: *urbem . . . sit gloriatus marmoream se relinquere, quam latericiam accepisset* (ed. LCL, trans. Edwards), on which see Favro, *Urban Image* and "Making Rome"; and Haselberger, *Urbem adornare*, on the Augustan transformation of city.

123. Vitruv. *De arch.* 1.*praef.* 2: *curam . . . habere . . . de opportunitate publicorum aedificiorum . . . ut maiestas imperii publicorum aedificiorum egregias haberet auctoritates* (trans. Granger LCL).

124. Vitruv. *De arch.* 1.*praef.* 3: *pro amplitudine rerum gestarum ut posteris memoriae traderentur* (trans. adapted Granger LCL).

125. Fears, "Theology of Victory at Rome," 804–824; McCormick, *Eternal Victory*, esp. 11–34; MacCormack, *Art and Ceremony*, esp. 41–42 on the "universal victoriousness of the emperor" in late antiquity; and Benoist, *Rome, le prince*, 241–273.

126. Wallace-Hadrill, *Rome's Cultural Revolution*, 275–312; Castrén, "*Vici* and *Insulae*," esp.

8–15; and, on the regionary catalogs, Purcell, "City of Rome," 425.

127. See Humphrey, *Roman Circuses*, 540–571 and 582–602, on other circuses in and around Rome; and Pisani Sartorio, "Le cirque de Maxence."

128. Arena, "*Pompa Circensis*," 86–92 at 91, and *Feste e rituali*, 80–93, for apposite remarks about the itinerary and imperial ideology, although the multiplication of imperial itineraries remains speculative.

129. Boin, *Ostia in Late Antiquity*, 146–147.

130. Dion. Hal. *Ant. Rom.* 4.61.4: τοῖς αὐτοῖς θεμελίοις ... εὑρέθη τῇ πολυτελείᾳ τῆς ὕλης μόνον διαλλάττων τοῦ ἀρχαίου, (trans. Cary LCL). The following references have been consulted on each site, building, or monument, which will only be cited to make a specific point (as previously, see Chapter 3 n. 46): D-S; P-A; Lugli, *Roma antica* and *Itinerario di Roma antica*; Nash, *Pictorial Dictionary of Ancient Rome*; Coarelli, *Foro Romano, Foro Boario*, and *Rome and Environs*; Richardson; LTUR; Claridge, *Rome*; Gros, *L'architecture romaine*; and Romano, "Digital Augustan Rome."

131. Tac. *Hist.* 3.72.2–3: *immensae postea populi Romani opes ornarent potius quam augerent. Isdem rursus vestigiis situm est* (LCL).

132. Cic. *Verr.* 2.4.69 and 2.5.48: *sicut apud maiores nostros factum est*; and Plin. *HN* 33.57, on which see Perry, "Same, but Different"; Flower, "Remembering and Forgetting"; and Gallia, *Remembering the Roman Republic*, 47–85, esp. 68.

133. Augustus, *RG* 20.1: *Capitolium ... opus impensa grandi refeci sine ulla inscriptione nominis mei* (ed. and trans. Cooley); and also Suet. *Aug.* 30.2, on which see Thein, "Augustan 'Rebuilding.'" My thanks to Alexander Thein for sharing this essay in advance of its publication.

134. Tac. *Hist.* 3.72.1: *Id facinus post conditam urbem luctuosissimum foedissimumque rei publicae populi Romani accidit ... sedem Iovis Optimi Maximi auspicato a maioribus pignus imperii conditam ... furore principum excindi* (trans. Moore LCL), on which see Edwards, *Writing Rome*, 74–82; Ash, "Victim and Voyeur," 229–236; and Gallia, *Remembering the Roman Republic*, esp. 48–53.

135. Tac. *Hist.* 4.53: *templum isdem vestigiis sisteretur: nolle deos mutari veterem formam* (trans. Moore LCL).

136. Tac. *Hist.* 4.53: *Altitudo aedibus adiecta: id solum religio adnuere et prioris templi magnificentiae defuisse credebatur* (trans. Moore LCL), on which see Darwall-Smith, *Emperors and Architecture*, 41–47 and 105–110; Wardle, "Vespasian, Helvidius Priscus"; and also Lindsay, "Vespasian and the City."

137. Suet. *Dom.* 5; Plut. *Publ.* 15.3–4; Zos. 5.38.5; and Procop. *Vand.* 1.5.4. Gallia, *Remembering the Roman Republic*, 69–73, argues that the Capitoline temple was credited to the Flavians alone after 69 CE, following hints in Tac. *Hist.* 3.72.3.

138. Gallia, *Remembering the Roman Republic*, 56–61 and 75–77, on destruction and loss of memory; and Jenkyns, "Memory of Rome," on the persistence of memory despite architectural changes.

139. See pp. 76, 197–198 and 223–224, on the *processus consularis*.

140. Dolansky, "*Togam Virilem Sumere*," 51–52.

141. Suet. *Aug.* 29.4–5: *ceteros principes viros saepe hortatus est, ut pro facultate quisque monimentis vel novis vel refectis et excultis urbem adornarent. Multaque a multis tunc extructa sunt, sicut ... a Munatio Planco aedes Saturni* (ed. LCL, trans. adapted Edwards). See Suet. *Vesp.* 8.5: Vespasian encouraging non-imperial rebuilding.

142. Dion. Hal. *Ant. Rom.* 1.34; and Macrob. *Sat.* 1.7.27 and 1.8.2.

143. Nora, "General Introduction," 1 (adapted to the singular); and see pp. 72–73.

144. Diod. Sic. 12.26.

145. Cic. *Att.* 4.16.7 (LCL 140): *isdem antiquis columnis*; Plin. *NH* 36.102; and Dio Cass. 49.42.2.

146. Tac. *Ann.* 3.72.1: *basilicam Pauli, Aemilia monimenta, propria pecunia firmaret ornaretque. ... more publica munificentia ... avitum decus recoluit* (ed. LCL, trans. Woodman); and Plin. *HN* 35.12: *M. Aemilius ... in basilica ... Aemilia ... [clupeos] posuit* (trans. Rackham LCL), on which see LTUR sv Basilica Aemilia, which disassociates the basilica Aemilia from the basilica Fulvia-Paulli, more commonly understood as the same basilica.

147. Tac. *Ann.* 13.58: *Ruminalem arborem in comitio, quae octingentos et triginta ante annos Remi Romulique infantiam texerat, mortuis ramalibus et arescente trunco deminutam prodigii loco habitum est, donec in novos fetus revivesceret* (ed. LCL, trans. adapted Woodman); and Plin. *HN*

15.77, on which see Hunt, "Keeping the Memory Alive"; and p. 84

148. Poulsen, "Dioscuri and Ruler Ideology"; and Sumi, "Monuments and Memory," esp. 183–186.
149. Val. Max. 9.5.ext.4 (see pp. 72–73).
150. Augustus, *RG* 19.1–2: *lupercal* . . . *feci* and 20.1: *Capitolium* . . . *refeci* (ed. Cooley), on which see Thein, "Augustan 'Rebuilding.'"
151. Ov. *Fast.* 2.411: *arbor erat: remanent vestigia.* Livy 1.4.5 maintains that the *ficus ruminalis* was still there in his day.
152. CIL 6.31200 = EDCS-17301035, on which see *Roman Statutes*, 545; and Lott, *Death and Dynasty*, 166–167 and 315–316.
153. Tac. *Ann.* 2.49.1: *deum aedis vetustate aut igni abolitas coeptasque ab Augusto dedicavit, Libero Liberaeque et Cereri iuxta circum maximum, quam A. Postumius dictator voverat* (ed. LCL, trans. Woodman).
154. Cassiod. *Var.* 3.51.4: *Sed mundi dominus ad potentiam suam opus extollens mirandam etiam Romanis fabricam in vallem Murciam tetendit Augustus* (ed. MGH, trans. Barnish TTH).
155. Plin. *HN* 36.102; Suet. *Iul.* 39.2; Augustus, *RG* 19: *pulvinar ad circum maximum* . . . *feci*; ναὸν πρὸς τῶι μεγάλωι ἱπποδρόμωι . . . ἐπόησα (ed. Cooley).
156. Plin. *Pan.* 51.3–4: *immensum latus circi templorum pulchritudinem provocat, digna populo victore gentium sedes, nec minus ipsa visenda, quam quae ex illa spectabuntur, visenda autem cum cetera specie* (trans. adapted Radice LCL).
157. Dio Cass. 68.7.2 (epitome): οὕτως γάρ που καὶ μεγαλόφρων καὶ μεγαλογνώμων ἔφυ ὥστε καὶ τῷ ἱπποδρόμῳ ἐπιγράψαι ὅτι ἐξαρκοῦντα αὐτὸν τῷ τῶν Ῥωμαίων δήμῳ ἐποίησεν, ἐπειδὴ διαφθαρέντα πη καὶ μείζω καὶ περικαλλέστερον ἐξειργάσατο (trans. Cary LCL).
158. Humphrey, *Roman Circuses*, 132–174; Marchet, "*Mittere mappam*"; and Cameron, *Circus Factions*, 157–192, on emperor and subjects at the races.
159. Suet. *Claud.* 21.3: *Circo vero Maximo marmoreis carceribus auratisque metis* (ed. LCL, trans. adapted Edwards); and see pp. 228–229 on the third-century CE *carceres*.
160. Holden, "Abduction of the Sabine Women," 125 and fig. 3; Toynbee, *Roman Medallions*, 185 n. 246; and Bergmann, "Pictorial Narratives," 383–384.
161. Augustus, *RG* 8.5: *m[ulta e]xempla maiorum* . . . *red[uxi et ipse] multarum rer[um exe]mpla imitanda pos[teris tradidi]* (ed. and trans. Cooley).
162. Clauss, "*Deus praesens.*"
163. Tac. *Ann.* 13.41.4: *consalutatus imperator Nero* . . . *statuaeque et arcus* . . . *decernuntur* and 15.18.1: *medio Capitolini montis* (ed. LCL, trans. Woodman). See Wallace-Hadrill, "Roman Arches," on shift from *fornix* to *arcus*. Marcus Aurelius also had an arch at the foot of the Capitoline likely near the intersection of the *clivus Argentarius* and the *via Lata* (P-A sv Arcus M. Aurelii and LTUR sv Arcus Marci Aurelii), but its location is disputed (Richardson sv Arcus M. Aurelii).
164. RIC 1^2 Nero #143–150, 392–393, 432–433, 498–500, and 573–575.
165. Suet. *Dom.* 13.2: *Ianos arcusque cum quadrigis et insignibus triumphorum per regiones urbis tantos ac tot exstruxit, ut cuidam Graece inscriptum sit: "Arci"* (ed. LCL, trans. Edwards).
166. Dio Cass. 68.1.1, on which see Varner, *Mutilation and Transformation*, 111–135, esp. 132–133; and Flower, *Art of Forgetting*, 234–262.
167. No road led under the arch, though the passage was paved according to Richardson sv Arcus Septimii Severii; and Laurence, "Streets and Facades," 409–410. Nonetheless, the *pompa circensis* could have passed through the arch.
168. Flower, "Sévères."
169. Beckmann, "Galleries on Honorary Arches"; and Macrob. *Sat.* 1.6.15: a spectator looking down on the gods from a domestic structure.
170. Tac. *Ann.* 2.41.1: *arcus propter aedem Saturni*; and LTUR sv Arcus Tiberii (Forum).
171. Plut. *Galb.* 24.4: χρυσοῦς . . . κίων, εἰς ὃν αἱ τετμημέναι τῆς Ἰταλίας ὁδοὶ πᾶσαι τελευτῶσιν (trans. Perrin LCL).
172. Suet. *Calig.* 34.1: *Statuas virorum inlustrium ab Augusto ex Capitolina area propter angustias in campum Martium* . . . *vetuitque posthac viventium cuiquam usquam statuam aut imaginem nisi consulto et auctore se poni* (ed. LCL, trans. Edwards).
173. Dio Cass. 60.25.2–3: ἐπειδή τε ἡ πόλις πολλῶν εἰκόνων ἐπληροῦτο (ἐξῆν γὰρ ἀνέδην τοῖς βουλομένοις ἐν γραφῇ καὶ ἐν χαλκῷ λίθῳ τε δημοσιεύεσθαί), τάς τε πλείους αὐτῶν ἑτέρωσέ ποι μετέθηκε, καὶ ἐς τὸ ἔπειτα ἀπηγόρευσε μηδενὶ ἰδιώτῃ, ᾧ ἂν μὴ ἡ βουλὴ ἐπιτρέψῃ, τοῦτο ποιεῖν ἐξεῖναι, πλὴν εἴ τις ἔργον τι ᾠκοδομηκὼς εἴη ἢ καὶ κατασκευάσαιτο: τούτοις γὰρ δή,

τοῖς τε συγγενέσιν αὐτῶν, ἵστασθαι ἐν τοῖς χωρίοις ἐκείνοις ἐφῆκε (trans. Cary LCL).

174. Eck, "Senatorial Self-Presentation" and "Emperor and Senatorial Aristocracy"; Hurlet, "Représentation(s) et autoreprésentation(s)"; and Weisweiler, "From Equality to Asymmetry," 321–324.
175. See Højte, *Roman Imperial Statue Bases*, 229–589, a catalog which lists eight for Augustus in Rome, two of which were in the Forum.
176. Dio Cass. 47.18.4 (n. 34 above).
177. Suet, *Iul.* 85.1: *solidam columnam prope viginti pedum lapidis Numidici* (ed. LCL, trans. Edwards), on which see Sumi, "Topography and Ideology," 211–217, whose reconstruction is followed here; and Koortbojian, *Divinization*, 26–27.
178. Dio Cass. 51.19.1.
179. Schol. Veronensia, Verg. *Aen.* 7.606: *iuxta aedem divi Iulii* (Teubner); and Scott, "Triple Arch of Augustus," on the via Sacra.
180. Coarelli, *Foro Romano*, 2.258–308, and *Rome and Environs*, 79–81.
181. Rich, "Augustus' Parthian Honors," 97–115.
182. The location of the *porticus* remains open to debate, e.g. Richarsdon sv Basilica Paulli (portico) and sv Porticus Gai et Luci (entrance) who offers both solutions, though the portico option is more commonly accepted. On the *fornix Fabianus*, see SHA *Gall.* 19.4.
183. Suet. *Aug.* 100.3: *pro aede Divi Iuli* (LCL); and Dio Cass. 56.34.4, on which see Price, "Noble Funerals"; and Sumi, "Topography and Ideology," 224–229.
184. See Beard, *Roman Triumph*, 61–67 and 72–80, on the *fasti Triumphales*.
185. Fishwick, "Temple of Divus Augustus."
186. Flower, "Sévères," 105–115.
187. *Curiosum: Regio XI. Circus Maximus: portam Trigeminam*; and *Notitia: Regio XI. Circus Maximus: Portam Trigeminam* (ed. Valentini and Zucchetti).
188. Arena, "Circo Massimo come microcosmo," and *Feste e Rituali*, 103–145.
189. Tert. *Spect.* 7.3: *daemoniorum conventus* (and 8.5: *daemonum concilium*) and 16: *furore ... tumultuosum ... caecum ... concitatum* (LCL). See Humphrey, *Roman Circuses*, 97–100 (arch) and 175–294 (central barrier); Green, "Gods in the Circus"; and Lim, "Inventing Secular Space," 61–70.
190. See pp. 89 above on the *pulvinar*. Fragments from the Severan *acta saecularium* (CIL 6.32332 = EDCS-20500154 and CIL 6.32333 = EDCS-20500155: *ebornei ... [ex]uvias in pulvinari*) suggest *exuviae* (and ivory statues [*ebornei* from *eburnus*]) were placed on the *pulvinar*, on which see Pighi, *De ludis saecularibus*, 172–173, 191, and 291, who considers the second fragment a description of the *pompa* to the Circus; and Madigan, *Ceremonial Sculptures*, 83.
191. CIL 6.9822 = ILS 7496 = EDCS-19400057: *C(aius) Iulius Epaphra / pomar(ius) de circo / maximo ante / pulvinar*; and CIL 6.9136 = ILS 7287 = EDCS-19000586: *Ti(berio) Claudio Sabino / sodales aerari(i) / a pulvinar(i)*, on which Ruggiero, *Dizionario epigrafico*, 1.312 (*sodales aerarii*); LTUR sv Pulvinar ad Circum Maximum; and Nelis-Clement, "métiers du cirque," 307 n. 164 (*pomarius*).
192. Suet. *Aug.* 45.1: *circenses ... spectabat ... ex pulvinari et quidem cum coniuge ac liberis sedens*, on which see Arena, *Feste e rituali*, 110–122. On emperors being visible in the right way, see Hekster, "Captured."
193. On the seating arrangements (of gods and emperors) and interconnections between traditional religion, imperial cult, and imperial power, see Hugoniot, "*puluinar*"; Rodriguez, "*puluinar*"; Golvin, "Réflexion relative"; and Dareggi, "Genesi e sviluppo."
194. Humphrey, *Roman Circuses*, 79–80.
195. Suet. *Claud.* 4.3: *ne quid faciat quod conspici et derideri possit. ... Spectare eum circenses ex pulvinari non placet nobis; expositus enim in fronte prima spectaculorum conspicietur* (ed. LCL, trans. adapted Edwards), on which see Coleman, "Public Entertainments," 335–336.
196. Suet. *Claud.* 27.2: *plebi per spectacula gremio aut ante se retinens assidue commendabat faustisque ominibus cum adclamantium turba prosequebatur* (ed. LCL, trans. Edwards).
197. Dio Cass. 61.16.4; and Plin. *Pan.* 51.5: *cubiculum principis ... in populo sedentem* (trans. adapted Radice LCL), on which see Roche, "*Panegyricus* and Monuments," 54–59; and Arena, *Feste e rituali*, 117–118. See also

pp. 149–150 for Nero's ritual failure while, seemingly, sitting in the *pulvinar*.

Five Behind "the veil of power"

1. After Gordon, "Veil of Power."
2. *Ei rei pompas et carpenta et tensas et exuvias a maioribus dicatas, elephantos et in pace, quibus numquam populus Romanus in acie usus sit, spectaculeis deservire nocturnis* (ed. Teubner, trans. adapted Davenport and Manley).
3. Juv. 10.81; and Fronto, *Principia Historiae* 20: *sciret populum Romanum duabus praecipue rebus, annona et spectaculeis, teneri; imperium non minus ludicreis quam serieis probari* (ed. Teubner, trans. adapted Davenport and Manley), on which see van den Hout, *Commentary*, 486–487.
4. Fronto, *ad M. Caes.* 2.4 (Teubner; *ad M. Caesar* 2.1 LCL) and *Ad amicos* 2.3: *Cum istis tamen doloribus in circum delatus sum. Rursum enim studio circensium teneor* (I was carried into the Circus even with this pain. I am again possessed by a passion for the circus games, ed. Teubner).
5. Yavetz, *Plebs and Princeps*, 103–129; Cameron, *Circus Factions*, 157–192, a classic; Aldrete, *Gestures and Acclamations*, 101–164; and Harries, "*Favor populi*."
6. On audience reactions/resistance, see Scott, *Domination and the Arts of Resistance*; Lincoln, *Authority*, 1–13; and Bell, *Spectacular Power*.
7. On imperial ritual failures in another context, see Icks, "Elevating the Unworthy Emperor."
8. Arena, *Feste e rituali*, 53–102, on the imperial *pompa circensis*; and Lendon, *Empire of Honour*, on the role of honor.
9. App. *B. Civ.* 2.16.106 (chapter 4 n. 16).
10. Cic. *Att.* 13.44.1: *O suavis tuas litteras! – etsi acerba pompa ... populum vero praeclarum, quod propter malum vicinum ne Victoriae quidem ploditur! ... pompa <me> deterret* (trans. Shackleton-Bailey LCL). On applause, see pp. 44–45; and 87–88; as well as 108–113, on Caesar.
11. Cic. *Att.* 14.14.1 (368 LCL): *coronatus Quintus noster Parilibus!* and 14.19.3 (372 LCL): *se coronam habuisse honoris Caesaris cause, posuisse luctus gratia* (trans. Shackleton-Bailey LCL), on which see Weinstock, *Divus Julius*, 367; and Sumi, *Ceremony and Power*, 118–119.
12. Cic. *Phil.* 2.110–111: *Quem is honorem maiorem consecutus erat quam ut haberet pulvinar, simulacrum, fastigium, flamimen? ... Quaeris placeatne mihi pulvinar esse, fastigium, flaminem. Mihi vero nihil istorum placet* (trans. adapted Shackleton-Bailey LCL), on which see Ferrary, "À propos de deux passages," 222–231. *Simulacrum* added to the second passage on the model of the first.
13. On celebrating and contesting power during games, see Benoist, *Fête*, 332–349.
14. Dio Cass. 48.19.2 (Sextus as Neptune) and 48.31.5 (circus crowd): ἐν ταῖς ἱπποδρομίαις κρότῳ τε πολλῷ τὸ τοῦ Ποσειδῶνος ἄγαλμα πομπεῦον ἐτίμων (trans. Cary LCL). On this conflict, see Welch, *Magnus Pius*, esp. 261–289; and pp. 110–111, on Caesar's comet.
15. See Cameron, *Bread and Circuses*; and nn. 5–6 above, on interactions between ruler and ruled at the Circus.
16. Suet. *Aug.* 16.2: *etiam invito Neptuno victoriam se adepturum, ac die circensium proximo sollemni pompae simulacrum dei detraxerit* (ed. LCL, trans. adapted Edwards).
17. Dio Cass. 48.31.5: ἐπεί τε ἡμέραις τισὶν οὐκ ἐσήχθη, τούς τε ἐν ταῖς ἀρχαῖς ὄντας λίθοις ἐκ τῆς ἀγορᾶς ἐξήλασαν καὶ ἐκείνων τὰς εἰκόνας κατέβαλον, καὶ τέλος, ἐπειδὴ μηδ' ὥς τι ἐπεραίνετο, σπουδῇ ἐπ' αὐτοὺς ὡς καὶ ἀποκτενοῦντές σφας ὥρμησαν (trans. Cary LCL). This reconstruction of events in Suetonius and Cassius Dio is uncertain, but reasonable, on which see Sumi, *Ceremony and Power*, 197.
18. Crowds during the empire "spoke" through image practices, processions, and desecrations, e.g. Tac. *Ann.* 5.4.3 and 14.61.1, and *Hist.* 2.55; and Plut. *Otho* 3.1, on which see Gregory, "Powerful Images," 88–98; and Varner, *Mutilation and Transformation*.
19. Bell, *Spectacular Power*, esp. 25–51 and 151–198; see p. 49 (performance); pp. 39–42 and 61–65 (ritual failure).
20. See Deniaux, "rue et l'opinion publique," on processions and public opinion in the late republic.
21. Suet. *Claud.* 4.3, 12.2, and 27.2; and see also p. 144
22. Dio Cass. 61.16.4 (epitome): οἱ ἐλέφαντες οἱ τὴν τοῦ Αὐγούστου ἁρμάμαξαν ἄγοντες ἐς μὲν τὸν ἱππόδρομον ἐσῆλθον καὶ μέχρι τῆς τῶν βουλευτῶν ἕδρας ἀφίκοντο, γενόμενοι δὲ ἐνταῦθα ἔστησαν (trans. Cary LCL). Golvin, "Réflexion relative"; and van den Berg, "*Pulvinar*," 264–265, argue that Nero was in the *pulvinar*.

23. Cassiod. *Var.* 10.30.
24. Dio Cass. 63.21.1 (epitome): Ἐκτελέσας δὲ ταῦτα ἱπποδρομίας ἐπήγγειλε, καὶ τοὺς στεφάνους, τούτους τε καὶ τοὺς ἄλλους πάντας ὅσους ἅρμασι νικήσας εἰλήφει, ἐς τὸν ἱππόδρομον ἐσήνεγκε καὶ τῷ ὀβελίσκῳ τῷ Αἰγυπτίῳ περιέθηκε (trans. Cary LCL), on which see Beard, *Roman Triumph*, 268–272; and pp. 130–132 (Elagabalus) and Suet. *Dom.* 13.2 (p. 140).
25. See pp. 64–65.
26. Suet. *Vesp.* 5.7 (see p. 122).
27. SHA *Sev.* 22.3: *die circensium cum tres Victoriolae more solito essent locatae gypseae cum palmis, media, quae ipsius nomine adscriptum orbem tenebat, vento icta de podio stans decidit et humi constitit; at quae Getae nomine inscripta erat, corruit et omnis comminuta est; illa vero, quae Bassiani titulum praeferebat, amissa palma venti turbine vix constitit* (trans. adapted Magie LCL).
28. Dio Cass. 79.8.1 (epitome): τῇ δὲ ἱπποδρομίᾳ τῇ τῆς τοῦ Σεουήρου ἀρχῆς ἕνεκα ποιουμένῃ κατέπεσε μὲν καὶ τὸ τοῦ Ἄρεως ἄγαλμα πομπεῦον (trans. Cary LCL).
29. Ando, *Matter of the Gods*, 13 (pp. 39–40).
30. Dio Cass. 60.6.4–5: Εἰθισμένου τε, εἰ καὶ ὁτιοῦν περὶ τὰς πανηγύρεις ἔξω τοῦ νενομισμένου πραχθείη, αὖθις αὐτάς, καθάπερ εἴρηταί μοι, γίγνεσθαι, καὶ πολλάκις τούτου καὶ τρίτον καὶ τέταρτον πέμπτον τε, καὶ δέκατον ἔστιν ὅτε, τὸ μέν τι κατὰ τύχην τὸ δὲ δὴ πλεῖστον ἐκ παρασκευῆς τῶν ὠφελουμένων ἀπ᾽ αὐτοῦ, συμβαίνοντος, νόμῳ μὲν ἔταξε μίαν ἡμέραν τοὺς ἀγῶνας τῶν ἵππων δεύτερον γίγνεσθαι, ἔργῳ δὲ καὶ τοῦτο ὡς πλήθει ἐπέσχεν: οὐδὲν γάρ τι ῥᾳδίως, ἅτε μηδὲν μέγα ἀποκερδαίνοντες, οἱ τεχνώμενοι αὐτὸ ἐπλημμέλουν (trans. Cary LCL); and, on *instauratio*, see further pp. 39–42 and 61–65.
31. Juv. 10.36–46: *quid si vidisset praetorem curribus altis / extantem et medii sublimem pulvere Circi / in tunica Iovis et pictae Sarrana ferentem / ex umeris aulaea togae magnaeque coronae / tantum orbem, quanto cervix non sufficit ulla? / quippe tenet sudans hanc publicus et, sibi consul / ne placeat, curru servus portatur eodem. / da nunc et volucrem, sceptro quae surgit eburno, / illinc cornicines, hinc praecedentia longi / agminis officia et niveos ad frena Quirites, / defossa in loculis quos sportula fecit amicos* (trans. adapted Braund LCL), on which see Keane, "Theatre, Spectacle," 269–273. On the religious importance of the games for Roman imperial elites, see Várhelyi, *Religion of Senators*, 94–97.
32. Plin. *HN* 33.11; and see pp. 25–28, on the "republican" *praeses*.
33. Tert. *De corona* 13.3–4: *gemmis et foliis ex auro, quercinis ab Iove, insignes ad deducendas tensas cum palmatis togis sumunt* (CCSL). To lead the *tensa* meant to conduct the circus procession (see p. 56).
34. Tert. *Apol.* 33.4: *"Respice post te! Hominem te memento!"* (LCL). On this phrase, the crown, the slave, see Versnel, *Triumphus*, 72–78; and esp. Beard, *The Roman Triumph*, 85–92.
35. Salomonson, *Chair, Sceptre and Wreath*, 96–102, and also 34–37 and 82–88, who argues that the republican *praeses* did not carry a scepter; while Alföldi, "[Review] Salomonson (J. W.)," 1077, connects Livy 5.41.1–2 to 5.41.9 to assert that he did.
36. Dio Cass. 59.7.4 (Chapter 4 n. 75); pp. 197–203 on imperial *quadrigae*; and cover image: a fourth-century consul in a *biga*.
37. Plin. *HN* 34.20: *Non vetus et bigarum celebratio in iis, qui praetura functi curru vecti essent per circum* (trans. adapted Rackham); and see Livy 45.1.7; and Dion. Hal. *Ant. Rom.* 5.57.5 (pp. 25–26), on chariots of the *praeses* in republican processions.
38. Humphrey, *Roman Circuses*, 248 (fourth century CE); Ronke #148 (second/third century CE); and Lo Monaco, "In processione al circo," 7 (mid-imperial).
39. Tac. *Ann.* 1.15.2: *per circum triumphali veste uterentur: curru vehi haud permissum* (ed. LCL, trans. adapted Woodman).
40. Dio. Cass. 56.46.5; and Tac. *Ann.* 1.15.2.
41. Himmelmann, *Typologische Untersuchungen*, 37; Ronke #200; *Imperii Insignia* S29; Fless, "Römische Prozessionen," #50; and Reinsberg, *Sarkophage* #5.
42. On equestrians, see pp. 28–29, 76, 81–82 and 84–85.
43. Plin. *Pan.* 92.5: *Nos sub oculis tuis augustior solito currus accipiet. nos inter secunda omina et vota certantia, quae praesenti tibi conferentur, vehemur alacres et incerti, ex utra parte maior auribus nostris accidat clamor* (trans. Radice LCL). The *currus* suggests a *pompa circensis* (instead of some sort of *processus consularis* which the ordinary consuls would have conducted on

foot or carried in a chair), on which see pp. 76, 197–198 and 223–224.

44. Juv. 11.193–197: *interea Megalesiacae spectacula mappae / Idaeum sollemne colunt, similisque triumpho / praeda caballorum praetor sedet ac, mihi pace / immensae nimiaeque licet si dicere plebis, / totam hodie Roman Circus capit* (trans. Braund LCL).

45. Sil. Ital. 16.314–316: *fluctuat aequoreo fremitu rabieque faventum, / carceribus nondum reseratis, mobile vulgus / atque fores oculis et limina servat equorum* (trans. Duff LCL).

46. Tert. *Spect.* 16.1–3: *Aspice populum ad id spectaculum iam cum furore venientem, iam tumultuosum, iam caecum, iam de sponsionibus concitatum. Tardus est illi praetor, semper oculi in urna eius cum sortibus volutantur. Dehinc ad signum anxii pendent, unius dementiae una vox est. Cognosce dementiam de vanitate: "misit" dicunt.* (trans. adapted Glover LCL), on which Marchet, "*Mittere mappam,*" esp. 295–300; and Nelis-Clément, "cirque romain," 445–453.

47. Lendon, *Empire of Honour,* on the game of honor. See pp. 28 and 89, on the race start; and pp. 36–37, on the importance of visibility.

48. Ronke #207 (end of third century CE); Humphrey, *Roman Circuses,* 145–147 (late empire); and Marchet, "*Mittere mappam,*" 300–311, on the predominance of *mappa* imagery in late antiquity, on which see further pp. 203–204 and 208–211.

49. See pp. 211–214.

50. André, "*ludi scaenici,*" 468–469; and see pp. 31–34, on *ludiones.*

51. Dion. Hal. *Ant. Rom.* 2.71.3–4 (chapter 1 n. 73; and n. 81 below).

52. RIC 2.1^2 Domitian #595–602, on which see Fless, "Römische Prozessionen," #21; and Sobocinski, "Visualizing Ceremony." Compare with Figures 8 and 9.

53. Bacchielli, "rilievo"; Fless, *Opferdiener und Kultmusiker,* 28–31 and pl. 11.1 and "Römische Prozessionen," #20. See also Fless, *Opferdiener und Kultmusiker,* 79–86 and pl. 9.1–2 and 10.1 and "Römische Prozessionen," #73, for additional images of *ludiones.*

54. Gnecchi 2: Antonino Pio #30.

55. Piganiol, *Jeux romains,* 23 n. 1, cites Lanciani and Visconti, "Le ville Tusculane," 209, for an inscription naming satyrs, fauns, maenads, Sileni, which I have been unable to locate in modern epigraphic corpora. La Rocca, "Sul circo flaminio," 111, also posits additions to the burlesque dancers.

56. Tert. *Spect.* 7.3 (n. 64 below).

57. Dio Cass. 75.4.1: *pompa circensis* and 74.4.5: funeral; SHA, *Gal.* 8.6 and *Aurel.* 34.4; and *Pan. Lat.* 5(8).8.4, on which see Waltzing, *Étude historique,* 1.239–241, 1.425, and 2.186–187; Nijf, *Civic World,* 191–206, on *collegia* in processions; and Liu, "Professional Associations," on *collegia* more broadly.

58. On the organization of the games, see Nelis-Clément, "métiers du cirque"; and Coleman and Nelis-Clément (ed.), *L'organisation des spectacles.*

59. Suet. *Aug.* 45.3: *Universum denique genus operas aliquas publico spectaculo praebentium etiam cura sua dignatus est* (ed. LCL, trans. Edwards).

60. Tert. *Spect.* 10.2 (n. 75 below): *dissignatore et haruspice* (LCL).

61. Hor. *Ep.* 1.7.6; Sen. *Ben.* 6.38.4; Toynbee, *Death and Burial,* 45; and Flower, *Ancestor Masks,* 99 and 116.

62. Plaut. *Poen.* 19–20; CIL 6.1074 = ILS 00456 = EDCS-17600022; and CIL 6.32332 = EDCS-20500154; Ps.-Acro, *Hor. Ep.* 1.7.6, on which see Lindsay, "Death-Pollution," 158–159.

63. *Dig.* 3.2.4.1, on which see Bodel, "Dealing with the Dead," 138–139.

64. Tert. *Spect.* 7.2–5: *Sed circensium paulo pompatior suggestus, quibus proprie hoc nomen: pompa praecedens, quorum sit in semetipsa probans de simulacrorum serie, de imaginum agmine, de curribus, de tensis, de armamaxis, de sedibus, de coronis, de exuviis. Quanta praeterea sacra, quanta sacrificia praecedant, intercedant, succedant, quot collegia, quot sacerdotia, quot officia moveantur, sciunt homines illius urbis, in qua daemoniorum conventus consedit. Ea si minore cura per provincias pro minoribus viribus administrantur, tamen omnes ubique circenses illuc deputandi, unde et petuntur, inde inquinantur, unde sumuntur. Nam et rivulus tenuis ex suo fonte et surculus modicus ex sua fronde qualitatem originis continet. Viderit ambitio sive frugalitas eius ** sit. Deum offendit qualiscumque pompa circi: etsi pauca simulacra circumferat, in uno idololatria est; etsi unam tensam trahat, Iovis tamen plaustrum est; quaevis idololatria sordide instructa vel modice, locuples et splendida est censu criminis sui* (trans. adapted Glover LCL).

65. Apul. *De deo Soc.* 14: *pro regionibus et cetera in sacris differunt longe varietate: pomparum agmina … item deorum effigiae et exuviae ….*

quae omnia pro cuiusque more loci sollemnia (ed. Teubner, trans. adapted Harrison).

66. CIL 2.3408 = EDCS-05502791: *Genio op(p)idi columnam / pompam ludosq(ue) / coiraverunt.* On epigraphic evidence for games in the Latin west, see Carter and Edmonson, "Spectacle in Rome, Italy, and the Provinces."

67. CIL 2.5439 (2^2.5.1022)= ILS 6087 = EDCS-20200004 = *Lex Coloniae Genetivae* 128.12 and 16–21: *II(vir) aed(ilis) pra<e>F(ectus) c(oloniae) G(enetivae) I(uliae) quicumque erit . . . / fiant e<i>qu[e] d(ecurionum) d(ecreto) suo quoque anno / ludos circenses, sacr[i]ficia pulvinariaque / facienda curent, que [a]d modum quitquit de iis / rebus, mag(istris) creandis, [lu]dis circensibus facien- / dis, sacrificiis procu[r]andis, pulvinaribus fa- / ciendis decuriones statuerint decreverint* (ed. and trans. adapted *Roman Statutes*, 415 and 430). See Chamberland, "mémoire des spectacles," on municipal Latin game-giver inscriptions.

68. Tert. *Ad nat.* 1.10 (chapter 4 n. 12 and p. 170) correlates *tensae* with *solisternia* (*sellisternia*) and *currus* (*elephantorum*) with *lectisternia.*

69. AE 1927 #158 = EDCS-12700139: *pompis et circinsibus cum corona laurea.*

70. CIL 10.6102 = ILS 6282 = EDCS-20800055: *tensae Minervae: / ex argenti libris centum,* on which see Duncan-Jones, "Epigraphic Survey of Costs," 197 and #492.

71. See Dodge, "Circuses in the Roman East" and "Venues for Spectacle and Sport," 564–565, on the distribution of circuses.

72. See Hellmann, *Lampes antiques* #289; Landes (ed.), *Le cirque* #31; and Szidat, *Teile eines historischen Frieses*, 33 and fig. 20, for other examples.

73. Zwierlein-Diehl, *Antike Gemmen in deutschen Sammlungen* #523 (Ceres); and Zazoff, *antiken Gemmen*, 329 n. 154 and 333 n. 195 (Livia).

74. Taylor, "*Sellisternium* and Theatrical *Pompa*," the fundamental study, and "Sellisternium and Theoxenia"; Hanson, *Roman Theater-Temples*, 80–92; and Madigan, *Ceremonial Sculptures*, 86–101. See also, Jory, "Continuity and Change"; and Beacham, *Spectacle Entertainments*, 27.

75. Tert. *Spect.* 7.1: *apparatus communes habeant necesse est de reatu generali idololatriae conditricis suae* and 10.2: *Apparatus etiam ex ea parte consortes, qua ad scaenam a templis et aris et illa infelicitate turis et sanguinis inter tibias et tubas itur duobus inquinatissimus arbitris funerum et sacrorum, dissignatore et haruspice* (trans. adapted Glover LCL); and also nn. 60–63 above, on the *dissignator.*

76. See pp. 9–11, 19–21 and 98–101 on gravity/levity, resonance/wonder, and ideal-type.

77. Ryberg, 98–99 n. 56; Humphrey, *Roman Circuses*, 193–194; Ronke #5; *Imperii insignia* C59; La Rocca, "Sul Circo Flaminio," 110–114; Fless, "Römische Prozessionen," #85; Lo Monaco, "In processione," 78–79; and Favro, "Festive Experience," 17–19. Fest. 436L suggests the presence of dancers during theatrical games, on which see Caldelli, "Associazioni di artisti," 141–146. Grimal, "théâtre à Rome," 253, suggests that actors featured in theater processions.

78. August. *De civ. D.* 2.26: *ante ipsum . . . delubrum . . . hinc meretriciam pompam, illinc virginem deam* (ed. Walsh).

79. Arn. *Adv. nat.* 7.33: *migratum ab lupanaribus in theatra* (CSEL), on which see Beacham, *Spectacle Entertainments*, 9–10; and Wiseman, "Games of Flora."

80. Apul. *Met.* 10.29: *Ad consaeptum caveae prosequente populo pompatico favore deducor* (ed. LCL, trans. adapted Walsh).

81. Dion. Hal. *Ant. Rom.* 2.71.3–4: ἐπιχώριον δὲ Ῥωμαίοις καὶ πάνυ τίμιον ὁ κουρητισμός, ὡς ἐκ πολλῶν μὲν καὶ ἄλλων ἐγὼ συμβάλλομαι, μάλιστα δ᾽ ἐκ τῶν περὶ τὰς πομπὰς τάς τε ἐν ἱπποδρόμῳ καὶ τὰς ἐν τοῖς θεάτροις γινομένας: ἐν ἁπάσαις γὰρ ταύταις πρόσηβοι κόροι χιτωνίσκους ἐνδεδυκότες ἐκπρεπεῖς κράνη καὶ ξίφη καὶ πάρμας ἔχοντες στοιχηδὸν πορεύονται (trans. adapted Cary LCL); chapter 1 n. 73 and n. 51 above.

82. Cic. *Har. resp.* 12.24: *ante templum in ipso matris magnae conspectu* (LCL), on which Lenaghan, *Commentary*, 120–121. See Hanson, *Roman Theater-Temples*, 9–26, on the proximity of the earliest performance locations to temples; and Goldberg, "Plautus on the Palatine," on performances in the Metroac sanctuary and the emergence of the theater procession. Jory, "Continuity and Change," notes that the theater of Pompey mimics the arrangements of the temple of Magna Mater: temple, cavea/stairs, stage. See Beacham, *Roman Theatre*, 56–84; and Sear, *Roman Theatres*, 54–67, on early Roman theaters.

83. Varro, *Eumenides* 150B: *cum illoc venio, video gallorum frequentiam in templo, qui dum e scena coronam adlatam imponeret aedilis signo deae, eam gallantes vario recinebant studio* (ed. and trans. Wiseman, *Catullus and His World*, 271), on which see Wiseman, *Catullus and His World*, 204–206 and 269–272 and *Cinna the Poet*, 159–160. Goldberg, "Plautus on the Palatine," 11; and Roller, *In Search of God the Mother*, 308, accept Wiseman's reconstruction. Romano, "Varrone e Cibele," 498; and "Rolle, "Il motivo del culto," 551–553, reconstruct this passage differently (as does the Teubner edition).
84. BMRRC #356.1, 409.2, and 431.1 (camel on reverse), on which see Roller, *In Search of God the Mother*, 289–290; and pp. 50–61 on the presence/representation of gods.
85. On *sellisternia* (objects displayed on chairs/thrones) more generally, see F. Hölscher, "Götterstatuen bei Lectisternien," in addition to n. 74 above.
86. CCCA 3.2, on which see Ryberg, 69–70; Fless, *Opferdiener und Kultmusiker*, 52–53, 70–78, and #22; Roller, *In Search of God the Mother*, 309–310; La Rocca, "troni dei nuovi dei," 88 n. 53; and Bell, "Revisiting the Pediment."
87. Roller, *In Search of God the Mother*, 288–289.
88. CCCA 7.39, on which see La Rocca, "troni dei nuovi dei," 88–89; and Madigan, *Ceremonial Sculptures*, 99–101. See also CCCA 7.184: a late third century CE marble relief of a throne with a hole on top for an object.
89. Ov. *Fast.* 4.326: *mira, sed et scaena testificata loquar* (trans. adapted Frazer/Goold LCL), on which see Wiseman, "Ovid and the Stage."
90. As suggested by Lucret. 4.79, a difficult passage which Taylor, "Lucretius," 148–149 reads as *patrum matrumque deorum(-que)* (fathers and mothers and gods); while Colin, "sénateurs et la mère des dieux," 348–349 has *patrum Matr<is>que Deorum* (senators and the Mother of the Gods), both of which put the gods and senators in the same seating area.
91. Dio Cass. 44.6.3 (chapter 4 n. 19). See Gebhard, "Theater and the City," on imperial power, gods, and the theater in the Greek east.
92. BMRRC #497.2 (see pp. 108–109); and RIC 2 Trajan #807. See also Florus 2.13.2.91: Caesar voted a crown to wear at the theater.
93. Dio Cass. 50.10.2 (Chapter 4 n. 21); and also 56.29.1 (pp. Chapter 4 n. 22)
94. See above pp. 148–149.
95. Dio Cass. 53.30.6 (see p. 118).
96. *Tab. Heb.* 50–54: *utiq(ue) ludis Augu[stalibus cum sedilia sodalium] / ponentur in theatris sellae curules Germanici Caesaris inter ea ponantur cu[m coronis querceis in memoriam] / eius sacerdoti, quae sellae sum templum divi Aug(usti) perfectum erit ex e<o> templo pr[oferantur et interea in templo] / Martis Ultoris reponantur en inde proferantur, quiq(ue) cumq(ue) eos ludos q(ui) s(upra) s(cripti) s(unt) fac[iendos curabit, is uti eae in the-] /atris ponantur et cum reponendae erunt in eo templo reponantur curet* (ed. *Roman Statutes*, 521, trans. adapted Lott, *Death and Dynasty*, 113), on which see Arena, *Feste e rituali*, 135–139, with a different reading of the evidence; and pp. 118–119.
97. Tac. *Ann.* 2.83.1: *sedes curules sacerdotum Augustalium locis superque eas querceae coronae statuerentur* (ed. LCL, trans. Woodman); and chapter 4 n. 63.
98. Tac. *Ann.* 4.9.2 (chapter 4 n. 65). See also CIL 6.31200.13, which Arena, *Feste e rituali*, 136 n. 134, reads as a possible epigraphic witness to Drusus' throne; while *Roman Statutes*, 547; Lott, *Death and Dynasty*, 166–167 and 316; and EDCS-17301035, prefer a name change for a section of theater seating on the model of Tac. *Ann.* 2.83.4.
99. Dio Cass. 58.4.3–4: κοινωνὸν τῶν φροντίδων ... δίφρους τε ἐπιχρύσους ἐς τὰ θέατρα ἀμφοῖν ἐσέφερον (trans. Cary LCL).
100. AE 1927 #158: *[–statu]a eius ut ponatur ludis omnibus in theatro*; or EDCS-12700139: *[–sell] a (?) eius ut ponatur ludis omnibus in theatro*; and p. 161 n. 69.
101. Dio Cass. 72.31.2 (epitome): ἐς τὸ θέατρον χρυσῆν εἰκόνα τῆς Φαυστίνης ἐπὶ δίφρου ἀεί, ὁσάκις γ᾿ ἂν ἐκεῖνος θεωρῇ, ἐσφέρεσθαί τε καὶ ἐν τῇ προεδρίᾳ ἐξ ἧς ζῶσα ἐθεᾶτο τίθεσθαι, καὶ περὶ αὐτὴν τὰς γυναῖκας τὰς δυνάμει προεχούσας συγκαθίζεσθαι (trans. Cary LCL); and see also p. 127 on Faustina II in the circus procession.
102. Dio Cass. 73.17.4 (epitome): ἡ ... λεοντῇ τό τε ῥόπαλον ... ἐν τοῖς θεάτροις ἐπὶ δίφρου

ἐπιχρύσου . . . ἐτίθετο (trans. adapted Cary LCL); and see p. 128

103. Dio Cass. 75.4.1 (epitome): ἐς τὰ λοιπὰ ἐκέλευσε θέατρα θρόνους τρεῖς καταχρύσους αὐτῷ ἐσκομίζεσθαι (trans. adapted Cary LCL); and see pp. 128–129 and Figure 36.
104. Tert. *Ad nat.* 1.10 (chapter 4 n. 12).
105. Ambrose, *Explanatio psalmorum* XII 43.55.3: *despicabiles aestimabantur, qui theatrum facti sunt huic mundo . . . quasi in pompa quadam circumferri* (they are considered contemptible, those who are made a theater to the world . . . as if carried about in a procession, ed. CSEL); and Auson. *Ephemeris* 8.4: *lati . . . pompa theatri* (LCL).
106. Webb, *Demons and Dancers*, 197–216, on Christians and late-antique theater.
107. Justinian, *Nov.* 105 (537 CE): πέμπτην γε ποιήσει πρόοδον τὴν ἐπὶ τὸ θέατρον ἄγοθσαν, ἣν πόρνας καλοῦθσιν, ἔωθα τοῖς ἐπι σκηνῆς γελωτοποιοῖς ἔσται χῶπα τραγῳδοῖς τε καὶ τοῖς ἐπι τῆς θυμέλης χοροῖς (*Quintum quoque faciet processum qui ad theatrum ducit, quem pornas vocant, ubi in scena ridiculorum est locus tragoedis et thymelicis choris*, ed. Schoell/Kroll); and pp. 203–204.
108. See pp. 186–191, on Christian (literate, elite) criticisms of the games.
109. Suet. *Tit.* 8.5: *Hos [delatores mandatoresque] assidue in Foro flagellis ac fustibus caesos ac novissime traductos per amphitheatri harenam* (ed. LCL, trans. adapted Edwards), on which see Coleman, "'Informers' on Parade."
110. Mart. *Spect.* 4.1–4: *Turba gravis paci placidaeque inimica quieti, / quae semper miseras sollicitabat opes, / traducta est †getulis† nec cepit harena nocentis* (trans. Shackleton-Bailey LCL).
111. Richardson, sv Amphitheatrum Flavium, argues the entrances on the major axes were for the *pompa* and performers.
112. Abaecherli, "Imperial Symbols"; and Taylor, "*Sellisternium* and Theatrical *Pompa*," both argue for the theater procession; while Damsky, "Throne and Curule Chair Types," proposes the inauguration of the Colosseum. See also La Rocca, "troni dei nuovi dei," 84–89; and F. Hölscher, "Götterstatuen bei Lectisternien," 38–39.
113. Thunderbolt: RIC 2.1^2 Titus #117–120 (Figure 50) and Domitian 4, 33–36, 68–72, and 101; and Helmet: RIC 2.1^2 Titus # 270–271 (Figure 51).
114. Wreath: RIC 2.1^2 Titus #106–109 (Figure 52) and Domitian 1, 8–11, 21–24, 46–50, and 95; Triangular object: RIC 2.1^2 Titus #124–125 (Figure 53) and Domitian 3 and 14–15 (triangular or semicircular); and Semicircular object: RIC 2.1^2 Titus #121–123 (Figure 54) and Domitian 14–15 (triangular or semicircular), 16–17, 31–32, 64–67, and 100.
115. Abaecherli, "Imperial Symbols," argues for *struppi* differentiated by sex; Damsky, "Throne and Curule Chair Types," backs of the thrones; and La Rocca, "troni dei nuovi dei," *struppi* contra chair backs.
116. RIC 2 Trajan #829–830 and 833; and RIC 2.1^2 Titus #184–186 and Domitian 131: images of the amphitheater.
117. RIC 3 Antoninus Pius #137; and see pp. 129–130.
118. See pp. 56–57, 89, 138, and 143.
119. Elkins, "Processions and Placement."
120. CIL 10.1074d = ILS 5053.4 = EDCS-11401167: 4, on which Jacobelli, *Gladiators at Pompeii*, 42–43.
121. Ryberg, 101–102 and figs. 50a-c; Ronke #6; *Imperii insignia* C15; La Regina (ed.), *Sangue e arena* #74; Fless, "Römische Prozessionen," #84; Jacobelli, *Gladiators at Pompeii*, 22–23 fig. 18 and 95–97 fig. 77; and *Trionfi Romani* I.3.4.
122. Bridel, "L'amphithéâtre d'Avenches."
123. Chapter 2 n. 65.
124. See pp. 53–54.
125. Guidetti, "Note sull'iconografia."
126. Ryberg, 100–101 and figs. 49a-b; Ronke #3; Compostella, "Iconografia, ideologia e status"; *Imperii insignia* C69; and, on the *Augustales* in general, Laird, *Civic Monuments and the* Augustales, esp. 19–24, on this monument.
127. Ryberg, 98–99 and fig. 47; Ronke #2; *Imperii insignia* C53; La Regina (ed.), *Sangue e arena* #72; and Clarke, *Art in the Lives of Ordinary Romans*, 143–152.
128. Ryberg, 150 and figs. 81d–e; Ronke #8; *Imperii insignia* C5; La Regina (ed.), *Sangue e arena* #21; and esp. Tuck, "Spectacle and Ideology," 257–264.
129. Prudent. *C. Symm.* 1.384–385: *illa amphitheatralis spectacula tristia pompae* (LCL); and Jiménez Sánchez, *Los juegos paganos*, 350–356.
130. N. 107 above.
131. Pp. 163–164 (nn. 78–80) and p. 96.
132. RIC 2.1^2 Titus #114–116; Mart. *Spect.* 20(17): *nostrum sentit et ille deum* (trans. Shackleton-Bailey LCL); and see pp. 115–117 on elephants.

133. See pp. 39–42, 61–65, and 147–152, on ritual rules, failures, and repetitions.
134. Ov. *Fast.* 4.392: *primaque ventosis palma petetur equis* (trans. Frazer/Gould).
135. Ov. *Am.* 3.2.65: *maxima ... spectacula* (trans. Henderson, "A Doo-Dah-Doo-Dah-Dey," 53). See Horsmann, *Wagenlenker*, 135–141, on charioteer inscriptions generally, and 147–154 on prize amounts; and pp. 27–28, 89, and 155–156, on the events after procession to the start of the races.
136. Balsdon, *Life and Leisure*, 316.
137. Thuillier, *sport dans la Rome antique*, 103–104; and Decker and Thuillier, *sport dans l'antiquité*, 210, argue that religious sentiment explains the prestige of the first race.
138. CIL 6.10048 = ILS 5287 = EDCS-19200318: lines 6–7: *Summa: quadriga agitavit annis XXIIII, missus ostio IIII CCLVII, / [vicit MCCC]CLXII, a pompa CX*; line 15: *[Dio]cles omnium agitatorum eminentissimus*; and lines 15–16: *praecessit omnium factionum agitatores qui unquam / [certaminibus ludorum ci]rcensium interfuerunt*; on which Horsmann, *Wagenlenker*, 194–198.
139. See pp. 3–4.
140. CIL 6.10047b = ILS 5288.3 = EDCS-19200317: lines 1–2: *in factione albata ... a pompa IIII ...* 5: *In factione veneta ... a pompa XXXV* and 7–8: *In factione prasina ... a pompa VI*; on which Horsmann, *Wagenlenker*, 226–228; and LTUR sv sepulcrum: P. Aelius Gutta Calpurnianus.

Six The *pompa circensis* in late antiquity

1. *Quamquam omnis superstitio penitus eruenda sit, tamen volumus, ut aedes templorum, quae extra muros sunt positae, intactae incorruptaeque consistant ... ex quibus populo romano praebeatur priscarum sollemnitas voluptatum [vel ludorum vel circensium vel agonum]* (342 CE) (trans. Pharr).
2. Tert. *Apol.* 38.4: *spectaculis vestris in tantum renuntiamus in quantum originibus eorum, quas scimus de superstitione conceptas ... Nihil enim nobis dictu, visu, auditu cum insania circi, cum inpudicitia theatri, cum atrocitate arenae* (trans. adapted Glover LCL).
3. On *divus* as blessed, see e.g. Hedrick, *History and Silence*, 2–3; Gradel, *Emperor Worship*, 356–369; and Bonamente, "Dall'imperatore divinizzato all'imperatore santo." See also Smith, "Imperial Court of the Late Roman Empire," for an overview of late Roman imperial ceremony.
4. Boin, "Late Antique *Divi*" and "Memory of 'Peter,'" argues for a variety of strategies of accommodation and resistance to imperial cult into the fifth century CE.
5. SHA *Maximini Duo* 26.2.
6. See pp. 94–97 and 132–134.
7. *[N]on spectacula visitis, non pompis interestis ... sacra certamina ... abhorretis* (LCL).
8. Min. Fel. *Oct.* 37.11: *merito malis voluptatibus et pompis vestris et spectaculis abstinemus* (LCL).
9. Tert. *Apol.* 42.7: *spectaculis non convenimus* (LCL). On Tertullian and Minucius Felix, see Price, "Latin Christian Apologetics." On Christian attitudes towards the games in the Latin west, see French, "Christian Emperors and Pagan Spectacles," 30–41; DeVoe, "Christians and the Games," esp. 134–165; Kahlos, *Debate and Dialogue*, 113–136; Lugaresi, "*Regio aliena*" and *teatro di Dio*, esp. 377–462 and 535–694; and Jiménez Sánchez, *juegos paganos*, esp. 269–316.
10. Tert. *Spect.* 3.1: *simplicior aut scrupulosior ... non significanter neque nominatim denuntietur servis dei abstinentia eiusmodi* (trans. adapted Glover LCL), on which see Rebillard, *Christians and their Many Identities*, esp. 20–23.
11. Novatian, *Spect.* 2.1: *Non pudet, inquam, non pudet fideles homines et christiani sibi nominis auctoritatem vindicantes superstitiones vanas gentilium cum spectaculis mixtas de scripturis caelestibus vindicare* (ed. CCSL, trans. DeSimone FC).
12. Harl, "dénonciation des festivités profanes," for the Greek East; and n. 9 above for Latin west.
13. On drawing boundaries, see Kahlos, "*Pompa diaboli*" and *Debate and Dialogue*, 126–136.
14. Tert. *Apol.* 38.4 (n. 2 above), re-arranged for rhetorical effect.
15. Tert. *Spect.* 8: *Proinde si Capitolium, si Serapeum sacrificator vel adorator intravero, a deo excidam, quemadmodum circum vel theatrum spectator* (trans. adapted Glover LCL), on which see Lugaresi, "*Regio Aliena*," 22–24.
16. Tert. *Spect.* 7.1 (see pp. 161–162 n. 75).
17. Novatian, *Spect.* 5.3–4: *quam vana sunt ipsa certamina, lites in coloribus, contentiones in curribus, favores in honoribus, gaudere quod equus velocior fuerit, maerere quod pigrior, annos pecoris computare, consules nosse, aetates discere, prosapiam designare, avos ipsos atavos que memorare. Quam hoc totum otiosum negotium, immo quam

turpiter ignominiosum! (ed. CCSL, trans. DeSimone FC).

18. Amm. Marc. 14.6.26: *memorabile nihil vel serium agi Romae permittunt* (LCL).
19. Ambrose, *Off.* 2.21.109: *ludis circensibus vel etiam theatralibus et muneribus gladiatoriis* (ed. Davidson).
20. Jer. *Ep.* 43.3: *Habeat sibi Roma suos tumultus, harena saeviat, circus insaniat, theatra luxurient* (trans. Wright LCL); and Aug. *Serm* 198.3*: turpitudinibus variis theatrorum, insania circi, crudelitate amphitheatri* (ed. Dolbeau #26, trans. adapted Hill), on both see Rebenich "*Insania circi.*"
21. Isid. *Etym.* 18.59.1: *Circensi insania . . . inpudicitia theatri . . . amphitheatri crudelitate . . . atrocitae arenae* (OCT); and, on the topos, see Jiménez Sánchez, "liturgie impériale," 182–183.
22. Tert. *Spect.* 7.2 (see pp. 159–160 n. 64).
23. Tert. *Spect.* 4.1, 4.3, 12.6, and 24.2 and *De corona* 3.2 and 13.7, on which see Waszink, "Pompa diaboli," who persuasively argues that *pompa diaboli* first implied the circus procession and then developed wider connotations. This view is commonly accepted, see e.g. Daniélou, *Bible and The Liturgy*, 28–29; Van Slyke, "Devil and His Pomps," 60; and Nelis-Clément, "Pompes et circonstances," 69–70.
24. Tert. *Spect.* 7.5 (chapter 5 n. 64).
25. Tert. *Spect.* 7.3 (chapter 5 n. 64); and pp. 88–89 and 96–97.
26. E.g. Ambrose, *Expositio psalmi CXVIII* 5.29; Prudent. *Psychomachia* 439–40; Quodvultdeus, *Serm.* 2.1 (*De Symbolo II*); and Caesarius, *Serm.* 12.4. *Pompa*, however, had long included pomp, display, and ostentation within its semantic range: e.g. Sen. *Ep.* 103.5: *sapere sine pompa* (wise without ostentation, ed. LCL), 110.15: *pompa pecuniae* (display of wealth, ed. LCL), and 110.17: *est pompa* (it is a show, ed. LCL).
27. Arn. *Adv. nat.* 4.31: *si rursus in sollemnibus ludis curriculisque divinis commissum omnes statim in religiones clamatis sacras, si ludius constitit aut tibicen repente conticuit aut si patrimus et matrimus ille qui vocitatur puer omiserit per ignorantiam lorum aut tensam tenere non potuit* (ed. CSEL, trans. adapted McCracken ACW), mocking Cic. *Har. resp.* 11.23 (see pp. 41 and 61–63).
28. See also Arn. *Adv. nat.* 6.7 for a similar misreading of the Capitoline *caput*; and also Isid. *Etym.* 15.2.31.
29. Lactant. *Div. Inst.* 2.16.16: *quotiens autem pericula impendent, ob aliquam se ineptam et levem causam profitentur iratos, sicut Iuno Varroni, quod formonsum puerum in tensa Iovis ad exuvias tenendas conlocaverat: et ob hanc causam Romanum nomen aput Cannas paene deletum est* (ed. CSEL, trans. adapted Bowen/Garnsey TTH), mocking Val. Max. 1.1.16 (see p. 64 n. 121).
30. Lactant. *Div. Inst.* 2.3.7: *quanto magis vulgus indoctum, quod pompis inanibus gaudet animisque puerilibus spectat omnia, oblectatur frivolis et specie simulacrorum capitur* (ed. CSEL, trans. adapted Bowen/Garnsey TTH).
31. See pp. 147–152.
32. Jer. *Ep.* 3.6: *fulgeat quilibet auro et pompaticis ferculis corusca ex sarcinis metalla radient* (ed. CSEL, trans. adapted Mierow ACW); see pp. 62–63 on *fercula* bearers; and 97–98, on *aurea Roma.*
33. Paulinus of Nola, *Carm.* 25.33: *Nec sit Christocolam fanatica pompa per urbem* (ed. CSEL, trans. adapted Walsh ACW).
34. Bachiarius, *Ad Januarium liber de reparatione lapsi: Qui vero captus est in rete vitiorum, et patienter inimicis suis, hoc est, venatoribus acquiescit, donec etiam recludatur in cavea, et ibi longo temporis spatio saginetur ad pompam* (PL 20 col. 1050B). On Bachiarus, see Kulikowski, "Identity of Bachiarius," (an Illyrian); and Dietz, *Wandering Monks, Virgins, and Pilgrims*, 65–66 (a Spaniard).
35. Salvian, *De gub. Dei* 6.3.15: *pompis athletis petaminariis pantomimis ceterisque portentis . . . de solis circorum ac theatrorum impuritatibus dico* (ed. CSEL, trans. O'Sullivan FC).
36. Caesarius, *Serm.* 12.4: *Omnia spectacula vel furiosa vel cruenta vel turpia, pompae diaboli sunt* (CCSL), and see also using the same phrase *Serm.* 89.5, 134.1, and 150.3, and, targeting circus and theater games, 141.4.
37. Novatian, *Spect.* 9.1: *Habet christianus spectacula meliora . . . mundi pulchritudinem* (CCSL).
38. Aug. *Serm.* 51.2: *Magnum spectaculum praebet oculis cordis integer animus, corpore dissipato* (ed. CCSL, trans. Hill), on which see Potter, "Martyrdom as Spectacle"; Castelli, *Martyrdom and Memory*, 104–133; Van Slyke, "Devil and His Pomps"; and Lugaresi, *teatro di Dio*, 693–694.
39. Aug. *Serm.* 280.2: *quid hoc spectaculo suavius?* (CCSL).

40. See e.g. Boin, "Hellenistic 'Judaism,'" on internal differences between militant and "accomodationist" Christians.
41. Rebillard, *Christians and their Many Identities*.
42. Jer. *Ep*. 69.9.4: *heri catechumenus, hodie pontifex; heri in amphitheatro, hodie in ecclesia; vespere in circo, mane in altari; dudum fautor histrionum, nunc virginum consecrator* (CSEL), on which see Adkin, "*Heri catechumenus, hodie pontifex*"; and Hunter, "The Raven Replies," esp. 183–186.
43. August. *Enn. Ps*. 39.9: *ecce aversus fuerit a circo, a theatro, ab amphitheatro* and 39.10: *pauci in comparatione multitudinis maiorum frequentiarum* (ed. CCSL, trans. adapted Boulding).
44. August. *Enn. Ps*. 80.2: *sunt enim multi non digne viventes baptismo quod perceperunt: quam multi enim baptizati hodie circum implere, quam istam basilicam maluerunt*! (ed. CCSL, trans. adapted Boulding); and see also *Serm*. 88.17, 301A.7, and *Enn. Ps*. 50.1, on Christians at games and shows, on which see Harries, "*Favor populi*"; and Kahlos, *Debate and Dialogue*, 127 n. 66, with a list of similar complaints.
45. Leo, *Serm*. 84.1: *Plus inpenditur daemoniis quam apostolis, et maiorem obtinent frequentiam insana spectacula quam beata martyria* (ed. CCSL, trans. adapted Freeland/Conway FC).
46. Markus, *End of Ancient Christianity*, 126–131; Salzman, "Leo in Rome" and "Leo's Liturgical Topography."
47. Salvian, *De gub. Dei* 6.4.20: *innumera Christianorum milia . . . bacchantur in circis* and 6.7.38: *ecclesia vacuatur circus impletur*! (CSEL).
48. Salvian, *De gub. Dei* 6.4.24 and 6.5.26: *Christo ergo (o amentia monstruosa!) Christo circenses offerimus et mimos* (CSEL), on which see Jiménez Sánchez, "*O amentia monstruosa*!" and "liturgie impériale."
49. Barnish, "Transformation and Survival"; Humphries, "Roman Senators and Absent Emperors"; Burgarella, "Il Senato"; Salzman, *Making of a Christian Aristocracy*, esp. 19–68; Chenault, "Rome Without Emperors"; and Weisweiler, "Price of Integration."
50. Brown, *Gentlemen and Officers*, 21–37; Matthews, *Western Aristocracies*, esp. 13–23; and Heather, "Senators and Senates."
51. Jones, *Later Romam Empire*, 523–562, esp. 554–557; Noble, "Roman Elite"; and esp. Wickham, *Framing the Early Middle Ages*, 155–168.
52. Symm. *Ep*. 1.52: *pars melior humani generis senatus* (ed. and trans. Salzman/Robert); on the heritage industry, see McLynn, "Crying Wolf"; and, generally, Samuels, "From *Theaters of Memory*"; on the festal calendar, Salzman, *On Roman Time*; and Machado, "City as Stage," 287–296; and, on the cost of games (and episcopal attempts to re-channel wealth), Fauvinet-Ranson, *Decor civitas, decor Italiae*, 417–423; and Brown, *Through the Eye of a Needle*, passim.
53. Lim, "People as Power," 267–275.
54. Bourdieu, *The Logic of Practice*, 112–121, on symbolic capital.
55. Olympiodorus fr. 41.2 (Blockley), on which see Matthews, *Western Aristocracies*, 277 and 384; Cameron and Schauer, "Last Consul," 139; Harries, "*Favor populi*"; Wickham, *Framing the Early Middle Ages*, 162–163; Cameron, *Last Pagans*, 790; Brown, *Through the Eye of a Needle*, 16–17 and 115–118; and Jones, "Organization of Spectacle," 305–306.
56. Asterius, *Anth. Lat*. 1.1^2, pp. 18–19 (Teubner): *tempore, quo penaces circo subiunximus atque / scenam euripo extulimus subitam / ut ludos currusque simul variumque ferarum / certamen iunctim Roma teneret ovans. / ternum quippe 'sofos' merui, terna agmina vulgi / per caveas plausus concinuere meos. / in pretium famae census iactura cucurrit, / nam laudis fructum talia damna ferunt. / Sic tot consumptas servant spectacula gazas, / festorumque trium permanet una dies, / Asteriumque suum vivax transmittit in aevum, / qui partas trabeis tam bene donat opes* (ed. Cameron, "Basilius, Mavortius, Asterius," 33 and trans. Cameron, *Last Pagans*, 791).
57. Markus, *End of Ancient Christianity*, 217.
58. Last consul: Fauvinet-Ranson, *Decor civitatis, decor Italiae*, 386; and Cameron, *Last Pagans*, 790 and "Basilius and his Diptych." Colosseum: Cassiod. *Var*. 5.42; Ward-Perkins, *Classical Antiquity to Middle Ages*, esp. 111–116; Tantillo, "*munera*"; and Orlandi, "loca del Colosseo," (last inscription). Circus: Procop. *Goth*. 7.37.4 presumably in the Circus Maximus, on which see e.g. Humphrey, *Roman Circuses*, 131 n. 297; and Ciancio Rossetta, "Circo Massimo."
59. Procop. *Anec*. 26.8, on which see Jones, "Organization of Spectacle," 312. MacMullen, *Roman Social Relations*, 61, on "sheer willingness." Brown, *Rise of Western Christendom*[2], 194–195; Wickham, *Framing the Early Middle Ages*, 203–211; and nn. 49–52

above, on the transformation of elites and their traditions.

60. CTh 6.4.4 (339 CE): *ad urbem Romam venire cum impensis, [qua]s ludi scaenicorum vel circensium ... cogantur* (trans. Pharr); reaffirmed by 6.4.7 (354 CE), but rescinded for Illyricum by 15.5.4 (424 CE). 15.7.13 (415 CE) compelled mime actresses to perform, amending, it seems, earlier laws exempting converts to Christianity (15.7.4 [380 CE]), so long as the convert did not return to her supposedly wanton ways (15.7.8 [381 CE]), on which see Soler, "L'état impérial romain."
61. CTh 6.4.7 (354 CE) restored penalties relaxed by 6.4.1–2 (329 and 327 CE); on planning ahead for expenses 6.4.22 (373 CE); and on curbing expenditures 15.9.1 (384 CE), which may haven been spurred by Symm. *Rel.* 8.2 per Barrow, *Prefect and Emperor*, 61–62 n. 2; and 15.9.2 (409 CE), on which see Giglio, "*munus* della pretura."
62. CTh 12.1.112 (386 CE): chief civic priests should be drawn from adherents of ancient Mediterranean traditional religions not Christianity (and so the contrary seems to have occurred); 12.1.145 (395 CE): *sacerdotales* allowed to provide games in Carthage; 12.1.176 (413 CE): *quicumque propter pompam illius diei Karthaginem forte convenerit, intra quinque dies ad propria rediturus ex eadem urbe discedat* (trans. adapted Pharr); and 16.10.20 (415 CE): "pagan" *sacerdotales* should return to their municipalities, on which see Chastagnol, "Sur les *sacerdotales* africains," on "pagan" and Christian *sacerdotales*; and Leone, *End of the Pagan City*, 11–14, 87–101, and 245–254, with additions by Boin, "Late Antique *Divi*," 156–157.
63. E.g. CTh 15.5.1 (372 CE) and 15.5.3 (409 CE).
64. See, generally, Fears, "Theology of Victory at Rome"; and, on the games specifically, Jiménez Sánchez, *juegos paganos*, 169–194.
65. Symm. *Rel.* 6.1–2: *ea iam quasi debita repetit ... [populus Romanus] orat igitur clementiam vestram, ut post illa subsidia, quae victui nostro largitas vestra praestavit, etiam curules ac scaenicas voluptates circo et Pompeianae caveae suggeratis* (ed. MGH, trans. Barrow), on which see Lim, "People as Power," 269–271, and "Inventing Secular Space," 74. See Fauvinet-Ranson, *Decor civitatis, decor Italiae*, 306–322 and 405–408, on Cassiod. *Var.* 1.27 and 1.30–32: spectacles and violence at Rome.
66. SHA *Marc.* 23.4: *absens populi Romani voluptates curari vehementer praecepit per ditissimos editores* (trans. adapted Rolfe LCL); and SHA *Sev.* 3.5: *ludos absens edidit* (LCL), on which see Lim, "People as Power," 271.
67. Exc. Val. (Anon. Val.) 12.60: *exhibens ludos circensium et amphitheatrum* (LCL). On games in Ostrogothic Italy, see Fauvinet-Ranson, *Decor civitatis, decor Italiae*, 379–440, and "spectacles traditionnels."
68. Amm. Marc. 28.4.28–29: *otiosam plebem ... et desidem* and 28.4.29: *eisque templum ... Circus est Maximus* (trans. adapted Rolfe LCL).
69. August. *De civ. D.* 1.32.4: *animos miserorum tantis obcaecavit tenebris, tanta deformitate foedavit, ut etiam modo ... romana urbe vastata, quos pestilentia ista possedit atque inde fugientes Carthaginem pervenire potuerunt, in theatris cotidie certatim pro histrionibus insanirent* (ed. and trans. adapted Walsh). See also *Expositio totius mundi* 61, on Carthaginians mad for *munera.*
70. Quodvultdeus, *Serm.* 11: *De tempore barbarico* 1.1.11: *cotidie frequentantur spectacula: sanguis hominum cotidie funditur in mundo, et insanientium voces crepitant in circo* (CCSL).
71. Salvian, *De gub. Dei* 6.12.69: *circumsonabant armis muros Cirtae atque Carthaginis populi barbarorum, et ecclesia Carthaginis insaniebat in circis luxuriabat in theatris* (ed. CSEL, trans. O'Sullivan FC), on which see Lim, "*Tribunus Voluptatum*," esp. 167–168; and Van Slyke, "Devil and His Pomps," on games in late-antique Carthage.
72. Hugoniot, "spectacles dans le royaume vandale."
73. Curran, *Pagan City and Christian Capital*, 230–236; and chapter 5 nn. 5 and 15.
74. Wistrand, *Entertainment and Violence* and "Change and Continuity"; and Mammel, "Ancient Critics."
75. See, on such influence, Brown, *Power and Persuasion*; on the role of the church in imperial politics e.g. Drake, *Constantine and the Bishops*, esp. 72–110, and "Church, Society and Political Power"; Rapp, *Holy Bishops*, esp. 260–273; and Lizzi Testa, "Late Antique Bishop"; and, on limited impact on imperial practice, which grew over time, Jacobs, "Time for Prayer."

76. On decline of sacrifice, see Bradbury, "Julian's Pagan Revival"; and Salzman, "End of Public Sacrifice."
77. On the "secularization" of the games, see French, "Christian Emperors and Pagan Spectacles," 30–81; Markus, *End of Ancient Christianity*, 107–121; Lim, "People as Power," "Christianization, Secularization," and "Inventing Secular Space"; Salzman, "Christianization of Sacred Time and Sacred Space"; Belayche, "Des lieux pour le 'profane'"; Soler, "*Ludi* et *munera*"; Jiménez Sánchez, *juegos paganos*, 317–330; and n. 85 below, with Benoist, "*Spectacula* et *romanitas*," who notes that the games remained religious for a long time.
78. Curran, *Pagan City and Christian Capital*, 161–217, on anti-"pagan" laws pertaining to Rome.
79. CTh 16.10.2 (341 CE): *Cesset superstitio, sacrificiorum aboleatur insania* (trans. Pharr).
80. CTh 16.10.4–13 (353–395 CE) 16.10.15 (396 CE), 16.10.17–18 (399 CE), 16.10.20 (415 CE), 16.10.23 (423 CE), and 16.10.25 (435 CE); and CJ 1.11.1–4, which repeat a number of these laws, while 1.11.7 (451 CE) and 1.11.10 (ca. 529–534 CE) extended the series into the mid sixth century CE, on which see Salzman, "'Superstitio' in the Codex Theodosianus"; Hunt, "Christianising the Roman Empire"; Bradbury, "Constantine and the Problem of Antipagan Legislation"; and Sandwell, "Outlawing 'Magic.'"
81. BNP 214–227.
82. CTh 16.10.6 (356 CE): *operam sacrificiis dare vel colere simulacra* (trans. Pharr).
83. CTh 16.10.8 (382 CE), 16.10.10 (391 CE), 16.10.12 (392 CE), 16.10.18 (399 CE), 16.10.19 (407 CE) = Sirm. 12; CJ 1.11.7 (451 CE); and 1.11.10 (ca. 529–534 CE).
84. CTh 16.10.8 (382 CE): *simulacra . . . artis pretio quam divinitate metienda* (trans. Pharr).
85. French, "Christian Emperors and Pagan Spectacles," 33–41; DeVoe, "Christians and the Games," 176–187; Lim, "People as Power," 268–269 and "Inventing Secular Space," 70–75; and Jiménez Sánchez, "*O amentia monstruosa!*" "liturgie impériale," and *juegos paganos*, 322–327.
86. CTh 16.10.17: *absque ullo sacrificio atque ulla superstitione damnabili* (trans. Pharr).
87. CTh 16.10.3 (342 CE): *Quamquam omnis superstitio penitus eruenda sit, tamen volumus, ut aedes templorum, quae extra muros sunt positae, intactae incorruptaeque consistant. Nam cum ex nonnullis vel ludorum vel circensium vel agonum origo fuerit exorta* (trans. Pharr); and n. 1 above.
88. CTh 2.8.22 (395 CE): *Sollemnes pagano[r]um superstitionis dies* (trans. Pharr).
89. CIL 1^2.1.XX-XXI: *Fasti Furii Dionysii Philocali et Polemii Silvii*, on which see Jiménez Sánchez "liturgie impériale," 184–185.
90. CTh 2.8.20 (392 CE): *Festis solis diebus circensium sunt inhibenda certamina, [q]uo Christianae legis veneranda mysteria nullus spectaculorum con[c]ursus avertat, praeter clementiae nostrae natalicios dies* (trans. Pharr, emphasis added). CTh 2.8.19 (389 CE) only restricts legal proceedings on certain days, including a litany of Christian holidays, while CJ 3.12.6.3 (389 CE) adds a prohibition of spectacles.
91. CTh 2.8.23 (399 CE).
92. CTh 2.8.24 (405 CE): *Religionis intuitu cavemus atque decernimus, ut [s]eptem diebus quadragesimae, septem paschalibus . . . natalis etiam die et epifa[n]iae spectacula non edantur* (trans. Pharr).
93. CTh 2.8.25 (409 CE).
94. CJ 3.12.9.2 (469 CE): *religiosi diei . . . obscaenis quemquam patimur voluptatibus detineri. Nihil eodem die sibi vindicet scaena theatralis aut circense certamen aut ferarum lacrimosa spectacula: etiam si in nostrum ortum aut natalem celebranda sollemnitas inciderit, differatur.*
95. Salzman, "Topography and Religion"; Soler, "*Ludi* et *munera*," 47–52; and Lim, "Inventing Secular Space," 73–74.
96. E.g. Cic. *Mur.* 77, defending public enjoyment of games.
97. Tac. *Ann.* 3.6.3 *Proin repeterent sollemnia, et quia ludorum Megalesium spectaculum suberat, etiam voluptates resumerent* (ed. LCL, trans. Woodman).
98. Tac. *Ann.* 4.62.2: *Adfluxere avidi talium, imperitante Tiberio procul voluptatibus habiti* (ed. LCL, trans. Woodman).
99. Apul. *Met.* 4.13: *publicas voluptates* (trans. adapted Hanson LCL).
100. CIL 14.3014 = ILS 6252 = EDCS-05800998; EDCS-01300250; and CIL 8.1483, 8.15505, 8.26546, 8.26639, and 8.26650 = EDCS-17900394: *agrum qui appellatur circus ad voluptatem po[p]uli rei publ(icae) remisit*, on which see Humphrey, *Roman Circuses*, 321–328 and Marcatilli, "*Agrum qui appellatur circus*," 313–316; and CIL 8.11340 = EDCS-25002177.

101. Tert. *Spect.* 29.3: *haec voluptates, haec spectacula* (LCL); and Min. Fel. *Oct.* 12.5: *honestis voluptatibus* (LCL and n. 7 above).
102. CJ 11.42.1; and SHA *Marc.* 23.4 (n. 66 above), *Gall.* 9.4, *Aurel.* 34.6, and *Prob* 19.1.
103. CTh 16.10.3 (nn. 1 and 87 above).
104. E.g. Cic. *Mur.* 77; and also CTh 15.7.3 (376 CE); CTh 15.7.5 (380 CE); and CTh 15.11.1 (414 CE).
105. CTh 15.7.6 (381 CE): *Equos, quos ad sollemne certamen . . . voluptates.*
106. CTh 15.10.2 (381 CE): *equos voluptatibus . . . necessaria antiqua et sollemni praebitione* (trans. Pharr).
107. CTh 15.9.2 (409 CE): *ludorum quidem, quibus moris est, intersint festivitati et oblectamentis favorem eliciant populorum* (trans. Pharr).
108. CTh 16.10.17 (399 CE): *absque ullo sacrificio atque ulla superstitione damnabili exhiberi populo voluptates secundum veterem consuetudinem* (trans. Pharr and n. 86 above).
109. CTh 15.7.13 (414 CE); and Cassiod. *Var.* 7.10: formula for appointment, on which see Lim, "*Tribunus voluptatum*," who argues that the office was created for Carthage; and Jiménez Sánchez, "*tribunus voluptatum*" and *juegos paganos*, 201–208, who argues for Rome. See also Fauvinet-Ranson, *Decor civitatis, decor Italiae*, 324–325 and 371–374, on Cassiodorus' letter; and Jiménez Sánchez, "Honorius," who argues that Honorius ramped up spectacle to deflect from troubled times.
110. Suet. *Tib.* 42.2: *officium instituit a voluptatibus* (ed. LCL, trans. Edwards); and Lim, "*Tribunus voluptatum*," 163–164, with further examples.
111. S. Pietro: CIL 6.8566 and 6.41420c = ICUR 2.4184 = EDCS-01000563; and S. Lorenzo FLM: CIL 6.8565 = ICUR 7.17617 = EDCS-18500213. See Jiménez Sánchez, "*tribunus voluptatum*" 96–97, for a catalog, to which add AE 2010 #1749 = EDCS-59600072 from Egypt. In the mid-fifth century CE at Ravenna, Peter Chrysologus, *Serm.* 155 and 155a, criticized those who hid idolatry behind amusements, on which see Arbesmann, "'Cervuli' and 'Anniculae,'" 111–113.
112. See esp. Curran, *Pagan City and Christian Capital*, 252–258, to whom the following section is greatly indebted.
113. Claud. *Cons. Hon. IV* 639–640: *semper venere triumphi /cum trabeis sequiturque tuos victoria fasces* (trans. adapted Platnauer LCL); and chapter 4 n. 125 and n. 64 above on ever-victorious emperors.
114. RIC 6 Roma #167 and 188 (on foot), 215 and 217 (elephants, Figure 59), and 216 and 264 (horses), on which see Stern, *Le calendrier de 354*, 152–164; and Bastien, "Remarques"; as well as Hölscher, *Victoria Romana*, 84–86; Ronke, 238–242; Bastien, *buste monétaire*, 1.282–283; and Curran, *Pagan City and Christian Capital*, 255, on consuls walking or being carried on chairs in a *processus consularis*, but riding in a *pompa circensis*. Mittag, "*Processus consularis*," esp. 448–451, also doubts that a consular emperor in *a quadriga* refers to the *processus consularis*, but notes there is no textual evidence for a consular *quadriga* during the *pompa circensis*. See Toynbee, *Roman Medallions*, 83–89; and Versnel, *Triumphus*, 302–303, who maintain that the consular *quadriga* coin-types pertain to the *processus consularis*. See too pp. 76 and 223–224 on the *processus consularis*.
115. E.g. Plut. *Mar.* 12.5: Marius; and Dio Cass. 48.4.5: L. Antonius and 55.8.2: Tiberius; and Versnel, *Triumphus*, esp. 284–303.
116. Euseb. *Hist. eccl.* 9.9 and *Vit. Const.* 1.33.1–41.2; Lactant. *De mort. pers.* 44.11; and CIL 6.1139 = ILS 694 = EDCS-17600785. Curran, *Pagan City and Christian Capital*, 76–90; and Kalas, *Restoration of the Roman Forum*, 47–74, trace Constantine's appropriation of Maxentian projects.
117. RIC 7 Trier #467–468 (Figure 60) and 469 (Victory and Constantine); and Toynbee, *Roman Medallions*, 52 and 88–89. See also RIC 7 Constantinople #1 and 103–106 and Nicomedia 164 and 170, images of Constantine in a horse *quadriga*.
118. Gnecchi 1: Diocleziano e Massimiano Erculeo #1–2; and Toynbee, *Roman Medallions*, 51–52 and 88. On the front-facing chariot in Roman art see Dunbabin, "Victorius Charioteer," 70–72.
119. See Latham, "Representing Ritual," briefly treating this shift.
120. RIC 2.1^2 Vespasian #1370–1372 (Figure 62) and 1383 (aureus).
121. Vespasian: RIC 2.1^2 #Vespasian 250, 364 (Figure 63), 388, 577, 595, and 1559; Titus: RIC 2.1^2 Vespasian #431, 451, 462, 475–476, 498, 611, and 635; Domitian: RIC 2.1^2 Vespasian #490 and 673: bust of Domitian on obverse and so likely Domitian in the *quadriga* on the reverse (contra RIC). Stern, *Le calendrier*

de 354, 161 n. 5, and Toynbee, *Roman Medallions*, 84, assign the origins of this imagery to the second century CE, while Bastien, "Remarques," traces it back to the Flavians.

122. RIC 2.1[2] Domitian #561, 700–701, 748–749, and 783.
123. RIC 2 Trajan #48, 72, 77, 86–87, 90, 137–141, and 458.
124. RIC 3 Antoninus Pius #93a–b, on which see Stern, *Le calendrier de 354*, 156–158 and pl. XXXI.4; and see also RIC 3 Antoninus Pius #161 (COS on obverse, but no reverse legend) and 766–767: Antoninus Pius alone.
125. RIC 3 Antoninus Pius #430, 491, 1246–1247 (COS on obverse, but SC on reverse), 1360, and 1364.
126. RIC 3 M. Aurelius #940, 1455, and 1505 (Verus alone, but SC on reverse).
127. RIC 3 M. Aurelius #1183 (Marcus Aurelius and Commodus), 1553, and 1563–1564, on which see Bastien, "Remarques," 26–27.
128. RIC 3 Commodus #213, 306, 319, 353, 376, 464, and 577 and, crowned by Victory, 558, 568, and 615.
129. RIC 4.1 Caracalla #77, 87, 103–104, 210, 499a (Figure 65), and 506.
130. Geta: RIC 4.1 Geta #28, 63 and 66; Macrinus: RIC 4.2 Macrinus #36, 47–48, 152–153, and 160–163 (all with Victory); Elagabalus: RIC 4.2 Elagabalus #35, 54–55, 170–171, 174–175, 180, 182–183, 308–313, 316–317, 331, and 337–338 without Victory and 26A, 36, and 296–298 with Victory; and Severus Alexander: RIC 4.2 Severus Alexander # 15–17, 56–56A, 98–99, 121, 384–385, 448, 452, 471, 495–498, and 499 (COS in legend, but accompanied by soldiers per RIC).
131. RIC 4.2 Maximinus: #2, 27–29 (Victory and 28 with a helmeted soldier), and 114 (Victory).
132. Gnecchi II: Gordiano Pio #27, on which see Perassi, "Medaglioni romani," 400–403; and Bergmann, "Pictorial Narratives," 379–380, who both see a triumphal procession; RIC 4.3 Gordian III #50B, 135 (Victory and soldiers), 139 (Victory), 173, 276A-B, 284, and 320–322 (Victory and 321–322 with soldiers).
133. Philip the Arab: Gnecchi 1: Filippo Padre #2 = RIC 4.3 Philip I #11; Trebonius Gallus and Volusian: RIC 4.3 Trebonius Gallus #98 (Victory and soldiers); Gallienus: RIC 5.1 Gallienus Joint Reign #313 (Victory) and RIC 5.1 Gallienus Sole Reign #20, 150, 154, 412–413, and 454 (Victory); Carinus: RIC 5.2 Carinus Augustus #226; Numerian: RIC 5.2 Numerianus Augustus #427; and Postumus: RIC 5.2 Postumus #256–257, on Postumus see Gricourt and Hollard, "date du quatrième consulat," who also agree that a consular emperor in a *quadriga* is a *pompa circensis*.
134. Gnecchi 2: Probo #12–13 (six horses) and 14 (*quadriga*); and RIC 5.2 Probus #1, 247, 579, 614–616, and 914: standard consular *quadriga*.
135. RIC 7 Constantinople #103–106 (Figure 67) and Nicomedia 170.
136. Constantius II: RIC 8 Thessalonica #145 and Antioch 77–78; Constantius II and Constans: RIC 8 Aquileia #42 (no *sparsio*, soldiers as groomsmen); Valentinian I: RIC 9 Mint of Constantinopolis #1 (Victory); Valentinian II: RIC 9 Treveri #89; and Eugenius: RIC 9 Treveri #100. Bastien, "Remarques," 28–29, argues that a series of six-horse chariot scenes (e.g. RIC 8 Antioch #67–68; RIC 9 Rome #25; and RIC 10 Arcadius #4–5) do not pertain to the *pompa circensis*.
137. Humphrey, *Roman Circuses*, 172, on the *carceres*; and Marchet, "*Mittere mappam*," on third-century CE *mappa* imagery.
138. RIC 6 Ticinum #56–57 (56a = Figure 68), Aquileia 63b–64, Serdica 10 and 14–15, and Alexandria 57–58. RIC 5.1 Tacitus #120 may have the emperor Tacitus holding a *mappa* on the obverse. On imperial busts and *mappae*, see Bastien, *buste monétaire*, 1.296–299 and 2. 535–540, who considers Diocletian the First example.
139. RIC 7 Trier #353, Siscia 132–133 and 139, Heraclea 14–49 (I^1 or J^1 obverse busts with *mappa* per p. 88), and p. 768: sv mappa (J^2), mappa and sceptre (J^3), mappa, sceptre, and globe (J^1) with examples for Constantine I, Constantine II, Crispus, Licinius, and Licinius II; RIC 8 T and Y obverse busts (not listed in index) and Antioch #204–206; RIC 9 p. 324: index sv mappa; RIC 10 pp. 494–496: sv emperor; and DOCLRE: Arcadius #72–74, Theodosius II 347, 370–376, 378, 391, and 428, Leo I 530–531 and 556–559, and in the west Valentinian III 836–838, 856, and 858. See pp. 208 with Figures 71–74 on "consular diptychs" with similar and longer-lived imagery.
140. Justinian, *Nov.* 105.*praef.* and 1 (see also pp. 170–171 and 177–178); CJ 12.3.2 (Majorian's law); and CTh 15.5.2 and 15.9.1 (earlier laws).

141. Theodosius II: RIC 10 Theodosius II #233–245 (237 = Figure 69); and DOCLRE Theodosius II #370–376, and 378, on which see Jiménez Sánchez, "liturgie impériale," 191–192. See also Bastien, *buste monétaire*, 1.300 and 2.527–528. RIC 9 Mint of Thessalonica #1–3 (364–367 CE) has an emperor holding a *mappa* on the obverse and the emperor holding a *labarum* (a Christian symbol) on the reverse, but seemingly only in the early fifth century CE did the two appear on the same side.

142. Valentinian III: RIC 10 Valentinian III #2033–2037 (2036 from Ravenna = Figure 70) and 2046 with empress; and DOCLRE Valentinian III #856 and 858. Interestingly RIC 10 Valentinian III #2032 (COS II in 426 CE) is very similar except that the scepter is topped by an eagle.

143. In coinage, such imagery seems to have faded earlier: e.g. RIC 10 Majorian #2601–2603 (Ravenna mint 457–461 CE); and RIC 10 Anthemius #2806 (Rome 468 CE).

144. John Malalas, *Chronographia* 13.8: ποιήσας ἑαυτῷ ἄλλην στήλην ξοάνου κεχρυσωμένην βαστάζουσαν τῇ δεξιά αὐτοῦ χειρὶ τὴν τύχην τῆς αὐτῆς πόλεως καὶ αὐτὴν κεχρυσωμένην, <ἣν> ἐκάλεσεν Ἄνθουσαν, κελεύσας κατὰ τὴν αὐτὴν ἡμέραν τοῦ γενεθλιακοῦ ἱππικοῦ εἰσιέναι τὴν αὐτὴν τοῦ ξοάνου στήλην διριγευομένην ὑπὸ τῶν στρατιωτῶν μετὰ χλαμύδων καὶ καμπαγίων, πάντων κατεχόντων κηρούς, καὶ περιέρχεσθαι τὸ σχῆμα τὸν ἄνω καμπτὸν καὶ ἔρχεσθαι εἰς τὸ σκάμμα κατέναντι τοῦ βασιλικοῦ καθίσματος, καὶ ἐγειρεσθαι τὸν κατὰ καιρὸν βασιλέα καὶ προσκυνεῖν, ὡς θεωρεῖ τὴν αὐτὴν στήλην Κωνσταντίνου καὶ τῆς τύχης τῆς πόλεως (ed. Thurn, trans. Jeffreys, Jeffreys, and Scott), on which see Curran, *Pagan City and Christian Capital*, 255–256; and Bardill, *Constantine, Divine Emperor*, 151–158. John Malalas, *Chronographia* 13.7 compares the *kathisma* to the place from which emperors watched games at Rome (the *pulvinar* presumably); and see also *Chronicon Pascale* 328 CE and 330 CE: *kathisma* at Constantinople and *pulvinar* at Rome.

145. Dagron, *Naissance d'une capitale*, 307–309 (winged victory); Bauer, "Urban Space and Ritual," 34–36; and Kantirea, "Imperial Birthday," 45–47; and see also the eighth-century CE *Parastaseis Syntomoi Chronikai* 5, 38, and 56, for (confused) accounts of statues in procession at the hippodrome.

146. Heather, "New Men," on the Constantinopolitan elite; and on the hippodrome and its rituals, see Cameron, *Circus Factions*, 230–270; and Dagron, *Naissance d'une capitale*, 320–347, and *L'hippodrome de Constantinople*.

147. Symm. *Rel.* 9.5: *elephantos regios per conferta agmina equorum nobilium pompa praecessit* (ed. MGH, trans. adapted Barrow); and p. 62, on Apollo's horses.

148. CTh 15.4.1 (425 CE): *in animis concurrentum mentisque secretis nostrum numen et laudes vigere demonstrent; excedens cultura hominum dignitatem superno numini reservetur* (trans. Pharr).

149. August. *De civ. D.* 2.26 (p. 163).

150. P. Oxy. 34.2707 and 79.5215; P. Bingen 128; and P. Harrauer 56, on which see Menci, "progamma circense"; Morelli, "Programma del circo"; Nelis-Clément, "métiers du cirque," 296–297; Günkel, "Entertainment," 45–48; and Decker, "Wagenrennen," 354–356.

151. Cameron, *Circus Factions*, 213–214; and Curran, *Pagan City and Christian Capital*, 258, on a procession of Victories. See also Mountford, "A Day at the Races."

152. On statues of Victory and emperors, see Lavan, "Political Talismans?" 445–450 (Victory) and 457–468 (Imperial statues); and Humphrey, *Roman Circuses*, 267–269, on Victory in the circus.

153. J. Assmann, *Cultural Memory and Early Civilization*, 76–78.

154. Hönle and Henze, *Amphitheater und Stadien*, 89, fig. 56; and Fless, "Römische Prozessionen," #49.

155. Sapelli, "Basilica di Gunio Basso"; and Kalas, "Architecture and Élite Identity," 284–288, on the basilica and its decoration.

156. Lepelley, "Du triomphe à la disparition"; and Cameron, *Circus Factions*, 230–270.

157. On the circus imagery, see Vespignani, "cerimoniale imperiale"; Olovsdotter, *Consular Image*, 88–90 and 123–127; Mariotti, "spettacoli"; Engemann, "Spiele spätantiker"; as well as Cameron, *Last Pagans*, 730–742 and "Origin, Context, and Function."

158. Delbrück, *Consulardiptychen* #56; Volbach, *Elfenbeinarbeiten* #54; and Olovsdotter, *Consular Image*, 16–20, noting that although

the magistrate was a suffect instead of an ordinary consul, the iconography coheres with other consular ivories.

159. Spier, "Lost Consular Diptych"; Marchet, "*Mittere mappam*," 308; van den Hoek, "Peter, Paul, and a Consul"; and van den Hoek and Hermann, *Pottery, Pavements, and Paradise*, 133–147.
160. Delbrück, *Consulardiptychen* #32; Volbach, *Elfenbeinarbeiten* #31; and Olovsdotter, *Consular Image*, 30–34 and 149–152.
161. Delbrück, *Consulardiptychen* #6; Volbach, *Elfenbeinarbeiten* #5; Olovsdotter, *Consular Image*, 34–38; Cameron and Schauer, "Last Consul"; and Cameron, *Last Pagans*, 790, and esp. "Basilius and his Diptych."
162. Ensoli and La Rocca (ed.), *Aurea Roma* 12–13; and Marchet, "*Mittere mappam*," nn. 91–92.
163. See pp. 28, 89, and 155–156, on the race start.
164. RIC 10 Valentinian III #2179 (Petronius Maximus); and *Kontorniat-Medallions* #461. See Mittag, *Alte Köpfe*, 71–93 (spectacles) and 182–214 (creators and functions); and Holden, "Abduction of the Sabine Women," 122–125 (function).
165. *Kontorniat-Medallions* #641; and Landes (ed.), *Le cirque* #52. The size indicators in Figure 77 has reversed the sides.
166. See pp. 180–181.
167. Fless, "Römische Prozessionen," #36; *Trionfi romani* I.3.2; Tortorella, "Processione trionfale e circense," 304–305 and #9; and Madigan, *Ceremonial Sculptures*, 45–47.
168. Himmelmann, *Typologische Untersuchungen*, 39; Ronke #185; Fless, "Römische Prozessionen," #34; Reinsberg, *Sarkophage* #37; *Trionfi romani* I.3.7; and Madigan, *Ceremonial Sculptures*, 43–45.
169. RIC 8 Rome #487–488, 500–502, and 508–509 (labeled a *tensa*). See Alföldi, *Festival of Isis*, 22, and pl. 16.19–25, and #56–57, 75–77, 84–85, 111, 114, 158, 207, 209, 264, 297, 305, 339, 343a, and 373 (*thensae/tensae* associated with consular games on January 3); and Cameron, *Last Pagans*, 691–698, on "pagan" medallions.
170. RIC 8 Rome #488 (*mappa*); but Alföldi, *Festival of Isis* #56, suggests a branch.
171. Lawrence, "Circus Relief at Foligno" (ca. 250–275 CE); Humphrey, *Roman Circuses*, 246–248 (fourth century CE); Ronke #208 (250–275 CE); Landes (ed.), *Le cirque* #79 (end of second century CE); and Curran, *Pagan City and Christian Capital*, 253–254 (third or fourth century CE). See also Lawrence, "Circus Relief at Foligno," 130–131 and figures 13–14; Humphrey, *Roman Circuses*, 202–203 fig. 102 and 278; Szidet, *Teile eines historischen Frieses*, 31 and 38–40, on a relief with a supposed *tensa* on the *euripus* under a rectangular structure next to the obelisk. It is, however, a *biga*, not a *quadriga*, and lacks a pediment, and so it may not be a *tensa*, despite its seeming rectilinearity and figural decoration.
172. Himmelmann, *Typologische Untersuchungen*, 40; Ronke #186; Szidat, *Teile eines historischen Frieses*, 31 and 53–54; and Fless, "Römische Prozessionen," #41. Menzel, "Elfenbeinrelief mit Tensa-Darstellung," discusses a small-scale ivory copy of this very image.
173. See pp. 111–112 (*tensa* iconography) and pp. 115–116 (relief).
174. Himmelmann, *Typologische Untersuchungen*, 37–42; Ronke #183; Fless, "Römische Prozessionen," #35; Reinsberg, *Sarkophage* #115; *Trionfi romani* I.3.5; and Madigan, *Ceremonial Sculptures*, 47–50.
175. Himmelmann, *Typologische Untersuchungen*, 38–39; Ronke #204; Reinsberg, *Sarkophage* #2 (and also #42 from Ostia with similar imagery); *Trionfi romani* I.3.6; and Madigan, *Ceremonial Sculptures*, 50–52. Magna Mater was apparently transported in a cart during the *lavatio*, e.g. Ov. *Fast.* 4.345; Serv. *Ad georg.* 1.163; and Amm. Marc. 23.3.7, on which see e.g. Roller, *In Search of God the Mother*, 274.
176. Delbrueck, *Consulardiptychen* #59; Volbach, *Elfenbeinarbeiten* #56; and Olovsdotter, *Consular Image*, 170–172.
177. Cracco Ruggini, "Apoteosi e politica senatoria"; MacCormack, *Art and Ceremony*, 138–144; and Arce, "Imperatori divinizzati."
178. Both Cracco Ruggini "Apoteosi e politica senatoria"; and Ensoli and La Rocca (ed.), *Aurea Roma* #207, associate the elephant cart with the *pompa circensis*; and Cameron, *Last Pagans*, 719–728, argues that the ivory commemorates Symmachus.
179. Macrob. *Sat.* 1.23.13: *vehitur enim simulacrum dei Heliupolitani ferculo, uti vehuntur in pompa ludorum circensium deorum simulacra* (trans. adapted Kaster LCL), on which see Cameron, "Date and Identity of Macrobius."
180. Peter Chrysologus, *Serm.* 155: *gentiles deos suos . . . trahunt, distrahunt, pertrahunt* (CCSL).

181. Peter Chrysologus, *Serm.* 155a: *tota daemonum pompa procedit, idolorum tota producitur officina. . . . Figurant Saturnum, faciunt Iovem, formant Herculem, exponunt cum vernantibus suis Dianam, circumducunt Vulcanum verbis anhelantem turpitudines suas, et plura, quorum, quia portenta sunt, nomina sunt tacenda; quorum deformitates* (ed. CCSL, trans. adapted Palardy FC).
182. Arbesmann, "'Cervuli' and 'Anniculae,'" 111–115, speculates that it was a reconfigured *pompa circensis*; while Scheid, "réjouissances," 360–363, argues that it was a New Year's public masquerade, on which see further Graf, "Fights about Festivals," 179–181; contra Cameron, *Last Pagans*, 787–788, who considers the masquerade private. See pp. 59–61 on the folkloric figures.
183. Brown, "Aspects of the Christianization"; Salzman, *Making of a Christian Aristocracy*; and Chenault, "Rome Without Emperors."
184. See McLynn, "Crying Wolf," on the importance of classical heritage into the late fifth century CE; and Latham, "Making of a Papal Rome" and "From Literal to Spiritual Soldiers."
185. RIC 10 Valentinian III #2171–2176, 2184–2185, and 2186; *Kontorniat-Medallions* #459, 463–466, 470–472, and 474 (whose descriptions differ from RIC); and Simpson, "Musicians and the Arena," 638.
186. Καίτοι ἀνθρώπων μάλιστα πάντων ὧν ἡμεῖς ἴσμεν φιλοπόλιδες Ῥωμαῖοι τυγχάνουσιν ὄντες, περιστέλλειν τε τὰ πάτρια πάντα καὶ διασώζεσθαι ἐν σπουδῇ ἔχουσιν, ὅπως δὴ μηδὲν ἀφανίζηται Ῥώμῃ τοῦ παλαιοῦ κόσμου. οἵ γε καὶ πολύν τινα βεβαρβαρωμένοι αἰῶνα τάς τε πόλεως διεσώσαντο οἰκοδομίας καὶ τῶν ἐγκαλλωπισμάτων τὰ πλεῖστα, ὅσα οἷόν τε ἦν χρόνῳ τε τοσούτῳ τὸ μῆκος καὶ τῷ ἀπαμελεῖσθαι δι' ἀρετὴν τῶν πεποιημένων ἀντέχειν. ἔτι μέντοι καὶ ὅσα μνημεῖα τοῦ γένους ἐλέλειπτο ἔτι, ἐν τοῖς καὶ ἡ ναῦς Αἰνείου, τοῦ τῆς πόλεως οἰκιστοῦ, καὶ εἰς τόδε κεῖται, θέαμα παντελῶς ἄπιστον (ed. LCL, trans. Dewing/Kaldellis); and Muth, "Rom in der Spätantike," on republican cultural memory in late antiquity.
187. In general, see Ward-Perkins, *Classical Antiquity to the Middle Ages*, 38–48, on the decline of classical public building, which Rome managed to stave off longer than elsewhere in Italy.
188. Machado, "Building the Past"; Kalas, "Writing and Restoration" and *Restoration of the Roman Forum*; and Iara, "Lingering Sacredness."
189. See Kalas, *Restoration of the Roman Forum*, esp. 8–20 and 47–103, on the concept and practice of restoration.
190. CTh 15.1.11: *Intra urbem Romam aeternam nullus iudicum novum opus informet, quotiens serenitatis nostrae arbitria cessabunt. Ea tamen instaurandi, quae iam deformibus ruinis intercidisse dicuntur, universis licentiam damus* (trans. Pharr).
191. CTh 15.1.19 (376 CE): *Nemo praefectorum urbis aliorumve iudicum, quos potestas in excelso locat, opus aliquod novum in urbe Roma inclyta moliatur, sed excolendis veteribus intendat animum* (trans. Pharr).
192. Nazarius, *Pan. Lat.* 4(10).35.4: *Celeberrima quaeque Urbis novis operibus enitescunt, nec obsoleta modo per vetustatem redivivo cultu insigniuntur, sed illa ipsa quae antehac magnificentissima putabantur nunc auri luce fulgentia indecoram maiorum parsimoniam prodiderunt* (ed. and trans. Nixon/Rodgers).
193. Procop. *Goth.* 7.22.9: Ῥώμη . . . μεγίστη τε καὶ ἀξιολογωτάτη (ed. LCL, trans. Dewing/Kaldellis).
194. Cassiod. *Var.* 8.31.7: *redeant igitur civitates in pristinum decus* (ed. MGH, trans. Barnish TTH).
195. Grig, "Imagining the Capitolium"; and Moralee, "Hill of Many Names."
196. Auson. *Ord. nob. urb.* 19.17: *aurea . . . Capitoli culmina* (LCL).
197. Amm. Marc. 16.10.14: *Iovis Tarpei delubra, quantum terrenis divina praecellunt* and 22.16.12: *Capitolium, quo se venerabilis Roma in aeternum attollit* (trans. adapted Rolfe LCL).
198. Cassiod. *Var.* 7.6.1: *Capitolia celsa conscendere hoc est humana ingenia superata vidisse* (MGH). Rome and the Capitol remained marvels, on which see Edwards, *Writing Rome*, esp. 96–102.
199. Lactant. *Div. Inst.* 1.11.49: *Capitolium suum id est summum caput religionum publicarum nihil esse aliud quam inane monumentum* (ed. CSEL, trans. Bowen/Garnsey).
200. Jer. *Ep.* 107.1: *Auratum squalet capitolium* (LCL).
201. Prudent. *C. Symm.* 1.579–586.
202. Paulinus of Nola, *Carm.* 19.68–70: *incusso Capitolia culmine nutant. / in vacuis simulacra tremunt squalentia templis / vocibus icta piis* (ed. CSEL, trans. adapted Walsh).

203. Zos. 5.38.5. The following references have been consulted on each site, building, or monument, which will only be cited to make a specific point (as previously, see chapter 3 n. 46 and chapter 4 n. 130): D-S; P-A; Lugli, *Roma antica* and *Itinerario di Roma antica*; Nash, *Pictorial Dictionary of Ancient Rome*; Coarelli, *Foro Romano, Foro Boario,* and *Rome and Environs*; Richardson; LTUR; Claridge, *Rome*; Gros, *L'architecture romaine*; and Romano, "Digital Augustan Rome."
204. Procop. *Vand.* 3.5.4: καὶ τοῦ τέγους τὴν ἡμίσειαν ἀφείλετο μοῖραν. τοῦτο δὲ τὸ τέγος χαλκοῦ μὲν τοῦ ἀρίστου ἐτύγχανεν ὄν, χρυσοῦ δὲ αὐτῷ ὑπερχυθέντος ἁδροῦ ὡς μάλιστα μεγαλοπρεπές τε καὶ θαύματος πολλοῦ ἄξιον διεφαίνετο (ed. LCL, trans. Dewing/Kaldellis).
205. Excerpta Sangallensia: *p. c. Iustini Aug. IIII anno. De Neapolim egressus Narsis ingressus Romam et deposuit palatii eius statuam et Capitolium* (Having left Naples and entered Rome, Narsis removed/deposited his statue from the Palatine and Capitolium, ed. MGH:AA *Chron. min.* 1.336), on which see P-A sv Iuppiter Optimus Maximus Capitolinus, Aedes; Richardson sv Iuppiter Optimus Maximus Capitolinus, Aedes; and LTUR sv Iuppiter Optimus Maximus Capitolinus, aedes (fasi tardo-Repubblicane e di età imperiale), which all cite this moment as the final spoliation of the temple, though the Latin is ambiguous.
206. CIL 6. 41318 = ILS 1222 = EDCS-01000445 = LSA-1416, on which see Salzman, *Making of a Christian Aristocracy*, 31–35; and Chenault, "Statues of Senators," 107–108, noting that senators were typically honored in the forum of Trajan.
207. Jer. *Ep.* 23.2: *ille, quem ante paucos dies dignitatum omnium culmina praecedebant, qui, quasi de subiectis hostibus triumpharet, Capitolinas ascendit arces, quem plausu quodam et tripudio populus romanus excepit* (CSEL).
208. Boethius, *Philos. Consol.* 2.3.25–30: *si quis rerum mortalium fructus ullum beatitudinis pondus habet, poteritne illius memoria lucis quantalibet ingruentium malorum mole deleri, cum duos pariter consules liberos tuos domo provehi sub frequentia patrum, sub plebis alacritate vidisti* (trans. Tester LCL); and, on the *processus consularis*, see pp. 76 and 197–198.
209. CIL 6.102 = ILS 4003 = EDCS-17200200 = LSA-1503, on which see Kahlos, "Restoration Policy"; and Bruggisser, "Sacro-saintes statues."
210. CIL 6.937 = ILS 3326 = EDCS-17301056: *Senatus populusque Romanus / incendio consumptum restituit.*
211. CIL 6.89 = ILS 3781 = EDCS-17200190: SPQR / *aedem Concordiae vetustate conlapsam / in meliorem faciem opere et cultu splendidiore restituit.*
212. On these restorations, see Ward-Perkins, *Classical Antiquity to Middle Ages*, 85–91; Machado, "Building the Past," esp. 169–170; and Kalas, "Writing and Restoration," 33–37, and *Restoration of the Roman Forum*, 125–140.
213. Kalas, *Restoration of Roman Forum*, 137–138, posits a possible restoration; though LTUR sv Castor, Aedes, Templum, suggests that it was in ruins in the fourth century CE.
214. Nora, "General Introduction," (see pp. 72–73 and 137).
215. For apposite remarks on the forum of Ostia, see Boin, *Ostia in Late Antiquity*, 145–154.
216. LTUR sv Vespasianus, Divus, Templum; and Symm. *Ep.* 5.54.3 (396–397 CE), on the column of Maenius.
217. On the Forum, Bauer, *Stadt, Platz und Denkmal*; Machado, "Building the Past"; and Kalas, *Restoration of the Roman Forum.*
218. J. Assmann, *Cultural Memory*, 76–78 and *Religion and Cultural Memory*, 24–30; and Gowing, *Empire and Memory*; and Gallia, *Remembering the Roman Republic*, on the memory of the republic.
219. Kalas, *Restoration of the Roman Forum*, 31–39, 41–45, and 85–87.
220. Machado, "Building the Past," 175–178; Spera, "realtà archeologica," 127–142; and Kalas, *Restoration of the Roman Forum*, 141–165.
221. CIL 6.1718 = ILS 5522 = EDCS-18100525: a post-410 CE renovation recalling the late-fourth-century CE construction of the *secretarium*.
222. CIL 6.1698 = ILS 1257 = EDCS-18100505 = LSA-342: *auctoritate, prudentia atq(ue) / eloquentia*, on which Chenault, "Statues of Senators," 112–115; and Weisweiler, "Inscribing Imperial Power," 314–316.
223. Curran, "Moving Statues"; Lepelley, "musée des statues divines"; Machado, "Building the Past," 179–185; Coates-Stephens, "Reuse of

Ancient Statuary"; and Kalas, *Restoration of the Roman Forum*, 105–124.

224. CIL 33856 = ILS 8935 = EDCS-24100628 = LSA-1388: *Marti Invicto patri / et aeternae urbis suae / conditoribus*; and Festus 184L: *lapis niger* as tomb of Romulus, on which see Curran, *Pagan City and Christian Capital*, 60–61; and Machado, "Religion as Antiquarianism," esp. 343.

225. E.g. RIC 6 Roma #189–190 (wolf with twins).

226. CIL 6.526 = ILS 3132 = EDCS-17300674 = LSA-791: *simulacrum Minerbae . . . pro / beatitudine temporis*, on which Machado, "Religion as Antiquarianism," 331–333; Kalas, "Writing and Restoration," 42–43; Lavan, "Political Talismans?" 455–457; and Iara, "Lingering Sacredness." See Stewart, *Statues in Roman Society*, 20–28; and Estienne, "*Simulacra deorum*," 258–259, on *simulacrum* as divine image.

227. Ambrose, *Ep.* 73.31 (18.31): *Non illis satis sunt lavacra, non porticus, non plateae occupatae simulacris?* (ed. CSEL, trans. adapted Liebeschuetz TTH).

228. Cassiod. *Var.* 7.13.1 (chapter 3 n. 79). On statues in the Forum, see Bauer, *Stadt, Platz und Denkmal*, 72–79 and 401–408; Niquet, *Monumenta virtutum titulique*, 20–22 and table 1; Kalas, "Writing and Restoration"; Chenault, "Statues of Senators"; Weisweiler, "Equality to Asymmetry"; *Visualizing Statues*; LSA; and n. 223 above.

229. CIL 6.10040 = EDCS-19200310: Polyclitus; CIL 6.10041 = EDCS-19200311: Praxiteles; and CIL 6.10042 = EDCS-19200312: Timarchus.

230. CIL 6. 1653a = EDCS-18100452 = LSA-1328: *curavit*; CIL 6.1653b = EDCS-18100453 = LSA-1329; CIL 6.1653c = EDCS-18100454 = LSA-1330; CIL 6.31880a = EDCS-18100455 = LSA-1331; CIL 6.31880b = EDCS-18100456; CIL 6.31881 = EDCS-18100457 = LSA-1332; CIL 6.37107 = EDCS-18100458 = LSA-1333 (in front of the basilica Aemilia); and CIL 6.37108 = EDCS-18100459 = LSA-1334, on which see Machado, "Building the Past," 179–185; and Kalas, *Restoration of the Roman Forum*, 111–117, on the basilica Aemilia; though LSA (Machado) places them further east. On the basilica Aemilia, see Spera, "realtà archeologica," 121–123; and Lipps, "Alarichs Goten," who casts doubt on the traditional story of the basilica.

231. CIL 6.1156b = ILS 5537 = EDCS-17600799 = LSA-1277; CIL 6.1658d = EDCS-18100466 = LSA-1342; CIL 6.31886 = EDCS-19900333 = LSA-1362, which all name the basilica Iulia; and CIL 6.3864a = ILS 9354 = EDCS-19900200 = LSA-1358; and CIL 6.3864b = EDCS-19900201 = LSA-1359, which both indicate an unidentified most celebrated location, but were found near the temple of Faustina and Antoninus Pius; and Chapter 3 n. 81 on famous and frequented places (*locus celeberrimus*).

232. CIL 6.1658a = EDCS-18100464 = LSA-1340; CIL 6.1658b = EDCS-18100465 = LSA-1341; CIL 6.1658e = EDCS-18100467: [. . . *prov*]*isis statuis* (having setting up statues), but not found in the Forum; CIL 6.41337 = EDCS-01000468 = LSA-1433; and CIL 6.41338 = EDCS-01000469 = LSA-1578: unknown original location. LSA (Machado) assigns many of these statue bases to the basilica Iulia, but Bauer, *Stadt, Platz und Denkmal*, 35; and Kalas, *Restoration of the Roman Forum*, 118–121, argue for the basilica Aemilia.

233. CIL 6.41394 = EDCS-01000529 = LSA-1524 (457–472 CE).

234. CIL 6.1779a = EDCS-18100594 = LSA-1409.

235. CIL 6.41398 = EDCS-01000534 = LSA-1525 (Petronius Maximus); and CIL 6.41344a = EDCS-01000477 = LSA-1797, on which see Machado, "Building the Past," 173–179; and Chenault, "Statues of Senators," esp. 124–129 and table D.

236. Rut. Nam. 1.575–578: *oblata mihi sancti genitoris imago, / Pisani proprio quam posuere foro. / laudibus amissi cogor lacrimare parentis: / fluxerunt madidis gaudia maesta genis* (trans. Duff LCL), on which see Machado, "Public Monuments," esp. 237–239; and, on statues in the Forum, pp. 79–80 (Gaius Gracchus wept in front of his father's statue, Plut. *C. Gracch.* 14.4) and p. 141.

237. Machado, "Building the Past," 161–173; Weisweiler, "Equality to Asymmetry," 332–336; and Kalas, *Restoration of the Roman Forum*, 75–103.

238. Constantine: CIL 6.1141 = ILS 698 = EDCS-17600787 = LSA-1263; Constantius: CIL 6.1158 = ILS 731 = EDCS-17600800 =

LSA-838; Theodosius: CIL 6.36959 = EDCS-19800531 = LSA-1374; Thermantia: CIL 6.36960 = ILS 8950 = EDCS-19800532 = LSA-2667; Valentinian II: CIL 6.3791a = EDCS-19000535 = LSA-1356; and Arcadius: CIL 6.3791b = ILS 789 = EDCS-19900156 = LSA-1357, on which Weisweiler, "Equality to Asymmetry," fig. 4; and Kalas, *Restoration of Roman Forum*, fig. 3.1.

239. CIL 6.41405 = EDCS-01000542. See Machado, "Building the Past," table 4; *Visualizing Statues*: chronological tab; and Chenault, "Statues of Senators," table D.

240. CIL 6.1730 = ILS 1277 = EDCS-18100539 = LSA-1436; and Claud. *Cons. Stil.* 1.116–122 and *Cons. Hon.* VI 578–583.

241. Coates-Stephens, "Reuse of Ancient Statuary," 183–184; and Machado, "Public Monuments," esp. 243–246.

242. Beckmann, "Galleries on Honorary Arches," 336.

243. See McLynn, "Crying Wolf," on the late-antique Lupercalia.

244. Cerrito, "Contributo."

245. Mulryan, "Temple of Flora."

246. *Curiosum Urbis Romae: XII Portas*; and *Notitia Urbis Romae: XII Portas* (ed. Valentini and Zucchetti). See also Plin. *HN* 3.66; and Obsequens 70, who both mentioned, but did not locate the twelve gates.

247. Smith (ed.), *Dictionary of Greek and Roman Antiquities* sv Circus suggests that the "entrance in the centre [was] called *porta pompae*; because it was the one through which the Circensian procession entered." Neither Humphrey, *Roman Circuses*, 132–151, esp. 136–137 and 141; nor LTUR sv Circus Maximus assign the larger, central gate a precise function; while Marcattili, *Circo Massimo*, 183, suggests ceremonial use.

248. Humphrey, *Roman Circuses*, 582–602; and Pisani Sartorio, "cirque de Maxence."

249. CIL 6.3038 = EDCS-19400038: *ad portas / ad pompas*. Baillie Reynolds, *Vigiles of Imperial Rome*, 55–58, argues that the seventh cohort was responsible for regio XI (the Circus); while Sablayrolles, *Libertinus miles*, 278–281 and 377: places the seventh cohort in the fourteenth and ninth regions in the third century CE, though jurisdictions could change, and notes that the firefighters provided illumination for some ritual procession.

250. Auson. *Ep.* 13.12: *excepto, medium quod patet ad stadium* (trans. adapted Evelyn-White LCL).

251. Sid. Apoll. *Carm.* 23.317 (written ca. 462–466 CE): *ianua consulumque sedes*; and Gillet, "Rome, Ravenna," esp. 142–148, on Valentinian's III's (the emperor under whom these races would have taken place) sojourns in Rome.

252. Claud. *Cons. Hon. VI* 616: *plebis adoratae ... fragor* (LCL); and Rut. Namat. 201: *attonitae resonant Circensibus aures* (LCL).

253. Humphrey, *Roman Circuses*, 126–131; Ciancio Rossetta, "Circo Massimo"; and Tantillo, "munera."

254. Aur. Vict. *Caes.* 40.27: *Circus Maximus excultus mirifice* (ed. Teubner, trans. Bird TTH); and Nazarius, *Pan. Lat.* 4(10).35.5: *sublimes porticus et rutilantes auro columnae* (ed. and trans. Nixon/Rodgers).

255. Amm. Marc. 17.4.15: *sphaera superponitur ahenea, aureis lamminis nitens* (trans. Rolfe LCL), on which see Humphrey, *Roman Circuses*, 287–289; and Marcattili, *Circo Massimo*, 233–239.

256. *Expositio totius mundi* 55.

257. Humprey, *Roman Circuses*, 246–254; and Curran, *Pagan City and Christian Capital*, 236–251.

258. Symm. *Rel.* 23.9: *ad circi secretarium*; CIL 6.40782a = EDCS-00900515 = LSA-1549 (statue base); CIL 6.40782b = EDCS-00900515 = LSA-1550 (statue base); CIL 6.1655b = EDCS-18100461 = LSA-1337 (statue base); and CIL 6.41388 = EDCS-01000522 (structural repairs), on which see Humphrey, *Roman Circuses*, 129; Curran, *Pagan City and Christian Capital*, 234–235; and Lim, "Inventing Secular Space," 71.

259. Bowes, "Christians in the Amphitheater," on the rarity of such installations; and see also Sales-Carbonell, "Roman Spectacle Buildings."

260. Procop. *Goth.* 7.37.4 (n. 58 above); and Cassiod. *Var.* 3.51, on which Fauvinet-Ranson, *Decor civitatis, decor italiae*, 329–344. See Jiménez Sánchez, *juegos paganos*, 331–335, on the decline of circus games in Rome and Italy.

261. *Kontorniat-Medallions* #182; Gnecchi 2: Constanzo II #16; Bergmann, "Pictorial Narratives," 383–384; and Holden, "Abduction of the Sabine Women," with a catalog.
262. Symm. Rel. 9.6: *fremitum Murciae vallis ... delenimenta circensium finitimorum conubium praestiterunt* (ed. MGH, trans. adapted Barrow).
263. See pp. 170–171 and 177–178.
264. Latham, "Making of a Papal Rome" and "From Literal to Spiritual."
265. Benjamin of Tudela, *Itinerary of Benjamin of Tudela*, 12–13 (trans. Adler), on which see Vespignani, *Simbolismo magia e sacralità dello spazio Circo*, 54 n. 121; and Dagron, *L'hippodrome*, 25–27.

BIBLIOGRAPHY

Abaecherli, Aline Louise. "*Fercula, carpenta*, and *tensae* in the Roman Procession." *Bollettino dell'Associazione Internazionale Studi Mediterranei* 6:1–28, 1935–1936.

Abaecherli, Aline Louise. "Imperial Symbols on Certain Flavian Coins." *Classical Philology* 30:131–140, 1935.

Adkin, Neil. "'*Heri catechumenus, hodie pontifex*' (Jerome, *Epist.* 69.9.4)." *Acta Classica* 36:113–117, 1993.

Adornato, Gianfranco. "L'area sacra di S. Omobono: Per una revisione dell documentazione archeologica." *Mélanges de l'École française de Rome: Antiquité* 115:809–835, 2003.

Alcock, Susan. *Archaeologies of the Greek Past: Landscape, Monuments, and Memories.* New York: Cambridge University Press, 2002.

Aldrete, Gregory. *Gestures and Acclamations in Ancient Rome.* Baltimore: Johns Hopkins University Press, 1999.

Alföldi, Andreas. *Caesar in 44 v. Chr.* Bonn: Habelt, 1985.

Alföldi, Andreas. "[Review] Divus Julius by Stefan Weinstock." *Gnomon* 47:154–179, 1975.

Alföldi, Andreas. *A Festival of Isis in Rome under the Christian Emperors of the IVth Century.* Budapest: Institute of Numismatics and Archeology of the Pázmány-University, 1937.

Alföldi, Andreas. "[Review] Salomonson (J. W.). *Chair, Sceptre and Wreath.*" *Revue belge de philologie et d'histoire* 37:1074–1078, 1959.

Alföldi, Andreas. *Die zwei Lorbeerbäume des Augustus.* Bonn: Habelt, 1973.

Amiotti, Gabriella. "Religione e politica nell'iniziazione romana: L'assunzione della toga virile." In *Religione e politica nel mondo antico*, edited by Marta Sordi, 131–140. Milan: Università Cattolica del Sacro Coure, 1981.

Ando, Clifford. *Imperial Ideology and Provincial Loyalty in the Roman Empire.* Berkeley: University of California Press, 2000.

Ando, Clifford. "Introduction to Part IV: Theology." In *Roman Religion*, edited by Clifford Ando, 141–146. Edinburgh: Edinburgh University Press, 2003.

Ando, Clifford. *The Matter of the Gods: Religion and the Roman Empire.* Berkeley: University of California Press, 2008.

Ando, Clifford. "The Ontology of Religious Institutions." *History of Religions* 50:54–79, 2010.

Ando, Clifford, ed. *Roman Religion.* Edinburgh: Edinburgh University Press, 2003.

André, Jacques. "Glanures de lexicologie latine." *Archivio glottologico italiano* 49:67–76, 1964.

André, J.–M. "Les *Ludi Scaenici* et la politique des spectacles au début de l'ère antonine." In *Actes du IXe Congrés (Rome 13–18 avril 1973) de l'Association Guillaume Budé*, edited by Association Guillaume Budé, 468–479. Paris: Les Belles Lettres, 1975.

Arata, Francesco Paolo. "Nuove considerazioni a proposito del Tempio di Giove Capitolino." *Mélanges de l'École française de Rome: Antiquité* 122:585–624, 2010.

Arbesmann, Rudolph. "The 'Cervuli' and 'Anniculae' in Caesarius of Arles." *Traditio* 35:89–119, 1979.

Arce, Javier. "Imperatori divinizzati." In *Aurea Roma: Dalla città pagana alla città cristiana*, edited by Serena Ensoli and Eugenio La Rocca, 244–248. Rome: "L'Erma" di Bretschneider, 2000.

Arena, Patrizia. "Il Circo Massimo come microcosmo dell'impero attraverso la ripartizione dei posti." In *Forme di aggregazione nel mondo romano*, edited by Elio Lo Cascio and Giovanna Daniela Merola, 31–48. Bari: Edipuglia, 2007.

Arena, Patrizia. *Feste e rituali a Roma: Il principe incontra il popolo nel Circo Massimo*. Bari: Edipuglia, 2010.

Arena, Patrizia. "The *Pompa Circensis* and the *Domus Augusta* (1st–2nd Century A.D.)." In *Ritual Dynamics and Religious Change in the Roman Empire*, edited by Olivier Hekster, Sebastian Schmidt-Hofner, and Christian Witschel, 77–93. Leiden: Brill, 2009.

Arena, Patrizia. "Si può parlare di una politica imperiale nel campo di rituali e cerimonie?" In *Interventi imperiali in campo economico e sociale: da Augusto al Tardoantico*, edited by Alfredina Storchi Marino and Giovanna Daniela Merola, 143–164. Bari: Edipuglia, 2009.

Ash, Rhiannon. "Victim and Voyeur: Rome as a Character in Tacitus' *Histories* 3." In *The Sites of Rome: Time, Space, and Memory*, edited by David Larmour and Diana Spencer, 211–237. New York: Oxford University Press, 2007.

Assmann, Aleida. *Cultural Memory and Western Civilization: Functions, Media, Archives*. New York: Cambridge University Press, 2011.

Assmann, Jan. "Communicative and Cultural Memory." In *Cultural Memory Studies: An International and Interdisciplinary Handbook*, edited by Astrid Erll and Ansgar Nünning, 109–118. Berlin: de Gruyter, 2008.

Assmann, Jan. *Cultural Memory and Early Civilization: Writing, Remembrance, and Political Imagination*. New York: Cambridge University Press, 2011.

Assmann, Jan. *Religion and Cultural Memory: Ten Studies*. Translated by Rodney Livingstone. Stanford: Stanford University Press, 2006.

Atchley, E. G. Cuthbert F. *A History of the Use of Incense in Divine Worship*. London: Longmans, Green and Co., 1909.

Auguet, Roland. *Cruelty and Civilization: The Roman Games*. New York: Routledge, 1972.

Auliard, Claudine. "La composition du cortège triomphal dans les rues de Rome: La marque des triomphateurs." In *La rue dans l'Antiquité: Définition, aménagement et devenir de l'Orient méditerranéen à la Gaule*, edited by Pascale Ballet, Nadine Dieudonné-Glad, and Catherine Saliou, 69–75. Rennes: Presses Universitaires de Rennes, 2008.

Auvray-Assayas, Clara. "Images mentales et représentations figurées: Penser les dieux au Ier siècle av. n. è." In *Images romaines: Actes de la table ronde organisée à l'École normale supérieure (24–26 octobre 1996)*, edited by Florence Dupont and Clara Auvray-Assayas, 299–310. Paris: Presses de l'École normale supérieure, 1998.

Bacchielli, Lidiano. "Un rilievo della collezione Castelli-Baldassini con rappresentazione di pompa trionfale." *Scienze dell'Antichità* 2:391–401, 1988.

Bahktin, Mikhail. *Rabelais and His World*. Translated by Hélène Iswolsky. Bloomington, IN: Indiana University Press, 1968.

Bailley, Donald Michael. *A Catalogue of the Lamps in the British Museum 2: Roman Lamps Made in Italy*. London: British Museum, 1980.

Baillie Reynolds, P. K. *The Vigiles of Imperial Rome*. London: Oxford University Press, 1926.

Ballet, Pascale, Nadine Dieudonné-Glad, and Catherine Saliou, ed. *La rue dans l'Antiquité: Définition, aménagement et devenir de l'Orient méditerranéen à la Gaule*. Rennes: Presses Universitaires de Rennes, 2008.

Balsdon, J. P. V. D. *Life and Leisure in Ancient Rome*. New York: McGraw-Hill, 1969.

Barchiesi, Alessandro, Jörg Rüpke, and Susan Stephens, ed. *Rituals in Ink: A Conference on Religion and Literary Production in Ancient Rome*. Munich: Franz Steiner, 2004.

Barchiesi, Alessandro and Walter Scheidel, ed. *The Oxford Handbook of Roman Studies*. New York: Oxford University Press, 2010.

Bardill, Jonathan. *Constantine, Divine Emperor of the Christian Golden Age*. New York: Cambridge University Press, 2012.

Barnish, S. J. B. "Transformation and Survival in the Western Senatorial Aristocracy, c. A.D. 400–700." *Papers of the British School at Rome* 56:120–155, 1988.

Barrow, R. H. *Prefect and Emperor: The Relationes of Symmachus A.D. 384*. Oxford: Clarendon Press, 1973.

Barton, Carlin. "Being in the Eyes: Shame and Sight in Ancient Rome." In *The Roman Gaze: Vision, Power and the Body*, edited by David Fredrick, 216–235. Baltimore, MD: Johns Hopkins University Press, 2002.

Bastien, Pierre. *Le buste monétaire des empereurs romains*. 3 vols. Wetteren: Éditions Numismatique Romaine, 1992.

Bastien, Pierre. "Remarques sur le *processus consularis* dans le monnayage romain." In *Italiam fato propugi: Hesperinaque venerunt litora: numismatic studies dedicated to Vladimir and Elvira Eliza Clain-Stefanelli*, edited by Richard Doty and Tony Hackens, 21–31. Louvain-la-Neuve: Département d'Archéologie et d'Histoire de l'Art, Séminaire de Numismatique Marcel Hoc, 1996.

Baudrillard, Jean. *Simulacra and Simulation*. Translated by Sheila Faria Glaser. Ann Arbor: University of Michigan Press, 1994.

Bauer, Franz Alto. *Stadt, Platz und Denkmal in der Spätantike: Untersuchungen zur Ausstattung des öffentlichen Raums in den spätantiken Städten Rom, Konstantinopel und Ephesos*. Mainz: Philip von Zabern, 1996.

Bauer, Franz Alto. "Urban Space and Ritual: Constantinople in Late Antiquity." *Acta ad archaeologiam et artium historiam pertinentia* 15:27–59, 2001.

Bayliss, Richard. "Usurping the Urban Image: The Experience of Ritual Topography in the Late Antique Cities of the Near East." In *TRAC 98: Proceedings of the Eighth Annual Theoretical Roman Archaeology Conference, Leicester 1998*, edited by Colin Forcey Patricia Baker, Sophia Jundi, and Robert Witcher, 59–71. Oxford: Oxbow Books, 1999.

Beacham, Richard. "The Emperor as Impresario: Producing the Pageantry of Power." In *The Cambridge Companion to the Age of Augustus*, edited by Karl Galinsky, 151–174. New York: Cambridge University Press, 2005.

Beacham, Richard. *The Roman Theatre and Its Audience*. Cambridge, MA: Harvard University Press, 1991.

Beacham, Richard. *Spectacle Entertainments of Early Imperial Rome*. New Haven: Yale University Press, 1999.

Beard, Mary. "Cicero and Divination: The Formation of a Latin Discourse." *Journal of Roman Studies* 76:33–46, 1986.

Beard, Mary. "A Complex of Times: No More Sheep on Romulus' Birthday." In *Roman Religion*, edited by Clifford Ando, 273–288. Edinburgh: Edinburgh University Press (original, 1987), 2003.

Beard, Mary. *Laughter in Ancient Rome: On Joking, Tickling, and Cracking Up*. Berkeley: University of California Press, 2014.

Beard, Mary. *The Roman Triumph*. Cambridge, MA: Harvard University Press, 2007.

Beard, Mary. "The Triumph of the Absurd: Roman Street Theatre." In *Rome the Cosmopolis*, edited by Catharine Edwards and Greg Woolf, 21–43. Cambridge: Cambridge University Press, 2003.

Beard, Mary. "Writing and Religion: *Ancient Literacy* and the Function of the Written Word in Roman Religion." In *Literacy in the Ancient World*, edited by John H. Humphrey, 35–58. Portsmouth, RI: Journal of Roman Archaeology, 1991.

Beard, Mary. "Writing Ritual: The Triumph of Ovid." In *Rituals in Ink: A Conference on Religion and Literary Production in Ancient Rome*, edited by Alessandro Barchiesi, Jörg Rüpke, and Susan Stephens, 115–126. Munich: Franz Steiner, 2004.

Beck, Hans. "Fabius Pictor, Quintus." In *The Encyclopedia of Ancient History*, edited by Roger Bagnall, Kai Brodersen, Craige B. Champion, Andrew Erskine, and Sabine Huebner, 2616–2618. Malden, MA: Wiley-Blackwell, 2013.

Beck, Hans. "Züge in die Ewigkeit. Prozessionen durch das republikanishe Rom." *Göttinger Forum für Altertumswissenschaft* 8:73–104, 2005.

Beck, Hans, Antonio Duplá, Martin Jehne, and Francisco Pina Polo, ed. *Consuls and* Res Publica*: Holding High Office in the Roman Republic*. New York: Cambridge University Press, 2011.

Beckmann, Martin. *Diva Faustina: Coinage and Cult in Rome and the Provinces*. New York: American Numismatic Society, 2012.

Beckmann, Martin. "Galleries on Honorary Arches in Rome." *Mitteilungen des Deutschen Archäologischen Instituts: Römische Abteilung* 116:331–341, 2010.

Behrwald, Ralf and Christian Witschel, ed. *Rom in der Spätantike: Historische Erinnerung in Städtischen Raum*. Stuttgart: Franz Steiner, 2012.

Belayche, Nicole. "Des lieux pour le 'profane' dans l'empire tardo-antique? Les fêtes entre *koinônia* sociale et espaces de rivalités religieuses." *Antiquité Tardive* 15:35–46, 2007.

Bell, Andrew. *Spectacular Power in the Greek and Roman City*. New York: Oxford University Press, 2004.

Bell, Catherine. "Performance." In *Critical Terms for Religious Studies*, edited by Mark C. Taylor, 205–224. Chicago: University of Chicago Press, 1998.

Bell, Catherine. *Ritual: Perspectives and Dimensions*. New York: Oxford University Press, 1997.

Bell, Catherine. *Ritual Theory, Ritual Practice*. New York: Oxford University Press, 1992.

Bell, Roslynne. "Revisiting the Pediment of the Palatine Metroön: A Vergilian Interpretation." *Papers of the British School at Rome* 77:65–99, 2009.

Bell, Sinclair. "Roman Chariot Racing: Charioteers, Factions, Spectators." In *A Companion to Sport and Spectacle in Greek and Roman Antiquity*, edited by Paul Christesen and Donald Kyle, 492–504. Malden, MA: Wiley-Blackwell, 2014.

Bendlin, Andreas. "Rituals of Beliefs? 'Religion' and the Religious Life of Rome." *Scripta Classica Israelica* 20:191–208, 2001.

Beneš, Carrie. "Whose SPQR? Sovereignty and Semiotics in Medieval Rome." *Speculum* 84:874–904, 2009.

Benoist, Stéphane. "L'espace urbain de Rome, comme lieu d'encadrement de la foule au premier siècle de l'Empire." In *La Rue, lieu de sociabilité? Rencontres de la Rue*, edited by Alain Leménorel, 215–223. Rouen: Université de Rouen, 1997.

Benoist, Stéphane. *La Fête à Rome au premier siècle de l'Empire: Recherches sur l'univers festif sous les règnes d'Auguste et des Julio-Claudiens*. Brussels: Latomus, 1999.

Benoist, Stéphane. "Images des dieux, images des hommes: Réflexions sur le 'culte impérial' au IIIe siècle." In *La "crise" de l'Empire romain de Marc Aurèle à Constantin: Mutations, continuités, ruptures*, edited by Marie-Henriette Quet, 27–64. Paris: Presses de l'université Paris-Sorbonne, 2006.

Benoist, Stéphane. "Le prince, les dieux et les hommes assemblés: réflexions sur les *spectacula* de la Rome impériale." In *La fête: La rencontre des dieux et des hommes: Actes du 2e colloque international de Paris, "La fête, la rencontre du sacré et du profane," organisé par les Cahiers Kubaba (Université de Paris I) et l'Institut catholique de Paris, 6 et 7 décembre 2002*, edited by Jorge Pérez Rey, Michel Mazoyer, Florence Malbran-Labat, and René Lebrun, 159–190. Paris: L'Harmattan, 2004.

Benoist, Stéphane. "Les processions dan la cité: de la mise en scène de l'espace urbain." In Roma illustrata: *Représentations de la ville*, edited by Philippe Fleury and Olivier Desbordes, 49–62. Caen: Presses universitaires de Caen, 2008.

Benoist, Stéphane. *Rome, le prince et la Cité: pouvior impérial et cérémonies publiques (Ier siècle av.—début du VIe siècle apr. J-C)*. Paris: Presses universitaires de France, 2005.

Benoist, Stéphane. "*Spectacula* et *romanitas*, du principat à l'empire Chrétien (note introductive)." In *Le jeux et les spectacles dans l'empire romain tardif et dans les royaumes barbares*, edited by Emmanuel Soler and Françoise Thelamon, 13–22. Rouen: Publications des universités de Rouen et du Havre, 2008.

Bergmann, Bettina. "Introduction: The Art of Ancient Spectacle." In *The Art of Ancient Spectacle*, edited by Bettina Bergmann and Christine Kondoleon, 9–35. Washington, D. C.: National Gallery of Art, 1999.

Bergmann, Bettina. "Pictorial Narratives of the Roman Circus." In *Le cirque romaine et son image*, edited by Jocelyne Nelis-Clément and Jean-Michel Roddaz, 361–391. Bourdeaux: Ausonius, 2008.

Bergmann, Bettina and Christine Kondoleon, ed. *The Art of Ancient Spectacle*. Washington, D. C.: National Gallery of Art, 1999.

Bernstein, Frank. "Complex Rituals: Games and Processions in Republican Rome." In *A Companion to Roman Religion*, edited by Jörg Rüpke, 222–234. Malden, MA: Wiley-Blackwell, 2007.

Bernstein, Frank. *Ludi publici: Untersuchgungen zur Entstehung und Entwicklung der öffentlichen Spiele im republikanische Rom*. Stuttgart: Frank Steiner, 1998.

Betts, Eleanor. "Towards a Multisensory Experience of Movement in the City of Rome." In *Rome, Ostia, Pompeii: Movement and Space*, edited by Ray Laurence and David Newsome, 118–132. New York: Oxford University Press, 2011.

Bodel, John. "Dealing with the Dead: Undertakers, Executioners and Potter's Fields in Ancient Rome." In *Death and Disease in the Ancient City*, edited by Valerie Hope and Eireann Marshall, 128–151. New York: Routledge, 2000.

Bodel, John. "Death on Display: Looking at Roman Funerals." In *The Art of Ancient Spectacle*, edited by Bettina Bergmann and Christine Kondoleon, 259–281. Washington, D. C.: National Gallery of Art, 1999.

Boin, Douglas. "Hellenistic 'Judaism' and the Social Origins of the 'Pagan-Christian' Debate." *Journal of Early Christian Studies* 22:167–196, 2014.

Boin, Douglas. "Late Antique *Divi* and Imperial Priests of the Late Fourth and Early Fifth Centuries." In *Pagans and Christians in Late Antique Rome: Conflict, Competition, and Coexistence in the Fourth Century*, edited by Michele Renée Salzman, Marianne Sághy, and Rita Lizzi Testa, 139–161. New York: Cambridge University Press, 2015.

Boin, Douglas. "The Memory of 'Peter' in Fourth-Century Rome: Church, Mausoleum, and Jupiter on the *Via Paenestina*." In *The Art of Empire: Christian Art in Its Imperial Context*, edited by Lee Jefferson and Robin Jensen, 87–114. Minneapolis, MN: Fortress Press, 2015.

Boin, Douglas. *Ostia in Late Antiquity*. New York: Cambridge University Press, 2013.

Bonamente, Giorgio. "Dall'imperatore divinizzato all'imperatore santo." In *Pagans and Christians in the Roman Empire: The Breaking of a Dialogue (IVth-VIth Century A.D.), Proceedings of the International Conference at the Monastery of Bose (October 2008)*, edited by Peter Brown and Rita Lizzi Testa, 339–370. Zürich: LIT, 2011.

Bonfante Warren, Larissa. "Roman Triumphs and Etruscan Kings: The Changing Face of the Triumph." *Journal of Roman Studies* 60:49–66, 1970.

Bonjour, Madeleine. *Terre natale: Études sur une composante affective de patriotisme romain*. Paris: Les Belles Lettres, 1975.

Bonnet, Corinne, Jörg Rüpke, and Paolo Scarpi, ed. *Religions Orientales – Culti Misterici: Neue Perspektiven – Nouvelles Perspectives – Prospettive Nuove*. Stuttgart: Franz Steiner, 2006.

Bourdieu, Pierre. *The Logic of Practice*. Translated by Richard Nice. Stanford: Stanford University Press, 1990.

Bourdieu, Pierre. *Outline of a Theory of Practice*. Translated by Richard Nice. Cambridge: Cambridge University Press, 1977.

Bowes, Kim. "Christians in the Amphitheater? The Christianization of Spectacle Buildings and Martyrial Memory." *Mélanges de l'École française de Rome: Moyen Âge* 126 (http://mefrm.revues.org/1807), 2014.

Boyancé, Pierre. "À propos de la *satura* dramatique." *Revue des études anciennes* 34:11–25, 1932.

Boyer, M. Christine. *The City of Collective Memory: Its Historical Imagery and Architectural Entertainments*. Cambridge, MA: MIT Press, 1994.

Bradbury, Scott. "Constantine and the Problem of Antipagan Legislation in the Fourth Century." *Classical Philology* 89:120–139, 1994.

Bradbury, Scott. "Julian's Pagan Revival and the Decline of Blood Sacrifice." *Phoenix* 49:331–356, 1995.

Brandt, J. Rasmus and Jon W. Iddeng, ed. *Greek and Roman Festivals: Content, Meaning, and Practice*. New York: Oxford University Press, 2012.

Bricault, Laurent and Francesca Prescendi. "Une 'théologie en images'?" In *Les religions orientales dans le monde grec et romain: Cent ans après Cumont (1906–2006): bilan historique et historiographique; Colloque de Rome, 16–18 Novembre 2006*, edited by C. Bonnet, V. Pirenne-Delforge and D. Praet, 63–79. Brussels: Belgisch Historisch Instituut te Rome, 2009.

Bridel, Philippe. "L'amphithéâtre d'Avenches: originalité de quelques aspects architecturaux et fonctionnels." *Études des Lettres* 1–2: 293–306, 2011.

Brint, Steven and Michele Renée Salzman. "Reflections on Political Space: The Roman Forum and Capitol Hill, Washington, D.C." *Places* 5:4–11, 1988.

Brodd, Jeffrey and Jonathan Reed, ed. *Rome and Religion: A Cross-Disciplinary Dialogue on the Imperial Cult*. Atlanta: Society of Biblical Literature, 2011.

Brown, Karen McCarthy. *Mama Lola: A Vodou Priestess in Brooklyn*. Berkeley: University of California Press, 1991.

Brown, Peter. "Aspects of the Christianization of the Roman Aristocracy." *Journal of Roman Studies* 51:1–11, 1961.

Brown, Peter. *Power and Persuasion: Towards a Christian Empire*. Madison, WI: University of Wisconsin Press, 1992.

Brown, Peter. *The Rise of Western Christendom: Triumph and Diversity, A.D. 200–1000*. 2nd ed. Malden, MA: Blackwell, 2003.

Brown, Peter. *Through the Eye of a Needle: Wealth, the Fall of Rome, and the Making of Christianity in the West, 350–550 AD*. Princeton: Princeton University Press, 2012.

Brown, T. S. *Gentlemen and Officers: Imperial Administration and Aristocratic Power in Byzantine Italy, A.D. 554–800*. London: British School at Rome, 1984.

Brugisser, Philippe. "'Sacro-saintes statues': Prétextat et la restauration du portique des *Dei consentes* à Rome." In *Rom in der Spätantike: Historische Erinnerung in städtischen Raum*, edited by Ralf Behrwald and Christian Witschel, 331–356. Stuttgart: Franz Steiner, 2012.

Bruit Zaidman, Louise and Pauline Schmitt Pantel. *Religion in the Ancient Greek City*. Translated by Paul Cartledge. New York: Cambridge University Press, 1992.

Brunt, P. A. "Philosophy and Religion in the Late Republic." In *Philosophia togata I: Essays on Philosophy and Roman Society*, edited by Miriam Griffin and Jonathan Barnes, 174–198. New York: Oxford University Press, 1989.

Buc, Philippe. *The Dangers of Ritual: Between Early Medieval Texts and Social Scientific Theory*. Princeton: Princeton University Press, 2002.

Buc, Philippe. "Ritual and Interpretation: The Early Medieval Case." *Early Medieval Europe* 9:183–210, 2000.

Burgarella, Filippo. "Il Senato." In *Roma nell'alto Medioevo: 27 aprile–1 maggio 2000*, 121–175. Spoleto: Centro italiano di studi sull'alto Medioevo, 2001.

Burkert, Walter. *Greek Religion*. Translated by John Raffan. *Cambridge, MA*: Harvard University Press, 1985.

Caldelli, Maria Letizia. "Associazioni di artisti a Roma: Una messa a punto." In *L'organisation des spectacles dans le monde Romain: Huit exposés suivis de discussions*, edited by Kathleen Coleman and Jocelyne Nelis-Clément, 131–166. Geneva: Fondation Hardt, 2012.

Calvino, Italo. *Invisible Cities*. Translated by William Weaver. New York: Harcourt, 1974.

Cameron, Alan. "Basilius and His Diptych Again: Career Titles, Seats in the Colosseum, and Issues of Stylistic Dating." *Journal of Roman Archaeology* 25:513–530, 2012.

Cameron, Alan. *Bread and Circuses: The Roman Emperor and His People*. London: King's College London, 1974.

Cameron, Alan. *Circus Factions: Blues and Greens at Rome and Byzantium*. Oxford: Clarendon Press, 1976.

Cameron, Alan. "The Date and Identity of Macrobius." *Journal of Roman Studies* 56:25–38, 1966.

Cameron, Alan. *The Last Pagans of Rome*. New York: Oxford University Press, 2011.

Cameron, Alan. "The Origin, Context, and Function of Consular Diptychs." *Journal of Roman Studies* 103:174–207, 2013.

Cameron, Alan and Diane Schauer. "The Last Consul: Basilius and His Diptych." *Journal of Roman Studies* 72:126–145, 1982.

Camillle, Michael. "Signs of the City: Place, Power, and Public Fantasy in Medieval Paris." In *Medieval Practices of Space*, edited by Barbara Hanawalt and Michal Kobialka, 1–36. Minneapolis, MN: University of Minnesota Press, 2000.

Cancik, Hubert. "Rome as Sacred Landscape: Varro and the End of Republican Religion in Rome." *Visible Religion* 4–5:250–265, 1985–1986.

Cancik, Hubert and Cancik-Lindemaier, Hildegard. "The Truth of Images: Cicero and Varro on Image Worship." In *Representation in Religion: Studies in Honor of Moshe Barasch*, edited by Jan Assmann and Albert I. Baumgarten, 43–61. Leiden: Brill, 2001.

Cancik, Hubert and Konrad Hitzl, ed. *Die Praxis der Herrscherverehrung in Rom und seinen Provinzen*. Tübingen: Mohr Siebeck, 2003.

Carson, Marvin. Introduction to *Transformative Power of Performance: A New Aesthetics*, by Erika Fischer-Lichte, 1–10. New York: Routledge, 2008.

Carson, Marvin. *Performance: A Critical Introduction*. 2nd ed. New York: Routledge, 2004.

Carter, Michael and Jonathan Edmondson. "Spectacle in Rome, Italy, and the Provinces." In *The Oxford Handbook of Roman Epigraphy*, edited by Christopher Bruun and Jonathan Edmondson, 537–558. New York: Oxford University Press, 2014.

Castelli, Elizabeth. *Martyrdom and Memory: Early Christian Culture Making*. New York: Columbia University Press, 2004.

Castrén, Paavo. "*Vici* and *Insulae*: The Homes and Addresses of the Romans." *Arctos* 34:7–21, 2000.

Cavalier, Laurence and Jacques des Courtils. "Degrés and gradins en bordure de rue: Aménagements pour les *pompai*?" In *La rue dans l'Antiquité: Définition, aménagement et devenir de l'Orient méditerranéen à la Gaule*, edited by Pascale Ballet, Nadine Dieudonné-Glad, and Catherine Saliou, 83–92. Rennes: Presses Universitaires de Rennes, 2008.

Çelik, Zeynep, Diane Favro, and Richard Ingersoll, ed. *Streets: Critical Perspectives on Public Space*. Berkeley: University of California Press, 1994.

Cerrito, Alessandra. "Contributo allo studio del *titulus Anastasiae*." In *Marmoribus vestita: Miscellanea in onore di Federico Guidobaldi*, edited by Olof Brandt and Philippe Pergola, 345–371. Vatican City: Pontificio Istituto di Archeologia Cristiana, 2011.

Certeau, Michel de. *The Practice of Everyday Life*. Translated by Steven Randall. Berkeley: University of California Press, 1984.

Chamberland, Guy. "La mémoire des spectacles: L'autoreprésentation des donateurs." In *L'organisation des spectacles dans le monde Romain: Huit exposés suivis de discussions*, edited by Kathleen Coleman and Jocelyne Nelis-Clément, 261–303. Geneva: Fondation Hardt, 2012.

Chaniotis, Angelos. "Processions in Hellenistic Cities: Contemporary Discourses and Ritual Dynamics." In *Cults, Creeds and Identities in the Greek City after the Classical Age*, edited by Onno van Nijf, Richard Alston, and Christina Williamson, 21–47. Leuven: Peeters, 2013.

Chaniotis, Angelos. "Rituals between Norms and Emotions: Rituals as Shared Experience and Memory." In *Ritual and Communication in the Greco-Roman World*, edited by Eftychia Stavrianopoulou, 211–238. Liége: Presses universitaires de Liége, 2006.

Chaniotis, Angelos, ed. *Ritual Dynamics in the Ancient Mediterranean: Agency, Emotion, Gender, Representation*. Stuttgart: Franz Steiner, 2011.

Chaniotis, Angelos. "Staging and Feeling the Presence of God: Emotion and Theatricality in Religious Celebrations in the Roman East." In *Panthée: Religious Transformations in the Roman Empire*, edited by Laurent Bricault and Corinne Bonnet, 169–189. Leiden: Brill, 2013.

Chankowski, Andrzej. "Processions et cérémonies d'accueil: Une image de la cité de la basse époque hellénistique?" In *Citoyenneté et participation à la basse époque hellénistique: Actes de la table ronde des 22 et 23 mai 2004, Paris BNF*, edited by Pierre Fröhlich and Christel Müller, 185–206. Geneva: Droz, 2005.

Chastagnol, André. "Sur les *sacerdotales* africains à la veille de l'invasion vandale." In *L'Africa romana: Atti del V Convegno di studio, 11–13 dicembre 1987, Sassari*, edited by Attilio Mastino, 101–110. Sassari: Università degli studi di Sassari, Dipartimento di Storia, 1987.

Chenault, Robert. "Rome without Emperors: The Revival of a Senatorial City in the Fourth Century CE." Ph.D., University of Michigan, 2008.

Chenault, Robert. "Statues of Senators in the Forum of Trajan and the Roman Forum in Late Antiquity." *Journal of Roman Studies* 102:103–132, 2012.

Christesen, Paul and Donald Kyle, ed. *A Companion to Sport and Spectacle in Greek and Roman Antiquity*. Malden, MA: Wiley-Blackwell, 2014.

Ciancio Rossetta, Paola. "Il Circo Massimo." In *Aurea Roma: Dalla città pagana alla città cristiana*, edited by Serena Ensoli and Eugenio La Rocca, 126–128. Rome: "L'Erma" di Bretschneider, 2000.

Ciancio Rossetto, Paola. "La ricostruzione architettonica del Circo Massimo: Dagli scavi alla maquette elettronica." In *Le cirque romaine et son image*, edited by Jocelyne Nelis-Clément and Jean-Michel Roddaz, 17–38. Bourdeaux: Ausonius, 2008.

Ciancio Rossetto, Paola and Marialetizia Bounfiglio. "Circo Massimo: Riflessioni e progetti." *Orizzonti* 8:19–41, 2007.

Claridge, Amanda. *Rome: An Oxford Archaeological Guide*. 2nd ed. New York: Oxford University Press, 2010.

Clarke, John. *Art in the Lives of Ordinary Romans: Visual Representation and Non-Elite Viewers in Italy, 100 B.C.–A.D. 315*. Berkeley: University of California Press, 2003.

Clavel-Lévêque, Monique. *L'Empire en jeux: Espace symbolique et pratique sociale dans le monde romain*. Paris: Editions du CNRS, 1984.

Clavel-Lévêque, Monique. "L'espace des jeux dans le monde romain: Hégémonie, symbolique et pratique sociale." *Aufstieg und Niedergang der römischen Welt II* 16. 3:2405–2563, 1986.

Coarelli, Filippo. *Il Foro Boario: Dalle origini alla fine della repubblica*. Rome: Quasar, 1988.

Coarelli, Filippo. *Il Foro Romano*. 2 vols. Rome: Quasar, 1983–1985.

Coarelli, Filippo. "I percorsi cerimoniali a Roma in età regia." In *Teseo e Romolo: Le origini di Atene e Roma a confronta*, edited by Emanuele Greco, 29–42. Athens: Scuola archeologica italiana di Atene, 2005.

Coarelli, Filippo. *Rome and Environs: An Archaeological Guide*. Translated by James Clauss and Daniel Harmon. Berkeley: University of California Press, 2007.

Coates-Stephens, Robert. "The Reuse of Ancient Statuary in Late Antique Rome and the End of the Statue Habit." In *Statuen in der Spätantike*, edited by Franz Alto Bauer and Christian Witschel, 171–188. Wiesbaden: Reichert, 2007.

Coleman, Kathleen. "'Informers' on Parade." In *The Art of Ancient Spectacle*, edited by Bettina Bergmann and Christine Kondoleon, 231–245. Washington, D. C.: National Gallery of Art, 1999.

Coleman, Kathleen. "Public Entertainments." In *The Oxford Handbook of Social Relations in the Roman World*, edited by Michael Peachin, 335–357. New York: Oxford University Press, 2011.

Coleman, Kathleen. "Spectacle." In *The Oxford Handbook of Roman Studies*, edited by Alessandro Barchiesi and Walter Scheidel, 651–670. New York: Oxford University Press, 2010.

Coleman, Kathleen and Jocelyne Nelis-Clément, ed. *L'organisation des spectacles dans le monde romain: Huit exposés suivis de discussions*. Geneva: Fondation Hardt, 2012.

Colin, Jean. "Les sénateurs et la mère des dieux aux Megalesia: Lucrèce, IV, 79 (d'après les mss de Leyde)." *Athenaeum* 32:346–355, 1954.

Compostella, Carla. "Iconografia, ideologia e status a Brixia nel I secolo D.C.: La lastra sepolcrale del seviro Anteros Asiaticus." *Rivista di archeologia* 13:59–75, 1989.

Connelly, Joan Breton. "Ritual Movement through Greek Sacred Space: Towards an Archaeology of Performance." In *Ritual Dynamics in the Ancient Mediterranean: Agency, Emotion, Gender, Representation*, edited by Angelos Chaniotis, 313–346. Stuttgart: Franz Steiner, 2011.

Corbeill, Anthony. *Nature Embodied: Gestures in Ancient Rome*. Princeton, NJ: Princeton University Press, 2004.

Cordier, Pierre and Valérie Huet. "Une 'théologie' en images? Isis et les autres: Introduction." In *Religions Orientales—Culti Misterici: Neue Perspektiven—Nouvelles Perspectives—Prospettive Nuove*, edited by Corinne Bonnet, Jörg Rüpke, and Paolo Scarpi, 65–73. Stuttgart: Franz Steiner, 2006.

Cornell, Tim. *The Beginnings of Rome: Italy and Rome from the Bronze Age to the Punic Wars (c. 1000–264 BC)*. New York: Routledge, 1995.

Cosgrove, Denis. *Social Formation and Symbolic Landscape*. Madison, WI: University of Wisconsin Press (original edition, 1984), 1998.

Cracco Ruggini, Lellia. "Apoteosi e politica senatoria nel IV s. D.C.: Il dittico dei Symmachi al British Museum." *Rivista storica italiana* 89:425–489, 1977.

Cracco Ruggini, Lellia. "Il paganesimo romano tra religione e politica (384–394 D.C.): per una reinterpretazione del 'Carmen contra paganos.'" *Memorie della Classe di Scienze morali e storiche dell'Accademia dei Lincei ser.* 8.23:3–141, 1979.

Crawford, Michael. *Roman Republican Coinage*. 2 vols. New York: Cambridge University Press, 1974.

Cristofani, Mauro, ed. *La grande Roma dei Tarquini: Roma, Palazzo delle Esposizioni 12 giugno—30 settembre 1990*. Rome: "L'Erma" di Bretschneider, 1990.

Crowther, N. B. "Greek Games in Republican Rome." *L'antiquité classique* 52:266–273, 1983.

Curran, John. "Moving Statues in Late Antique Rome: Problems of Perspective."*Art History* 17:46–58, 1994.

Curran, John. *Pagan City and Christian Capital: Rome in the Fourth Century*. Oxford: Clarendon Press, 2000.

Dagron, Gilbert. *L'hippodrome de Constantinople: Jeux, peuple et politique*. Paris: Gallimard, 2011.

Dagron, Gilbert. *Naissance d'une capitale: Constantinople et ses institutions de 330 à 451*. 2nd ed. Paris: Presses universitaires de France, 1984.

Damsky, Ben. "The Throne and Curule Chair Types of Titus and Domitian." *Revue suisse de numismatique* 74:59–70, 1995.

Daniélou, Jean. *The Bible and the Liturgy*. Notre Dame, IN: University of Notre Dame Press, 1956.

Dareggi, Gianna. "Genesi e sviluppo della tipo logiato imperiale nelle raffigurazioni degli edifici circensi." *Mélanges de l'École française de Rome: Antiquité* 103:71–89, 1991.

Darnton, Robert. *The Great Cat Massacre and Other Episodes in French Cultural History*. New York: Basic Books, 1984.

Darwall-Smith. *Emperors and Architecture: A Study of Flavian Rome*. Brussels: Latomus, 1996.

Davis, Susan. *Parades and Power: Street Theatre in Nineteenth-Century Philadelphia*. Berkeley: University of California Press, 1986.

Decker, Wolfgang. "Wagenrennen im römischen Ägypten." In *Le cirque romaine et son image*, edited by Jocelyne Nelis-Clément and Jean-Michel Roddaz, 347–358. Bourdeaux: Ausonius, 2008.

Decker, Wolfgang and Jean-Paul Thuillier. *Le sport dans l'antiquité: Égypte, Gréce, Rome*. Paris: Picard, 2004.

Delbrück, Richard. *Die Consulardiptychen und verwandte Denkmäler*. Berlin: de Gruyter, 1929.

Demougin, Ségolène. *L'ordre équestre sous les Julio-Claudiens*. Rome: École française de Rome, 1988.

Demougin, Ségolène, Hubert Devijver, and Marie-Thérèse Raepsaet-Charlier, ed. *L'ordre équestre: histoire d'une aristocratie (IIe siècle av. J.-C.–IIIe siècle ap. J.-C.): actes du colloque international (Bruxelles-Leuven, 5–7 octobre 1995).* Rome: École Française de Rome, 1999.

Deniaux, Elizabeth. "La rue et l'opinion publique à Rome et en Italie (Ier siècle avant J.-C.)." In *La Rue, lieu de sociabilité? Rencontres de la Rue*, edited by Alain Leménorel, 207–213. Rouen: Université de Rouen, 1997.

Devallet, Georges. "*Pompa circensis* et constitution d'un espace ludique romain." In *Lalies: Actes des sessions de linguistique et littérature VII*, 299–305. Paris: Presse de l'École Normale Supérieure, 1989.

DeVoe, Richard. "The Christians and the Games: The Relationship between Christianity and the Roman Games from the First through the Fifth Centuries, A.D." Ph.D., Texas Tech University, 1987.

Dietz, Maribel. *Wandering Monks, Virgins, and Pilgrims: Ascetic Travel in the Mediterreanean World, A.D. 300–800.* Philadelphia: University of Pennsylvania Press, 2005.

Dodge, Hazel. "Circuses in the Roman East: A Reappraisal." In *Le cirque romaine et son image*, edited by Jocelyne Nelis-Clément and Jean-Michel Roddaz, 133–146. Bourdeaux: Ausonius, 2008.

Dodge, Hazel. "Venues for Spectacle and Sport (Other Than Amphitheaters) in the Roman World." In *A Companion to Sport and Spectacle in Greek and Roman Antiquity*, edited by Paul Christesen and Donald Kyle, 561–577. Malden, MA: Wiley-Blackwell, 2014.

Dolansky, Fanny. "*Togam Virilem Sumere*: Coming of Age in the Roman World." In *Roman Dress and the Fabrics of Roman Culture*, edited by Jonathan Edmondson and Alison Keith, 47–70. Toronto: University of Toronto Press, 2008.

Doukellis, Panagiotis. "Από την έννομη τάξη και τις ανομίες στο Δοξαστικό της Πόλης: μια ανάγνωση της κατά Διονύσιο Ἀλικαρνασσέα *pompa circensis*." *Annuario della Scuola Archeologica di Atene e delle Missioni Italiane in Oriente* Ser. 3a 9:583–597, 2009.

Drake, H. A. "The Church, Society, and Political Power." In *The Cambridge History of Christianity: Constantine to c. 600*, edited by Augustine Casiday and Frederick Norris, 403–428. New York: Cambridge University Press, 2007.

Drake, H. A. *Constantine and the Bishops: The Politics of Intolerance.* Baltimore: Johns Hopkins University Press, 2000.

Dunbabin, Katherine. "The Victorious Charioteer on Mosaics and Related Monuments." *American Journal of Archaeology* 86:65–89, 1982.

Duncan-Jones, Richard. "An Epigraphic Survey of Costs in Roman Italy." *Papers of the British School at Rome* 33:189–306, 1965.

Dupont, Florence. *Daily Life in Ancient Rome.* Translated by Christopher Woodall. Cambridge, MA: Blackwell, 1992.

Dupont, Florence. "Ludions, *lydioi*: Les danseurs de la *pompa circensis*: exégese et discours sur l'origine des jeux a Rome." In *Spectacles sportifs et scéniques dans le monde étrusco-italique: Actes de la table ronde*, 189–210. Rome: École française de Rome, 1993.

Dupont, Florence. "*Pompa* et *carmina* ludiques." *Cahiers du groupe interdisciplinaire du théâtre antique* 3:75–81, 1987.

Dupont, Florence and Clara Auvray-Assayas, ed. *Images romaines: Actes de la table ronde organisée à l'École normale supérieure (24–26 octobre 1996).* Paris: Presses de l'École normale supérieure, 1998.

Durand, Jean-Louis and John Scheid. "'Rites' et 'Religion': Remarques sur certains préjugés des historiens de la religion des Grecs et des Romains." *Archives des sciences sociales des religions* 85:23–43, 1994.

Dušanić, Slobodan. "*Loci Constitutionum Fixarum.*" *Epigraphica* 46:91–115, 1984.

Eck, Werner. "Emperor and Senatorial Aristocracy in Competition for Public Space." In *The Emperor and Rome: Space, Representation, and Ritual*, edited by Björn Ewald and Carlos Noreña, 89–110.

New York: Cambridge University Press, 2010.

Eck, Werner. "Senatorial Self-Presentation: Developments in the Augustan Period." In *Caesar Augustus: Seven Aspects*, edited by Fergus Millar and Erich Segal, 129–167. Oxford: Clarendon Press, 1984.

Eder, Walter. "Augustus and the Power of Tradition: The Augustan Principate as Binding Link between Republic and Empire." In *Between Republic and Empire: Interpretations of Augustus and His Principate*, edited by Kurt Raaflaub and Mark Toher, 71–122. Berkeley: University of California Press, 1990.

Eder, Walter. "Augustus and the Power of Tradition." In *The Cambridge Companion to the Age of Augustus*, edited by Karl Galinsky, 13–32. New York: Cambridge University Press, 2005.

Edmondson, Jonathan. "The Cultural Politics of Public Spectacle in Rome and the Greek East, 167–166 BCE." In *The Art of Ancient Spectacle*, edited by Bettina Bergmann and Christine Kondoleon, 77–95. Washington, D. C.: National Gallery of Art, 1999.

Edmondson, Jonathan. "Public Spectacles and Roman Social Relations." In *Ludi Romani: Espectáculos en Hispania Romana (Museo Nacional de Arte Romano, Mérida, 29 de julio–13 de octubre, 2002)*, edited by Trinidad Nogales Basarrate and Angeles Castellano Hernández, 42–63. Mérida: Museo Nacional de Arte Romano, 2002.

Edwards, Catharine. "Imaginaires de l'image de Rome ou comment (se) représenter Rome?" In *Images romaines: Actes de la table ronde organisée à l'École normale supérieure (24–26 octobre 1996)*, edited by Florence Dupont and Clara Auvray-Assayas, 235–245. Paris: Presses de l'École normale supérieure, 1998.

Edwards, Catharine. *Writing Rome: Textual Approaches to the City*. Cambridge: Cambridge University Press, 1996.

Edwards, Catharine and Greg Woolf, ed. *Rome the Cosmopolis*. New York: Cambridge University Press, 2003.

Elkins, Nathan. "The Procession and Placement of Imperial Cult Images in the Colosseum." *Papers of the British School in Rome* 82:73–107, 2014.

Elsner, Jaś. *Roman Eyes: Visuality and Subjectivity in Art and Text*. Princeton: Princeton University Press, 2007.

Elsner, Jaś. "Rome as Palimpsest: The City in Architecture and the Imagination."*Apollo* 140:18–22, 1994.

Engemann, Josef. "Die Spiele spätantiker Senatoren und Consuln, ihre Diptychen und ihre Geschenke." In *Spätantike und byzantinische Elfenbeinbildwerke im Diskurs*, edited by Anthony Cutler, Gudrun Bühl, and Arne Effenberger, 730–742. Wiesbaden: Reichert, 2008.

Ensoli, Serena and Eugenio La Rocca, ed. *Aurea Roma: Dalla città pagana alla città cristiana*. Rome: "L'Erma" di Bretschneider, 2000.

Erdkamp, Paul, ed. *The Cambridge Companion to Ancient Rome*. New York: Cambridge University Press, 2013.

Erll, Astrid. *Memory in Culture*. Translated by Sara Young. New York: Palgrave Macmillan, 2011.

Estienne, Sylvia. "Les dévots du Capitole: Le 'culte des images' dans la Rome impériale, entre rites et superstition." *Melanges de l'École Française de Rome: Antiquité* 113:189–210, 2001.

Estienne, Sylvia. "Image et culte: pratiques 'romaines'/influences 'orientales'?" In *Religions Orientales—Culti Misterici: Neue Perspektiven—Nouvelles Perspectives—Prospettive Nuove*, edited by Corinne Bonnet, Jörg Rüpke, and Paolo Scarpi, 147–158. Stuttgart: Franz Steiner, 2006.

Estienne, Sylvia. "*Simulacra deorum versus ornamenta aedium*: The Status of Divine Images in the Temples of Rome." In *Divine Images and Human Imaginations in Ancient Greece and Rome*, edited by Joannis Mylonopoulos, 257–271. Leiden: Brill, 2010.

Estienne, Sylvia. "Statues de dieux 'isolées' et lieux de culte: l'exemple de Rome." *Cahiers du Centre Gustave Glotz* 8:81–96, 1997.

Evans-Pritchard, E. E. "From *The Nuer: A Description of the Modes of Livelihood and Political Institutions of a Nilotic People.*"

In *The Collective Memory Reader*, edited by Vered Vinitzky-Seroussi, Jeffrey Olick, and Daniel Levy, 168–172. New York: Oxford University Press, 2011.

Fauvinet-Ranson, Valérie. *Decor civitatis, decor Italiae: Monuments, travaux publics et spectacles au VIe siècle d'après les Variae de Cassiodore.* Bari: Edipuglia, 2006.

Fauvinet-Ranson, Valérie. "Les spectacles traditionnels dans l'Italie ostrogothique d'après les *Variae* de Cassiodore." In *Le jeux et les spectacles dans l'empire romain tardif et dans les royaumes barbares*, edited by Emmanuel Soler and Françoise Thelamon, 143–160. Rouen: Publications des universités de Rouen et du Havre, 2008.

Favro, Diane. "The City Is a Living Thing: The Performative Role of an Urban Site in Ancient Rome, the Vallis Murcia." In *The Art of Ancient Spectacle*, edited by Bettina Bergmann and Christine Kondoleon, 205–219. Washington, D. C.: National Gallery of Art, 1999.

Favro, Diane. "The Festive Experience: Roman Processions in the Urban Context." In *Festival Architecture*, edited by Sarah Bonnemaison and Christine Macy, 10–42. New York: Routledge, 2008.

Favro, Diane. "The iconiCITY of ancient Rome." *Urban History* 33.1:20–38, 2006.

Favro, Diane. "Making Rome a World City." In *The Cambridge Companion to the Age of Augustus*, edited by Karl Galinsky, 234–263. New York: Cambridge University Press, 2005.

Favro, Diane. "Moving Events: Curating the Memory of the Roman Triumph." In *Memoria Romana: Memory in Rome and Rome in Memory*, edited by Karl Galinsky, 85–101. Ann Arbor: University of Michigan Press for the American Academy in Rome, 2014.

Favro, Diane. "Reading the Augustan City." In *Narrative and Event in Ancient Art*, edited by Peter Holliday, 230–257. Cambridge: Cambridge University Press, 1993.

Favro, Diane. "The Roman Forum and Roman Memory." *Places* 5.1:17–24, 1988.

Favro, Diane. "The Street Triumphant: The Urban Impact of Roman Triumphal Parades." In *Streets: Perspectives on Public Space*, edited by Zeynep Çelik, Diane Favro, and Richard Ingersoll, 151–164. Berkeley: University of California Press, 1994.

Favro, Diane. *The Urban Image of Augustan Rome.* Cambridge: Cambridge University Press, 1996.

Fears, J. Rufus. "The Cult of Jupiter and Roman Imperial Ideology." *Aufstieg und Niedergang der römischen Welt II* 17.1:3–141, 1981.

Fears, J. Rufus. "The Theology of Victory at Rome: Approaches and Problems."*Aufstieg und Niedergang der römischen Welt II* 17.2:736–826, 1981.

Feeney, Denis. *Literature and Religion at Rome: Cultures, Contexts, and Beliefs.* New York: Cambridge University Press, 1998.

Feldherr, Andrew. *Spectacle and Society in Livy's History.* Berkeley: University of California Press, 1998.

Feldman, Cecelia. "Bodies in Motion: Civic Ritual and Place-Making in Roman Ephesus." In *Making Roman Places, Past and Present: Papers Presented at the First Critical Roman Archaeology Conference Held at Stanford University in March 2008*, edited by Darian Marie Totten and Kathryn Lafrenz Samuels, 50–64. Portsmouth, RI: Journal of Roman Archaeology, 2012.

Fentress, James and Chris Wickham. *Social Memory.* Cambridge, MA: Blackwell, 1992.

Ferrary, Jean-Louis. "À propos de deux passages des Philippiques (1,11–13 et 2,110): Remarques sur les honneurs rendus à César en 45–44 et sur la politique d'Antoine après les Ides de Mars." *Archiv für Religionsgeschichte* 1:215–232, 1999.

Ferrary, Jean-Louis. "À propos des pouvoirs et des honneurs décernés à César entre 48 et 44." In *Cesare: precursore o visionario? Atti del convegno internazionale, Cividale del Friuli, 17–19 settembre 2009*, edited by Gianpaolo Urso, 9–30. Pisa: ETS, 2010.

Fishwick, Duncan. "The Deification of Claudius." *Classical Quarterly* 52:341–349, 2002.

Fishwick, Duncan. "*Hastiferi*." *Journal of Roman Studies* 57.1/2:142–160, 1967.

Fishwick, Duncan. *The Imperial Cult in the Latin West*. 3 vols. Leiden: Brill, 1987–2005.

Fishwick, Duncan. "On the Temple of Divus Augustus." *Phoenix* 46:232–255, 2002.

Flaig, Egon. *Ritualisierte Politik: Zeichen, Gesten und Herrschaft im Alten Rom*. Göttingen: Vandenhoeck & Ruprecht, 2004.

Fless, Friederike. *Opferdiener und Kultmusiker auf stadtrömischen historischen Reliefs: Untersuchungen zur Ikonographie, Funktion und Benennung*. Mainz: Philipp von Zabern, 1995.

Fless, Friederike. "Römische Prozessionen." In *Thesaurus cultus et rituum antiquorum (ThesCRA) I: Processions, Sacrifices, Libations, Fumigations, Dedications*, 33–58. Los Angeles: J. Paul Getty Museum, 2004.

Fless, Friederike and Katja Moede. "Music and Dance: Forms of Representation in Pictorial and Written Sources." In *A Companion to Roman Religion*, edited by Jörg Rüpke, 249–262. Malden, MA: Wiley-Blackwell, 2007.

Flower, Harriet I. *Ancestor Masks and Aristocratic Power in Roman Culture*. Oxford: Clarendon Press, 1996.

Flower, Harriet I. *The Art of Forgetting: Disgrace and Oblivion in Roman Political Culture*. Chapel Hill, NC: University of North Carolina Press, 2006.

Flower, Harriet I. "Élite Self-Representation in Rome." In *The Oxford Handbook of Social Relations in the Roman World*, edited by Michael Peachin, 271–285. New York: Oxford University Press, 2011.

Flower, Harriet I. "Remembering and Forgetting Temple Destruction: The Destruction of the Temple of Jupiter Optimus Maximus in 83 BC." In *Antiquity in Antiquity: Jewish and Christian Pasts in the Greco-Roman World*, edited by Gregg Gardner and Kevin Osterloh, 74–92. Tübingen: Mohr Siebeck, 2008.

Flower, Harriet I. "Les Sévères et l'usage de la memoria: l'arcus du Forum Boarium à Rome." In *Un discours en images de la condamnation de mémoire*, edited by Stéphane Benoist and Anne Daguet-Gagey, 97–115. Metz: Centre Régional Universitaire Lorrain d'Histoire, Site de Metz, 2008.

Flower, Harriet I. "Spectacle and Political Culture in the Roman Republic." In *The Cambridge Companion to the Roman Republic*, edited by Harriet I. Flower. New York: Cambridge University Press, 2004.

Foertmeyer. "The Dating of the Pompe of Ptolemy II Philadelphus." *Historia* 37:90–104, 1988.

Frank, Richard. *Scholae Palatinae: The Palace Guards of the Later Roman Empire*. Rome: American Academy in Rome, 1969.

Frankfurter, David. *Religion in Roman Egypt: Assimilation and Resistance*. Princeton: Princeton University Press, 1998.

Fraschetti, Augusto. *Roma e il principe*. Rome: Laterza, 1990.

Freedberg, David. *The Power of Images: Studies in the History and Theory of Response*. Chicago: University of Chicago Press, 1989.

French, Dorothea. "Christian Emperors and Pagan Spectacles: The Secularization of the *Ludi* A.D. 382–525." Ph.D., University of California, Berkeley, 1985.

Freud, Sigmund. "The 'Uncanny.'" In *The Standard Edition of the Complete Psychological Works of Sigmund Freud, Volume 17*, edited by James Strachey, 217–252. London: Hogarth Press, 1955.

Friedländer, Ludwig. "Les jeux." In *Le culte chez les romains*, edited by Joachim Marquardt, 247–349. Paris: E. Thorin, 1890.

Fulminante, Francesca. *The Urbanisation of Rome and Latium Vetus: From the Bronze Age to the Archaic Era*. New York: Cambridge University Press, 2014.

Gabba, Emilio. *Dionysius and The History of Archaic Rome*. Berkeley: University of California Press, 1991.

Gaertner, Jan Felix. "Livy's Camillus and the Political Discourse of the Late Republic." *Journal of Roman Studies* 98:27–52, 2008.

Gailliot, Antoine. "Une impiété volontaire? La procession des jeux et le problème de *l'instauratio*." In *Rituels et transgressions de l'Antiquité à nos jours*, edited by Geneviève Hoffmann and

Antoine Gailliot, 89–96. Amiens: Encrage, 2009.

Gailliot, Antoine. "La place de *l'editor* dans la procession des jeux." *Cahiers "Mondes anciens."* 2011. http://mondesanciens.revues.org/634

Galinsky, Karl, ed. *The Cambridge Companion to the Age of Augustus*. New York: Cambridge University Press, 2005.

Galinsky, Karl, ed. *Memoria Romana: Memory in Rome and Rome in Memory*. Ann Arbor, MI: University of Michigan Press, 2014.

Gallia, Andrew. *Remembering the Roman Republic: Culture, Politics and History under the Principate*. New York: Cambridge University Press, 2012.

Garelli-François, Marie-Hélène. "Ludions, homéristes ou pantomimes? (Sénèque, *Ep.* 117; Fronton, éd. Naber p. 158)." *Revue des études anciennes* 102.3–4:501–508, 2000.

Gebhard, Elizabeth. "The Theater and the City." In *Roman Theater and Society: E. Togo Salmon Papers I*, edited by William Slater, 113–127. Ann Arbor, MI: University of Michigan Press, 1996.

Gee, Emma. "Cicero's Astronomy." *Classical Quarterly* 51:520–536, 2001.

Gernentz, Wilhelm. *Laudes Romae*. Rostock: Adler, 1918.

Giglio, Stefano. "Il *munus* della pretura a Roma e a Costantinopli nel corso del tardo impero romano." *Antiquité Tardive* 15:65–88, 2007.

Gillet, Andrew. "Rome, Ravenna and the Last Western Emperors." *Papers of the British School at Rome* 69:131–167, 2001.

Ginsburg, Judith. *Representing Agrippina: Constructions of Female Power in the Early Roman Empire*. New York: Oxford University Press, 2006.

Goffman, Erving. *The Presentation of Self in Everyday Life*. New York: Anchor Books, 1959.

Goldberg, Sander. "Plautus on the Palatine." *Journal of Roman Studies* 88:1–20, 1998.

Golvin, Jean-Claude. "Réflexion relative aux questions soulevées par l'étude du *pulvinar* et de la *spina* du Circus Maximus." In *Le cirque romaine et son image*, edited by Jocelyne Nelis-Clément and Jean-Michel Roddaz, 79–87. Bourdeaux: Ausonius, 2008.

Gordon, Richard. "The Real and the Imaginary: Production and Religion in the Graeco-Roman World." *Art History* 2.1:5–34, 1979.

Gordon, Richard. "The Veil of Power: Emperors, Sacrificers and Benefactors." In *Pagan Priests: Religion and Power in the Ancient World*, edited by Mary Beard and John North, 201–231. Ithaca, NY: Cornell University Press, 1990.

Gowers, Emily. "The Anatomy of Rome from Capitol to Cloaca." *Journal of Roman Studies* 85:23–32, 1995.

Gowing, Alain. *Empire and Memory: The Representation of the Republic in Imperial Culture*. New York: Cambridge University Press, 2005.

Gowing, Alain. "Rome and the Ruin of Memory." *Mouseion* ser. 3.8:451–467, 2008.

Gradel, Ittai. *Emperor Worship and Roman Religion*. Oxford: Clarendon Press, 2002.

Graf, Fritz. "Fights about Festivals: Libanius and John Chrysostom on the *Kalendae Ianuariae* in Antioch." *Archiv für Religionsgeschichte* 13:175–186, 2012.

Graf, Fritz. "What Is New about Greek Sacrifice?" In *Kykeon: Studies in Honour of H.S. Versnel*, edited by H.W. Singor, H.F.J. Horstmanshoff, F.T. Van Straten, and J.H.M. Strubbe, 113–125. Leiden: Brill, 2002.

Green, Carin. "The Gods in the Circus." In *New Perspectives on Etruria and Early Rome: In Honor of Richard Daniel de Puma*, edited by Sinclair Bell and Helen Nagy, 65–78. Madison, WI: University of Wisconsin Press, 2009.

Greenblatt, Stephen. *Renaissance Self-Fashioning: From More to Shakespeare*. Chicago: University of Chicago Press, 1980.

Greenblatt, Stephen. "Resonance and Wonder." In *Exhibiting Cultures: The Poetics and Politics of Museum Display*, edited by Ivan Karp and Steven Lavine, 42–56. Washington, D.C.: Smithsonian Institution Press, 1991.

Gregory, Andrew. "'Powerful Images': Responses to Portraits and the Political Uses of Images in Rome." *Journal of Roman Archaeology* 7:80–99, 1994.

Gricourt, Daniel and Dominique Hollard. "La date du quatrième consulat de Postume: à propos d'un document numismatique méconnu." *Revue numismatique* 36:66–75, 1994.

Grig, Lucy. "Imagining the Capitolium in Late Antiquity." In *The Power of Religion in Late Antiquity: Select Papers from the Seventh Biennial Shifting Frontiers in Late Antiquity Conference*, edited by Andrew Cain and Noel Lenski, 279–292. Burlington, VT: Ashgate, 2009.

Grimal, Pierre. "Le théâtre à Rome." In *Actes du IXe Congrés (Rome 13–18 avril 1973) de l'Association Guillaume Budé*, edited by Association Guillaume Budé, 251–305. Paris: Les Belles Lettres, 1975.

Grimes, Ronald. "Infelicitous Performances and Ritual Criticism." *Semeia* 43:103–122, 1988.

Grimes, Ronald. *Ritual Criticism: Case Studies in Its Practice, Essays on Its Theory*. Columbia, SC: University of South Carolina Press, 1990.

Grønne, Claus. "The Architectural Terracottas." In *The Temple of Castor and Pollux: The Pre-Augustan Temple Phases with Related Decorative Elements*, edited by Inge Nielsen and Birte Poulsen, 157–176. Rome: Edizioni de Luca, 1992.

Gros, Pierre. *L'architecture romaine: du début du IIIe siècle av. J.-C. à la fin du Haut-Empire*. Vol. 1. Paris: Picard, 2011.

Gruet, Brice. *La rue à Rome, miroir de la ville: Entre l'émotion et la norme*. Paris: Presses de l'université Paris-Sorbonne, 2006.

Guaglianone, Antonio. "Cic. *De harusp. resp.* XI 23, 3, Arn. *Adver. nat.* IV 31, 19 (*terram e tensam*)." *Rivista di Studi Classici* 14:109–110, 1966.

Guidetti, Fabio. "Note sull'iconografia di un rilievo funerario da Amiternum: Modelli e scelte figurative di un liberto municipale." *Archaeologia Classica* 7.57:387–403, 2006.

Guidetti, Fabio. "*Tensam non tenuit*: Cicerone, Arnobio e il modo di condurre i carri sacri." *Studi Classici et Orientali* 55:233–248, 2009.

Guittard, Charles. "Invocations et structures théologiques dans la prière à Rome," *Revue des études latines* 76:71–92, 1998.

Gunderson, Erik. "The Ideology of the Arena." *Classical Antiquity* 15:113–151, 1996.

Günkel, Ute. "Entertainment im römischen Reich: der Zirkus." In *Spiel am Nil: Unterhaltung im Alten Ägypten*, edited by Harald Froschauer and Hermann Harrauer, 45–58. Wien: Phoibos, 2004.

Habetzeder, Julia. "Marsyas in the Garden? Small-Scale Sculptures Referring to the Marsyas in the Forum." *Opuscula* 3:163–178, 2010.

Halbwachs, Maurice. *On Collective Memory*. Translated by Lewis Coser. Chicago: University of Chicago Press, 1992.

Hanson, John Arthur. *Roman Theater-Temples*. Princeton: Princeton University Press, 1959.

Hardie, Philip. *Ovid's Poetics of Illusion*. New York: Cambridge University Press, 2002.

Harl, Marguerite. "La dénonciation des festivités profanes dans le discours épiscopal et monastique, en Orient chrétien, à la fin du IVe siècle." In *La fête, pratique et discours: d'Alexandrie hellénistique à la mission de Besançon*, 123–147. Paris: Les Belles Lettres, 1981.

Harmon, Daniel. "The Religious Significance of the Games in the Roman Age." In *The Archaeology of the Olympics: The Olympics and Other Festivals in Antiquity*, edited by Wendy Rashke, 236–255. Madison, WI: University of Wisconsin Press, 1988.

Harries, Jill. "*Favor populi*: Pagans, Christians and Public Entertainment in Late Antique Italy." In *Bread and Circuses: Euergetism and Municipal Patronage in Roman Italy*, edited by Kathryn Lomas and Tim Cornell, 125–141. New York: Routledge, 2003.

Harris, William V., ed. *The Transformation of the* Urbs Roma *in Late Antiquity*. Portsmouth, RI: Journal of Roman Archaeology, 1999.

Haselberger, Lothar. *Urbem adornare: die Stadt Rom und ihre Gestaltumwandlung unter Augustus: Rome's Urban Metamorphosis under Augustus.*

Translated by Alexander Thein. Portsmouth, RI: Journal of Roman Archaeology, 2007.

Hazzard, R. A. *Imagination of a Monarchy: Studies in Ptolemaic Propaganda*. Toronto: University of Toronto Press, 2000.

Heather, Peter. "New Men for New Constantines? Creating an Imperial Elite in the Eastern Mediterranean." In *New Constantines: The Rhythm of Imperial Renewal in Byzantium, 4th–13th Centuries*, edited by Paul Magdalino, 11–33. Brookfield, VT: Ashgate, 1994.

Heather, Peter. "Senators and Senates." In *The Cambridge Ancient History, Volume XIII: The Late Empire, A.D. 337–425*, edited by Averil Cameron and Peter Garnsey, 184–210. New York: Cambridge University Press, 1998.

Hedrick, Charles. *History and Silence: Purge and Rehabilitation of Memory in Late Antiquity*. Austin: University of Texas Press, 2000.

Hekster, Olivier. "Captured in the Gaze of Power: Visibility, Games, and Roman Imperial Representation." In *Imaginary Kings: Royal Images in the Ancient Near East, Greece and Rome*, edited by Olivier Hekster and Richard Fowler, 157–176. Stuttgart: Franz Steiner, 2005.

Hekster, Olivier. "Honouring Ancestors: The Dynamic of Deification." In *Ritual Dynamics and Religious Change in the Roman Empire*, edited by Olivier Hekster, Sebastian Schmidt-Hofner, and Christian Witschel 95–110. Leiden: Brill, 2009.

Hekster, Oliver, Sebastian Schmidt-Hofner, and Christian Witschel, ed. *Ritual Dynamics and Religious Change in the Roman Empire*. Leiden: Brill, 2009.

Hellmann, Marie-Christine. *Lampes antiques de la Bibliothèque Nationale II: Fonds général: Lampes pré-romaines et romaines*. Paris: Bibliothèque Nationale de France, 1987.

Henderson, John. "A Doo-Dah-Doo-Dah-Dey at the Races: Ovid *Amores* 3.2 and the Personal Politics of the *Circus Maximus*." *Classical Antiquity* 21.1:41–65, 2002.

Herz, Peter. "Diva Drusilla: Ägyptisches und Römisches im Herrscherkult zur Zeit Caligulas." *Historia* 30:324–336, 1981.

Hickson Hahn, Frances. "Performing the Sacred: Prayers and Hymns." In *A Companion to Roman Religion*, edited by Jörg Rüpke, 235–248. Malden, MA: Wiley-Blackwell, 2007.

Himmelmann, Nikolaus. *Typologische Untersuchungen an Römischen Sarkophagreliefs des 3. und 4. Jahrhunderts n. Chr.* Mainz: Philipp von Zabern, 1973.

Hinard, François. "Rome dans Rome: La ville définie par les procédures administratives et les pratiques sociales." In *Rome: l'espace urbain et ses représentations*, edited by François Hinard and Manuel Royo, 31–54. Paris: Presse de l'université de Paris-Sorbonne, 1991.

Hitzl, Konrad. "Kultstätten und Praxis des Kaiserkults anhand van Fallbeispieln." In *Die Praxis der Herrscherverehrung in Rom und seinen Provinzen*, edited by Hubert Cancik and Konrad Hitzl, 97–127. Tübingen: Mohr Siebeck, 2003.

Højte, Jakob Munk. *Roman Imperial Statue Bases from Augustus to Commodus*. Aarhus: Aarhus University Press, 2005.

Holden, Antonia. "The Abduction of the Sabine Women in Context: The Iconography on Late Antique Contorniate Medallions." *American Journal of Archaeology* 1112:121–142, 2008.

Hölkeskamp, Karl-Joachim. "Capitol, Comitium und Forum: Öffentliche Räume, sakrale Topographie und Erinnerungslandschaften der römischen Republik." In *Studien zu antiken Identitäten*, edited by Stefan Faller, 97–132. Würzburg: Ergon, 2001.

Hölkeskamp, Karl-Joachim. "Hierarchie und Konsens: *Pompae* in der politischen Kultur der römischen Republik." In *Machtfragen: Zur kulturellen Repräsentation und Konstruktion von Macht in Antike, Mittelalter und Neuzeit*, edited by A.H. Arweiler and B.M. Gauly, 79–126. Stuttgart: Franz Steiner, 2008.

Hölkeskamp, Karl-Joachim. "History and Collective Memory in the Middle Republic." In *A Companion to the Roman Republic*, edited by Nathan Rosenstein and Robert Morstein-Marx, 478–495. Malden, MA: Wiley-Blackwell, 2006.

Hölkeskamp, Karl-Joachim. "Images of Power: Memory, Myth and Monuments in the Roman Republic." *Scripta Classica Israelica* 24:249–271, 2005.

Hölkeskamp, Karl-Joachim. "In Defense of Concepts, Categories, and Other Abstractions: Remarks on a Theory of Memory (in the Making)." In *Memoria Romana: Memory in Rome and Rome in Memory*, edited by Karl Galinsky, 63–70. Ann Arbor: University of Michigan Press for the American Academy in Rome, 2014.

Hölkeskamp, Karl-Joachim. "Pomp und Prozessionen. Rituale und Zeremonien in der politischen Kultur der römischen Republik." *Jahrbuch des Historischen Kollegs* 2006:35–72, 2007.

Hölkeskamp, Karl-Joachim. "Rituali e cerimonie 'alla romana': Nouve prospettive sulla cultura politica dell'età repubblicana." *Studi storici* 47.2:319–363, 2006.

Hölkeskamp, Karl-Joachim. "The Roman Republic as Theatre of Power: The Consuls as Leading Actors." In *Consuls and* Res Publica*: Holding High Office in the Roman Republic*, edited by Hans Beck, Antonio Duplá, Martin Jehne, and Francisco Pina Polo, 161–181. New York: Cambridge University Press, 2011.

Hölkeskamp, Karl-Joachim. *Senatus Populusque Romanus: Die politische Kultur der Republik—Dimensionen und Deutungen*. Stuttgart: Franz Steiner, 2004.

Holleran, Claire. *Shopping in Ancient Rome: The Retail Trade in the Late Republic and the Principate*. Oxford: Oxford University Press, 2012.

Holleran, Claire. "Street Life in Ancient Rome." In *Rome, Ostia, Pompeii: Movement and Space*, edited by Ray Laurence and David Newsome, 245–261. New York: Oxford University Press, 2011.

Holliday, Peter. *The Origins of Roman Historical Commemoration in the Visual Arts*. Cambridge: Cambridge University Press, 2002.

Hollinshead, Mary. "Monumental Steps and the Shaping of Ceremony." In *Architecture of the Sacred: Space, Ritual, and Experience from Classical Greece to Byzantium*, edited by Bonna Wescoat and Robert Ousterhout, 27–65. New York: Cambridge University Press, 2012.

Hölscher, Fernande. "Das Capitol: das Haupt der Welt." In *Erinnerungsorte der Antike: Die römische Welt*, edited by Elke Stein-Hölkeskamp and Karl-Joachim Hölkeskamp, 75–99. Munich: C.H. Beck, 2006.

Hölscher, Fernande. "Götterstatuen bei Lectisternien und Theoxenien?" In *Römische Bilderwelten: Von der Wirklichkeit zum Bild und zurück: Kolloquium der Gerda Henkel Stiftung am Deutschen Archäologischen Institut Rom 15.-17.3.2004*, edited by Fernande Hölscher and Tonio Hölscher, 27–40. Heidelberg: Verlag Archäologie und Geschichte, 2007.

Hölscher, Tonio. "Die Alten vor Augen: Politische Denkmäler und öffentliches Gedächtnis im republikanischen Rom." In *Institutionalität und Symbolisierung: Verstetigungen kultureller Ordnungsmuster in Vergangenheit und Gegenwart*, edited by Gert Melville, 183–211. Köln-Weimar-Wien: Böhlau, 2001.

Hölscher, Tonio. "Das Forum Romanum: Die monumentale Geschichte Roms." In *Erinnerungsorte der Antike: Die römische Welt*, edited by Elke Stein-Hölkeskamp and Karl-Joachim Hölkeskamp, 100–122. Munich: C.H. Beck, 2006.

Hölscher, Tonio. "The Transformation of Victory into Power: From Event to Structure." In *Representations of War in Ancient Rome*, edited by Sheila Dillon and Katherine Welch, 27–48. New York: Cambridge University Press, 2006.

Hölscher, Tonio. *Victoria Romana: Archäologische Untersuchungen zur Geschichte und Wesenart der römischen Siegesgöttin von den Anfängen bis zum Ende des 3. Jhs. n. Chr.* Mainz: Philipp von Zabern, 1967.

Hönle, Augusta and Anton Henze. *Römische Amphitheater und Stadien: Gladiatorenkampfe und Circusspiele*. Zurich and Freiburg: Atlantis, 1981.

Hope, Valerie and Eireann Marshall, ed. *Death and Disease in the Ancient City*. New York: Routledge, 2000.

Hopkins, John. "The Capitoline Temple and the Effects of Monumentality on Roman Temple

Design." In *Monumentality in Etruscan and Early Roman Architecture: Ideology and Innovation*, edited by Michael Thomas and Gretchen Meyers, 111–138. Austin, TX: University of Texas Press, 2012.

Hopkins, John. "The Cloaca Maxima and the Monumental Manipulation of Water in Archaic Rome." *The Waters of Rome* 4:1–15, 2007.

Hopkins, John. "The Colossal Temple of Jupiter Optimus Maximus in Archaic Rome." In *Arqueología de la construcción II. Los procesos constructivos en el mundo romano: Italia y provincias orientales*, edited by Stefano Camporeale, Hélène Dessales, and Antonio Pizzo, 15–33. Mérida: Instituto de Arqueología de Mérida, 2010.

Hopkins, John. "The Creation of the Forum and the Making of Monumental Rome." In *Papers on Italian Urbanism in the First Millenium B.C.*, edited by Elizabeth Robinson, 29–61. Portsmouth, RI: Journal of Roman Archaeology, 2014.

Hopkins, John. "The 'Sacred Sewer': Tradition and Religion in the Cloaca Maxima." In *Rome, Pollution, and Propriety: Dirt, Disease, and Hygiene in the Eternal City from Antiquity to Modernity*, edited by Mark Bradley and Kenneth Stow, 81–102. New York: Cambridge University Press, 2012.

Hopkins, Keith. "From Violence to Blessing: Symbols and Rituals in Ancient Rome." In *City States in Classical Antiquity and Medieval Italy*, edited by Anthony Molho, Kurt Raaflaub, and Julia Emlen, 479–498. Ann Arbor, MI: University of Michigan Press, 1991.

Hörig, Monika and Elmar Schwertheim, ed. *Corpus cultus Iovis Dolicheni (CCID)*. Leiden: Brill, 1987.

Horsfall, Nicholas. "The Cultural Horizons of the *Plebs Romana*." *Memoirs of the American Academy in Rome* 41:101–119, 1996.

Horsfall, Nicholas. *The Culture of the Roman Plebs*. London: Duckworth, 2003.

Horsmann, Gerhard. *Die Wagenlenker der römischen Kaiserzeit: Untersuchungen zu ihrer sozialen Stellung*. Stuttgart: Franz Steiner, 1998.

Hugoniot, Christophe. "Le *pulvinar* du Grand Cirque, le Prince et les jeux." In *Pouvoir et religion dans le monde romain: En hommage à Jean-Pierre Martin*, edited by X. Loriot Annie Vigourt, A. Bérenger-Badel, and B. Klein, 213–230. Paris: Presses de l'université Paris-Sorbonne, 2006.

Hugoniot, Christophe. "Les spectacles dans le royaume vandale." In *Le jeux et les spectacles dans l'empire romain tardif et dans les royaumes barbares*, edited by Emmanuel Soler and Françoise Thelamon, 161–204. Rouen: Publications des universités de Rouen et du Havre, 2008.

Humphrey, John. *Roman Circuses: Arenas for Chariot Racing*. London: Batsford, 1986.

Humphries, Mark. "Roman Senators and Absent Emperors in Late Antiquity." *Acta ad Archaeologiam et Artium Historiam Pertinentia* 17.3:27–46, 2003.

Hunt, Alisa. "Keeping Memory Alive: The Physical Continuity of the *Ficus Ruminalis*." In *Memory and Urban Religion in the Ancient World*, edited by Juliette Harrisson Martin Bommas, Phoebe Roy, and Elena Theodorakopolous, 111–128. New York: Bloomsbury, 2012.

Hunt, David. "Christianising the Roman Empire: The Evidence of the Code." In *The Theodosian Code: Studies in the Imperial Law of Late Antiquity*, edited by Jill Harries and Ian Wood, 143–158. Ithaca, NY: Cornell University Press, 1993.

Hunter, David. "The Raven Replies: Ambrose's *Letter to the Church at Vercelli* (*Ep. ex.coll.* 14) and the Criticisms of Jerome." In *Jerome of Stridon: His Life, Writings and Legacy*, edited by Andrew Cain and Josef Lössl, 175–189. Burlington, VT: Ashgate, 2009.

Hurlet, Frédéric. "Représentation(s) et autoreprésentation(s) de l'aristocratie romaine." *Perspective* 1:159–166, 2012.

Hurlet, Frédéric and Bernard Mineo, ed. *Le principat d'Auguste: Réalités et représentations du pouvoir autour de la* Res publica restituta. Rennes: Presses universitaires de Rennes, 2009.

Hüsken, Ute. "Ritual Dynamics and Ritual Failure." In *When Rituals Go Wrong: Mistakes, Failures, and the Dynamics of Ritual*, edited by Ute Hüsken, 337–366. Leiden: Brill, 2007.

Hüsken, Ute, ed. *When Rituals Go Wrong: Mistakes, Failures, and the Dynamics of Ritual* Leiden: Brill, 2007.

Iara, Kristine. "Lingering Sacredness: The Persistence of Pagan Sacredness in the Forum Romanum in Late Antiquity." In *Religious Practices and Christianization of the Late Antique City (4th–7th cent.)*, edited by Aude Busine, 141–165. Leiden: Brill, 2015.

Icks, Martijn. *The Crimes of Elagabalus: The Life and Legacy of Rome's Decadent Boy Emperor*. Cambridge, MA: Harvard University Press, 2012.

Icks, Martijn. "Elevating the Unworthy Emperor: Ritual Failure in Roman Historiography." In *Ritual Dynamics in the Ancient Mediterranean: Agency, Emotion, Gender, Representation*, edited by Angelos Chaniotis, 347–376. Stuttgart: Franz Steiner, 2011.

Iossif, Panagiotis, Andrzej Chankowski, and Catharine Lorber, ed. *More than Men, Less than Gods: Studies on Royal Cult and Imperial Cult: Proceedings of the International Colloquium Organized by the Belgian School at Athens (November 1–2, 2007)*. Leuven: Peeters, 2011.

Iossif, Panagiotis and Catharine Lorber. "More than Men, Less than Gods: Concluding Thoughts and New Perspectives." In *More than Men, Less than Gods: Studies on Royal Cult and Imperial Cult: Proceedings of the International Colloquium Organized by the Belgian School at Athens (November 1–2, 2007)*, edited by Andrzej Chankowski, Panagiotis Iossif, and Catharine Lorber, 691–710. Leuven: Peeters, 2011.

Itgenshorst, Tanja. "Roman Commanders and Hellenistic Kings: On the 'Hellenization' of the Republican Triumph." *Ancient Society* 36:51–68, 2006.

Itgenshorst, Tanja. *Tota illa pompa: Der Triumph in der römischen Republik*. Göttingen: Vandenhoeck & Ruprecht, 2005.

Jacobelli, Luciana. *Gladiators at Pompeii*. Los Angeles: J. Paul Getty Museum, 2003.

Jacobs, Ine. "A Time for Prayer and a Time for Pleasure: Christianity's Struggle with the Secular World." In *Religion and Conflict in Antiquity*, edited by David Engels and Peter Van Nuffelen, 192–219. Brussels: Latomus, 2014.

Jaeger, Mary. *Livy's Written Rome*. Ann Arbor, MI: University of Michigan Press, 1997.

Jannot, Jean-René. "Les danseurs de la *pompa* du cirque: Témoinages textuels et iconographiques." *Revue des études latines* 70:56–68, 1992.

Jenkyns, Richard. *God, Space, and City in the Roman Imagination*. New York: Oxford University Press, 2013.

Jenkyns, Richard. "The Memory of Rome in Rome." In *Memoria Romana: Memory in Rome and Rome in Memory*, edited by Karl Galinsky, 15–26. Ann Arbor: University of Michigan Press for the American Academy in Rome, 2014.

Jiménez Sanchez, Juan Antonio. "Honorius, un souverain 'ludique'?" In *Le jeux et les spectacles dans l'empire romain tardif et dans les royaumes barbares*, edited by Emmanuel Soler and Françoise Thelamon, 123–142. Rouen: Publications des universités de Rouen et du Havre, 2008.

Jiménez Sánchez, Juan Antonio. *Los juegos paganos en la Roma cristiana*. Treviso/Rome: Fondazione Benetton Studi Ricerche/Viella, 2010.

Jiménez Sánchez, Juan Antonio. "La liturgie impériale et les jeux durant l'antiquité tardive: Entre paganisme et christianisme." In *Figures d'empire, fragments de mémoire: Pouvoirs et identités dans le monde romain impérial (IIe s. av. n. è.–VIe s. ap. n. è.)*, edited by Anne Daguet-Gagey, Stéphane Benoist, and Christine Hoët-van Cauwenberghe, 181–193. Villeneuve d'Ascq: Presses universitaires du Septentrion, 2011.

Jiménez Sánchez, Juan Antonio. "'*O amentia monstruosa*!' A propósito de la cristianización de la liturgia imperial y del ritual circense durante el siglo V." *Cristianesimo nella storia* 24:23–39, 2003.

Jiménez Sanchez, Juan Antonio. "Le *tribunus voluptatum*, un fonctionnaire au service du plaisir populaire." *Antiquité Tardive* 15:89–98, 2007.

Jones, A. H. M. *The Later Roman Empire 284–602: A Social, Economic, and Administrative Survery*. 2 vols. Baltimore: Johns Hopkins University Press, 1964.

Jones, Christopher. "The Organization of Spectacle in Late Antiquity." In *L'organisation des spectacles dans le monde Romain: Huit exposés suivis de discussions*, edited by Kathleen Coleman and Jocelyne Nelis-Clément, 305–328. Geneva: Fondation Hardt, 2012.

Jones, Christopher. "Processional Colors." In *The Art of Ancient Spectacle*, edited by Bettina Bergmann and Christine Kondoleon, 247–257. Washington, D. C.: National Gallery of Art, 1999.

Jory, E. J. "Continuity and Change in the Roman Theater." In *Studies in Honour of T. B. L. Webster*, edited by J. T. Hooker, J. H. Betts, and J. R. Green, 143–152. Bristol: Bristol Classical Press, 1986.

Jucker, Hans. "Zum Carpentum-Sesterz der Agrippina maior." In *Forschungen und Funde: Festschrift Bernhard Neutsch*, edited by Brianna Otto, Fritz Krinzinger, and Elisabeth Walde-Psenner, 205–217. Innsbruck: Verlag des Instituts für Sprachwissenschaft der Universität Innsbruck, 1980.

Jullian, Camille. "*Processus consularis*." *Revue de philologie, de littérature et d'histoire anciennes* 7:145–163, 1883.

Junkelmann, Marcus. "On the Starting Line with Ben Hur: Chariot Racing in the Circus Maximus." In *Gladiators and Caesars: The Power of Spectacle In Ancient Rome*, edited by Eckart Köhne, Cornelia Ewigleben, and Ralph Jackson, 86–102. Berkeley: University of California Press, 2000.

Kahlos, Maijastina. *Debate and Dialogue: Christian and Pagan Cultures c. 360–430*. Burlington, VT: Ashgate, 2007.

Kahlos, Maijastina. "*Pompa diaboli*: The Grey Area of Urban Festivals in the Fourth and Fifth Centuries." In *Studies In Latin Literature and Roman History XII*. Brussels: Latomus, 2005.

Kahlos, Maijastina. "The Restoration Policy of Vettius Agorius Praetextatus." *Arctos* 29:39–47, 1995.

Kaiser, Alan. "Cart Traffic Flow in Pompeii and Rome." In *Rome, Ostia, Pompeii: Movement and Space*, edited by Ray Laurence and David Newsome, 174–193. New York: Oxford University Press, 2011.

Kaiser, Alan. *Roman Urban Street Networks*. New York: Routledge, 2011.

Kalas, Gregor. "Architecture and Élite Identity in Late Antique Rome: Appropriating the Past at Sant'Andrea Catabarbara." *Papers of the British School at Rome* 81:279–302, 2013.

Kalas, Gregor. *The Restoration of the Roman Forum in Late Antiquity: Transforming Public Space*. Austin, TX: University of Texas Press, 2015.

Kalas, Gregor. "Writing and Restoration in Rome: Inscriptions, Statues and the Late Antique Preservation of Buildings." In *Cities, Texts and Social Networks 400–1500: Experiences and Perceptions of Medieval Urban Space*, edited by Anne Lester, Caroline Goodson, and Carol Symes, 21–43. Burlington, VT: Ashgate, 2010.

Kantirea, Maria. "Imperial Birthday Rituals in Late Antiquity." In *Court Ceremonies and Rituals of Power in Byzantium and the Medieval Mediterranean: Comparative Perspectives*, edited by Stavroula Constantinou, Alexander Beihammer, and Maria Parani 37–50. Leiden: Brill, 2013.

Keane, Catherine Clare. "Theatre, Spectacle, and the Satirist in Juvenal." *Phoenix* 57:257–275, 2003.

Kienast, Dietmar. "Diva Domitilla." *Zeitschrift für Papyrologie und Epigraphik* 76:141–147, 1989.

King, Charles. "The Organization of Roman Religious Beliefs." *Classical Antiquity* 22:275–312, 2003.

Kondratieff, Eric. "The Coinage and Column of C. Duilius: Innovations in Iconography in Large and Small Media in the Middle Republic." *Scripta Classica Israelica* 23:1–39, 2004.

Kontokosta, Anne Hrychuck. "Reconsidering the Arches (*fornices*) of the Roman

Republic." *Journal of Roman Archaeology* 26:7–35, 2013.

Koortbojian, Michael. *The Divinization of Caesar and Augustus: Precedents, Consequences, Implications*. New York: Cambridge University Press, 2013.

Koziol, Geoffrey. "Review Article: The Dangers of Polemic: Is Ritual Still an Interesting Topic of Historical Study?" *Early Medieval Europe* 11.4:367–388, 2002.

Kulikowski, Michael. "The Identity of Bachiarius." *Medieval Prosopography* 24:3–14, 2003.

La Regina, Adriano, ed. *Lexicon Topographicum Urbis Romae – Suburbium*. 5 vols. Rome: Quasar, 2001–2008.

La Regina, Adriano, ed. *Sangue e Arena*. Milan: Electa, 2001.

La Rocca, Eugenio. "Art and Representation." In *The Oxford Handbook of Roman Studies*, edited by Alessandro Barchiesi and Walter Scheidel, 309–348. New York: Oxford University Press, 2010.

La Rocca, Eugenio. "Sul Circo Flaminio." *Archeologia Laziale* 12:103–119, 1995.

La Rocca, Eugenio. "I troni dei nuovi dei." In *Culto imperial: política y poder*, edited by Trinidad Nogales and Julián González, 76–104. Rome: "L'Erma" di Bretschneider, 2007.

Laird, Margaret. *Civic Monuments and the* Augustales *in Roman Italy*. New York: Cambridge University Press, 2015.

Lanciani, Rodolfo and Carlo Visconti. "Le ville Tusculane." *Bullettino della Commissione Archeologica Comunale in Roma* 12:172–217, 1884.

Landes, Christian, ed. *Le cirque et les courses de chars Rome—Byzance: Catalogue de l'exposition*. Lattes: Imago, 1990.

Larmour, David and Diana Spencer. "Introduction – *Roma, recepta*: A Topography of the Imagination." In *The Sites of Rome: Time, Space, and Memory*, edited by David Larmour and Diana Spencer, 1–60. New York: Oxford University Press, 2007.

Larmour, David and Diana Spencer, ed. *The Sites of Rome: Time, Space, and Memory*. New York: Oxford University Press, 2007.

Latham, Jacob A. "From Literal to Spiritual Soldiers of Christ: Disputed Episcopal Elections and the Advent of Christian Processions in Late Antique Rome." *Church History* 81:298–327, 2012.

Latham, Jacob A. "The Making of a Papal Rome: Gregory I and the *letania septiformis*." In *The Power of Religion in Late Antiquity: Select Papers from the Seventh Biennial Shifting Frontiers in Late Antiquity Conference*, edited by Andrew Cain and Noel Lenski, 293–304. Burlington, VT: Ashgate, 2009.

Latham, Jacob A. "Performing Theology: Imagining the Gods in the *Pompa Circensis*." *History of Religions* 54:288–317, 2015.

Latham, Jacob A. "Representing Ritual, Christianizing the *Pompa Circensis*: Imperial Spectacle at Rome in a Christianizing Empire." In *The Art of Empire: Christian Art in Its Imperial Context*, edited by Lee Jefferson and Robin Jensen, 197–224. Minneapolis: Fortress Press, 2015.

Latte, Kurt. *Römische Religionsgeschichte*. Munich: C. H. Beck, 1960.

Laurence, Ray. "City Traffic and the Archaelogy of Roman Streets from Pompeii to Rome." In *Stadtverkehr in der antiken Welt: Internationales Kolloquium zur 175-Jahrfeier des Deutschen Archäologischen Instituts Rom, 21. bis 23. April 2004*, edited by Dieter Mertens, 87–106. Wiesbaden: Reichert, 2008.

Laurence, Ray. "Emperors, Nature and the City: Rome's Ritual Landscape." *Accordia Research Papers* 4:79–87, 1993.

Laurence, Ray. "Streets and Facades." In *A Companion to Roman Architecture*, edited by Roger Ulrich and Caroline Quenemoen, 399–411. Malden, MA: Wiley-Blackwell, 2014.

Laurence, Ray and David Newsome, ed. *Rome, Ostia, Pompeii: Movement and Space*. New York: Oxford University Press, 2011.

Lavan, Luke. "Political Talismans? Residual 'Pagan' Statues in Late Antique Public Space." In *The Archaeology of Late Antique "Paganism,"* edited by Luke Lavan and Michael Mulryan, 439–477. Leiden: Brill, 2011.

Lavan, Luke and Michael Mulryan, ed. *The Archaeology of Late Antiquity "Paganism."* Leiden: Brill, 2011.

Lawrence, Marion. "The Circus Relief at Foligno." In *Ricerche sull'Umbria tardoantica e preromanica: Atti del secondo convegno dei studi Umbri*, 119–135. Gubbio: Centro di Studi Umbri, 1965.

Le Bonniec, Henri. *Le culte de Cérès à Rome des origines à la fin de la République.* Paris: C. Klincksieck, 1958.

Le Bonniec, Henri. "Une faute rituelle dans la *pompa* des jeux." In *Mélanges de philosophie, de littérature et d'histoire ancienne offerts à Pierre Boyancé*, 505–511. Rome: École française de Rome, 1974.

Leach, Eleanor. *The Rhetoric of Space: Literary and Artistic Representations of Landscape in Republican and Augustan Rome.* Princeton: Princeton University Press, 1988.

Lebek, Wolfgang Dieter. "Die circensischen Ehrungen für Germanicus und das Referat des Tacitus im Lichte von Tab. Siar. frg. II, col. c 2–11." *Zeitschrift für Papyrologie und Epigraphik* 73:249–274, 1988.

Lebek, Wolfgang Dieter. "Intenzione e composizione della 'Rogatio Valeria Aurelia.'" *Zeitschrift für Papyrologie und Epigraphik* 98:77–95, 1993.

Lebek, Wolfgang Dieter. "Kritik und Exegese zu Tab. Heb. cap. 5 (Z. 50–54) und Tac. Ann. 2,83,1." *Zeitschrift für Papyrologie und Epigraphik* 73:275–280, 1988.

Lehmann, Yves. *Varron théologien et philosophe romain.* Brussels: Latomus, 1997.

Leménorel, Alain, ed. *La rue, lieu de sociabilité? Rencontres de la rue.* Rouen: Université de Rouen, 1997.

Lenaghan, John O. *A Commentary on Cicero's Oration* De Haruspicum Responso. The Hague: Mouton, 1969.

Lendon, Jon. *Empire of Honour: The Art of Government in the Roman World.* New York: Oxford University Press, 1997.

Leone, Anna. *The End of the Pagan City: Religion, Economy, and Urbanism in Late Antique North Africa.* Oxford: Oxford University Press, 2013.

Lepelley, Claude. "Du triomphe à la disparition: Le destin de l'ordre équestre de Dioclétien à Théodose." In *L'ordre équestre: Histoire d'une aristocratie (IIe siècle av. J.-C.–IIIe siècle ap. J.-C.): Actes du colloque international (Bruxelles-Leuven, 5–7 octobre 1995)*, edited by Ségolène Demougin, Hubert Devijver, and Marie-Thérèse Raepsaet-Charlier, 629–646. Rome: École Française de Rome, 1999.

Lepelley, Claude. "Le musée des statues divines: La volonté de sauvegarder la patrimonie artistique païen à l'époque théodosienne." *Cahiers archéologiques* 42:5–15, 1994.

Leppin, Harmut. "Between Marginality and Celebrity: Entertainers and Entertainments in Roman Society." In *The Oxford Handbook of Social Relations in the Roman World*, edited by Michael Peachin, 660–678. New York: Oxford University Press, 2011.

Letzner, Wolfram. *Der römische Circus: Massenunterhaltung im Römischen Reich.* Mainz: Philipp von Zabern, 2009.

Levene, D. S. "Defining the Divine in Rome." *Transactions of the American Philological Association* 142:41–81, 2012.

Levene, D. S. *Religion in Livy.* Leiden: Brill, 1993.

Levick, Barbara. *Faustina I and II: Imperial Women of the Golden Age.* New York: Oxford University Press, 2014.

Lim, Richard. "Christianization, Secularization, and the Transformation of Public Life." In *A Companion to Late Antiquity*, edited by Philip Rousseau and Jutta Raithel, 497–511. Malden, MA: Wiley-Blackwell, 2009.

Lim, Richard. "In the 'Temple of Laughter': Visual and Literary Representations of Spectators at Roman Games." In *The Art of Ancient Spectacle*, edited by Bettina Bergmann and Christine Kondoleon, 343–365. Washington, D. C.: National Gallery of Art, 1999.

Lim, Richard. "Inventing Secular Space in the Late Antique City: Reading the Circus Maximus." In *Rom in der Spätantike: Historische Erinnerung in Städtischen Raum*, edited by Ralf Behrwald and Christian Witschel, 61–82. Stuttgart: Franz Steiner, 2012.

Lim, Richard. "People as Power: Games, Munificence and Contested Topography." In *The Transformations of the* Urbs Roma *in*

Late Antiquity, edited by W. V. Harris, 265–281. Portsmouth, R. I.: Journal of Roman Archaeology, 1999.

Lim, Richard. "The *Tribunus Voluptatum* in the Later Roman Empire." *Memoirs of the American Academy in Rome* 41:163–173, 1996.

Lincoln, Bruce. "On Ritual, Change, and Marked Categories." *Journal of the American Academy of Religion* 68:487–510, 2000.

Linder, M. and John Scheid. "Quand croire c'est faire: Le problème de la croyance dans la Rome ancienne." *Archives des sciences sociales des religions* 81:47–61, 1993.

Lindsay, Hugh. "Death-Pollution and Funerals in the City of Rome." In *Death and Disease in the Ancient City*, edited by Valerie Hope and Eireann Marshall, 152–172. New York: Routledge, 2000.

Lindsay, Hugh. "Vespasian and the City of Rome: The Centrality of the Capitolium." *Acta Classica* 53:165–180, 2010.

Ling, Roger. "A Stranger in Town: Finding the Way in an Ancient City." *Greece and Rome* 37:204–214, 1990.

Ling, Roger. "Street Plaques at Pompeii." In *Architecture and Architectural Sculpture in the Roman Empire*, edited by Martin Henig, 51–66. New York: Cambridge University Press, 1990.

Lipps, Johannes. "Alarichs Goten auf dem Forum Romanum? Überlegungen zu Gestalt, Chronologie und Verständnis der spätantiken Platzanlage." In *The Sack of Rome in 410 AD: The Event, Its Context and Its Impact*, edited by Carlos Machado, Johannes Lipps, and Philipp von Rummel, 103–122. Wiesbaden: Reichert, 2013.

Liu, Jinyu. "Professional Associations." In *The Cambridge Companion to Ancient Rome*, edited by Paul Erdkamp, 352–368. New York: Cambridge University Press, 2013.

Lizzi Testa, Rita. "The Late Antique Bishop: Image and Reality." In *A Companion to Late Antiquity*, edited by Philip Rousseau and Jutta Raithel, 525–538. Malden, MA: Wiley-Blackwell, 2009.

Lo Monaco, Annalisa. "In processione al Circo." In *Trionfi romani*, edited by Eugenio La Rocca and Stefano Tortorella, 76–83. Milan: Electa, 2008.

Long, Charlotte R. *The Twelve Gods of Greece and Rome*. Leiden: Brill, 1987.

Lott, J. Bert. *Death and Dynasty in Early Imperial Rome: Key Sources, with Text, Translation, and Commentary*. New York: Cambridge University Press, 2012.

Lovatt, Helen. "Statius on Parade: Performing Argive Identity in *Thebaid* 6.268–95." *Cambridge Classical Journal* 53:72–95, 2007.

Lozano, Fernando. "*Divi Augusti* and *Theoi Sebastoi*: Roman Initiatives and Greek Answers." *Classical Quarterly* 57:139–152, 2007.

Lucchi, Gabrielle. "Sul significato del carpentum nella monetazione romana imperiale." *Rivista italiana di numismatica e scienze affini* 68:131–143, 1968.

Lugaresi, Leonardo. "*Regio aliena:* L'attegiamento della chiesa verso i loughi di spettacolo nella città tardoantica." *Antiquité Tardive* 15:21–34, 2007.

Lugaresi, Leonardo. *Il teatro di Dio: Il problema degli spettacoli nel cristianesimo antico (II-IV secolo)*. Brescia: Morcelliana, 2008.

Lugli, Giuseppe. *Itinerario di Roma antica*. Milan: Periodici scientifici, 1970.

Lugli, Giuseppe. *Roma antica: Il centro monumentale*. Rome: Bardi, 1946.

Lynch, Kevin. *The Image of the City*. Cambridge, MA: MIT Press, 1960.

Lynch, Kevin. "Reconsidering *The Image of the City*." In *City Sense and City Design: Writings and Projects of Kevin Lynch*, edited by Tridib Banerjee and Michael Southworth, 247–256. Cambridge, MA: MIT Press (original 1984), 1990.

MacCormack, Sabine. *Art and Ceremony in Late Antiquity*. Berkeley: University of California Press, 1981.

MacCormack, Sabine. "*Loca Sancta*: The Organization of Sacred Topography in Late Antiquity." In *Roman Religion*, edited by Clifford Ando, 252–272. Edinburgh: Edinburgh University Press (original in R. Ousterhout, ed., *The Blessings of Pilgrimage*. Urbana, Il: University of Illinois Press, 1990), 2003.

MacDonald, William. *The Architecture of the Roman Empire, Volume II: An Urban Appraisal.* New Haven: Yale University Press, 1986.

Machado, Carlos. "Building the Past: Monuments and Memory in the *Forum Romanum*." In *Social and Political Life in Late Antiquity*, edited by William Bowden, Adam Gutteridge, and Carlos Machado, 157–192. Leiden: Brill, 2006.

Machado, Carlos. "The City as Stage: Aristocratic Commemorations in Late Antique Rome." In *Les frontières du profane dans l'antiquité tardive*, edited by Éric Rebillard and Claire Sotinel, 287–317. Rome: École française de Rome, 2010.

Machado, Carlos. "Public Monuments and Civic Life: The End of the Statue Habit in Italy." In *Le trasformazioni del V secolo: L'Italia, i barbari e l'Occidente romano: Atti del seminario di Poggibonsi, 18–20 ottobre 2007*, edited by Paolo Delogu and Stefano Gasparri, 237–257. Turnhout: Brepols, 2010.

Machado, Carlos. "Religion as Antiquarianism: Pagan Dedications in Late Antique Rome." In *Dediche sacre nel mondo Greco-Romano: Diffusione, funzioni, tipologie*, edited by John Bodel and Mika Kajava, 331–354. Rome: Institutum Romanum Finlandiae, 2009.

Maclean, Rose. "People on the Margins of Roman Spectacle." In *A Companion to Sport and Spectacle in Greek and Roman Antiquity*, edited by Paul Christesen and Donald Kyle, 578–589. Malden, MA: Wiley-Blackwell, 2014.

MacMullen, Ramsey. *Paganism in the Roman Empire.* New Haven: Yale University Press, 1981.

MacMullen, Ramsey. *Roman Social Relations, 50 B.C. to A.D. 284.* New Haven: Yale University Press, 1974.

Mader, Gottfried. "Triumphal Elephants and Political Circus at Plutarch, *Pomp.* 14.6." *Classical World* 99:397–403, 2006.

Madigan, Brian. *The Ceremonial Sculptures of the Roman Gods.* Leiden: Brill, 2013.

Malmberg, Simon. "Finding Your Way in the Subura." In *TRAC 2008: Proceedings of the Eighteenth Annual Theoretical Roman Archaeology Conference, Amsterdam 2008*, edited by Stijn Heeren, Mark Driessen, Joep Hendriks, Fleur Kemmers, and Ronald Visser, 39–51. Oxford: Oxbow Books, 2009.

Mammel, Kathryn. "Ancient Critics of Roman Sport and Spectacle." In *A Companion to Sport and Spectacle in Greek and Roman Antiquity*, edited by Paul Christesen and Donald Kyle, 603–616. Malden, MA: Wiley-Blackwell, 2014.

Manuwald, Gesine. *Roman Republican Theatre.* New York: Cambridge University Press, 2011.

Marcattili, Francesco. "*Agrum qui appellatur circus* (ILAfr, 527): Postilla sul circo di Assisi." *Ostraka* 16:311–317, 2007.

Marcattili, Francesco. *Circo Massimo: Architetture, funzioni, culti, ideologia.* Rome: "L'Erma" di Bretschneider, 2009.

Marcattili, Francesco. "Pulvinar." In *Thesaurus Cultus et Rituum Antiquorum (ThesCRA) IV: Cult Places, Representations of Cult Places*, edited by Lexicon Iconographicum Mythologiae Classicae (LIMC), 306–307. Los Angeles: Getty Publications, 2005.

Marchet, Gwénaëlle. "*Mittere mappam* (Mart. 12.28.9): Du signal de départ à la théologie imperiale (Ier a.C.-VIIe p.C)." In *Le cirque romain et son image*, edited by Jocelyne Nelis-Clément and Jean-Michel Roddaz, 291–317. Bourdeaux: Ausonius, 2008.

Marco Simón, Francisco. "Ritual Participation and Collective Identity in the Roman Republic: *Census* and *Lustrum*." In *Repúblicas y ciudadanos: Modelos de participación cívica en el mundo antiguo*, edited by Francisco Marco Simón, Francisco Pina Polo, and José Remesal Rodríguez, 153–166. Barcelona: Publicacions i Edicions de la Universitat de Barcelona, 2006.

Mariotti, Valeria. "Gli spettacoli in epoca tardoantica: I dittici come fonte iconografica." In *Eburnea diptycha: I dittici d'avorio tra Antichità e Medioevo*, edited by Massimiliano David, 245–268. Bari: Edipuglia, 2005.

Markus, R. A. *The End of Ancient Christianity.* New York: Cambridge University Press, 1990.

Marquardt, Joachim. *Römische Staatsverwaltung.* Leipzig: S. Hirzel, 1885.

Martin, Susan. "Transportation and the Law in the City of Rome." In *Rome and Her Monuments: Essays on the City and Literature of Rome in Honor of Katherine A. Geffcken*, edited by Sheila Dickison and Judith Hallet, 193–213. Wauconda, IL: Bolchazy-Carducci, 2000.

Massa-Pairault, Françoise-Hélène. "Aspects idéologique des *ludi*." In *Spectacles sportifs et scéniques dans le monde étrusco-italique: Actes de la table ronde*, 247–279. Rome: École française de Rome, 1993.

Matthews, John F. *Western Aristocracies and Imperial Court, AD 364–425*. Oxford: Oxford University Press, 1975.

Mattingly, Harold. "The Consecration of Faustina the Elder and Her Daughter." *Harvard Theological Review* 41:147–151, 1948.

Mauss, Marcel. *The Gift: The Form and Reason for Exchange in Archaic Societies*. Translated by W. D. Halls. New York: Norton, 1990.

McCormick, Michael. *Eternal Victory: Triumphal Rulership in Late Antiquity, Byzantium and the Early Medieval West*. New York: Maison des Sciences de l'Homme and Cambridge University Press, 1986.

McGinn, Bernard. "*Regina quondam* ..." *Speculum* 83:817–839, 2008.

McIntyre, Gwynaeth. "Constructing a Family: Representations of the Women of the Roman Imperial Family."*Acta Patristica et Byzantina* 21:109–120, 2010.

McLynn, Neil. "Crying Wolf: The Pope and the Lupercalia." *Journal of Roman Studies* 98:161–175, 2008.

Menci, Giovanna. "Un progamma circense." In *Papyri in honorem Johannis Bingen octogenarii (P. Bingen)*, edited by Henri Melaerts, 523–527. Leuven: Peeters, 2000.

Menzel, Heinz. "Elfenbeinrelief mit Tensa-Darstellung im Römisch-Germanisch Zentralmuseum." *Mainzer Zeitschrift* 44/45: 58–62, 1949/50.

Meslin, Michel. *La fête des kalendes de janvier dans l'empire romain*. Brussels: Latomus, 1970.

Michels, Agnes Kirsopp. "The Topography and Interpretation of the Lupercal." *Transactions of the American Philological Association* 84:35–59, 1953.

Miles, Gary. *Livy: Reconstructing Early Rome*. Ithaca, NY: Cornell University Press, 1995.

Millar, Fergus. *The Crowd in Rome in the Late Republic*. Ann Arbor, MI: University of Michigan Press, 1998.

Mittag, Peter Franz. *Alte Köpfe in neuen Händen: Urheber und Funktion der Kontorniaten*. Bonn: Habelt, 1999.

Mittag, Peter Franz. "*Processus consularis, Adventus* und Herrschaftsjubiläum: Zur Verwendung von Triumphsymbolik in der mittleren Kaiserzeit." *Hermes* 137:447–462, 2009.

Molin, Michel. "Le char à Rome, véhicule de l'idéologie impériale." In *Images et représentations du pouvoir et de l'ordre social dans l'antiquité: Actes du colloque, Angers, 28–29 mai 1999*, edited by Michel Molin, 291–300. Paris: Boccard, 2001.

Momigliano, Arnaldo. *On Pagans, Jews, and Christians*. Hanover, NH: Wesleyan University Press, 1987.

Mommsen, Theodor. "Die *ludi magni* und *romani*." *Rheinisches Museum für Philologie* 14:79–87, 1859.

Monti, Salvatore. "*Instauratio ludorum*." *Rendiconti dell'Accademia di Archeologia, Lettere e Belle Arti di Napoli* 24–25:155–179, 1949–1950.

Moore, Timothy. "*Palliata Togata*: Plautus, *Curculio* 462–86." *American Journal of Philology* 112:343–362, 1991.

Moralee, Jason. "A Hill of Many Names: The Capitolium from Late Antiquity to the Middle Ages." *Acta ad archaeologiam et artium historiam pertinentia* 26: 47–70, 2013.

Morelli, Federico. "Programma del circo (senza corse?)." In *Wiener Papyri als Festgabe zum 60. Geburtstag von Hermann Harrauer (P. Harrauer)*, edited by Bernhard Palme, 201–206. Vienna: Holzhausens, 2001.

Mountford, Margaret. "A Day at the Races in Byzantine Oxyrhynchus." *Egyptian Archaeology: The Bulletin of the Egypt Exploration Society* 41:5–7, 2012.

Mulryan, Michael. "The Temple of Flora or Venus by the Circus Maximus and the New Christian Topography: The 'Pagan Revival' in

Action?" In *The Archaeology of Late Antique "Paganism,"* edited by Luke Lavan and Michael Mulryan, 209–227. Leiden: Brill, 2011.

Mumford, Lewis. *The City in History: Its Origins, Its Transformations, and Its Prospects.* New York: Harcourt, Brace & World, 1961.

Mura Sommella, Anna. "L'area sacra di S. Omobono: La decorazione architettonica del tempio arcaico." *La parola del passato* 32: 62–128, 1977.

Mura Sommella, Anna. "Il tempio di Giove Capitolino: Una nuova proposta di lettura." *Annali della Fondazione per il Museo Claudio Faina* 16:333–372, 2009.

Muth, Susanne. "Rom in der Spätantike: Die Stadt als Erinnerungslandschaft." In *Erinnerungsorte der Antike: Die römische Welt,* edited by Elke Stein-Hölkeskamp and Karl-Joachim Hölkeskamp, 438–456. Munich: C.H. Beck, 2006.

Naerebout, F. "*Das Reich Tanzt*... Dance in the Roman Empire and Its Discontents." In *Ritual Dynamics and Religious Change in the Roman Empire,* edited by O. Hekster, S. Schmidt-Hofner, and C. Witschel, 143–158. Leiden: Brill, 2009.

Nash, Ernest. *Pictorial Dictionary of Ancient Rome.* London: Zwemmer, 1961–1962.

Nelis, Damien. "Caesar, the Circus and the Charioteer in Vergil's *Georgics.*" In *Le cirque romaine et son image,* edited by Jocelyne Nelis-Clément and Jean-Michel Roddaz, 497–520. Bourdeaux: Ausonius, 2008.

Nelis, Damien and Jocelyn Nelis-Clément. "Vergil, *Georgics* 1.1–42 and the *pompa circensis.*" *Dictynna* 8 http://dictynna.revues.org/730, 2011.

Nelis-Clément, Jocelyne. "Le cirque romain et son paysage sonore." In *Le cirque romaine et son image,* edited by Jocelyne Nelis-Clément and Jean-Michel Roddaz, 431–457. Bourdeaux: Ausonius, 2008.

Nelis-Clément, Jocelyne. "Les métiers du cirque, de Rome à Byzance: Entre texte et image." *Cahiers du Centre Gustave Glotz* 13:265–303, 2002.

Nelis-Clément, Jocelyne. "Pompes et circonstances: Cérémonies et rituels, de Fribourg à Rome." In *Epigraphie romaine et historiographie antique et moderne: Actes de la journée d'études en mémoire du Prof. ém. T. Zawadzki (28 octobre 2011),* edited by Olivier Curty, 53–72. Fribourg: RERO DOC (Bibliothèque Cantonale and Universitaire de Fribourg), 2013.

Nelis-Clément, Jocelyne and Jean-Michel Roddaz, ed. *Le cirque romain et son image.* Bourdeaux: Ausonius 2008.

Newsome, David. "Introduction: Making Movement Meaningful." In *Rome, Ostia, Pompeii: Movement and Space,* edited by Ray Laurence and David Newsome, 1–54. New York: Oxford University Press, 2011.

Newsome, David. "Movement and Fora in Rome (the Late Republic to the First Century CE)." In *Rome, Ostia, Pompeii: Movement and Space,* edited by Ray Laurence and David Newsome, 290–311. New York: Oxford University Press, 2011.

Nicolet, Claude. *L'ordre équestre à l'époque républicaine (312–43 av. J.-C.).* Paris: Boccard, 1966.

Nicolet, Claude. *Space, Geography and Politics in the Early Roman Empire.* Translated by Hélène Leclerc. Ann Arbor: University of Michigan Press, 1991.

Nicolet, Claude. *The World of the Citizen in Republican Rome.* Translated by P. S. Falla. Berkeley: University of California Press, 1980.

Nielsen, Inge. "The Forum Paving and the Temple of Castor and Pollux." *Analecta Romana Instituti Danici* 19:89–104, 1990.

Nijf, Onno M. van. *The Civic World of Profesional Associations in the Roman East.* Leiden: Brill, 1997.

Niquet, Heike. *Monumenta virtutum titulique: Senatorische Selbstdarstellung im spätantiken Rom im Spiegel der epigraphischen Denkmäler.* Stuttgart: Franz Steiner, 2000.

Noble, Thomas F. X. "The Roman Elite from Constantine to Charlemagne." *Acta ad Archaeologiam et Artium Historiam Pertinentia* 17:13–25, 2003.

Nogales, Trinidad and Julián González, ed. *Culto imperial: Política y poder.* Rome: "L'Erma" di Bretschneider, 2007.

Nora, Pierre. "General Introduction: Between Memory and History." In *Realms of Memory: The Construction of the French Past*, edited by Pierre Nora, 1–20. New York: Columbia University Press, 1996.

Noreña, Carlos. *Imperial Ideals in the Roman West: Representation, Circulation, Power*. New York: Cambridge University Press, 2011.

North, John. "Caesar at the Lupercalia." *Journal of Roman Studies* 98:144–160, 2008.

North, John. "Praesens Divus: *Divus Julius* by S. Weinstock." *Journal of Roman Studies* 65:171–177, 1975.

North, John and Neil McLynn. "Postscript to the Lupercalia: From Caesar to Andromachus." *Journal of Roman Studies* 98:176–181, 2008.

O'Daly, Gerard. *Augustine's City of God: A Reader's Guide*. Oxford: Oxford University Press, 1999.

O'Sullivan, Timothy. "Augustan Literary Tours: Walking and Reading the City." In *The Moving City: Processions, Passages and Promenades in Ancient Rome*, edited by Ida Östenberg, Simon Malmberg, and Jonas Bjønebye, 111–122. New York: Bloomsbury, 2015.

O'Sullivan, Timothy. *Walking in Roman Culture*. New York: Cambridge University Press, 2011.

Olgilvie, R. M. *A Commentary on Livy, Books 1–5*. Oxford: Clarendon Press, 1965.

Olick, Jeffrey, Vered Vinitzky-Seroussi, and Daniel Levy. "Introduction." In *The Collective Memory Reader*, edited by Jeffrey Olick, Vered Vinitzky-Seroussi, and Daniel Levy, 3–62. New York: Oxford University Press, 2011.

Olick, Jeffrey, Vered Vinitzky-Seroussi, and Daniel Levy, ed. *The Collective Memory Reader*. New York: Oxford University Press, 2011.

Olovsdotter, Cecilia. *The Consular Image: An Iconological Study of the Consular Diptychs*. Oxford: British Archaeological Reports, 2005.

Orlandi, Silvia. "I *loca* del Colosseo." In *Sangue e Arena*, edited by Adriano La Regina, 89–103. Milan: Electa, 2001.

Orlin, Eric. "Augustan Religion and the Reshaping of Roman Memory." *Arethusa* 40:73–92, 2007.

Orlin, Eric. *Foreign Cults in Rome: Creating a Roman Empire*. New York: Oxford, 2010.

Osgood, Josiah. *Claudius Caesar: Image and Power in the Early Roman Empire*. New York: Cambridge University Press, 2011.

Östenberg, Ida. "*Circum metas fertur*: An Alternative Reading of the Triumphal Route." *Historia* 59:303–320, 2010.

Östenberg, Ida. "Power Walks: Aristocratic Escorted Movements in Republican Rome." In *The Moving City: Processions, Passages and Promenades in Ancient Rome*, edited by Ida Östenberg, Simon Malmberg, and Jonas Bjønebye, 13–22. New York: Bloomsbury, 2015.

Östenberg, Ida. *Staging the World: Spoils, Captives, and Representations in the Roman Triumphal Procession*. New York: Oxford University Press, 2009.

Östenberg, Ida, Simon Malmberg, and Jonas Bjønebye, ed. *The Moving City: Processions, Passages and Promenades in Ancient Rome* New York: Bloomsbury, 2015.

Owens, William. "Plautus' *Stichus* and the Political Crisis of 200 B.C." *American Journal of Philology* 121:385–407, 2000.

Pagnotta, Maria Antonietta. "Carpentum: Privilegio del carro e roulo sociale della matrona romana." *Annali della Facoltà di Lettere e Filosofia, Università di Perugia* 15:157–170, 1977–1978.

Pandey, Nandini. "Caesar's Comet, the Julian Star, and the Invention of Augustus." *Transactions of the American Philological Association* 143:405–449, 2013.

Papi, Emanuele. "La *turba inpia*: Artigianti e commercianti del Foro Romano e dintorni (I sec. a.C.—64 d.C.)." *Journal of Roman Archaeology* 15:45–62, 2002.

Paradisi, Donatella. *Il Campidoglio: Storie, personaggi e monumenti del mitico colle di Roma*. Rome: Rendina, 2004.

Parker, Holt. "The Observed of All Observers: Spectacle, Applause, and Cultural Poetics in the Roman Theater Audience." In *The Art of*

Ancient Spectacle, edited by Bettina Bergmann and Christine Kondoleon, 163–179. Washington, D. C.: National Gallery of Art, 1999.

Peachin, Michael, ed. *The Oxford Handbook of Social Relations in the Roman World*. New York: Oxford University Press, 2011.

Péché, Valérie and Christophe Vendries. *Musique et spectacles dans la Rome antique et dans l'Occident romain sous la République et le Haut-Empire*. Paris: Errance, 2001.

Peppel, Matthias. "Gott oder Mensch? Kaiserverehrung und Herrschaftskontrolle." In *Die Praxis der Herrscherverehrung in Rom und seinen Provinzen*, edited by Hubert Cancik and Konrad Hitzl, 69–95. Tübingen: Mohr Siebeck, 2003.

Perassi, Claudia. "Medaglioni romani dedicati alla celebrazione dei ludi circensi." *Rivista italiana di numismatica e scienze affini* 95:385–412, 1993.

Perry, Ellen. "The Same, but Different: The Temple of Jupiter Optimus Maximus Through Time." In *Architecture of the Sacred: Space, Ritual, and Experience from Classical Greece to Byzantium*, edited by Bonna Wescoat and Robert Ousterhout, 175–200. New York: Cambridge University Press, 2012.

Piacente, Luigi. "*Peregrini ac superbi vehiculi* (Symm. *Rel.* 4,1)." *Classica & Christiana* 1:173–186, 2006.

Pietrangeli, Carlo, ed. *I monumenti dei culti orientali: Cataloghi dei musei comunali di Roma 1*. Rome, 1951.

Piganiol, André. *Recherches sur les jeux romains: Notes d'archéologie e d'histoire religeuse*. Strasbourg: Librarie Istra, 1923.

Piganiol, André. "Les sens religieux des jeux antiques." In *Scripta Varia II: Les origines de Rome et la République*, edited by André Chastagnol, Raymond Bloch, Raymond Chevallier, and Maurice Renard, 158–174. Brussels: Latomus, 1973.

Pighi, Giovanni. *De ludis saecularibus populi romani Quiritum*. Milan: Società Editrice 'Vita e Pensiero', 1941.

Pina Polo, Francisco. *The Consul at Rome: The Civil Functions of the Consuls in the Roman Republic*. New York: Cambridge University Press, 2011.

Pina Polo, Francisco. "Consuls as *curatores pacis deorum*." In *Consuls and* Res Publica*: Holding High Office in the Roman Republic*, edited by Hans Beck, Antonio Duplá, Martin Jehne, and Francisco Pina Polo, 97–115. New York: Cambridge University Press, 2011.

Pisani Sartorio, Giuseppina. "Le cirque de Maxence et les cirque de l'Italie antique." In *Le cirque romaine et son image*, edited by Jocelyne Nelis-Clément and Jean-Michel Roddaz, 47–78. Bourdeaux: Ausonius, 2008.

Pisani Sartorio, Giuseppina. *Mezzi di trasporto e traffico*. Rome: Quasar, 1988.

Plass, Paul. *The Game of Death in Ancient Rome: Arena Sport and Political Suicide*. Madison, WI: University of Wisconsin Press 1995.

Polverini, Leandro. "Donne al circo." In *Le cirque romaine et son image*, edited by Jocelyne Nelis-Clément and Jean-Michel Roddaz, 469–474. Bourdeaux: Ausonius, 2008.

Porte, Danielle. "Note sur les *luperci nudi*." In *Italie prèromaine et la Rome rèpublicaine: Mélanges offerts à Jacques Heurgon*, 817–824. Rome: École française de Rome, 1976.

Portefaix, Lilian. "Ancient Ephesus: Processions as Media of Religious and Secular Propaganda." In *The Problem of Ritual: Based on Papers at the Symposium on Religious Rites held at Åbo, Finland, on the 13th–16th of August 1991*, edited by Tore Ahlbäck, 195–210. Åbo: Donner Institute, 1993.

Potter, David. "Entertainers in the Roman Empire." In *Life, Death, and Entertainment in the Roman Empire*, edited by David Potter and David Mattingly, 280–372. Ann Arbor, MI: University of Michigan Press, 2010.

Potter, David. "Martyrdom as Spectacle." In *Theater and Society in the Classical World*, edited by Ruth Scodel, 53–87. Ann Arbor, MI: University of Michigan Press, 1993.

Poulsen, Birte. "The Dioscuri and Ruler Ideology." *Symbolae Osloenses* 66:119–146, 1991.

Prescendi, Francesca. "Children and the Transmission of Religious Knowledge." In *Children, Memory, and Family Identity in Roman Culture*, edited by Véronique Dasen and Thomas Späth, 73–93. New York: Oxford University Press, 2010.

Price, Simon R. F. "From Noble Funerals to Divine Cult." In *Rituals of Royalty: Power and Ceremonial in Traditional Societies*, edited by David Cannadine and Simon R. F. Price. New York: Cambridge University Press, 1987.

Price, Simon R. F. "Gods and Emperors: The Greek Language of the Roman Imperial Cult." *Journal of Hellenic Studies* 104:79–95, 1984.

Price, Simon R. F. "Latin Christian Apologetics: Minucius Felix, Tertullian, and Cyprian." In *Apologetics in the Roman Empire: Pagans, Jews, and Christians*, edited by Martin Goodman, Mark Edwards, Simon Price, and Christopher Rowland, 105–129. New York: Oxford University Press, 1999.

Price, Simon R. F. *Rituals and Power: The Roman Imperial Cult in Asia Minor*. New York: Cambridge University Press, 1984.

Purcell, Nicholas. "Becoming Historical: The Roman Case." In *Myth, History and Culture in Republican Rome: Studies in Honour of T. P. Wiseman*, edited by David Braund and Christopher Gill, 12–40. Exeter: University of Exeter Press, 2003.

Purcell, Nicholas. "The City of Rome." In *The Legacy of Rome: A New Appraisal*, edited by Richard Jenkyns, 421–453. New York: Oxford University Press, 1992.

Raaflaub, Kurt. "Romulus und die Wölfin: Roms Anfänge zwischen Mythos und Geschichte." In *Erinnerungsorte der Antike: Die römische Welt*, edited by Elke Stein-Hölkeskamp and Karl-Joachim Hölkeskamp, 18–39. Munich: C.H. Beck, 2006.

Ramsey, John and A. Lewis Licht. *The Comet of 44 B.C. and Caesar's Funeral Games*. Atlanta, GA: Scholars Press, 1997.

Rapp, Claudia. *Holy Bishops in Late Antiquity: The Nature of Christian Leadership in an Age of Transition*. Berkeley: University of California Press, 2005.

Rappaport, Roy. *Ritual and Religion in the Making of Humanity*. New York: Cambridge University Press, 1999.

Rawson, Elizabeth. "*Discrimina ordinum*: The *Lex Julia Theatralis*." *Papers of the British School at Rome* 55:83–114, 1987.

Rawson, Elizabeth. *Intellectual Life in the Late Roman Republic*. Baltimore: Johns Hopkins University Press, 1985.

Rea, Jennifer. *Legendary Rome: Myth, Monuments, and Memory on the Palatine and Capitoline*. London: Duckworth, 2007.

Rebecchi, Fernando. "Per l'iconografia della *transvectio equitum*: Altre considerazioni e nouvi documenti." In *L'ordre équestre: Histoire d'une aristocratie (IIe siècle av. J.-C.–IIIe siècle ap. J.-C.): Actes du colloque international (Bruxelles-Leuven, 5–7 octobre 1995)*, edited by Ségolène Demougin, Hubert Devijver, and Marie-Thérèse Raepsaet-Charlier, 191–214. Rome: École Française de Rome, 1999.

Rebenich, Stefan. "*Insania circi*: Eine Tertullianreminiszenz bei Hieronymus und Augustin." *Latomus* 53:155–158, 1994.

Rebillard, Éric. *Christians and Their Many Identities in Late Antiquity, North Africa, 200—450 CE*. Ithaca, NY: Cornell University Press, 2012.

Reinsberg, Carola. *Die Sarkophage mit den Darstellungen aus dem Menschenleben: Dritter teil: Vita Romana*. Berlin: Gebr. Mann, 2006.

Rice, E. E. *The Grand Procession of Ptolemy Philadelphus*. New York: Oxford University Press, 1983.

Rich, J. W. "Augustus' Parthian Honors, the Temple of Mars Ultor and the Arch in the Forum Romanum." *Papers of the British School at Rome* 66:71–128, 1998.

Ricoeur, Paul. *Time and Narrative*. Translated by Kathleen McLaughlin and David Pellauer. 3 vols. Chicago: University of Chicago Press, 1984.

Ridley, Ronald. "Unbridgeable Gaps: The Capitoline Temple at Rome." *Bullettino della Commissione Archeologica Comunale in Roma* 106:83–104, 2005.

Rives, James. *Religion in the Roman Empire*. Malden, MA: Blackwell, 2007.

Robertson, Anne. *Roman Imperial Coins in the Hunter Coin Cabinet, University of Glasgow*. 5 vols. London: University of Glasgow, 1962–1982.

Robinson, O.F. *Ancient Rome: City Planning and Administration*. New York: Routledge, 1992.

Roche, Paul. "The *Panegyricus* and the Monuments of Rome." In *Pliny's Praise: The* Panegyricus *in the Roman World*, edited by Paul Roche, 45–66. New York: Cambridge University Press, 2011.

Rodriguez, Connie. "The *puluinar* at the *Circus Maximus*: Worship of Augustus in Rome?" *Latomus* 64:619–625, 2005.

Rodríguez-Mayorgas, Ana. "*Annales Maximi*: Writing, Memory, and Religious Performance in the Roman Republic." In *Sacred Words: Orality, Literacy, and Religion*, edited by Josine Blok, A. P. M. H. Lardinois, and Marc van der Poel, 235–254. Leiden: Brill, 2011.

Rodríguez-Mayorgas, Ana. *La memoria de Roma: Oralidad, escritura e historia en la República romana*. Oxford: John and Erica Hedges Ltd, 2007.

Rodríguez-Mayorgas, Ana. "Romulus, Aeneas and the Cultural Memory of the Roman Republic." *Athenaeum* 98:89–109, 2010.

Rogers, Guy. *The Sacred Identity of Ephesos: Foundation Myths of a Roman City*. New York: Routledge, 1991.

Rolle, Alessandra. "Il motivo del culto cibelico nelle *Eumenides* di Varrone." *Maia* 61:545–563, 2009.

Roller, Lynn. *In Search of God the Mother: The Cult of Anatolian Cybele*. Berkeley: University of California Press, 1999.

Roman, Luke. "Martial and the City of Rome." *Journal of Roman Studies* 100:88–117, 2010.

Romano, D. "Varrone e Cibele." In *Atti congresso internazionale di studi varroniani: Rieti settembre 1974*, 495–506. Rieti: Centro di studi varroniani, 1976.

Romano, David Gilman. "Digital Augustan Rome." (http://digitalaugustanrome.org/), 2008–2016.

Rose, Peter. "Spectators and Spectator Comfort in Roman Entertainment Buildings: A Study in Functional Design." *Papers of the British School at Rome* 73:93–130, 2005.

Rosenstein, Nathan. "Aristocratic Values." In *A Companion to the Roman Republic*, edited by Nathan Rosenstein and Robert Morstein-Marx, 365–382. Malden, MA: Wiley-Blackwell, 2006.

Rosenstein, Nathan and Robert Morstein-Marx, ed. *A Companion to the Roman Republic*. Malden, MA: Wiley-Blackwell, 2006.

Rosso, Emmanuelle. "Culte imperial et image dynastique: Les *divi* et *divae* de la *Gens Flavia*." In *Culto imperial: política y poder*, edited by Trinidad Nogales and Julián González, 126–151. Rome: "L'Erma" di Bretschneider, 2007.

Rousseau, Philip and Jutta Raithel, ed. *A Companion to Late Antiquity*. Malden, MA: Wiley-Blackwell, 2009.

Rowan, Clare. *Under Divine Auspices: Divine Ideology and the Visualisation of Imperial Power in the Severan Period*. New York: Cambridge University Press, 2012.

Rowe, Greg. *Princes and Political Cultures: The New Tiberian Senatorial Decrees*. Ann Arbor, MI: University of Michigan Press, 2002.

Ruggiero, Ettore de. *Dizionario epigrafico di antichità romane*. Vol. 1. Rome: Istituto Italiano per la Storia Antica, 1895.

Rüpke, Jörg. "Acta aut agenda: Relations between Script and Performance." In *Rituals in Ink: A Conference on Religion and Literary Production in Ancient Rome*, edited by Alessandro Barchiesi, Jörg Rüpke, and Susan Stephens, 23–44. Stuttgart: Franz Steiner, 2004.

Rüpke, Jörg, ed. *A Companion to Roman Religion*. Malden, MA: Wiley-Blackwell, 2007.

Rüpke, Jörg. "Public and Publicity: Long-Term Changes in Religious Festivals during the Roman Republic." In *Greek and Roman Festivals: Content, Meaning, and Practice*, edited by J. Rasmus Brandt and Jon W. Iddeng, 305–322. New York: Oxford University Press, 2012.

Rüpke, Jörg. *Religion in Republican Rome: Rationalization and Religious Change*. Philadelphia: University of Pennsylvania Press, 2012.

Rüpke, Jörg. *Religion of the Romans*. Translated by Richard Gordon. Malden, MA: Polity, 2007.

Rüpke, Jörg. "Representation or Presence? Picturing the Divine in Ancient Rome." *Archiv für Religionsgeschichte* 12:181–196, 2010.

Rüpke, Jörg. "Tempel, Daten, Rituale: Die Götter als Langzeitgedächtnis der Gesellschaft." In *Erinnerungsorte der Antike: Die römische Welt*, edited by Elke Stein-Hölkeskamp and Karl-Joachim Hölkeskamp, 554–569. Munich: C.H. Beck, 2006.

Rüpke, Jörg. "Triumphator and Ancestor Rituals between Symbolic Anthropology and Magic." *Numen* 53:251–289, 2006.

Rüpke, Jörg. "Varro's *Tria Genera Theologiae*: Religious Thinking in the Late Republic." *Ordia Prima* 4:107–129, 2005.

Sablayrolles, Robert. *Libertinus miles: Les cohortes de vigiles*. Rome: École Française de Rome, 1996.

Sales-Carbonell, Jordina. "Roman Spectacle Buildings as a Setting for Martyrdom and Its Consequences in the Christian Architecture." *Journal of Ancient History and Archeology* 1:8–21, 2014.

Salomonson, Jan Willem. *Chair, Sceptre and Wreath: Historical Aspects of Their Representation on Some Roman Sepulchral Monuments*. Amsterdam: E. Harms, 1956.

Salzman, Michele Renée. "The Christianization of Sacred Time and Sacred Space." In *The Transformations of the* Urbs Roma *in Late Antiquity*, edited by W. V. Harris, 123–134. Portsmouth, R. I.: Journal of Roman Archaeology, 1999.

Salzman, Michele Renée. "The End of Public Sacrifice: Changing Definitions of Sacrifice in Post-Constantinian Rome and Italy." In *Ancient Mediterranean Sacrifice*, edited by Jennifer Knust and Zsuzsanna Várhelyi, 167–183. New York: Oxford University Press, 2011.

Salzman, Michele Renée. "Leo in Rome: The Evolution of Episcopal Authority in the Fifth Century." In *Istituzioni, carismi ed esercizio del potere (IV-VI secolo d.C.)*, edited by Giorgio Bonamente and Rita Lizzi Testa, 343–356. Bari: Edipuglia, 2010.

Salzman, Michele Renée. "Leo's Liturgical Topography: Contestations for Space in Fifth-Century Rome." *Journal of Roman Studies* 103:208–232, 2013.

Salzman, Michele Renée. *The Making of a Christian Aristocracy: Social and Religious Change in the Western Roman Empire*. Cambridge, MA: Harvard University Press, 2002.

Salzman, Michele Renée. *On Roman Time: The Codex-Calendar of 354 and the Rhythms of Urban Life in Late Antiquity*. Berkeley: University of California Press, 1990.

Salzman, Michele Renée. "'Superstitio' in the Codex Theodosianus and the Persecution of Pagans." *Vigiliae Christianae* 41:172–188, 1987.

Salzman, Michele Renée. "Topography and Religion in 4th-c Rome." *Journal of Roman Archaeology* 16:689–692, 2003.

Samuels, Raphael. "From *Theatres of Memory*." In *The Collective Memory Reader*, edited by Jeffrey Olick, Vered Vinitzky-Seroussi, and Daniel Levy, 261–264. New York: Oxford University Press, 2011.

Sandwell, Isabella. "Outlawing 'Magic' or Outlawing 'Religion'? Libanius and the Theodosian Code as Evidence for Legislation against 'Pagan' Practices." In *The Spread of Christianity in the First Four Centuries: Essays in Explanation*, edited by W. V. Harris, 87–123. Leiden: Brill, 2005.

Santucci, Anna. "22. Rilievo frammentario con pompa trionfale." In *La raccolta di antichità Baldassine-Castelli: Itinerario tra Roma, Terni e Pesaro*, edited by Valeria Purcaro Maria Elisa Micheli, and Anna Santucci, 196–197. Pisa: Edizioni ETS, 2007.

Sapelli, Marina. "La Basilica di Gunio Basso." In *Aurea Roma: Dalla città pagana alla città cristiana*, edited by Serena Ensoli and Eugenio La Rocca, 137–139. Rome: "L'Erma" di Bretschneider, 2000.

Schäfer, Thomas. "Römisches Relief mit Tensa." *Bulletin du Musée Hongrois des Beaux-Arts* 96:31–49, 2002.

Scheid, John. "Cults, Myths, and Politics at the Beginning of the Empire." In *Roman Religion*, edited by Clifford Ando, 117–138. Edinburgh: Edinburgh University Press, 2003.

Scheid, John. "Le délit religieux dans la Rome tardo-républicaine." In *Le délit religieux dans la cité antique: Actes de la table ronde de Rome (6–7 avril 1978)*, 117–171. Rome: École Française de Rome, 1981.

Scheid, John. "Les dieux du Capitole: Un exemple des structures théologiques des sanctuaires romains." In *Théorie et pratique de l'architecture romaine: La norme et l'expérimentation*, edited by X. Lafon and G. Sauron, 93–100. Aix-en-Provence: Publications de l'université de Provence, 2005.

Scheid, John. "The Expiation of Impieties Committed without Intention and the Formation of Roman Theology." In *Transformations of the Inner Self in Ancient Religions*, edited by Jan Assmann and Guy Stroumsa, 331–347. Leiden: Brill, 1999.

Scheid, John. "The Festivals of the Forum Boarium Area: Reflections on the Construction of Complex Representations of Roman Identity." In *Greek and Roman Festivals: Content, Meaning, and Practice*, edited by J. Rasmus Brandt and Jon W. Iddeng, 289–304. New York: Oxford University Press, 2012.

Scheid, John. "Le flamine de Jupiter, les Vestales et le général triomphant: Variations romaines sur le thème de la figuration des dieux." In *Corps des dieux*, edited by C. Malamoud and J.P. Vernant, 213–230. Paris: Gallimard, 1986.

Scheid, John. "Hierarchy and Structure in Roman Polytheism: Roman Methods of Conceiving Action." In *Roman Religion*, edited by Clifford Ando, 164–189. Edinburgh: Edinburgh University Press, 2003.

Scheid, John. *An Introduction to Roman Religion*. Translated by Janet Lloyd. Bloomington, IN: Indiana University Press, 2003.

Scheid, John. "Polytheism Impossible; or the Empty Gods: Reasons behind a Void in the History of Roman Religion." *History and Anthropology* 3:303–325, 1987.

Scheid, John. *Quand croire, c'est faire: Les rites sacrificiels des romains*. Paris: Aubier, 2005.

Scheid, John. "Les réjouissances des calendes de janvier d'après le sermon Dolbeau 26: Nouvelles lumières sur une fête mal connue." In *Augustin Prédicateur (395–411): Actes du colloque international de Chantilly (5–7 septembre 1996)*, edited by Goulven Madec, 353–365. Paris: Institut d'Études Augustiniennes, 1998.

Scheid, John. "Religion romaine et spiritualité." *Archiv für Religionsgeschichte* 5:198–209, 2003.

Scheid, John. "Rituel et écriture à Rome." In *Essais sur le rituel II*, edited by Ann-Marie Blondeau, 1–15. Louvain: Peeters, 1990.

Scheid, John. "Roman Animal Sacrifice and the System of Being." In *Greek and Roman Animal Sacrifice: Ancient Victims, Modern Observers*, edited by Christopher A. Faraone and F. S. Naiden, 84–95. New York: Cambridge University Press, 2012.

Scheid, John. "Les sens des rites. L'exemple romain." In *Rites et croyances dans les religions du monde romain*, edited by John Scheid, 39–71. Geneva: Fondation Hardt, 2007.

Scheid, John. "Théologie romaine et représentation de l'action au début de l'Empire." In *Antike Mythen: Medien, Transformationen und Konstruktionen*, edited by Christine Walde and Ueli Dill, 122–131. Berlin: de Gruyter, 2009.

Schieffelin, Edward. "Introduction." In *When Rituals Go Wrong: Mistakes, Failures, and the Dynamics of Ritual*, edited by Ute Hüsken, 1–20. Leiden: Brill, 2007.

Schieffelin, Edward. "On Failure and Performance: Throwing the Medium Out of the Seance." In *The Performance of Healing*, edited by Carol Laderman and Marina Roseman, 59–89. New York: Routledge, 1996.

Schieffelin, Edward. "Performance and the Cultural Construction of Reality." *American Ethnologist* 12:707–724, 1985.

Schieffelin, Edward. "Problematizing Performance." In *Ritual, Performance, Media*, edited by Felicia Hughes-Freeland, 194–207. New York: Routledge, 1998.

Schultze, Clemence. "Authority, Originality and Competence in the *Roman Archaeology* of

Dionysius of Halicarnassus." *Histos* 4:6–49, 2000.

Schultze, Clemence. "Dionysius of Halicarnassus: Greek Origins and Roman Games (*AR* 7. 70–73)." In *Games and Festivals in Classical Antiquity: Proceedings of the Conference held in Edinburgh, 10–12 July 2000*, edited by Sinclair Bell and Glenys Davies, 93–105. Oxford: Archeopress, 2004.

Scott, James C. *Domination and the Arts of Resistance: Hidden Transcripts*. New Haven: Yale University Press, 1990.

Scott, R. T. "The Triple Arch of Augustus and the Roman Triumph." *Journal of Roman Archaeology* 13:183–191, 2000.

Scullard, H. H. *The Elephant in the Greek and Roman World*. Ithaca, NY: Cornell University Press, 1974.

Sear, Frank. *Roman Theatres: An Architectural Study*. New York: Oxford University Press, 2006.

Seelentag, Gunnar. *Taten und Tugenden Traians: Herrschaftsdarstellung im Principat*. Stuttgart: Franz Steiner, 2004.

Sehlmeyer, Markus. *Stadtrömische Ehrenstatuen der republikanischen Zeit: Historizität und Kontext von Symbolen nobilitären Standesbewusstseins*. Stuttgart: Franz Steiner, 1999.

Shelton, Jo-Ann. "Elephants, Pompey, and the Reports of Popular Displeasure in 55 BC." In *Veritatis Amicitiaeque Causa: Essays in Honor of Anna Lydia Motto and John R. Clark*, edited by Edmund Cueva and Shannon Byrne, 231–271. Wauconda, IL: Bolchazy-Carducci, 1999.

Simpson, C. J. "Musicians and the Arena: Dancers and the Hippodrome." *Latomus* 59:633–639, 2000.

Small, Jocelyn Penny. *Cacus and Marsyas in Etrusco-Roman Legend*. Princeton: Princeton University Press, 1982.

Smith, Jonathan Z. *Imagining Religion: From Babylon to Jonestown*. Chicago: University of Chicago Press, 1982.

Smith, Jonathan Z. *Map Is Not Territory*. Chicago: University of Chicago Press, 1978.

Smith, Jonathan Z. *To Take Place: Toward Theory in Ritual*. Chicago: University of Chicago Press, 1987.

Smith, Rowland. "The Imperial Court of the Late Roman Empire, c. AD 300–c. AD 450." In *The Court and Court Societies in Ancient Monarchies*, edited by Anthony Spawforth, 157–232. New York: Cambridge University Press, 2007.

Smith, William, William Wayte, and G. E. Marindin, ed. *A Dictionary of Greek and Roman Antiquities*. London: John Murray, 1890.

Sobocinski, Melanie Grunow. "Visualizing Architecture Then and Now: Mimesis and the Capitoline Temple of Jupiter Optimus Maximus." In *A Companion to Roman Architecture*, edited by Roger Ulrich and Caroline Quenemoen, 446–461. Malden, MA: Wiley-Blackwell, 2014.

Sobocinski, Melanie Grunow. "Visualizing Ceremony: The Design and Audience of the Ludi Saeculares Coinage of Domitian." *American Journal of Archaeology* 110:581–602, 2006.

Soler, Emmanuel. "L'état impérial romain face au baptême et aux pénuries d'acteurs et d'actrices, dans l'antiquité tardive." *Antiquité Tardive* 15:47–58, 2007.

Soler, Emmanuel. "*Ludi* et *munera*, le vocabulaire des spectacles dans le Code Théodosien." In *Le jeux et les spectacles dans l'empire romain tardif et dans les royaumes barbares*, edited by Emmanuel Soler and Françoise Thelamon, 37–68. Rouen: Publications des universités de Rouen et du Havre, 2008.

Soler, Emmanuel and Françoise Thelamon, ed. *Le jeux et les spectacles dans l'empire romain tardif et dans les royaumes barbares*. Rouen: Publications des universités de Rouen et du Havre, 2008.

Spaeth, Barbette. *The Roman Goddess Ceres*. Austin, TX: University of Texas Press, 1996.

Spencer, Diana. "Movement and the Linguistic Turn: Reading Varro's *De Lingua Latina*." In *Rome, Ostia, Pompeii: Movement and Space*, edited by Ray Laurence and David Newsome, 57–80. New York: Oxford University Press, 2011.

Spencer, Diana. "Rome at a Gallop: Livy, on Not Gazing, Jumping, or Toppling into the

Void." In *The Sites of Rome: Time, Space, and Memory*, edited by David Larmour and Diana Spencer, 61–101. New York: Oxford University Press, 2007.

Spencer, Diana. "Urban Flux: Varro's Rome-in-Progress." In *The Moving City: Processions, Passages and Promenades in Ancient Rome*, edited by Ida Östenberg, Simon Malmberg, and Jonas Bjønebye, 99–110. New York: Bloomsbury, 2015.

Spera, Lucrezia. "La realtà archeologica: Restauro degli edifici pubblici e riassetto urbano dopo il sacco." In *Roma e il sacco del 410: Realtà, interpretazione, mito*, edited by Gianluca Pilara, Angelo Di Berardino, and Lucrezia Spera, 113–155. Rome: Institutum Patristicum Augustinianum, 2012.

Spier, Jeffrey. "A Lost Consular Diptych of Anicius Auchenius Bassus (A.D. 408) on the Mould for an ARS Plaque." *Journal of Roman Archaeology* 16:350–354, 2003.

Stamper, John. *The Architecture of Roman Temples: The Republic to the Middle Empire*. New York: Cambridge University Press, 2005.

Stamper, John. "Urban Sanctuaries: The Early Republic to Augustus." In *A Companion to Roman Architecture*, edited by Roger Ulrich and Carolione Quemenoen, 207–227. Malden, MA: Wiley-Blackwell, 2014.

Stein-Hölkeskamp, Elke and Karl-Joachim Hölkeskamp, ed. *Erinnerungs der Antike: Die römische Welt*. Munich: C.H. Beck, 2006.

Steiner, Deborah Tarn. *Images in Mind: Statues in Archaic and Classical Greek Literature and Thought*. Princeton: Princeton University Press, 2001.

Stern, Henri. *Le calendrier de 354: Étude sur son texte et sur ses illustrations*. Paris: Guenther, 1953.

Stewart, Peter. *Statues in Roman Society: Representation and Response*. New York: Oxford University Press, 2003.

Strong, Mrs. Arthur. "Sepuchral Relief of a Priest of Bellona." *Papers of the British School at Rome* 9:205–213, 1920.

Sumi, Geoffrey. *Ceremony and Power: Performing Politics in Rome between Republic and Empire*. Ann Arbor, MI: University of Michigan Press, 2005.

Sumi, Geoffrey. "Monuments and Memory: The Aedes Castoris in the Formation of Augustan Ideology." *Classical Quarterly* 59:167–186, 2009.

Sumi, Geoffrey. "Topography and Ideology: Caesar's Monument and the Aedes Divi Iulii in Augustan Rome." *Classical Quarterly* 61:205–229, 2011.

Szidat, Sabine. *Teile eines historischen Frieses in der Casa de Pilatos in Sevilla mit einem Exkurs zur Tensa*. Munich: Hieronymus, 1997.

Tagliafico, Moira. "Ludiones, ludi saeculare e ludi scaenici." *Aevum* 68.1:51–57, 1994.

Tanner, Jeremy. "Portraits, Power, and Patronage in the Late Roman Republic." *Journal of Roman Studies* 90:18–50, 2000.

Tantillo, Ignazio. "I *munera* in età tardoantica." In *Aurea Roma: Dalla città pagana alla città cristiana*, edited by Serena Ensoli and Eugenio La Rocca, 120–125. Rome: "L'Erma" di Bretschneider, 2000.

Taussig, Michael. "Viscerality, Faith, and Skepticism: Another Theory of Magic." In *In Near Ruins: Cultural Theory at the End of the Century*, edited by Nicholas Dirks, 221–256. Minneapolis, MN: University of Minnesota Press, 1998.

Taylor, Lilly Ross. *The Divinity of the Roman Emperor*. Middletown, CT: American Philological Association, 1931.

Taylor, Lilly Ross. "Lucretius on the Roman Theater." In *Studies in Honour of Gilbert Norwood*, edited by Mary White, 147–155. Toronto: University of Toronto Press, 1952.

Taylor, Lilly Ross. "On the Chronology of Cicero's Letters to Atticus, Book XIII." *Classical Philology* 32:228–240, 1937.

Taylor, Lilly Ross. "The Opportunities for Dramatic Performances in the Time of Plautus and Terence." *Transactions and Proceedings of the American Philological Association* 68:284–304, 1937.

Taylor, Lilly Ross. "The *Sellisternium* and the Theatrical *Pompa*." *Classical Philology* 30.2:122–130, 1935.

Taylor, Lilly Ross. "Sellisternium and Theoxenia." In *Atti del VIII congresso internazionale di storia delle religioni (Roma 17–23 aprile 1955)*, 349–350. Rome: Sansoni, 1956.

Taylor, Lilly Ross. "*Seviri Equitum Romanorum* and Municipal *Seviri*: A Study in Pre-Military Training among the Romans." *Journal of Roman Studies* 14:158–171, 1924.

Thein, Alexander. "The Augustan 'Rebuilding' of the Capitolium." In *Ruin or Renewal? Places and the Transformation of Memory in the City of Rome*, edited by J. Richardson, M. García Morcillo, and F. Santangelo, 135–156. Rome: Quasar, 2016.

Thein, Alexander. "Capitoline Jupiter and the Historiography of Roman World Rule." *Histos* 8:284–319, 2014.

Thomas, E. "Ovid at the Races: *Amores* III.2; *Ars amatoria* 1.35–164." In *Hommages à M. Renard*, edited by Jacqueline Bibauw, 710–724. Brussels: Latomus, 1969.

Thompson, Dorothy. "Philadelphus' Procession: Dynastic Power in a Mediterranean Context." In *Politics, Administration and Society in the Hellenistic and Roman World: Proceedings of the International Colloquium, Bertinoro 19–24 July 1997*, edited by Leon Mooren, 365–388. Leuven: Peeters, 2000.

Thuillier, Jean-Paul. "Denys d'Halicarnasse et le jeux romains (*Antiquités Romaines* VII, 72–3)." *Melanges de l'École française de Rome: Antiquité* 87:563–581, 1975.

Thuillier, Jean-Paul. "Les jeux dans les premiers livres des *Antiquités romains*." *Melanges de l'École française de Rome: Antiquité* 101:229–242, 1989.

Thuillier, Jean-Paul. *Le sport dans la Rome antique*. Paris: Editions Errance, 1996.

Tilburg, Cornelius van. *Traffic and Congestion in the Roman Empire*. New York: Routledge, 2007.

Toher, Mark. "Octavian's Arrival in Rome, 44 B.C." *Classical Quarterly* 54:174–184, 2004.

Torlone, Zara Martirosova. "Writing Arenas: Roman Authors and Their Games." In *A Companion to Sport and Spectacle in Greek and Roman Antiquity*, edited by Paul Christesen and Donald Kyle, 412–421. Malden, MA: Wiley-Blackwell, 2014.

Tortorella, Stefano. "*Luperci* e *Lupercalia*: La documentazione archeologica." In *Roma: Romolo, Remo e la fondazione della città*, edited by Andrea Carandini and Rosanna Cappelli, 244–255. Milan: Electa, 2000.

Tortorella, Stefano. "Processione trionfale e circense sulle lastre Campana." In *Le perle e il filo: A Mario Torelli per i suoi settanta anni*, edited by Sabrina Boldrini, Simonetta Angiolillo, Paolo Braconi et al, 301–322. Venosa (Potenza): Osanna, 2008.

Toynbee, Jocelyn M. C. *Animals in Roman Life and Art*. Ithaca, NY: Cornell University Press, 1973.

Toynbee, Jocelyn M. C. *Death and Burial in the Roman World*. Baltimore, MD: Johns Hopkins University Press, 1971.

Toynbee, Jocelyn M. C. *Roman Medallions*. New York: American Numismatic Society, 1944.

Trifiló, Francesco. "Power, Architecture and Community in the Distribution of Honorary Statues in Roman Public Space." In *TRAC 2007: Proceedings of the Seventeenth Annual Theoretical Roman Archaeology Conference, London 2007*, edited by Corisande Fenwick and Meredith Wiggins, 109–120. Oxford: Oxbow Books, 2008.

Tuck, Steven. "Spectacle and Ideology in the Relief Decorations of the *Anfiteatro Campano* at Capua." *Journal of Roman Archaeology* 20:255–272, 2007.

Turcan, Robert. *Religion Romaine*. 2 vols. Leiden: Brill, 1988.

Valli, Barbara. "*Lupercis nudis lustratur antiquum oppidum palatinum*: alcune reflessioni sui *Lupercalia*." *Florentia* 2:101–154, 2007.

Valli, Barbara. "I percorsi delle processioni nella Roma antica: *ludi saeculares* and funerali imperiali." *Fragmenta* 1:33–59, 2007.

van den Berg, Christopher. "The *Pulvinar* in Roman Culture." *Transactions of the American Philological Association* 138:239–273, 2008.

van den Hoek, Annewies. "Peter, Paul, and a Consul: Recent Discoveries in African Red

Slip Ware." *Zeitschrift für antikes Christentum* 9:197–246, 2006.

van den Hoek, Annewies and John Hermann. *Pottery, Pavements, and Paradise: Iconographic and Textual Studies on Late Antiquity.* Leiden: Brill, 2013.

van den Hout, Michael P. J. *A Commentary on the Letters of M. Cornelius Fronto.* Leiden: Brill, 1999.

Van Slyke, Daniel. "The Devil and His Pomps in Fifth-Century Carthage: Renouncing Spectacula with Spectacular Imagery." *Dumbarton Oaks Papers* 59:53–72, 2005.

Várhelyi, Zsuzsanna. *The Religon of Senators in the Roman Empire.* New York: Cambridge University Press, 2010.

Varner, Eric. *Mutilation and Transformation:* Damnatio Memoriae *and Roman Imperial Portraiture.* Leiden: Brill, 2004.

Vasaly, Ann. *Representations: Images of the World in Ciceronian Oratory.* Berkeley: University of California Press, 1993.

Vernant, Jean-Pierre. "From the 'Presentification' of the Invisible to the Imitation of Appearance." In *Mortals and Immortals: Collected Essays,* edited by Froma I. Zeitlin, 151–163. Princeton: Princeton University Press, 1991.

Versnel, Hendrik Simon. *Coping with the Gods: Wayward Readings in Greek Theology.* Leiden: Brill, 2011.

Versnel, Hendrik Simon. "Divus Julius by S. Weinstock." *Mnemosyne* 29: 99–102, 1976.

Versnel, Hendrik Simon. *Inconsistencies in Greek and Roman Religion.* 2 vols. Leiden: Brill 1990, 1993.

Versnel, Hendrik Simon. "Red (Herring?): Comments on a New Theory Concerning the Origin of the Triumph." *Numen* 53:290–326, 2006.

Versnel, Hendrik Simon. *Triumphus: An Inquiry into the Origin, Development and Meaning of the Roman Triumph.* Leiden: Brill, 1970.

Vespignani, Giorgio. "Il cerimoniale imperiale nel circo (secoli IV-VI): La iconografia nei dittici eburnei." *Bizantinistica* 4:13–37, 2002.

Vespignani, Giorgio. *Simbolismo magia e sacralità dello spazio circo.* Bologna: Scarabeo, 1994.

Veyne, Paul. *Bread and Circuses: Historical Sociology and Political Pluralism.* Translated by Brian Pearce. New York: Allen Lane, Penguin (original 1976), 1990.

Veyne, Paul. *Did the Greeks Believe in Their Myths? An Essay on the Constitutive Imagination.* Translated by Paula Wissig. Chicago: University of Chicago Press, 1988.

Veyne, Paul. "Iconographie de la *transvectio equitum* et des Lupercales." *Revue des études anciennes* 62:100–112, 1960.

Volbach, Wolfgang Fritz. *Elfenbeinarbeiten der Spätantike und des frühen Mittelalters.* 2nd ed. Mainz: Verlag des römischen-germanischen Zentralmuseums, 1952.

Volpe, R. and E. M. Loreti. "L'Arco di Domiziano con quadrighe di elefanti." In *La terra degli elefanti: Atti del 1° congresso internazionale,* edited by P. Gioia, G. Cavarretta, M. Mussi, and M. R. Palombo, 407–410. Rome: Consiglio Nazionale delle Ricerche, 2001.

Vout, Caroline. "Sizing Up Rome, or Theorizing the Overview." In *The Sites of Rome: Time, Space, and Memory,* edited by David Larmour and Diana Spencer, 295–322. New York: Oxford University Press, 2007.

Walbank, F. W. "Two Hellenistic Processions: A Matter of Self-Definition." *Scripta Classica Israelica* 15:119–130, 1996.

Wallace-Hadrill, Andrew. "Civilis Princeps: Between Citizen and King." *Journal of Roman Studies* 72:32–48, 1982.

Wallace-Hadrill, Andrew. "Image and Authority in the Coinage of Augustus." *Journal of Roman Studies* 76:66–87, 1986.

Wallace-Hadrill, Andrew. "Roman Arches and Greek Honours: The Language of Power at Rome." *Proceedings of the Cambridge Philological Society* 36:143–181, 1990.

Wallace-Hadrill, Andrew. *Rome's Cultural Revolution.* New York: Cambridge University Press, 2008.

Waltzing, Jean-Pierre. *Étude historique sur les corporations professionnelles chez les Romains depuis les origines jusqu'à la chute de l'Empire d'Occident.* 4 vols. Louvain: Peeters, 1895–1900.

Ward-Perkins, Bryan. *From Classical Antiquity to the Middle Ages: Urban Public Building in*

Northern and Central Italy, AD 300–850. New York: Oxford University Press, 1984.
Wardle, David. "Vespasian, Helvidius Priscus and the Restoration of the Capitol." *Historia* 45:208–222, 1996.
Waszink, J. H. "Pompa Diaboli." *Vigiliae Christianae* 1:13–41, 1947.
Webb, Ruth. *Demons and Dancers: Performance in Late Antiquity*. Cambridge, MA: Harvard University Press, 2008.
Weber, Max. "'Objectivity' in Social Science and Social Policy." In *Max Weber on the Methodology of the Social Sciences*, translated and edited by Edward Shils and Henry Finch, 49–112. Glencoe, IL: Free Press, 1949.
Weinstock, Stefan. *Divus Julius*. Oxford: Clarendon Press, 1971.
Weinstock, Stefan. "The Image and the Chair of Germanicus." *Journal of Roman Studies* 47:144–154, 1957.
Weisweiler, John. "From Equality to Asymmetry: Honorific Statues, Imperial Power and Senatorial Identity in Late-Antique Rome." *Journal of Roman Archaeology* 25:319–350, 2012.
Weisweiler, John. "Inscribing Imperial Power: Letters from Emperors in Late-Antique Rome." In *Rom in der Spätantike: Historische Erinnerung in Städtischen Raum*, edited by Ralf Behrwald and Christian Witschel, 309–329. Stuttgart: Franz Steiner, 2012.
Weisweiler, John. "The Price of Integration: State and Élite in Symmachus' Correspondance." In *Der wiederkehrende Leviathan: Staatlichkeit und Staatswerdung in Spätantike und Früher Neuzeit*, edited by Sebastian Schmidt-Hofner, Peter Eich, and Christian Wieland, 343–373. Heidelberg: Universitätsverlag Winter, 2011.
Welch, Kathryn. *Magnus Pius: Sextus Pompeius and the Transformation of the Roman Republic*. Swansea: Classical Press of Wales, 2012.
Welch, Kathryn. "The Roman Arena in Late-Republican Italy: A New Interpretation." *Journal of Roman Archaeology* 7:59–80, 1994.
Welch, Tara. *The Elegiac Cityscape: Propertius and the Meaning of Roman Monuments*. Columbus, OH: Ohio State University Press, 2005.
Welch, Tara. "Elegy and the Monuments." In *A Companion to Roman Love Elegy*, edited by Barbara K. Gold, 103–118. Malden, MA: Wiley-Blackwell, 2012.
Wescoat, Bonna and Robert Ousterhout, ed. *Architecture of the Sacred: Space, Ritual, and Experience from Classical Greece to Byzantium*. New York: Cambridge University Press, 2012.
Wickham, Chris. *Framing the Early Middle Ages: Europe and the Mediterranean, 400–800*. New York: Oxford University Press, 2005.
Wikander, Charlotte. "Pomp and Circumstance: The Procession of Ptolemaios II." *Opuscula Atheniensia* 19:143–150, 1992.
Wiseman, T. P. *Catullus and His World: A Reappraisal*. Cambridge: Cambridge University Press, 1985.
Wiseman, T. P. *Cinna the Poet, and Other Roman Essays*. Leicester: Leicester University Press, 1974.
Wiseman, T. P. "The Games of Flora." In *The Art of Ancient Spectacle*, edited by Bettina Bergmann and Christine Kondoleon, 195–203. Washington, D. C.: National Gallery of Art, 1999.
Wiseman, T. P. "The God of the Lupercal." *Journal of Roman Studies* 85:1–22, 1995.
Wiseman, T. P. *Historiography and Imagination: Eight Essays on Roman Culture*. Exeter: University of Exeter Press, 1994.
Wiseman, T. P. *The Myths of Rome*. Exeter: University of Exeter Press, 2004.
Wiseman, T. P. *New Men in the Roman Senate, 139 B.C.–A. D. 14*. London: Oxford University Press, 1971.
Wiseman, T. P. "Ovid and the Stage." In *Ovid's* Fasti: *Historical Readings at Its Bimillenium*, edited by Geraldine Herbert-Brown, 275–299. New York: Oxford University Press, 2002.
Wiseman, T. P. "Popular Memory." In *Memoria Romana: Memory in Rome and Rome in Memory*, edited by Karl Galinsky, 43–62. Ann Arbor: University of Michigan Press for the American Academy in Rome, 2014.
Wiseman, T. P. *Remembering the Roman People: Essays on Late-Republican Politics and Literature*. New York: Oxford University Press, 2010.
Wiseman, T. P. *Roman Drama and Roman History*. Exeter: University of Exeter Press, 1998.

Wistrand, Magnus. "Change and Continuity: Some Observations on Tertullian's *De spectaculis* and Pagan Views on Entertainment." In *Tongues and Texts Unlimited: Studies in Honour of Tore Janson on the Occasion of His Sixtieth Anniversary*, edited by Peter af Trampe, 298–307. Stockholm: Stockholms Universitet, Institutionen för klassiska språk, 2000.

Wistrand, Magnus. *Entertainment and Violence in Ancient Rome: The Attitude of Roman Writers of the First Century A.D.* Götenburg, Sweden: Acta Universitatis Gothoburgensis, 1992.

Wood, Susan. "Diva Drusilla Panthea and the Sisters of Caligula." *American Journal of Archaeology* 99:457–482, 1995.

Wood, Susan. *Imperial Women: A Study in Public Images, 40 B.C.–A.D. 68.* Leiden: Brill, 2001.

Wood, Susan. "Who Was Diva Domitilla? Some Thoughts on the Public Images of the Flavian Women." *American Journal of Archaeology* 114:45–57, 2010.

Woodman, A. J. "Not a Funeral Note: Tacitus, *Annals* 1.8.5–6." *Classical Quarterly* 52:629–632, 2002.

Woolf, Greg. "Reading and Religion in Rome." In *Reflections on Religious Individuality: Greco-Roman and Judaeo-Christian Texts and Practices*, edited by Jörg Rüpke and Wolfgang Spickermann, 193–208. Berlin: de Gruyter, 2012.

Yavetz, Zvi. *Plebs and Princeps.* Oxford: Clarendon Press, 1969.

Yegül, Fikret. "The Street Experience of Ancient Ephesus." In *Streets: Critical Perspectives on Public Space*, edited by Zeynep Çelik, Diane Favro, and Richard Ingersoll, 95–110. Berkeley: University of California Press, 1994.

Zaleski, John. "Religion and Roman Spectacle." In *A Companion to Sport and Spectacle in Greek and Roman Antiquity*, edited by Paul Christesen and Donald Kyle, 590–602. Malden, MA: Wiley-Blackwell, 2014.

Zanker, Paul. *The Power of Images in the Age of Augustus.* Translated by Alan Shapiro. Ann Arbor, MI: University of Michigan Press, 1988.

Zarmakoupi, Mantha. "Public Entertainment Structures." In *A Companion to the Archaeology of the Roman Republic*, edited by Jane DeRose Evans, 33–49. Malden, MA: Wiley-Blackwell, 2013.

Zazoff, Peter. *Die antiken Gemmen.* Munich: Beck, 1983.

Ziółkowski, Adam. "Ritual Cleaning-Up of the City: From the Lupercalia to the Argei." *Ancient Society* 29:191–218, 1998–1999.

Zwierlein-Diehl, Erika. *Antike Gemmen in deutschen Sammlungen II: Staatliche Museen, Preußischer Kulturbesitz: Antikenabteilung Berlin.* Munich: Prestel, 1969.

INDEX